Arabs and Berbers

This book is published for the Center
on International Race Relations in
their *Race and Nations Series*. The
Center seeks the wider recognition of
the role of race in international affairs,
and through its research and teaching
programs develops a systematic
analysis of race in American foreign
relations.

Arabs and Berbers

FROM TRIBE TO NATION IN NORTH AFRICA

EDITED BY

Ernest Gellner

AND

Charles Micaud

Lexington Books
D.C. Heath and Company
Lexington, Massachusetts
Toronto   London

CONTENTS

PREFACE   9

INTRODUCTION   *Ernest Gellner*   11

PART ONE   **The traditional base**

1 The tribe in modern Morocco: two case studies   25
  David M. Hart

2 Political and religious organization of the Berbers of the
  central High Atlas   59
  Ernest Gellner

3 The socio-political organization of a Berber *Taraf* tribe:
  pre-protectorate Morocco   67
  Amal R. Vinogradov

4 Berber imperialism: the Ait Atta expansion in southeast
  Morocco   85
  Ross E. Dunn

5 Local politics and state intervention: northeast Morocco
  from 1870 to 1970   109
  J. David Seddon

6 The Mzab   141
  E. A. Alport

PART TWO   **Ethnicity and nation**

7 The social and conceptual framework of Arab–Berber
  relations in central Morocco   155
  Lawrence Rosen

8 The image of the Moroccan state in French ethnolo-
  gical literature: a new look at the origin of Lyautey's
  Berber policy   175
  Edmund Burke III

9 The impact of the *Dahir Berbère* in Salé   201
  Kenneth Brown

10 The Berbers and the rise of Moroccan nationalism   217
  Louis-Jean Duclos

11 Tribalism, trade and politics: the transformation of the
    Swasa of Morocco   231
    John Waterbury

12 The neo-makhzan and the Berbers   259
    Abdaslam Ben Kaddour

13 Note on the role of the Berbers in the early days of
    Moroccan independence   269
    A. Coram

14 The political evolution of the Berbers in independent
    Morocco   277
    Octave Marais

15 The Berbers in the Algerian political elite   285
    William B. Quandt

PART THREE **Ethnicity and social change**

16 Traditionalism through ultra-modernism   307
    Jeanne Favret

17 Berber migrants in Casablanca   325
    André Adam

18 Social change among the Tuareg   345
    Jeremy H. Keenan

19 Patterns of rural rebellion in Morocco during the early
    years of independence   361
    Ernest Gellner

20 Political authority and social stratification in Mauritania   375
    C. C. Stewart

PART FOUR **The coup of 10 July 1971**

21 The coup manqué   397
    John Waterbury

22 The Berbers and the coup   425
    A. Coram

23 Berbers and the Moroccan political system after the
    coup   431
    Octave Marais

CONCLUSION *Charles Micaud*   433

INDEX   441

ILLUSTRATIONS

FIGURES

3.1 Typical segmentary organization among the Beni Mtir   71
4.1 Segmentation of the Ait Khabbash   87
15.1 Berbers within the Algerian elite: the revolutionary period   293
15.2 Berbers within the Algerian elite: the Ben Bella and Boumedienne periods   300

MAPS

0.1 North-West Africa with regions of Berber speech   16–17
4.1 Ait Atta expansion   91
4.2 The Ziz Valley and Tafilalt   94
5.1 Morocco   110
5.2 Province of Nador, northeast Morocco   111
5.3 Distribution of tribes in northeast Morocco   112
18.1 West-Central Sahara   346
18.2 Ahaggar   347
21.1 Morocco and the coup of 1971   408

PREFACE

We acknowledge our indebtedness to the Center for International Race Relations at the University of Denver which made this book possible. Besides exploring the significance of ethnicity in the process of nationbuilding and modernization in North Africa, the present volume makes available contributions by scholars with an intimate knowledge of various aspects of North African society, contributions that might otherwise not reach the large audience they deserve. We hope that the many case studies brought together here will give students of North Africa a unique and many-sided background for understanding a complex society, in which traditional structures and values continue to play a major role. Except for five reprints of articles, listed in the following paragraph, the contributions appear for the first time. All articles (except of course those of Part Four) were completed well before the Moroccan events of July 1971. We have judged it preferable to retain the coherence of analysis and argument, rather than attempt any last-minute injection of new illustrative material.

We thank the following for permission to reprint: the Editor of *Man* for *The Mzab* by E. A. Alport; the Editorial Board of *Archives européennes de sociologie* for *Traditionalism through Ultra-modernism* by Jeanne Favret; Dr Alan Horton and the American Universities Field Staff for *The Coup Manqué* by John Waterbury; the Editorial Board of the *European Journal of Sociology* for *Patterns of Rural Rebellion in Morocco during the Early Years of Independence* by Ernest Gellner; and to the International African Institute for the map on pp. 16–17. *Political and Religious Organization of the Berbers of the Central High Atlas* by Ernest Gellner was orginally presented at the World Anthropological Congress in Moscow in 1964.

We are grateful to Miss Adrian Adams for her excellent translation of the manuscripts received in French; to Mrs Thelma O'Brien for her invaluable secretarial assistance to Professor Gellner; and to Susan Gellner for putting in a very great deal of work on the Index. We also acknowledge our gratitude to the contributors of the volume, who agreed so readily to participate in this team effort.

E. G. and C. M.

Ernest Gellner   Introduction

North Africa—the island of the West, as the Arabs call it—enclosed by the sea
and the Sahara, is a distinctive world of its own, notwithstanding all affinities it
also has with the Middle East, southern Europe and West Africa. Whether by
accident or for some deep-seated geopolitical reasons, it has tended to be linked
with the East rather than Europe, except at such times as the East itself was over-
shadowed by Europe: the North African coast was under Phoenician, Byzantine
or Arab influence, except for later Roman and modern colonial times.

The present volume is concerned with modern North Africa and the problem
of nationalism and political development. Hence it is worth singling out, by way
of background, the distinctive features of the entire region.

North Africa, or the Maghreb ('the West', in Arabic) shares Muslim and
Arabic civilization with the Middle East. But it differs from it in a number of
significant ways. For one thing, the Maghreb is much less diversified and
pluralistic, in either an ethnic or a religious sense, than is the Middle East proper.
The Middle East proper reflects its own complex religious history, and the survival and intrusion of very numerous ethnic groups, by constituting a religious
and linguistic patchwork. Not so the Maghreb: within its Muslim community,
religious homogeneity is almost complete. Linguistic diversity is limited to two
groups of dialects—Arab and Berber. (The two languages are of course totally
distinct from each other.) It is curious that the Muslim–Christian dialogue should
have had such different end-results at either end of the Mediterranean: in the
East, diversity faces diversity, and in the West, homogeneity faces homogeneity.

Whatever the explanation, the consequence is that North African civilization
does not, like the Middle East, consist of 'enclaves'—to use Dr Louise Sweet's
expression—of inward-turned communities, often openly displaying their
religious or cultural idiosyncrasy. Such diversity as is found in North Africa is,
above all, *discreet*: it does not underscore or advertise its idiosyncrasies, which
remain hidden under the nearly all-embracing cloak of Sunni Islam of the Maliki
rite.[1] Of course there is *de facto* religious diversity, manifested in the proliferation
of saint cults, religious brotherhoods, and differences in religious style of various
milieux: but these differences stop short, considerably short, of an avowed
separation or schism, and L.-J. Duclos even claims that through their repetition
of similar themes and solutions in diverse localities, these fragmented movements
actually make a contribution to a sense of national unity. In any case, the

[1] The only non-Sunni Muslims in North Africa are two small pockets of Kharejite
Ibadis, concentrated in their desert retreat in Mzab in southern Algeria, and on the island
of Djerba in southern Tunisia. Within the Sunni community, adherence to the Maliki
rite is universal, except for a small number of non-Malikis, surviving from the days of
Ottoman suzerainty in the Eastern part of North Africa.

differences remain muted. It may be said, for instance, that the trauma of 1930, described by Kenneth Brown, which shocked urban Moroccans into a new nationalism when the French underwrote Berber customary law, arose not from the *existence* of a doubtfully orthodox Berber custom—this the bourgeoisie knew full well, and perhaps even exaggerated—but from its overt *recognition*, black on white, on the statute book. To publish it was a kind of indiscretion. It is not a sin as such which makes a scandal, but its brazen publication.

This discretion, the relatively muted tone in which divergences are articulated, also extends to differences in language and culture. (I am not saying that North Africans refrain from violent conflict, which would not be true at all, but only that, within the Muslim community, divergences in *practice* or *language* are not dramatically symbolized or clearly perceived.) To begin with, there are only two linguistic categories—Arabic and Berber. Note that they are indeed categories, not corporate groups. Neither has ever acted or felt as one unit. They are also mere categories in another sense—each is a mere cluster of dialects, such that within each group, mutual intelligibility may not be taken for granted. Within the Arabic group of dialects, however, there is the unity springing from a shared relation to written and classical Arabic and to religion. Within the Berber group, there is nothing corresponding to this—only, once again, the shared faith and consequently the shared use of *Arabic* as the language of writing, sacred or secular. (The use of Arabic script for writing in Berber exists, but is very rare.)

Still, the perceptible differences between Arabic-speakers and Berber-speakers does exist. Social perception is a subtle and complex thing, as Lawrence Rosen shows, but it cannot altogether ignore so blatant and striking a distinction. But it can make it the object of this curious and unconscious social discretion. This discretion is helped by the fact that the North African folk vision of the world is articulated entirely from within Islam: the limits of Islam are the limits of the world. What is non-Islamic is seen *through* the categories which Islam itself brought along. North Africans are not, as are the Persians for instance, a Muslim people who have embraced the Faith but retained a memory stretching beyond its coming, so that their own cultural identity is not co-extensive with Islam. On the contrary, North African folk consciousness does not reach out beyond the limits of Islam. When it refers to pre-Islamic proto-populations, it does not characterize them further nor identify with them, even if it credits them with the contribution of an ancestress or two to tribal genealogies. To say all this is not, of course, to say that everything in folk culture is 'properly' Islamic and would be endorsed as such by an urban learned Muslim theologian: not at all. It merely means that the elements in folk life are all locally re-interpreted in Koranic terms, which thus set a limit to the historic horizon.[1]

---

[1] Elements in folk culture which are not properly Islamic—i.e. could not be shown to be Islamic by criteria that would satisfy a literate, genuine Muslim scholar—may but need not necessarily be *pre*-Islamic, contrary to the methodological assumption of some ethnologists. Could one assemble all features of English life which a puritan theologian would refuse to class as Christian, and treat the resulting collection as a picture of pre-Christian Anglo-Saxon life?

This of course already makes it hard to *see* the Berbers at all, as they do not figure in the Koran or the Judeo-Christian background which it recognizes. It is of course possible, in time-honored fashion, to attach the Berbers to that background, by forging genealogical links with some personages within it. Thus Ibn Khaldun attaches them to Goliath. How widely accepted such beliefs were in his time it is hard to tell: they do not appear to have survived as living beliefs into the present.

It would of course be an exaggeration to say that Berbers and their language are an invisible social fact. You cannot ignore, or ignore altogether, something as conspicuous as that a man speaks, or even speaks exclusively, an unintelligible and difficult language. The urban Arab notes it with contempt, irritation or, sometimes, with fear. But the displeasure does not congeal around some permanent and central idea. The Berber tribesman is a menace *qua* tribesman, not *qua* speaker of a gibberish-sounding language. As tribesman, he might also be an ally. His morals are suspect as those of a rustic ignoramus and not, once again, in virtue of his speech. So, the difference which exists in linguistic fact and history is not underscored, for it lacks a connection with any of those ideas in terms of which men do see their world. (The vacillations and initial formlessness of the French image of the Moroccan Berber, described by Edmund Burke, may at least in part be due to the lack of an adequate pre-existing stereotype of Berber society.) There are of course limits to what 'our thinking can make so' or what it can obscure. But it can 'make so' a good deal. For instance, a Berber who credits himself with an Arabic genealogy simply does not ask himself how he comes to be speaking Berber rather than Arabic. In particular, the fact that Berbers are the original population of North Africa, preceding Arabs and Islam, simply is not mirrored in the folk mind. The Berber sees himself as a member of this or that tribe, within an Islamically-conceived and permeated world—and *not* as a member of a linguistically defined ethnic group, in a world in which Islam is but one thing among others.

There are interesting regional differences in the extent to which folk consciousness possesses concepts for grasping Berberism at all. In the central High Atlas of Morocco, where Berbers are numerous and important, the concepts are generally lacking; in southern Tunisia, where the number of Berber villages is very small and without political significance, the awareness is much clearer. The explanation of this paradox is simple. In Tunisia, the idea of Berber speech is linked to the Ibadi heresy (though in fact even in southern Tunisia, not all Berbers are Ibadi heretics, and in the Berber world at large, such dissidents are as rare as they are in the Arab world). But this provides the idea of Berberism in Tunisia with a kind of grip on the symbolism in terms of which the world is seen. (Alport gives us an account of the background and condition, as it was till the early 1950s, of the one other Berber-speaking Ibadi community, in what is now Algerian Sahara. But even this community tended to be seen as *Ibadi* rather than Berber.) Saints' shrines are the very stuff of local folk memory and consciousness, and a typical southern Tunisian saint will be credited with having displaced the local heretics—*and* Berbers—much as a coastal saint in Morocco will be credited with having fought off the Christians, and a saint in the High

Atlas with having helped displace the mythical 'Portuguese' proto-inhabitants. Whether in fact the linguistic Arabization of southern Tunisia was linked to a religious reconversion or expulsion of Kharejite dissidents, historians may be able to tell us: folk legends certainly claim it is so. The consequence of this is that the *idea* of a Berber here at least has an ideological role, which in most other places it lacks.

Of course, it is possible to find signs of Berber consciousness, and of consciousness *of* Berbers, in the course of North African history. Ibn Khaldun was fully aware of them (though his handling of ethnic concepts is none too assured). A medieval heresy proclaimed a Koran in Berber, a seventeenth-century religious movement was opposed to 'all those who do not speak Berber', and Dadda Atta, the putative ancestor of the important Ait Atta tribe, is proudly claimed by his descendants to have been a *Berraber*. (This is a most remarkable tribe. David Hart and Ross Dunn explain its great achievement, which was to coordinate complex pastoral, judicial and military activities over a large population and an enormous territory, while using institutional devices drawn exclusively from the equipment of a segmentary, 'acephalous' society.) But the striking thing about these signs is not their occurrence, but their rarity.

Thus a North African, looking around for a sign by which to identify or characterize a friend or an enemy, will, as Lawrence Rosen shows, find plenty close to hand, and some on the distant horizon: close to hand, a shared ancestor, an affinal link, pasture rights, a shared saint or pilgrimage, or, if necessary, an *ad hoc* sacrificial meal to ratify an alliance and an obligation. On the horizon, there is Islam and the faiths from which it knowingly distinguishes itself. It is the middle ground which is somewhat poor in distinguishing marks that are either clear or well sustained by interest or injury. Yet it is in this middle ground that a new ethnic nationalism or irredentism would need to find principles of identification. It would not be easy to find them. There are, it is true, two languages, or rather two groups of dialects. But one group is too firmly linked to the shared faith which has already defined the first, easily available nationalism; while the other is a purely folk matter, not served by script or scribe class, nor ever made normative by convention or the elevation of one dialect to a dominant position.

It is thus, then, that the Maghreb differs from the Middle East: it is not quite such a plural society, rich in self-conscious enclaves. It may be, indeed it is, segmented, but it is religiously *gleichgeschaltet* in a way which tolerates differences that are muted and restrained. The linguistic differences which do exist lack an anchorage, a *prise*, in local concepts, and also lack socio-political stimulus, as so many of the contributors—Waterbury, Coram, Marais, Quandt, Favret, Adam— all document.

It may be worth noting that the Berbers were not at first the only *prima facie* candidates for a separatist nationalism. History had left behind Jewish and Negro minorities, and, since the colonial period, also an European-Christian one. The conflict of decolonization was of course as much a war between communities, as a war against the colonial government. But the Europeans chose exile rather then either assimilation or a struggle for partition, and no *laager* state remains behind as the heritage of the colonial period. Similarly, very little remains by now of the Jewish community. This leaves the Negroid communities of the southern oases. As André Adam and David Hart mention, color racism does exist, but whatever tensions this may generate, it does not have profound political consequences. As the contemporary theoretician of color racism, Mr Enoch Powell, tells us, numbers are of the essence of the thing: and the colored population of the Maghreb simply is not numerous enough to present this problem.

It is at this point that the Maghreb differs so much from the West African Saharan border zones, with which it otherwise has so much in common. In these regions, the accidents of colonial cartography have left behind a series of states in which whites dominate blacks (Sudan republic, Mauritania) or *vice versa* (Chad, Mali). Two of the contributors, Jeremy Keenan and Charles Stewart, describe situations that are in striking contrast both to each other and to the Maghreb proper. In the central Sahara, bequeathed to modern Algeria, a Berber nomadic warrior aristrocracy has had to bow to the egalitarianism of the Algerian republic. In the western Sahara, Mauritania, object of Moroccan claims, but now an independent state, a complex system of stratified tribes—Arab warriors on top, religion-oriented tribes of Berber origin a little below—dominated a sedentary Negro population, and survives in a modern guise into the present.

North African society is also distinctive in its political culture. From a political viewpoint, societies can be classified according to the extent and manner in which the central government can impose its will on their members. Assertions to the contrary notwithstanding, there can be no question of classifying the traditional North African state as an 'oriental tyranny' in the 'hydraulic' sense, or as a 'bureaucratic empire'. Generally speaking, local authorities were not bureaucratic nominees, but autonomous power-holders who had their position ratified from the center. Amal Vinogradov, David Hart, Ross Dunn, David Seddon and others highlight this fact. Taxes did not flow smoothly but often had to be collected by special military expeditions. Quite different were the towns—centers of learning, trade, and garrisons—which were normally too frightened of the tribes to be a threat to the central power. (The pirate town of Salé was an interesting exception at one time, and for a time constituted a kind of civic republic.) A peripatetic court and army, based on the towns, only partially controlled a tribal countryside, where groups were hostile or allied to it according to circumstance. (Dunn's, Seddon's and Vinogradov's chapters describe the complexities of this game.)

The lack of unity inherent in this system was however in some measure compensated, as L.-J. Duclos stresses, not merely by the shared Muslim faith but above all by its specific and characteristic local institutions, the complex and ramified network of religious brotherhoods and saint cults, with their regular pilgrimages and loose but extensive hierarchies. They facilitated contacts, commercial and other, the flow of information, and made possible mediation and arbitration, and thus fostered a very real sense of cultural continuity, in an environment in which this end could hardly be attained by central law-enforcement.

The European variant of such a loose system was of course 'feudalism'. But

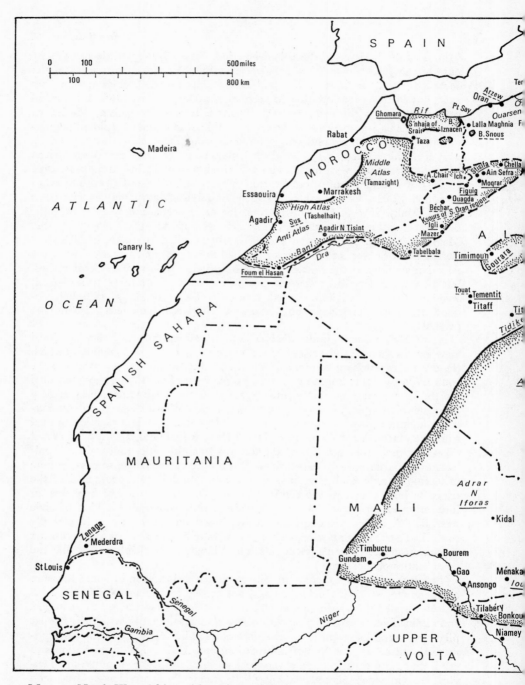

Map o.1 North-West Africa with regions of Berber speech. Areas of Berber speech are mark
line indicates plurality of languages. Recent social changes and population movements ha

MEDITERRANEAN SEA

GREECE

SICILY

Malta

CRETE

Algiers
Bejaïa
Blida
aoua
Metmata
Kabylie
Constantine
Tunis
et el Had
Batna
(Chaouia)
Aurès
TUNISIA
Biskra
Tmagourt
Sened
O.Righ
Taguijiout
Zraoua
Djerba I.
Touggourt
Tamezret
Chnini
Douiret
Zuara
Mzab
Ngousa
Ouargla
Djebel Nefusa

RIA

TRIPOLITANIA

Ghadamès

Sokna

Augila

Siwa

CYRENAICA

Timasinin
(Ft. Flatters)

Fezzan

LIBYA

midir

Ajjer
Ghat

Djanet

Ahaggar
Tamanrasset

UAREGS

Aïr

NIGER

Agadès

CHAD

en

Tahoua
Tanout

Madaoua
Maradi
Zinder
Lake
Chad

NIGERIA

International
boundary

Berber-speaking
areas

a black line, and names of isolated Berber-speaking pockets are underlined. A discontinuous
bably reduced the extent of Berber-speaking regions, especially in urban centres.

the traditional Maghrebin system was profoundly different from this: it threw up no permanent ruling class of warriors. Instead, it was tribal. The maintenance of order hinged everywhere on the presence of local groups, generally (though not universally) self-defined in kin terms, in which virtually all adult males were warriors, and which maintained order by a complex system of balance of power, or rather balances, operating simultaneously at various levels of size. To function properly, the system required mediators and arbitrators, and these were provided by religion in the form of holy lineages or personages, who were exempt from the warrior or at least feuding ethos of the tribes (though not from the genealogical manner of conceiving groups, and defining rights and duties). These lineages were the only 'aristocracy' in any permanent sense, for within the ordinary tribes there were only temporary notables, rather than any permanent stratification. The holy lineages however did not combine to form a church or any other kind of large body: like the tribes, whose spiritual shepherds they were, they remained fragmented.

This system differs from European feudalism in kind, but also differs from traditional Middle Eastern society in degree. Though two of the three Maghrebin states were at one time under Ottoman suzerainty, nevertheless the Maghreb never experienced a centralized state as effective as the Ottoman empire was in its heartlands. (Tunisia was probably the most effectively centralized of the traditional North African states.) It did not know a powerful state superimposed on a patchwork of diverse communities, keeping the peace amongst them and extracting taxes from them. Moreover, there was no middle area of oppressed, subdued peasants, intervening between town and tribe. Instead, tribal life extended to the city walls.[1] The relative absence of pluralism and the weakness of the state were perhaps connected: the Maghrebin state was perched precariously on top of a mass of tribal communities which resembled each other, and which indulged in such qualitative diversity as existed only with restraint and discretion, as indicated.

A typical institution within this loose system were the famous moieties, *leff*s or *soff*s, the division of the countryside into two opposed camps, whose balanced power helped to maintain some degree of peace. These divisions could be linked to central government by being articulated in terms of support of rival erstwhile claimants to the throne (as in Tunisia), or on the contrary they could be purely local. My own belief is that under this kind of binary terminology, two quite different types of institution could be found—or perhaps one should say, two polar opposites, with a spectrum of intermediate possibilities. At one end of the spectrum, there was something like a settled sedentary population, in well-defined valleys, with a segmentary organization. In this context, a *leff* system would be a region-wide system of two opposed alliances, differing from the segmentary system (of which it is but a variant) only by a certain number of features: (*a*) One particular level of size of segmentation receives special stress, for the alliance chooses its units at that level. (*b*) The alliance has a chequer-board pattern on the map—neighbors are enemies, but neighbors-but-one are

[1] Cf. E. Burke III, 'Morocco and the Near East. Reflections on some basic differences', *Archives européennes de sociologie*, Vol. x, 1969, No. 2.

allies. (*c*) Being region-wide, the alliance cuts across the genealogical or territorial criteria of the ordinary 'segmentary' pyramids of nested units. (*d*) The system strictly requires (unlike ordinary segmentation) that there should be, at that level, two parties and two parties *only*. In this kind of *leff*, the members of a league are groups (in principle, groups of a certain prescribed size, or rather at a given level of the segmentary ladder), and not individuals.

By contrast, there are what might be called loose *leff*s, which are more likely to arise when, say, nomadism, interference by the central power and partial imposition of government, intrusion by foreigners, or dynastic strife, all jointly or severally disrupt the stability of local groups. In this kind of context, networks of patronage arise, in which patrons and clients exchange protection for support, in a manner more fluid and opportunistic, and less bound by previous kin or territorial designations. In the end, only two such networks survive, by absorbing or eliminating rivalry, and face each other. The situation explored in northeastern Morocco by David Seddon, covering a period when domestic governmental intrusion, rival pretenders and foreign interests were all making their contribution to instability, seems to exemplify this kind of *leff*. Vinogradov's material may exemplify an intermediate position. The distinction I am making is as it were ideal-typical: some opportunism and patronage no doubt also occurred even in highly sedentarized Kabylia or the western High Atlas at the time of conflicts of *soffs* or *leffs*, and kin links were not wholly disregarded in northeast Morocco even at a time of disputed succession. Nevertheless, this distinction between *kinds* of binary political opposition needs to be borne in mind.

How was this system affected by the colonial period and the impact of modernity? It is of course impossible to trace here in detail the varied fate of the three countries, though the contributors do supply concrete and detailed views of specific regions and problems. The Maghreb naturally shared in the diffusion of the well-known general characteristics preceding or accompanying 'modernization'—a population explosion, dissemination of the developmental ideal, selective erosion of old structures, a revaluation of old values, the emergence of partially new elites. More specifically, the agent of modernity in North Africa was initially France. I believe the impact of French culture in North Africa to be profound and permanent. In his heart, the North African knows not merely that God speaks Arabic, but also that modernity speaks French. The Arabic and French cultures share what might be called an imperial or absolutist or world-pervading character—each of them possesses a kind of brilliance which lead them to absorb the souls of those who internalize them, and to fill out their world. In some curious way, for North Africa these two total visions are complementary rather than rivals. (I remember a little chieftain in the Atlas telling me that there were three languages in the world—Arabic, French and Berber.) Unlike Turkey, North Africa does not suffer from any violent conflict between political modernism and religious fundamentalism. As Kenneth Brown's contribution shows, nationalism, fusing modernism and puritanism, could even forge a link between otherwise hostile generations. Nationalism was born of a puritan reforming strain in Islam, and was at its inception hostile to folk religion, which it saw as a perversion of the faith, as L.-J. Duclos reminds us. Its other source of inspiration came to be the French Left, but these two scholastic theologies co-exist with far less tension than one might logically expect. Whatever the explanation, North African elites are relatively homogeneous, as John Waterbury has shown for Morocco[1], and their divisions tend to depend more on the current state of the game and the opportunities it offers, than on any deep, fundamental or ideological splits.

But one major innovation has been brought in by the modern world—the effectiveness of government, as Waterbury, Seddon, Favret, Keenan and others stress. The old stalemate between the central power and tribalism has been overcome. This is all the more striking insofar as many of the older structures survive, not necessarily from inertia, but also because they often find new functions, as Adam and Waterbury demonstrate. But they no longer usurp the political role, though they may take part in the new political game.

On their approaches to modernity, societies need to overcome (at least) two painful humps, the political and the economic—the establishment of effective government and the development of a growing, industrial economy. The classical political philosophers were preoccupied with the first hump, twentieth-century sociologists with the second. Basically, contemporary North Africa has overcome the first, but not the second. Of course there has been some economic growth, even striking growth, but certainly not enough to create a new equilibrium, a viable society, one liberating the masses from shanty-towns or from rural backwaters, which are tolerated but as interim solutions, as Favret and Adam describe. The consequence of political development without adequate economic development has been the situation in which, to simplify a little, there are now two North African dreams—official employment, and labor migration; a job with government or a job abroad . . . Adam, Favret, Alport and Waterbury tell us much about internal economic migration—and about those who stay behind—while Ben Kaddour, Coram, Marais and Quandt describe the competition for political spoils, especially at a higher level.

This brings us back to our central theme, nationality and politics. Neither of the two archetypal experiences of the modern Maghrebi—labor or trade migration, or maneuvering for political administrative position—are likely to lead his thoughts to a new nationalism, to the redrawing of the boundaries of loyalty in terms of a new, hitherto unhighlighted criteria. He experiences either fate qua Maghrebin Muslim, not qua Arab or Berber. The old, narrow, intimate kin or local links may still be of great use and be reactivated for all kinds of purposes, but they are too narrow for some new nationalism; whereas on the wider horizon, a man will inevitably be aware of his identity as a Muslim, impossible to confuse in most cases with a non-Muslim; but in between, in the middle ground, there will be little to attract or retain his attention.[2]

---

[1] Cf. John Waterbury, *The Commander of the Faithful*, London & Chicago, 1969.

[2] I have attempted elsewhere to spell out a theory of modern nationalism, distinguishing it from group loyalties in general, and specifying the criteria which help to determine just where, and within what boundaries, a new nationalism is likely to crystallize. Cf. *Thought and Change*, London & Chicago, 1965, and also Anthony D. Smith, *Theories of Nationalism*, London & New York, 1971.

Thus the cultural boundary which holds his attention is the one which separates him as a Muslim and North African from others with whom he knows himself not to be interchangeable—in other words, anti-colonial nationalism makes sense. This point of course leaves open the question of the *intra-* or *inter-*Maghrebin loyalties. As in most of Africa, the political units inherited from colonialism have maintained themselves. They did not specifically benefit from the considerations adduced in this analysis, though they do benefit from the increased importance of government and of political patronage. But this is a different theme: insofar as they have been hostile to each other, the Maghrebin states have invoked (at most) historical or ideological considerations, but never ethnic ones.

The conclusion—internal ethnic nationalism or irredentism is not a major force in the Maghreb—is hard to demonstrate in the abstract; it can only be documented by concrete individual studies. The contributors to this volume have done just this, for a wide variety of milieux. The consensus, noted by Charles Micaud, may perhaps arouse the reader's suspicions. The unusual spectacle of a large group of historians and social scientists actually in agreement must make one wonder. The nervous reader may feel reassured when he sees, under this overall agreement, ample specific disagreements amongst the contributors. The editors have not sought to impose any homogeneity of view or outlook—merely to present the available facts and ideas. If any viewpoint remains unrepresented, this is certainly not due to any editorial desire to exclude it.

Part 1 The Traditional Base

1

David M. Hart

**The Tribe in Modern Morocco:
Two Case Studies**

I

This paper will examine the nature and role of the tribe and of the concept of tribalism in a 'developing' North African Muslim nation, Morocco. It will discuss the notion of the Moroccan tribe or *qabila* both in general terms and in relation to the wider (and changing) society of which the tribe is part. It will, furthermore, illustrate this discussion with case materials drawn principally from two specific tribal groups, located at opposite ends of the country: the Aith Waryaghar (or the 'Beni Ouriaghel') of the Central Rif (El-Hoceima Province, properly, al-Husaima) and the Ait Atta of the South-Central Atlas, Jbil Saghru mountains and adjacent Saharan oases (Provinces of Beni Mellal, Ouarzazate and Ksar es Souk). These two tribal groups both happen to be Berber-speaking, although their languages are not mutually comprehensible; they are both essentially mountain-dwelling; and they are both highly tribal, in the sense of the word to be employed here. None the less, their responses to the economic, social and political changes set in motion by the French and Spanish Protectorates have been very different; and thus they emerge as two entirely separate points on the available spectrum of tribes and social change.

Before such a discussion can be launched, however, it is appropriate to define what is meant by the term 'tribe'. A standard definition in a text-book of social anthropology states that 'a tribe may be defined as a politically coherent and autonomous group occupying or claiming a particular territory'.[1] This is all very well, as far as it goes, but it asks more questions than it answers, e.g. *how* coherent and *how* autonomous, and what are the relevant factors making for such cohesion and autonomy? No mention, furthermore, is made of the group's relations with similar groups, and with a wider society, such as a central government. Therefore, for present purposes, it can be rejected out of hand.

Equally misleading, for Morocco anyhow, is the French administrative approach, one which has been espoused by at least one American political scientist.[2] This consists of totting up all the named tribal groups on the Moroccan map and simply announcing that there are some 600 of them. Such a procedure displays a fatal ignorance of the *kinds* of units being totted up: for in Morocco a group which is labeled in Arabic as *qabila* or in Berber by the cognate *taqbilt* may range in size from a tiny cluster of hamlets dotting one or two mountain slopes to a huge (though not necessarily amorphous) unit covering most of a whole province or even spilling over into other neighboring provinces.

It is well to begin, therefore, by agreeing with Gellner[3] that all Moroccan (and

[1] *Notes and Queries in Anthropology*, 6th edn., London, 1954, p. 66.
[2] Douglas E. Ashford, *Political Change in Morocco*, Princeton, 1961, p. 186.
[3] Ernest Gellner, 'Saints of the Atlas', in Julian Pitt-Rivers, ed., *Mediterranean Countrymen*, The Hague, 1963, pp. 145–58; and 'Tribalism and social change in North Africa',

indeed all North African and Middle Eastern) tribes are at once characterized by two qualities: *segmentation* and *marginalism*. The first is a structural attribute, and the second a situational one, with respect to the wider non-tribal society of what has become the nation-state in question. The first point was never grasped by the French administration, and the second has only been dimly perceived by most anthropologists (for whom the first principle, on the other hand, is a professional tool), who have, especially in writing on Black Africa and elsewhere, been accustomed to treat tribal systems as final political units more or less islands unto themselves. In a Muslim context, the two factors coexist: tribesmen and non-tribesmen share a common Islamic cultural heritage, and the criterion of relevance here is that tribes have always been extremely aware both of other tribes and of towns and cities, and *vice versa*. In Morocco, they have also always been equally aware of the distinction between 'Arabs' and 'Berbers'. It is these latter considerations that will now be dealt with; and the questions of segmentation and marginalism will then be discussed briefly in the light of the tribe and the wider society.

In 1912, when France and Spain established their respective protectorates over Morocco, the country was cross-cut by three basic axes: (1) an Arab–Berber axis, (2) an urban–tribal axis, and (3) a *makhzan–siba* axis. Each of these will now be considered in turn, in its contributing role to the total structural backdrop.

The first axis, Arab–Berber, is linguistic. Arabic is the national language of the country, but it is only spoken at most by three-fifths of a total population of 13 million. Berber is another language entirely, or rather another group of closely related languages; and in Morocco it is spoken by three different and territorially discontinuous blocks of tribes (Rifians, Middle/Central Atlas Berbers, and Susis). Arabic perforce becomes the means of communication between any member of one of these three groups and a member of another, when it is realized that the three languages are by no means entirely mutually comprehensible (although they have many common elements—the situation is rather like Norwegian, Swedish and Danish). As Bousquet[1] has pointed out, the geographical fractionalization of Berber speech areas across the map of North Africa has always been a barrier not only to linguistic comprehensibility, but even more to any concept of 'Berber nationhood'. Although 'Berber' and 'tribal' are by no means coterminous (given the existence of numerous 'Arab' tribes as well), it is significant that both the Moroccan and the French stereotypes of these terms have, for entirely different reasons in each case, tended to make them so. It is certainly undeniable that Berbers represent, in a 'tribal' sense, the autochthonous as well as the most change-resistant elements of the population; and this is so even when one considers the amazing adaptations on the part of Susi (or Soussi) grocers to a modern economy.[2]

---

in William H. Lewis, ed., *French-Speaking Africa: the Search for Identity*, New York, 1965, pp. 107–18.

[1] G.-H. Bousquet, *Les Berbères*, series 'Que Sais-Je?', No. 718, Paris, 1957, *passim*.

[2] Cf. E. A. Alport, 'The Ammeln', *Journal of the Royal Anthropological Institute*, Vol. 94, Part 2, 1964, pp. 160–71, for a most illuminating discussion of this problem.

The second axis, labeled 'urban-tribal' rather than 'urban-rural' (for it is axiomatic that in Morocco before 1912 'rural' and 'tribal' were one and the same, except for the negroid cultivators, known as Haratin, in the Saharan oases who are probably not tribally organized), is socio-economic. All the cities were and are Arabic-speaking, but the tribes were roughly half and half, with Arabic-speaking groups tending to be nearer the urban centers, and Berber-speaking tribes tending to be further removed from urban influences. With certain exceptions,[1] the generalization of 'Arabs in the Plains; Berbers in the Mountains' still holds good today.

The final axis, *makhzan–siba*, was political in character, and here some contextual explanation is required. The unifying thread through all of Morocco was religious: it was and is Orthodox Sunnite Islam of the Malikite rite (barring a small and largely but not entirely urban Jewish minority). Political power was dynastic and centered in the Sultan (a direct descendant of the Prophet Muhammad) who was in theory the spiritual and temporal head of the whole Moroccan Muslim community. The Sultan was surrounded by a large court and numerous ministers, and by a standing army which also served as a tax-collecting force. As the Sultan, in order to keep the peace in his domain, had to be on the move continuously, crossing tribal territory to get from one urban center to another, the court and the army moved with him. All the urban centers and the predominantly Arab tribal lands surrounding them were entirely under government control; and they were therefore known as *bled el-makhzan*, or government land. The inhabitants of the *bled el-makhzan* not only did not fail to pay taxes to the Sultan when called upon to do so, but furnished the backbone of his army.

In terms of geography, the *bled el-makhzan* covered the Atlantic Coastal Plain and adjacent plains regions of Morocco only, considerably less than half the surface area of the country. Most of what remains in Morocco is either mountains or desert, and virtually all of this was *bled es-siba*, or 'land of dissidence' and 'disorder'. The *bled es-siba* was the reverse side of the coin of the *bled el-makhzan*; and it is noteworthy that both sides explicitly conceptualized themselves and each other in these terms. (In the Rif, for example, the long period of disorder *before* Abd el-Krim was known as the *Ripublik*, or *République*, but the idea behind this concept is exactly the same as that of *bled es-siba*, and it has absolutely nothing to do with and does not in any way refer to Abd el-Krim's own personal creation of a 'Rifian Republican State' in 1923.)[2] The *bled es-siba* was entirely tribal, of course, and most of it happened to be Berber in speech. In it, the Sultan was acknowledged to be *only* the spiritual head of the country, *not* the temporal head; for despite numerous punitive expeditions on an almost annual basis, the free tribesmen in the land of dissidence seldom if ever paid their taxes

[1] At least two such exceptions are the Arabic-speaking Jbala mountaineers in the northwest, and the Bedouins of the Western Sahara. Cf. my articles on both peoples: 'Tribal and place names among the Arabo-Berbers of Northwestern Morocco', *Hespéris-Tamuda*, I, 3, 1960, pp. 457–511; and 'The social structure of the Rgibat Bedouins of the Western Sahara', *Middle East Journal*, xv, 4, 1962, pp. 515–27.

[2] This temporary and wartime measure is referred to by Rifians (and in Arabic) either as *Jibha Rifiya* ('(the) Rifian Front') or as *r-hkam n-Abd r-Krim* ('Abd el-Krim's Command').

to the central government. And two of the core groups in what was *siba* territory are the two mentioned at the beginning of this report, the Aith Waryaghar and the Ait Atta, neither of whom had ever known *makhzan*-established authority before pacification (i.e. by the Spaniards in 1926 in the first instance, and by the French conquest completed in 1933 in the second).

The difference then between *makhzan* and *siba* was essentially one of payment or 'withholding' of taxes; and the polar relationship between these two concepts is without any doubt the central fact of the political sociology of pre-Protectorate Morocco. In a persuasive work by Mohammed Lahbabi,[1] the whole question has been presented as a more or less Rousseauesque situation of 'Social Contract', for one could opt to be within the pale or beyond it (the latter, to use Gellner's expression, through a 'partial opting-out'[2]) and the issue hinged squarely on the parallel notion of 'Government by Consent of the Governed'. Indeed, in the *siba* case, the partial opting-out was socially if not legally recognized by the Sultan himself as Commander of the Faithful, those Faithful who made up the Wider Society.

II

It is now appropriate to consider the relevance of the concepts of segmentation, or segmentary tribalism, and, later, of marginalism, in the light of the foregoing.

The first of these is hardly known, perhaps, outside the field of social anthropology, and it was developed by E. E. Evans-Pritchard, today the senior social anthropologist in England, in his pioneer work *The Nuer* (Oxford, 1940). Of greater import to the present article, however, in his refinement of the concept in a subsequent work on the Bedouin tribes of Cyrenaica:

> Each section of a tribe, from the smallest to the largest, has its shaikh or shaikhs. The tribal system, typical of segmentary structures everywhere, is a system of *balanced opposition between tribes and tribal sections* [our italics] from the largest to the smallest divisions, and there cannot therefore be any single authority in a tribe. *Authority is distributed at every point of the tribal structure* [our italics] and political leadership is limited to situations in which a tribe or a segment of it acts corporately. With a tribe this only happens in war or in dealings with an outside authority which for its own purposes recognizes the tribe as an administrative unit. There cannot, obviously, be any absolute authority vested in a single shaikh of a tribe when the fundamental principle of tribal structure is opposition between its segments, and in such segmentary systems there is no state and no government as we understand these institutions; and criminal law is absent and civil law exists in only a very rudimentary form. *Consequently the exact status of a shaikh can only be defined in terms of a complicated network of kinship ties and structural relations* [our italics]. It is

[1] *Le Gouvernement marocain à l'aube du XXᵉ siècle*, Rabat, 1958, pp. 41 sq.
[2] Ernest Gellner, 'Patterns of rural rebellion in Morocco', *Archives européennes de sociologie*, III, 1962, pp. 297–311.

only necessary here to emphasize that his social position is unformalized and that he must in no sense be regarded as a ruler or administrator. Bedouin respect their shaikhs, but they do not regard them as superiors. Rather, their influence and wealth are considered as capital to be drawn on for the benefit of whoever is in need of them. So long as a shaikhly family can keep their prestige, derived from the strength of their section [i.e. of the tribe], their wealth, their traditional place in Bedouin society, and the character of their leading members, so long only are they regarded as shaikhs of whatever the grade may be.[1]

This passage sums up the characteristics of a segmentary society extremely well, but it needs some explanation for an audience untrained in social anthropology. In the first place, as stated, *all* North African tribes, whether Arab or Berber, are segmentary, and very much so; and a corollary of this is that their segments are usually named or labeled agnatically, in accordance with the prevailing system of patrilineal descent from a common male ancestor (though just as often, too, they may be territorially named and based, even though the segmentary and agnatic principles remain constant and the same). There are of course differences in the nomenclature—an Arabic-speaking tribe may be referred to as *Ulad X* or *Bni X*, 'children' or 'sons' of X, whereas a Berber-speaking one may be referred to correspondingly as *Ait X*, having the same meaning as in the Arabic, as well as that of 'people' of X.

What this means is that X may refer to a common agnatic ancestor, whether or not he is genealogically traceable, or to a place, a tribal point of origin. In both cases, however, the process of subdivision through time and space which is known as segmentation remains the same; and the three basic principles behind it are very easy to grasp. Each tribe, whether bearing the name of a putative common ancestor or that of a traditional point of origin, is segmented into X number of maximal segments or clans (in Morocco, seldom more than five)[2]; each of these is in turn subsegmented into Y number of major segments or subclans; and each of these is in its turn subsegmented into Z number of lineages, which in their turn may themselves be subsegmented again and again and again down to the level of the elementary family of father, mother and unmarried children. The difference between a *clan* and a *lineage* is that in the former, its members recognize descent from a given (patrilineal or agnatic) ancestor but are not capable of tracing such descent step by step, genealogically; whereas in the latter, always a smaller group in number of living members, such descent is *always* traceable, by definition. *Subclans* occur when a clan itself subdivides or

---

[1] E. E. Evans-Pritchard, *The Sanusi of Cyrenaica*, Oxford, 1949, pp. 59–60.

[2] For a discussion of the function and significance of five primary segments into Moroccan tribal group, see my articles, 'Emilio Blanco Izaga and the Berbers of the Central Rif', *Tamuda*, VI, 2, 1958, pp. 171–237, and 'Clan, lignage et communauté locale dans une tribu rifaine', in *Douars et centres ruraux*, special issue of *Revue marocaine de géographie*, No. 8, 1965, pp. 25–33. A later elaboration of 'five fifths' as a structural and ideological principle is also to be found in my 'Segmentary systems and the role of "five fifths" in tribal Morocco', *Revue de l'occident musulman et de la Méditerranée*, III, 1, 1967, pp. 35–65.

segments into two or more sub-units from the ancestors of which descent is likewise not genealogically traceable.

The second basic principle of the system is that of balance and opposition between segments, a principle which parallels, on a very much smaller scale, the 'balance of power' concept of political science. It may be put this way: although the descendants of two brothers, A and B, may fight against each other, they join together if attacked by the descendants of that brother's cousin, C, because, although A, B and C all go back to the same agnatic ancestor D, none the less A and B are more closely related to each other than either one of them is to C. In other words, the same principle which separates segments at a lower level joins them together at a higher one; and an Arab proverb expresses this very concretely: 'I against my brothers; my brothers and I against our cousins; my cousins and brothers and I against the world.'

This brings up the third basic principle in classical segmentary systems: the extreme diffusion of political authority, what John Middleton and David Tait, in their *Tribes Without Rulers* (London, 1958) have referred to as 'acephaly'. In most segmentary societies, balance and opposition between segments is the primary element for maintenance of order in the absence of an organized or centralized chieftainship. And, as already indicated in the passage from Evans-Pritchard, an Arab shaikh may be technically a 'chief', but he is in fact only a *primus inter pares*. Elections were held annually for clan chiefs of Berbers in the Central Atlas, and even for top chiefs of the whole tribe amongst the Ait Atta. But these top chiefs were only elected in wartime and they could easily be impeached for bad conduct before their year's term of office was up—for political power lay essentially in the hands of the tribal or clan council, itself by definition an acephalous body. Balance and opposition between segments implies egalitarianism between them as well, and egalitarianism is such a marked feature of the Berber social system in general that the competition, in the Rif, for instance, between council-members of equal standing at the clan or tribal level was savage indeed, manifesting itself principally in a tremendously complicated network of inter- (and even intra-) lineage bloodfeuds and inter-clan warfare.

Given a segmentary system with a resulting diffusion of political authority, loyalty and cohesion, at any level of segmentation, are conditioned by the next level above it, for the external enemy is the agent of cohesion. Thus a lineage can only exist as against other lineages of the same order of segmentation, a clan can only exist as against other clans of the same order, and a tribe can only exist as against other tribes. Balance, opposition and distribution of authority at all levels are maintained more or less consistently throughout the system.

In this sense, then, loyalties are expressed in an expanding series of concentric circles: the individual in his elementary family, this family within the lineage, the lineage within the subclan, the subclan within the clan, and the clan within the tribe (as Evans-Pritchard pointed out in *The Nuer*). Any loyalty therefore is directly relevant to membership in the group involved in a given situation of conflict and to the size of this group. Complete division of a household may separate full brothers, while agnatic cousins may fight over boundaries in a field; two agnatic lineages may come to blows over rights to irrigation water separating or dividing such fields; and two villages or two subclans, say, may fire shots over priority use of pasture or grazing lands held in common. And most important of all, such a system of concentric segmentary circles minimizes the need for leadership, especially amongst Berber tribes, where one finds invariably either councils or annually elected and rotating chiefs, or both. In Arab tribes the upper-level shaikhs generally come from certain specific lineages or clans, and to this extent chieftainship is hereditary; but the chief is still little more (barring certain exceptions) than the No. 1 man in his own peer group, with the others all right behind him. It is not much of an oversimplification to say that, in general, the names which are 'remembered' in Moroccan tribal leadership, such as Muha u-Hammu of the Middle Atlas Zayan, Abd el-Krim of the Aith Waryagher in the Rif, and the Grand Caids of the Western Atlas (the Gundafi, the Mtuggi and the Glawi) were men who catapulted into power through external conditions or threats, and once such power was in their hands, they were opportunistic enough to hold onto it. Under normal circumstances (and this is so even today), the diffusion of power, leadership and authority is very great indeed. A 'leader' in a local lineage context may be quite submerged in a clan context, and a clan leader may be equally submerged in a tribal context. It is for this reason that when one asks about 'tribal leadership' or 'who were or are leaders', one is given a plethora of names; and it is very rare that a single individual stands out. The result is that most of them are in effect ciphers who cancel each other out (in Berber regions in particular), and one is back where one started, with segmentary systems and their concomitants of balance, opposition and acephaly.

III

Above and beyond the previous considerations, and before a discussion of the question of marginalism, each tribe has a given name and a given territory; and each clan within the tribe has its own corresponding name and corresponding sub-territory, so that the overall system of tribal land ownership[1] is in effect nothing but the segmentary system—which is genealogically conceived, in terms of time—flopped down spatially onto the ground.

The linguistic axis of Arab–Berber cuts across certain features of the tribal system already referred to: many Arabic-speaking tribes, for instance, conceive of themselves as descended from common ancestors, but some (particularly in the northwestern mountains of Jbala and Ghmara) are built up on a toponomy principle, with *heterogeneous clans* having merely come in and occupied territory which eventually became that of the tribe in question. The same is true of Berber tribes: those in the northern Rif[2] and those in the southern Western Atlas,

[1] The internal dichotomy within a clan or village between individually-owned gardens or orchards and collectively-owned pastureland is only of incidental relevance to the present discussion.

[2] Cf. Hart, op. cit. The principle of heterogeneous clans holds true for all of the tribal regions of the Moroccan North, without exception, including the Aith Waryaghar of the Rif.

Anti-Atlas and Sous regions[1] tend as well to be organized on the heterogeneous clan principle; while those in the Middle, Central and Eastern Atlases tend to be organized on the principle of *common ancestry*.[2]

There are thus two principles of definition involved in the classification of the *type* of segmentation of Moroccan tribes. Both of these depend on the base-level conception the tribesmen in question have of themselves: whether their group is held together through primarily territorial considerations (i.e. heterogeneous clans) or whether the principle of common agnatic ancestry is dominant. As we shall see, the Rifian Aith Waryaghar fall into the first category and the southern Berbers of Ait Atta into the second; and under the one a Moroccan tribal system is fully as segmentary as under the other.

In general terms, an economic correlation can be made here, as Montagne came close to pointing out, in a brilliant if often wrong-headed study many years ago.[3] It is this: that the bulk of the tribes, whether Arabic- or Berber-speaking, which are organized on the heterogeneous-clan principle are sedentary agriculturists who live the year round in fixed houses, while the bulk of those organized on the common-ancestor principle, again whether Arab or Berber, are either transhumant or fully nomadic. (By 'transhumant', a useful word which has crept into the Anglo-Saxon anthropological lexicon from the French, is meant that the people in question make two well-defined moves per year: up into the mountains to pasture their sheep and live in tents during the spring, and back into the lower valleys where their permanent houses are located, in the autumn.)

However, it should be borne in mind that since all Moroccan tribes are segmentary structures, they all, whether settled, transhumant or nomadic, have clan and lineage segments as common vertical characteristics in time, while the horizontal territorial counterparts of these, in space, are either villages or camping units, or (for transhumant groups) both.

Another feature common to most if not all Moroccan tribes is the existence, in their midst, of resident holy men (most not only claiming descent from the Prophet but possessing genealogical evidence, either written in Arabic or in their heads, to back up this claim, which in some cases is manifestly false) who form lineages or even whole clans apart from the tribal lay community. The job of these holy lineages is the arbitration of conflicts (for which their members receive suitable 'perks' either through a portion of the fines imposed, or through donations and offerings), both inside and outside the tribe. Such conflicts, in tribal Morocco before the Protectorate, were very much the order of the day.

It can be, and has been, argued that feuds and wars, far from promoting a disintegration of segmentary systems, provided in fact a major stimulus to keep them going;[4] and this state of affairs led French and Spanish investigators of a

[1] An excellent example is the Seksawa, studied in depth by Jacques Berque. Cf. his *Structures sociales du Haut Atlas*, Paris, 1955, *passim*. The Ammeln, studied by Alport, op. cit., in less detail, seem to exhibit the same clan heterogeneity.

[2] Exceptions in the Central and South Central Atlas (and adjacent Saharan oasis regions) are Ait Bu Gmaz, Ait Siddrat and Ait Murghad.

[3] Robert Montagne, *Les Berbères et le makhzen dans le sud du Maroc*, Paris, 1930, pp. 149, 181 (note 1).

[4] William H. Lewis, 'Feuding and social change in Morocco', *Journal of Conflict*

generation ago to categorize tribal systems as systems of 'organized anarchy'.[1] This is hardly the right label, for anarchy implies a total lack of government, but these observers, in their own way, were nevertheless on the right track. They would have been very much more so, however, if they had realized, which they did not, that such 'organized anarchy' is nothing more nor less than the diffusion of political power inherent in all segmentary societies. However, as the notion of segmentation was quite unfamiliar to them, they had to grope along with the conceptual tools at their command.

Another observation can be made here:[2] nomadic and transhumant tribes tend to engage in *inter*-tribal warfare and to keep their conflicts externalized to this extent, while amongst sedentary tribes feuds were generally *intra*-tribal in character, and conflicts were internal. In the Rif, for example, each tribe was literally split in half, and when the two halves were not fighting against each other, feuding continued just as intensively on a lower level, among the lineages of a single clan, for instance, some on one side and some on the other. (One lineage, usually a humble one of little account, generally remained neutral and buried the dead of each of the feuding groups.)

This splitting in half of whole tribes for purposes of alliance and war is called *leff*, and the moieties thereby created in each tribe are in essence *one* variant form of the segmentary system. They must *not*, however, be confused *with* segmentary systems; and although Montagne[3] worked out a checkerboard-style system of *leff* alliances for the whole of the Western Atlas and the Anti-Atlas, his *leff*-theory, which was not based on the concept of segmentation, was greatly hampered because it could not explain why or how conflict could occur *within* each *leff*. The Rifian system as I have described it[4] differed from the Western Atlas system as described by Montagne in that each tribe was a terminal unit unto itself, in effect. It was only the neighboring clans of neighboring tribes who could be drawn into conflict with or against one or other of the moieties of the warring tribe; and these neighboring clans provided the outer limits of each system, which I conceive as a series of interlocking concentric circles, a very different phenomenon from the Montagne checkerboard analogy, which theoretically had *no* limits (although it certainly had in fact). Alliances of this type in any case

---

Resolution, Vol. 5, No. 1, 1961, pp. 43–54, in which abundant reference is made to D. M. Hart, 'An ethnographic survey of the Rifian tribe of Aith Waryaghar', *Tamuda*, II, 1, 1954, pp. 51–86. However, the classic exposition of this thesis is contained in Max Gluckman, *Custom and Conflict in Africa*, Oxford, 1959, Ch. 1, 'The Peace in the Feud'.

[1] Robert Montagne, *La Vie sociale et la vie politique des Berbères*, Paris, 1931, p. 74; and Col. Emilio Blanco Izaga, *Conferencia sobre Derecho Consuetudinario Rifeño*, unpublished mss., 1935. At present, I have assembled and translated the writings, published and unpublished, of Col. Blanco on Rifian social structure, to be published as a separate monograph and as an outgrowth of my earlier article, op. cit., on the same subject.

[2] This and the previous generalization about the principle of heterogeneous clans as opposed to that of common ancestry are both taken from my unpublished lecture given in 1963 to members of the Smith-Mundt Foundation entitled 'Tribalism: the skeleton in the Moroccan closet'.

[3] Montagne, op. cit., 1930, *passim*.

[4] Hart, op. cit.

2

seem to have been confined to sedentary agricultural mountain tribes (Rif, Western Atlas, Anti-Atlas); and alliances elsewhere assumed far more of an *ad hoc* character.

In this system of what can now be discerned to be *armed* opposition between in principle equal segments, only the lineages whose members practiced despised trades (blacksmiths, minstrels, etc.) as well as only the holier of the holy men, refrained from fighting; the rank and file, as it were, of the holy clans fought themselves, though not as a rule with outsiders. The holier holy men, in their white robes and the emanation of their *baraka*, the 'blessing' God gave them to endow them with their ability as miracle-workers (an ability not possessed by the rank and file), lived up to the prestigious status and role ascribed to them by the community by seeing to it that feuds and wars were interrupted by seasonal truces for harvesting, etc. At the same time, however, they received a healthy 'rake-off' through annual offerings from their constituents as well as (in the Rif) a cut off the top when fines for murder were imposed by the tribal council. (The saints could not exist without the lay tribesmen, and *vice versa*. Gellner describes the situation very well by saying that in a Moroccan tribal context, *vox dei* is in reality *vox populi*,[1] for saints are 'elected', in a long-drawn-out process lasting over generations, by the tribal community where they reside and operate.)

IV

Murder, in Moroccan tribal society, under certain controllable circumstances, was indeed punished (though tribal society had no jails and little or nothing which in the West would be recognized as 'law enforcement'). This point, to which we will return, brings up another important feature of tribal organization all over Morocco, the institution of the *souk*, or weekly market. Almost every tribal group in the country (except for very small groups which may share a market) has its own market; and the word *souk* (Arabic *suq*) in each case is followed by the name of the day of the week on which it is held and then by the name of the tribe or clan in question. Market day before Independence could be any day of the week, but since the resistance in the early 1950s, Friday markets have been proscribed by the Istiqlal as being contrary to the spirit of the Muslim day of rest. Market day is for social intercourse as well as trade. In any market, tribesmen see friends and fellow-tribesmen, and even people from neighboring tribes, and exchange news. Above all, market day is a day of peace. The tribal or clan council meets in or near the market to see that the peace is kept, and also to deliberate on issues that have come up during the week. Thus the market has a political function. Very often associated with a market, too, is a saint's tomb where donations may be made or oaths sworn.

Markets vary greatly in size according, generally, to (1) whether they serve merely one or two clans or act as points of exchange for several tribes jointly, and (2) the population density of the area in which they are located. Generally, also,

[1] Ernest Gellner, *Saints of the Atlas*, London & Chicago, 1969.

all objects bought and sold (animals, vegetables, fruits, utensils, etc.) in a market are located in the same place every week, especially since the French and Spanish Protectorates converted markets into effective points of tribal control.[1] Before protectorate times, the site of a market showed little or nothing to indicate its character as a market; but when the Spaniards established their *interventor* posts and the French their Affaires Indigènes bureaux at tribal market sites, a natural result was that permanent shops began to be built all along the four edges of the market site itself, which thus became more or less walled in, even though in the open air. Slaughterhouses were built, and with the improvement of overland communications, there is scarcely a market in Morocco today which cannot be reached by truck or even by bus.

In the flatter regions where markets are large (Atlantic Coastal Plain, Zemmour region between Rabat and Meknes, Eastern Rif around Nador, etc.) many markets have today grown into what Troin calls 'rural centers'[2] in which the accent on surrounding shops is now almost as strong as it is on the market itself. But such rural centers are not as yet characteristic of most of the mountain markets, either in the Central Rif or in the Central Atlas, a fact which is certainly partly a result of geography. Berber mountaineers in general are still more 'tribally oriented' than Arab plainsmen, and the tribal system in the mountains has certainly undergone less change.

However, it is a mistake to assume, for instance, that any tribal group is autarchic or economically self-sufficient, for both the segmentary system and the traditional place of the tribe in the wider society have always militated against this. An extreme case is provided by the Ait Abdi, Berber transhumants of the Kusar Plateau, the roof of Morocco at an altitude of 11,000 feet in the Central Atlas. They have almost no agriculture, only sheep, goats and camels (which they keep on the ground floors of their homes during the winter), they are snowed in on their plateau for a long period each year, and during the summer they scurry back and forth to markets down below, selling their very good sheep for grain reserves which they transport on their camels back to the plateau before the winter sets in.

As Mikesell has convincingly demonstrated, each market has four main functions: (1) distribution of local products, (2) exchange of rural surplus or specialties for urban goods, (3) circulation of articles such as pottery and millstones from villages which specialize in making them, and (4) dissemination of foreign imports. The large markets differ from the smaller in their greater stress on the latter functions and are generally located, moreover, at the convergence of communication lines and on the frontiers of complementary production zones.[3]

---

[1] For a penetrating analysis of this point, see Walter Fogg, 'Villages, tribal markets and towns: some considerations concerning urban development in the Spanish and international zones of Morocco', *The Sociological Review*, XXXII, 1940, pp. 85–107.

[2] J.-F. Troin, 'Une nouvelle génération de centres ruraux au Maroc: les agglomérations commerciales' and 'Excursions: trois exemples de centres ruraux en pays Zemmour', in *Douars et centres ruraux* conference volume, *Revue de géographie du Maroc*, No. 8, 1965, pp. 109–17, 118–32.

[3] Marvin W. Mikesell, *Northern Morocco: a Cultural Geography*, University of California Publications in Geography, No. 14, Berkeley & Los Angeles, 1961, p. 91.

(The foreign imports have of course decreased greatly in Morocco since Mikesel wrote, but his analysis holds good even so.)

To return now to the socio-political character of markets, Benet is thoroughly justified in referring, for instance, to Berber markets in the highlands as 'explosive'.[1] Reference has already been made to the fact that market day in a feuding society was the one day of peace during the week. In the Rif, any man who murdered another on any of the paths leading to the market, on market day, had to pay not only blood money to his victim's agnates (which the latter generally did not accept, preferring to take vengeance either on the person of the murderer or on that of one of his own agnatic kinsmen), but in addition a prohibitively heavy fine to the tribal council. This fine was split up equally amongst the council-members of the clans to whom the market belonged. And if the murder was committed in the market itself, the fine was doubled, because the peace of the market had been 'broken', as Berbers say. If a murderer was unable to pay, the councillors descended upon him in a body, burned his house, cut down his trees and confiscated his livestock. Not only this, but he himself had to flee to another tribe to escape the wrath of his victim's kinsmen.[2]

Woundings, too, were fined accordingly, and the council also imposed fines for the theft of livestock (although in the Rif theft of animals was as uncommon as murder was common; it is far more current in the Central Atlas, where sheep abound, and where, too, the mode of proof or trial by collective oath reached its greatest development, as will shortly be shown). The council, among Rifians and Western Atlas Berbers, was the body politic, and an acephalous one in that no one member of it was deemed superior to any other, though individual members often tried to become so. Before the advent of Abd el-Krim in the one area and of the Glawi in the other—both of whom exemplified Montagne's thesis of the 'rise to personal power'[3]—decision-making never rested in the hands of a single individual, and segmentary self-help prevailed. In all the sedentary tribal regions, political power tended to be extremely diffuse and de-centralized; and generally speaking, it was only amongst certain rural Arab groups that a *caid* could 'eat' a whole tribe. Amongst the Berber transhumants of the Middle and Central Atlas, a totally different system obtained, but the end result was the same extreme diffusion. Here there were annual elections of chiefs in which the clan whose turn it was to provide the chief that year would remove itself from the other assembled clans, whose members did the electing. This system was discovered by Gellner and labeled by him 'rotation and complementarity': if one year it was A's turn to provide the chief, B, C, D and E did the electing; the next year, when B's turn came up, A, C, D and E did the electing; the following year, when C's turn arrived, A, B, D and E elected, and

[1] Francisco Benet, 'Explosive markets: the Berber highlands', in Karl Polanyi, Conrad M. Arensberg and Harry W. Pearson, *Trade and Market in the Early Empires*, Glencoe, 1957, pp. 188–217.
[2] Cf. Hart, op. cit., 1954. The Rifian tribe of the Aith Waryaghar is also the center of a phenomenon unique in Morocco, that of women's markets which men may not attend; but these fall outside the purview of this article.
[3] Montagne, op cit., 1930.

so on.[1] The Ait Atta are a noteworthy case in point, in their annual elections for top chief which were held in their 'capital' at Igharm Amazdar in the Jbil Saghru until 1927;[2] but even here it often seems to have been the case that the top chief was activated only in wartime (though opinions differ), and both annual rotation and the penalty of immediate dismissal for any abuse of power are indications of the essentially ephemeral character of the office.

V

Certain institutional differences between Arabic and Berber speakers have by now begun to emerge, and it is useful to consider a few more. In cases of suspected murder and suspected theft, an Arabic-speaking tribesman had to take oath in the mosque on the Koran to attest his innocence. A Berber from the Rif also took (and takes) oath in the mosque on the Koran in the same way, but before Abd el-Krim (who between 1921 and 1926 was responsible, as I have indicated,[3] for changing a great deal of Rifian custom), he did so with 5 of his close agnatic kinsmen (making 6 co-jurors in all) for minor matters and with 11 close kinsmen (making 12 co-jurors in all) in a case of suspected murder; and if the homicide involved men of different tribes, the party under suspicion had to produce 50 co-jurors. A Berber from the Central Atlas had to produce 10 co-jurors (himself and 9 agnates) in case of theft,[4] and 40 (himself and 39 agnates, some of whom he generally had to obtain from nearby lineage groups through sacrifice) in case of murder; but the difference here was that oaths were always sworn at saints' tombs in front of a lay oath-administrator, and never on the Koran. Oath-takings by their very nature were an extremely public affair, and if the plaintiff at the oath requested it, onlookers often heckled the accused and his co-jurors in order to trip them up. If the defendant or any of his agnates failed to pronounce or repeat the oath correctly, it became as 'broken' as the Rifian markets above, and he had to pay. Some tribes in this region even had Supreme Courts of Appeal, the Ait Atta being an outstanding example; and two further refinements of the system were (1) the existence of accusing as well as of denying oaths, and (2) the privilege available to a man who became angry with his own lineage-mates of changing to another lineage and thus another co-jurant group by sacrificing a sheep, without losing his property rights in his lineage of origin.

The Moroccan tribal world was and is very definitely a man's world in which women took and take little or no part, at least on the surface. None the less, the division of labor by sex is very unequal: women work far harder and longer than men do; and in the realm of magic—potions, poisons, etc.—their influence is of

[1] Gellner, op. cit., 1963.

[2] Capt. Georges Spillmann, *Les Ait Atta du Sahara et la pacification du Haut Dra*, Publications de l'Institut des Hautes Etudes Marocaines, XXIX, Rabat, 1936, pp. 55, 61.

[3] Hart, op. cit., 1954, 1958, 1965.

[4] These 10 agnates also accompanied their kinsman in ritual flight to an enemy tribe if he had murdered somebody in his own tribe; but they returned home after three days to treat for peace. If the victim's kin refused to accept blood money, the murderer had to stay in exile forever.

course tremendous. In the social structure, women, handed around in marriage from one lineage to the next within a given clan, or, more rarely, given to their agnatic cousins in their own lineage, or married out into another clan or tribe, provided links of alliance in which they themselves, being passive instruments of policy, had little or no choice or voice—and these links were continuously reinforced through subsequent marriages. The Koran, for instance, says that daughters inherit half what sons do, and it absolutely forbids a wife to divorce her husband, who on the other hand can divorce *her* with ease. The situation with respect to divorce is entirely unilateral, but divorce is not in fact as common as might be expected, nor, for that matter, are polygamous marriages; the great bulk of Moroccan tribesmen are monogamous, largely for economic reasons if for no other, even though they are permitted as many as four wives. But Berbers in the Central Atlas show two variants here, which in the long run actually balance each other out: wives in some tribes (Ait Atta, Ait Hadiddu) may divorce their husbands (in the Ait Hadiddu no strings are attached, but in the Ait Atta the husbands may forbid their ex-wives to remarry a set number of men with whom they suspect the wives of having carried on)—but the balance is made up in inheritance. Here daughters get nothing at all; and in fact, if there are no sons, the brothers of the deceased, after his widow gets her customary one-eighth of the inheritance or after she is remarried to a younger brother (a common practice both in the Rif and amongst the Ait Atta), take over his daughters lock, stock and barrel.

VI

Such in general terms was the fabric of tribal society in Morocco before 1912, and only one final point needs to be made before the picture is brought up to date. This concerns the marginalism of Moroccan tribes, and the tribal relationship to the wider society. The tribes themselves, first of all, are thoroughly aware of their own marginal position, and they always have been. The most characteristic expression of this awareness (particularly among Berbers) was their partial but voluntary opting out of the wider political system, as discussed above: dissidence through unwillingness to pay the Sultan's taxes. The tribes were and are, again, fully aware of their own place on the spectrum of, so to speak, dissident tribe—tax-paying tribe—town—city—central government; and today this kind of awareness is stronger than ever before. What Halpern says in a rather different (but none the less Moroccan) context applies equally well to the tribe and the wider society at the present time:

> Is a man born in Fes to give his first loyalty to his wife and children (to one wife or to several, to his daughters no less than his sons), or to his father, his tribe, to Fes, to Morocco, to the king, to the Istiqlal Party, or to its offshoot the National Union of Popular Forces, to North Africa, to France, to the Arabs, to Islam, to God, to humanity, to himself alone? This problem never arose with such scope and complexity before the modern age. The hierarchy

of loyalties was clear. Ideally, and usually also in practice, it began with one's loyalty to the head of the family, who determined the next link. New loyalties are in competition, and the nation itself, even in the Middle East's sovereign states, remains a promise rather than fulfillment.[1]

The above may be 'jumping the gun', to some extent, for what is to follow, but in pre-1912 Morocco it is very clear that in the tribal regions the widest terminal loyalty was to the widest agnatic group, in this series of concentric circles, which was capable of corporate action; and it was seldom if ever that such a group embraced any unit wider than the tribe itself. It is also significant that operationally such a group was generally restricted to the clan within the tribe or the lineage within the clan, according to the segmentary context of the conflict. Today, immediate terminal loyalties are equally narrow; but the wider loyalties have been brought more into a national framework, mainly because administration by higher authorities has caused compartmentation. It is worth while to consider how this came about, as the tribal picture is brought up to date.

In the North Zone, because Abd el-Krim, who later became something of a nationalist hero, had already introduced very considerable changes amongst the tribes of the Rif—outlawing feuds, knocking out the feuding pillboxes which formerly stood near every house, decollectivizing oaths, etc.—so that the Spaniards, after his surrender to the French in 1926, merely took over where he left off. As he himself had been a *qadi*, or Muslim judge, he had substituted the Sharia (Muslim Law) in every domain where custom had previously reigned supreme, and the Spanish administration merely perpetuated the reforms he had introduced. The French, however, magnified the differences between Arabs and Berbers in their much larger zone to the point where, in 1930 with the promulgation of the famous Berber Dahir, Divide-and-Rule seemed to become official policy. This policy confirmed and stressed the differences between Berber custom (as manifested through such institutions as collective oaths, priority rights of agnates over land and women, the special treatment accorded to both inheritance and divorce laws, etc.) and Muslim law. Thus the Berber Dahir and what it stood for was the real impetus to Arab nationalism in Morocco, a nationalism which eventually embraced Berbers as well.

This nationalism, over the course of the next two decades, became more and more articulate in the cities; but in the Atlas mountains, French army officers saw to it that Berber custom was kept in the Deep Freeze, and that the tribesmen themselves, through their *caids*, were kept in isolation. In the Spanish Zone, aside from the Spanish Civil War, which Rifian troops virtually won for Franco, the situation was essentially the same; and nationalism remained an ugly urban phenomenon.

One point of significance should be made about the administrative framework of both protectorates: the *caids*, all of them, whether Berber or Arab, *primi inter pares* in their own tribes, were frozen by the protectorate authorities at the top of the tribal political ladder, so to speak. Their opposite numbers, the French

[1] Manfred Halpern, *The Politics of Social Change in the Middle East and North Africa*, Princeton, 1963, pp. 200–1.

and Spanish army captains, were on the other hand at the bottoms of their own administrative ladders, whose tops reached back to Rabat and Tetuan, the two protectorate capitals where the French and Spanish proconsuls were located, respectively. There were thus two quite separate chains of command, with the bottom of one parallel to the top of the other; but they did not touch. This situation was to be radically altered after independence.

The nationalist storm, of course, broke in the cities in the early 1950s, led by the Istiqlal Party with the support of a large detribalized urban proletariat—a proletariat which, ever since 1936 and the security of the *Pax Gallica*, had been increasing by leaps and bounds.[1] It did not, however, spread to the countryside until mid-1955, almost the eve of independence. The French, right up to the very end, believed implicitly in a myth of their own making: that the Berbers— who were all assumed to be under the dictatorial command of the Glawi, the head of the Glawa tribe in the Western Atlas and the French-created Pasha of Marrakesh as well—would remain loyal to them. Yet on 1 October 1955, it was Berbers from the Igzinnayen in the Moroccan Army of Liberation in the Rif who simultaneously attacked the three French outposts of Aknul, Burid and Tizi Usli; and within two months, the Glawi himself, now repentant, about-faced and declared his loyalty to King Muhammad V, who soon returned to Rabat, amid immense acclaim, from exile in Madagascar. This was, ironically, the Glawi's last act before his death, which occurred before the year was out.

VII

With the granting by France of Independence to Morocco in 1956 (Spain reluctantly had to follow suit in her zone), one of the first things that happened, naturally enough, was that the Berber Dahir of 1930 was rescinded. The title of *caid* was still retained in the rural areas; but now, after the transfer of power in 1956, the incumbents were Moroccan government employees from the newly-created Ministry of the Interior in Rabat. Besides being, as a rule, representatives of the new elite rather than members of the tribe itself, they served both as local *caids* and as tribal administrators, the latter posts having been formerly held by French or Spanish army officers or civil controllers.

It should be noted that in both protectorates, very few of the local *caids* who had been appointed by France and Spain survived the transfer of power after independence; their jobs were given to loyal servitors of the nationalist movement. Furthermore, the effective integration of the ex-Spanish Zone, the North Zone, into the rest of the country was not accomplished until 1958; and in 1956, of course, Rabat and not Tetuan became the capital.

In the new and now single chain of command in the tribal areas, the highest local official was now the shaikh, usually not a tribal headman but the headman of only a single clan or group of clans within the tribe. The tribal *caid* had been eliminated as a vestige of colonialism, and a newer, younger and generally

---

[1] Robert Montagne *et al.*, *La Naissance du prolétariat morocain : enquête collective, 1948–1950*, Cahiers de l'Afrique et de l'Asie, III, Paris, 1950.

urbanized Moroccan, with some training in bureaucratic technique, took his place. This fact not only tended to bring the tribes more within the orbit of the central government in Rabat (even though, paradoxically, it had been France and to a lesser extent Spain that had effectively *conquered* tribal Morocco), but it also tended to reduce those situations in which a whole tribe, *qua* tribe, could act corporately. Now, under the shaikh as the highest local or tribal official, there was only the village *mqaddim*.

This was, as Gellner has suggested,[1] an administrative change of crucial importance, and its most tangible result was perhaps that through a now unified chain of command, a tribal *shaikh* or *mqaddim*, had a pipeline back to Rabat which he had never had earlier. If he had a friend at court, his position was of course strengthened. Thus the whole tribal system was drawn into the arena of national politics, and the first manifestation of this, one which was to have very important repercussions in the tribal areas, was that everybody enthusiastically espoused the cause of the Istiqlal Party which had been so instrumental in gaining independence for Morocco.

But the Istiqlal, then the major and now the senior political party in the country, was not to retain an uncontested dominance; and within two years the pluralistic heritage of Moroccan society at large came to the fore once again. For a number of reasons, centering mostly around maladministration and insufficient representation at court, a disenchantment with the Istiqlal, particularly strong in Berber-speaking areas, became general in 1958. By early in the following year two other major parties had emerged, the National Union of Popular Forces and the Popular Movement. Both of these gained numerous adherents amongst Berbers, especially the latter party, to all appearances primarily a Berber Party and headed by Mahjub Ahardan from Oulmes (properly Ulmas) in the Middle Atlas. By 1963 the Popular Movement had merged with one or two lesser parties to form a right-wing coalition backing the monarchy and the 1962 Constitution, which were then under attack from both the Istiqlal and the National Union of Popular Forces. As the *leff* alliances in Berber tribal systems had done, the alliances and emphases of the newer political parties had shifted, and every change in governmental composition became yet another round of 'musical chairs'.

The effects of these various phenomena will be considered in more detail further on, as they apply to the Aith Waryaghar of the Rif and to the Ait Atta of the South-Central Atlas. It is only necessary to emphasize here that in the tribal regions present-day party cleavages almost always follow traditional lines, which were generally local manifestations of the segmentary system.

The post-independence period has also seen the creation of the so-called 'rural communes', some 800 of them over all of Morocco. The object of these communes, a creation of the Ministry of the Interior dating from 1958, appears at least in part to be an avowed substitution of this new administrative unit for the tribe as a focus of local loyalty, intended to undermine the whole tribal system. However, one reason this intention has failed thus far is that boundaries

---

[1] Gellner. 'Patterns of rural rebellion in Morocco during the early years of Independence', *European Journal of Sociology*, 1962. Reproduced as Chapter 19 of this book (pp. 361–74).
2*

of communes often follow clan borders, or even borders those of the tribe itself, if it is small. It should be noted that clans were inappropriately called 'fractions' by the protectorate governments, an error that persists even today. Each commune has its head, assisted by one or two *khalifas*, and a variable number of communal council members from each of the constituent clans, depending on its size. It is in charge of maintaining tribal markets, collecting the tithe for the poor which is one of the five 'pillars' of Islam, and building bridges, drinking fountains, minor roads, and other public works within the commune territory. Since present-day Moroccan administration calls for separation of powers, heads of communes are in no way subject to the new *caids*, who themselves are not subject to the rural *qadis*, or Muslim judges, serving under the Ministry of Justice.

The effectiveness of the rural commune scheme has so far been only moderate, greatest perhaps in the Atlantic Coastal Plains and least in the Rif and in the Central Atlas, where Berber speech, Berber tribalism and Berber values still prevail, even though custom is no longer king. This is not to imply that individual communes in Berber regions have not made considerable local improvements; but it is safe to say that it will be many years before the idea of commune supplants that of tribe or clan in these regions.

Under the French, officers of the corps of the Affairs Indigènes studied the Berber language for as many hours per week, sometimes, as they did Arabic, in the old Institut des Hautes Etudes Marocaines in Rabat; and as a reaction, for several years after independence 'Berber' in Rabat was considered a dirty word.[1] This is no longer so, however, and French-educated Berbers in particular point to their origins with great pride. Even educated Moroccan Arabs have now come to admit, albeit somewhat grudgingly, that the Berber base of the Maghreb is what gives the area its uniqueness *vis-à-vis* the rest of the Arab world.

Last but not least, the post-independence period has been characterized by a series of tribal revolts, all of which, very significantly, have taken place in areas of Berber speech: in the Tafilalt in 1956–57, in the Rif in 1958–59, and in the Central Atlas in 1960. None have occurred, as yet, since then; but this fact underscores the 'developing' character of Moroccan society, for rural and tribal political attitudes in the new national framework are of a 'wait and see' variety. They depend just as much on a rise in the price of sugar, for instance—since heavily-sugared green mint tea is the national beverage—as on provincial underadministration or maladministration. As Gellner has remarked,[2] these revolts have seemed in some ways inexplicable: the one in the Rif was in part a result of underadministration, so Rifians say (though inadequate governmental representation was certainly another cause, and very closely linked to this); and the one in the Central Atlas was proclaimed in favor of Abdallah Ibrahim, who happened at the very time to be Prime Minister. These are not in any sense nativistic or revitalization movements, and although they have occurred in just those areas where dissidence and non-payment of taxes to the central govern-

---

[1] For an excellent exposition of this phenomenon, cf. Jean Ougrour, 'Le Fait berbère: essai de démystification', in *L'Homme au Maghreb après l'Indépendance*, special issue of *Confluent*, Nos. 23–4, October 1962, pp. 617–34.

[2] Gellner, 'Patterns of rural rebellion', op. cit.

ment was the normal state of affairs before 1912, the pattern they reveal is, owing to the French unification of Morocco during the protectorate, of a very different character. They are indeed an assertion of tribal personality, but within a new and national framework. Through the channels of the multiplicity of political parties, most present-day tribal leaders have easy access to the capital, a fact which has shown up in the leniency, by and large, of their treatment after capture in the event of rebellion. Their heads do *not* adorn the walls or windows of the concrete-and-glass building of the Ministry of the Interior; and the penchant of both post-independence kings for general amnesties granted to political prisoners at the occasion of religious feasts is famous. The real national political struggle is still to come, and thus the tribal rebellions which have occurred so far assume only the proportions of local dress rehearsals. They seem to be part and parcel of a new national game in which tribes, towns, political parties, labor unions, the government in or out of power, the army and the monarchy are all jockeying for position. The pluralism of the wider national society is of crucial importance in this connection.

Given the total framework outlined above, it is now appropriate to discuss recent political developments amongst the Rifian Aith Waryaghar and the Ait Atta of the Far South in the light of this whole problem of Tribe *versus* Wider Society.

VIII

According to the Moroccan census of 1960, the Aith Waryaghar tribe of the Central Rif (Province of El-Hoceima) was the largest tribe in the North Zone, numbering 75,895 souls. They live in the back country behind El-Hoceima itself, their territory going south some seventy kilometers to and including the Jbil Hmam massif, whence, according to their traditions, they originated. They are sedentary agriculturists, tribal farmers, and the area they live in is one of the most densely populated in rural Morocco (over 120 people per square kilometer in the Plain of El-Hoceima, though less than that in the southern mountains of the tribe). Even though they grow a surprising variety of crops, with barley and figs as the staples, the soil is infertile and has to feed too many people. The traditional responses of the Aith Waryaghar both to the poverty of their terrain and to an expanding population (today twice what it was in 1926 when Abd el-Krim surrendered) have been bloodfeuding and labor migration. These are mentioned in that order, for the bloodfeuding has presumably gone on since time immemorial, reaching a refinement and complexity rare even in tribal Morocco, while the labor migration began around the turn of the century or shortly before, when French *colon* farmers in western Algeria found that migrant Rifian labor was very much superior to the local work force in stamina and productivity. And the migrant Rifian labor continued, from then until 1955 when the Algerian War caused the Moroccan–Algerian frontier to close down.

Abd el-Krim had outlawed feuds in 1921 and the Spaniards had confiscated the Rifians' rifles in 1926; but the period of 1930–55 saw the flowering of Rifian

labor migration, with continual remittances sent back to the laborers' families in
the Rif through special Rifian couriers. The old values of the feud had become
transmuted and integrated into those of labor migration. If during the period
before Abd el-Krim, a young man, in order to prove himself, had to shoot down
an enemy, he had, during the Spanish Protectorate, to find a temporary job
on the farm of some *colon* in the Oran region of Algeria. This is clearly evident
from the total body of songs sung at Rifian weddings.[1]

I have, in three publications, dealt in considerable detail with various aspects
of the traditional social structure of the Aith Waryaghar;[2] and it is therefore not
worth while expanding upon this subject here, beyond saying that the population
is segmented into five heterogeneous and internally discontinuous clan groups
(here called 'fifths'), the essential function of which was the division of fines five
ways among the councillors in the event of murder committed in any of the tribal
markets, in the same terms and context as discussed in Section IV. The moiety
or *leff* system of hostile dual factions as discussed in Section III also applied, and
in this particular instance it cross-cut the clan system so that politically, two
clans out of the total of five were themselves halved and their component
subclans were on opposite sides of the fence. Apart from this, small temporary
leff alliances were made among subclans and lineages when the larger permanent
*leff*s were not activated (they were 'permanent' in that they always assumed the
same shape when called into play); and for this reason, in my 1965 article (op.
cit.), I have characterized the whole sociopolitical system as a paradox: a system
of disequilibrium in equilibrium.

The significant reforms of Abd el-Krim have already been mentioned in
Section VI, as well as the fact that the Spaniards essentially took over the Rif
where he left off at the time he was defeated. Only three more points need to be
made in this general connection. First of all, Abd el-Krim was not merely the only
Rifian from the Aith Waryaghar or any other tribe whose fame has become world-
wide, he has been (and this is more important in the present context) the only
real Rifian *leader* in history, the only Rifian with a personal 'charisma', the only
Rifian whom outside events catapulted to the top of a highly segmentary and
acephalous society—a society in which leadership as known in the West does not
exist at all and in which the only instrument of political power, as well as that
acting as a check on its abuse, is the tribal council. Beside his name, the names of
other Rifians before and since his time, feuding members of ineffectual councils,
pale into insignificance.

Secondly, the most important of the reforms that Abd el-Krim effected revolved around the firm implantation of the Sharia, of Muslim law, in all domains
which had previously been regulated by custom; for before his time, only
questions dealing with land and water, marriage or divorce came under the
jurisdiction of the *qadi*. Under Abd el-Krim every form of legal behavior was
now subject to Sharia regulations, and this persisted under the Spanish administration with only one change: murder, theft and adultery cases were now subject
to the Spanish protectorate government. As the Rifians of the Aith Waryaghar

[1] Hart, op. cit., 1958.
[2] Hart, op. cit., 1954, 1958, 1965.

are notoriously violent, hard-headed, unruly and perhaps more jealous of their women than any other tribe in Morocco, fights over land and water rights abound in this day, and murders of either party or both parties caught in adultery by injured husbands still occur. These last received only token jail sentences under the Spaniards, but appear to be dealt with more severely today by the independent Moroccan Government.

The Spaniards maintained a single top *caid* over Beni Ouriaghel (where none, in truth, had existed before Abd el-Krim's time), but in 1935, when they created this same *caid* Pasha of the new town of El-Hoceima, they again implicitly recognized the segmentary nature of the tribe by dividing it into three caidates, each one headed by a *caid* of equal status, with clan *shaikhs*, subclan *mqaddims* and village *jaris* under him. Each caidate also had its Spanish military *interventor*, with a top *interventor comarcal* for the whole of the Aith Waryaghar; the latter was lodged in the building which had replaced Abd el-Krim's old headquarters at Ajdir, overlooking the Bay of El-Hoceima. As stated above, the *caid* was at the top of his ladder, the *interventor* at the bottom of his, and this situation persisted until independence. The Spanish economic development of the region was very slight indeed, almost nil, but on the credit side, the same can be said about Spanish interference in internal tribal affairs. However, in a sense, the clan 'juntas' which they created in 1952 were forerunners of the later 'rural communes'.

The part played by the Aith Waryaghar in the Independence Movement was negligible compared with that played by their southern—and French-Zone—neighbors of the Igzinnayen. During the Moroccan Army of Liberation campaign in the Rif in late 1955, the Aith Waryaghar clans bordering Igzinnayen territory freely harbored fugitives and combatants from the fighting area; and the Spaniards turned a blind eye to this, just as they had turned a blind eye to the existence of Army of Liberation training camps, etc., near Nador all through 1954, when arms were being smuggled into the French Zone. Active participation by members of the Aith Waryaghar in the fight against the French, however, was almost nil, though the *interventors* were warned in directives from Tetuan that Waryaghar-land could become a prize danger zone. Early in 1956 feeling rose against one of the Spanish *interventors*, who was removed from office for having fired on a group of people who came into a market wanting to kill one of the tribal *caids*. Apart from this incident, however, the transfer of power in the region seems to have been accomplished fairly smoothly. In fact, the Aith Ammarth, southwestern neighbors of the Aith Waryaghar and located in what was then the Spanish Zone, gave far more real assistance to the Army of Liberation than the Aith Waryaghar themselves did.

As soon as power had been transferred, the Istiqlal Party was quick in establishing a foothold, and was enthusiastically welcomed all over the region. None the less, discontent soon set in when the Aith Waryaghar realized not only that none of their own people were being appointed to the new local and provincial administration, but that these posts were all, virtually without exception, from that of provincial governor on down, being filled by South-Zone French-speaking Istiqlal supporters. As another very tangible legacy of the Spanish administration had been that a considerable number of Aith Waryaghar men had learned to speak passable or even fluent Spanish (for the Spaniards did not bother to learn Rifian), it galled them that French-speaking Arabs from the South Zone, of whose existence they had previously been but dimly aware, had now come up from nowhere to fill the key jobs. The fact that one of the first governors of the province after independence was a Casablanca Negro did not help matters; for, as I have said (Hart, op. cit., 1954, 1965), a major reason why the Aith Waryaghar, alone in the Rif, rose unanimously against the Pretender Bu Hmara in 1908 and defeated his army on the banks of the Nkur river had been not so much that they favored the Sultan as that the Pretender's army was commanded by a Negro.

By the time Independence came, moreover, the Algerian border had been closed to Rifian and Moroccan labor migration; and here was another source of discontent, for migrant labor had brought considerable revenue to the region for the last two or three decades, whereas the result now was virtually total unemployment.

IX

For these reasons, by 1957–58 most Rifians were disenchanted with the Istiqlal Party and its officials, who had given them neither jobs nor what they deemed adequate political representation. One result was that the Democratic Independence Party began to gain a strong opposition foothold in the region, though Rabat officially ignored its existence there. A young and entirely unofficial spokesman from the segmentary ranks of the Aith Waryaghar now emerged: Muhammad nj-Hajj Sillam n-Muh Amzzyan, from the large clan of the Aith Bu Ayyash. He had been a minor subclan shaikh under the Spaniards, but, like all the other tribal authorities installed by them, had lost his job with independence. It was soon realized in retrospect that the Spaniards at least had administered the tribe through its own people, which the new independent administration was most emphatically *not* doing; and Muhammad nj-Hajj Sillam was the *primus inter pares* in the ranks of the disgruntled, as well as the local tribal head of the Democratic Independence Party (PDI).

The eighteen-point program for the Rif which he and two other members of the Aith Waryaghar (Abd s-Sadaq Sharrat Khattabi and Abd el-Krim's son Rashid) submitted to King Muhammad V in Rabat on 11 November 1958 is interesting in retrospect; and from early in 1966, a checklist against the various points indicates clearly to what extent the program was achieved:

1. Evacuation of all foreign troops from Morocco. (This did not at the time affect the US bases, but the objective was none the less realized within four years, insofar as French and Spanish troops were concerned.)

2. Formation of a popular government *with a wide base* (my italics: first part achieved in part, second part not at all).

3. *Abolition of political parties* (my italics) and formation of a government of

national union. (First part will probably never be achieved, though second part has been, at least once.)

4. Local recruitment of local civil servants. (By 1962, most lower-echelon civil servants were certainly locally recruited.)

5. Freedom for all political prisoners. (Political prisoners were very numerous at the time the document was drafted; but by mid-1965 there were none at all.)

6. *Return of Abd el-Krim to Morocco.* (This was the most important point of all, and the granting of all other requests except this would have been deemed unacceptable. Abd el-Krim had from his surrender in 1926 been detained on Réunion Island until 1947, when en route to France he jumped ship in Egypt and simply stayed there. In his declining years, he wrote articles attacking colonialism and the vestiges of foreign troops in Morocco. But Abd el-Krim was not to see Morocco again, for he died in Cairo in February 1963.)

7. *Guarantees to dissidents against reprisals.* (My italics. This may have been responsible in part for the general leniency shown by the Moroccan Government to tribal rebels since Independence.)

8. Choice of capable judges (by which, obviously, was meant Rifian ones).

9. Reorganization of the Ministry of Justice (as the South Zone *qadis* then in the Rif were notoriously inept).

10. Bringing of criminals to justice (by which one assumes that the 'criminals' concerned were in fact individuals in government service).

11. A Rifian to be given an important post in the Moroccan Government. (No Rifian from the Aith Waryaghar, at least, has as yet been given such a post, but Gen. Mzzyan is from Nador and Col. Medbuh from the Igzinnayen.)

12. Operation Plow to be extended to the Rif. (Operation Plow was already on its last legs in 1958 and never did reach the Rif; but currently a large agricultural development scheme there, the DERRO Project, has fully supplanted it.)

13. Tax reductions for all of Morocco, especially the Rif. (The *tartib* tax on agricultural produce was officially abolished in 1961, but the Rifians for two years thereafter were still in arrears on previous payments.)

14. Creation of an ambitious program against unemployment (not yet).

15. Creation of scholarships for Rifian students (today only in a very undeveloped stage).

16. Rapid Arabization of education all over Morocco. (Rifians deplore, then and now, the use of French in the ex-Spanish Zone, but this still continues, of course, and Arabization is still more a hope than a reality.)

17. Creation of more rural schools. (Emphatically *yes*, the answer is here, after King al-Hasan's Opération Ecole of 1963.)

18. Reopening of the Lycée in El-Hoceima. (It was closed down early in 1958 and many students were jailed. It has long since, of course, been reopened, so that this is a purely topical question—and like many questions once timely, today outdated.)

However, by the time this program had been presented to the king, the Rifian Revolt had already been in progress about three weeks; and Muhammad nj-Hajj Sillam was 'in charge' of it, if such a statement can be made about any one person. The first overt act of rebellion occurred on 25 October 1958, when the Istiqlal Party office at the post of Beni Hadifa was stormed by irate tribesmen and the incumbent very badly beaten up; the *mukhaznis* (Makhzen Mobile) of the bureau were overpowered, and a few rifles were taken. The same thing happened at the post of Imzuren, and in l-Arba Tawrirt there was a fight at the bureau as well. (These were the three posts of the three former Spanish caidates of the Aith Waryaghar.)

The most extraordinary feature of this revolt, the worst one which has yet occurred in Independent Morocco, is how poorly armed the Aith Waryaghar were. Only the merest handful of the rebels had rifles, for the ban on rifles imposed by the Spaniards after the Abd el-Krim war was continued through the post-independence period; the rest were armed only with billhooks (the standard tool for cutting brushwood, with a long wooden handle and a curved iron head, ending in a point) and stones. However, the Aith Waryaghar are remarkably accurate stone-throwers, and a billhook in their hands becomes a formidable weapon at close quarters. And, thus armed, they took to the massif of Jbil Hmam (1,930 meters at its peak), the core of the tribal territory.

It was at this point that the insurrection became a real rebellion. All the Central Rifian tribes were involved, but at the first broadcast appeal by the king for them to return to their homes, they all did so—except for the Aith Waryaghar, who alone stayed up in their mountains refusing either to return to their houses and autumn plowing or to attend their weekly markets. A show of force was necessary, and even though Aith Waryaghar spokesmen said that their only quarrel was with the Istiqlal Party, not with the newly-formed Royal Army or with the Monarchy, the army was none the less sent in. The military aspects of the campaign as the largest exercise yet attempted by the neophyte Royal Army in establishing internal security have been adequately described by Zartman,[1] and need not be recapitulated here. It is only necessary to record that the then Crown Prince Mulay al-Hasan proved himself as a field commander after taking personal charge of the Royal Army's show of force in encircling El-Hoceima, when the Aith Waryaghar refused to obey the king's warning that a 'cruel punishment' would await them if they had not returned to their local communities by 7 January 1959.

[1] I. William Zartman, *Morocco: Problems of New Power*, New York, 1964, pp. 86–91.

They did not return; and they received the cruel punishment in good measure. But at times they gave as good as they got: on one occasion the Crown Prince's personal aeroplane, on attempting to land at Imzuren, was greeted by several bursts of rifle fire, and it is said that General Oufqir himself (then a colonel) took part in the army attack on the airstrip defenders. On other occasions, Royal Army troops subsequently attempting to clamber up the mountains of the Jbil Hmam were greeted with very accurate volleys of rocks thrown by the furious Aith Waryaghar. But in the end, after January 1959, the toughest month of the campaign, the Aith Waryaghar took a sound drubbing; and they will not forget it for a long, long time. They came down from the hills sullenly, with displeasure and rancor, just as they had done when Abd el-Krim surrendered. They had been bad boys, and the army had soundly spanked them; and thereupon both the army and the Crown Prince became two more targets of their muttered opprobrium, as well as the Istiqlal Party. Muhammad nj-Hajj Sillam had fled to Spain, with a number of other prominent men from the Aith Waryaghar, before the army was able to capture him. The other men all returned to El-Hoceima with a royal pardon in 1962, but Muhammad nj-Hajj Sillam was condemned to death *in absentia*. (The situation quite resembled that of an unpardoned Berber murderer fleeing with his agnates to an enemy tribe in the Central Atlas. Thus even here his behavior was traditional in character; and it should be added that he was in no way the charismatic figure that Abd el-Krim was. Indeed, after the revolt was over, the Aith Waryaghar themselves criticized him and sneered at him.)

The Province of El-Hoceima was now subjected to military government for at least the next two years, as a result of the revolt; and perhaps the most outstanding effect of this was the complete and absolute abolition of political parties in the area of insurrection, if not in the whole province. (Paradoxically, it will be recalled that this in any case was a major objective in the eighteen-point program which the Aith Waryaghar spokesmen had presented to King Muhammad V.) The revolt was finished by the end of January 1959, and from then until the present day the Aith Waryaghar have been notable for their complete and voluntary abstention from political party activities of any kind, an abstention which has, indeed, been carried to the point of marked lack of participation in other issues with political significance: in particular, the series of local and national elections which began on 29 May 1960. Fully congruent both with this non-participation and with their tremendous jealousy about the honor of their women was the fact that, although women all over Morocco were vigorously encouraged to vote in elections (one man, one vote now became also one woman, one vote), the participation rate of Aith Waryaghar women was nil; and the total tribal average for the first election of eligible participant voters was thus only 43 percent, the very lowest in the country.

This attitude of non-participation is nothing new. Rifians in general and Aith Waryaghar in particular, even in times of *siba* dissidence, have always been fully aware of the *Gharb*—the 'Arab West' of Morocco—and have always distrusted it; and therefore what Gellner calls 'partial opting out' of the wider society is still fully inherent in their terminal loyalties. They are proud to the point of arrogance of being Aith Waryaghar and of the reputation they have for fighting; they detest the Royal Army for having 'pricked their balloon'; and they are condescending in the extreme in their attitude toward all non-Rifian Moroccans. Other Moroccans are quite aware of this sneering condescension, this seeming superiority complex on the part of poor tribesmen from a backward province—and it irks them. The mistrust is mutual, and the kindest thing South Zone military administrators have to say about the Aith Waryaghar is that they are incredibly hard-headed.

Their terminal loyalties have now, given their increased awareness, passed the boundaries of their own tribe (of course the *best* of all Rifian tribes, in their eyes) to include the Rif and the North Zone as a whole. None the less, their antagonism to anything emanating from the South Zone is normally extremely marked,[1] and they are patiently licking their wounds and hurt pride incurred during the revolt. Nothing would please them more than to see the small North Zone tail wag the large South Zone dog; they have always been politically aware, but invariably in terms of self-interest only. And loyalties have in recent times expanded to the point they have only because active intra-tribal and intra-clan feuding is a thing of the past, though the values associated with it have not changed. The belief of the Aith Waryaghar in their own uniqueness is such that their position in the national political arena might be likened to a game of touch football among small boys, in which one boy sulkily refuses to play. As their revolt very clearly showed, though the stimuli were fully modern, the Aith Waryaghar responses to them were thoroughly traditional.

As has been reiterated throughout this paper, leadership in segmentary societies, given the nature of such societies, is negligible and, barring crises, indeed entirely dormant; and this is certainly the case with the Aith Waryaghar of today. There are of course a number of men, all of whom held positions of responsibility under the Spaniards, and all of whom come from well-reputed lineages in the tribe,[2] who because of greater wealth and greater political acumen than the rank and file have achieved a certain measure of respect in this highly egalitarian society. But these men, even today, are still *primi inter pares*, and to what extent any of them might truly become leaders—which at the moment they are not—would only be seen in a crisis.

The political orientation and attitudes of the Aith Waryaghar have already

[1] The only exception to date has been during the Moroccan–Algerian border war of 1963, in which Aith Waryaghar sentiments were with Morocco (though again, sometimes, grudgingly).

[2] Mikki n-Sriman, the ex Pasha of El-Hoceima; Sidi Mhammad Bu Rjila, also El-Hociema; Si Bu Azza, at present a *caid* in Targuist; and Shaikh Mzzyan, who resides in Tetuan and is a cousin of Muhammad nj-Hajj Sillam: these men are all examples. They all fled to Spain at the end of the Rifian Revolt, but have all been back in Morocco since 1962–1963. The sons of Abd el-Krim are of course to be numbered in this group as well; they have achieved a certain respect, but they have nothing resembling the charismatic qualities of their late father. Among the 'intellectuals' of Aith Waryaghar must also be numbered the *caids* and other administrative officials they have given to present-day Morocco: Caid Bu Ayyashi in Tetuan and al-Ughlidi in Jibha, for example. As it is rare to find French-speaking individuals amongst the Aith Waryaghar, it is also rare to find them as officials in the South Zone.

been discussed; and their isolation from the rest of Moroccan political life was fostered by Moroccan army occupation, with a military governor and military super-caids and caids, for two or three years after the revolt, the army itself being theoretically above politics. The attitude of 'once bitten, twice shy' still remains; but by its very refusal to participate and to 'play the game' even though the province is now entirely under civilian control, this corner of the Rif is still a potential danger-spot, and the Aith Waryaghar are biding their time. Plain-clothes policemen (called 'secret police' by the tribesmen), many of them now Rifians themselves, generally show up in force at tribal markets, along with members of the Royal Gendarmerie.

Many younger men now wear elements of Western clothing, but this is at best only the merest external index of acculturation; and the hard infrastructural core has remained remarkably intact. The only development since the revolt which the Aith Waryaghar and indeed all Rifians have wholeheartedly espoused has been a new upsurge of labor migration, since 1961, in an entirely new direction: Western Europe. West Germany until very recently was the favored spot because salaries there were highest and housing and working conditions were best; and the work that migrant Rifian laborers gravitated toward was of course entirely industrial in character, ranging from beer breweries to automobile assembly plants. But at the moment Holland and Belgium are in the lead, although France and England, even, both have their share of Rifian workers as well; and the current complaint is that the Moroccan government is far too reluctant to issue passports. Rifians are now saying that the Rif would become empty remarkably fast if all young men could obtain working passports for abroad—and the fact that not enough people get them is yet another source of discontent. The poverty and infertility of the Rif has become aggravated today through an expanding population. Feuds no longer take care of any of the surplus, and labor migration is still too restricted to affect more than a fraction of it. These factors, as well, contribute to the mistrust of the Aith Waryaghar for the rest of Morocco; and they are factors that show the other side of the coin of non-politicalism.

X

The Ait Atta are Berbers in speech as much as the Rifian Aith Waryaghar, if not more; but their Berber language is a different one, and in many other crucial respects they are also utterly dissimilar. Whereas the Aith Waryaghar show a heavy population density in their one tribal area in a single province, the Ait Atta show a thin population spread out over three South Moroccan provinces, i.e. Beni Mellal (properly Bni Mallal), Ouarzazate (properly Warzazat), and Ksar es-Souk (properly Qsar s-Suq); and within these three provinces they depend on no less than nineteen different administrative bureaux, and they number, at an educated guess based on the 1960 Moroccan census materials, somewhat less than 150,000 souls. One northern group, the Ait Atta n-Umalu, near the Bin l-Widan Lake (Beni Mellal Province), is completely cut off from the rest; and in their case alone, the transhumance of the others has given way to complete sedentarization.[1]

The huge territory covered by the Ait Atta ranges from the holly-oak area of the Middle Atlas to the date-palm oases of the south; but their heartland, from which they radiated in all directions, is the Jbil Saghru. Unlike that of the Aith Waryaghar, the segmentary system of the Ait Atta is based upon the principle of common descent from a single sixteenth-century ancestor, Dadda ('Grandfather') Atta; but like the Aith Waryaghar, the Ait Atta are for political purposes organized into five clan-groups of 'fifths'; and in three of these five cases, several clans have recombined to produce a single 'fifth'.[2] However, in the Ait Atta case, as I have shown elsewhere,[3] the function of this top-level segmentation into five 'fifths' was entirely different from the division-of-fines function in the Aith Waryaghar: it was, rather, to provide the top chief of the whole 'super-tribe' of the Ait Atta by the system of 'rotation and complementarity' mentioned in Section IV above. Furthermore, the degree of clan discontinuity and reduplication is far greater even than in Waryaghar-land; and thus there are members of the Ait Bu Iknifen subclan located at no less than seven distinct points in the total Ait Atta territory.

The basic references to the sociopolitical structure of the Ait Atta have already been made in Sections IV–V; here it is only necessary to say that at a tumble-down series of *qsur* called Igharm Amazdar, in the center of the Jbil Saghru, they had their tribal 'capital', where the top chiefs, before 1926–27, were elected and where their Supreme Court of Appeal was held until 1956. This court of appeal, to which Ait Atta from the length and breadth of their tribal territory brought cases or differences of opinion which could not be solved locally, consisted of six men, rechosen for each case from among the three localized Ait Atta sub-clans at Igharm Amazdar. If the six arbiters were not agreed among themselves in what was an open session until the French built the courthouse building (now a rural school), six more were brought in, making twelve; and if these twelve still did not agree, another six were brought in, making eighteen; and if the vote amongst these eighteen members of the court was still at a deadlock, nine to nine, the local chief of the three resident subclans (chosen himself by the rotation and complementarity process) would be brought in to tip the balance either way, at ten to nine.

The Ait Atta only occasionally feuded amongst themselves; their enemies— Ait Murghad, Ait Siddrat, etc.—were almost always people of other tribes, and therefore, although they too, like the Aith Waryaghar, were in perpetual conflict, their conflicts were largely externalized. However, unlike that of the Aith

[1] J. H. Jager Gerlings and D. J. Jongmans, 'The Ait Atta, from nomadic to settled life', *Royal Tropical Institute No. CXV, Department of Physical and Cultural Anthropology, No. 50*, Amsterdam, 1955, take as their central thesis the entirely mistaken idea that all Ait Atta are becoming sedentarized. They regard the existence of permanent houses as an index of sedentarization, and quite overlook the fact that the coexistence of permanent houses and agriculture plus tents and sheep produces *transhumance*.

[2] Cf. Spillmann, op. cit., pp. 74 sq.

[3] D. M. Hart, 'Segmentary systems and the role of five "fifths" in Tribal Morocco', op. cit.

Waryaghar, the total radius of the Ait Atta social system embraced Berber tribes of more or less equal standing, and in the desert, Bedouin Arab tribes (one of which, the Arib, stood in a relationship of fiefdom to them), and in the oases, Jews and Haratin. In other words, in pre-protectorate times, the social relations of the Ait Atta covered a wide and complex range of divergent ethnic groups,[1] which those of the Aith Waryaghar did not. The Jews, who performed valuable services such as jewelry-making, sought safety in humility; and now that there are almost none left, owing to recent emigration to Israel, they no longer count in any case. The relations with other Berber tribes and with the Bedouin Arab tribes in the desert to the south were always hostile; and the only groups that were respected were the holy clans whose members received donations and adjudicated disputes.

XI

The Haratin, however, are another problem. They are a very old, negroid and non-tribal population who live in village clusters along all the southern rivers, the Dra, the Dads and the Tudgha, from which in fact they take their names (Ait Dra, Ait Dads, Ait Tudgha). They are sedentary agriculturists, well-diggers and date cultivators, and they are perhaps the most numerous single element of the population in the Moroccan Deep South. They live either in communities consisting of themselves alone, or in communities that are also inhabited by white Berbers, generally Ait Atta or Ait Murghad. The cleavage in these latter communities is almost always very strongly marked, for the Ait Atta, Ait Murghad and other Berber tribes despise the Haratin and never intermarry among them. (The only instance of a racially mixed community known to the writer is that of the Ait Unir at Bu Maln n-Dads, where the Ait Atta have become thoroughly Haratinized not only racially but in customs and institutions as well. They have long since lost the traditional system of electing chiefs by rotation and complementarity, for instance; and they constitute a glaring exception in every way to a general rule.) Each Hartani (singular of Haratin) in such a case had his individual Ait Atta protector, and in return for protection against raids from the Ait Siddrat or Ait Murghad tribes (the traditional enemies of the Ait Atta, as mentioned above), the Hartani cultivated his Atta master's fields and date gardens and generally received one-fifth of the crop. The Ait Murghad and Ait Siddrat also of course had their own Haratin, who were similarly organized and protected.

The Ait Atta show the same egalitarianism among themselves which is common to all Berber societies and is a direct result of the tribal and segmentary systems; but in any egalitarian society some people are always 'more equal' than others, and in this particular one the Haratin, both literally and figuratively, are simply beyond the pale. The Atta-Haratin relationship is based upon a premise of inequality; and in this sense the Ait Atta are without question the biggest

[1] D. Jacques-Meunié, 'Hiérarchie sociale au Maroc présaharien', *Hespéris*, XLV, Nos. 3-4, 1958, pp. 239-69; also, same author, 'Les oasis des Lektaoua et des Mehamid: institutions traditionelles des Draoua', *Hespéris*, XXXIV, Nos. 3-4, 1947, pp. 397-429.

racists in the Moroccan South. They, white tribally-organized transhumant Berbers who traditionally always bore arms, despise the Haratin for being (1) negroid, (2) non-tribal, (3) sedentary and agricultural, and (4) inexperienced in bearing arms. Ait Atta even say that before the protectorate it was common practice for a man who had just acquired a new rifle to try it out on a Hartani. Today, however, the relationship between the two groups is subtly changing, and in a way which the Ait Atta do not like at all. The extent of this change will be discussed further on in its proper place.

The pacification by the French of Ait Atta territory was long and hard, and was accomplished only after the savage Battle of Bu Gafr in the heart of the Jbil Saghru in February–March 1933, a battle which the Ait Atta say was won for the French by other Ait Atta who had started soldiering in the goums (the most prestige-laden troops, all of them Berbers, among the various Franco-Moroccan native military units. There are many ex-goumiers among the Ait Atta who are veterans of the campaigns in Italy, France and Germany during World War II, for example). Typically, the man who spearheaded Ait Atta resistance to the French, Assu u-Baslam, was made Caid of Ikniwn Bureau by them, a post he held continuously from 1933 until his death in 1960. He was thus one of a tiny handful of tribal *caids* who survived the transfer of power in 1956.

This fact indicates at once that one Ait Atta institution the French did away with at the outset was the annual changing of chiefs by rotation and complementarity. However, they retained all the others through their emphasis on the Berber Dahir and their retention of Customary law: the collective oath, the priority rights of agnates over land and women, and the specifically Berber dispositions about inheritance and divorce, for instance, were all integrally retained until independence. During the whole of the French period, Berber custom was dominant and Islamic law recessive.

The role of the Ait Atta in the Nationalist Movement toward independence was very negligible indeed, although Gellner states that one of the chiefs of the Ait Atta n-Umalu in the Beni Mellal Province was jailed by the French for nationalist activities in the early 1950s,[1] as a very few of the Aith Waryaghar had also been, by the Spaniards, at the same time.

More important was what happened after independence was achieved, and the very first thing was that the Berber Dahir was rescinded. The Ait Atta and other Central Atlas Berber tribes now came under the sway of Muslim law. Collective oaths were individualized, the extended priority rights of agnates over land and women were greatly reduced, and Muslim stipulations regarding inheritance and divorce regulations were enforced. The customary tribunals and the old Ait Atta Supreme Court were abolished, and *qadis* were sent in to all the major markets and previous French Affaires Indigènes centers of control over the Ait Atta. The latter, today, are still more partial to their custom in such matters than they are to the law of Islam, and there has been a great lack of understanding between these Berber tribesmen and the Muslim authorities who minister to their legal needs.

Independence also brought in its wake the emergence of political parties; and

[1] Gellner, op. cit.

ever since it became legal and open, the majority of the Ait Atta have been adherents of the Berber Party, Mahjub Ahardan's Popular Movement. It is of considerable interest in this connection to note that the Haratin, by contrast, were wooed by the National Union of Popular Forces; and thus the old cleavage between the groups continues to exist in modern dress and modern idiom. (However, this political cleavage may not now be as apparent as it was in 1962–63, given the great curtailment by the government of the activities of this particular party.) Another factor here is that the Haratin, in those areas where they live on their own and without Ait Atta, are, through labor migration to Marrakesh and Casablanca, becoming wealthier; and those who live in communities under Atta domination have come to realize this and want to follow suit. The Ait Atta themselves are fully aware of this problem, and they do not like it in the least, as the Haratin are slipping from their grasp, economically. They say that they themselves are becoming poorer, while the Haratin, who were previously nobodies, are becoming richer. Furthermore, as the Moroccan Constitution of 1962 proclaimed all Moroccans equal in the sight of the law, this present legal equality of Ait Atta and Haratin is one of the greatest potential danger points in the Moroccan Deep South, where racism has always been a basic sociopolitical fact.

The intensity of terminal loyalties of the Ait Atta is much like that of the Aith Waryaghar, and depends on which units happen to be in conflict. For example, at Tilmist near Zawiya Ahansal in the Central Atlas (Beni Mellal Province), there is a group of resident Ait Bu Iknifen, a major Atta subclan. Now, given the discontinuity and reduplication of clans and subclans over Atta territory, Tilmist is only one out of some seven places within this territory where Ait Bu Iknifen are to be found. Tilmist also acts as the summer pasturing grounds of other Ait Bu Iknifen who come up from the south on transhumance; and because the original agreement between Dadda Atta, the ancestor of the Ait Atta, and Sidi Said Ahansal, the founder of Zawiya Ahansal, in the sixteenth century was vague and imprecise over certain crucial points, there are, to this day, conflicts between the two groups of Ait Bu Iknifen which often end in fights and brawling, with killed and wounded, over the grazing rights in this area. The matter goes up every summer to the gubernatorial level in Beni Mellal, but it is quite unsolvable.[1]

The fact that no top chiefs have existed among the Ait Atta since 1926 has of course also reduced the degree of effectiveness of this huge tribe as a whole; but, again as a whole, the Ait Atta have a tremendously strong common sentiment and 'we-feeling', particularly as manifested in their common opposition to the Ait Siddrat and the Ait Yafilman tribes (i.e. Ait Murghad, Ait Hadiddu, Ait Izdig and Ait Yihya, a loose confederacy formed in the seventeenth century for the sole purpose of fighting against the Ait Atta). Their feeling about Arabs and urban Moroccans in general is one of complete detestation, and although they feel just the same way about the Haratin, they recognize that the Arabs and urban Moroccans represent more of a threat to them. They are equally conscious of their 'Berber-ness', and identify themselves with the Zayan, Ait Mguild and

[1] Gellner, op. cit., 1965

Ait Sukhman tribes of the Middle Atlas through membership in Ahardan's Popular Movement. None the less, their loyalty to the Monarchy is equally without question.

As to leadership among the Ait Atta at present (apart from the present—from early 1966—governor of Ouarzazate, who is one of them), the segmentary system again discourages anything but diffusion of power, while of course the central government is the main agency for checking the emergence of any leadership other than that imposed by itself. However, though continually stressing this same fact himself, one man has emerged who is universally liked and respected by the Ait Atta: Ali, the son of Hajj Assu u-Baslam, who since 1961, a year after his father's death, has been *caid* at Ikniwn in the Jbil Saghru (Ouarzazate Province). If any man today is the No. 1 man among the Ait Atta, it is he, and although initially his prestige was a reflection of that of his father, which was tremendous, he has since then gained a great deal on his own. He surrounds himself entirely with Ait Atta personnel, e.g. his driver and his *mkhaznis*; he is scrupulously fair in his dealings with them, and though an easy informality obtains in his relations with his fellow tribesmen, there is none the less no doubt that it is he who commands. He has a great sense of humor and a strong notion of 'fair play'. He is one of very few Ait Atta who speak Arabic, and he has two French-speaking sons, one at the date of writing acting as his father's clerical secretary at the bureau and the other in school in Marrakesh.

The Caid Ali took office as *caid* in his late thirties or early forties, and it seems reasonable to assume that he will hold the position until his death, for just after being appointed *caid* he took a special oath with King al-Hasan II in Rabat to pledge his friendship and support, as well as those of his tribesmen, to the monarchy. He also has a special dispensation, one might call it, from the king, to dress traditionally; and like all the rest of the Ait Atta he is never seen without long white shirt, burnous and turban, though his sons wear Western clothing. His values are exactly those of his fellow-tribesmen raised to a slightly higher power; and although not himself a member of the Popular Movement, he is extremely sympathetic to it and to Ahardan. His loyalty to the monarchy seems beyond question, as is his sympathy toward anyone interested in the Ait Atta and their problems. Although he is just one *caid* among many in Ait Atta territory, his bailiwick at Ikniwn covers all the Jbil Saghru and the old Atta capital at Igharm Amazdar as well as the old battleground of Bu Gafr—the heartland of the Ait Atta, in brief. (It goes without saying that anyone ever dealing with this tribe should approach them through him!)

Labor migration among the Ait Atta is almost non-existent. They have a huge territory but they do not move from it; and even on transhumance they almost never have to cross the territory of other tribes—who refer to them as 'flies', both because they are so numerous, and because their men's burnouses and all of their women's clothing as well are black. (It is common among other tribes in the region, when a fly drops into someone's mint tea, to hear them say, 'Another w-Atta just died.')[1] This fact certainly contributes to their extreme resistance to social change and modernization, as does the fact that they have an extra-

[1] *w-Atta*: sing. of *Ait Atta*.

ordinarily rich corpus of custom, to which they are still enormously attached. It is only legally defunct today, and by no means entirely so in practice. In such resistance to change, greater here than in any other part of Morocco perhaps, they might well be considered a prototypical Berber tribe, at the base level of the spectrum.

XII

The two cases which have just been discussed clearly indicate that in present-day Morocco 'tribalism' and 'Berberism' are becoming synonymous, even though such was by no means the case before the establishment of the protectorate. The Moroccan mountains have acted as a strong preserver of segmentary tribal structures of the kind outlined above; and to the contrary, where tribal systems as such are beginning to break down is in the plains, with the development of large agricultural cooperatives and other similar projects. The influx to the cities has of course produced the phenomenon of a detribalized urban proletariat, over the course of two generations; and the unemployed slough-off from the urban *bidonvilles* or shanty-towns is in turn producing rural shanty-towns in some of the coastal regions (Rummani is one such). The result is that the detribalized individual returns home and has as much difficulty readjusting to old tribal ways as he had originally in adjusting to urban ones; and he is thus caught between two fires.

The Ammeln, Idaw-Gnidif and other Berber-speaking tribes in the Anti-Atlas provide an interesting example of a complete adjustment to a modern economy, but likewise one in which the tribal frame of reference has in no way changed. These are the famous 'Susi *épicier*' or 'grocer' tribes, whose members own and operate grocery-stores in all the major Moroccan cities in such a way that A manages the store for six months, and is then free to return home when relieved by his brother B. A young man from the Ammeln of Tafrawt (Agadir Province) who goes to look for work in Casablanca always starts on the lowest rung of the grocery store run by one of his agnates. These are very much 'family businesses', but the thrift of the 'Soussi' is so proverbial that some of them, who run their own bus-lines from Casablanca to Tafrawt in the Anti-Atlas non-stop, have become multimillionaires. Nobody who has a business going in Casablanca or Tangier, for example, would ever dream of relinquishing his house or property in the Ammeln valley, to which all of them eventually retire.

This leads to a final observation: that what with labor migration and the urban grocery stores, for example, tribalism in itself constitutes no inherent impediment to progress (even though planners of schemes such as the 'rural commune' system may think it does). Such impediments, indeed, are more to be found under conditions of detribalization, in which individuals are completely uprooted from the security of the kinship and segmentary systems in which they once had a place.

Even though, if a pseudo-evolutionary sequence is postulated, detribalization appears to be a necessary step in the direction of urbanization, urbanization and modernization are hardly the same thing. The poverty in any shanty-town is far greater than in the poorest tribe, both quantitatively and qualitatively; and the miserable squalor of a discontented urban proletariat is far more apt to light the fuse to set off a powder-keg than any tribe (even in the Rif). This was abundantly proved during the initial overt manifestations of Moroccan nationalism in the early 1950s, and it could happen once again; for despite government efforts to improve housing and living conditions, the *bidonville* population is today greater than ever. Whether as former wolves (in Gellner's analogy)[2] the tribes in general would once again become the tame sheep-dogs of the administration is entirely another matter.

[2] Gellner, op. cit., 1962, and op. cit., 1965.

2
Political and Religious Organization of the Berbers of the Central High Atlas[1]

Ernest Gellner

Strictly speaking, one should not say 'political *and* religious organization' when discussing central Moroccan Berber tribes: their political and religious organization is closely interdependent. Yet, at the same time, they are not identical: the sacred and the secular elements are distinct.

The crucial politico-religious institution of these tribes is the *agurram* (pl. *igurramen*), the hereditary holy man. In popular French literature, these men are referred to as *marabouts*, a term whose usage is rather similar to the anglicized word dervish. These are the 'saints' of Islam. Whereas in Christianity, sanctity, like the age of miracles, has come to be a kind of retrospective phenomenon ('Miracles don't happen nowadays', Bernard Shaw makes one of the characters observe in *Saint Joan*), in traditional Muslim society it remained an ever-contemporary one, experienced in the present tense and not merely in the past. The hereditary nature of much of this sanctity ensured, or helped to ensure, an adequate supply of it.

The effective social reality expressed in terms of Muslim sanctity differs of course a great deal in various contexts—urban, rural, tribal, centrally administered or dissident, etc., The form found in central Morocco, in the extensive Berber-speaking mountainous area where the Middle and High Atlas flow into each other, represents, I believe, in very clear outline, one particular extreme on the available spectrum. This is so because, in such an area, two (related) forces were present only in a minimal form, or not at all: (*a*) official, genuinely literate Islam, and (*b*) central government.

The area in question was purely tribal, and free from central administration, until its conquest by the French, nominally on behalf of the Moroccan monarchy, in 1933. Between 1933 and the winter of 1955/6, the area was under indirect French military rule: French district officers, who were military men seconded to a special administrative service, ruled the region through, more or less, its traditional institutions, though these were considerably adapted and as it were stylized in the interests of administrative convenience and efficiency. Still, this arrangement meant that traditional institutions, which had survived untouched until 1933, were placed in a kind of sociological ice-box, which preserved them at least sufficiently to enable a social anthropologist to understand both their old functioning, and its transformation. (At least, I fondly hope this is the case.) It was only in 1956, with Moroccan independence, that the area was incorporated in the national Moroccan state, which took little or no official cognizance of the tribal structures. The field work on which this paper is based was carried out both under the French, and under the independent Moroccan administration.[2]

[1] Originally presented at World Anthropological Congress, Moscow, 1964.
[2] In fact, several somewhat different independent administrations and their impact on

Before discussing the sociopolitical role of the *igurramen* in Berber tribal society of central Morocco, it is best to define an *agurram*, as conceived and recognized by the society of which he is part. An *agurram* is one who:

i) possesses the appropriate descent from other *igurramen*, and ultimately traces his supposed descent from the Prophet. (He is thus also a *sharif*.)

ii) possesses *baraka*, divine grace and approval, which manifests itself in further ways, such as:

iii) material prosperity, and

iv) magical powers. Moreover, he is:

v) generous and hospitable, conspicuously so, and above all, in a spontaneous, uncalculating manner. He is, in theory:

vi) pious and well-versed in Koranic matters, which, after all, he is supposed (by tribal, 'genealogical' reasoning) to exemplify automatically, for is he not the Prophet's flesh and blood?

vii) He is pacific. He does not fight, feud, or, by extension, litigate.

viii) He secludes his womenfolk. Tends not to divorce, nor give away daughters in marriage to lay tribesmen.

This is the ideal. Needless to say, the criteria I have listed are not listed in any such formal manner by the tribesmen who actually employ the concept defined. But these are the criteria which are applied or invoked or both. In practice, as with most concepts whether in simple or in complex societies, it is enough for an object or person to satisfy *some* of the criteria, to fall into the category in question.

The above definition needs to be complemented by another and briefer one: a person is an *agurram* in virtue of being held to be one. This, of course, is something the concept has in common with many other social categorizations: they are really attributions, at least in part, but they masquerade as objective characterizations, independent of human will. (And, indeed, they generally are independent of any one individual will.) They thus help endow the social world, in some sense man-made, with the aura of external necessity. What is imposed by such independent necessity is more easily born. No man deliberates about what could not be otherwise, Aristotle observed (not quite accurately): many systems of concepts have succeeded in making things at least appear as if they could not be otherwise.

The manner in which the two definitions—simple ascription, and possession of some or all of the listed characteristics—complement each other, is fairly obvious. A person who is believed to be an *agurram* will be credited with *baraka*, with the appropriate genealogy (when he claims to possess it, the claim will be accepted and respected), with magical powers, etc. Thus, the ascription generates the reality, by a fairly simple process, in the mind, or rather the minds, of the

---

the tribal population were observed. In the early years after Independence, the new local Moroccan administration tended to consist of adherents of the Left tendency in the national movement: after an unsuccessful little tribal rising in 1960, by a tribal group whose leader was affiliated to the leftist party, these administrators—some of whom had been implicated in the rising—were removed, and replaced by Moroccan military officers of Royalist loyalties. One wheel had turned full circle: a military administration returned. Later on, administration became once again civilian.

fellow-members of the society. The formulation in the plural is important: for any one individual, the fact that all others see and recognize the characteristics in question, endows them with a genuine objective reality.

But this is not the only process by which ascription itself generates the characteristics ascribed. There is also a process involving more material and tangible things which are conditions of sustenance and survival. A person who is believed to be an *agurram*, who is an effective one in other words, receives religious donations in virtue of his status, and hence can satisfy the 'objective' criteria of *agurram*-hood, notably prosperity, and the willingness to entertain generously. An effective *agurram* will also be respected and indeed revered by the tribesmen, and thus be able to satisfy another condition, namely pacificity: he will not need to ensure his safety by self-defence, by taking part in alliances, by being ready to feud and to belong to feuding groups.

Thus circular processes result in the genuine acquisition of the necessary characteristics by those credited with *agurram* status, while of course the acquisition of the characteristics justifies and reinforces the attribution of the status.

One further important fact about *igurramen*: the supply always exceeds demand. The egalitarian principles of Berber inheritance, the equality of brethren and the absence of any strong presumption of primogeniture, are one factor ensuring excess of supply (through natural increase). There are others. This fact has important consequences: the lay tribesmen who avail themselves of the services of *igurramen*, and who revere them, have, in the long run, a certain choice as to whose services they are to employ, as to just whom they are to revere. This means that *igurramen*, effective or aspiring, must compete for the reverence and client-ship of the tribesmen. This in turn means that they must please them. This places a very definite limit on the power of *igurramen*, however much revered. Ultimately, an *agurram* is such in virtue of the will of the people, even although in the eyes of the people, he is such in virtue of divine and hence independent approval. *Vox dei* is really *vox populi*. But this dependence on the 'popular will' of the lay, non-holy surrounding tribes clearly limits the possible courses of action and policy of the holy men. Most authority depends on a mixture of force and consent. But *igurramen* have no force of their own, being a small minority and moreover being, by the very definition of their role, pacific. Thus in this society, consent is relatively far more important a factor, and force far less so, in explaining the position of such permanent leadership (i.e. the saints) as exists.[1] This is a curious fact about a society which is otherwise anarchic and feud-addicted. But it is only superficially paradoxical.

Leaving the *igurramen* for a moment, let us turn to the surrounding 'lay', ordinary tribes. (The *igurramen* form less than 5 percent of the population, and effective ones, much less.)

These ordinary tribes, making up the majority of the population, are segmentary in organization. In other words, they are composed, in a rather

---

[1] The threat of violence does of course exist, but it comes not from the *igurramen*, but from other lay tribes, who in turn have nothing, physically, to fear from the *igurramen* themselves, but only from other tribesmen in turn, and so on.

symmetrical manner, of subgroups resembling each other, without specialization and without any one of them possessing political or other priority. Each of these subgroups is subdivided further and in a similarly symmetrical manner, and so on, until ultimate family units are reached. In general, these groups, subgroups, etc. conceptualize themselves in a genealogical manner:[1] a very distant supposed ancestor defines (or rather descent from him defines) membership of the largest group, descent from (say) his supposed sons defines membership of the next 'level' of group-size, and so on. Note that in contrast to the excessive stress on the importance of moieties in Berber organization by some writers, the sub-divisions in central Morocco[2] are not necessarily or predominantly cases of a kind of binary fission: a tribe is as likely to subdivide into three, four, five, or sometimes more subclans. The number two has no preeminence.

These tribes are very segmentary—more so, I believe, that many societies often invoked as examples of segmentary organization. The diffusion of power, a certain egalitarianism, is carried very far indeed. Nevertheless, the lay tribes do have some form of political leadership, though of a minimal kind. They have chiefs, *imgharen* (sing. *amghar*: this term signifies both 'chief', and 'old man', in which respect it of course resembles the Arabic shaikh. But, characteristically, it is not extended to leaders of religious organizations. To my knowledge, *imgharen* are always lay.)

The mode of election of these lay chiefs is highly significant. They are, first of all, elective, and they are elected for one year only. They are elected in a manner I call 'Rotation and Complementarity'.[3] Suppose a tribe consists of three subclans, A, B and C. This year, it will be the turn of A to supply the chief. This also means, however, that the men of A cease to be electors: during the year when they are all potential candidates, none of them have the vote. It is the men of B and C who are the electors. The subsequent year, when B supplies the chiefs, similarly its men are without the franchise, and A and C do the electing, and so forth.

It need hardly be stated that in a society of this kind, there are no formal rules specifying the precise nature of the majority required (such as 51 percent, or two-thirds, etc.). Elections end in unanimity. This does not prevent them being hard 'fought' and negotiated before the decision is reached. But in the end, each subgroup must accept the leader who seems to be getting the majority, and thereby ratify his election and recognize his authority. (The alternative is opting out of the larger group altogether. This can also happen: whole clans, like individual tribesmen, can transfer their allegiance through the ritual of 'making a sacrifice to' a new group, thereby obtaining admission.)

The consequences of this mode of election are obvious. Notwithstanding protestations one may hear about the great amount of respect due to a chief,

---

[1] But this is not universally so, contrary to what is sometimes asserted: at the 'higher' levels, i.e. with regard to the larger groupings, group membership is sometimes also conceived territorially, without the aid of any genealogical beliefs.

[2] And, I believe, elsewhere—in for instance the work of D. M. Hart on Rifian tribes, to be published.

[3] Though rotation alone has been noticed and reported before, e.g. by Said Guennoun for the 'Middle Atlas' proper, as far as I know no one has noticed or reported the system in full, including complementarity. Yet it is of very great interest.

and draconic rules of customary law penalizing anyone who defies a chief (confiscation of all goods and their distribution amongst the other tribesmen), the
power of such highly impermanent chiefs, 'lame ducks' from the very start of
their term of office, dependent on the suffrage of the rival clans, cannot be very
great. Moreover, they cannot supply the continuity, which is a part of effective
leadership. Who or what does? And another problem: given that *imgharen* are
almost[1] the only form of leadership supplied from within the lay tribes, who is to
supervise the election of the new chief when the old one is at the end of his office?

The principal political institution internal to the lay tribes has been described:
elective annual chieftaincy, observing the rules of 'Rotation and Complementarity'. One other crucial institution needs also to be specified—the chief judicial
process, trial by collective oath. This is the main method of terminating (or
rather, in practice, of terminating temporarily) conflict, without recourse to
physical violence.

The procedure is as follows. Suppose that a man is accused of an offence (say
theft, rape, murder) by a member of another group. The man accused can clear
himself of the accusation by testifying, and getting his agnates to testify, according to a fixed formula, in a sacred place, that he is innocent. He testifies first,
and is followed by his agnates in order of proximity of relationship (which
corresponds to the order in which they have a claim to inheriting his property
should he die). Women are of course excluded from being such co-jurors, as are
paupers. The number of co-jurors required depends on the gravity of the
offence: a theft of a sheep might call for two, rape for four, the murder of a
woman twenty, of a man, forty.

The rules are complex and vary from tribe to tribe, but a characteristic set of
rules would be this: the oath is 'broken', defeated (i.e. the accused found
'guilty') if even one of the co-jurors refuses to testify or slips up while testifying.
(*N.B.* the co-jurors are not witnesses. They do not necessarily know whether the
accused is or is not guilty. They are rather guarantors, to this and the other
world, of the good faith of the man who wishes to establish his innocence.) If
defeated through the defection of one or more of their party, the co-juring group
becomes liable for the compensation appropriate for the offence in question, to
be paid to the injured and accusing groups, the amount theoretically pre-
determined by customary law (and, in practice, subject to adjustment by negotiation). Within the defeated party, it is the minority who become liable for raising
the required compensation: if the majority stood by the alleged culprit, it is the
recusant minority, who failed to testify, who pay. If the majority decline, it is the
minority who stood by the culprit, who are now financially co-responsible with
him. (The compensation tends to be in sheep, not in money.)

[1] There are slight qualifications. The tribes are segmentary. Hence, one might very well
and appropriately ask—at just which level of segmentation does this process of rotation
occur? Answer: it occurs at a number of levels at one. To this extent, the system is
indeed complicated. Wheels rotate within wheels. A further qualification: in addition to
the chiefs, there may be special chiefs, also elected (and also in a manner observing
'Rotation and Complementarity'), who have special responsibilities such as Chief of the
Market, or Chief of the Collective Storehouse.

The theory is of course that this form of trial has supernatural sanctions. False testimony will be punished supernaturally. Otherwise, it would of course be too easy for kinsmen always to stand by the accused kinsman, testify him out of his predicament. Group loyalty would be stronger than any abstract concerns with justice.

I have argued elsewhere that the working of this legal procedure does not presuppose that the tribesmen live in such dread of the supernatural that they dare not perjure themselves. They do not live in quite such an effective dread— though, on the other hand, they are not in any conscious or overt sense sceptical either. The working of the oath does not really depend on the firmness of faith and the fear of God. It depends rather on the general structure of segmentary societies. There is conflict or opposition inside each of the groups in conflict, as well as between them. Inside as well as out, there is no concentration of power, no center of authority capable of enforcing order and cohesion. One of the few means available to a group, for the disciplining of an unruly member or sub-group, short of violence, is to let them down at the collective oath. This, and the loss incurred, may on occasion be preferable to allowing the group to become repeatedly involved in external conflict through the acts of some member.[1]

But to make testimony, and the possible perjury, into a serious act, it is necessary that it be not merely solemn, but also very public: whether or not the co-juror is frightened of sanctions emanating from the Other World, what he does must be well publicized in this one. It must be done in some neutral territory where communications meet and news travel, and where his act will come to the notice of other groups. Otherwise, the solemn testimony of the juror is of little value to the accusing group. Anyone might have the courage to perjure himself privately: but in the presence of a very wide audience, one is risking rather more. How is this necessary publicity assured?

The pieces of the jigsaw I have delineated fit together neatly, as of course was intended. Discontinuous lay leadership presupposes continuity somewhere else. The lay elections need to be supervised, morally guaranteed, by some party which is itself not in the running and which is bound to be neutral with regard to them. Similarly, some neutral, and morally authoritative framework is required for the holding of the collective oath, and indeed some kind of intermediary is required for the negotiations which precede it. (Collective oath, like the violent conflict of which it is an alternative—the oath is the continuation of the feud by other means—is a last resort. In negotiations, the demand for the oath, and the offer to perform it, are cards one holds in one's hand, but does not always play.)

The *igurramen* provide this neutral and morally authoritative ground, as it were, both in the literal sense (their villages are sanctuary), and in the extended,

---

[1] I have described the kind of collective oath which is centered on one man and his alleged deed; and in which consequently co-jurors are selected by agnatic proximity to him. Conflict can also arise about matters which concern groups as a whole—e.g. pasture boundaries. Then co-jurors are selected by seniority and 'weight', as it were, in the tribe, and not by proximity to any one man, for in such cases there is no such man.

human sense. The elections are held at their settlements, as are important collective oaths.[1]

I have singled out two institutions, in any case crucial for the tribes, which also highlight the manner in which the holy lineages, as it were professional and sacred outsiders, make possible the working of the tribal constitution—with its remarkable diffusion of power, its egalitarianism, its absence or minimal development of political and judicial specialization. There are also many other ways in which the *igurramen* perform such mediating functions: they facilitate trade (the tribes, contrary to a widespread stereotype of tribal life, are not economically autarchic), they arrange resettlement of exiled murderers, they arrange the pairings of tribal segments of diverse tribes for purposes of hospitality and as it were mutual consular services, etc.

They are not members of the tribes. They live on the frontiers between tribes (thereby, incidentally, helping to guarantee those frontiers), belonging to neither. Leo Africanus crossed the central High Atlas and reported with contempt that amongst these tribes, 'no one has any competence (political, legal) with regard to anything whatever'. This, as we have seen, is not quite true: but to the extent which it approximates the truth, this absence of political specialization amongst the lay tribes, is made possible by the functions assumed by the *igurramen*.

Of course, in addition to the structural functions described, the *igurramen* also aid the tribes in their Islamic identification. The *igurramen* are credited with being descendants of the Prophet: reverence for them and respect for their spoken word are a substitute, for illiterate tribesmen, for acquaintance with the Book which, in principle, a scriptural religion would seem to require, and which of course is not open to them. This substitute is, moreover, from the viewpoint of such tribesmen, superior to the real thing: it does not presuppose subjection to the verdict of the Book-learned men of the towns or, worse still, of those urban rulers who stand behind the literate judges.

The tribesmen revered the holy lineages instead, with a fervor sufficient to make some observers suppose one could speak of a 'maraboutic state', a hagiarchy in the mountains. If we dignify their authority with the designation of 'state', it is such only with serious qualifications: it is a state without real boundaries. *Igurramen* are not characteristically located within tribes, but between them: one settlement of *igurramen* will arbitrate a dispute between tribes A and B, and another settlement, a dispute between B and C, and so on. Is tribe B subject to the first or the second settlement of *igurramen*? No answer can be given. Again this region is one of extensive transhumance, and the same tribal groupings will be clients, or subjects, of different saintly groups at different times of the year.

Vis-à-vis any individual or small tribal group, the saints are enormously powerful, for they speak with the authority of all the other tribesmen who revere them: they can, and sometime did, as it were anathemize a given group, and

[1] As indicated, the number of co-jurors required depends on the gravity of the offence. Minor disputes can be settled by a local oath, at the mosque or a local shrine which is not graced by a settlement of *igurramen*: but disputes involving ten or more co-jurors, must go up to the holy men's shrine.

3

thus give *carte blanche* to all the others to despoil them, which they can then proceed to do. But *vis-à-vis* the tribes as a whole, or large blocks of them, the *igurramen* are really powerless: any unpopular policies or decisions on their part are liable to lead to a transfer of reverence by the tribes to the ever-ready *agurram* rivals (often cousins or distant cousins of the currently 'reigning' ones, ready in the wings for any opportunity). Thus the real power of these professional neutrals, arbitrators, mediators, is rather limited.[1]

In its pure form, this system survived till 1933. Its subsequent transformation is another story.

[1] In the central Atlas, the most striking example of *agurram* influence were the saints of Ahansal. Their principal settlement was near the point where the territories of four very large tribal groupings meet, and where seasonal transhumance rights are at their most complex—an ideal place for mediation, and one where it was most needed. The material on which this article is based is now available in full detail in *Saints of the Atlas* (London & Chicago, 1969).

3

Amal R. Vinogradov

The Socio-political Organization of a Berber 'Taraf' Tribe: Pre-Protectorate Morocco[1]

This chapter will reconstruct the socio-political organization of the Beni Mtir,[2] a Berber-speaking tribe located in the plains south of Meknes and astride the last northern ridges of the Middle Atlas. The Beni Mtir were a *taraf*[3] tribe (from the Arabic *qabail al taraf*) having been located on the edge of *bled el-makhzan* (the Pale, the land controlled by government) at the limits of the government's effective power and reach. The Beni Mtir existed in that politically transitional zone beyond which started the land of *siba* (dissidence). Needless to say, the tribe's political status varied with the actual ability of the *makhzan* (central government) to dominate the region. An examination of the tribe's history indicates that the relation of the Beni Mtir to the Alawi dynasty alternated between states of active hostility and outright war to ones of temporary alliance and sporadic submission.[4] The Beni Mtir were also in an ecologically transitional zone, inhabiting the *dir* or the slopes that join the foothills of the Middle Atlas to the nearby plains. Along with other *dir* tribes such as the Ait Seghrouchen, Ait Youssi and Gerouan, the Beni Mtir were transhumants utilizing the complementary zones of the mountains and the plains in their seasonal migrations. These *dir* tribes, all *tamazight* speakers, formed the vanguard of the historical migratory movement that carried waves of semi-nomadic populations from the dry southeastern part of Morocco to its humid and fertile northwest plains. Beginning with 1860, the Beni Mtir were in the backyard of the *makhzan*; not far from the royal cities of Fes and Meknes. Behind them on the upper ridges of the Middle Atlas surged the powerful and turbulent Beni Mguild confederation. The encroachment of the Beni Mtir on the rich Sais plain coincided with a period of relative weakness of the Alawi *makhzan*. Geographically close to the urban-based Arab culture, the Beni Mtir, unlike other Berber tribes (namely sections of the

[1] This paper is part of a dissertation on the evolution of the Beni Mtir. I wish to thank the Center for Near Eastern and North African Studies, the University of Michigan, for the fellowship that made the research possible.
[2] The Beni Mtir are also known by their Berber name of Ait Ndir. This duality of their name reflects their cultural and geographical position at the edge of the Arab–Berber zones. They now refer to themselves as Beni Mtir or Mtiris adding occasionally that this is the Arabic version of their real name, Ait Ndir. In other contexts, however, they will 'prove' their Arab origins and affiliations by pointing out the existence of an Arab tribe called the Beni Mtir in Tunis of which they once formed a part.

[3] The Arabic word *taraf* simply means 'edge'. I use it here in order to underline the fact that for the period under consideration, the Beni Mtir were located on the edge of the area that was effectively governed by the *makhzan*, or central government.

[4] For a history of the Beni Mtir and the region, see al-Nasiri, *Kitabal-Istiqsa*; Commdt. Ed. Arnaud, 'La région de Meknès', *Bulletin de la Société de Géog. du Maroc* (1916), No. 2, pp. 47–105; Abes, *Les Aïth Ndhir*, Paris, 1918 (pub. du Comité d'études berbères de Rabat).

Mjatt and Gerouan), maintained a remarkable purity of their own institutions and language. Socially, there was very little Arabization.[1] It is as if their very position in the gallery overlooking the Arabized world of Morocco and their political opposition to the *guish* (privileged, tax-exempt, government-supporting) tribes protecting the Sais plain, made them emphasize their Berberism and independence. This Berber independence was made possible by obstinately maintaining their key institutions: semi-nomadism, collective ownership of land, and their own *urf* (customary law) in opposition to the *sharia* (Koranic law).[2] By resisting sedenterization and full-time agriculture on the rich Sais plain, they also resisted being incorporated into the exploitive network of the *makhzan*. This choice 'to be independent' expressed itself in the structural adaptation of the human group, the two major features of which were a complete absence of individual property in land and a high degree of flexibility and pragmatism in the application of the principles of tribal affiliation and cohesion.

The ebb and flow of the *makhzan*'s power and effective domination in the area made for the emergence of an extremely functional social organization, one trimmed to basic essentials and capable of accommodating several structural alternatives without loss of its basic nature. Strong sultans such as Moulay Hasan (1874–94) attempted to settle the tribe, divide it into manageable administrative units for tax purposes and appoint non-tribal *caids*[3] to collect the tax. But as soon as the sultan died, the Beni Mtir, taking advantage of the chaotic period that usually followed, invariably kicked out the imposed *caids*, withheld the tax, elected their own chiefs, and reverted to their favourite occupation, highway robbery.[4] This patterned instability (what the French elegantly called 'stubborn anarchy') persisted until the French occupation of the region in 1912. Within years of their surrender and the establishment of a French administrative system, the distinctive features of the Beni Mtir's tribal

---

[1] This is not to deny that both ethnic groups shared a common metaphysical world view; if this were not the case, the Berbers would not have accepted the *sharifs* with their religious charisma (*baraka*) who came to play such a crucial role in the social structure of the tribes. This shared metaphysical outlook enabled the Berbers to accept the *sharifs* (or those who claimed such status) as mediators, healers, or advisers and made of the Berber and Arab tribes a potential reservoir for dynasties.

[2] A detailed analysis of the evolution of land tenure and land use among the Beni Mtir has been made by the author in a doctoral dissertation entitled, *From Ordered Anarchy to Confusing Order : the Evolution of a Berber Tribe*. It should be pointed out here that *all land* among the Beni Mtir was collectively owned, including the cultivated areas. After the establishment of the Protectorate, the French divided part of the collective land among the Mtiri households and gave it to them in *mulk* (private ownership).

[3] A *caid* is an administrative officer appointed or confirmed by the sultan to rule over a tribe or section. The *caid* was usually a notable from the tribe, although the sultan could and often did appoint men who were complete strangers to the tribe.

[4] The Beni Mtir had a notorious reputation as bandits and rebels. They themselves admit to practising banditry in times of the weakness of the *makhzan*. Their favored position astride both the internal Meknes–Marrakesh route and on the edge of the Meknes–Fes route rendered banditry lucrative. This outright banditry is not to be confused with the institutionalized protection (*mezraq*) which consisted of the payment of a toll tax by the travellers in tribal territory in return for their safety.

organization disappeared. The purpose of this paper, therefore, is to demonstrate the specific adaptation of a *taraf* tribe to the political environment of which the proximity of the *makhzan* formed the most prominent feature. I contend that part of this adaptation was in terms of a highly flexible and pragmatic socio-political organization that was a variant on a common Middle Atlas model. The Beni Mtir offer an interesting example of what Ernest Gellner has called 'dissident tribalism'; a group organized such that it could reject the political domination of the *makhzan* without denying the moral and religious superiority of the sultan.

WHAT WAS A BENI MTIR TRIBE?

The Beni Mtir divide all Moroccan tribes into three categories: (1) *guish*, the tribes who were allied to the *makhzan*; (2) *nayiba*, the tribes who were too weak to resist the *makhzan*; (3) *taryazt*, the tribes who were free and independent.[1] They themselves were always a *taryazt* tribe: 'we came from the south and fought our way through the mountains with the guns (*bilbarood*), and we took this land with the gun. We kept it with our guns and later we were driven off it only with the cannon (*nfad*)'.[2] However, this pride in their past independence does not translate itself into any concrete knowledge of their tribal structure or history. Tradition is minimal in the society and what there is does not explain origins nor does it validate structural relationships. 'People call us Ait Ndir; and it is our name. It is the same way that we call other groups near us Ait Youssi or Zayan.' Others, more sophisticated would say, 'There must have been a man called Ndir who was our ancestor and the founder of this tribe, but we really do not know anything about him except that he must have lived in the south because that is where we came from.' One legend prevalent in the region is the following:

> At the time of the Prophet, there lived three brothers, one of whom was called Ndir. One brother died and then Ndir killed the other brother. The *jmaa* (tribal assembly) met and decided that Ndir should be put to death for having committed the crime of fratricide. But he ran away and came to Tunis. However, he did not stay in Tunis for a long time, but left and made his way to the Maghreb and came to the south near the town of *Rish* where he married a *tamazight* (Berber) woman and became the founder of the Ait Ndir.

The name Beni Mtir is Arabic and they say that it was given to them by a *sharif* from Fes who reputedly exclaimed 'hadi mashi Ait Ndir, hadi albla kaytir' ('This is no tribe of Ait Ndir, this is the scourge, plague, affliction, that flies'). This was in reference to their notorious banditry and mobility on horse-

---

[1] The *nayiba* was a replacement tax that certain tribes paid the *makhzan* in return for their use of domain land. These tribes were made to furnish contingents to the sultan, but this was not on any regular basis. *Taryazt* is from the tamazight word *aryaz* meaning man, also manly, free.

[2] In reference to the French army that used heavy cannons against the Beni Mtir.

back as they retreated into the mountains. 'And from that day on, the name stuck to us and came to replace our Berber name.'[1]

The Beni Mtir are patrilineal and segmentary. They refer to themselves as a *taqbilt*, the term being the *tamazight* form of the Arabic word *qabila*: tribe and/or confederation. They do not claim any common descent from one ancestor and their usual reply to the question, 'Why are you a *taqbilt*?' is, 'Because we share an area in common, have one dialect (i.e. speak differently from the way the Zayan and Gerouan) and have our own *qaida* (custom).' The term *taqbilt* among the Beni Mtir is reserved for the supreme unit with which the individual identifies and is never utilized in a sliding segmentary fashion, i.e. relative to context as is reported for other Middle Atlas tribes. This usage seems to hold true for all the *dir* tribes and may reflect the political ascendancy of that level of organization (confederation) in their chronic wars with the *makhzan*.

The term *taqbilt*, therefore, connotes the largest political framework that encompasses a number of contiguous groups all exploiting a common ecological area, in this case, the complementary zones of transhumance, the plateau and the plain. The major role of the *taqbilt* was to safeguard the strategic and economic area necessary for the proper functioning of these groups as well as to represent their common interest *vis-à-vis* other groups of the same order.

There are ten primary divisions within the *taqbilt*. These are named, territorially localized segments of equal structural order called *ikhsan* (sing. *ighs*). The French refer to this level of segmentation as 'fraction' and it has been translated as 'clans'.[2] The word *ighs* means 'bone' in tamazight and the Bein Mtir who tend to be bilingual in Arabic use the terms *fekhda* (lit. 'thigh') and *ferqa* (division) when speaking of this level. *Ighs* is the Mtiri segmentary designate par excellence. It is used to refer to all subsequent tribal subdivisions, regardless of size and rank, although at lower levels they generally substitute the dimunitive form *tighst* (pl. *tikhsatin*). The ten *ighsan* of the Beni Mtir are:

Ait Iqqedaren
Ait Bourzouine
Ait Sliman
Ait Lahsen ou Shaib
Ait Boubidman
Ait Ourtindi
Ait Hammad
Ait Ouallal Bittit
Ait Harzallah
Ait Naaman

[1] The Beni Mtir do not know how the expression 'kaytir' came to be their name of 'Mtir'; they simply say that 'it has to do with us being like the *tir*, or bird'. It is likely that the name Beni Mtir was derived by prefixing the feminine particle of belonging, /m/, to the noun *tir* (bird). The feminine possessive in this case agrees in gender with the word *qabila* or tribe; thus one gets *qabilat mtir*, or the tribe that belongs to the birds, or of the birds.

[2] Ernest Gellner, *Saints of the Atlas*, London & Chicago, 1969, p. 93; Abes, op. cit., p. 40.

The above are the original and 'real' sections to which the French later added two more: Ait Ayash and Ait Lahsen ou Youssef. The Beni Mtir point out that the Ait Ayash are a fraction of the Ait Ayash of the Anseghmir. In 1803, Moulay Sliman defeated the Ait Idrassen confederation and in the aftermath detached a section of the Ait Ayash and brought it to the Sais. It was made a *guish* tribe and settled south of Fes, where it is today. The Ait Lahcen ou Youssef is a recent

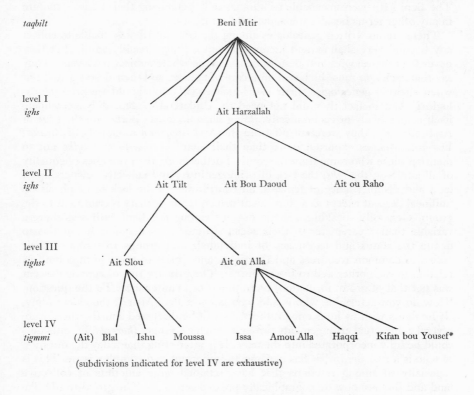

(subdivisions indicated for level IV are exhaustive)

* Kifan bou Yousef is composed today exclusively of *Shurfa* Boukili families.

Fig. 3.1 Typical segmentary organization among the Beni Mtir

composite group made up of some Ait Naaman families and some Mjatt who were relocated by the French on land owned originally by the Naaman.

Figure 3.1 illustrates a typical segmentary organization among the Beni Mtir. The usual depth varies between three and four levels; younger informants are completely ignorant of levels III and IV, whereas older ones tend to disagree on which *tigmmi* are to be included in what *tighst*. Most of the *ikhsan* on levels II and III tend to bear names that imply agnatic descent, but in the absence of genealogies, they serve only for identification purposes. Apart from the primary sections (level I), all others above the level of *tigmmi* can be considered as contingent groups, since as far as I could ascertain they had no jural, political or ritual functions. They are logically there by virtue of the segmentary principle, but remained structurally and functionally latent. They may be considered as nominal descent groups, since above the level of the douar, putative common descent is the generalized deduction from the possession of the common name. The Beni Mtir were incapable of idiomatically perceiving their social structure in any other terms besides the agnatic descent ones.

There are no written genealogies among the tribe and I was unable to collect any beyond very shallow and incomplete ones. Elders readily admit that they never kept genealogies and besides consider the whole subject irrelevant. They say that each *ighs* must be based on a core of agnates and their descendants, but when eliciting genealogies, their usual answer is 'Why should we keep genealogies?' And in fact they did not need to. Unilateral descent did not validate itself ceremonially or economically. Being selfconsciously Berber on the edge of Arab territory, they were cut off from the Arab-*sharifian* monopoly of *baraka*; Fes and Meknes exported more than their share of *sharif*s and *fqih*s not to mention those who came from the south. Furthermore, the principles of equality of all adults in the *ighs*, the lack of primogeniture, and collective ownership of land and disinheritance of females, all contributed to the lack of emphasis on unilineal descent except as a convenient principle for primary recruitment to the group. Generally speaking, agnatic descent among the Beni Mtir was more a variable than a parameter of their social structure. Its major function was to define the status and legitimacy of individuals and groups in terms of their access to common resources and the rights and duties of these groups both in relation to each other and to the resources. The primary role of agnatic descent was not that of group formation, recruitment or maintenance. To the question, 'How do you determine who is and who is not a Beni Mtir?', the elders reply, 'If he fights with us he is our brother.' As will be discussed shortly, there were several contractual arrangements through which a stranger (*barrani*, lit. outsider) could be fully incorporated into the tribe. It is interesting that today the question of who is a real Beni Mtir has become an important and complex issue. This is especially so among fractions that have retained large amounts of collective land and that are now demographically pressed for space. The group would like to divide this joint patrimony, and in its self-interest is seeking to flush out all the 'strangers' and bar them from access to the land. As an old man of Ait Harzallah said, 'In the old days, people came from other tribes, made the *tamghrust* [sacrifice], and we let them settle on our land. In time they took their guns and fought by our side and they became our brothers. Now everybody is selfish and people point out this and that *takhamt* [lit. 'tent', but term is still used to refer to an extended family] and say they are not genuine Harzallawis; we remember their grandfather who came from the Rif and was allowed to squat on our land. He did not even make the *tamghrust*. They cannot be counted among us [meaning they cannot be considered as members of the group when it comes to division of collective land]. This is *hshuma* ['shame'] and against *qaida* ['custom']. But then things have changed and many of us who never have farmed in our lives are obliged to take up the plow and break the rocks for a living.'

The ten clans may be considered corporate to the extent that they were permanently constituted land-owning units.[1] Mtiris insist that there were and always will be ten *ikhsan* (clans) to their *taqbilt*. The land was considered the collective property of all male members of the *ighs*, who had only usufruct rights to it. It was called *tamazirt n jmat* (the land of the collectivity or group). If a man left his clan territory for a period of time, he held residual rights to it which could be activated upon his return, but if he left his family behind, they were considered as 'using his share'. Women had no independent legal status in the society; their access to resources was by virtue of their being mothers, wives and daughters of the men. Under certain circumstances, though, they could constitute a sort of 'carrier' of tribal rights, and could serve as links to perpetuate the patrilineal family in the absence of males.[2] There were two ways in which this was done, the *amhars* and *amazzal* relationships. A widowed woman with young sons might find a man whom she married informally (i.e. without the public sacrifice) and who then became the head of her family. She then operated an independent household, i.e. without being incorporated into her former husband's household, and any children born to her out of the new marriage were considered ('counted on') her deceased husband's. In other words, the new sons retained rights to the collective property of the clan of the former husband regardless of the actual affiliation of the progenitor, who was known as *amazzal*. The second arrangement was more formalized. A man, who might be an outsider to the *taqbilt* came to the *jmaa* (assembly) of a douar and made a sacrifice (*tamghrust*). He asked to become an *amhars* of someone in the group (*amhars*: one who is watched or guarded). One of those present agreed to be his sponsor and a contract period between the two was then decided upon publicly. This usually ranged between two to six years. During this time, the *amhars* lived near his patron, who usually gave him a daughter or niece in marriage. Any children born were considered as belonging to the mother, i.e. to the patron's lineage. The *amhars* was not allowed to marry a second wife until his contract period was over; and should he die, his accumulated goods went to his patron. If at the end of the contract period, the man decided to move away, he had to leave his wife and children behind. But should he decide to stay permanently, he was 'adopted' into the group. The *amhars* took a sheep and sacrificed it in front of the *jmaa* of the douar and declared his desire to join them 'as a free man'. They then gave him a piece of land where he could set up an independent household with his wife and children. But before he did that, he paid the bride price to his former patron and thus achieved full status. He then could sit in the *jmaa*, carry arms and participate in wars; he also became liable for the payment of the *diyya* (blood money) like any other member of the douar.

Both the *amazzal* and the *amhars* were considered as *amzaid*, i.e. people who

[1] The term clan is used here to refer to a compromise kin group which is both unilineal and residential.

[2] This need not be literally true. Informants say that if the *takhamt* has only a few males, it is weak (*d'eef*) and must therefore be augmented.

3*

were added to the original group. A slight social stigma was attached to the status since it implied that the *amzaid* lacked full *aryazen* (manly, gun-carrying tribesman) status in his own tribe. However, subsequent personal success and prestige could obliterate the initial *miskin* (abject, servile) stigma. Children of *amzaids* who were later incorporated into the douars suffered no handicaps whatsoever.

Apart from the Koranic injunctions, the Beni Mtir had no preferential or proscribed marriage rules. They knew of the Arab tribes' preference for the father's brother's daughter, but stated that it was not their way (*abrid*) or custom (*qaida*). The best marriages were those within the clan since 'we share the same customs and there is less likelihood for the woman to run away'. Clans who bordered other tribes often exchanged wives with them, e.g. the Iqeddaren exchanged women with the Irklaouen fraction of the Beni Mguild. But this was simply a function of proximity and personal preference rather than any systematic alliance-making activity. In general, marriage was not a pivotal institution in the society and women were not considered a terribly important commodity. Often they were 'inherited' along with other movable property. Mtiri women claim that their status is better today, since under the *sharia* they can at least appoint a *wakil* (representative) who will represent their interest in court and disputes.

The lack of preferred marriage patterns among the tribe resulted in the absence of common genealogical unity at any level above that of the extended family or the minimal lineage. This, and the practice of open recruitment into the agnatic descent group, rendered them structurally flexible. Logically, one could elevate the descent-organized segmentary constructs among the Beni Mtir into a model of the social system, but it would not be referable to anything real or relevant to the Mtiris themselves, or to the functioning of their society. This is not to deny the idiomatic prevalence of kinship terminology and concepts. For example, no matter what the original form of incorporation into the group, in time it will be reinterpreted in agnatic terms.

The *tigmmi* was the smallest and the most viable segment among the Beni Mtir. French writers rightly refer to it as the cell at the base of the social organization. The term *tigmmi*, which is completely replaced today by *douar*, referred to a group of tents that camped together. Their number varied between 14 and 25. Mtiris say that the ideal *tigmmi* should have had no less than 20 adult men, which was usually enough to repel a sudden raid. A *tigmmi* of less than 13 men was considered 'weak' and should have either increased its number, or joined up with another one. An extended family which formed one economic household was considered one *takhamt* (tent) regardless of its actual size; thus the Mtiris use the term for tent coupled to an individual's name to mean 'the household of so and so'. For example, *Ait ukham Haddou ou Ali* refers to an extended family headed by Haddou ou Ali. The family owned all the animals in common and exploited one share of the irrigated land. Upon the death of Haddou, it could break up and form as many *takhamts* as Haddou had sons; or these might decide not to divide and to stay together as one household. A group of closely related *takhamts* formed a *rif*. The number of *rifs* varied with the size of the *tigmmi* and they say that when a *rif* grew too large, it simply broke away to form a new *tigmmi*. This new *tigmmi* became a replica of the original one; no genealogical depth was added.

The actual composition of the *tigmmi* varied seasonally. In winter and when the group was in the lowland, it conformed closely to the ideal model. A *tigmmi* would consist of an agnatically related group, of three to four generations in depth, that had definite jural character since it was liable for the payment of a joint *diyya* (blood money) and was directed by an assembly. In summer, though, greater flexibility was displayed; an original *douar* may split up and each *rif* could band with a different group. These would spend the summer months together as nomads in the higher pastures. These temporary camp units were based on personal preferences, affinal ties, and economic cooperation. The Beni Mtir had institutionalized means for forging these non-descent based units and some of these will be discussed further on.

Each *tigmmi* was allotted an area on the plain. This area was then divided up among the different households.[1] Plots were divided equally regardless of the actual size of the household or the number of draft animals that it possessed. In theory, these plots were rotated annually, but in practice this was not done until some drastic change in the douar's composition necessitated a redivision. It could be pointed out that the Mtiris possessed more arable land than they could utilize, and that agriculture was anyway a subsidiary activity in their total economy. The French counted 18,099 Beni Mtir in the year 1915. These were spread out over an area totalling approximately 1,500 square kilometers, giving them a rough density of 12 people per square kilometer. Their occupation of the area in the plain was normally precarious and conditional since they could be and often were driven off it by the sultans. However, their hold on their territory in the plateau was more tenacious and significant to them in terms of pasture for their animals and the strategic function of the area in case of retreat. This grazing area (*agdal*) was never divided up but was exploited jointly by all the *tigmmi*.[2]

The *tigmmi* constituted the most visible and critical level of organization among the Beni Mtir; it was the unit where the jural, kinship and territorial principles of the society intersected. *Tigmmi*s had remarkable degree of autonomy; they resembled tribes in miniature. Only when the group was at war did they recede in importance to give way to the level that was the most operative politically, the *ighs*.

The day-to-day affairs of the *tigmmi* were directed by an informal assembly of men, the *jmaa*. All adult males in the douar were theoretically eligible to sit on the assembly; the insane, sick, women and children were excluded. So were the *barrani*s, the outsiders. In practice, however, a usual *jmaa n tigmmi* consisted of five to seven older men who had authority and commanded respect in their

---

[1] The normal procedure was for the *jmaa* of the douar to go into the fields, survey the area, and then divide it *bilhabl*, using a rope for measurement.

[2] I have been using the term douar to mean *tigmmi*. Today, the term douar is used indiscriminately to refer to all types of rural settlements in Morocco. See the special issue of the *Revue de géographie*, No. 8, 1965.

community. The Mtiris call them *akhatar* (pl. *ikhataren*). These met irregularly to deal with problems as they came up. Since most activities were routine, the major function of the *jmaa* was the regulation and containment of conflict. French ethnographers tend to elevate the *jmaa* into a specialized political institution with defined roles and functions. In fact, the *jmaa* did not constitute a specialized political body, but was simply the extention of the patriarchal kinship system. It was not so much a well-defined institution as a mode of expression of the solidarity of the small agnatically based group; it had no regular meeting days and no hierarchy. It functioned through the tacit agreement of the whole group. An *akhatar n jmat* (or as they call him an *ajemmai*, one who is a member of the *jmaa*) was neither elected nor appointed to his position. He was there 'naturally', because of the sum total of all the roles he played in his community which made of him a natural and informal leader and spokesman for the group. The *jmaa* functioned as both a judicial and administrative body; it allocated collective land, oversaw division of water for irrigation, collected money for a passing *sharif*, and officiated at marriages and inheritance ceremonies. Above all, it served as guardian of the *qaida* or the customary way of life of the community.[1]

The *jmaa* of the *ighs* was composed of members coopted from the *jmaas* of each *douar*. This *jmaa* usually numbered eighteen to twenty persons. Members met irregularly to handle matters that affected the whole clan; hence their duties were mainly political in nature. They decided on alliances, concluded peace pacts (*hana*) and coordinated the summer grazing movements of the douars. When necessary, they negotiated with tribes that pastured on territory of the Beni Mtir during severe winters, groups such as the Beni Mguild and the Seghrouchen. They also elected the *amghar* (chief) for the whole clan. 'The *akhatars* met in a tent; they sacrificed and ate sheep. They then talked and went outside, so everybody could see them and chose one among themselves to be the *amghar*.[2] Then each *akhatar* took some grass and put it on him saying "We have chosen you our *amghar* and we shall obey you." The *amghar* then turned and said "Give me the *amasais* (the respondents) who will be responsible for you, and we sent him those that he wanted. The *amghar* was chosen from war to war.' Actually, each *ighs* usually nominated one person for the position of *amghar*, and if the *jmaa* did not agree on a choice then they selected by lot (*ghir illan*).[3]

The *amasai* was a person chosen by the douar to 'speak for them' and to be responsible for their behavior to the *amghar*. At the same time, he must be

[1] Mtiris use the term *qaida* (Arabic custom) and *abrid* (Berber road, way) to refer to the traditional way of life of the tribe. The terms *izref* and *urf* are used to refer to the customary laws that safeguard and embody these traditions.

[2] Informants always mentioned 'going outside, so all can see' as an integral part of all ceremonies and group meetings. This public witness as validation was no doubt necessary in an illiterate society.

[3] There seems to have been no systematic method for electing the *amghar* among the Beni Mtir, certainly nothing like the rotation and complementarity mentioned by Gellner for the central High Atlas (Gellner, op. cit., p. 81). In cases where the members of the *jmaa* disagreed on a candidate, they took a number of straws of equal length and included a short one among them. Then each *ajemmai* pulled a straw and the man who got the short one got to name the *amghar*.

acceptable to the *amghar*. Mtiris usually use the Arabic term *dhamen* (guarantor) to refer to the *amasai*. 'The *amasai* made sure that he was chosen by everybody in the *tigmmi*. He then told them, "now you have to obey me", and they said, "yes, we have chosen you and we shall obey you". The *amasai* stood responsible for his *douar* to the *amghar*; when the *amghar* gave an order, especially in war-time, he had to be obeyed. If a man disobeyed, then the *amghar* ordered his *amasai* (the man's) to burn his tent or to cut his wife's hair in public. *Amasis* left their *silham* (outer garment) with the *amghar*; if they failed in their duties or made trouble the women dyed them *henna* (yellow) and exhibited them outside the tent. This was *ar* (grave shame).'

Each clan usually had one *amghar*; it did happen that two powerful leaders might contest the title; the clan would then split into factions. Beni Mtir tended to refer to their *amghars* as *amghar el-barood* (the war chief) rather than *amghar n touya* (chief of the grass), which is the usual form among the Middle Atlas tribes in general.[1] 'L'*amghar* n'est pas rétribué. Pour le dédommager de ses peines, de sa responsabilité et des frais d'hospitalité qu'exigent ses fonctions, il jouit de certains avantages. Les groupements désignent en effet des hommes qui exécutent ce qu'on appelle "les corvées d'*amghar*"; on lui laboure ses champes, on moisonne et on dépique sa récolte . . . on porte son courrier à sa destination, on garde ses tentes. De plus, il touche les amendes (en berbère: *izmaz*) infligées à ceux qui contreviennent à la coutume, désobéissent à l'*amghar* ou à ses sub-ordonnés . . . le taux des amendes est assez élevé en temps de guerre. L'*amghar* n'hésite pas à confisquer les biens du délinquant, à brûler sa tente, à raser les cheveux de sa femme en public.'[2]

In theory there was a *jmaa* for the whole *taqbilt* whose members were coopted from the *jmaas* of each clan, and this would in turn choose a paramount *amghar* who was usually called *amghar n touya*. But despite the fact that in the mono-graph written by Abes on the Beni Mtir, such a *jmaa* and an *amghar* are men-tioned (p. 45), I was not able to pinpoint any one historical time that this 'logical' extention of the socio-political model did in fact operate. The Beni Mtir do not seem to have ever fought as one corporate unit; the usual pattern was for a clan or two to fight (against Gerouan or Dkhissa) while the remaining clans 'stood behind them, in their backs' giving them tacit support and aid. In such cases, one of the *amghars* involved would take over as the supreme commander (or one would be chosen on the spur of the moment) and he would be assisted by the most influential and prestigious *ikhataren*. Needless to say, one can hardly exaggerate the importance of the personal charisma and character of the leaders in this ill-defined role and in the context of a nebulous shifting field of power. The closest that the Beni Mtir came to fighting as one unit, at least within historical memory, was in the years 1908–9, and even then the leadership was in the hands of two *amghars*. As the tribesmen themselves say 'the word (*klamm*) of the whole *taqbilt* was entrusted to two people: Aqqa Boubidmani and Mokhtar el-Hammadi'. These two leaders became the spokesmen for the tribe.

---

[1] Mtiris know of the term *amghar n touya* and some used it, but the rule was to use *amghar el-barood*, or simply *amghar*.

[2] Abes, op. cit., pp. 45–6.

There is no doubt that despite the disproportionate amount of power given an *amghar*, he was still considered to be the embodiment of the collective will of the tribe and the symbol of its latent solidarity.

Perhaps the following story will elucidate both the attitude to the *amghar* and the relative position of the status itself. 'The *caid* Haddou ben Grin and all those of the tribe who were allied with him were with Siddi Rahu in the mountains fighting the French. They then started to raid us, their cousins.[1] We got tired of this and all of us got together, all the different *ikhsan* (clans) went to Bou Semsel and chose Hajj el-Boubidmani to be our *amghar*. This then meant that all the other *caid*s including Hadou ben Grin became as if they were the *amasai*s of the newly chosen *amghar*. We then went out against Sidi Rahu and the Mtiris with him and chased them until we reached Tichoukt (in Seghrouchen territory). We did not rely on the French to fight for us.'

Apart from the *shurfa*, there were no distinctions of rank within the society itself. The Beni Mtir maintained a special relationship with *zawiya* Boukili which is located north of Ksar el-Souk in the territory of Ait Izdig. Boukili *shurfa* traveled (and still do) every summer to the territory of the Beni Mtir to collect their share (*ushr*) of the harvest. Some lingered to mediate conflict and lend their moral presence to alliances. They also wrote love-potions for the tribesmen and dispensed curing services. No one knows exactly when this symbiotic relationship started between the *zawiya* and the tribe, but they claim that it dates back to the time when the tribe was still in the south.[2] In fact, one whole *douar* among the Ait Harzallah (Kifan bou Yousef) is composed entirely of *shurfa* Boukilis, who have been settled among the Harzallah for at least a hundred years. These are inactive *shurfa* with no manifest *baraka*. In the old days they refrained from carrying arms, but otherwise were hardly distinguishable from the rest. A certain amount of deference is granted to them today by older Mtiris and they themselves make feeble attempts at confirming their separate rank. Thus they tend to be endogamous, seclude their women, and forbid them from mingling with crowds at public celebrations.

Positions of status were few and, apart from the *amghar*'s, highly generalized. In all, personal character was of real and paramount importance since it was relevant to the requirements of leadership: self-confidence, dignity, exercise of judgment and responsibility. All leaders were subsumed under the category of *ikhetaren*, out of which were chosen the *amghar*s, *amasai*s and *ajemmai*s (those who sit in the *jmaa*). All *ikhetaren*, almost by definition, commanded great personal prestige and enjoyed public trust. These served as their weapons in the

[1] The majority of the Beni Mtir had submitted to the French at this time since it was harvest time on the plain and they did not dare leave their crops to be burned by the French army.

[2] A story gathered by Mr John Chiapuris among the Ait Hadiddu explains the origin of the relationship in this way: 'The Ait Ndir (Beni Mtir) were a wicked and mischievous tribe. One day all the saints gathered to read the *fatiha* and to plan how to eliminate the Ait Ndir. Only Sidi Boukil spoke up for them and asked the saints to spare them, he promised that he will try to control them. Because of this, the Ait Ndir visit the *zawiya* of Sidi Boukil, which is located higher than the river Ziz near Rish. They offer the saint sheep, mules, butter and grain.'

absence of ritual sanctions and coersive power. Whenever the *jmaa* of any level met, members had to be present unless they had valid reasons for absence. Complete attendance was necessary to lend the weight of general concensus to resolutions; those individuals who failed to appear had to kill a sheep and host the *jmaa* for a day.

Even though the *amghar* did monopolize the right to exercise certain extremes of force, such as burning a tent or cutting the hair of women, his position was nevertheless one of relative authority and not of arbitrary power. The *jmaa* was always evaluating his performance and when necessary could remove him. 'Good' *amghar*s have been known to last ten years, whereas 'bad' ones could be impeached immediately. Distortions in this flexibility were often the result of the *makhzan*'s interference. 'We had this *amghar* whom the *jmaa* had elected. One day he sent for an *amasai* and told him "go to your people and get me twenty mounted men with guns. I need them." We were not at war, and the *amasai* went and told the other people. The *ikhetaren* then got up and came to the *kashbah* of el-Hajeb to see why the *amghar* was giving such orders. They found him with 200 *askar* (soldiers) that the sultan has sent him. Now they knew that he was a real *caid* and nobody could disobey, not with two hundred soldiers at his command.'

THE DYNAMICS OF INTRA-TRIBAL RELATIONSHIPS

'A good war justifies any cause'

The normal relationship between the *ikhsan* was one of mutual suspicion and hostility since they were rivals for land and the right to protect the travelers and caravans that passed through the tribal territory. Warfare expressed the political legitimacy of the *ighs* and it therefore necessarily mobilized all individuals within the territory of the clan. It also formed the only occasion on which the cohesion of the whole group became visible.[1] As mentioned earlier, the harshest measures were dealt out to those who disobeyed the *amghar* or who refused to fight. Since the tribe had no high centralized authority to mediate and end the continual raids and warring between its primary segments (they themselves say that a supreme *amghar* tended always to favor his own group), they resorted to outsiders: *shurfa*, famous arbitrators from nearby tribes and often times the sultan himself.

We had been fighting among ourselves for a long time and we were tired; but we could not agree. So a delegation of notables went to Fes to seek the audience of the sultan Moulay Hasan. He met them and said to them 'Why is it that you the Beni Mtir are always fighting among yourselves; the news had reached me that you make the roads unsafe for caravans, your fields rest fallow and your crops unharvested while you fight; why do you do this?'

[1] The clan territory was considered an extension of the solidarity of the human group itself, and a measure of its strength. In other words, an affirmation of their right to be. Mtiris say 'Our land was our strength'.

Then one of the notables present, the *caid* Hammou el-Hajj said, 'Mawlana, it may be we fight because the clans [*afkhad*] are all intermingled on the land' and the sultan said, 'Why don't you go back and separate the different *afkhad*s and put each one on its own territory with its own boundaries.' And the notables thought it was a good idea and when they came back here, they did just that. They got together all the *jmaa*s and worked out the boundaries; and from that day all the Iqeddaren are on this land and all the Harzallah are on that. And they did not fight as much because of the advice of the sultan, who was a wise man.[1]

The Beni Mtir know of the word *leff* (which is the usual North African term for alliance) but do not use it. They say that it is an Arabic word which simply means alliance, the power that an individual or group can muster in case of a quarrel. They have their own word for alliance: *thamunt* or *thumint*.[2] The Beni Mtir use *thamunt* in a generic fashion to mean 'an alliance'; they then differentiate between several kinds of alliances each involving its own sanctions and responsibilities. The most important of these alliances was the *tada*.

In reply to a question about the number of clans in the tribe, an old and intelligent informant replied

Well, you could say there are five and you could say there are ten. It all depends on how you look at it. If you are looking from above, then we are five and I will show you how.

He then proceeded to count in pairs, 'Ait Hammad and Ait Harzallah, Ait Boubidman and Air Ourtindi, Ait Sliman and Ait Bourzouine, Ait Lahcen ou Shaib and Ait Iqeddar, Ait Oullal and Ait Naaman. Now each of these pairs had a *thamunt* between them, therefore we could be considered five divisions.' The *thamunt* implied mutual assistance and the sharing of clan territory. Each of the pairs mentioned occupied a different altitude and the alliance obviously functioned therefore to provide the necessary complementarity of areas for transhumance. Furthermore, this vague alliance pattern among the clans precipitated itself into an overall dual division of the tribe into two halves, what the Mtiris call the *Ait Omnasf*.[3] Thus one *Ait Omnasf* was made up of the fractions of Ouallal, Naaman, Harzallah, Boubidman, Hammad and Ourtindi as opposed to the other Ait Omnasf made up of the Iqeddaren, Bourzouine, Lahcen ou Chaib, Sliman and the Ayash. These also corresponded very roughly to an east–west geographical division.

---

[1] Regardless of the authenticity of the story, related to me by an informant of Ait Sliman, it does illustrate one of the many roles that sultans played in the life of the tribes It also shows the tribesmen's own view of their history. Both written and oral history indicate that the Beni Mtir clans were already localized in their territories before the reign of Moulay Hasan, but Berbers tend to peg all remembered events from their past unto the reign of the few really famous sultans, thus collapsing time.

[2] Etymologically, the word *thamunt* or its *thumint*, may be derived either from the verb *amn*, with its Arabic meaning 'safety', or 'security', or from the tamazight verb *mun* meaning 'to accompany'. Either way, makes semantic sense.

[3] *Omnasf* mans half.

It is claimed that when wars occurred intratribally, the clans fell back on the Omnasf division, each having to respect its position on one or the other side of the dual arrangement. However, if war was with a stranger, outside the tribe, the *Omnasf* ceased to operate. In other words, the upper limits of the *thamunt* was the tribe itself, and alliances never extended beyond the *taqbilt*. But it would be too easy to assume that this dualism was a permanent structure which functioned all the time. What seems to have happened was this, two or three powerful clans, always ranged on the opposite sides of the *Omnasf*, would compete for the leadership of the confederation, and the other less powerful ones would be drawn into their orbits and ranged themselves on one side or the other depending on the nature of the issues and their range. For example, informants would always place the Iqeddaren against the Harzallah and the Bourzouine against the Naaman,[1] then they would hesitate about the rest of the clans, different informants giving different versions of the division. They would usually conclude by adding that there was nothing sacred or permanent about these alliances, and that they tended to change with the intratribal wars.

When fighting each other, the clan that suffered the most caualties usually asked for *aman* or *hana* (peace). As soon as the fighting was stopped, the *amghar*s involved went out and counted the casualties on both sides. The dead cancelled out each other, and the clan that was left with the most dead had to be compensated by the victors. Blood money (*diyya*) was paid to the relatives of those who were killed in much the same way as if this were an intraclan murder. I am of the opinion that all intratribal fighting resembled the feud, rather than war. In other words, it was viewed as blood revenge within a political community rather than as armed conflict between autonomous political communities. Viewed thus, the necessity to settle the credit–debit balance of human life through *diyya* becomes clear. Only in this way could they prevent the perpetuation of a state of feud which would be intolerable since it would interfere with the necessary automatic coalescing of the confederation in the likelihood of an attack by an outsider. After all, this was the whole *raison d'être* of the confederation which was nothing more than a pattern of military defense units that managed to accommodate internal differences in the face of external threats.

There was a gain in interclan fighting, albeit a subtle one. The clan that inflicted more casualties and forced its antagonist to ask for peace, gained moral credit among the totality of the Beni Mtir, prestige and status that could be exploited when the victorious clan desired to initiate an alliance, exploit a certain pasture or challenge a *caid*. Therefore, the financial loss they suffered in paying the *diyya* was more than compensated for in terms of prestige and persuasive force within the confederation.

To recapitulate, despite the ephemeral nature of the *thamunt*s (alliances) among the Beni Mtir, they did function to extend the sphere of mutual protection and cooperation among the different segments of the society. For example, a special kind of alliance was that of the *taymat* (from Berber *aytma*: brothers). The *taymat* was a voluntary pact of friendship between two individuals that need not involve their respective families. *Taymat* implied mutual assistance,

[1] These specific clans had the reputation of being very strong and belligerent.

economic cooperation such as breeding sheep and aiding in harvest, and the exchange of hospitality and women in marriage. The ceremony sealing the pact involved the sharing of food but no sacrifice, although the participants often recited the *fatiha* (the first chapter of the Koran) together in order to lend solemnity to the occasion.[1]

An important kind of alliance was the *tada*.[2] The Mtiris differentiate two kinds of *tadas* (*tada biljouj*), the inner (*dakhlaniya*) and the upper (*foqaniya*). The *tada dakkhlaniya* was a freely contracted alliance between two *rifs* or two *douars*; they did not need to be of the same *taqbilt*. 'When these decided to make a *tada*, they spread the word around and then on the agreed day, they took their tents and pitched them together on high ground, so everyone could see. Then they took the slippers of all the men who wanted to enter this *tada* and threw them in the middle of the gathering, mixing them up. Each man from one group retrieved his slipper with a mate from the other group's slippers. They then found the owner of the mate and the two men embraced and called each other Ait ou tada. Afterwards they sat and shared a meal together. This *tada* was very important and lasted from one child to the next (meaning from one generation to the next). If anyone broke the rules of the *tada*, God punished them.' The *tada* was taken very seriously by the participants. It implied mutual aid and trust and guaranteed entrée and hospitality among the *tigmmi*s.

The second *tada*, the *tada foqaniya*, was an alliance concluded between two clans. In this case, the *jmaa*s involved met in a tent, sacrificed sheep and feasted each other. 'Then they gave their word to each other, preferably in the presence of a *sharif*. This *tada* also lasted till the death of all the participants. For example, we, the Iqeddaren, have a *tada* with the Ait Hammad that is still going on today, and it will end only when my friends and I die.'[3] Clans that had a *tada* between them were forbidden to intermarry for the duration of the *tada*. The major function of this alliance was the regulation of theft and adultery, violations of which were believed to be punished automatically through supernatural sanctions. However, the *tada* did not impose the obligation of mutual assistance in intratribal war. When asked about the contradictions and possible strains resulting from this, an informant said, 'It is like this. We, the Iqeddaren, have a *tada* with Ait Hammad, but we fall on opposite sides of the *Omnasf*. Now, if we find ourselves in a fight, we will try to avoid shooting at each other. We will send word and say that our men will be behind such and such a rock and the Hammad will stay away from that place. If anyone of them becomes our prisoner, or is wounded, we treat him well and send him to his people.' Even though, in theory, the *tada*s were binding from one generation to the next, there seem to

---

[1] For reasons of space, I have left out a whole class of alliances known collectively as *amur*. The *mezraq* came under this category.

[2] The verb *tad* means 'to nurse' in tamazight and Beni Mtiris say that at one time in their past, certain *tada*s involved ceremonies of colactation. The participants exchanged milk that was obtained from nursing mothers of the respective groups involved. See G. Marcy, 'L'Alliance par collactation (*tada*) chez les Berbères du Maroc central', *Revue africaine*, Vol. II, pp. 957–73.

[3] My informant was a very old man who insisted that this *tada* was still operative today, much to the disbelief and amusement of the young tribesmen who were present.

have been ways of revoking them. Informants said that if the *ou tada*s found themselves breaking too many of the rules, such as allowing many cows to wander over boundaries, or abducting women from the *ou tada* clan, then the *ikhetaren* might decide that their *tada* should be suspended. Otherwise they would run the risk of incurring supernatural wrath. But this must have occurred very rarely, for I was unable to find anyone who could describe such a revocation ceremony.

It should be clear from the above brief description that it is both arbitrary and unrewarding to conceive of the socio-political system of the Beni Mtir in exclusively segmentary or alliance terms. A more realistic interpretation would be to view it in terms of a dynamic interplay of the two models. An alliance could reinforce the lineage, contradict it, or even replace it altogether. Many times, a segment had to make a choice between respecting lineage solidarity or upholding its own political interests. This was obvious from the reaction of the tribe to the French invasion, when 'cousins' joined different factions and started to raid each other. Therefore, one may safely say that although agnatic segmentation, or its ideology in this case, defined broadly the spheres of political cooperation and the level at which conflict was to be evaluated and dealt with, it did not determine them. The function of the different alliances was to provide alternatives in the case of the failure of lineage cohesion.

I may add in conclusion that the 'order' of this society proves a difficult one to describe. One is struck by the contradictions, general amorphousness, and the overlapping of the units underlying its organization. These units were dynamic and can only be defined adequately in terms of outside events which were often negative in nature, a feud, a war, or a raid. The segments did not come together along any discernible structural lines for weddings, religious ceremonies or economic activities. As with all tribal societies, the social organization among the Beni Mtir was idealized in terms of the kinship system and its various extensions, of which the *ighs* was the most important since it was the level at which kinship and political spheres met. On the other hand one must not exaggerate the role of 'tribalism' in the daily life of the individual Mtiri, who seemed to have retained a remarkable freedom in interpreting and manipulating his socio-political universe.

4

Berber Imperialism: the Ait Atta Expansion in Southeast Morocco

Ross E. Dunn

The migratory movement of pastoral populations has been a continuous theme in the history of Morocco and the western Sahara for almost a thousand years. Beginning with the Almoravid explosion out of the Mauritanian desert in the eleventh century, the major thrust of these movements has been from the fringes of the Sahara northward into the Atlas and beyond to the fertile Atlantic coastal plains. The Saharan environment was a constant factor in setting in motion tribal migrations. Extended periods of drought, famine, and epidemic, alternating with population growth too great for the limited resources of the steppes and oases, periodically forced herding groups to seek new homes. The more abundant pastures on and beyond the slopes of the Atlas invariably attracted them toward the north.

The movements generated on the margins of the desert, if involving large numbers, eventually produced population congestion in the High Atlas pastures. As a result, mountain tribes, themselves grandsons of desert-dwellers, were forced to advance still further. The effect over the centuries was a kind of recurring bumping action with both Arabic- and Berber-speaking tribes pushing one another ever closer to the northwestern coast. The Berber collectivity known as the Zummur (Zemmour), for example, left the pre-Sahara by the sixteenth century, finally settling in their present location in the hinterland of Rabat–Salé only at the end of the nineteenth. The stages of tribal migrations were accomplished in a variety of ways, sometimes by aggressive expansion, sometimes by gradual infiltration and nomadic drift, sometimes even at the invitation of the Moroccan Sultan, who used the services of one predatory tribe to halt the expansion of another. In any case these sporadic but persistent movements help account for the continually changing territorial pattern of Morocco's tribes, some expanding, some contracting or even disappearing, but none remaining static. And it was of course in the process of interaction between pastoral groups or between them and the sedentary and urban populations that Morocco's unique institutions for regulating social and political relations were hammered out.[1]

---

[1] For a summary discussion of tribal migrations and their causes, see Marcel Lesne, 'Les Zemmour: Essai d'histoire tribale', *Revue de l'occident musulman et de la Méditerranée*, No. 3, 1967, pp. 97–132.

The term 'Southeast Morocco' is used throughout this chapter to designate territory which today lies partially within the boundaries of the Republic of Algeria. During the nineteenth century, the Sultan of Morocco claimed sovereignty over Touat. In religio-legal terms, in fact, his sovereignty had no definable territorial limits. Furthermore, all the populations from Tafilalt to Touat regarded themselves as living within the frontiers of the Sharifian Muslim community. One can argue that in terms of the western definition of the state, the people of Touat and the northwestern Sahara were not subjects of the

The expansion of the Berber-speaking Ait Atta, while not involving a significant northward migration, is an important chapter in the history of the Saharanborn tribal movements. The tribe's birthplace was the Jbel Saghro mountains, a relatively low chain extending from southwest to northeast in the pre-Saharan belt just south of the central High Atlas. In the thirteenth century, Arabs of the Maqil group, the westward vanguard of the Bani Hilal migrations from Egypt, arrived in southern Morocco, forcing a dispersal of the indigenous Berber tribes. In the sixteenth century, according to Spillmann's account, some of these Berber groups joined into a political federation under the leadership of the warrior Dadda Atta in order to resist Arab domination. The Maqil tribes, however, were beginning to leave the Saghro region by the late fourteenth century, some of them moving northward across the Atlas, others pushing southwestward into the Seguiet al-Hamra and Mauritania. The new aggregate, therefore, may have begun to form during the fifteenth century, even though Dadda Atta himself lived in the sixteenth. Moreover, it may have been more an offensive league aimed at occupying and controlling abandoned territory than a defensive alliance against Arab oppression.[1]

The commonality of the Saghro Berbers was articulated in terms of their real or putative descent from Dadda ('Ancestor') Atta and his forty warrior grandsons. Thus the federation became a tribe, the Ait Atta, or 'people of Atta'. As it grew, it evolved the pattern of segmentary organization which is common to all Moroccan tribes. That is, the entire body was divided into five primary sections (*khums*, pl. *khmas*), each primary section into subtribes (*taqbilts*), and so on through subdivisions of clan (*ighs amaggran*), lineage (*ighs ahzzan*), and sublineage. Each unit at every level of segmentation defined itself by the assertion of

Sultan. But one can hardly make a case for their being part of French Algeria before 1900 or even 1912. The term 'Southeast Morocco', therefore, is used in the sense that Moroccans would have understood it before the Protectorate.

A National Defense Education Act Title VI Fellowship and grants from the University of Wisconsin supported research in Morocco and France in 1966–7. A grant from the San Diego State University Foundation helped finance a return to Morocco during the summer of 1969.

[1] Georges Spillmann, *Les Ait Atta du Sahara et la pacification du Haut Dra*, Rabat, 1936, pp. 32, 33, 40, 41. This book is the only general ethnographic study of the Ait Atta, though a much more comprehensive work by D. M. Hart is forthcoming.

On the Maqil migrations, see George S. Colin, 'Origine arabe des grands mouvements de population berbère dans le Moyen-Atlas', *Hespéris*, Vol. 25, 1938, pp. 265–8; and Robert Montagne, *La Civilisation du désert*, Paris, 1947, pp. 248–52.

The evidence concerning the origin in time of the Ait Atta is meager and contradictory. According to one legend, Dadda Atta was a contemporary and ally of Sidi Said Ahansal, who founded the *zawiya* of Ahansal in the High Atlas about 1400 (Ernest Gellner, *Saints of the Atlas*, London & Chicago, 1969, pp. xxi, 174–6). According to another, he was the pupil and friend of Mawlay Abdallah bin al-Husayn, the patron saint of the tribe, who supposedly died in 1568 (Spillmann, op. cit., p. 68). David Hart (personal communication) accepts the later version, claiming that a computation of the named generations between Sidi Said and his twentieth-century descendants places him in the sixteenth century with Mawlay Abdallah, not in the early fifteenth. Even so, the emergence of a new Berber grouping in the Saghro could have predated the life of the Atta's structural ancestor.

common descent from an ancestor (whose name was usually also that of the group) having a place on the family tree of Dadda Atta. The units at each level had generally the same political or economic functions, though corporate action was habitual only at the lineage level or below.

In the early days a large portion of the tribe probably united from time to time to defend its mountain pastures. But by the seventeenth century population growth (and perhaps recurrent drought) necessitated expansion into the steppe lands surrounding the Saghro. This drive for new territory strengthened tribal cohesion against outsiders and encouraged the development of institutions serving greater political and military unity. To facilitate corporate action and check internal conflict, the Atta devised the office of supreme chief (*amghar n-ufilla*). His functions were to serve as liaison among the various units of the

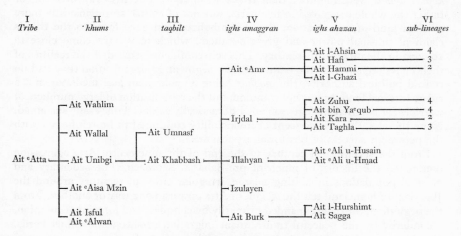

Fig. 4.1   Segmentation of the Ait Khabbash

tribe, to act as spokesman in relations with outsiders, to coordinate trans-humance patterns, to mediate or arbitrate minor disputes, and to organize and possibly lead in time of war.[1]

Each year representatives of the entire tribe gathered at a special location in the Jbel Saghro to elect the *amghar*. For this purpose, the five-way division of the tribe, the 'five fifths', or *khams khmas*, came into play. (The five segments were Ait Wahlim, Ait Wallal, Ait Isful–Ait Alwan, Ait Aisa Mzin, and Ait Unibgi.) Two major rules governed the election. First, the office rotated every year from one *khums* to another in succession. That is, each *khums* ideally provided the *amghar* once every five years. In practice, an exceptionally effective leader might hold office for a longer period, and conversely, a poor or unlucky one might be removed from office at any time. Secondly, the men of the *khums* which was to provide the candidates did not participate in the election but sat in a circle while

[1] Gellner, op. cit., pp. 81–7; Spillmann, op. cit., p. 58.

the members of the other four *khmas* made the decision by a general vote. This electoral procedure was duplicated on other occasions at the clan level where the chiefs of each subtribe (*taqbilt*) were chosen. The system of rotation and cross-election was designed primarily to prevent the emergence of dominant power groups or tyrants. But more than that, the annual electoral conclave of all sections of the tribe (or of the clans of each *taqbilt*), which were widely scattered in small herding units most of the year, reaffirmed their unity and delineated their distinctive political identity *vis-à-vis* all strangers.

The 'five fifths' organization developed an ideological value as well. The members of the tribe came to assert that the very possession of *khams khmas*, aside from its specific function in electing the *amghar*, conferred upon them collectively extraordinary military power. According to them, tribes with *khams khmas* were mightier than tribes without it. The five-way division, or rather the whole conceived in five parts, was not of course an intrinsically more efficient kind of organization. But it symbolized and gave force to the tribe's claim of unusual power and great numbers, which may have come close to 100,000 in the nineteenth century. This self-confidence exceeded the realities of their cohesion, since by the nature of their segmentary organization they had no central political authority, the *amghar* being a spokesman and mediator, not a ruler. Internal feuding was not common, but the mobilization of large numbers of warriors for external warfare was not automatically achieved nor easily sustained. None the less, this self-concept of invincibility continued to be reinforced with the persistent success of territorial expansion.[1]

From the seventeenth century to the end of the nineteenth, Atta aggression dominated the history of much of pre-Saharan Morocco. The sedentary and pastoral populations inhabiting a large, irregular circle of territory around the Jbel Saghro homeland felt the weight of Atta power in one way or another. From the beginning, the tribe expanded primarily by conquest and forceful occupation, secondarily by the peaceful transhumant migration of sheep and camel herds. On some occasions Atta warriors operated in armies of a few thousand men, comprising both horsemen and infantry. Large forces, however, came together only for specific campaigns and disbanded as soon as the major battle was over. More often small, spontaneously organized war parties operated beyond the home territory, commandeering livestock from other pastoral groups, raiding for dates and other booty in the pre-Saharan oases, and in general preparing the way for later occupation or political overlordship.

The initial thrust may have been toward the Atlas slopes since the most favorable pasturelands lay in that direction. A small number of deep, narrow river valleys gave access to the mountains. By these routes, however, the expansion achieved only limited success owing to the resistance of other Berber-speaking tribes which had preceded them during the fifteenth or sixteenth

[1] David M. Hart, 'Segmentary systems and the role of "five fifths" in tribal Morocco', *Revue de l'occident musulman et de la Méditerranée*, No. 3, 1967, pp. 82–92; Gellner, op. cit., pp. 81–104. Gellner, and Hart after him, calls the electoral system 'rotation and complementarity', The organizational principle of *khams khmas* was found among a number of Moroccan tribes, though the specific function varied widely.

centuries. To stand fast against Atta pressure, which was applied along a front of more than 100 miles from the Ziz valley in the east to the Dadès in the west, these tribes banded together in a defensive confederation known as the Ait Yafalman, the 'people who seek the peace'. Raids, skirmishes, and pitched battles between the Atta and Yafalman forces went on incessantly from the seventeenth into the twentieth century. During his passage along the southern fringe of the High Atlas in 1884, Charles de Foucauld received fresh reports of a bloody battle between 8,600 Ait Atta and 12,700 Ait Mirghad, one of the principal Yafalman tribes. Losses were estimated at 1,600 for the Atta and 400 for the Ait Mirghad. The *causus belli* on that occasion was the Atta's seizure of a number of *qsars*, or walled villages, belonging to the Mirghad in the Wad Gheris valley.[1]

The Ait Yafalman successfully thwarted Atta penetration into the High Atlas everywhere except up the Dadès valley, which cuts into the mountains directly north of the Saghro. From the upper Dadès, Atta groups representing four of the *khmas* pushed northwestward, establishing settlements deep in the mountains and even north of the Atlas divide.[2] If the Yafalman tribes had been less successful in blockading them, it is likely the Atta would have infiltrated the high country in much greater numbers or even migrated out of the pre-Sahara altogether.

At any rate, the way was clearer for expansion to the south and east. Southwest of the Saghro they pushed as far as the lower valley of the Wad Dra. In the date-growing oases along the river, various sub-tribal groups established protection agreements (*raaya*) with several sedentary communities, comprised of black or racially mixed cultivators. The terms of these pacts centered upon Atta guardian-ship of palm groves in return for a percentage of the harvest and rights to grazing land in and around the oasis.[3]

Penetration directly south of the Saghro was limited to the part-time occupa-tion of winter pastures in the northern desert. In another way, however, the arm of Atta power extended a great deal further. As late as the first decade of the twentieth century, large raiding parties of anywhere from 50 to 1,000 men made forays deep into the Sahara, sometimes all the way to the vicinity of the Niger river. The targets of these *razzias* were the camel-herding tribes of the Sahara, such as the Rguibat, and the Barabish, and sometimes even Black sedentary communities of the western Sudan. Such long-distance expeditions were of course extremely hazardous, especially if the raiding party was itself attacked a long way from home ground. But when successful, these bands returned with

[1] Charles de Foucauld, *Reconnaissance au Maroc*, Paris, 1939, p. 381.

[2] One segment is located near the *zawiya* (center for Sufi saints) of Ahansal in the heart of the High Atlas. In fact, the entire tribe has long had close ties with the saints of Ahansal (Gellner, op. cit., pp. 172–8). A conglomerate Atta group inhabits a limited region around Ouaouizarht on the northern side of the Atlas (Spillmann, op. cit., p. 36).

[3] See F. de la Chapelle, 'Une cité de l'Oued Dra sous la protectorate des nomades', *Hespéris*, Vol. 29, 1929, pp. 29–42; and D. Jacques-Meunié, 'Les oases des Lektaoua et des Mehamid', *Hespéris*, Vol. 34, 1947, pp. 397–429. The most thorough unpublished work is Niclausse, *Rapports entre nomades et sédentaires dans le coude du Draa : la raia*, Centre des Hautes Etudes d'Administration Musulmane (CHEAM), No. 2306, 1954.

highly valued camels and until the end of the nineteenth century with slaves.[1]

The existence of French archives and published material relating to the Algero-Moroccan border region permits a more detailed reconstruction of the Atta offensive east and southeast of the Saghro. This theater of expansion, the most important during the later eighteenth and the nineteenth centuries, extended from the region of the lower Wad Ziz, eastward onto the Hammada of the Guir (an extensive plateau east of the Ziz), and southeastward as far as the Touat oasis complex in the north central Sahara.

Both sedentary and nomadic populations were living in this region when the first Atta contingents arrived. The Wad Ziz was one of several rivers which flowed sporadically from the High Atlas southward into the desert. A long, thin, intermittent line of date-palm groves and *qsars* followed the river valley. About forty miles south of the mountains the stream flowed out onto a broad alluvial plain and the great oasis of Tafilalt. The sedentary cultivators living along the narrow stretch of the valley were mostly Berber speakers, while in Tafilalt they were mostly Arabs. These Arab farmers claimed descent from Maqil who, over a period of time after the thirteenth century, gave up pastoralism for irrigation agriculture. Tafilalt was also the location of Sijilmasa, the celebrated northern *entrepôt* of the trans-Saharan trade. More precisely, it was the location of Sijilmasa's ruins, for by the early nineteenth century a nearby center, Abou Am, had replaced it as the principal market in the region.

Ait Izdig and Ait Mirghad Berbers, members of the Ait Yafalman confederation, herded their sheep over a wide band of territory on both sides of the Ziz and deep into the mountains. In the nineteenth century they did not move very far south of the slopes, though the Atta may have pushed them out of the steppe lands around the lower stretch of the river. The Dawi Mani, a transhumant Arab tribe whose political and economic center was the grain-producing flood plain of the Wad Guir about ninety miles southeast of Tafilalt, occupied the Hammada part of the year. They also owned palm groves and traded regularly in Tafilalt. The desert south of the Hammada was sparsely inhabited as far south as Touat, an immense agricultural area and a major crossroads of trade. The *qsar*-dwellers of Touat included both Arabs and Berbers, with Tuareg living in the southernmost district.

During the course of the nineteenth century, the vast region between the lower Ziz and Touat became in large measure an Atta sphere of influence. The incursion was almost exclusively the work of a single section of the tribe, the Ait

---

[1] 'Notes sur les rezzou marocains', Institut de France, *Fonds Auguste Terrier*, LXI (5951), 1907. The Dawi Mani, the eastern neighbors of the Ait Atta, also participated in trans-Saharan raids. The following descriptions could apply in general to both them and the Atta. Mercier, 'Une Harka des Doui Menia et Ouled Djerir vers le Sahel (asût 1904 à février 1905)', *Renseignements coloniaux*, No. 7, July 1905, pp. 265–7; Archives du Gouvernement Général de l'Algérie (AGGA), 22H.27, Dossier (D.) Lyautey to Jonnart, 3 June 1910, No. 561, Doury, 'Harkas des Doui-Menia: considérations d'ensemble', 10 January 1910. The Ait Khabbash section of the Atta may have been the only one to participate regularly in Saharan raiding, since they were the only ones to keep large numbers of camels for transport or riding.

Khabbash. This group was one of the several *taqbilt*s into which the Atta were segmented at the level immediately below the 'fifth'. The Ait Khabbash, together with one other *taqbilt*, the Ait Umnasf, combined to form the Ait Unibgi, one of the 'five fifths'. In daily life the sentiment of corporate identity was much stronger among members of the *taqbilt* than within the *khums* as a whole. Each *taqbilt*, unlike the *khums*, had its own chief, whom the component clans elected every year according to the rules of rotation and cross-election (see Map 4.1).[1]

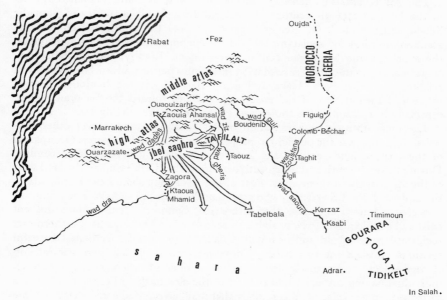

Map 4.1   Ait Atta expansion

While small Ait Khabbash groups lived in the Dadès valley and near the lower Dra, most of the *taqbilt*, numbering perhaps ten thousand, migrated during the seventeenth or eighteenth century into the steppe lands east of the lower Ziz valley and south of Tafilalt. Whereas the other Atta sections were almost exclusively sheep herders, some living in houses during the winter months, the Ait Khabbash favored the camel and, perhaps with some exceptions, lived under the tent all the year round. Like all pre-Saharan transhumants, they led their herds and flocks northward in summer and deeper into the desert in winter. But because of their reliance on the camel, they were clearly the most mobile, most 'nomadic' of the Atta breed.

They also boasted a reputation for being the most warlike. Raiding and other harassments against sedentary populations probably started in the Ziz valley and

[1] Interview with al-Hajj Hda l'Allah, Adi u Brahim, and Baha Ardwi, Ait Khabbash, Merzouga (north of Taouz), 6 August 1969; Spillmann, op. cit., pp. 92–4; Hart, op. cit., pp. 86–90.

Tafilalt in the later eighteenth century and spread to Touat in the nineteenth. In a sense, their devotion to the camel and their penetration so far east of the Saghro homeland set them apart from the rest of the tribe. On the other hand, their membership in the *khams khmas*, their sense of being part of a great, un-stoppable design of conquest, gave them a self-concept of invincibility. This idealization certainly surpassed the reality of their fiercest exploits, but their victims in many cases undoubtedly shared their view.[1]

The Ait Khabbash offensive was not, however, as some French observers in the later nineteenth century characterized it, simply a matter of nomadic 'blood and thunder'. Of greater importance than the violence itself was the resultant political and social impact both on the populations of the region and on the *makhzan*, the Moroccan central government. Locally, the Ait Khabbash aggression led to the emergence of new, sometimes permanent, social and political relationships with both Arabs and other Berbers. At the 'national' level it influenced formulation of the *makhzan*'s policies toward the Saharan region, especially in relation to the southward expansion of French Algeria.

The most obtrusive manifestation of Ait Khabbash power over other pre-Saharan groups was the outright appropriation of land and property. Occupation of the pasture lands around the Ziz valley actually generated little conflict. During the eighteenth and nineteenth centuries, the Khabbash had the land west of the Ziz largely to themselves. East of the river they shared the Hammada of the Guir with the Dawi Mani, who grazed both sheep and camels. The pasturage was sparse but so extensive that inter-tribal boundary demarcations did not exist and conflicts over grazing rights were isolated and infrequent. Furthermore, reciprocal pacts of aid and hospitality, called *tata* or *tada*, facilitated peaceful relations between the two tribes. These agreements, which were common in Berber society, were made between the member of whole clans, with each individual having a special *tata* partner in the clan of the other tribe. *Tata* was formalized in a special ritual ceremony that may have varied somewhat from one group to another. Essentially, the members of each clan placed their right shoe in a pile. Then each individual chose his *tata* partner by drawing a shoe from the pile of the other clan. A local saint was sometimes present to sanctify the pact. *Tata* brothers (and symbolic blood brotherhood was at least vaguely implied) agreed to give refuge to one another and to perform other acts of assistance. Failure to meet these obligations could have the consequence of tribal dishonor. This institution was a kind of diplomatic bridge between tribes

[1] See Spillmann, op. cit., pp. 92, 93. The earliest recorded date I have seen for Atta involvement in the Ziz valley is 1783–84. Sultan Sidi Muhammad either evicted them or negotiated their departure from Tafilalt after they had become involved on the side of the *khalifa* (governor) in a feud with local *shurfa*. Aboulqasem ben Ahmed Ezziani (trans. O. Houdas), *Le Maroc de 1631 à 1812* (extracted from *Al-tarjaman al-muarib an duwal al-mashriq wa al-maghrib*), Paris, 1886, p. 153; Eugène Fumey, 'Chronique de la dynastie alaouite du Maroc' (translation of Ahmed Ennasiri Esslaoui, *Kitab al-Istiqsa*), *Archives marocaines*, Vol. 9, 1906, pp. 336–9; H. Dastugue, 'Quelques mots au sujet de Tafilet et de Sidjilmassa', *Bulletin de la Société de Géographie de Paris*, Vol. 13, April 1867, pp. 364, 365. A conflict in Tafilalt between the Ait Atta and the Ait Izdig led to the destruction of the *kasba* of Sijilmasa and the final abandonment of the *entrepôt*. The city, however, had been in decline for a long time (Dastugue, op. cit., pp. 371, 372).

especially useful when herds mingled in the same area, local disputes broke out between families, or safe passage was needed while traveling. *Tada* implied a recognition that numerous points of tension existed between the two tribes and provided one effective method for easing them.[1]

In the Ziz valley no such *modus vivendi* was worked out. In two major districts of Tafilalt (Tanijiout in the northeast and Safalat in the southwest) and along a stretch of the valley further north known as the Rteb, Atta assailants seized several *qsars* outright and established permanent control. While the Ait Khabbash operated exclusively in Tafilalt, the Ait Umnasf, the other and much smaller *taqbilt* of the Ait Unibgi *khums*, also participated in the Rteb offensive. Both groups would probably have taken possession of other villages in the valley both north and south of the Rteb were it not for the resistance of Ait Yafalman tribes. The Ait Izdig and Ait Mirghad to the north and the Arab Sabbah, a small Arabic-speaking sedentary tribe living between the Rteb and Tafilalt, prevented further incursions. This was accomplished, however, only at the price of raiding and skirmishing that was, according to one Khabbashi informant, 'like the rising of the sun'.[2]

The main objective of the Atta in attacking sedentary populations was seizure of the extensive groves of date palms, with their associated gardens, grain fields and fruit trees, surrounding and sustaining the villages. Dates, along with grain and milk, were the basic staples of the Atta diet. Under more peaceful circumstances, they, like other pastoral groups, bought their dates from the sedentary growers or at the local markets. Some owned their own trees individually or in groves in one oasis or another. Other men, who for some reason had little wealth in livestock, obtained dates from *qsar*-dwellers in return for standing guard over the groves during harvest season, an agreement known both in the Ziz and the Dra valleys as *raaya*.[3]

[1] *Tata* between the Ait Khabbash and the Dawi Mani is noted by Capt. Regnault, *Notice sur les Ait Khabbach*, AGGA, 30H.12, D. Pourparlers avec les Beni M'hamed et les Ait Khabbach à Beni Abbès, 29 February 1904. F. Albert ('Les Oulad Djerir', *Bulletin de la Société de Géographie et d'Archéologie d'Oran*, Vol. 25, October–December 1905, pp. 393, 394) gives a list of correspondent *tata* clans for the Ait Khabbash and the Awlad Jarir, a small Arab tribe politically associated with the Dawi Mani. Informants of both the Ait Khabbash (Hamid al-Qarawi, Lahsin u-Rahma, and Baha Ardwi, Taouz, 27 July 1967) and the Dawi Mani (al-Hashmi bin Abd al-Karim, Abd al-Karim Butahir, Muhammad bin Amsifi, and al-Hajj bin Hamid bin Salah, Ghorfa district of Tafilalt, 24 July 1967) confirmed that *tata* existed between them, though it is not clear that *all* the clans in each tribe had such a relationship in the nineteenth century.

The basic discussion of *tata* is G. Marcy, 'L'Alliance par colactation (tâda) chez les Berbères du Maroc central', *Revue africaine*, Vol. 2, No. 2, 1936, pp. 957–73. See also H. Bruno and G.-H. Bousquet, 'Contribution à l'étude des pactes de protection et l'alliance chez les Berbères du Maroc central', *Hespéris*, Vol. 33, 1946, pp. 353–70; Spillmann, op. cit., pp. 50–2; Lesne, op. cit., pp. 144, 145; Gellner, op. cit., p. 137.

[2] Interview with u-Rahma Ali u-Assu and Lahsin n-Ait l-Hajj, Aufous (Rteb), 31 July 1967.

[3] *Raaya* between the Atta and sedentary communities appears to have been more prevalent in the Dra valley where almost everyone was involved in such a relationship. Informants in the Ziz area consistently asserted that only poor men got their dates in this way. Interview with Idir, Hada Hammu, and Asu Brahim, Ait Khabbash, Mesguida (Tanijiout district of Tafilalt), 2 August 1969; interview: Merzouga, 6 August 1969.

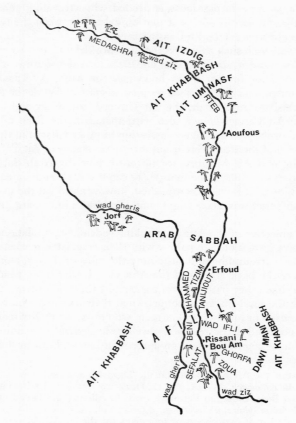

Map 4.2   The Ziz valley and Tafilalt

The *qsars* which the Atta occupied in both the Rteb (about sixteen as of 1913) and Tafilalt (three in Tanijiout district and a few more on the outskirts of Safalat) had populations composed of five general social categories. All the sedentary inhabitants of the Ziz valley belonged to one or another of these. At the top in prestige, though not necessarily power, were the sanctified lineages of *shurfa* (sing. *sharif*) and *murabtin* (sing. *murabit*). The *shurfa* were those individuals generally accepted as being descended from the Prophet Muhammad through the line of either Mawlay Idris, the founder of the first Arab dynasty in Morocco in the eighth century, or Mawlay Ali *Sharif*, the progenitor of the Alawite line of sultans. The Alawite *shurfa* were by far the larger group in the valley, numbering several thousand. *Murabtin* were the descendants of reputed holy men whose ascetic and pious lives usually sparked the formation of a saint cult and an associated center of religious learning and mystical practice (*zawiya*). In Tafilalt a few *murabtin* lineages played a special and crucial role in political life as neutral mediators or arbitrators of disputes or feuds.

The largest segment of the population were independent cultivators, who owned the greatest share of land and palms in most of the *qsar*s. In the Rteb these were mainly families of the Ait Izdig. The bulk of the tribe, living further north, practised transhumance, but the Rteb groups, or most of them, were living in houses year round by the nineteenth century. In Tafilalt the farmers were known as *ahrar*, or freemen. The *ahrar* identified socially with a particular *qsar* and district (of which there were seven in Tafilalt) but did not reckon kinship beyond the lineage level. A few lineages generally shared a single *qsar*, each occupying its own quarter. Two *ahrar* groups, however, counted themselves as tribes, being descended from a common ancestor and segmented at higher levels than the lineage. The Bani Mhammad, who resided in the northern district of the same name, were segmented into three sub-tribes and, below them, into a series of clans and lineages. The Arab Sabbah, who lived just north of the Tafilalt plain along the banks of the Wad Ziz and the Wad Gheris, had a similar social organization. All the *ahrar* groups, while not possessing the impressive lineages, the prestige, and the pious demeanor of the *shurfa* and *murabtin*, put great stock in their lineage organization, which served to verify the 'whiteness' of their blood and separated them from the debased *haratin*.

The origin of the *haratin* class is still a subject of debate, but they are generally believed to be the descendants of black, immigrant slaves who intermarried with the Berber population. Most had dark skin and negroid features. Although they were legally free men and could own real property, almost all of them worked as *khammas* laborers for the white Arabs or Berbers, receiving for their toil a fifth or less of the harvests. Pride of ancestry was lacking, lineal descent being traced no more than three generations. *Haratin* families were dispersed throughout the oasis.

The slave population, the fourth category, probably numbered no more than a few hundred at the end of the nineteenth century. Nomadic groups in the area around Tafilalt owned most of them, employing them as domestics or as shepherds.

At the bottom of the social ladder and, as non-Muslims, outside of the spectrum altogether, were the Jews. Perhaps about 6,000 of them lived in Tafilalt in the nineteenth century.[1] Jewish families inhabited a number of *qsar*s, the largest concentration being the *mallah* (Jewish quarter) of Rissani. Jews did not, of course, participate in the political and social life of the Muslim community, but neither were they persecuted in normal times. As almost everywhere else in Morocco, most of them found their professional niche as merchants, jewelry makers, or cobblers.[2]

The manner in which the Atta invaders treated the sedentary inhabitants after seizing a *qsar* varied widely from one place to the next, depending in part

---

[1] Gerhard Rohlfs, who visited Tafilalt in the 1860s, estimated the Jewish population at 6,000. Quoted in Oskar Lenz, *Timbouctou*, Paris, 1886, p. 302.

[2] On social structure in pre-Saharan Morocco, see D. Jacques-Meunié, 'Hiérarchie sociale au Maroc présaharien', *Hespéris*, Vol. 45, 1958, pp. 239–70.

on the kind of resistance they encountered. Documentation on this question is limited, but a certain pattern can be discerned. Members of the previously dominant groups were sometimes either killed or evicted. In the Rteb, the Atta expelled all or most of the Ait Izdig and *shurfa* families and simply confiscated their property, leaving them to seek refuge with their kin in other districts. In one *qsar* in Tafilalt, according to Khabbash informants, only those people who resisted were forced to leave. Many, including a few *shurfa* families, were allowed to stay and retain their property.[1]

It is likely that in all the *qsars* many of the *haratin*, as well as the Jewish families, remained. Since the Atta warriors were averse to tilling the soil and, at first anyway, were absent with their herds part of the year, the *haratin* were needed to tend the palm groves as much as before the seizure. In one of the *qsars* and very likely all of them, the *haratin* insured their personal security by becoming protégés of the Atta on an individual or family basis. The entreating *hartani* agreed to work for an Atta family in return for protection and a percentage of the crops. This relationship became formal when the *hartani* sacrificed a sheep or other animal before the house of the Atta men. This act (*dabiha*) carried with it a conditional curse, since it would be shame (*ar*) in the eyes of God for the dominant party to refuse. It is almost certain that the Jews living in these villages performed *dabiha* as well, since no Jew in southern Morocco was without a Muslim patron. In fact, *dabiha*, involving shame compulsion, was practised widely in Morocco in various types of situations as a method of sanctioning and defining relations between people of unequal power, fortune, or social position.[2]

While the Atta seized direct control of many villages in the Ziz valley, they exercised less blatant domination over other groups through special alliances, toll collection, or extortion. In Tafilalt the Ait Khabbash formed a permanent alliance with the Bani Mhammad, one of the sedentary Arabic-speaking tribes inhabiting the northern district of the same name. The tribe was segmented into three sub-tribes (Awlad Sadan, al-Ghadar, and Zanata), and each of these was divided further at the clan and lineage levels. Like the other *ahrar* of Tafilalt, the Bani Mhammad were at least in part descendants of Maqil nomads. The fact that they (and the Arab Sabbah as well) had a more ramified kinship structure than the others may mean simply that the process of 'sedentarization' had not been going on for so long. The principal corporate function of the tribe was the

---

[1] Dr Linarès ('Voyage au Tafilalt avec S.M. le Sultan Moulay Hassan en 1893', extracted from *Bulletin de l'Institut d'Hygiène du Maroc*, Nos. 3 and 4, 1932, pp. 48, 49) gives a brief but vivid account of the Atta penetration of the Rteb, which was still proceeding when he passed through in 1893. Also Denoun (Officer-Interprète, Colomb–Béchar), *Essai de monographie de la tribu berbère des Ait Atta*, AGGA, 22H.27, 7 April 1913, p. 1; interview: Aoufous, 31 July 1967. On Atta attacks in Tafilalt, Gerhard Rohlfs, *Adventures in Morocco and Journeys through the Oases of Draa and Tafilalet*, London, 1874, pp. 17, 35; interview with Sidi al-Arabi bin Maruf, Tabouasamt (Safalat district of Tafilalt), 4 August 1969; interview: Mesguida, 2 August 1969.

[2] Interview: Mesguida, 2 August 1969. The concept of *ar* in social relations is discussed in Edward Westermarck, *Ritual and Belief in Morocco*, London, 1926, Vol. 1, pp. 518–64. Anyone could make use of *dabiha* to compel another to grant a request. The act did not necessarily imply a state of inequality between the two parties.

annual election of a paramount *shaykh*, something the other *ahrar* groups of Tafilalt, who identified themselves with a district, never did.[1]

Probably during the later eighteenth century, the Ait Khabbash launched a campaign against the Bani Mhammad, resulting sooner or later in their surrender. Perhaps because the Bani Mhammad still preserved a strong tribal structure and may have been partially nomadic, the Ait Khabbash did not subordinate them through *dabiha*, but rather united with them in a pact known in the region as *tafargant* (interdiction). The initiating ritual involved the exchange of milk from lactating mothers. *Tafargant* was actually a variation of *tata*, but its terms were considered more binding, more sacred, than those of the 'shoe exchange' pact. *Tafargant* stipulated not only peaceful relations and mutual aid but also strict prohibition on marriage between the two tribes. This taboo implied symbolic brotherhood between them, but it may also have had the practical function of eliminating one major cause of tension.[2]

Despite the apparently reciprocal nature of the pact, the Bani Mhammad henceforth became junior partners of the Ait Khabbash. Indeed, they became partially integrated into the greater Atta political organization. While never providing the paramount chief of the *khams khmas*, they did participate in his yearly election as part of the Ait Unibgui fifth. They also used the same electoral system internally, choosing their *shaykh al-am* (chief of the year) by the method of rotation and cross-election among the component clans. The *shaykh*'s duties were similar to those of the Atta chiefs. He nominated a representative (*mazrag*) in each *qsar* as his liaison with its council (*jamaa*).[3]

The *tafargant* alliance, the only formal and permanent one the Ait Khabbash took part in during the nineteenth century, also had an economic dimension. The Bani Mhammad were not only farmers, but also the merchants *par excellence* on the trade route between Tafilalt and Touat. Until about the middle of the century, they also regularly organized and accompanied caravans bound for Timbuktu and were especially distinguished as slave dealers.[4] Although the decline of the trans-Saharan trade through Abou Am (Sijilmasa's successor) later in the century may have sent some of them back to their palm groves, the tribe continued to lead in supplying Touat with European tea, sugar, and manufactures. They obtained these goods in Abou Am from other merchants who brought them over the Atlas from Fes or Marrakesh.[5]

Following their alliance with the Ait Khabbash, the two tribes entered into a

[1] Denoun, op. cit., pp. 1, 8–10, 25; interview with Lagid bin al-Madani, *qsar* Ouled l'Imam (Bani Mhammad district), 25 July 1967. The origins and sedentarization of the Arab Sabbah, whose history may be very similar to that of the Bani Mhammad, are discussed in Henriet, *Un Problème de l'extrême-sud marocain: répercussions de sa situation politique et sociale sur son relévement économique*, CHEAM, No. 6, 1937, pp. 41, 42.

[2] Spillmann, op. cit., pp. 50–2; interview: Taouz, 27 July 1967.

[3] Spillmann, op. cit., p. 96; Denoun, op. cit., p. 25.

[4] Capt. Berriau, *Contribution à l'étude de la région du Sud-Ouest*, French Ministry of War Archives, Service Historique de l'Armée (SHA), Carton (C.) Algérie 19; L. Mercier, 'Notice économique sur le Tafilalet', *Renseignements coloniaux*, No. 6, June 1905, pp. 215, 217, 218; interview: Bani Mhammad, 25 July 1967.

[5] Augustin Bernard and N. Lacroix, *L'Évolution du nomadisme en Algérie*, Paris, 1906, p. 225; interview: Bani Mhammad, 25 July 1967.

4

highly successful commercial partnership: the Bani Mhammad supplied the merchants and capital, the Ait Khabbash provided the guards, the drivers, and most of the transport camels. Other traders, such as the merchants of Touat and *shurfa* of Tafilalt, did not enjoy the same protection and privileges as the Bani Mhammad. Sometimes they 'hitchhiked' with Bani Mhammad caravans. Those who set out on their own usually found themselves paying a toll (*zattata*) to cross Ait Khabbash territory or even serving up their merchandise at the point of a gun.[1] Since the Ait Khabbash controlled the main Tafilalt–Touat route, they could have plundered caravans at will. But even though French observers usually portrayed them as incorrigible *coupeurs de route*, they were generally much more interested in expanding commerce in league with the Bani Mhammad than in hindering or destroying it through brigandage. In short, their commercial activities represented a positive and not insignificant aspect of their penetration east of the Ziz.

The northeastern limit of Ait Khabbash power was the *qsar* of Boudenib, a minor date-producing center on the Wad Guir inhabited by several *shurfa* families and *haratin*. About 1893 a feud broke out between two *shurfa* factions over political control of the oasis. When one faction rallied the support of Ait Izdig and other outsiders from the upper Guir region, the other party called on the aid of the Ait Khabbash, who arrived 900 strong. This extension of the conflict was clearly not the activation of any pre-existing binary alliance structure, but it was a good example, often noted in Saharan politics, of two rival sedentary groups recruiting nomadic 'hired guns' to serve as their *force de frappe*. The Khabbash warriors drove off several attacks on the *qsar* by the opposing alliance, then demanded, as the price of their support, the settlement of 300 of their number in one section of the oasis. These 300, families too poor to continue transhumance, eventually constructed a second *qsar* there and named it Taouz, after a major Khabbash watering-place south of Tafilalt.[2] It should be pointed out, however, that the new residents did not try to commandeer the oasis as they did elsewhere, but rather settled down apparently without bringing catastrophe on the other inhabitants. Arbitrary transfers of property, though, almost certainly took place.[3]

[1] Lt Huot, *Notice succinct sur les Beraber*, AGGA, 30H.3, D. Enquête sur les rapports qui existent entre les indigènes algériens et les tribus du territoire marocain, 18 October 1902, pp. 10–13; A. G. P. Martin, *Quatre siècles d'histoire marocaine*, Paris, 1923, pp. 147, 148.

[2] Capt Canavy, 'Les Régions du Haut-Guir et de l'Oued Haïber', *Renseignements coloniaux*, No. 5, May 1905, p. 127; Augustin Bernard, *Les Confins algéro-marocains*, Paris, 1911, p. 86.

[3] Atta intervention by 'invasion' was also the pattern in Mesguida in the Tanijiout district of Tafilalt. Here, according to Ait Khabbash informants (interview: Mesguida, 2 August 1969), the *ahrar* and *haratin* inhabitants invited ten Khabbash families to move in in order to protect them against attacks by the Arab Sabbah. Within a year the Atta residents, having been unjustly locked out of the *qsar* and robbed of their property by some of the cultivators, brought in a large force, which evicted and confiscated the property of the guilty parties. Today, Mesguida is a full-fledged Ait Khabbash *qsar*. The Atta version of the story, of course, may be rather one-sided, providing a convenient justification for what could have been a dragonnade.

In Touat, especially the two northern districts of Gourara and Touat proper, extortion was the principal feature of relations between the Ait Khabbash and the *qsar*-dwelling population. As early as 1808, Atta groups or individuals were making treaties (*khawa*, meaning literally 'brotherhood') with various villages. In one early case, spokesmen for the Sefians and Ihamids, the two competing political groupings of Touat, agreed to maintain peace in the oases under the guardianship of the Atta. In other cases the Atta (the Ait Khabbash in all or most cases) offered protection of the land and property of certain *qsar*s in return for an annual payment of money.[1] Early in the century these relations appear to have been genuinely based on parity and mutual interest. But in the 1830s, as the Ait Khabbash became stronger and more numerous in the region, their position began to harden. With the complicity of the Bani Mhammad they began launching raids against *qsar*s and following them up with demands for 'protection money'. To avoid being pillaged or having their palms cut down, most of the cultivators who were intimidated in this way resigned themselves to paying a regular tribute. The Dawi Mani and the Ghanamna, the two important Arab tribes of the region, joined the Ait Khabbash in tyrannizing the *qsar*-dwellers, with each small group of nomads setting up its own sphere of influence and extortion. This situation lasted until the French occupied Touat in 1900.[2]

The Sultan of Morocco no more ignored the Atta expansion than did the populations lying directly in its path. Since the time of Mawlay Ismail, who died in 1727, no Sultan succeeded regularly in collecting taxes or calling up military contingents south of the High Atlas. *Makhzan* military expeditions, sometimes led by the Sultan, crossed the mountains only a few times during the later eighteenth and the nineteenth centuries. On the other hand, both the *makhzan* and the southern populations had a stake in keeping open the lines of political intercourse. Despite the absence of real political authority, the Sultan did claim sovereignty over the entire western Sahara as *amir al-muminin*, or head of the Muslim community. His capacity to exert influence in the south by issuing seals and letters of investiture to local political leaders and by mediating or arbitrating disputes contributed to his prestige throughout Morocco. In turn, most southern groups, including the populations of Touat, recognized the Sultan's religious authority, believing him, as a *sharif*, to retain the *baraka*, or divine grace, which brought munificence and good fortune on the community of believers. Thus, local leaders sought association with the Sultan through political investiture (while in reality depending solely on their followers for authority), and disputing families, villages, and even tribes sent their cases to the Sultan or *makhzan* judges for adjudication.

Lurking just beneath these manifestations of *makhzan* 'presence', however, was the continual threat that a local power group would become strong and aggressive enough to disrupt the flow of trade, make a mockery of Sultanic

[1] Martin, op. cit., pp. 124, 125, 130, 147. Martin's work on Touat is based largely on Arabic documents which he examined and translated while serving there as an Affaires Indigènes officer.

[2] Ibid., pp. 153–60, 287, 288.

sovereignty in the south, and even champion another *sharif* as pretender to the throne. The Atta expansion represented a menace of his kind. A number of Alawite Sultans attempted in one way or another to contain the Atta offensive, especially in the east. Mawlay Ismail, who had the most active Saharan policy, in 1678 crushed a southern rebellion raised by three of his brothers with the aid of Atta forces.[1] In 1783–84, Sultan Sidi Muhammad sent an expedition to Tafilalt to put down a rebellious *khalifa*, the Sharifian governor of the region, who had laid seige to Sijilmasa with Atta support.[2] In 1841, Mawlay Abd al-Rahman sent letters to 'Arabs' in the southeast, probably the Dawi Mani, urging them to attack the Atta as punishment for their raids on villages and caravans in Touat.[3] It is clear that military confrontations with the Atta had no permanent effect owing to their local military preponderance and the extreme difficulty of marching armies across the Atlas. Only an examination of the *makhzan* archives will show to what extent these Sultans negotiated with the Atta or tried to undermine their power in other ways.

Relations between the Atta, especially Ait Khabbash, and Sultan Mawlay Hassan (1873–94) can be pieced together in somewhat more detail because of the availability of French archives and published material dealing with the Algero-Moroccan frontier zone. During this period, the problem of Atta power became closely linked to that of European imperialist pressure on Morocco. The acceleration of European commercial and political penetration absorbed practically all the considerable energies of Mawlay Hassan and conditioned his internal as well as diplomatic policies. His overriding objective was to check this external influence while at the same time achieving sufficient stability and control to convince the powers of Morocco's right to independence.

In the east the creeping advance of French military forces toward the Algerian pre-Sahara threatened Mawlay Hassan's prestige both at home and in the European chanceries by nullifying his claims to sovereignty over the northwestern Sahara. Since the 1870s, French expansionists had been promoting various schemes for the occupation of Touat and even Tafilalt as a prelude to construction of a trans-Saharan railroad. Mawlay Hassan responded to this threat by intensifying *makhzan* political involvement in the southeast. He appointed and invested local *caids*, exchanged official delegations and correspondence, and made verbal assurances of his capacity to protect his most distant subjects from French aggression. He also made direct appeals to other European powers to support his claims against France.[4]

In 1890 Great Britain gave its assent to French expansion into the Sahara. During the following two years, a flurry of public debate on the Touat issue coupled with a series of French probing operations south of their military frontier (in the Saharan Atlas) led Mawlay Hassan to conclude that an invasion

[1] Fumey, op. cit. (Esslaoui, *Kitab al-Istiqsa*), p. 80; Georges Spillmann, *Districts et tribus de la haute vallée du Draa*, Paris, 1931, p. 61.

[2] See note 10.

[3] Martin, op. cit., pp. 157, 158.

[4] Ibid., pp. 223, 236, 249, 255–7, 267–70. The Touat question in European diplomacy is discussed in Pierre Guillen, *L'Allemagne et le Maroc*, Paris, 1967, *passim*; and in Jean-Louis Miège, *Le Maroc et l'Europe*, Paris, 1963, Vol. 4, pp. 249–55.

of the central Sahara was imminent. In response, he undertook to lead an army and his entire court from Fes to Tafilalt, a journey across the mountains of more than 400 miles. Tafilalt was the seventeenth-century cradle of the Alawite dynasty and the burial place of its founder, Mawlay Ali Sharif. Being also the homeland of the Alawite *shurfa* and place of exile of politically troublesome members of the family, it was a potential 'hotspot' for rebellion against the encumbent ruler. By moving the central government there (the first sultan-led expedition to the lower Ziz since 1816), Mawlay Hassan aimed to demonstrate his willingness and ability to assert his authority anywhere in his domains and to buttress the loyalty of the southeastern populations in the face of French imperialism. More specifically, he intended to put a stop to the incessant, internecine skirmishing, which was betraying the absence of *makhzan* power and which could provide the French with an excuse for invading Tafilalt under the guise of intervention to restore law and order on the Algero-Moroccan frontier.

The success of the journey depended heavily on the behavior of the Ait Khabbash, who were themselves aware of the French threat to their local hegemony. Most of Mawlay Hassan's predecessors appear to have sided with the victims of Atta aggression, at times supporting the Ait Yafalman tribes as a kind of mountain buffer against Atta penetration up the southern slopes. Mawlay Hassan, however, broke with tradition and adopted a genuinely conciliatory position toward the Ait Khabbash, realizing that in this case their cooperation would better serve his ends than a hazardous punitive operation. During 1892, a number of Atta delegations (mainly Ait Khabbash), as well as *shurfa* and other groups from Tafilalt, visited the royal court in Fes. While not investing Atta *caid*s, a frequent procedure during audiences with tribal personages, he did confer with them to obtain assurances of their quiescence when the expedition reached the lower Ziz. He also toyed with the idea of journeying all the way to Touat and may have discussed the possibility of using the Ait Khabbash as his escort. Another point of discussion was a contingency plan for having the Atta attack the Ait Izdig from the south when the expedition approached from the opposite direction.[1] Although for unrelated reasons the Ait Izdig received the Sultan peacefully, this proposed pincer movement against an Ait Yafalman affiliate indicates Mawlay Hassan's flexibility and ingenuity in dealing with tribes far from his center of power.

The Sultan and his gigantic retinue arrived in Tafilalt in the fall of 1893 to find the expected conditions of political strife. Dr Linarès, the French physician who accompanied the expedition, attested that:

the Ait Atta are invading little by little, but in a continuous manner, the region of Tafilalt. The least quarrel, the smallest altercation between a Filali and an Attaoui is the point of departure for an armed struggle in which the Ait

[1] SHA, C. Maroc c6, D. Mission Militaire (1892), Cauchemez to Min. of War, Rapport du mois de Mars 1892, No. 71; Rapport du mois de Mai 1892, No. 79; Rapport du mois de Juin 1892, No. 83. SHA, C. Maroc c7, D. Mission Militaire (1893), Cauchemez to Min. of War, Rapport du mois d'Avril 1893, No. 106. Linarès, 'Voyage au Tafilalet . . .', pp. 417–420.

Atta clan, more warlike and cohesive than the Filali clan, always has the upper hand.[1]

Since some of Tafilalt's population, notably the Bani Mhammad and some of the Dawi Mani, supported the Atta aggression, Linarès' reference to the Filali clan certainly refers mainly to members of the Ait Yafalman group, including the whole population of the Safalat district, the Arab Sabbah, and *ad hoc* bands of Ait Mirghad and Ait Izdig who came into the oasis to join the fray.[2]

Mawlay Hassan spent much of his time in Tafilalt trying to mediate or arbitrate specific disputes involving the Ait Khabbash in order to restore a measure of calm.[3] Local parties, which might have been expected to act as go-betweens, were in this situation not very effective. *Murabtin* of the Sidi al-Ghazi lineage, probably the most important mediational agency in Tafilalt, did intervene in some instances, but only to bring a temporary end to violence, never a lasting peace.[4] Both Alawite and Idrisi *shurfa* sometimes performed mediational services in Morocco. The *shurfa* community of Tafilalt, however, was too large and too factionalized (as it often was elsewhere) to remain aloof from the conflict. Instead, one faction condoned the Atta penetration, probably out of expediency, while another group sided with the Ait Yafalman, knowing that the Ait Khabbash were not disposed to spare property because it belonged to the Sultan's kinsmen.[5]

Mawlay Rashid, the Sharifian governor (*khalifa*) of Tafilalt and head of the local *shurfa* community, might also have been expected to check violence related to the Atta offensive. He did represent the only over-arching governmental authority in the oasis. French observers in the nineteenth century tended to belittle his political role (as they did any *makhzan* official), but in fact he was instructed to do little more than to represent the central government in the dynasty's birthplace. In other words, the presence of a *khalifa* in Tafilalt, the only others being in Marrakesh and Fes, reflected the religious and ideological significance of the location rather than the size and importance of the *makhzan* administration there. Only a few dozen soldiers and *shurfa* subalterns assisted him as he went about administering the land and treasure belonging to the dynasty, policing the market at Abou Am, and serving as a liaison between the palace and the *shurfa* or other groups in the region. Real government in Tafilalt

---

[1] Linarès, op. cit., p. 48.

[2] The informant in Safalat (interview: *qsar* Tabouasamt, 4 August 1969) stated that his district was in fact part of the Ait Yafalman confederation and that the member tribes in the area always aided them in their defense against the Ait Khabbash.

[3] SHA, C. Maroc c7, D. Mission Militaire (1893), Schlumburger to Min. of War, 1 January 1894, No. 8; Walter B. Harris, *Tafilet*, London, 1895, pp. 243–5. Harris was a British journalist who joined the Sultan's expedition in Tafilalt. Linarès, op. cit., pp. 50–2.

[4] Spillmann, op. cit., p. 70; interview with Muhammad Tuhani, *zawiya* Sidi al-Ghazi, 25 July 1967; interview: Tabouasamt, 4 August 1969, and Mesguida, 2 August 1969.

[5] Evidence for the existence of two *shurfa* parties, one pro-Atta, the other pro-Yafalman, is contained in a large number of French reports from both the frontier zone and the military mission in Morocco concerning the period of especially intense feuding between 1896 and 1900. One informant (Tabouasamt, 4 August 1969) in Safalat affirmed that *murabtin* rather than *shurfa* always mediated conflicts in that district.

was in the hands of the *jamaa*s of each *qsar*, all of which were politically autonomous. District wide councils met on special occasions, but none existed for the oasis as a whole.[1]

Since Mawlay Rashid was incapable of forcing the Ait Khabbash either to retreat or negotiate, he bent with the wind and, at least during much of his career, allied himself with their interests. He even recruited Khabbash warriors from time to time to carry out administrative orders that would otherwise be ignored.[2] Consequently, he was in no position to serve as a political broker between them and the *qsar*-dwellers or the Ait Yafalman.

Since Mawlay Hassan only stayed in Tafilalt for three weeks, his success in restoring peace was only transitory. He also abandoned the trip to Touat and largely failed to strengthen ties with the political leaders of that region. Probably his greatest achievement was his preservation of good relations with the Ait Atta, which prevented the expedition from ending in the military disaster which some French observers predicted. Unfortunately, he died soon after recrossing the Atlas, and Ba Ahmad, his successor, gave the Saharan problem a much lower priority. The Regent did send representatives to Tafilalt toward the end of the century, but they failed to check the feuding which was especially violent between 1896 and 1900.[3]

Thus, the Ait Khabbash were still very much outward bound when a French column marched into Touat in late 1899. This event, however, marked the zenith of Atta expansion in the east. Whereas the Sultans had been unable to check their power either by force or negotiation, the French army virtually obliterated it in the course of thirty-three years of pacification. Despite strong resistance by most of the tribe, the French offensive, first from Algeria to the banks of the Ziz, later southward over the Atlas, forced the war bands to retreat back towards the Saghro homeland. Submission to French authority came section by section, even family by family. Ironically, Atta power was finally broken in 1933 where it had first been nurtured—at the battle of Bou Gafer in

[1] Interview with Mawlay Ali (an elderly son of Mawlay Rashid), *qsar* Moulay Abdelhakem (Tafilalt), 4 August 1969. The role of the *khalifa* in Tafilalt is also discussed in Berriau, *Contribution à l'étude de la région du sud-ouest*; A. Le Chalelier, *Notes sur les villes et tribus du Maroc: Tafilelet—Tizimmi—Er-Reteb—Medghara*, Paris, 1903, p. 12; Maurice Bernard, 'Le Tafilala', *Renseignements coloniaux*, No. 10, October 1927, p. 391; Vicard, 'Le Territoire de Bou Denib avant et pendant la guerre: la dernier soulèvement du Tafilalet, 1918–1919', *Bulletin de la Société de Géographie d'Alger*, 1921, p. 10.

[2] Mawlay Ali (interview: *qsar* Moulay Abdelhakem, 4 August 1969) affirmed that the *khalifa* used the Ait Atta, as well as the Dawi Mani and Bani Mhammad, to execute *makhzan* orders. In 1895, for example, the *makhzan* sent instructions to Tafilalt to the effect that the Ghanamna, a nomadic tribe inhabiting a small area north of Touat, should be chastized for attacking and pillaging a caravan on its way to Fes carrying a government *caid*. A force of Atta and Dawi Mani (one report said 1,100 of them) were recruited to do the job. The Ghanamna were subsequently decimated and a number of them taken to Fez in chains. SHA, C. Maroc C9, D. Mission Militaire (1895), Schlumberger to Min. of War, Rapport d'Avril 1895, No. 14; Rapport d'Août 1895, No. 33; Martin, op. cit., pp. 274–8.

[3] The French occupation of Touat in 1899–1900 prompted a temporary end to Atta-related skirmishing in Tafilalt while the tribes sought ways, for the most part unsuccessfully, to unify against the European threat.

the eastern end of the Saghro. Only remnants of the Ait Khabbash, who had begun their retreat from Touat in 1900, held out several months longer. A ragtag band withdrew ahead of the French advance, traveling more than a hundred miles west of the Dra, an exodus that revealed the depth and rigidity of the war mentality which had governed the tribe since its founding.[1]

The coming of the Protectorate administration resulted in the stabilization though little diminution of the tribe's territorial spread. The Ait Khabbash ceased their visits to Touat after 1900, but they remained in Boudenib, the Rteb, and Tafilalt. Although the social changes of the Protectorate led many of the Atta to give up pastoralism, many continue to herd camels and sheep, following the same transhumance patterns they did before the French came. But warfare is outlawed, the supreme chief is no longer elected, and the strong bonds of *khams khmas* exist largely in the realm of reminiscence.

Ait Atta aggression dominated the history of much of pre-Saharan Morocco from the seventeenth century until 1900, when French aggression summarily replaced it. The causes of the expansion and the reasons for its long endurance may never be thoroughly understood. But the early phases of it, like the other major tribal movements, resulted from a chronic imbalance between population and resources, probably related to long periods of drought. The natural course of Atta expansion, or what could have been migration, was toward the greener Atlas pastures. The Ait Yafalman alliance, however, proved to be a highly effective if not decisive barrier against another tide of surplus desert dwellers. With the northern routes blocked (except in the area of gradual infiltration northwest of the Dadès), the only alternative for the Atta was to abandon migration and simply to fan out, that is, to take possession of enough pre-Saharan and mountain territory to bring population and resources back into equilibrium. The enduring success of this program west, south, and east of the Saghro permitted the tribe to continue to grow.

The movement of the Ait Khabbash and Ait Umnasf into the steppe lands on both sides of the lower Ziz was probably accomplished more by peaceful nomadic drift than by purposeful conquest over other pastoralists. The Ait Khabbash initially may have forced Ait Izdig or Ait Mirghad out of desert fringe pastures and deeper into the mountains. But conflict between the Atta and other tribes over grazing land was apparently not intense in the eighteenth and nineteenth centuries. The Ait Khabbash made no concerted effort to achieve exclusive occupation of land east of the Ziz, but rather shared the Hammada of the Guir with the Dawi Mani without generating unresolvable tensions.

Most of the conflict involving the Ait Khabbash occurred in the oases, reflecting the fact that their aggression was directed much more toward the control of agricultural resources than toward the occupation of territory for herding. All the Atta sections inhabiting the pre-Sahara came to depend on dates and other oasis products almost as much as did the *qsar*-dwellers. Since the extent of

[1] On the pacification of the Atta during the Protectorate, see Spillmann, op. cit., pp. 99–168.

arable land, unlike pasture, was strictly limited, nomads and sedentaries either had to share the harvests or battle for them. More often than not, mutual dependence, involving regular, peaceful exchange of goods and services, characterized their relations. The Atta purchased land and maintained it with *haratin*, traded their meat and wool in the market place for dates and grain, and guarded palm groves in return for a share of the harvest through *raaya* agreements. But in spite of this essential symbiosis between desert and sown, the Atta never regarded cultivators, Berber or Arab, white or black, as their social or political equals. To them, with their military prowess, their tribal *élan*, and their acute sense of racial superiority over sedentary Arabs as well as over *haratin*, all men of the soil were to be despised and coerced. The Atta did not hesitate to use force in one form or another when they wanted a larger share of the resources than they could conveniently secure through reciprocity. Were it not for the French intervention, the pattern of aggression against individual *qsar*s in the Ziz valley and Touat would probably have continued long after 1900 and even spread to centers further east. One Ait Khabbash informant, looking back on better days, boasted that, except for the French 'counter-offensive', the Atta would have swept across Algeria!

In the long run, however, the tribe aimed to exploit agriculture and commerce, not to obliterate them. A general policy of aimless rapine and pillage would ultimately have undermined (and at times perhaps did) their more profitable activities in trade, collection of tribute and tolls, and supervision of *haratin* labor. Therefore, acts of violence, though almost continuous in the region during the nineteenth century, were often restrained and always selective. They were also fragmented and episodic, since neither the Ait Khabbash nor the Ait Unibgui *khums* as a whole operated as a single, disciplined military unit, but rather in independent, uncoordinated, spontaneously organized war bands varying greatly in size. Atta sections other than the Ait Khabbash, the Ait Umnasf (in the Rteb), and, in a sense, the Bani Mhammad, took no part in later expansion to the east and southeast, other than as small groups or individuals. Except in the earlier centuries, the 'five fifths' did not fight as one against outsiders. In fact, were it not for the election of the supreme *amghar* and the pervasive ideological function of *khams khmas*, it is possible that by the end of the nineteenth century Ait Khabbash membership in the Atta political-genealogical structure would have been purely vestigial.

Another notable aspect of the Ait Khabbash expansion is the degree to which inter-tribal relations cut across ethno-linguistic boundaries. A look at the ethnographic map of the Algero-Moroccan frontier region reveals a rather clearcut transition from the territory of Berber-speaking to Arabophone transhumant populations. The Berber heartland of central and southern Morocco extends eastward as far as the extremity of the High Atlas and the Hammada of the Guir. Beyond there, the tribes are Arab all the way to eastern Algeria. Thus Ait Atta, Ait Izdig, and Ait Seghrushin (in the upper Guir region) faced Dawi Mani, Awlad Jarir, Bani Gil, and Awlad al-Haj. Tafilalt was almost an Arab island in a Berber sea, while the reverse situation prevailed in and around the oasis of Figuig, 150 miles to the east.

4*

It should be clear from the pattern of alliance and opposition in Ait Khabbash politics that ethno-linguistic differences had little direct impact on political behavior. The Ait Khabbash were continually at swords point with the Ait Yafalman tribes, whereas they developed *tata* ties with the Dawi Mani and Awlad Jarir and formed a permanent alliance of blood brotherhood (or rather big brotherhood) with the Bani Mhammad. Language may have posed little obstacle to Arab–Berber alliance since many of the Atta learned Arabic primarily for reasons of trade. The schema of inter-tribal alliances and hostilities, then, must be explained in terms of on-going economic interests and political expediences, not on the basis of ethnic dichotomies. The notion of endemic Arab–Berber antagonism is much more the abstract creation of French colonial theorists than the result of careful ethnographic research among the tribes (see Edmund Burke, Chapter 8).

Relations between the Ait Atta and Mawlay Hassan suggests a further conclusion on the nature of the Moroccan political system in the nineteenth century. Henri Terrasse, the French historian of Morocco, conceived of the country as divided into two mutually antagonist zones, the *bled el-makhzan*, or country of the *makhzan*, and the *bled es-siba*, or country of dissidence. According to his scheme, relations between the two zones centered upon the efforts of the *makhzan* to submit dissident populations to its authority, that is, to force them to accept administrative officials, pay taxes, and provide conscripts for the Sultan's army.[1]

Other students of Moroccan history, writing both before and after Terrasse, have suggested a more subtle conceptualization.[2] They have not rejected the *makhzan-siba* approach out of hand, but only modified it to a degree. The principal revision is the idea that some tribes and communities were only partially or irregularly subjected to government rule and, therefore, could not permanently or precisely be placed in either the *makhzan* or *siba* category. These marginal groups generally lived just beyond the heartland of *makhzan* control, usually thought of as a triangle bounded by Rabat, Fes, and Marrakesh. The extent of their autonomy depended upon the relative strength or weakness of the Sultan in power at the time. According to the revised model, then, the Moroccan political community constituted three zones rather than two: a central core where the government exercised regular authority, a fluctuating belt where control was intermittent and uncertain, and a third zone, mainly the high mountains and southern deserts, where it was hardly ever imposed. The tribes and towns of all three zones were politically united only in their recognition of the Sultan as leader of all Muslims. On the other hand, merchants, pilgrims, saintly mediators, and transhumant nomads moved regularly between one zone and another, thus

[1] H. Terrasse, *Histoire du Maroc des origines à l'établissement du protectorat français*, Casablanca, 1950, Vol. 2, pp. 356–8.

[2] See Edward Doutté, 'Les Marocains et la société marocaine', *Revue générale des sciences pures et appliquées*, Vol. 14, No. 7, 1903, p. 386; G. Salmon, 'Essai sur l'histoire politique du nord-marocain', *Archives marocaines*, Vol. 2, 1905, p. 1; and Eugène Aubin (Descos), *Le Maroc d'aujourd'hui*, Paris, 1913, pp. 238–41, 245. For more recent views, see Mohamed Lahbabi, *La Gouvernement marocain à l'aube de XXe siècle*, Rabat, 1958; and Gellner, op. cit., pp. 1–5, 23–6.

welding the country together through a network of commercial, political, and social relationships.

This more flexible model is certainly an improvement over that of Terrasse, but it is still useful only up to a point. It is weak in its implied assumption that the imposition of and resistance to central authority was the only prominent issue in contacts between the *makhzan* and the rural populations. It does not show how the prestige of the Sultan, as *Imam* and *Sharif al-baraka*, could be translated into political influence affecting tribal politics in a variety of ways. In other words, the *makhzan-siba* approach does not do justice to the dynamic and multifarious character of relations between the government and the tribes.

In the Southeast, for example, the Sultan almost never achieved real political authority over any of the tribes and oasis communities (including his own *shurfa* kinsmen) during the nineteenth century. Yet to state only that these groups were dissident does not reveal anything about the significant 'diplomatic' exchanges regularly being transmitted back and forth across the Atlas. Various local issues—the Atta expansion, the decline in commerce, feuding in Tafilalt, the approach of the French—determined the intensity and seriousness of these exchanges, rather than the linear distance of a group from the northern capital. The populations of Touat, for instance, were eminently free of *makhzan* control, yet the flow of letters and delegations between their villages and the Sultan's court during the later nineteenth century shows that they were hardly isolated from or indifferent to *makhzan* politics. Furthermore, tribes living equidistant from the capital did not necessarily follow an identical course in relations with it. During the reigns of Mawlay Hassan and Mawlay Abd al-Aziz, the quality of exchanges with the Ait Atta were notably different from those with the neighboring Dawi Mani, whose *caid*s received on several occasions official investitures and seals from the Sultan, something the Atta leaders never did.

It is unfortunate that both European and North African writers have in recent years expended so much effort attempting to prove or disprove the claims of *makhzan* sovereignty in the trans-Atlas regions—using criteria applicable to the Western nation-state. Pre-occupation with the location of international frontiers before the Protectorate has been at the expense of the potentially more fruitful study of the *makhzan*'s role in tribal politics as both mediator and manipulator. Conversely, the impact of events and trends south of the Atlas upon the *makhzan*'s power and prestige throughout the country deserves closer attention. In short, the shopworn themes of rural dissidence and *makhzan* debility should be de-emphasized in favor of more refined analyses of the nature and import of political interplay, whatever its form, between the Sultan and his far-flung subjects.

5

Local Politics and State Intervention: Northeast Morocco from 1870 to 1970

J. David Seddon

The absorbtion of the *bilad as-siba* into the *bilad al-makhzan* represents a revolution whose consequences are as far-reaching as those of the signing of the protectorate treaty, or of the gaining of independence, or of all the changes, taken singly or collectively, which have taken place in Morocco since 1956. This revolution was some twenty-two years in the making, but its net result was to render anomalous the traditional patterns of government. The *makhzan* no longer needed an army to collect taxes, and, in any case, it was not permitted one under the terms of the protectorate agreement. The formerly nomadic court took up fixed residence in Rabat, and there grew up about it a sophisticated administrative apparatus whose heart was the Direction of the Interior and Political Affairs. At the other end of the scale, the tribes could no longer attack one another with impunity, nor could they feasibly challenge the central authorities.

John Waterbury, *The Commander of the Faithful.*

INTRODUCTION

1. In this essay we examine some of the changes in political organization that have taken place over the last hundred years in the northeast of Morocco. We are interested primarily in the alterations that have come about as a result of increasing governmental and administrative control over the rural areas and of the gradual penetration of State (*makhzan*) institutions into the countryside.

Our analysis is based on the detailed investigation of two tribes in what is now the province of Nador: the Berber-speaking Ait bu Ifrur (Beni bu Ifrur) and the Arabic-speaking Ulad Stut,[1] and the discussion presented here refers directly only to Nador province, although there is good evidence to suggest

[1] The fieldwork upon which this discussion is based was carried out between March 1968 and December 1969 as part of a longer-term project directed by Robert T. Holt, of the Center for Comparative Studies in Technological Development and Social Change, at the University of Minnesota, and entitled *The Lower Moulouya Irrigation Project: an Analysis of the Social Structural Constraints on Capital Formation and Entreprenurial Development in Peasant Communities.* My colleague, Raymond Jamous, worked with the Ait bu Ifrur, and I with the Ulad Stut. I am extremely grateful to Professor Holt and to Raymond Jamous for their support and assistance; also to Professor Ernest Gellner for his comments on the original manuscript of this chapter. Much of the discussion is based on combined work by Jamous and myself, but I am responsible for the form and presentation and any shortcomings are mine alone. A brief preliminary report is to be found in J. D. Seddon, 'Social and economic change in Northeast Morocco', *Current Anthropology*, 1971.

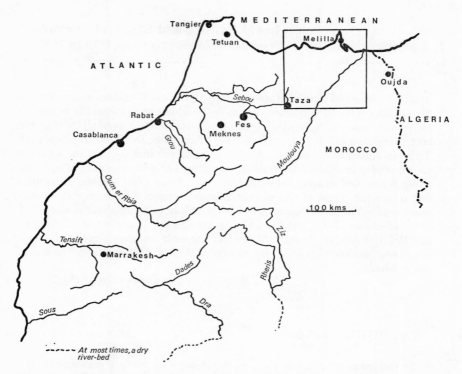

Map 5.1   Morocco indicating area of the province of Nador

that many of the features of political organization in this region, both past and present, resemble those found elsewhere in the northeast.[1]

2. John Waterbury has recently suggested, in his study of the Moroccan political elite, that 'contemporary political behaviour in Morocco has been historically conditioned, or is at least derivative to a substantial degree from the country's past and its traditional social institutions', and that, while the colonial occupation between 1912 and 1956 totally disrupted the governmental and administrative continuity, it 'brought about no correspondingly profound changes in the political style of Moroccans'.[2]

Although it is possible to argue that certain aspects of the national 'political culture' have remained little affected by over a century of European commercial, political and military penetration, we believe that the foundations of wealth and

[1] Specifically among the Beni Snassen tribes to the east and southeast, and probably also the Ait Waryaghel to the west. For a discussion of the latter tribe, see D. M. Hart, *Conflicting Models of a Berber Tribal Structure in the Moroccan Rif: the Segmentary and Alliance Systems of the Aith Warryaghar* (ms. 1970).

[2] J. Waterbury, *The Commander of the Faithful: the Moroccan Political Elite, a Study of Segmented Politics*, London, 1970, p.34.

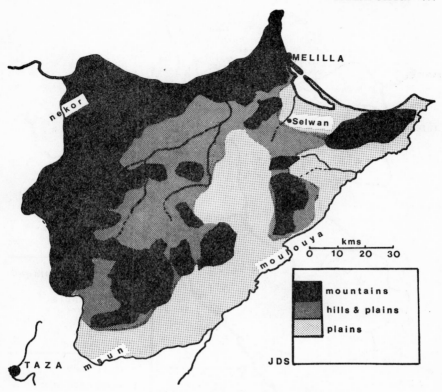

MELILLA

ne/kor

●Selwan

kms
0 10 20 30

mountains

hills & plains

plains

TAZA

mou/ouya

m/sun

JDS

Map 5.2   Province of Nador, northeast Morocco

power in the countryside have been altered so radically over the last eighty or so years that the whole nature of political organization (as well as certain elements of the political culture) in the rural areas has undergone a fundamental change.

3. We cannot give here a complete and detailed account of the complex process of economic and political change that took place in the northeast of Morocco between 1870 and 1970, and what follows is a highly simplified analysis, in which certain variables have been isolated to produce a brief study in terms of comparative statics.[1] The discussion is divided into a number of sections, representing 'stages' or 'periods': 1860–90 (the 'traditional' situation); 1890–1908 (the pre-colonial period); 1909–56 (the Spanish occupation); 1956–60 (the first years of independence); and 1960–70 (the 'present' situation), in which the crucial variable is the extent to which the sociopolitical 'environment' provided the possibility of accumulating enduring power and wealth (see

[1] A major disadvantage of comparative statics is that the time factor remains external to the model itself; a more realistic and sophisticated model could be constructed.

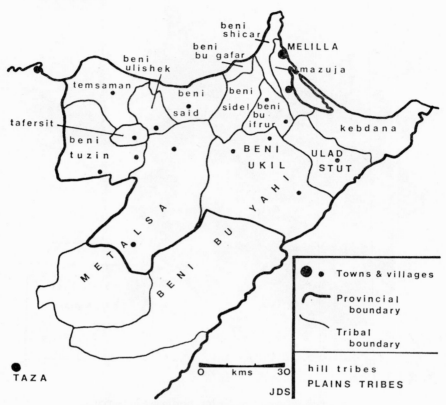

Map 5.3   Distribution of tribes in northeast Morocco

Table 5.1). We argue that, whereas in 1870 the key to a successful political career, among the tribes of the northeast, was the maintenance of a large following, in 1970 the ambitious man in the rural areas attempts rather to develop a relationship of dependence and 'clientship' with the administration (or *makhzan*).

4. The region under consideration lies in the extreme northeast of Morocco, bordering the Mediterranean. In 1970 it is some six hours by bus from Fes; of 1870 it was many days' journey from the same town, which was then the seat in government and one of the centers of the *makhzan*, where the Sultan held court. Defined administratively today as the province of Nador, the region may also be conceived of geographically as bounded by rivers and mountains: by the great Moulouya river to the east and southeast, by the Msun—a tributary of the Moulouya—to the south and southwest, and by the river Nekor to the west. Across the Moulouya, in what used to be the French zone during the colonial period, are the Beni Snassen mountains, and the high ground in the west of the province marks the easternmost extension of the Rif mountain range, which runs along the northern coastline of Morocco (see Maps 5.1 and 5.2).

Table 5.1   Brief Chronology of Events Affecting Politics in Northeast Morocco

International/National		*Regional*
French invade and begin to occupy Algeria	— 1830	
	1840s —	Labour migration from the eastern Rif into Algeria begins
Moroccan army defeated by the French at Isly	— 1844	
	1850s —	Active hostility between the Spanish in Melilla and the surrounding tribes
War between Spain and Morocco	— 1859	
Morocco defeated and obliged to pay large indemnity. Treaty included agreement to allow the Spanish to enlarge Melilla	— 1860	
	1891–3 —	Increased tension between the Spanish in Melilla and the surrounding tribes as Melilla is enlarged and fortified. Fighting breaks out. Spanish troops reinforced from the mainland. The tribes sue for peace
(i) Agreement between Morocco and Spain regarding Melilla incidents (ii) Death of Moulai Hassan. Abdel Aziz, youngest son of Moulai Hassan, proclaimed Sultan in Fes. Opposition both within the *makhzan* and throughout the country. Outbreaks of revolt.	— 1894 —	*Makhzan* garrison sent to the northeast. Base established at Selwan
Bu Hmara raises rebellion near Fes	— 1901	
	1903 —	Bu Hmara comes to the northeast and set ups his *makhzan* at Selwan after chasing official garrison toward Melilla. Claims to be Mohamed, brother of Abdel Aziz and finds local support
The Act of Algeciras	— 1906	
Hafid, brother of Abdel Aziz proclaimed Sultan in Marrakesh	— 1907	
	1908 —	Bu Hmara chased from Selwan by his former supporters after dealings with Europeans
French occupy Casablanca in the west and Oujda in the east, and control the surrounding regions	—1907–10—	Moulouya river effective boundary between French and Spanish zones of operations
	1909–12—	Spanish use Melilla as a bridgehead for penetration of the northeast
Moulai Hafid signs the Protectorate treaty and abdicates. Yussef, brother of Abdel Aziz and Hafid becomes Sultan	— 1912	
Spanish given 'Protectorate' in the north	— 1913	

Table 5·1 (*cont.*)

International/National		*Regional*
	1921 —	Crushing defeat of Spanish by the tribesmen followers of Abd el-Krim, at Anual. Retreat of Spanish in northeast to Melilla
French forces join with Spanish in the areas north of Fes	— 1924	
Muhammed, son of Yussef, succeeds the deceased Sultan	— 1927 —	Submission of all rebellious tribes of the Rif after final defeat of Abd el-Krim
Spanish civil war. Many Riffians fight for Franco	—1936–9	
Founding of Istiqlal (Independence) Party	— 1944	
Sultan Muhammed exiled for his sympathies with Istiqlal	— 1953	
Formation of the Liberation army Return of Muhammed, as king	— 1955 —	Liberation army active in northeast. Halt of labour migration to Algeria by French authorities
Independence and reunification	— 1956/7	
Growth and proliferation of political parties	— 1936–8	
	1958–9—	Rebellions in the northeast, based on those tribes that had most strongly supported Abd el-Krim. Crushed by *makhzan* columns
King becomes Prime Minister First elections for rural communes' councils	— 1960 —	Province of Nador: rural communes merely follow or subdivide tribal boundaries (areas)
Hassan, son of Muhammed, becomes king on his father's death	— 1961	
Parliament established	— 1962	
Harrassment of political parties, especially UNFP. Border conflict with Algeria	— 1963 —	Purges of suspected UNFP members. Cessation of large-scale labour migration into Algeria. Labour migration to Europe begins
Suspension of Parliament and declaration of state of exception	— 1965	
Rural elections	— 1969 —	Local elections clearly controlled and 'rigged'. Majority of candidates defined as 'neutrals', i.e. non-party but *makhzan*-approved
New constitution and elections	— 1970	

The relatively mountainous coastal area in the north of the region gives way, as one progresses south, to low hills, and finally to uneven plains. Average rainfall decreases away from the coast and falls from between 700 mm and 400 mm in the north, to as low as 200 mm in the extreme south. Population density reflects these climatic and geomorphological differences, ranging from *c.* 130 per square kilometer in the north, to *c.* 15 per square kilometer in the south. Demographic variation within the region is related, not only to climate and physical geography, but also to the pattern of economic organization among the different tribes before the Spanish occupation, proximity to Melilla (the only town in the vicinity until *c.* 1930), and the growth, since 1910, of several village-market centers.[1]

At the present time the great majority of the rural population is composed of settled agriculturalists, living, for the most part, in relatively scattered homesteads in the hills and foothills, keeping some goats and sheep (and cattle in some cases) and cultivating wheat and barley. Until the mid-1930s, however, four of the tribes were primarily pastoral, living in tents and keeping camels and sheep, growing barley and wheat in certain limited areas and ranging over the plains and lower hills for grazing. (See Map 5.3 and Table 5.2.) These four

Table 5.2

Circle	Rural commune	Annexe/Tribe	Language	Total population	Population density
L'Uta	Zaio	Ulad Stut	Arabic	10,500	24
	Ras el-Ma	Kebdana	Berber	30,700	50
	Qariet Arkeman	Kebdana			
	Hassi Berkan	Beni bu Yahi	Berber		
		Beni Ukil	Arabic	18,800	15
	Tistutin	Beni bu Yahi			
		Beni Ukil			
	Driush	Metalsa	Berber	28,100	17
	Ain Zohra	Metalsa			
Gelaia	Nador	(Mazuja)		18,500	
	Ferkhana	Mazuja	Berber	28,000	126
	Had Beni Shicar	Berber	Berber	21,500	127
	Iazanen	Beni bu Gafar	Berber	8,300	131
	Tleta Jbel	Beni Sidel	Berber	22,900	73
	Tleta l'Uta	Beni Sidel			
	Selwan	Beni bu Ifrur	Berber	25,200	123
	Beni bu Ifrur	Beni bu Ifrur			
Rif	Dar Kebdani	Beni Said	Berber	31,700	78
	Tazarhin	Beni Said			
	Ben Tiyeb	Beni Ulishek	Berber	22,100	100
	Mehayast	Beni Ulishek	Berber		
	Kemis Temsaman	Temsaman	Berber	36,800	87
	Budinar	Temsaman			
	Trugut	Temsaman			
	Ijermauas	Beni Tuzin	Berber	39,000	64
	Midar	Benit Tuzin			
	Tleta d'Azlef	Beni Tuzin			
	Tafersit	Tafersit	Berber	8,200	130

(*N.B.* Population figures taken from Mennesson, 1961, and refer to 1957.)

[1] For further details, see J. F. Troin, 'Le Nord-est du Maroc: mise au point régionale', *Revue de géographie du Maroc*, No. 12, Paris, 1967.

tribes retain certain features, primarily in their economic organization, which distinguish them from the other groups of the region.

Of the fifteen tribal groups in the province of Nador only two are not Berber-speaking: the Beni Ukil, all of whom claim to be *shorfa*,[1] and the Ulad Stut. Despite a certain cultural distinctiveness as 'Arabs' in a predominantly 'Berber' area, these groups show no radical differences in social structure and social organization, at the present time, from the other groups in the region. Although significant differences existed in the past, and continue to exist, as a result of ecological and historical factors, we consider the analysis which follows to be of general validity for the whole area.[2]

1860–90: THE TRIBES, THE *MAKHZAN* AND THE EUROPEANS

1. The tribes of the northeast, like those elsewhere in Morocco,[3] were never autonomous or isolated entities, either politically or culturally, and the majority of individuals living in the northeast were linked in a variety of ways with others from outside the tribe, the region, and even from outside Morocco. The vast complexity of inter-personal and inter-group relations might crudely be summarized as involving tribesman and tribesman, tribesman and townsman, tribesman and *makhzan*, tribesman and foreigner.

2. Tribesman was linked to tribesman by virtue of their common participation in the social life of the region: kinship, marriage alliances and friendship, the shifting pattern of political coalitions and the membership of religious groups, as well as commercial enterprise and a wide range of economic contract associations, provided bases for cooperation and interaction, whether within the tribe or between members of different tribes.[4] Although there were no towns or villages, apart from Spanish Melilla, inter-tribal markets enabled tribesmen to exchange produce from different ecological zones within the region on an organized basis, and also served a more general social function as meeting places, centers for the

---

[1] Among all the tribes of the region were small groups claiming to be *shorfa*, some of which were Beni Ukil in origin; the Beni Ukil being the only tribe in which all members claimed to be *shorfa*. In this chapter we have not discussed the important role of the *shorfa* in tribal politics as mediators and peacemakers. We note only that with the penetration of the *makhzan* and state institutions into the countryside and the associated control of open violence, the role of the *sherif* has become redundant.

[2] A more detailed and through investigation of the differences between tribes is under way.

[3] See, for example, K. Brown and *The Social History of a Moroccan Town, Salé, 1830–1930*, unpublished Ph.D. dissertation, University of California, Los Angeles, 1969, pp. 120, 124, 129, 131; Ernest Gellner, *Saints of the Atlas*, London & Chicago, 1969, pp. 2–3; Waterbury, op. cit., p. 29.

[4] For a brief summary of some of these 'linking mechanisms', see B. C. Hoffman, *The Structure of Traditional Moroccan Rural Society*, The Hague, 1967, pp. 99–105, 130–41. Also J. D. Seddon, 'Economic change and family structures in a Moroccan rural commune', unpublished paper given to the Social Anthropology and Sociology Conference held in Nicosia, Cyprus, in September 1970 (forthcoming).

exchange of news and information, and as informal courts for the consideration of various 'offences'.[1]

Social interaction was not always peaceful, and fighting, both within the tribe and between tribes, was common. Raiding was a recognized way of increasing one's wealth, while at the same time demonstrating personal courage and the size of one's following; feuds between groups within the tribe, disputes between kinsmen over the ownership of land or livestock, and enmity between individuals over matters of 'honor' were endemic throughout the area during this period.

3. The nearest towns were Melilla, Oujda, Taza and Fes. Commerce with Melilla, although limited in 1860, increased during the latter part of the nineteenth century, especially between 1880 and 1909, and included the unofficial sale of arms by the Spanish garrison to the surrounding tribesmen.[2] Goods imported through Melilla also found their way into Algeria and even further east, for labor migration from the eastern Rif to Algeria began as early as the 1840s, and tribesmen from this region used their connections in the newly-occupied French territory to indulge in trade and commerce as well as large-scale smuggling. Some tribesmen went as far afield as Fes to buy foreign imported goods and to sell their local produce, both animal and vegetable, although an important market for livestock lay closer at hand near Taza. Iron ore was exported from the region and other goods, including arms and ammunition were smuggled in off the coast for sale in the hinterland.[3]

The region came, in theory, under the jurisdiction of the Pasha of Oujda, the highest representative of the *makhzan* in the whole of the northeast of Morocco, but, in practice, although certain contacts were usually maintained with the *makhzan* by at least some of the tribesmen, the area was by no means under *makhzan* control and the tribes frequently refused to pay taxes.

4. Much has been written about tribal dissidence (*siba*) in Morocco, and one often obtains the impression that whole tribes or tribal confederations stood in a more or less permanent relation of hostility and opposition to the Sultan and his *makhzan*. This was certainly not the case in the northeast, and it was probably not so in other parts of Morocco. First, the objective was seldom to attack the *makhzan* or to overthrow the Sultan; rather it was to escape his secular arm, and to avoid his taxes and his local officials. The tribes often distinguished between Sultan and *makhzan*, regarding the former with religious veneration and the latter with contempt. Secondly, the tribes were not economically self-sufficient

[1] See W. Fogg, 'The Suq: a study in the human geography of Morocco', *Geography*, Vol. 17, 1932. 'Villages and suqs in the High Atlas Mountains of Morocco', *Scottish Geographical Magazine*, Vol. 51, No. 3, 1935. 'The importance of tribal markets in the commercial life of the countryside of northwest Morocco', *Africa*, Vol. 12, No. 4, 1939. Also F. Benet, 'Explosive Markets: the Berber Highlands', Arensberg and Polanyi (eds), *Trade and Markets in the Early Empires*, New York, 1957; M. W. Mikesell, 'The role of tribal markets in Morocco', *Geographical Review*, XLVIII, October 1958, pp. 494–511; and Hoffman, op. cit., pp. 79–92.

[2] See Payne, *Politics and the Military in Modern Spain*, London, 1967, p. 630.

[3] For a more detailed discussion of the economic situation in the northeast between 1870 and 1890, see J. D. Seddon, 'Modern economic and political change in northeast Morocco: the northeast up to 1912', unpublished paper given to the research seminar of the Department of Anthropology and Sociology, SOAS, University of London, 1970.

and could afford to cut off vital economic exchanges with urban markets only on a short-term basis. Thirdly, factionalism within the tribes generally prevented a long-term united front, and it was in the interests of the *makhzan*, ever on its guard against the possibility of major rebellions and permanent hostility in the countryside, to maintain diverse relations with different individuals within the tribes and to promote internal factionalism by granting and withdrawing recognition of tribal leaders, and their major opponents.

In this way the *makhzan*, although remote and with little direct control over the distant tribesmen, was often able to exert an indirect influence over local politics and administration by subtle manipulation and intrigue, calming with promises, withholding favors, blocking economic exchange and soothing with tactful mediation, rather than attempting direct military intervention in every case. This was generally the wiser course of action, for the *makhzan* forces could never be sure of military success against rebellious tribesmen in little-known and difficult terrain. The *makhzan* had, in fact, never maintained more than a relative monopoly of coercive means within the country, and, during the last three decades of the nineteenth century, the spread of fast-loading rifles through-out the tribal areas resulted in the loss, on the part of the *makhzan*, of its hitherto significant superiority of fire-power.[1] This factor alone made the effective control of the tribes excessively difficult at a time when the *makhzan* had need of all its authority and power to levy taxes and impose fines in order to repay national debts and to attempt financial reforms.[2]

5. The gradual weakening of the *makhzan*'s grasp on the economic and political affairs of Morocco may be regarded as largely the result of the activities of the Europeans in North Africa. The large-scale commercial penetration of Morocco,[3] the political maneuvering of the western European powers for footholds in North Africa,[4] and, in some cases, direct military action against the forces of the *makhzan*,[5] resulted in economic and financial crises, political upheaval, and a widespread recognition throughout the country of the inability of the Sultan, the *makhzan* and the army to deal either with internal dissidence and rebellion or with growing foreign intervention.[6]

6. European activities affected all parts of Morocco, either directly or in-directly,[7] but nowhere is the importance of the complex interaction between Europeans, *makhzan* and tribes clearer than in the northeast. A few examples will suffice.

During the first part of the nineteenth century the Riffians had maintained a

---

[1] Not only in this area (see J.-L. Miège, *Le Maroc et l'Europe*, Paris, 1961–3, Vol. 4, p. 106) but elsewhere. See, for references, Hoffman, op. cit., p. 98.

[2] See J. Brignon *et al.*, *Histoire du Maroc*, Casablanca, 1967, pp. 304–27.

[3] See Brignon *et al.*, op. cit., pp. 270–310; Miège, op. cit., *passim*.

[4] Miège, op. cit., Vol. 2, pp. 19–33, 191–220, 261–86, 307–412; Vol. 3, pp. 159–96, 263–92; Vol. 4, pp. 13–87, 170–284.

[5] Brignon *et al.*, op. cit., pp. 285, 290.

[6] Brignon *et al.*, op. cit., pp. 304–21; Miège, op. cit., Vol. 2, pp. 22–40, 349–82; Vol. 3, pp. 197–234, 343–69, 419–68; Vol. 4, pp. 88–170.

[7] There is no space here to document this assertion fully, and we merely refer to Miège, op. cit., Vol. 2, pp. 39–189 and note the comment on pp. 136–7.

variety of broadly 'commercial' activities along the Mediterranean coast, either together with Europeans, or else directed against them.[1] In the period from 1830 to 1850 the conflict between the French and the Algerian tribes, together with the absence of all customs control between the French-occupied territories and those retained by the Algerians, or in Morocco, encouraged the development of a substantial 'commercial' network throughout the Rif.[2] Abdelqader, leader of the resistance against the French in Algeria, received supplies, including arms and ammunition, from England, via Gibraltar and northeast Morocco. He had many contacts in the eastern Rif, and two governors of Melilla were recalled to Spain after their association with agents of Abdelqader were discovered.[3] In 1847, the Moroccan *makhzan*, subject to increasing pressure from the French to support their actions against the Algerian tribes, sent three columns to the northeast and dislodged Abdelqader from the old fortress of Selwan (see Map 5.2), to which he had retreated with his loyal supporters, and, no doubt, with the assistance of the local tribes.

Spain occupied several towns along the Mediterranean coast, of which Melilla was the most important. The population of Melilla was provisioned largely from the Spanish mainland and relations with the surrounding tribesmen were uneasy and often hostile, although some tribesmen bought and sold at the market in the Spanish town. In 1854, the military governor of Melilla began an active campaign against the tribes and increased the number of armed sorties.[4] In August 1859 an agreement was signed between Spain and Morocco, allowing the Spanish to increase the territory of Melilla, but incidents around Ceuta (another Spanish-owned enclave) provided an excuse for both countries, between whom relations had been growing increasingly strained, to enter into open war.[5] The Spanish landed near Ceuta and occupied Tetuan in February 1860. Losses were heavy and the costs considerable on both sides, but revolts in other parts of Morocco seriously affected the ability of the *makhzan* to wage an effective campaign.

The peace treaty of 1860–61, signed after the Moroccan defeat, included clauses concerning the territories of Ceuta and Melilla, which were to be enlarged substantially; but the opposition of the Gelaia tribes (see Table 5.2) to the expansion of Melilla nearly ruined the negotiations, and only a combination of Spanish threats, *makhzan* promises, and the intervention and influence of the holy *sherif* of Wazzan was sufficient to calm the tribesmen. In 1891 a boundary commission was sent to demarcate the area granted in 1860 for the enlargement of Melilla, and the construction of a network of small forts along the periphery was planned as a defence against the possible incursions of the surrounding tribes. The siting of one of the blockhouses, too close to a local shrine, however, aroused the Moroccans to tear down the walls. Subsequent hostilities brought Morocco and Spain once again to the brink of outright war, and by 1893 there were some

---

[1] Miège, op. cit., Vol. 2, p. 294. Also for reference to piratc activities off the Rif coast, see Miège, Vol. 2, pp. 308, 326.

[2] Miège, op. cit., Vol. 2, pp. 158–60.

[3] Ibid., pp. 160–1, 200, 202.

[4] Ibid., p. 353.

[5] Ibid., 357–93.

22,000 Spanish troops in Melilla. The Spanish display of force quieted the tribes and a truce was established. In 1894 the Sultan signed a treaty in which he optimistically promised to disarm the hostile tribesmen and punish them; he also allowed the Spanish to station troops on territory technically under Moroccan sovereignty.[1]

There is evidence that Germany also was interested, during this period, in establishing a presence in northeast Morocco;[2] and British boats were regularly seen off the coast, near the mouth of the Moulouya, from as early as 1859.[3]

1860–90: TRIBAL POLITICS

1. From 1860 to 1893–4 local political organization was relatively self-contained, despite the multiplicity of relations existing between tribesmen and the *makhzan*, between tribesmen and Europeans. A would-be leader and successful local politician might attempt to make use of his connections with the *makhzan* or with Europeans, but he relied, for the most part, for the acquisition and maintenance of wealth and power on the support of a following drawn from among his agnates and other kinsmen, but also including a number of unrelated dependants, friends and allies. Whether one considers the settled farmers of the northern part of the region, or the transhumant pastoralists of the southern plains, the political game was broadly the same. Differences arose largely out of the differential significance of land (always a scarce good among the settled, densely-populated agriculturalists), and flocks (highly mobile, highly prized and subject to much raiding).

2. Two principles, or models, of political alliance and opposition were recognized, which appear, at first sight, in some way contradictory. The first involved the conceptualization and explanation of sociopolitical relations in terms of a 'segmentary lineage model', and the second was based on the concept of *elfuf* (sing. *leff*), which may be translated, in this context, as 'factions' or 'coalitions'.[4]

In the first of these models, descent or residence in a particular locality determined the status of individuals, their political and other alignments, and their membership of a series of increasingly inclusive 'segments', from the family to the tribe. As in all such systems, as described by social anthropologists, authority and power was conceived as vested in the total system and in the balance and opposition of homogeneous and 'identical' segments, and, as in other

---

[1] For fuller descriptions of the events around Melilla between 1891–4, see T. Garcia Figueras, *Marruecos : la accion de Espana en el Norte de Africa*, Madrid, 1941, pp. 93–7; A. Llanos y Alcarez, *Melilla, Historia de la Campana de Africa en 1893–4*, Madrid, 1894; Payne, op. cit., pp. 61–4; J. P. Val D'Eremao, 'Melilla and the Moors', *Imperial and Asiatic Quarterly Review*, Vol. 7, No. 13, 1894.

[2] Miège, op. cit., Vol. 4, pp. 25, 180–1; L. Voinot, *Oujda et son Amalat*, Oran, 1912, p. 454.

[3] Miège, op. cit., Vol. 3, pp. 71–2, 169.

[4] See J. D. Seddon, 'Kinship, friendship and factions', *Annales marocaines de sociologie*, 1969.

such systems, the kinship ideology, in terms of which the segments were defined, was that of patrilineal (agnatic) descent.[1]

In the second, no single basis of recruitment or membership was particularly stressed, although the idiom of kinship was widely used, and both alliance and opposition were contextual and contingent. The similarities between the *elfuf* of northeast Morocco and factions, as analysed by sociologists, are striking. Although, in any given socio-cultural context, certain sorts of ties may be given greater emphasis than others, factions are defined, first, by the absence of a single clear principle in the organization of support, and secondly, by their relative impermanence and the possibility of a rapid turn-over of individual supporters and a degree of 'unreliability' in the strength and direction of support.[2] It has recently been suggested that 'the distinctive feature of these factional conflicts, which sets them off from conflicts in a segmentary lineage system, is that the conflicting groups change in composition owing to "transference of persons from one faction to another, loss and replenishment in the followings of leading men"'.[3]

3. These two models of alliance and opposition could, depending on circumstance, appear to complement each other, or to contradict each other. Occasionally, the well-worn Arab proverb—I against my brothers; my brothers and I against our cousins; my brothers, my cousins and I against the world—would apply, providing a pattern of alliance and opposition according to the segmentary lineage model. It was possible to find members of a single patrilineage in one *leff*, or faction, but it was equally possible to find them split between two *elfuf*, opposing each other as members of hostile factions.

In fact, the two principles of recruitment to political groupings were of different orders; leaders could emerge, for instance, without causing major conceptual confusion, because the 'segmentary lineage model' was not, in the final analysis, considered to provide a total explanation of all political behaviour and it was recognized, by some at least, that the 'segmentary lineage model' could be used, or even manipulated, as an explanation and justification for the membership of certain individuals in (or their recruitment to) a *leff*, without necessarily accounting for the total composition of the *leff*.

Tribesmen were aware that, while the 'segmentary lineage model' provided a

[1] For discussion of the features of such 'systems', see E. Durkheim, *The Division of Labour in Society*, New York, 1968, p. 178; E. E. Evans-Pritchard, *The Nuer*, Oxford, 1940; E. E. Evans-Pritchard, *The Sanusi of Cyrenaica*, Oxford, 1949; J. Favret, 'Relations de dépendance et de violence dans la Kabylie pré-coloniale', *L'Homme*, No. 3, 1968; Gellner, op. cit., pp. 35–69; D. M. Hart, 'Segmentary systems and the role of the "five fifths" in tribal Morocco', *Revue de l'occident musulman et de la Méditerranée*, No. 3, 1. trimetre, 1967; R. Jamous, 'Réflexions sur la segmentarité et le mariage arabe', *Annales marocaines de sociologie*, 1969, pp. 21–7; E. L. Peters, 'The proliferation of segments in the lineage of the Bedouin of Cyrenaica', *Journal of the Royal Anthropological Institute*, Vol. 90, 1960; E. L. Peters, 'Some structural aspects of the feud among the camel-herding Bedouin of Cyrenaica', *Africa*, Vol. 37, No. 3, 1967.

[2] See R. Firth, 'Introduction to factions in Indian and Overseas Indian Societies', *British Journal of Sociology*, Vol. 8, 1957, pp. 291–5.

[3] R. W. Nicholas, 'Factions: a comparative analysis', p. 24, in Banton (ed), *Political Systems and the Distribution of Power*, London, 1965.

reasonable shorthand and stereotyped 'explanation' of patterns of alliance and opposition, it did not really explain the actualities of political behavior.[1] Rather, it could be used as a rallying cry, or principle of recruitment, among others, in the complex and difficult game of forming, affirming or breaking political alliances and coalitions within the '*leff* model'. In certain circumstances it was possible to account for all the members of a *leff* in terms of the segmentary lineage model; in others it was not. A similar situation appears to have existed in pre-colonial Kabylia (in Algeria), and also, probably, in the central Rif.[2]

4. To remain at the level of 'models' and 'principles' prevents any real understanding of how, and in what circumstances, certain choices were possible and were made, of the process whereby men grow to wealth and power, of the features of leadership, of who were the followers, and of what were the limitations on success. In order to understand the way in which the game was played, and thus to reach some comprehension of the 'rules' or limits, we must consider the smallest arena for political power defined in terms of the ideology of agnatic descent, the lineage. For it was here that a man's struggle for power began, and it was here that disputes over land, water, animals, women and honor were most heated and most acrimonious.

Political action took place, for the most part, within a specific ecological, demographic and sociological context, certain of whose features exerted significant constraints and limitations on political behavior and, by so doing, provided the 'underlying structure of the game'.[3] These included: extreme variability of rainfall, temperature, etc., both in time (throughout the year and from year to year), and in space (throughout the region); a resultant uncertainty regarding the distribution, at any one time, of the major sources of wealth—crops and animals; high fertility and high mortality rates; the possibility of polygamy and the relative facility of divorce. It would appear that the fundamental similarity of political organization among the tribes of the northeast is associated with these features, as well as with the fact that, despite certain socio-cultural and economic differences, members of all the tribal groups had (1) limited access to sources of wealth outside the normal area of socio-economic activity (i.e. outside the region)[4] (2) limited access to sources of authority and power outside the normal area of sociopolitical activity (i.e. outside the region); and (3) a tendency, as a result of

[1] Peters has drawn attention to the fact that 'the segmentary lineage model' is a 'conscious model' construed by the people themselves, and that it does not explain the actualities of political behavior. See Peters, 'Some structural aspects of the feud . . .'; also Evans-Pritchard, *The Nuer*, p. 138, where the same structural point is made, and Seddon, 'Kinship, friendship and factions', pp. 58–64.

[3] See Favret, op. cit., and the works of D. M. Hart.

[2] The usefulness of considering political organization in terms of game theory is argued cogently in F. G. Bailey, *Stratagems and Spoils*, London, 1969. For a highly relevant discussion see F. Barth, 'Segmentary opposition and the theory of games; a study of Pathan organisation', *Journal of the Royal Anthropological Institute*, Vol. 89, 1959, pp. 5–21.

[4] We do not consider, largely for lack of information, the significance of labor migration to Algeria, although this would have constituted an important extra input of wealth, from outside the region, and is likely to have affected the balance of power to some extent.

these two major factors to consider the distribution of both wealth and power in terms of a zero-sum game.[1]

5. In order to achieve, or to maintain, a position of power and wealth within the lineage, within the tribe, or even within the region as a whole, a man sought to attain a number of goals, most of which were closely related, subject to considerable uncertainty, and could be considered both as ends, in themselves, or as means to further ends. Political and economic success depended on the ability to gather and to keep a large following, and it could be said that the overall aim and final goal of an ambitious man was to attract and maintain such a following. Short-term goals could be seen as means to this final end, or, in the case of a less successful man, could remain goals. Ultimate success was related to the ability of an individual to plan and follow an effective 'path'.[2]

A large number of contingent factors controlled and affected the 'paths' taken by particular individuals, but one of the prerequisites for success was the ability to control and even manipulate one's closest agnates, for it was from these that one could expect the initial hostility and opposition to a budding political career, and the search by one individual of wealth and power, at the expense of others.[3] It was also necessary to build up a following of 'clients' by offering them employment, or economic assistance of some sort; by entering into one of a variety of possible economic contracts with them;[4] by providing protection for them and their families (or lineage), and a safe refuge; and, very generally, by establishing a relationship of inequality, involving indebtedness and obligation, promoting interdependence of leader–patron and follower–client in such a way that even the poorest were cultivated as supporters and enjoyed a minimum of security and well-being, as long as they attached themselves to a sufficiently powerful patron.[5] Thirdly, it was essential to construct a widespread network of strategic alliances and 'friendships', as between equals.

6. Although it is not possible to examine here the whole range of strategies available for use in the search for power and wealth, we should draw attention to two significant and related phenomena. The first concerns the control exerted by an individual over the direction or marriages contracted by members of his lineage, and the second the direction and nature of certain political alliances contracted between leaders of lineages. the relationship between political and marriage alliance was always a close one, in the northeast of Morocco as elsewhere in the 'Arab' world, and it would seem that discussions of marriage

[1] A situation in which any increase in wealth and power to one person or group must mean a corresponding loss to some other person or group.

[2] The inter-relatedness of the factors which contributed to a man's success makes analysis difficult. The relationship between means and ends is not always clear. A somewhat similar situation is that of the *agurram* of the central High Atlas as described by Gellner, op. cit., pp. 74–7.

[3] See P. Pascon, 'La Main-d'œuvre et l'emploi dans le secteur traditionnel', *Bulletin économique et social du Maroc*, Nos. 101–2, 1966, p. 134; Waterbury, op. cit., p. 75.

[4] See Hoffman, op. cit., pp. 130–7.

[5] In fact, the poor man tended to be a more reliable dependant and supporter than any other, for his indebtedness was greater and the chances of his becoming a serious rival were smaller. For the importance of indebtedness in Moroccan politics, see Waterbury, op. cit., p. 77.

patterns in North Africa and the Middle East, by sociologists, have, with some exceptions, tended to pay too little attention to the dynamic and constantly changing relationship between lineage endogamy and lineage exogamy in terms of responses by individuals in positions of power to changes in the political and economic environment.[1]

A man who had ambitions within his own lineage, as the first major step to wider political power, might seek to marry (himself) or to marry his own children outside the lineage, and frequently outside the tribe, in order to extend the range of possible allies. At the same time, it was in his interests if co-members of the lineage could be persuaded to marry within the group, so that their affines were also his agnates, and therefore within the group and more easily controllable, rather than outside his growing area of authority and influence. It appears, from the analysis of lineages in the region, that those lineages forming the core of an important leader's following tended to have a higher proportion of endogamous marriages than those without leaders or split by internal quarrels and dissension. Marriage, it should be noted, was no guarantee of political alliance and there were many instances in which affines found themselves involved in conflict situations on opposite sides, but it increased the possibility of a profitable connection. Conversely, divorce proceedings did not necessarily signal the deterioration of relations between the groups involved, although, in practice, it frequently did. Thus endogamy and exogamy reflect past and present maneuvering and the location of leaders, among other things.

Alliance and opposition between lineages tended to manifest itself in a geographical form. Leaders of lineages, or of smaller factions, might, if successful at this level, attempt to achieve power in the wider community—the crowning success being to control a sufficiently large and cohesive following in the region as to be recognized as 'overall leader' by the Sultan in distant Fes, and to be named as *caid* of one or more tribes and, thereby, as local representative of the *makhzan*.[2] Coalitions between members of different lineages and between leaders resulted from the struggle for clients, patrons and allies throughout the

[1] See the discussions beginning with F. Barth, 'Father's brother's daughter marriage in Kurdistan', *Southwestern Journal of Anthropology*, Vol. 10, 1954, pp. 164–71, to which the most recent contributions are R. F. Murphy and L. Kasdan, 'Agnation and endogamy: some further considerations', *Southwestern Journal of Anthropology*, Vol. 23, No. 1, 1957, pp. 1–13; Peters, 'Some structural aspects of the feud . . .'; A. Cohen, *Arab Border-villages in Israel*, Manchester, 1965; Jamous, 'Réflexions sur la segmentarité et le mariage arabe'; H. Rosenfeld, 'The contradictions between property, kinship and power as reflected in the marriage system of an Arab village', in Peristiany (ed), *Contributions to Mediterranean Sociology*, Paris & The Hague, 1968.
It is interesting to note that *elfuf* appear to have been endogamous both in the northeast of Morocco and in Kabylia. See P. Bourdieu, 'The sentiment of honour in Kabyle Society', in Peristiany (ed), *Honour and Shame: the Values of Mediterranean Society*, London, 1965, pp. 236–7.
[2] Although an object of envy and enmity for the less successful, and therefore, both personally and politically insecure, the *caid* was in a position to act as intermediary between the Sultan and the tribe. This could be a profitable role to play. See Waterbury, op. cit., p. 25. Also compare the situation of the *caid* in Morocco with that of the chief among the Pathans, as described by Barth, 'Segmentary opposition and the theory of games . . .', p. 13.

region and from the attempts on the part of faction leaders to reduce the power of their adversaries' rivals by tempting or forcing away their supporters.[1] At the same time as they tried to reduce their adversaries by drawing away their support from below (clients and dependants), faction leaders would seek support from above (bigger leaders or the *makhzan*), thus becoming clients themselves, to some extent, or, more profitably, from certain of those considered their peers (as allies and 'friends'). They would establish alliances with other leaders whose own support was drawn from a population sufficiently remote geographically and distant politically as to remove the immediate possibility of direct conflict over resources, human or material, within the region. This meant that economic and political alliances were made generally with groups at a distance, occasionally even in other tribes, while those groups nearest by tended to be the most hostile of competition.[2]

7. The pattern of opposition and alliance resulting from this would resemble, on the ground, the famous 'checkerboard' of political alliances described by Montagne for the south of Morocco, although the *elfuf* of northeast Morocco were relatively impermanent, constantly changing coalitions and alliances, and never constituted anything like the coherent political structure resulting from a 'system' of moieties like that Montagne perceived.[3] It would seem that the *elfuf* in the northeast do not conform to the descriptions and analyses provided by sociologists to explain '*leff* organization' elsewhere in Morocco, but whether this reflects a real difference, or results from the different views of the observers, remains to be seen.[4]

8. The *leff* as a faction in a pervasive competition for power appears to have been a specific aspect of a more general and loosely defined phenomenon: any association of persons in a conflict situation. Quarrels over rights to land, or as a result of raiding and thefts; family or lineage disputes over property or questions of honor; antagonism over access to water-holes or wells, and arguments arising out of differences of opinion with regard to economic agreements, might all result in inter-group or inter-personal hostility and subsequently in the development of significant political cleavages. Divisions of this sort were intrinsically of a

[1] The delicate business of weakening one's rival without attracting such a large number of followers that one's own support-group becomes too big to be able to maintain unity effectively is described by both Barth, ibid., pp. 17–18, and Waterbury, ibid., pp. 65–6, 76.

[2] A somewhat similar phenomenon has been noted among the Bedouin of Cyrenaica. See Peters, 'Some structural aspects of the feud . . .', p. 274.

[3] All informants in the northeast agreed that it was possible to change alliances with reasonable facility and there seems to have existed a fair degree of what Waterbury has termed 'value-neutrality regarding group membership'. We have suggested that the *elfuf* of the northeast are best considered as factions or coalitions, and, although factionalism was pervasive throughout the region and there tended to polarize into two blocs over any issue or in any particular struggle, one cannot really talk of a 'political system or structure' in terms of a more or less permanent pattern of *leff* alliances.

[4] We are prepared, at this stage, to do no more than suggest—although we hope to go much further than this in the near future—that in other areas of Morocco our analysis will hold true. There are strong suggestions in the writings of Montagne of a difference between his formal position and his substantive material about the dynamics of political action. See R. Montagne, *Les Berbères et le makhzen dans le sud du Maroc*, Paris, 1930; and *La Vie sociale et la vie politique des Berbères*, Paris, 1931 (especially pp. 45–114).

different kind from the longer-term, essentially political coalition, although they could, and often did, provide some of the action-sets from which the *leff* quasi-groups or factions were built up.[1]

We have pointed out how necessary it was for an aspirant leader first to control his own family and lineage, and that lineage co-members frequently provided the core of a following and of a *leff*. We have also attempted to show how the segmentary lineage model can be seen as (1) a conscious model, providing a short-hand or stereotyped explanation of political organization, and (2) a ready-made justification, based on an ideology of agnatic descent, for recruitment to and membership of a *leff*. According to the model, and to some extent in practice, the lineage could act as a group with a collective responsibility. In most instances of inter-group hostility the members of a lineage were supposed to come to one another's defence and assistance, and allies in the *leff* were to be called upon only in need.

In the case of a homicide involving members of two different lineages the members of each lineage were supposed to exact, or pay, as the case may be, blood money (*dia*) as a sort of fine imposed by equals, or to take vengeance, if no settlement could be reached peacefully. In theory, it was the closest male relative to the victim who was obliged to avenge his agnate by killing the killer, or, if that was for some reason impossible, a close kinsman of the killer. Often, in practice, any member of the victim's lineage might take revenge on any member of the killer's lineage. If this method of obtaining 'justice' by the taking of a single 'life for a life' did not bring an end to the matter a feud between the two lineages might develop[2] or an outbreak of more general hostilities, in which all possible support was sought by each party and as a result of which two bitterly opposed groups developed.

If the two lineages were generally in the same *leff* a number of possibilities existed at this stage. The least strong group might be forced to leave the area and seek refuge elsewhere, probably in another tribe; or else the lineage of the killer might fragment into the supporters of the killer and those who resented his action and were not prepared to support his cause; or, thirdly, a way might be found to have the killer assassinated anonymously (usually by a hired gunman or by a lowly client). The unreliability of political support in this region was related to the unwillingness of individuals to commit themselves absolutely to any one group or cause and their usual attempts to 'hedge their bets'.[3] One important consequence of this was that individuals shifted their allegiance (and, among the transhumant tent-dwellers at least, their place of residence) with relative ease from group to group. A fourth possibility existed whereby the

[1] The concepts action-set and quasi-group are derived from an article: A. C. Meyer, 'The significance of quasi-groups in the study of complex societies', in Banton, op. cit.

[2] What is meant here by a state of feud is a set of relationships between two groups which are characterized by hostility whenever two or more of their members meet. These hostilities are, in theory, of a sort which cannot be terminated without the intervention of some outside authority. See Peters, 'Some structural aspects of the feud . . .', p. 262. Vengeance needs to be distinguished from feud, for a vengeance killing may be the means whereby a settlement of hostilities is made possible. See Peters, ibid., p. 265.

[3] See Waterbury, op. cit., p. 75.

lineage, or those supporting the killer, might leave the *leff* and join the opposing faction.

Weak lineages rarely attempted to exact the blood-money from stronger lineages, unless supported by some outside source of authority or power,[1] for the reaction might be extremely violent and result in the physical annihilation of the lineage making the demands. The debt remained, however, and unless the stronger lineage could, in some way, satisfy the weaker, and thus enable them to retain their honor, revenge was merely delayed or postponed until the balance of power altered, sometimes a generation or more later. The uncertainty and precarious nature of wealth and political power provided strong incentives for the larger and more cohesive groups to maintain amicable relations with their weaker fellow-tribesmen and hopes for the weaker groups of some day attaining a position of strength themselves.

9. Interdependence between the strong and the weak was to be found within the group as well as between groups. The position of leader, whether of lineage or of *leff*, was highly desirable, carrying with it, not only power and wealth, but also prestige and honor. The position, however, was precarious and even dangerous; a leader stood to lose, not only his following but also his life. And, in fact, few leaders lived to enjoy old age; more commonly they died fighting or were murdered, either by a rival or by a dependant. Some were obliged to flee the region as their support dwindled and their followers deserted them; and a few were imprisoned in Fes when visiting the court.

The difficulties of leadership lay less in dealing with threats from outside the group, given a degree of cohesion in the coalition, than in preventing fragmentation and desertion. The heterogeneity of the following and their motives contributed to these difficulties.[2] In addition to managing his following the leader was often obliged to act as mediator and arbitrator in quarrels and disputes within the *leff* and also to control the marriage alliances of members of the *leff* insofar as he was able.

If the nature of authority and power was unstable and uncertain during a leader's life time, his death generally resulted in the disintegration of the *leff* and the decline of his own lineage. A powerful leader would generally be father to many sons, between whom his property was supposedly divided at his death. Quarrels over inheritance and the struggle for 'succession' commonly reduced the previously united lineage to a multiplicity of small groups, each one seeking its own advantage at the expense of all the others, as men strove to keep for

[1] A strong leader of an uninvolved group, or a respected *sherif*, could provide such a source of authority.

[2] The bases of recruitment to factions 'are usually structurally diverse—they may rest upon kin ties, patron-client relations, religious or politico-economic ties or any combinations of these . . .' (Firth, op. cit., p. 292). Participants in a *leff* alliance may have sought no more than security, access to the generosity of a powerful and wealthy man and the prestige of belonging to his entourage; they may also have been hostile but impotent agnates or else rivals, awaiting the fullness of time before making a bid to dislodge the current leader; they may have been genuine supporters of a man believed to be a worthy and honourable leader, or, finally, leaders in their own right of smaller factions, operating in a different arena and thus no immediate threat to the more powerful leader.

themselves the resources, both material and human, so successfully cultivated and maintained by the deceased leader. One way in which this situation could, in theory, be avoided was by the selection of one son as heir apparent; but reluctance to share their wealth and power, fear of competition from the chosen one, and a concern to keep the loyalty of the other sons, prevented most men from choosing this path.

1890–1908: BU HMARA AND THE *MAKHZAN* IN THE NORTHEAST

1. From 1860 to 1893 contacts between the *makhzan* and the local tribes had been relatively slight, but after the incidents around Melilla in the years 1891–93, mentioned above, a garrison was sent to maintain order in the region. According to informants, this garrison not only fulfilled the function of border-guard between the Spanish in Melilla and the tribes, but also participated actively in local politics. Certain of the leaders (among the Gelaia, in particular) used their good relations with this 'force' from outside the region to bolster their position within the lineage and the tribe, and kept on friendly terms, if possible, with the officers of the garrison.

The presence of this small garrison, badly-paid and poorly disciplined as its soldiers were, and dependent as it was on maintaining amicable relations with the surrounding tribes for its very existence, changed the balance of power in the region but little and hardly affected the structure of the political game. It did provide, however, to a greater degree than did the *makhzan* in Fes, or even further away, a certain amount of contact with organized forces deriving their authority and income from their association with the *makhzan*. It perhaps made a little more real to the leaders in the region the possibility of achieving a certain stability in power and wealth, and hinted that this might be obtained better through a relationship of some sort with a relatively permanent authority from outside the region than through the maintenance of a following or through the manipulation of a regional network of alliances.

2. In 1903 a new development in the region resulted from the appearance in the northeast of the rebel against the Sultan, Bu Hmara. The death of the Sultan Moulai Hassan in 1894 and that of his Grand Vizir, Ba Ahmed, six years later, had considerably weakened the control exerted by the *makhzan* over the country; one sign of the weakness at the centre was the rash of major rebellions throughout Morocco at this period, of which that raised by Bu Hmara among the chronically restive tribes east of Fes, around Taza,[2] was one of the longest and perhaps the most dangerous.

Already successful in raising the tribes against the young Sultan Moulai

[2] Accounts of the rise and fall of Bu Hmara are to be found in E. Maldonado, *El Rogui*, Melilla, 1949; L. Arnaud, *Au Temps des 'Mehallas' : le Maroc de 1860 à 1912*, Casablanca, 1952; E. Aubin, *Le Maroc d'aujourd'hui*, Paris, 1913; F. Weisberger, *Au Seuil du Maroc moderne*, Rabat, 1947; M. LeGlay, *La Mort du Rogui*, Paris, 1926; A. Maitrot de la Motte Capron, 'Le Rogui', *Bulletin de la Société de Géographie d'Alger*, Algiers, 1929.

Abdel Aziz, and having spent a short while in Algeria, Bu Hmara came to the northeast in 1903 and established himself in the fortress (*qasbah*) at Selwan, between the territories of the Ait bu Ifrur and the Ulad Stut. The official garrison of the *makhzan* was defeated without much difficulty and forced to retreat toward Melilla, and Bu Hmara set up his own rival *makhzan* in Selwan, as he had done in Taza, claiming to be Moulai M'Hammed, brother to Abdel Aziz and rightful heir to the throne.

The changes brought about by the established presence of Bu Hmara's 'army' in the region and the effectively *makhzan*-like nature of his control over the greater part of the population were considerable. While it was still important for local leaders to maintain control over their kinsmen and personal following, and to contract alliances as in the past, the factors involved were different, and power (and therefore wealth) rapidly became associated with the ability to create and maintain good relations with Bu Hmara (or, for those who refused to accept his authority, with Moulai Abdel Aziz, who kept a considerable following in the Beni Snassen mountains to the east, around Oujda).

Local leaders came to depend, to a large extent, for their authority with the tribesmen on their relations with Bu Hmara and his '*makhzan*'; but, although the new 'Sultan of the northeast' had assistance from outside the region[1] and a credible claim to the throne, he was, in turn, and to a considerable degree, dependent on the local leaders for support from below and for the recruitment and maintenance of a following. The new '*makhzan*' had need of soldiers to wage war against Abdel Aziz and *his* following and to increase its control over the tribes of the northeast. These soldiers were recruited through the local leaders, who thereby reinforced their position with Bu Hmara; on the other hand, the leaders could increase their control over their followers and clients (of whom they clearly still had need) by virtue of their relationship with the new '*makhzan*', and tended to grow more powerful.

Support for Bu Hmara, on the other hand, and for Abdel Aziz, on the other, frequently split the tribes and smaller tribal segments,[2] these cleavages reflecting old rivalries, enmities and alliances from the days before there were two 'sultans' and two '*makhzan*s', rather than any deep-seated loyalties to either of these two 'great patrons'. Bu Hmara found support as long as he looked like either achieving his stated aim of replacing Moulai Abdel Aziz and becoming Sultan of all Morocco, or else maintaining his position as 'Sultan of the northeast'. The size of his following, throughout his career, put the limit on his effectiveness and depended, in its turn, on a number of factors, of which the most significant were: his credibility as a potential Sultan or major regional leader, his success in military encounters, his ability to draw on resources from outside the region and beyond the grasp of lesser men, his performance as a patron toward the more influential local leaders and the provision of a satisfactory 'administration' in the

---

[1] There is some evidence to suggest that Bu Hmara received help, not only from the Spanish, but also from certain French businessmen in Oran between *c.* 1902–8. Details of Spanish aid to the Pretender are given in *Espana en sus Heroes*, No. 1.

[2] In some cases virtually whole tribes stood opposed to Bu Hmara, as did the Kebdana in 1907 and 1908. See *Espana en sus Heroes*, No. 1.

5

area, and, finally, his ability to reconcile the conflicting demands and pressures from the Europeans providing him with financial and material assistance, and the tribesmen providing man-power and support from below.

It is clear that his expulsion from Selwan in 1908, by the tribesmen who had previously welcomed and supported him, was the result of his failure to give satisfaction on a number of these counts. His defeat in September by the Ait Waryaghel tribe of the central Rif, at the river Nekor, and news of his dealings with the French and Spanish, which involved, among other things, the sale of mining rights in tribal areas, contributed largely to his downfall.

3. The appearance of the *makhzan* garrison in the region of 1893, followed by the presence of the two '*makhzan*s' in the general vicinity between 1903 and 1908 first complicated and finally changed the political game in the area. New sources of support and profitable alliances had developed, it is true, and, in the broadest sense, the game of 'hedging bets' continued unabated. But the forces involved were rapidly becoming significantly different and not only had the dimensions and complexity of the game increased, but the goals sought by ambitious men, the ways in which they sought those goals, and the very nature and underlying structure of the game was substantially altered. The advantages, even for local leaders, of becoming clients of the *makhzan*, in order to emerge as the local patrons and as brokers between tribes and *makhzan* of material and less tangible goods, were clearer and more immediately relevant to local politics than they ever had been before.

In fact, two very different games appear to have coexisted during this period, one of which (the second) was to become dominant under the Spanish 'protectorate' and administration. The first involved the construction of flexible alliances between equals and the acquisition of a sizable following; this was associated with the insecurity and unpredictability of the social and natural environment and the resultant instability in the distribution of wealth and power. The extreme difficulty of accumulating wealth, or of maintaining a position of political superiority over more than a relatively short period explains the degree of interdependence between the more and the less powerful, between the richer and the poorer individuals, families and lineages within the area, and the need for the leaders to establish and cherish support from below and from equals. The second involved the creation and maintenance of relations with a powerful and relatively stable organization, in order to receive benefits in return for services rendered; in this game even the local leaders strove for recognition from above and hoped thereby to achieve key positions as brokers, or political entrepreneurs, in a much wider arena by virtue of their dominant role in local politics, while men from families that had been insignificant in 'traditional' times sought new opportunities for improving their status through connections with the 'authorities' whose strength was not based on local support.

1909–56: THE SPANISH OCCUPATION

1. The Act of Algeciras, signed in 1906, placed Morocco under the protection

of several of the European powers, but with France and Spain as effective holders of mandates over the southern and northern parts of Morocco respectively.[1] Both Spain and France regarded the agreements and bilateral treaties which preceded and led up to the Act as 'go-signs', and began active physical penetration of their respective 'zones'. At first both powers maintained the fiction that they were 'acting on behalf of the Sultan' and Spanish penetration into the northeast, in the campaign of 1909–10, was explained as 'punitive action against the dissident tribes'.[2]

Spanish expansion from the bridgehead at Melilla into the Moroccan hinterland continued unofficially through 1911 and 1912 until the French occupation of Fes in August 1911 brought about the official end of the Moroccan Sultanate as an independent polity when the Sultan signed, on 30 March 1912, the treaty which turned a *de facto* military invasion and occupation by both Spain and France into a recognized 'presence' and Protectorate. An agreement with the Sultan giving Spain the right to supervise and 'protect' the northern territory was arranged in November 1912 and signed by the Sultan in Marrakesh in May 1913.

2. The government of the Spanish Protectorate was to be administered by a deputy of the Sultan, called his *khalif*, with the 'traditional' hierarchy of administrators, judges and local officials. Spanish authorities, however, nominated the *khalif* and intervened at all levels in the government and administration of the Protectorate.[3] It was not until July 1927, however, that 'Spanish Morocco' existed in fact, as it had since 1913 on paper, because for fourteen years after the creation of the Protectorate there was resistance by the tribes and intermittent fighting throughout the 'zone' (especially in the central Rif) and the Spanish were unable to control effectively all of northern Morocco.[4]

During the years from 1909 to 1927 the 'traditional' and 'pre-colonial'

[1] See E. R. Anderson, *The First Moroccan Crisis*, Chicago, 1930; J. H. Campoamore, *La Actitud de Espana ante la cuestion de Marruecos (1901–4)*, Madrid, 1951; C. Peyreigne, *Les Influences européennes au Maroc avant la Conférence d'Algeciras*, Toulouse, 1908; E. Vidal, *La Politique de l'Espagne au Maroc*, Montpellier, 1913. Also, Payne, op. cit., p. 102, and Figueras, op. cit., pp. 101–5.

[2] See *Espana en sus Heroes*, No. 1. This explanation for Spanish activities was maintained in the face of a massive troop build-up in 1909, an official visit by the King of Spain and review of the troops in December 1910, and a visit in October 1911 by the Spanish Minister of War who gave the order to expand the zone of occupation westward. For useful accounts of the campaign of 1909–10, see Gallego Ramos, *La Campana del Rif (1909)*, Madrid, n.d.; Payne, op. cit., pp. 105–12; A. Riera, *Espana en Africa: Cronica de la Campana de 1909*, Barcelona, 1910; V. Ruiz Albeniz, *El Riff*, Madrid, 1912; V. Ruis Albeniz, *Espana en el Riff*, Madrid, 1921.

For the operations between 1911 and 1912, see Central del Ejercito Estado Mayor, *Historia de las Campanas de Marruecos* (2 vols), Madrid, 1947, pp. 378–566.

Extremely useful accounts of the whole 1908–27 period are found in the journal *Espana en sus Heroes*, Vols. 1–9, 18–20, 24–7.

[3] There are many sources of accounts both of the official administrative and political organization of the Spanish zone and of the difficulties of pacifying the region between 1913 and 1927. See, for convenience, Payne, op. cit., pp. 488–90, where a number of references are given.

[4] See D. S. Woolman, *Rebels in the Rif: Abd el Krim and the Rif Rebellion*, London, 1969, pp. 55–214.

political game of forming alliances between equals, maneuvering for support from clients and followers and competing for essentially limited wealth and power, on the basis of resources that could be accumulated only with difficulty and never invested,[1] was changing radically as the area under effective Spanish control grew. From 1927 onwards, until the mid-1950s, the Spanish colonial administration so controlled the political and economic life of the 'zone' that, in effect, 'the Blad l-Makhzan, for the first time in history, included all of northern Morocco . . .'[2] and there was, for the first time, no apparent alternative for an ambitious tribesman but to operate through the *makhzan* or with *makhzan* approval. Looking back, one can agree that 'the absorbtion of the *bilad as-siba* into the *bilad al-makhzan* represents a revolution whose consequences are as far-reaching as those of the signing of the protectorate treaty, or the gaining of independence . . .'[3]

3. In certain crucial respects 1927 marks the beginning of a new era for local politics in the northeast, for, from this time onwards, with the exception of a short period between 1954 and 1960, the *makhzan* has so deeply penetrated and controlled local political activities that the only real 'path' to wealth and power within the region has been the cultivation of good relations with the *makhzan*, whether under colonial rule or under an independent Moroccan government.

4. As early as the 1930s there were attempts to create a political movement in the Spanish zone, linked to the growing nationalist movement in the French territory, and whose aims focused upon the complete independence of the 'northern zone' and of Morocco. Efforts were made to recruit support among the tribes of the Rif, but these met with little success, for a variety of reasons.[4] None of the political parties that developed in the Spanish zone ever managed to obtain a popular base among the tribes,[5] and it was not until the emergence of the Liberation Army in 1954 that tribesmen in the northeast were provided with the opportunity of becoming involved once again in active, and frequently violent, politics.[6] Even then, it was only with the tacit agreement and support of

[1] The only form of 'investment' was 'effective and directed spending'. The leader acted as an agent of redistribution or 'pooling' in the local economy. For a discussion of redistribution and its relationship to wealth and power, see M. Sahlins, 'The sociology of primitive exchange' in Banton (ed), *The Relevence of Models for Social Anthropology*, London, 1965. In a situation where social credit and social debt were so crucial the concept of social investment is not alien.

[2] Woolman, op. cit., p. 214.

[3] Waterbury, op. cit., p. 35.

[4] Partly because these efforts were spasmodic and often half-hearted, the nationalists being, for the most part, from the better-off families of the urban northwest and tending to look down somewhat on the tribesmen, partly because many of the tribesmen were, or had been, soldiers in Franco's armies in the Spanish Civil War and were reluctant to oppose the *makhzan* that kept and paid them. They did have some limited success. For a discussion of the political parties in the north, see D. E. Ashford, *Political Change in Morocco*, Princeton, 1961, pp. 45–56.

[5] While it is maintained that the Istiqlal party had a following of 100,000 it seems doubtful if this number represents more than the sum total of those offering a minimal and uncommitted support. See Ashford, ibid., p. 56.

[6] The Liberation Army was always active in the northeast and the main training centre was near Nador. See Ashford, ibid., pp. 157–84; Waterbury, op. cit., pp. 204–8.

colonial administration in the Spanish zone that the north could act as a training ground and base for the operations of the Liberation Army, which were directed primarily at the French-occupied territories.[1]

5. Toward the end of 1955 the French announced that the exiled Sultan, Muhammad V, would be allowed to return to Rabat, that political reforms would be inaugurated and a native Moroccan government formed. In December 1955 Franco officially claimed that Morocco was not yet ready for independence and a wave of strikes, demonstrations and terrorist acts broke out. Despite attempts to separate the local Moroccan government in Tetuan from the Sultan's administration in Rabat, and to control the outbursts of the population in the towns and in the countryside,[2] it became clear during the first few months of 1956 that if France really intended to grant independence to its zone, the Spanish regime had little choice but to follow suit. And the independence treaty for the north of Morocco was signed in Madrid at the beginning of April.[3]

1956–60: THE FIRST YEARS OF INDEPENDENCE

1. 'The formal structure of Moroccan government and administration changed little during the first three years of independence',[4] and in the early months of independence Morocco continued to use almost the identical central organization as the old French Protectorate. Although the *makhzan* as the central administrative agency of the Moroccan government was outmoded by the changes introduced during the Protectorate, it continued in a new form as the office of the King, the Royal Cabinet and the Secretary General of the government.[5]

2. During those first few years, however, the growth and proliferation of political parties provided a new element in Moroccan politics.[6] Their development not only introduced the possibility of alternative lines of communication between 'centre' and 'periphery' and between urban and rural politicians, but also provided a hope for the rural population of participating in the national polity and the suggestion that the masses, although as individuals poor and without power, could, by joining such national institutions, affect the policies and actions of the central authorities—the *makhzan*.

Very real attempts were made by the various political parties in the years just after independence to acquire substantial rural support. Indeed, the leader of the

---

[1] Ashford, op. cit., pp. 45–55.

[2] Ashford, op. cit., p. 55; Payne, op. cit., p. 441.

[3] See Payne, op. cit., p. 441. For brief discussion of the events leading up to the signing of the independence agreement, see Ashford, *Political Change in Morocco*, pp. 86–92; an anonymous article in the *American Journal of International Law*, 'France–Morocco: joint declaration: diplomatic accord', pp. 676–87; M. Howe, 'The birth of the Moroccan Nation', *Middle East Journal*, Vol. 10, No. 1, winter 1956; Landau, *Mohammed V, King of Morocco*; Landau, *Hassan II, King of Morocco*.

[4] Ashford, *Political Change in Morocco*, p. 93.

[5] Ibid., pp. 93–4.

[6] See Ashford, ibid., pp. 57–156, 194–343; Rézette, *Les Partis politiques marocains*; Waterbury, op. cit., pp. 169–265.

left-wing UNFP, Ben Barka,[1] could still hope, in 1959, at the time of the formal scission of the Istiqlal (or Independence) Party, for 'a synthesis of the three great forces of Morocco, the trade unionists, the peasantry, and the resistance',[2] believing that in this way a bridge could be built between the urban and the rural masses.

The success of the parties was limited, for, if a tribesman did join, it was rare that his support remained firm and wholly committed. Also, the fact that the parties tended to be urban based, with urban leadership and national programs made it difficult for the rural population to identify with them and to distinguish always between the political party and the *makhzan*.[3]

3. The vast majority of the Moroccan people believed that independence meant not only the achievement of a new international status, but also the end of all the controls that had been placed on them by the colonial regimes. To the extent that the administration after independence followed the pattern of highly centralized, authoritarian control which characterized the French and Spanish systems, the population saw little difference between independence and colonial rule.[4] Nowhere was this more true than in the ex-Spanish zone and in the Rif.[5]

General dissidence grew in the tribal areas, especially in the more remote and underdeveloped areas,[6] as the rural population perceived that the departure of the Europeans had not provided them with the benefits, either material or political, that they had expected, and that the political parties were incapable of really improving local conditions, while the new *makhzan* had other priorities. The rural masses were not being integrated effectively into the new nation and they resented it.[7] Particularly resentful were the tribes of the northeast who rose up in arms during 1958 and 1959, and were only subdued when the king's son led a force of 20,000 Royal Army troops into the area. Specific complaints by the 'pacified' tribesmen included references to administrative injustices and inadequacy and to the interference by political parties in the administration and in judicial affairs. More general dissatisfaction was expressed with regard to unemployment, fiscal injustice, lack of hospitals, roads, schools and agricultural credit.[8]

4. The suppression of the various tribal uprisings throughout Morocco during

[1] Union Nationale des Forces Populaires. See Waterbury, ibid., pp. 169–232.

[2] Waterbury, ibid., p. 217.

[3] See Ashford, ibid., pp. 196–202; Waterbury, ibid., p. 57.

[4] Ashford, ibid., p. 157.

[5] In the province of Nador, for example, 'the annexes (administrative divisions) correspond almost exactly with the pre-colonial tribal divisions, despite the avowed intention of the government on independence to create new administrative units that would cut across tribal boundaries' (Seddon, 'Economic change and family structures in a Moroccan rural commune', p. 8). The annexes also correspond to the Spanish administrative divisions.

[6] Ashford, ibid., pp. 211–12. 'Rabat could hardly have been ignorant of the depletion of tribal food reserves over the summer so that many areas were at a near-starvation diet level by fall' (p. 212).

[7] There were uprisings in separate regions all over the country. See Ashford, ibid., pp. 212–13.

[8] Waterbury, ibid., pp. 235–43.

1959 by Royal Army troops marks the end of a short phase (of three years) during which popular participation in the process of 'nation-building' had been encouraged, verbally at least, and the beginning of a period of increasing control over the nation's political life, from the centre, by the king and the *makhzan*. Control was achieved in the rural areas by a combination of the Royal Army and the Ministry of the Interior, in the urban areas, and more specifically among the country's elite, by means of a complex system of patronage, organized by the king.[1] After May 1960, when the king became prime minister, all governmental posts of any importance were filled by royal decree. When Muhammad V died, his son, Hassan, became king and prime minister; by March 1961 the king was prime minister, minister of defence, minister of agriculture and minister of the interior.

1960–70: STATE CONTROL AND LOCAL POLITICS

1. Despite the rapidly increasing control of political life throughout Morocco by the king and his *makhzan* an appearance of democratic participation was clearly necessary, and in May 1960 the first elections were held throughout the country for the newly created local communes. In the rural areas these were supposed to draw upon pre-colonial tribal institutions and yet to provide a framework for the development of democratic local government and of community self-awareness;[2] the participation of the political parties in the elections was not discouraged.[3]

2. From 1958 onwards the strength of the Istiqlal Party, that had led the country into independence, was gradually reduced both by the emergence of rival parties and by the machinations of the Palace among the elite and in the administration. The development of a major split in the Istiqlal, which resulted in the establishment, in 1959, of the UNFP, further weakened the major political party. In the elections of 1960, however, the Istiqlal won about 40 percent of all seats in the local councils, on a nation-wide basis, the Mouvement Populaire about 7 percent and the UNFP 23 percent.[4] (In the rural areas the electoral campaigns generally amounted to a series of confrontations between local individuals without much reference to party adherence, although the strength of the Mouvement Populaire in the province of Nador was quite marked.)[5]

3. The success of the left-wing party, in particular, was seen as a threat to the control over the political process required by the king, and in July 1963 the

[1] Waterbury, ibid., pp. 267–98.

[2] D. E. Ashford, *National Development and Local Reform: Political Participation in Morocco, Tunisia and Pakistan*, Princeton, 1967, pp. 23–59; A. Cherkaoui, *Le Contrôle de l'état sur la commune*, Rabat, 1968, *passim*.

[3] P. Chambergeat, 'Les elections communales marocaines du mai 29, 1960', *Revue française de science politique*, No. 1, Vol. 11, March 1961, pp. 89–117.

[4] Waterbury, ibid., p. 219.

[5] One of the reasons for this local strength was that the origins of the Mouvement Populaire were closely associated with the development of the Liberation Army in the post-independence years.

UNFP leaders began to debate the advisability of running candidates in the forthcoming local elections, because they believed that the legislative elections had been rigged, and that the local authorities (representatives of the Ministry of the Interior) were doing all they could to hinder 'undesirable' candidates from registering in the commune elections.[1] The elections went ahead, despite 'the rather heavy-handed tactics of the Palace to obstruct the voting in rural areas . . .'[2] but by the end of 1963 many of the political parties were suffering harassment, and the UNFP leaders were charged with treason and conspiring to overthrow the king.[3]

4. King Hassan was as concerned as his father to maintain the appearance of democracy and in June 1961 the Charter of Fundamental Rights was issued, followed in November 1962 by the promulgation of a new constitution. In fact, the National Assembly created by this document was virtually without power and the associated institutional structure extremely complex; the main result was to increase even further the power of the king.[4] Even the elaborate façade of parliamentary democracy failed to satisfy the Palace; the king was not able to achieve a workable majority within the parliament and in June 1965 he suspended it. 'Throughout the short life of Parliament, and ever since, the king has consistently belittled the notion of formal democracy, describing it as an impediment to the struggle against need and misery. He has unequivocally stated the incompatibility between Parliament and true democracy. When he suspended Parliament in June 1965, he said that if he had allowed the empty debates to continue, Morocco's democracy, moral values, dignity and will to create would have been shaken.'[5]

It is against such a general background in which the *makhzan*, in the general sense (but particularly the Ministries of the Interior and Justice, the army and the police, the Royal Cabinet and the press as the essential instruments of royal control), dominates all political activity throughout the country that one should consider the position of the rural communes and the state of local politics in the 1960s.

5. In the Speech from the Throne, Muhammad V spoke of 'the creation of democratic institutions based on free elections', and when the first Cabinet was installed in December 1955, he defined as one of its goals the laying of the foundations of a new regime which was to enable the people to administer their own affairs by means of local assemblies and a parliament.[6] But even as late as 1967 it was possible to observe that 'the Moroccan government has achieved little in the way of fundamental change at the local level to hasten the developmental process'.[7] The major reason for this is that mass participation in any process of development at the local level, whether primarily political or primarily economic, is seen as a threat to the *status quo*, and the creation of the rural communes should

[1] Waterbury, ibid., pp. 224–5.
[2] Ashford, *National Development and Local Reform . . .* , p. 352.
[3] Ashford, ibid., p. 352; Waterbury, ibid., pp. 293–5.
[4] Ashford, ibid., pp. 349–52.
[5] Waterbury, ibid., p. 157.
[6] See Ashford, *National Development and Local Reform . . .* , pp. 33–4.
[7] Ashford, ibid., p. 23.

be seen as a response to 'partisan demands for monarchical concessions',[1] rather than as a serious attempt to bring about any radical change in the countryside.

6. Between 1960 and 1970 it has become clear that tribal dissidence and rebellion is no longer possible and that even the most remote regions are within reach of a highly effective *makhzan*, which uses not only the time-honored method of sending troops into the trouble areas after the incidents but also a hierarchy of local administrators that penetrates into the smallest *duar*, village or tribal segment, together with a combination of the Gendarmerie Royale, informers and the local and provincial court system, to prevent incidents from ever arising.

Ambitious men among the 'tribes' of the northeast,[2] as elsewhere, have come to realize, over the past decade, and especially since the purges of 1963, that virtually the only source of power and wealth lies in the maintenance of good relations with the *makhzan*, whether with the local authorities, or, if possible, with persons in the provincial, or even national, capital. The political parties provided little in the way of alternative avenues to power or of alternative sources of wealth and prestige, for the vast majority, even before 1963, and now it has become inadvisable to admit to having any strong political interests at all. The strength of the *makhzan*'s grip on the countryside is exemplified in its relation to the rural commune.

7. The sole unqualified power given to the commune council is that of discussing the communal budget, and, given the local community's dependence on subsidies from the central government, and often an unfamiliarity with budget procedures, even this power is more apparent than real. The council may express its approval on fifteen further matters, after they have first been approved by superior authorities, but these concern minor economic problems rather than administration or politics; and, in fact, councils are expressly forbidden to formulate views 'of a political character or foreign to objects of local interest'.[3] In addition, the control exerted by the local authority (the *caid*) over the agenda, the direction of the discussion and even the conclusions and decisions of the council meeting is considerable.[4] While the president of the rural commune council may request the administration to execute certain of the decisions taken in council, frequently it is only the *caid* who is able to take the responsibility of execution. At a higher level, the governor may annul any decision taken by the council of which he does not approve.

8. Much of this control over the actions and deliberations of the rural commune council appears redundant when it is appreciated that the elections for the council are strictly controlled by the local authorities, and those elected are rarely other than the candidates approved by the administration (*makhzan*) in

[1] Ashford, ibid., pp. 46–7.
[2] It is questionable whether the use of the term 'tribe' has any sociological significance today in the province of Nador, although certain 'tribal' institutions are certainly fostered by the local authorities.
[3] See A. Cherkaoui, *Le Contrôle de l'état sur la commune*, Rabat, 1968.
[4] See S. Ben Bachir, *L'Administration locale du Maroc*, pp. 150–63; A. Cherkaoui, ibid., pp. 34–5.
5*

the first place.[1] Manipulation of the electoral lists, refusal to register certain candidates on various grounds, the use of veiled (and often not so veiled) threats, as well as promises of future rewards and requests not to cause 'trouble and conflict' within the *duar* or the voting constituency by opposing the 'chosen' candidate, are all methods widely used by the local authorities to control the selection of candidates. Other similar pressures are used to ensure that the voters behave in the desired fashion.[2]

9. The control over political activities in the countryside is not, of course, as simple as this brief outline would suggest. The local authorities themselves, for instance, are carefully chosen and appointed by their superiors. Below the level of governor, in the province of Nador, the majority of administrative officials are of the region, if not of the 'tribe', that they administer, but are generally chosen from among those who took no part in politics between 1956 and 1958. Some were active, though not important leaders, in the resistance, but some held administrative posts under the Spanish. What appears to be sought is the individual who is loyal to the *makhzan* and relatively apolitical, and it is stressed that the only organization upon which they can rely for support and advancement is the administration in which they serve. In addition to the supervision of *caid* by *caid-mumtez*, and *caid-mumtez* by *amel* (governor), the local authorities are kept under surveillance by the Gendarmerie Royale and other independent agents.

Candidates for the rural commune council chosen by the local authorities must not reflect badly on the *caid* or *caid-mumtez* himself and selection is very careful. The candidates are generally clients, in some way, of the local authority, or possibly relatives. Here again, however, the situation may be more complex, and it is possible to find a candidate for election in the region who is a client of a higher authority in the administration (at the provincial level, or maybe even in the capital) standing against a candidate chosen by the *caid* or the governor.[3]

Political organization in the rural communes of Nador province at the present time is best seen in terms of a complex pattern of patron–client relations that cluster around the major source of power and authority in the countryside: the administration and the Ministry of the Interior, but also include certain collateral organizations that lead eventually to the capital and the Palace. In this way the individual in the most distant *duar* or village is caught up in the game and forced to conform to the new pattern of political activity if he desires any degree of economic or 'political' success, or even if he merely wishes to maintain a reasonable style of life.

10. An ambitious man can no longer acquire or maintain a following unless he himself has patrons in the administration; he has become a broker rather than a leader, and a patron only by virtue of his support and recognition from above.

---

[1] Ashford, *National Development and Local Reform* . . . , pp. 55, 352; P. Chambergeat, 'Les Elections communales au Maroc', *Annuaire de l'Afrique du nord*, Vol. 2, 1963, pp. 102–3; Waterbury, ibid., pp. 224–5.

[2] See the reactions to the elections in 1969 in the national press during October, particularly the Istiqlal organ, *L'Opinion*. Also in Lamalif, 1969, pp. 2–5.

[3] For further detailed discussion of relations between the local inhabitants and the administration, in one particular tribal group, see R. Jamous, *Les Rapports politiques et economiques actuels dans une tribu du Rif orientale (Maroc)*, ms., 1970, pp. 39–64.

Both the political and economic context have changed so radically that the pre-colonial 'game' of alliances and coalitions within the tribe or region is no longer necessary, or even possible, although certain aspects of political style and 'political culture' are slow to alter. The sociopolitical context has become visibly larger and more complex, and yet it has also become, in some ways, both simpler and less uncertain. It is difficult even for the ambitious man to manipulate his 'environment', and the lives of the masses appear to them to a large extent controlled by factors beyond their vision and certainly beyond their influence.

Old patterns of interdependence between the various sectors of the local 'community' are rapidly disappearing. With a stable and all-controlling *makhzan* and the development of modern financial institutions the accumulation of both wealth and power is possible for the small minority looked upon with favor by the *makhzan*, and the need to cultivate even one's poorer relatives and fellow-'tribesmen' as a form of social investment and insurance is now hardly necessary. The distinction between the richer and the poorer, the more and the less powerful, is growing fast and the gap between them is becoming larger.[1]

11. The stability of the present political system should not, however, be over-estimated. Dissatisfaction is also growing, both in the countryside and in the towns, and the economic and political stagnation which has existed in Morocco since 1960/61 is increasingly associated with the attempts of the elite, and more specifically of the king, to maintain equilibrium at all costs. Even in the rural areas, like the northeast, where all forms of economic and political organization are closely controlled, there is open resentment of the *makhzan*'s undisguised constraint on individual behavior, and attempts to maintain the façade of democratic participation by the holding of 'elections' and the announcement of a new Constitution appear less and less convincing to the population.[2]

[1] See Seddon, 'Economic change and family structures in a Moroccan rural commune'.
[2] See, for example, the comments of the opposition press over the periods of local elections and the reports of incidents throughout the country during 1969 and 1970.

E. A. Alport

About 560 kilometers south of Algiers, and extending for about 250 kilometers further south, there lies a region of limestone in the Sahara which is known as the Shebka. The word signifies a net in Arabic, and the reason for this is that the ground of bare stone has been eroded into a criss-cross network or maze of short ravines and clefts. Roughly in the center of this barren wilderness, the bed of the river Mzab forms a valley between low, yellowish hills, and in the lower part of this valley lie five cities, perched on the slopes, or on higher ground in the river-bed. They are built fairly close together so that from each it is easy to see one or two of the others. They were all founded in the eleventh century A.D., they are all surrounded by stout walls, and each is crowned by the minaret of its mosque, shaped like an obelisk and lacking any kind of decoration.

Their total population is about 30,000, of whom Ghardaya, the capital, contains half. Next in importance comes the city of Beni Isguen, with 5,000 inhabitants, while the smaller cities of Melika, Bou Noura, and El-Ateuf share about 10,000 between them. Ghardaya is also the center of one of the four large military and administrative territories into which southern Algeria is divided, and the only one of the five cities that has admitted Europeans, Arabs, Jews, and other foreign elements—not within its walls, but within its precincts;[2] the others remain completely homogeneous and, with one small exception at Melika, untouched by alien habitations.

The river Mzab, from which the district takes its name, flows very rarely, rising only about once in twelve or thirteen years. Rainfalls or showers are not quite so rare, but there are years without any precipitation from the atmosphere, and one or two heavy showers in a year are regarded as a blessing. Water is found at depths varying between 8 and 55 meters and has to be drawn from wells. One is therefore almost astonished to find palm-gardens at a short distance from each city, maintaining by constant labour, and to discover whole towns of summer-houses among the date-palms and fruit trees, not lightly built as bungalows, but constructed with stone in the same way as the town-houses.[3]

Besides the five cities in the valley, the confederation of the Mzab, as it is sometimes called, comprises three other places: the oasis of Berriane, 47 kilometers to the north; the city of Guerrara, 99 kilometers to the northeast; and, nearer to the Mzab valley, the oasis of Medili, partly owned by Mozabites, but inhabited by the sedentary Shaamba from the large Arab nomad tribe of that name.

The Mozabites are peculiar in several respects. They represent a small Berber

---

[1] First published in *Man*, Vol. 84, 1954, pp. 34–44.

[2] The foreign elements number about 10,000; the original population is Berber by descent and language (E. Doutté and E. F. Gautier, *Enquête sur la dispersion de la langue berbère en Algérie*, Algiers, 1913, p. 139).

[3] J. Brunhes, *Human Geography*, London, 1952. Translation by E. F. Row of *La Géographie humaine* (eds Mme Jean-Brunhes Delamarre and P. Deffontaines), Paris, 1942.

island in a vast Arab sea; they are the only city-dwellers in the Sahara; they practise a fierce and exclusive form of Islamic puritanism, not unlike that of the Wahabi of Arabia, but in an *urban* and not a *tribal* frame of society; and they have kept their institutions intact, only giving up their political status as independent republics and becoming part of the territory of Algerian France, as it then was.

Why do they live in such a remote and barren place? How can they afford to keep gardens and summer-houses at great expense? How were they able to withstand, for a thousand years, the vicissitudes of sedentary life in the Sahara, and, even more surprisingly, the impact of twentieth-century competitive civilization?

To find the answer to these questions one must begin by tracing the history of the Beni Mzab back to the period of the Arab conquest of North Africa in the seventh and eighth centuries, as it is recorded, for example, by Ibn Khaldun[1] and others.[2] At that time bitter quarrels and feuds were being fought out in Arabia among the Prophet Muhammad's successors, and a sect of nonconformists, the Kharijites, gained considerable influence for a short period. Their political and religious teaching was republican, democratic, puritan, and fundamentalist, and in all these respects they were radically opposed to the orthodox and absolutist Caliphate at whose hands they suffered a series of defeats which led to their practical disappearance in Arabia by the beginning of the eighth century.

The Kharijites disappeared, but they were not extinguished. Ali, the Prophet's son-in-law, crushed their first revolt under Abd el-Wahb, but they found another leader in Abdalla ibn Ibad, who gave their passionately held beliefs the form of doctrine and the rules of conduct.

The original and immediate cause for their disaffection was that Ali had been prepared to accept arbitration between himself and the other pretender to the succession, Muawiya. To the fundamentalists among his followers, compromise or arbitration in this case was inadmissible. There was one law and one law only: the Koran. According to a fundamentalist interpretation of the Koran, arbitration is applicable in two cases only: in the case of conflict between husband and wife (Koran IV. 39) and in the case of killing of game while on pilgrimage, when certain compensation becomes due (Koran V. 96). No other differences can be resolved by arbitration. Any action is either right or wrong. If wrong, it must be resisted, 'with the hand, with the tongue, or with the heart' (a rule based on Koran III. 106).

Secondly, and of like importance, was the fundamentalist belief that all Muslims were equal, and that the office of Shaikh el-Islam, or Caliph, or Imam should be an elected and not an hereditary one.

[1] Baron M. de Slane, *Histoire des Berbères et des dynasties musulmanes de l'Afrique septentrionale par Ibn Kaldoun*. Translation of *Kitab al Ibar* by Baron MacGluckin de Slane, 4 vols, Algiers, 1853–6. Reprinted in 5 vols, ed P. Casanova, Paris, 1927.

[2] E. Masqueray, *Chronique d'Abou Zakaria*, translated with a commentary by E. Masqueray, Algiers, 1879; B. Lewis, *The Arabs in History*, London, 1950; Ch.-A. Julien, *Histoire de l'Afrique du nord, de la conquête à 1830*, 2nd edn rev. by R. Le Tourneau, Paris, 1952.

Based upon these two propositions, that all Muslims are equal, and that any action is either right or wrong, the principle tenets of Ibadi doctrine are (Masqueray 1879, preface):

(1) That the law is laid down once and for all time in the Koran, that therefore it is essential not only to know the Koran, but to understand it; also that prayers must not merely be repeated but understood.

(2) That there is only one way of being righteous, any other ways being sinful and leading to certain damnation.

(3) That sin can never be expiated or forgiven; and that punishment by the law can only have secular and not spiritual or redeeming effect.

(4) That Works are as important as Faith; that sinners are damned whether they are true believers or not; and that a man's conduct in this world determines precisely his position in the next.

(5) And, finally, that since all Muslims are equal, luxurious living and ostentation by some is sinful; that no man can command who is not expressly elected to do so; that a man should live soberly and modestly, shunning all stimulants and intoxicants including music and dancing; and that he should practise charity and strict honesty in his personal and business dealings.

Abdalla ibn Ibad, during whose lifetime the Kharijites or Dissenters were persecuted, cut down in battle, oppressed, and killed, taught that there were four states or ways in which true believers could achieve Grace: (i) the State of Defense in protecting their faith; (ii) the State of Devotion in its practice; (iii) the State of Glory in its victory; and (iv) the State of Secrecy when its concealment became a duty.

A story or two may illustrate the stoic faith of these Puritans: Rahan, one of those who revolted against Ali, was captured, his hands and feet were cut off and his enemy, Ibn Ziyad, asked him 'What do you think now?' 'I think,' he replied, 'that you have spoiled my life in this world, and that I have spoiled yours in the next.' Another, Arua, when asked by the same Ibn Ziyad to choose his own torture, replied 'Choose the form of your eternal damnation yourself!'

The State of Secrecy had been reached. The dissenters could meet only in small conventicles, where they comforted and helped one another and made converts when possible. One such conventicle, or *halqa*, from Bosra, decided to emigrate in order to escape persecution, to preach the pure doctrine, and to seek the State of Glory in North Africa.

There, the Ibadi doctrine fell on fertile ground. The Arab conquest of the Maghreb (the West) had been slow and difficult. After fifty years of campaigns and of expeditions organized from Egypt and Damascus, Byzantine power was at last broken, and by A.D. 698 all the Greek fortresses of the coastal belt from Carthage to Ceuta as well as those of the interior were in the hands of Arab governors. But the Berber population of the plains, the high plateaux and the mountains, from Tripolitania and the Jebel Nefus in the east to the Sus and the Anti-Atlas in the west, remained largely unsubdued. Great tales and legends are told of heroic Berber resistance under chieftains like Kossila and Kahina, the Jewish queen of the Aures mountains. However, from their firm bases on the coast, the Arab governors, who frequently took advantage of inter-tribal feuds between Berber leaders, succeeded in obtaining the submission and also the conversion of ever-increasing numbers of Berber tribes.

In matters of religion the Berbers had never been too difficult. The tribes in the interior remained largely pagan and idolatrous, but many in the mountains had adopted Judaism, and in the coastal plains Christianity had found entry under the Romans. But already under Roman and later under Byzantine rule, the christianized Berbers were given to sectarianism. Byzantine governors in particular had great trouble with the Donatists and the Circoncellions, sects that professed an equalitarian and primitive creed, revolted against their bishops, and refused to pay taxes.

In their efforts at converting the Berber tribes to Islam, the Arabs were aided, on the one hand, by the successful invasion of Spain (A.D. 709), which almost immediately brought to their side large numbers of Berbers eager to take part in battle, conquest, and loot—this, of course, they could do only as soldiers of the Prophet—and, on the other hand, by the rule, based on Koranic law, that Muslims were exempted from certain land and poll taxes that non-Muslims had to pay. Conversions under those circumstances were largely a matter of form and were mostly regarded as such by Arab governors, who continued or resumed the exaction of these taxes from their fresh co-religionists. Revolts and apostasies naturally followed, and so did repressions. The situation was complicated by quarrels and fights between the Arab governors themselves, who had not failed to import their old tribal feuds and hostilities from Arabia, and repeatedly called to their aid native forces in order to gain a local advantage.

It was in the midst of this state of affairs that the Ibadi *halqa* from Bosra arrived, led by a young Persian nobleman, Ibn Rustem. They quickly collected a following of Berbers who at last found in these Arabs other Muslims by whom they were treated and regarded as equals. The Berbers, who had been Christian sectarians and rebels under Byzantine rule, became Muslim sectarians and rebels under the Caliphs. As Bernard[1] put it, Islamic Calvinism found in North Africa its Scotland.

Soon Ibn Rustem was strong enough to be considered worth an alliance, and he was called in to put down a palace revolution that had upset the city of Kairouan. He proceeded to occupy Kairouan himself and held it for four years until an army sent from Egypt obliged him and his followers to give way. They left Kairouan and trekked for 700 miles, going west all the time, until they reached a place in the mountains of western Algeria, situated at 3,000 feet, by a pass leading from the highlands of the Tell Atlas down to the fertile coastal plain. There was an ancient Berber settlement in this place, based upon a Roman camp, and near it in A.D. 761 Ibn Rustem founded the city of Tahert, or Tiaret, which became the capital of the so-called kingdom of Tiaret, comprising a good deal of present-day Algeria, and which, according to Ibn Khaldun,[2] lasted for a century and a half.

It was a kingdom without a king—it was a theocracy. Ibn Rustem and his successors took the title of Imam, leader of prayer; and the people, unlike the

[1] A. Bernard, *Le Maroc*, Paris, 1932, p. 89.
[2] de Slane, op. cit., pp. 242–3.

Children of Israel, did not demand a king. No ass was lost, no Saul anointed! Merchants and artisans of different persuasions brought wealth and affluence, and they and their trade were protected; but the Imam and his band of elect continued to live an austere and simple life, devoted to the study of the law and the sciences, especially astronomy. No family or tribe arrogated to itself the spoils of power or office, which was the rule practically everywhere else in the Muslim world. All Muslims were equal. The Imam was surrounded by his theologians, and his acts of government were performed with their advice and moral support.[1] It is not possible here to study this theocracy beyond mentioning these few of its principal features. In A.D. 909 Tiaret, and with it the State of Glory, was suddenly destroyed by an army of orthodox Muslim fanatics, believers in the hereditary succession of the Prophet, who later were to lift the Fatimid dynasty onto the throne of Egypt.

The Ibadites of Tiaret that were not killed or dispersed began under their Imam another long trek, this time southeast, into the Sahara. They crossed 400 miles of steppe and desert and finally reached Ouargla, a large oasis south of Touggourt, where an Ibadi community had settled earlier and where the refugees from Tiaret started to build the new city of Sedrata.[2] The Imam who had led them renounced his leadership and returned to private life; and from that moment the religious as well as the secular authority of this Ibadi community rested in the hands of its clergy. As his final act the last Imam proclaimed the State of Secrecy by which the Ibadites separated themselves from the heterodox world and decided to live entirely on their own, instead of in mixed communities.

Sedrata was not a very safe place. It lay in the open desert, only a few days' march away from other centers of population, and it was within striking distance of powerful Negro kingdoms in the south. It grew and prospered, thanks to the industry and application of its citizens and its position on a main caravan route from the southwest to the northeast; it also attracted Ibadi communities from other parts of North Africa; but the sectarians looked for a safer place and soon found it, only some 120 miles to the northwest, in the region of the Shebka that was avoided, even by nomads, because it was lifeless and afforded no grazing.[3] In the year A.D. 1011 men from Sedrata founded El-Ateuf, the first city of the Mzab; thirty years later Bou Noura and Melika were built, then Beni Isguen further up the valley; and finally Ghardaya in A.D. 1053. The precaution proved to be wise, for in A.D. 1075 Sedrata was destroyed by a hostile Berber tribe.

These, then, are the five cities of the Mzab valley. It can now be understood how they came to be founded in this particular location. But it will be necessary to examine whether they really are cities in the accepted sense, and not just fortified places. After all, there are numberless fortified places, or *ksour*, all over North Africa.[4] In what way do those of the Mzab differ from the others? Nearly

[1] A. de C. Motylinski, 'Chronique d'Ibn Saghir sur les imams de Tahert. Texte et traduction', *Act. XIV. Int. Orient. Congr.*, Algiers, 1905, III, pp. 3–132, Paris, 1908.

[2] M. van Berchem, 'Deux campagnes de fouilles à Sedrata (1951–1952)', *Trav. Inst. Rech. sahar.* 3, 1953, pp. 123–38.

[3] A Bernard, *Afrique septentrionale et occidentale*, 2 vols, Paris, 1937–8.

[4] It should be noted that *ksar*, plural *ksour*, is the French transcription of the word as it is spoken in the Maghreb instead of the correct *qsar* (plural *qusur*).

all the Berber *ksour* have two features in common: every *ksar* is inhabited by people standing in some kind of blood-relationship to one another as members of the same tribe, or clan, or family—always excepting Jews or slaves attached to many of the *ksour*; and they are nearly all dependent upon a higher authority, be it a local chieftain, a territorial ruler, or a nomad tribe. There are indeed some placed in Kabylia and the Aures where Berber families or clans not necessarily related have moved together constituting townships with a form of local self-government; the cities of the Mzab, however, were each founded not by several families, but by several *groups* of families who continue to this day their separate identities but who gave up their juridical and executive tribal powers to the higher political entity of the city. These family-groups, or *qabail*, correspond closely to the ancient Roman *curiae* which were each composed of several *gentes*; and the city, called *arsh*, corresponds to the Roman *urbs* in its political sense, or to the Greek *polis*.[1]

Not all the families or clans that founded the cities have survived; but the *qabail* or family-groups have.[2] For instance, the *arsh* of Ghardaya is based upon two *qabail*, the Ouled Ammi Aissa and the Ouled Ba Sliman, each occupying a ward in the city. The Ouled Ammi Aissa are composed of three *hashair* or clans, two of which came from the west and one from Sedrata. The two from the west have their own burial ground near the tomb of a western marabout, or saint. The other *qabila*, the Ouled Ba Sliman, consists of two clans, each of a different origin. Beni Isguen has three *qabail*, one of which is from Sedrata, the second composed of *hashair* from the Atlas, and the third of later migrants grouped in five *hashair* of different origins and integrated into the city under the name of Ouled Anan. Bou Noura has two *qabail*, but one of them consists now of a single *hashira*, which occupies half the city, while the other is composed of seven *hashair*. A comparatively recent document, the chronicle of a new city, dating from A.D. 1613, when, for reasons of overpopulation and civil strife, a number of families left Ghardaya and went to found Guerrara, opens with the declaration: 'The Ouled Betamer composed of six *hashair*, and the Ouled Ben Brahim and the Ouled Debbat, each consisting of one *hashira*, found this city and make certain laws.'[3]

The social structure of the Mzab city has been compared with the Roman *urbs* or the Greek *polis* in their early stages. Another comparison can be made with Italian city-states of the Renaissance. The *qabail* not only jealously guard their separate identities, they frequently used to assert them by force of arms, and the *sofs*[4] or bloody quarrels between the wards or between leading families in

---

[1] E. Masqueray, *Formations des cités chez les populations sédentaires de l'Algérie*, Paris, 1886, p. 221.

[2] 'Le mot *qebila* signifie au Mzab toujours un groupe politique dépendant d'un autre plus considérable, une fraction en un mot' (E. Masqueray, 1886, op. cit., p. 175).

[3] The Chronicle of Shaikh Sliman ibn Abdalla (Masqueray, ibid., p. 176). A. de C. Motylinski, *Guerara depuis sa fondation*, Algiers, 1885, gives a translation of another and later chronicle. Here the names differ from those quoted above, but the account of the city's foundation is very similar.

[4] The word means 'party' and, by extension, 'party quarrels' (J. Huguet, 'Les Soffs', *Rev. Ec. Anthrop. Paris*, 13, 1903, p. 94). See also A. Bernard, *Le Maroc*, Paris, 1932, p. 219.

different *qabail* or factions in different cities were as notorious in the Mzab as were the fights between the Pazzi and the Medici in Florence, or between the *contrade* of Siena.

Although the *qabail* are strong vestiges of tribal organization, they retain no political or administrative rights within the city.[1] Each *qabila* elects a magistrate, or *kebir*, and one or two sheriffs, or *muqaddemin*. The magistrates collectively pass sentences and impose fines, and the sheriffs execute judgments, keep the city's accounts, and receive strangers. Each individual, no matter from which ward, enjoys the protection of, and is subject to, city law, and the authorities are responsible for the peace of the city as a whole. Besides the officers of the law, every *qabila* elects a number of elders, each from a different *hashira* who, together with the magistrates and the sheriffs, form the *jamaa*, or assembly. This assembly is summoned by the magistrates only in exceptional circumstances or for special reasons like important litigation, public security or the making or revision of laws. It is a legislating body and a high court at the same time, and an immemorial institution among all Berber tribes. However, in the Mzab it is powerless by itself; it may meet only in the mosque and in the presence of the *halqa* or conventicle of the learned clerks whose chief, the shaikh of the mosque, presides. Of the lay members, only the magistrates have the right to speak. The elders' part is to listen and to give assent. The mosque is, in fact, the government of the city; the authority of the clergy is supreme. The higher clergy, or clerks of the first degree, setting an example of the State of Secrecy, hold themselves aloof from the day-to-day management of affairs; but nothing of any importance can take place without their consent. The laity are associated with acts of government through their elected representatives in the assembly which must be consulted; but in a conflict of opinion it is always the clergy who have the last word, for they have at their disposal two powerful weapons—excommunication against the individual, and, against the community, the sit-down strike: in grave cases the clerks lock themselves up in their mosque; there are no prayers, no funerals can be held, no benedictions, purifications, circumcisions, marriages, no teaching—in fact, the whole life of the community comes to a standstill.

So the theocracy of Tiaret and Sedrata continues in the Mzab, and through it the Puritan doctrine of the sect is upheld in all its severity. The *qawanin*, or laws of the cities, abound in proscriptions of vanity, ostentation, levity, and pleasure.[2] Here, for example, is the *qanun* of the city of Melika regulating the expenses for a wedding[3]:

> For the preparation of a wedding-feast no more than two slaves in the house of the bridegroom and two slaves in the house of the bride shall be employed. In neither of the two houses shall musical instruments be played. The Negress who is sent with the dish of *ghedara* shall have one measure of corn: the

[1] Nevertheless, their local cohesion is strictly safeguarded. Property may be sold only to members of the same *sof* which, in this context, means the *qabila* and its assimilated families inhabiting the same ward (R. Capot-Rey, *Le Sahara français*, Paris, 1953, p. 244).

[2] A *qanun* of Beni Isguen punishes him who boasts of his descent from an ancient family (M. Morand, *Etudes de droit musulman algérien*, Algiers, 1910, p. 440).

[3] Masqueray, 1886, op. cit., pp. 62–3.

ghedara must not contain eggs, neither must it contain saffron, and it must not be made with *ajid*-flour. All these things are forbidden. Also forbidden is the use of a mule or a horse for conveying the bride: she shall walk on foot. No flute-player shall enter the house of the bridegroom and no one shall smoke in his house, for tobacco is hateful. The Negress who carries the bread to the house of the bridge shall be given two small measures of corn. The bread of the seventh day must not exceed one small measure of corn: the bridegroom shall give in exchange half a real, no more.[1] The servant who fetches the dish of *refis* [a sweet made of dates and semolina] shall receive from the hand of her mistress one mouthful of it, no more. The woman who remains with the bride shall be given one-eighth of a real. Flute-players and slaves shall not make music in the city, and within the city-walls it is forbidden to let off firearms. After the bride has entered the house of the bridegroom, it is forbidden to send her food, be it dates, or corn, or any other victual, and the *ghedara* made by the mother-in-law on the first day must not exceed the measure of eight dishes. The mother-in-law shall not offer any food to the friends of her son-in-law, nor shall she make nor send him any *refis* on the day she receives his presents.

Whosoever does any of these things shall be subjected to the censure of the Faithful.

Given by the Assembly of the people of Melika, clerics and laymen, the first day of *rejeb* of the year 1108 after the *Hijra* of the Prophet (A.D. 1697).

It has been mentioned that the cities of the Mzab form what is sometimes called a confederation. This must not be understood in the sense of a political union. There are no federal organs of government, no constitution, and no federal council. The union of the cities is founded in their common history and their common dangers, and both these are the consequences of their common faith. This sectarian faith, the state of secrecy in which it is practised and the self-denial which its puritan doctrine demands, produce an inordinate pride in its adepts. They call themselves 'God's Family', in other words the Chosen People. Nothing will normally induce a Mozabite to part from his community and mix with others whom he deems so much beneath himself—not the hard and barren ground where his ancestors took refuge, not the fact that he has to spend half his life away from home to earn his living (as will presently be explained), not his neighbor's jealousy and hatred, nor even the banishment he may suffer for a murder he may have committed in pursuit of a *sof*. There may be disunity among the cities through their autonomy and conflicting interests; there may be violence and hostility among citizens: but stronger than all dissociating influences are the unity created by the pressure of the control the community exercises over all its members for the sake of the doctrine, and the social cohesion produced by the energy—one might say the high temperature—of this religious sect. Indeed, any lowering of the temperature, any concession or relaxation of the religious and moral doctrine, must, in this artificially created society—existing in an artificially

[1] A Spanish real was worth approximately one florin. See Morand (1910, pp. 427-8) on the real, its history in North Africa, its various coinages, its value, etc.

created living space—entail gradual disintegration and loss of identity. This, in fact, is happening in the island of Jerba where the old and important Mozabite community, under the influence of easy living conditions and the relaxation of rules, is slowly dwindling.[1] In other words, if doctrine no longer separated the Mozabite from other people, there would be no particular reason why he should go on living in the Mzab rather than elsewhere—on the coast, for instance, or in some other practical and less costly surroundings.[2]

Since the soil of the Oued Mzab had to be created, because there was practically none to begin with, it was clear from the start that the only salvation of the Mozabite communities lay in trade. Of this they had centuries of experience, first in Tiaret where they were placed between the stock-breeding plateaux and the agricultural plains of the coastal Tell; and then in Sedrata which lay on the route connecting the western Sudan and the Niger valley with the Mediterranean, through the oases of the Rhir and the Jerid. The Mzab was less favorably placed, in fact that is why it was chosen as a retreat; so—although a north–south route through their valley was gradually established by the Beni Mzab—it became necessary to trade elsewhere and send the proceeds home. Puritans make good business men: a high standard of literacy, necessary in order to study the holy scriptures; a high standard of honesty as part of the doctrine; a disciplined will, which is the essence of Puritanism, and the avoidance of dissipation make successful trading almost inevitable.[3] From the earliest times of their settlement in the valley, Mozabites went to the north trading in slaves, hides, wool, and livestock from the Sahara, and in produce, commodities, and imported groceries from the coast and the ports. Nowadays, they dominate the trade in textiles and groceries in Algeria and Tunisia and they are very large property owners in the cities and the countryside of the Tell as well as in the oases of southern Algeria.[4]

In the normal course of events, a small boy would be sent or taken by his father to his own or a friend's business in the north to learn to trade.[5] He is brought home to the Mzab at the age of between fourteen and sixteen to marry, then returns to the north and pays periodical visits to his home until he has made enough capital to take things easier, look after his family and his property, and concern himself earnestly with his salvation. Since he cannot spend money on luxuries, he makes investments, he marries frequently but never more than one wife at a time (which, of course, means a fresh payment for every wife), he endows his mosque so that the clergy is kept and every child can be taught, and—last but not least—he improves his garden and his summer-house, which is

[1] M. Mercier, *Etude sur le waqf abadhite et ses applications au Mzab*, Algiers, 1927, p. 11.

[2] M. Weber, *Wirtschaft und Gesellschaft*, 3 vols, II. *Grundriss der Sozialökonomik*, III. Abt., Tübingen, Mohr; R. H. Tawney, *Religion and the Rise of Capitalism. A Historical Study*, London, 1926, p. 201.

[3] M. Mercier (*La Civilisation urbaine au Mzab*, Algiers, 1922), in this context, points out the effect of 'une logique collective et emotionelle', as opposed to practical individual reasoning.

[4] L. Vigourus, 'L'Émigration mozabite dans les villes du Tell algérien', *Trav. Inst.Rech. Sahar.*, 3, pp. 87–102.

[5] It is estimated that about 5,000 Mozabites, or about one-sixth, are absent from their homes every year (Capot-Rey, ibid., p. 161).

costly, because it needs constant care and the employment of servants and animals to draw water, keep the water-channels in repair, add fresh soil and fertilizers, and look after the plants and trees. 'The Mozabite,' said Gautier,[1] 'is a shrewd business man from the Tell who—at ruinous expense—keeps a country-house in the Sahara.'[2]

Judging by appearances, this would seem true. But nothing is quite what it seems in the Mzab. The State of Secrecy still obtains, and although there may not be very much more to hide now, it was not so long ago that little was known about the Beni Mzab except that one met them everywhere. In 1878 Émile Masqueray visited the Mzab and, as the first outsider of any race or creed, was allowed to see and then to copy one of the important Mozabite books, the *Chronicle* of Abu Zakaria.[3] Some years later he was given insight into the *qawanin*, or written laws of the Mzab,[4] and thus opened up the Mzab as a field of study. In 1882 France annexed the Mzab and made Ghardaya the military headquarters of a territory stretching from Jelfa in the north to El-Golea in the south. The Beni Mzab cooperated willingly with the French administration, and accepted nominated *caids*, French law-courts, mission-schools, and hospitals, while the French, of course, respected their religious practices and customs, including that of locking the gates of their cities every night when the strangers had left.[5]

It was not until 1925, when Mlle Goichon came to live in the Mzab, gained the confidence of some women, and was able to study family life, that any particulars concerning the life of women and small children became known at all. And incidentally, stories of massacres, assassinations, and religious upheavals came to light that had happened during the preceding thirty or forty years without ever so much as a murmur reaching the world outside.

The role of the women is determined by one fundamental law: no Mozabite woman is ever allowed to leave the Mzab.[6] Apart from the hived-off colonies, no Mozabite woman is found in any other place. William Marçais, in his preface to Mlle Goichon's important work, calls the women the armature of Mozabite society; they do, indeed, hold it together, since a man cannot take his family when he goes away and would lose it altogether if he did not return. The women of the Mzab are, therefore, in a very special sense the guardians of the hearth not only of the family but of the whole city; and since young wives of the age of twelve or thirteen can hardly be expected to run a family and a household in a fully responsible manner, the city-fathers set up an authority whose duty it is to supervise the conduct of the women and to see that they observe the laws

[1] E. F. Gautier, *Le Sahara*, Paris, 1923, p. 153.

[2] See also le lieutenant Charlet-Cozon, 'Les palmiers du Mzab, *Bull. Soc. Géog. Alger (Afr. N.)*, 9, 1905, pp. 11–87; Capot-Rey, op. cit., p. 230.

[3] Masqueray, 1879, op. cit.

[4] In the Mzab, these laws although not codified, are written down and registered, while in the Berber townships of the Aures and in Kabylia, where religious government is absent, they are preserved by oral tradition only (Masqueray, ibid., p. 50).

[5] N.-J. Robin, *Le Mzab et son annexion à la France*, Algiers, 1884.

[6] A.-M. Goichon, *La Vie féminine au Mzab, étude de sociologie musulmane*, 2 vols, Paris, 1927–31 (with a preface by W. Marcais). This law is discussed by E. Zeys (*Législation mozabite, son origine, ses sources. son présent, son avenir*, Algiers, 1886), Morand (ibid., Chapter 11) and other authorities.

strictly and that the children are brought up in the correct way. This authority is vested in the guild or order of women who wash and lay out the bodies of the dead—in French, *les laveuses des morts*.[1]

The women who fill this office, which is unpaid and highly respectable, are chosen by the clerks from among the most virtuous, capable, and intelligent matrons of the town. Their influence on family life is all-pervading, and they are feared and respected, because they have access to every house, they must be consulted on all occasions, and they have the disciplinary power of excommunication, delegated to them by the *halqa*. It may be believed that they do their duty conscientiously, methodically, and strictly.

Their principal function is to teach. The dogma that all Muslims are equal includes women, who have therefore to be taught to understand the Koran and to understand their prayers, for prayers merely recited do not go to heaven.[2] They have also to be taught something of the laws and the history of their city and sect. Women do not go to the mosque, so the *laveuses* lead their prayers and occasionally preach to them. They are really female clergy, dons, and provost-marshals, all in one.

There are five *laveuses* in Ghardaya. There are also five men in this city who perform the same pious office on the bodies of men. The *laveuses* deal only with women, dead and alive. Once a year, the *laveuses* from the five cities of the Mzab meet in conference to exchange information, learn from one another's experiences, revise old regulations, and define any modern transgressions or deviations from proper behavior.

Every detail in the conduct of a woman is regulated: her dress, her ornaments, her hair style, her use of cosmetics (which is allowed in certain ways, forbidden in others), and her deportment in the street (provided she is allowed to leave the house). She must not show her hand to a man when paying in a shop; it must be covered by a corner of her garment. She may not dance, nor sing at a feast, although singing at work is allowed if the text is approved. She is forbidden to weep over the body of a dead person (be it her own child or mother)—Arab weeping-women are engaged to do that, Mozabite women remain silent. She must not raise her voice in laughter, in conversation, or when calling someone— one calls by clapping one's hands. She is forbidden to speak from roof-terrace to roof-terrace, and so on.

Children are reared in equally precise and strict ways. For example, a baby is made to stand upright in its second month; it is exercised by being held up by the feet, head downwards, and having its back and sides slapped; it is rocked on the left knee, the mother's left foot resting on the right knee. The baby is carried on the arms while it is in swaddling-clothes, and later astride on the left hip— never on the mother's back.

A Mozabite woman may not marry a stranger, but men are allowed to marry women of other races and creeds, including Christians and Jewesses.[3] She

[1] Goichon, op. cit., pp. 220 ff.
[2] Masqueray, 1886, op. cit., p. 57.
[3] Except in Beni Isguen, the 'holy city', where marriage with a non-Mozabite woman entails banishment (Morand, ibid., p. 442).

retains her father's surname, but in all other respects passes into the family of her husband. In the husband's absence it is his mother who supervises the household, lives in the house if possible, and exercises authority.

Shortly after the annexation of the Mzab by France, European observers began to speculate how long the mediaeval and reactionary society of the pentapolis could survive close contact with the progressive, scientific, and rational forces of the modern age. E. Zeys, a lawyer and humanist, advocated annulment of the law prohibiting the emigration of women and looked forward to the emigration of whole families from the inhospitable valley and to the 'victory of civilization'.[1] Dr Amat, army physician and scientist, who gave the first accurate account of the valley and its people, predicted the rapid decadence of the Mzab for economic and social reasons. He argued that the loss of the slave trade, improved transport, and above all the newly-found security would tempt the people from their walled cities in the desert and draw them to the easier and more comfortable life in the fertile regions of North Africa.[2]

It has already been suggested that the determination of the Beni Mzab not to mingle with the population of the country, but to maintain their homes and families in the desert and to wish to die and be buried in their native valley, is founded on pride in their exceptional faith, in the sacrifices which this demands, and on the superior attitude toward the world which it engenders. However, a traditional social group on the defence could not resist the pressure of twentieth-century Western civilization by will-power alone; it would have to dispose of considerable material, spiritual, and intellectual resources, to make good that defence. Does Mozabite society possess these resources?

If it is true to say that tribal and traditional societies succumb to Western influence principally through poverty, ignorance, and inferior organization, it follows that the Beni Mzab are protected by their wealth, education, and privileged urban government. They are sufficiently in command of modern commercial practice and capitalist procedure to hold their own in highly competitive markets, they have long been familiar with European ways and languages, and their domestic authorities, who admit no strangers, have to contend only with traditional problems. But these meritorious or fortunate circumstances would be of little avail without the spiritual strength of this community. As in the case of Calvinism and its insistence on personal responsibility, discipline, and asceticism, the acquisition of wealth is not allowed to become merely an instrument of individual advantage, but remains a moral duty with the aim of glorifying God and sustaining the community. So the Mzab is still a theocracy and a society of equals.

---

[1] Zeys, op. cit., p. 54.
[2] C. Amat, *Le Mzab et les Mzabites*, Paris, 1888.

Part 2 Ethnicity and Nation

7

Lawrence Rosen

The Social and Conceptual Framework of Arab–Berber Relations in Central Morocco[1]

In the vast literature compiled by French travelers, administrators, and ethnographers on the structure of Moroccan society it has generally been assumed that the divisions of the Moroccan population into Arabs and Berbers constitutes a distinction of primary and obvious importance. 'Arab' and 'Berber' have been regarded as mutually exclusive categories useful not only to the outsider's understanding of Moroccan society and culture but characteristic of the Moroccan's own perceptions and behavior. Instead of questioning how ethnicity[2] fits into the larger system through which each Moroccan's social identity is established and made significant, the validity and utility of this distinction has almost always been taken for granted. This tendency to avoid systematic analysis of the Arab–Berber distinction appears to stem both from French colonial attitudes to the Moroccan population and the failure to apply appropriate conceptual tools to the study of this problem.

The French view of the composition and relative importance of the different sectors of the Moroccan population was itself subject to significant alteration over the course of the Protectorate. In the first few years of domination the French, though increasingly aware of the linguistic and social differences between Arabs and Berbers, considered the primary lines of division within Moroccan society to be those separating the people under government control from those who, for whatever reason, were actively engaged in opposing the policies of the Sultan and his 'protectors'. As more was learned about the Berbers and more functionaries of the Office of Native Affairs took up residence in their territories the Berbers were seen less as anarchic and uncivilized tribesmen than as proud warriors whose manly qualities should constrain one's sincere admiration. Increasingly, too, the French became aware of the real and imagined differences between Berbers and Arabs, particularly as they bore on the structure of Berber political organization and the apparent differences in attachment to the

[1] Research for this study was carried out under grants from the National Institutes of Health and Center for International Comparative Studies at the University of Illinois. In addition to thanking these foundations the author would like to express his gratitude to the following persons for their comments and suggestions on an earlier version of this paper: Robert McC. Adams, Leonard Binder, Kenneth Brown, Edmund Burke, Lloyd A. Fallers, Ernest Gellner, and especially Clifford and Hildred Geertz.
[2] The terms 'ethnicity' and 'ethnic identity' are used throughout this paper only in the sense of a segment of a population distinguished by certain characteristics, customs, or language, and not in the sense of nationhood or persistent treatment by others as if the grouping so defined were an undifferentiated whole. For a discussion of some of the technical rather than simply descriptive usages to which the term 'ethnic' and subsidiary concepts have been put in recent anthropological literature see Raoul Naroll, 'On Ethnic Unit Classification', *Current Anthropology*, Vol. 5, No. 4, October 1964, pp. 283–312.

Islamic religion. The issuance of the Berber *dahir* in 1930, which allowed Berber communities to remain under their own customary laws instead of the formal Islamic *sharia*, was only the most notorious (and disastrous) consequence of the French belief that Arab–Berber differences were so great as to permit a real divide-and-conquer policy. For as the nationalist activities of the following decades clearly indicated, this division was not nearly so sharp as the French had thought it to be.

The French also failed to consider the ways in which Arab or Berber identity as such was really a factor in certain aspects of Moroccan social life because they lacked certain sociological concepts that would have allowed them to abstract individual features from the undifferentiated whole of a community's social life. In particular, they lacked a modern concept of culture as an integrated system of symbols in terms of which people conceive of themselves and the world around them and by means of which this experience is articulated into an ordered and meaningful whole.[1] Failing to distinguish the ways in which Moroccans of different social backgrounds conceived of one another as kinds of persons and the situations in which these cultural concepts informed their specific actions toward one another, French ethnographers tended to see Moroccan society as composed of a set of individually homogeneous units whose members related toward one another as representatives of various corporate entities. 'Berber' and 'Arab', therefore, stood as glosses for separate groupings whose concomitant identities as rural *v*. urban, 'dissident' *v*. 'loyalist' could usually serve as well to typify the relevant factor in each grouping's identity.

Since the advent of national independence in 1956, the Moroccan government itself has tended to avoid characterizing the differences between Arabs and Berbers as a significant axis of division within the country. This avoidance is, of course, not without its political rationale and implications. Accordingly, there is a tendency for outside observers to feel that the present government's view, no less than that maintained by the colonial government itself at various times, is either an attempt to gloss over an underlying difficulty or represents a conscious attempt to re-phrase the question of Arab–Berber differences for the purposes of contemporary political policy.

Such a view would, however, be a gross oversimplification not only of the political strategies of the present Moroccan government but of the realities of Moroccan social life itself. It is true that particular groups of Arabs and Berbers have at times organized themselves into separate political organizations, and it is equally true that many individuals feel a greater degree of commonality with members of their own ethnic group than with outsiders. But what is not always appreciated is the fact that the lines of social cohesion in Morocco are highly diversified and that ethnicity constitutes only one, and not necessarily the most important, basis of any Moroccan's social identity. If a proper assessment of the place and importance of ethnic identity in Morocco is to be undertaken two

---

[1] I am indebted to Professor Clifford Geertz for this point. For a definition and illustration of the anthropological concept of culture see Clifford Geertz, 'Ritual and Social Change: A Javanese Example', *American Anthropologist*, Vol. 59, No. 1, February 1957, pp. 32–54.

separate but related questions must be given careful consideration. First, we must ask where ethnic identity as such fits into the broader range of categories in terms of which an individual's overall social identity is established: what other relationships contribute to a man's social placement and what place does ethnicity occupy in this larger scheme? Secondly, if we then factor out ethnic identity for separate consideration, which of any man's actions can we say are affected by his recognition of himself or another as an Arab or a Berber, in what situations does this identification take precedence, and how does this distinction relate back to the totality of his social relations?

To raise these questions, to consider ethnic identity in its overall social and cultural context while at the same time allowing for it to be treated as a distinct category, presents a significant methodological problem. For the purposes of this chapter, however, the description and analysis of data can be divided into three major sections. In order to place ethnic identity in its proper context and in order to indicate its relative importance the first section will deal with the multiple sources of an individual's social identity and will attempt to show that almost all of the major indices by which a Moroccan is placed cut across the boundaries of ethnic identity as such. If ethnic identity thus takes on less primacy as an axis of social identity and affiliation the question will still remain as to the exact importance ethnicity does or appears to possess in a series of particular situations. Thus the second part of the chapter will consider the relative importance of ethnic identity alone in such illustrative social contexts as the formation of clientele relationships, political alliances, and inter-ethnic marriages. Finally, we shall explore, within a broader theoretical framework, some of the characteristic functions ethnic identity serves in the multi-dimensional context of Moroccan social life, the mechanisms through which this identity is ordered and communicated, and the extent to which further studies of Moroccan society and culture profit or suffer from a concentration on ethnicity as a major axis of social differentiation.

As a focus for studying these aspects of Arab–Berber identity reference will be made throughout to materials collected in the central Moroccan city and region of Sefrou. Sefrou is a city of about 25,000 people located fifteen miles south of Fes in an irrigated zone transitional between the largely Arab inhabited grainlands of the central plain and the predominantly Berber inhabited pasturelands of the Ait Yusi 'tribe' that begin just south of the city in the Middle Atlas mountains. The city itself has a core of old Arab families but in recent years it has also become the home for a number of Berber and Arab immigrants from the surrounding countryside. Most of the Berbers of the region speak good colloquial Arabic as well as their native Berber dialect, and almost all of the rural people go into town regularly to visit relatives and deal in the local marketplace. Taken as a whole, then, the city is quite heterogeneous in character. And taken as individuals the inhabitants of the city and region alike draw on a multiplicity of social relations and personal attributes for the establishment of their own social identities.

THE SOCIAL FOUNDATIONS OF PERSONAL IDENTITY

The distinction between Arab and Berber is only one of a number of different features in terms of which any particular Moroccan may be identified. Ties of kinship and residence, occupation and personal affiliations all serve as additional indices of personal identification. As the Moroccans themselves see it the fundamental basis of a man's identity can be said to derive from that social and physical milieu from which he draws his personal sustenance. Sustenance here refers both to the geographical and occupational basis of one's physical well-being and the other persons with whom one is engaged in this quest for well-being. The initial sources of a man's nurture will, of course, be set by the circumstances of his birth and with it the definition of his social and geographical origins. Insofar as he continues to work out his sustenance in this area and with this relatively confined group of persons, the original sources of his sustenance and consequent social identity may remain roughly the same throughout his life. But insofar as it is also both possible and likely that the social and physical sources of his nurture may be altered over the years, so too the content of any man's identity may change accordingly. Indeed, it is true for even the most sedentary individuals in this society that none of the rules which order relationships with others are so rigid or exclusive that the overwhelming majority of social ties will be defined, for example, by kinship or residence alone. Rather, even for the person who spends most of his lifetime living and working with others related to him by blood, there is a wide latitude permitted in these relationships, and he can actually choose, or contract, particular kinds of relationships with his kinsmen just as, in the absence of strong sanctions to the contrary, he can contract such ties with outsiders.

The constant focus in Moroccan society is not, therefore, on corporate groups but on individuals; not on the sanctions through which behavior can be channelled and limited but on arranging associations wherever they appear most advantageous; not on a widely ramified set of solidary groupings of which one is a member but on the customary ways in which personal ties to others can be contracted. Inherent ties offer a significant basis for establishing such dyadic bonds but as each bond is developed and each personal trait displayed a multiplicity of components contribute to one's individual social identity. Thus even in a man's identity as a member of a family, an occupation category, or a resident of a particular region or quarter the primary focus is not on his group affiliations as such but on the personal traits embodied in and the personal ties formed around each particular individual.

Like ties of kinship, occupation, residence and so on, inherent ties to other members of a particular ethnic division contribute to but do not wholly typify a given individual. In general terms this distinction between Arab and Berber is easily drawn, the main discriminant being that of language: an Arab is someone who speaks Arabic but not one of the Berber dialects while a Berber is someone who speaks a form of Berber whether or not he also speaks Arabic. Although certain social and cultural features may tend to be found more often among particular groups of one ethnic division as opposed to another, the fact remains that for virtually any given feature—with the obvious exception of language—there are as many differences within each ethnic division as there are similarities between segments of each of them. For certain quantifiable features this assertion can be sustained by reference to a few statistics from the 1960 census of Sefrou.[1]

It can be shown, for example, that in the Sefrou area Berbers are not all rural dwellers: 14 percent of the population of Sefrou are of Berber origin; those Berbers living in the city are not just men: the male/female ratio for rural-born Berbers is 0·98; not all of the Berbers are recent immigrants to the city: two-thirds arrived before 1955; they are not grouped into particular quarters of the city but tend to be scattered throughout almost all neighborhoods; Berber men of rural origins tend to hold jobs that pay as well as those occupied by Arab men born in the city itself; although they tend to rent entire houses more often (55%) than Sefrou-born Arabs (38%) and tend toward greater unemployment (35% as opposed to 19% for Sefrou-born Arabs), in both cases the figures for rural-born Berbers and rural-born Arabs are quite comparable; and although rural-born Arab and Berber men are more illiterate (70 and 72% respectively) than Sefrou-born Arab men (46%), and proportionately few of their children are enrolled in school, one must bear in mind too that the number of men under thirty is disproportionately low for Berbers (27%) and rural-born Arabs (33%) as compared with the Sefrou-born Arabs (43%). For almost any quantitative index, then, the differences in economic status, residential placement, and employment do not indicate a sharp polarity between Arabs and Berbers. Similarly if one were to trace such qualitative factors as attitudes toward the monarchy, modernization, or religious beliefs one would not discover a sharp dichotomy along lines of ethnicity or rural versus urban residence. Even in matters of dress, physical appearance and accent, it is not always easy for a Moroccan to discern another's ethnic identity with certainty. Thus one must probe for the extent to which such differences are actually relevant to the relations between any two persons and how that particular bit of information articulates with the data concerning other aspects of a man's social identity.

The question we shall want to raise, then, is what one man really knows when he knows another's ethnic affiliations. If, as we have already indicated, people in this part of Morocco do not at all times relate to one another in such a way that ethnicity is an equally important and relevant factor—if, indeed, personal identity derives as much from family ties, residence, occupation, associates, and individual attributes—it will prove valuable to look at some of the specific contexts in which these various factors are brought into play. In particular, one can look for the bearing of ethnicity on such relationships as those established through clientele relations, alignment in a specific election, and the formation of marriages across ethnic lines.

[1] Statistics cited here are derived from a 100 percent sampling of the raw census forms that were programed for computer analysis by Hildred Geertz and summarized in her mimeographed compendium, *A Profile of a Moroccan Town: Sefrou 1960*. At that time there were 17,583 Moslems, 3,041 Jews, and 172 Frenchmen living in the city.

ARENAS OF ARAB–BERBER INTERACTION

Clientele relationships

In the rather fluid social structure characteristic of both Arabs and Berbers in the Sefrou region, in which one builds on various inherent ties through a multiplicity of personally contracted alliances, almost all social relations are characterized by a rather high degree of competitiveness and even jealousy. Through ingratiation and role bargaining, manipulating intermediaries and performing 'favors', each man plays on the expectation of some form of reciprocation to form a wide network of supporters and dependents whose potential aid will serve as a hedge against a host of natural and sociological uncertainties. The contracting of such social debts is, however, carried out with a certain element of caution. Men are particularly wary of becoming obliged to another if they feel that, in the absence of such cross-cutting ties as kinship or common residence, they will have no alternative channels through which to modify the demands of their social or financial creditors. It is not, therefore, a question of avoiding involvement in a web of indebtedness, for without such ties a social existence could hardly be maintained. Rather, the trick is to arrange ties in order to gain the highest possible degree of predictability, if not control, over the actions of others.

In the specific context of a bazaar economy such as that of Sefrou this avoidance of undesirable obligations is coupled with the need to deal effectively in the marketplace. Lacking detailed knowledge of the quality of particular goods, their purchase price by the dealer, and the consequent worth of various items presented for the bargainer's consideration, it is often the case that for certain major goods a man chooses the seller to deal with rather than the goods as such. In the purchase of such items as cloth, meat, furniture, and the services of a barber, people often form clientele relationships with particular merchants in order to have some personal basis for relying on the quality of the supplier's goods or services and in order to obtain more favorable prices. Some indication of the other's personal reliability must, therefore, be sought in establishing this kind of relationship. The expectation of exclusive patronage in return for high quality, low priced merchandise or the extension of purchasing credit is, of course, of great importance to the establishment of an ongoing clientele relationship. But of at least equal importance—since what a person is buying is a relationship with a particular man rather than a simple commodity—is the quest for a basis of relationship with the other as a total personality. Ties of common background, similar residence, equivalent attitudes, or some such common bond may supply the necessary degree of assurance that the other's actions can indeed be induced to conform to their ideal. The absence of such a basis for a personal bond of reliability may inhibit or strain the establishment of a lasting clientele relationship. And it is the absence of such a basis of commonality that often puts a strain on relations between Arab merchants and their potential Berber clientele.

Initially at least there is often a tendency on the part of an Arab businessman and a Berber client for each to regard the other with a certain degree of antipathy.

Berber countrymen often feel that the urban Arab merchant is trying to get the better of them while the merchant himself often considers the Berber as a country bumpkin of questionable intelligence and morality. In fact, these gross stereotypes are almost always capable of being superseded once a face-to-face relationship is actually established, but in the absence of additional cross-cutting ties an element of distrust often tends to persist. Berbers express a certain reluctance to become financially or socially indebted to an urban Arab merchant knowing that because he cannot be relied upon to treat them as fellow kinsmen or neighbors he will be less vulnerable to the constraints implicit, at least ideally, in these latter forms of relationship. Accordingly, in the past, when there were numerous Jewish merchants in Sefrou, Berbers clearly preferred dealing with them because the Jews were socially non-competitive, linked in a clearly symbiotic relationship with the Muslims, and interested mainly in straightforward economic relations with the Berbers. As the Jews have moved out of the city many of their shops have been taken over by Berbers now residing in town and there is a tendency for them to acquire clienteles composed in great part of those with whom they share common social bonds.[1]

Ethnicity, then, is a factor but by no means either the sole or even necessarily the primary factor associated with patron–client relations. The main consideration is the whole personality of a man as perceived by another, and in this perception and evaluation ethnic identity is only one among a number of crucial variables. There are those who prefer to play on the ideals of mutual aid implicit in any common social bond in order to obtain a favored bargaining position. Others avoid compounding obligations within their own social groupings preferring instead to deal with people who are not closely related to them by blood or social origins. Clientele relations often operate, therefore, as if the ethnic distinction were irrelevant, and insofar as it may be superseded by a personal tie and a personal evaluation of one another's whole social personality it may indeed recede into virtual irrelevance. But as a baseline for perceiving the lines of association with an unknown merchant, a difference in ethnicity also tends to project an image of uncertain and perhaps uncontrollable reliability whose precise impact is as difficult to measure as it is a somewhat ambiguous yet real factor in the perception by Arabs and Berbers of the initial bases of their economic relationships with one another.

Political alignment: a case study

After independence in 1956, political parties became a major vehicle through which members of the electorate sought to gain access to the national decision-making apparatus or through which they sought to acquire certain patronage

---

[1] For a description of Moslem–Jewish relations in Morocco with particular reference to their intermediate position between Arabs and Berbers see my article 'A Moroccan Jewish Community During the Middle Eastern Crisis', *The American Scholar*, Vol. 37, No. 3, 1968, pp. 435–51.

6

benefits. Although at first politically active Berbers worked largely within the context of the Istiqlal political party—and during the actual struggle for independence within the Army of Liberation as well—many of them supported the Mouvement Populaire (which was formed in 1957 but not granted immediate legal recognition) because they felt that it more adequately represented their needs than the urban Arab-dominated parties then in existence. The Mouvement Populaire, as a Berber-oriented party, has since received the support of a large number of Berber electors in subsequent political undertakings, but this does not mean that Berbers uniformly support the party as a simple function of their ethnic identity. Indeed, since a host of factors besides ethnicity are usually involved, it often happens that when elections do occur there is some crossing of party lines. Such was the case, for instance, in the parliamentary election of the Sefrou district in 1963.

At that time candidates were put forward from each of the three main parties, the two most important being Istiqlal and FDIC (Front pour la Défense des Institutions Constitutionelles). This latter was an *ad hoc* coalition, including the Mouvement Populaire, devoted to the support of the king and his programs. The FDIC candidate for this constituency was, moreover, a government minister, a distant relative of the king (and thus an Alawite *sharif*), and brother of the *pasha* (appointed mayor) of the city of Sefrou itself. The Istiqlal candidate, on the other hand, was the director of the local poorhouse. More importantly, though, he was a local man with numerous local connections as opposed to the FDIC candidate, an outsider to this particular region. All of the candidates involved were, however, Arabs.

Now in theory the Berbers, who generally voice strong support for the Mouvement Populaire and whose leaders had been urged by party officials to support the FDIC candidate, should have voted quite solidly for the coalition candidate. In fact, a large number did. However, a very substantial number of Berbers felt that the FDIC candidate, being an outsider, would be wholly concerned with his ministerial duties and would not be as amenable to sharing the benefits of his office with the electorate as might his opponent. Consequently, for reasons that had little to do with either their Berber identity or their general support of the 'Berber Party' in other circumstances, many Berbers chose to cross over and vote for the candidate from the urban Arab-dominated Istiqlal Party. And because he also drew heavy support from other rural groups as well, the Istiqlal candidate did, in fact, win the election.

In this particular situation no one felt that the lines being drawn were those of Arabs versus Berbers in any sense. Had one of the candidates been a Berber perhaps the situation would have been different, but when such instances have occurred at other times it has also not been primarily in these terms that the elections were contested or the voters aligned.[1] In more general terms, one can note that, as Joan Vincent has put it

[1] For an example of such an election see my article 'Rural Political Process and National Political Structure in Morroco', in Richard T. Antoun and Iliya Harik (eds), *Rural Politics and Social Change in the Middle East*, Bloomington (in press).

... cultural pluralism becomes politically relevant only when differential access to positions of differing advantage is institutionalized in ethnic terms. The mere existence of social or cultural categories in the population is not enough to account for political cleavages: there must be politicization of ethnicity before we can talk of 'the politics of ethnicity'. Ethnicity *per se* is a cultural not a political variable. We must inquire, therefore, into the *process* of politicizing ethnicity and the ideology that validates it.[1]

In the Sefrou region—and for that matter throughout most of Morocco—the politicization of ethnicity, at least as it is expressed in electoral events, has never proceeded very far. In this particular locale the reason seems to lie in the fact that people prefer to be free to contract personal ties wherever they seem most advantageous rather than to allow momentary social or political alliances to form barriers across which such personal ties cannot be contracted at will. The emphasis is on personal networks of affiliation in which ethnicity is but one among a number of factors, and there are few people in the Sefrou area who are willing to sacrifice long-term eventualities to the binding exigencies of a short-term alliance. Elections in Morocco are, of course, rather rare events and it might therefore prove more fruitful to consider the politics of ethnicity in terms of the lines of political influence (for jobs, patronage, etc.) rather than the lines of voting support alone. None the less, on the basis of impressions rather than detailed data, it appears that ethnic lines are less a factor than ties of kinship, residence, and personally contracted bonds of association. In electoral politics proper, as in the axes of political influence, ethnicity is not a major factor in Sefrou, but as situations vary its relative centrality, at least as an idiom of expressing alignment, could conceivably shift as well.

Intermarriage between Arabs and Berbers

If there is only a certain hesitancy associated with economic relations between Arabs and Berbers and even less associated with political events there is, by contrast, a sharper sort of barrier of interaction associated with marriage between members of each group. The figures on this are quite clear. As Table 7.1 indicates, in 1960 in the city of Sefrou proper less than one married couple in eight (11·3%) was composed of partners of different ethnic backgrounds. Within this group marriages between Berber men and Arab women are found to occur three times more often (8·6%) than unions between Arab men and Berber women (2·7%). The figures thus reveal not only a high rate of ethnic endogamy but sustain the impression gained from many informants that some Berber men regard marriage to Arab wives as a form of 'marrying up' socially.

[1] Anthropology and Political Development', in Colin Leys (ed), *Politics and Change in Developing Countries*, Cambridge, 1969, p. 52.

Table 7.1   Marriages between Arabs and Berbers in Sefrou (1960 Census)

	Arab men		Berber men		Totals
Arab women	96·5	N = 1403	38·7	N = 160	N = 1563
		89·8		10·2	100
Berber women	3·5	N = 51	61·3	N = 253	N = 304
		16·8		83·2	100
	100	N = 1454	100	N = 413	N = 1867

Note: Figures in the upper left-hand corner of each quadrant represent the percentage of men of each category married to women of each category while figures in the lower right-hand corners represent the percentage of women of each category married to men of each category. Numbers of couples sampled are indicated in the upper right-hand corners. Source: compiled from data in Hildred Geertz, *A Profile of a Moroccan Town : Sefrou 1960*, Tables 2.8.1–2.8.3 (mimeographed).

These figures can, however, give a misleading impression of both the extent of ethnic group endogamy and its relative importance when a series of more discriminating indices are taken into account. The figures in Table 7.1 do not, for example, take into account such factors as economic background, residence, or length of time the various parties have lived in Sefrou. They do not show the frequency with which urban Arab men marry Arab women of rural origins, or whether the Berber men who marry Sefrou Arab women come from equal or higher economic backgrounds. When, however, we look at the gross figures concerned with the rates of endogamy for groups defined in terms of residential origins it becomes clear that there is a general tendency for a person to marry members not only of his own ethnic group but persons with whom he shares certain other characteristics, particularly social origins (Table 7.2). Thus, the rates of ethnic group endogamy alone do not prove that ethnicity (as opposed, say, to economic background, residential origins, etc.) is the really crucial factor, but when one also considers certain qualitative data for each form of endogamy a good case can indeed be made for ethnic identity alone being a significant if not all-pervasive factor in the selection of mates.

Table 7.2   Social group endogamy in Sefrou (1960 Census percentages)

	Sefrou-born Arabs	Rural-born Arabs	Rural-born Berbers
Men marrying women of their own social group	83·4	63·0	62·9
Women marrying men of their own social group	71·7	71·9	79·1
Percentage of total population	34·9	23·4	12·1

Source: Hildred Geertz, op. cit., Tables 2.8.1 – 2.8.2.

In the case of ethnic group endogamy the attitudes expressed by informants make these figures quite understandable. Berbers often attribute their reluctance to marry their daughters to Arabs to the fact that Arab men seclude their women and do not allow them the freedom to which Berber women are accustomed among their own people. Arabs, in turn, regard Berbers as less cultivated and, given the freedom of their women, too used to dealing freely with members of the opposite sex to be trusted around their own women. The women in an Arab bride's family are reluctant to have as in-laws women who will speak another language and possess different backgrounds from their own, while Berber men often find it preferable to shore up existing relations with fellow kinsmen through the endogamous marriage of a son or daughter. A wide range of reasons is, then, given by all the relatives of the principals for prefering one mate or another, but unless the person is a close neighbor or associate about whose homelife one has some detailed knowledge there is a clear tendency to avoid inter-ethnic marriages. The statistics themselves do not permit us to say that ethnicity is the only factor involved here, but there can be no doubt that it is indeed a significant contributing factor.

AN ANALYSIS OF ARAB–BERBER RELATIONS

For students of North African society the distinction between Arab and Berber has always appeared obvious and useful. It categorizes large numbers of people into discrete entities distinguished and labeled in the same ways in which the subjects themselves appear to handle the situation. In fact, however, the Arab–Berber distinction is generally drawn at a higher level of abstraction and reified into a more significant axis of division than the data itself would sustain. It is true that in central Morocco, for example, the terms *chleuh* (berber) and *arab*[1] are used in normal conversation, but the two are neither strict polar opposites nor more importantly, the main level at which others are perceived or relationships formed. The Berbers of any region of Morocco do not express or enact solidarity with all those who speak their dialect of Berber (much less with those speaking other forms of the language) as opposed to Arab speakers, and within any particular locale there are few situations in which people can be shown to be relating to one another simply as Arabs or Berbers rather than in terms of a much finer set of discriminants refering to family ties, occupation, residence, and economic level. What one must not do, therefore, is take the distinction Arab versus Berber as the initial or end point of one's investigation. Rather than just assuming its validity or primacy it is perhaps preferable to ask the question: What sort of information do the people of central Morocco communicate to one another about the various sources of their personal identities and what does the knowledge of another's ethnic background actually contribute to the way in which a man is perceived and related to by others in a series of different social

[1] The term *arab* can, in theory, also signify any rural dweller regardless of his ethnicity, although in actual practice the usual term for a person living in the countryside is *arubi*.

situations? Phrasing the question in this way allows us to avoid any presuppositions about the importance of ethnicity in the overall conceptual and relational scheme while at the same time allowing us to factor it out for separate investigation when such an exercise seems appropriate.

We can begin our own attempt at such an analysis by recalling some of the points we raised earlier about the social sources of a man's personal identity. Here we saw that ethnicity was only one among a series of identities ranging from ancestral origins and the subdivision of an extended kin group, through personal nicknames, occupation, quarter of residence, and ethnic background, to identity based on the city or region in which a man now lives and indeed his identity as a Moroccan and a Muslim. Each of these identifications has relevance in different situations but this does not mean that there is a simple hierarchy of situations precisely and uniquely correlated with some level of identification. For all of these features find their touchstone not in a set of discrete and ever more highly ramified corporate groupings but constitute bits of information cumulated and realized within each individual person. In Sefrou society, the primary focus is on the particular pattern of features cohering in a single individual, and since relations are mainly between two persons rather than two groups (or individuals simply as representatives of two groups) it is the cumulation of personal ties and traits, defined and perceived through the distinctively Moroccan cultural screen, that constitutes the essential focus when two Moroccans confront one another. Of course, as situations vary certain features of overall social identity may take on more importance—at least in the eyes of particular kinds of beholders—than they do in other contexts. And this is as true, say, for family identity or educational background as for ethnic group affiliations. One can, therefore, choose any one of these features and run it through a series of situational tests in order to determine the relative importance of a given feature for the conduct of the participants. This was done in the second section of our paper when the feature of ethnic identity was considered in a series of specific situational contexts.

Thus when we looked at the importance of ethnic identity in the formation of clientele relations several important factors became evident: first, that such relations involve risking a certain degree of personal independence and reliability as well as hard cash; secondly, that in risking trust and independence it is desirable to possess those additional checks on the other's behavior that may be supplied by common bonds of kinship, residence, or conceptual orientation; and, thirdly, that the absence of such cross-cutting ties may be strong enough to impede but not fully prohibit inter-ethnic clientele relations, particularly those between rural Berbers and urban Arab merchants. In the political domain, the quest for influence, jobs, education, and government loans may lead Berbers to identify broadly with one political party and Arabs with another. However, in electoral situations, the emphasis on the whole of any candidate's traits and ties, the present disillusionment with (and government encouraged disinterest in) political party organization generally, and the tendency not to allow momentary political alliances to prevent a man from forming ties wherever they seem most advantageous all contribute to the politically selective force exercised by the ethnic distinction. Finally, in the case of intermarriage, where the symbols of cultural distinctiveness express different conceptions of the role of women and the preferred composition of the household proper, a much more forceful barrier exists which is capable of seriously impeding the rate of interaction. In sum, then, when we choose ethnicity as the feature to be tested by situational analysis it is clear that in no case is it the only variable operative and indeed— even in the case of intermarriage, where all social groups were seen to be highly endogamous—it seldom appears to be the major factor at work influencing specific behavior.

If we may tentatively conclude that ethnicity is only one among a series of factors operative in various situations and that it serves as only one among a set of social identifiers we can then ask the question: just what does this piece of information about a man contribute generally to another's perception of and relationship to him? What is really learned from knowing a man's ethnic identity and how does it relate to the process of information gathering that also includes reference to other features of his total social identification? As an initial step in the direction of answering these questions it might prove useful to consider a distinction drawn by the philosopher-sociologist, Alfred Schutz.

Briefly stated, Schutz argues that in any society one can make an analytic distinction between persons (called consociates) who actually confront one another in intimate face-to-face relations and persons (designated by Schutz as contemporaries) who are defined almost wholly by the structural positions they occupy *vis-à-vis* one another. The former are treated as total personalities whose individual characteristics are of vital importance, whereas the latter, defined mainly by the roles they play, are regarded as more stereotyped and anonymous occupants of particular positions.[1] More interesting still is the fact that for all the analytical distinction that can be made between these two types of persons in every society, certain cultures tend to treat both categories as if they were in fact kinds of only one of these types. In Bali, for example, people tend to categorize even their closest associates in an all-pervasive scheme of role and status positions such that it is the structural category rather than the whole personality of another that constitutes the primary indicator for one's perception of and relationship to a given individual.[2] By contrast, Moroccans tend to regard all persons, whether or not they have actually come into face-to-face contact, as kinds of consociates, persons who possess distinct and multidimensional personalities and with whom one is actually or potentially linked not in a set of particulate structural roles but in the totality of one's individuality.[3] Instead of trying to establish their respective positions through the elaboration of definitive titles, names, or other structural indicators, Moroccans utilize the information about one another's

[1] Alfred Schutz, *Collected Papers*, Vol. I, The Hague, 1962, pp. 15–19; and *The Phenomenology of the Social World*, Evanston, 1967, pp. 139–214.

[2] Clifford Geertz, *Person, Time, and Conduct in Bali: an Essay in Cultural Analysis*, Yale University Southeast Asian Studies Cultural Report Series No. 14, New Haven, 1966.

[3] For an application of this concept to relations between Moslems and Jews in Morocco see my 'Moslem-Jewish relations in a Moroccan city', *International Journal of Middle East Studies* (in press).

social backgrounds—and particularly that which refers to the individuals through whom such links, however tenuous, can be found to bind them together—to explore the bases on which their particular relationship can be worked out within the overall chain of consociation that unites all individuals together into a single community of men.

This emphasis on consociate relationships is relevant to the consideration of any feature of social identity including the particular topic with which we are concerned here, namely Arab–Berber relations. For it can be argued that since it is the regularized ways in which individuals form various personal and contractual ties with one another that constitute the major focus of Moroccan social structure, knowledge of another's ethnicity serves to supply certain baseline data about another's most probable characteristics, ties with others, and customary ways of forming new face-to-face relations with others. The minimal, baseline information derived from the knowledge of another's ethnic background contributes, therefore, to the transition to that second level of conceptualization in which a particular consociate relationship is formed. In other words, the information supplied by a knowledge of ethnic affiliation, though it remains a relatively incomplete means of typifying another person, does indicate the bases upon which the implicit relation of intimate and personal consociation can be made manifest as an actual dyadic bond. The existence of this second stage of conceptualization, treated here under the rubric of consociation, thereby utilizes the baseline information of ethnicity, residence, kin bonds, and so on but places primary emphasis on the superordinate level of perception and relationship in which all men have the potential for forming contractual ties with one another without being limited by ethnic origins or any other single feature of their overall social identities.

If the image of consociation indicates the role a knowledge of ethnic identity plays in the two-stages process of cultural conceptualization, it remains necessary, at the very least, to probe further into the actual mechanisms through which this information is communicated and ordered. When, for example, two people of different ethnic backgrounds encounter one another directly what are the characteristics into which each inquires, what sort of form does this exchange of information take, and what do both the form and content of this communication tell us about the relative importance of ethnicity and its relation to the other aspects of one's social identity? Again, a great deal depends on the context in which we choose to study such an exchange of information and space does not allow us to look at the full range of non-verbal factors associated with each man's perception and evaluation of another. As a touchstone for the argument to be developed here, we might, however, begin with a model conversation similar to those that often occur between two strangers, in this case an urban Arab merchant and his potential Berber client:

B   As-alamu alaikum.
A   W-alaikum salam.
B   Do you have any material for children's clothing?
A   Look, I have all kinds.

B How much is this one?

A Sixty rials per meter.

B That's a great deal. Give me a reasonable price.

A How much do you say it is?

B Forty, no more.

A Oh no, this is good cloth—first quality.

B Forty is enough; even Moulay Ali sells it for that.

A Oh, you know Moulay Ali?

B Sure. And his cousin Moulay Hamed. I buy a lot of groceries from Moulay Hamed. I'm a good client.

A He has some farmland near your settlement?

B No, his land is over by Kerruz, along the river. I live a few kilometers away, beyond the Ait Yahya settlement.

A Then you are from the Ait Mohand? [a Berber tribal segment].

B That's right.

A I know people there: Moha ou Hadou and his brother Hamou.

B Oh yes? They are here today. We came together to sell some sheep.

A Is there enough grazing for all your sheep this year?

B Not by our settlement. I keep mine with relatives in the hills. Except for those I sell Si Mustapha, the butcher. He's a good friend of mine.

A I buy from him myself. You know everyone in town.

B Of course. So how much for the cloth?

A Look, my brother, I'll do you a favor. Take it for forty-five.

B Is this really good cloth?

A Absolutely. On my ancestor Moulay Idriss, it is so.

B All right. Wrap it up. And if you give me good prices I'll buy from you regularly.

A Inshallah ('God willing').

B Inshallah.

This conversation is, of course, rather idealized. In fact the actual process of discerning another's background, characteristics, connections, etc. would be far more elaborate, discontinuous, and subtle. Each would inquire of third parties about the other and would thus gain a feel for the other's reliability and usefulness to oneself. However, after experience with many such encounters continuing over long periods of time and taking place in a variety of different situations one begins to note certain features about the form of communication being carried out and the way in which the quest for information about ethnicity and other social identifiers accords with the ideas expressed on this general subject by the educator-linguist, Basil Bernstein.

Bernstein argues that the particular forms of social relations that are operative in any one society give rise to rather different linguistic codes through which individuals transmit vital information about themselves. The codes, in turn, serve to orient the speakers toward certain kinds of relationships that bind them together. Specifically, Bernstein says, two main kinds of codes can be distinguished. Restricted codes arise from situations in which a tightly-knit group of

6*

individuals—such as a prison community, a group of adolescents, or the members of an academic department—possess an 'extensive set of closely shared identifications, self-consciously held by the members'.[1] In the case of restricted code usage,

> . . . the speech is played out against a backdrop of assumptions common to the speakers, against a set of closely shared interests and identifications, against a system of shared expectations; in short, it presupposes a local cultural identity which reduces the need for the speakers to express their intent verbally and to make it explicit.[2]

Because they share so many assumptions those using a restricted code in any given situation are, in the context of this constraining form of communication, indicating their relative role and status positions far more than they are probing into one another's total personalities. Thus, 'the unique meaning of the individual is likely to be implicit'[3] in the communication and the more restricted the communication the less one can predict another's individual attributes. One has only to think of the almost ritualized forms of communication at cocktail parties, diplomatic occasions, religious events, or the shorthand idioms of a group of specialists to find examples of such usage.

An elaborated code, on the other hand,

> . . . will develop to the extent that the discrete intent of the other person may *not* be taken for granted. Inasmuch as the other person's intent may not be taken for granted, then the speaker is forced to expand and elaborate his meanings, with the consequence that he chooses more carefully among syntactic and vocabulary options.[4]

An elaborated code thus 'encourages the speaker to focus upon the other person as an experience different from his own. An elaborated code is *person* rather than status oriented'.[5] Indeed, in so far as an elaborated code is not, like a restricted code, 'refracted through the implications of the status arrangements',[6] it permits a far more highly ramified concept not only of others but also of one's own self as a distinctive personality.

Now if one looks at the relations between Arabs and Berbers in the Sefrou region in terms of Bernstein's distinctions several important features can be noted. As our schematic conversation shows, in their initial contacts with and conceptualizations of one another an Arab and a Berber are, fundamentally, dealing in terms of a rather restricted code. From the form of greeting and

[1] Basil Bernstein, 'Elaborated and restricted codes: their social origins and some consequences', in John J. Gumperz and Dell Hymes (eds), *The Ethnography of Communication*, American Anthropologist Special Publication, Vol. 66, No. 6, Part 2 (December 1964), p. 61.

[2] Ibid., p. 60.

[3] Basil Bernstein, 'A socio-linguistic approach to social learning', *Penguin Survey of the Social Sciences 1965*, Harmondsworth and Baltimore, 1965, p. 156.

[4] Basil Bernstein, 'Elaborated and restricted codes', op. cit., p. 63.

[5] Ibid.

[6] Basil Bernstein, 'A socio-linguistic approach', op. cit., p. 161.

the recognition of one's dress and accent, through the routinized inquiry into the sources of one another's nurture (place of residence, occupation, etc.), to the inquiry into who one knows and what intermediate persons fill in the missing links between oneself and the other an almost set scenario is played out. However, once this restricted code has indicated the bases of another's social identity and the grounds that are now perceived for establishing a face-to-face, personal relationship the possibility exists for using a more elaborated code that probes into the other's overall personality and tests for the kinds of relationships that can be formed with him. And since it is the social relationship that precedes the entire communication, namely one in which all individuals are seen as linked in consociate forms that merely need to be uncovered, movement into an elaborated code is an almost inevitable result. Thus, even in what may seem the most casual of interactions—say, in the communication between a buyer and a seller—the initial use of a restricted code to determine the bases for further interaction is quickly superseded by the use of an elaborate code to discover a desirable form of interpersonal relationship. The choice and timing involved in the use of different codes elicits, stabilizes, strengthens, and models one person's orientations toward another. Ethnicity, then, defines, through the mediation of a restricted code, the bases on which an elaborated code can be implemented for establishing a particular kind of consociate relationship with men of quite different ethnic backgrounds.

Bernstein himself has suggested that 'the ability to switch codes controls the ability to switch roles',[1] and indeed there is a sense in which the emphasis of one's ethnic affiliation can be regarded as the playing of a role. F. K. Lehman, for example, argues quite convincingly that in Burma 'ethnic categories are formally like roles'[2] and that given the political plurality of the country it is to the advantage of ethnic minorities to possess several ambiguous identities that can be enacted, like roles, as the situation varies. In so far as Berbers or Arabs may indeed identify with members of their own grouping one can, perhaps, say that ethnic identity is at times given a role-like quality in Morocco. But in most instances ethnicity is used simply to establish what another's most probable traits and ties are and how a personal bond of consociation, colored but in no sense wholly determined by ethnic background, can now be established. Only in such instances as intermarriage, where cultural differences apparently restrict rather free intermingling, does a significant barrier to full interaction exist. But even this eventuality may be as much a function of differences of education, economics, and urban–rural residence as of ethnicity as such.

In sum, then, ethnicity in this part of contemporary Morocco, is a factor of quite differential importance, a factor that varies with situational contexts and the additional affiliations by which each of the participants is characterized. Identity as a Berber or an Arab is not, however, in almost any context an all-pervasive typification in terms of which one views and relates to another person.

[1] Ibid., p. 157.
[2] F. K. Lehman, 'Ethnic categories in Burma and the theory of social systems', in Peter Kunstadter (ed), *Southeast Asian Tribes, Minorities, and Nations*, Princeton, 1967, pp. 106–7.

Each of the social groupings is only quite imperfectly isolated in reality and hence only quite imperfectly isolable for analytic study. Nor are the categories themselves seen as mutually exclusive: those rural Arabs living in the territory of the Ait Yusi Berber 'tribe', for example, see no contradiction between the fact that they are Arab-speakers and the fact that they identify themselves and are identified by others as Ait Yusi. Similarly, Berbers living among Arab-speakers in an urban environment see no more inherent a contradiction between their cultural identification as Berbers and the dominant Arab culture of the city than does a person of Irish or Italian descent necessarily regard the cultural features he displays as a member of a particular ethnic group as inherently opposed to his identity as an American citizen. To speak, therefore, of the Arabization of Berbers as if they had to dispense with their identity as the latter to achieve inclusion as a member of the former is to fail to appreciate that the two categories are simply not totally antithetical to begin with.[1]

Indeed, as we have argued, the primary emphasis in this society seems to be placed on the regularized ways in which two individuals can contract a personal bond of affiliation in order to secure the bases of their own well-being. In order for each person to take fullest advantage of the contractual social ties available to him he seeks information about others that is relevant to an understanding of who that person is and how he does or may relate to people like himself. Identity as a Berber or an Arab supplies some of this information, for each man starts not only with a generalized stereotype of other kinds of people but an awareness that people of different backgrounds tend to possess different kinds of traits and ties and tend, therefore, to form relationships with others in terms of specific customary ways. Through the use of a restricted linguistic code this fundamental information is communicated to others. But almost immediately this fundamental data, this baseline conceptualization, gives way to a more elaborated, open-ended probe into the totality of the other's social personality. The possibility of such a probe is not only a necessary consequence of the fact that all men see themselves as linked in a chain of face-to-face relations that knows no totally impermeable barriers, but itself serves to establish the basis on which any particular dyadic relation is going to be formed. Thus the recognition of a common friend, an experience in the army, difficulty finding a job, or a broadly similar geographical origin may serve as a basis for a personal relationship as patron–client, political ally, or potential go-between. Once a slightly more than

[1] A popular stereotype, found most often among the contemporary urban Arab elite, is noted by the Lacoutures when they argue that: 'To be Berber is, quite simply to be *not yet Arabized* . . . Perhaps only one [trait] is common to all the Berber-speakers: the taste for opposition, above all verbal; for contradictory debate. This hardly facilitates the formation of a constant and constructive policy towards them.' Jean and Simone Lacouture, *Le Maroc à l'épreuve* (Ch. iv, 'Comment peut-on être Berbère?'), Paris, 1958, pp. 83, 96 (original italics). Increased migration to the cities and the achievement of higher levels of education will doubtless result in greater absorption by the Berbers of Arabic language forms, but to characterize this as a shift in ethnic identity is to fail to appreciate that Arab and Berber are simply not mutually exclusive categories in the first instance. On the broader relations between language and social identity in North Africa see Charles F. Gallagher, 'Language and identity', in Leon Carl Brown (ed), *State and Society in Independent North Africa*, Washington, D.C., 1966, pp. 73–96.

casual acquaintance has been established this delving into another's being will progress through a highly ramified series of conceptual categorizations influenced but not necessarily fully determined at any point by the facts of any one particular trait or tie.

Treated as an ordered system of categories in terms of which the experience of another is perceived and articulated, ethnic identity serves to indicate some of the bases of possible relationship to those who choose to actualize such latent bonds while it defines in rather vague and minimal detail the essential features of those members of the opposite ethnic group with whom a direct tie of consociation has yet to be realized. Ethnicity, like other social indicators in Morocco, distinguishes men as kinds of persons without at the same time separating them from rather full social intercourse. Indeed, in so far as there is a clear tendency to resist the establishment of any sharp lines of affiliation and identification in this part of Morocco, all studies that confront the question of Arab–Berber relations are forced to view them as the Moroccans themselves do— as contingent and partial rather than complete and pervasive features of each man's social identity. To approach the question of social relations in Morocco mainly in terms of ethnic differences is to perpetuate the same error of misplaced concreteness of which the French themselves were so guilty:[1] it is to give a reified and primary status to a distinction which, in actual operation, is of more ambiguous and subsidiary importance. By considering ethnicity as just one of the features that can be factored out for analysis without having its particular importance unnecessarily exaggerated, and by concentrating primarily on the overall system into which such a feature fits one can avoid dichotomizing the categories 'Berber' and 'Arab' and appreciate how each of these attributes relates to the whole conceptual and relational scheme so characteristic of contemporary Moroccan society.[2]

[1] This mistaken reification of the Arab–Berber distinction, like that between the *bled es-siba* and the *bled el-makhzan*, developed only in the years just prior to and following the establishment of the Protectorate. Earlier investigators appear to have been able to approach the Moroccan system with somewhat less rigid presuppositions. Thus, at the turn of the century E. Doutté was able to write: '... le vocable de "berbère" n'a de sens précis qu'en linguistique où il désigne un ensemble de dialectes étroitement unis par des caractères communs et c'est vraisemblablement dans ce sens qu'il fût pris à l'origine. On peut donc si l'on veut répartir les Africains en berberophones et arabophones; en nomades et en sédentaires; en nombreux types anatomiques distincts: mais la classification ethnique, en arabe et en berbère ne correspond à aucun fait concret susceptible d'être précisé.' 'Une Mission d'études au Maroc. Rapport sommaire d'ensemble renseignements coloniaux', *Bulletin du Comité de l'Afrique Française*, No. 8, 1901, p. 166.

[2] As Jacques Berque has put it: 'The analysis of Maghrib societies requires, not a distinction between what may be "Berber", "Arab", or "French", but criteria that would trace, with respect to the Maghrib personality, the greater or lesser coherence or dynamism achieved in the integration of heterogeneous characteristics and in the respones of a group to its milieu.' 'The rural system of the Maghrib', in Leon Carl Brown, op. cit., p.194.

8
The Image of the Moroccan State in French Ethnological Literature: a New Look at the Origin of Lyautey's Berber Policy

Edmund Burke III

The image of the native and of native society in the European colonial mind has long been a good indicator of the prejudices and pre-suppositions with which the colonizer approached the subject people. Books like Philip D. Curtin's *The Image of Africa: British Ideas and Action, 1780–1850* have accustomed us to examine these images for the insights which they give us into the mind of the colonizer, and of the ways in which these stereotyped views of the colonized people influenced the planning of policy toward them. During the early period of European penetration into Africa which Curtin deals with, the prejudices and stereotypes remained relatively close to the surface. Later, with the coming of a more self-confident style of imperialism toward the end of the nineteenth century, and the invention of such concepts as dual mandate, these prejudices became less obvious, although still important. Their impact can be observed, for example, in the pragmatic, empirical, 'scientific' system of native administration adopted by the French in Morocco during the years 1912–1919. The Morocco of Lyautey, in fact, forms an especially good laboratory within which to study the curious inter-relations between colonial sociology, native policy, and French perceptions of Morocco.

The image of Morocco which one finds in French ethnological literature has been characterized by a composite stereotype about the nature of the Moroccan state and Moroccan society. In general this view of Morocco and the Moroccan past has emphasized the division of the realm into two zones, one where the central government (the *makhzan*) was supreme, taxes were collected, governors governed, and laws were respected, and the other where the central government was impotent, and unruly tribes devoted their time to feuding and banditry. Under the rubric of *Bled el-makhzan* and *Bled es-siba*, the portrait of a regime divided between contradictory tendencies toward autocratic order and anarchy, in which neither was able to gain the upper hand has gained widespread acceptance.[1] Closely interwoven with this image has been a second one, a view of a profound ethnic split in Moroccan society between Arabs and Berbers. The course of Moroccan history before the protectorate was seen as the efforts of the Arab government forces to impose themselves upon the Berber dissidents. A more detailed examination of the major elements of this compound stereotype of Morocco will be undertaken here. On the whole this image of Morocco was the product of the colonial period, and while it still remains a persuasive one in some respects, it has not gone without criticism.

[1] The powerful influence of the concept can be seen for example in Carleton Coon, *Caravan: the Story of the Middle East*, New York, 1958, pp. 309–23, where it is used to explain the course of Middle Eastern history.

In the first flush of enthusiasm following decolonization, Moroccan nationalists proposed a counter-image of the Moroccan state, which denied the importance of the dichotomous divisions which played such a role in colonial historiography. The image which they suggested in its place was one of a quasi-democratic and constitutional monarchy, where the choice of sultan was ratified by the signing of the *bay'a*, a proclamation drawn up by the corps of religious scholars (*ulama*), and the urban notables and tribal chiefs. According to this view the Moroccan monarchy was not only elective, it was also conditional, since restrictions on the power of the sultan could be written into the *bay'a* document itself. The early revisionist historians also emphasized the significance of the various modernization schemes which had been adopted by the *makhzan* during the nineteenth century, and suggested that if Morocco had not been brutally conquered by France in 1912, it would have achieved a modern political form on its own.[1] This counter-view of Morocco has not gained much acceptance among professional historians, however, and it has recently been implicitly repudiated in a new Moroccan history textbook.[2] Thus the first attempts to present a new image of Morocco's past and to destroy the existing stereotypes must be judged a failure— although one with which it is possible to sympathize. French stereotypes, however, cannot be challenged by the mere erection of an opposing set of Moroccan stereotypes about the nature of the Moroccan state and Moroccan society. The effort to decolonize Moroccan history will call for careful research into the Moroccan past and a firm historical judgment, and can only be achieved as part of the wider search for authenticity on the part of Moroccan historians and Moroccan society as a whole. In this way the struggle for Morocco's past will rejoin the newly independent nations' search for a viable national culture. Such an effort is not my task here.

This study springs instead from the conviction that before a revised image of Morocco can be generated, it may be more fruitful to examine the image of Morocco in French ethnological literature, its origins, development, and influence. The study which follows will therefore seek to answer the question of how the present dichotomous view of Morocco came to dominate the literature. It will then go on to trace the impact of this image upon policy, with special reference to the development of France's Berber policy in Morocco. While not a detailed study of Berber policy *per se*, this essay is conceived of as a necessary preliminary to a further exploration of this topic—one which seeks to place Berber policy within the larger framework of the complicated interaction of colonial ideology, French policy, and French scholarship on Morocco.

Before beginning the investigation of the various phases which the development of a composite stereotype about the nature of Moroccan society went through, it may be well to examine the constituent elements of this stereotype

---

[1] Mohamed Lahbabi, *Le Gouvernement marocain à l'aube de XXᵉ siècle*, Rabat, 1957; and Abdelaziz Benabdullah, *Les Grands Courants de la civilization du Maghreb*, Tangier, 1957. On these books, see the review article of Ernest Gellner, 'The struggle for Morocco's past', *Middle East Journal*, 1961, pp. 79–90.

[2] Jean Brignon *et al.*, *Histoire du Maroc*, Paris, 1966, makes but little mention of the revisionist thesis.

as they emerge from the classic work on Moroccan history, Henri Terrasse's *Histoire du Maroc*.[1] The conceptions which we will insist upon here include the following: the nature of the Islamic state and of the sultan's authority, the notion of Berber and Arab, the notion of *makhzan* and *siba*, the nature of Moroccan Islam (and the role of *sharif*s, marabouts, and Sufi brotherhoods), and the idea of Morocco's isolation and backwardness. These conceptions fit together into a coherent image of pre-protectorate Moroccan society which, as will be seen, was not without its influence on the development of the protectorate and the policy toward the Berbers which was adopted under the protectorate. This overall image of Morocco we may call the Moroccan Vulgate.[2]

Terrasse's Morocco, for all of the strong points of that otherwise admirable work, is the Morocco of the Moroccan Vulgate, presented with vividness and style. According to Terrasse, the pre-colonial Moroccan state can be divided into *bled el-makhzan* and *bled es-siba*. The former zone he portrays as constituting 'neither a firm bloc nor a coherent force; it was only the coalition, maintained by force, of the directing and profiting elements—the *makhzan* and the guich (Ar. *jaysh*, or military) tribes—in passive resignation'.[3] *Bled es-siba*, on the other hand, is portrayed as profoundly divided by the ancient rivalries of clans, tribes and *leff*s (moieties), marked by feuding, and incapable of opposing a coherent resistance to the *makhzan*.[4] The leitmotif of Moroccan politics before the coming of the French consisted of the ceaseless efforts of the *makhzan* to impose its authority upon the rebellious tribes of *siba*-land, and their constant defense of their independence.[5] Islam was unable to supply the 'moral unity' which would have enabled the sultans to bring about the political unity of the country.[6] The *makhzan–siba* division, moreover, coincided with a profound ethnic cleavage of Moroccan society into Arab and Berber.[7] The Berbers, whom Terrasse sees as the original inhabitants of the country, were only superficially Islamicized and retained the core of their old natural paganism, as expressed in a host of superstitious practices and the heterodox nature of their Islam. They opposed Islamic law, and the establishment of *makhzan* administration among them. Instead, they settled disputes through application of their own customary laws, and regulated their society by tribal councils, or *jama'a* which were marked by a democratic spirit.[8] They were preferred to retain their own language and customs, rather than come under the domination of the central government. According to Terrasse, the clash of *makhzan* and *siba* was therefore far more than one between administrators and rebels. Rather, it was the continuation of a profound and

---

[1] Henri Terrasse, *Histoire du Maroc*, Casablanca, 1950, 2 vols.

[2] The concept of a Moroccan Vulgate has been derived from the conception of an Algerian Vulgate put forward by Charles-Robert Ageron as a means of describing the colonial stereotypes about Algerian society. Cf. his important essay, 'La France a-t-elle eu une politique Kabyle?' *Revue historique*, CCXXIII (1960), pp. 311–52, and its later reworking in his thesis, *Les Algériens musulmans et la France*, Paris, 1968, 2 vols.

[3] Terrasse, op. cit. II, p. 357.

[4] Ibid.

[5] Ibid., pp. 357–8.

[6] Ibid., p. 423.

[7] Ibid., p. 433.

[8] Ibid., pp. 307, 410.

age-old dispute between Arabo-Islamic civilization and the ancient Berber race.[1] Only the weakness of the *makhzan* and the divisions amongst the Berbers kept one side or the other from triumphing. A kind of weak Moroccan empire was maintained in being because while the sultan did not enjoy political sovereignty over the Berbers, he was respected and venerated by them as a religious leader, so that they would willingly follow his lead in a holy war against European invaders, for example.[2] Still, Morocco had never been a nation at any time in its history, and only under the Almoravids and Almohads had it ever been a state.[3] In the end, Terrasse asserts, the precarious equilibrium between the two sides had persisted largely because of the isolation of Morocco. The apparent anomaly of a society which was marked by no significant change or development Terrasse explains by the idea that Morocco was 'fiercely withdrawn into itself'.[4] Thus partly by accident, partly by design, Morocco arrived at the twentieth century with the form of a medieval Muslim monarchy. This, in brief, is the Moroccan Vulgate in its fully developed form. But when did it come into being, and how did it affect the development of the protectorate?

THE PARADOX: EARLY VIEWS OF MOROCCO (1900–1904)

Before 1904 the image of Morocco which was presented in French journals like the *Bulletin* of the Comité de l'Afrique Française (the most important of the periodicals devoted to colonial affairs) was remarkably undogmatic, tentative, and flexible. With the exception of a few travelers' reports, and the observations of French diplomats posted to Morocco (who rarely traveled), France possessed surprisingly little reliable information on Morocco in 1900, when the Moroccan Question was first broached by the French occupation of the Touat oasis complex in the central Sahara.[5] Between 1900 and 1904, the major outlines of the Moroccan state and of Moroccan society were unveiled by French scholars following a series of study missions to Morocco sponsored by the Comité de l'Afrique Française. The dominant figure of these early expeditions to Morocco was sociologist-ethnologist Edmond Doutté, who between 1900 and 1904 made three missions to Morocco, chiefly traveling through the province of Marrakesh. He was to make two more major expeditions to Morocco in the years which followed. Intellectually, Doutté had been strongly influenced by Emile Durkheim and Sir James Frazer, and was a recognized student of Algerian Islam.[6] Up

[1] Ibid., pp. 412, 418, 433.
[2] Ibid., pp. 362–3.
[3] Ibid., p. 422.
[4] Ibid., p. 361.
[5] Among the travelers' reports, one especially is worth citing, Charles de Foucauld, *Reconnaissances au Maroc, 1883–1884*, Paris, 1888. The one exception to his general paucity of information was the Algero-Moroccan border zone, where the remarkable work of H. M. P. Lamartinière and N. Lacroix, *Documents pour servir à l'étude du nord-ouest africain*, Algiers, 1894–7, 4 vols, stands out.
[6] Doutté is one of the most underrated students of Moroccan society, known chiefly for his books *Marrakech*, Paris, 1905, and *En Tribu*, Paris, 1914, which do not do him justice. The reports of his missions published in *Renseignements coloniaux*, supplement to *Afrique française* from 1901 show him in a much better light.

until 1904 the published reports of Doutté's findings on Morocco constituted the most complete description of Moroccan provincial society available. The other major student of Morocco during the early period of French involvement was a young diplomat attached to the staff of the Tangier Legation, Eugène Aubin Descos. He wrote what is still regarded as the best single book on pre-protectorate Morocco, the classic, *Le Maroc d'aujourd'hui*.[1] Especially considering that he knew no Arabic, Descos's book is a remarkable effort, demonstrating his keen powers of observation and shrewd judgments with every page. Both his book and Doutté's reports are still remarkable for their lack of preconceived ideas about the nature of Moroccan society. Two other individuals should perhaps be mentioned as contributing to French views of Morocco prior to 1905: Augustin Bernard, an expert on eastern Morocco[2] and the Marquis de Segonzac, an explorer who traveled through the Rif mountains, the Middle Atlas, and the Sous valley.[3] Neither was to have much of a role in shaping French ideas about Morocco during the period 1900 to 1904, however.

One of the paradoxes which the student of Moroccan history who has been raised on the brusque dichotomous formulations of the Moroccan Vulgate must confront is how this image could have come into being when the early work on Morocco shows such sensitivity to nuance. The discussion of the division of Morocco into *makhzan* and *siba*, for example, which one finds in Doutté or Aubin is a far cry from later dogmatisms on the subject. 'The expression of *blad el-makhzan* opposed to that of *blad es-siba* is not correct,' Doutté wrote in 1901, 'for all of Morocco under different forms and to varying degrees undergoes the action of the *makhzan*. . . .' He went on to point out the folly of attempting to draw a map of Morocco with the dissident and submitted zones marked off, because the European notion of empire differs profoundly from the Muslim conception. Europeans think in terms of territorial limits, while Muslims think in terms of the submission of a population to the sultan.[4] The result of this misunderstanding, Doutté continued, has been to generate considerable confusion and conflict over the frontier between Algeria and Morocco. A similar theme was taken up by Aubin: the Moroccan state was portrayed by him as a vague federation held together by Islam and the operation of the *makhzan*. Despite the conflicts which went on between the central authorities and the tribes and the continued efforts of the sultans to preserve and expand the territory which paid taxes to them, 'even in the most distant parts of *bled es-siba*, there is no tribe which is not in relations with the *makhzan*.' These relations continue even while the battle between the two rages.[5] While a European might interpret the persistent conflict between the *makhzan* and the tribes as mere anarchy, Doutté was of a different opinion: 'all this is not disorder, but an order;

[1] Eugene Aubin (Descos), *Le Maroc d'aujourd'hui*, Paris, 1903. It has been translated into English under the title *Morocco Today*.

[2] Augustin Bernard, 'Une mission au Maroc. Rapport à M. le Gouverneur General de l'Algérie', *Renseignements coloniaux*, 1904, No. 10. Also author of *Le Maroc*, Paris, 1909, the first general manual on Morocco.

[3] Marquis de Segonzac, *Voyages au Maroc, 1899–1901*, Paris, 1904.

[4] E. Doutté, 'Une mission d'études', *Renseignements coloniaux*, 1901, p. 171.

[5] Aubin, op. cit., pp. 241 (quote), 238–9.

in this apparent chaos all the living forces ended up by finding an equilibrium: the play of classes and of parties of all kinds resulted in a kind of social stasis which constitutes a durable state, as much in the tribes as in the cities'.[1] The final judgment of Aubin was similar: 'if there is no government whose organization appears more simple than that of Morocco, there is none the less none whose operation is more complicated. It is a veritable group of little autonomous states, toward which the *makhzan* must proceed according to a diplomacy appropriate for each one.'[2] The result of the analysis of these two men, was therefore to emphasize: (1) that the *makhzan–siba* division was inadequate to explain the relationship between the sultan and the dissident tribes, and (2) that as an Islamic state, the conception of the nature of the empire and of the ruler's authority differed considerably from European notions of territorial sovereignty. We shall see below what became of this carefully nuanced and balanced view.

The study of Morocco had from the beginning emphasized the presence of a large percentage of Berber-speaking peoples among its inhabitants. Yet in 1900 little was known of them, or of their society. Under the circumstances, therefore, it might have been natural for Frenchmen familiar with the Berber-speaking Kabyles of Algeria to have assumed that the Moroccan Berbers were essentially similar to their Algerian cousins. To some extent, indeed, some of the early commentators on Morocco were tempted to make just such a connection—the reports of de Segonzac on the Berber tribes of the Middle Atlas made some such vague attempt, and there are hints of it also in Aubin (who none the less had little to say on the subject, having traveled but little among the Berber tribes of *bled es-siba*).[3] The tone which was set for the study of Morocco's Berber populations by the chief French student of the subject, Edmond Doutté, was however largely free from the obstinate romanticism of the French Kabylophiles. Instead of insisting upon the distinction between Arabs and Berbers in Morocco, Doutté minimized it: 'As much in Morocco as in Algeria the ethnic division of natives in "Arabs" and "Berbers" is a vain distinction, because no criteria can be invoked on which to base this distinction.'[4] One can find Arab speakers who used to speak Berber and *vice versa*, and one can find nomads and sedentaries among both groups. 'The word "Berber" has no precise sense except a linguistic one where it designates a group of dialects closely allied by common character. . . . One can thus if one wishes divide Africans into berberophones and arabophones; into nomads and sedentaries; into numerous anatomical types; but the ethnic classification into Arab and Berber corresponds to no concrete fact capable of being singled out.'[5] The absence of the familiar Berber–Arab stereotypes in these observations helps set off Doutté's views from the majority of those which were to be expressed in the next two decades. To be fair, however, it should be noted that Doutté himself was to some degree influenced by prevailing Kabylophile attitudes, for he frankly disliked Arabs, and feared the results of Arabization

[1] Doutté, op. cit., p. 172.
[2] Aubin, op. cit., p. 245.
[3] de Segonzac, op. cit., and Aubin, op. cit., p. 52.
[4] Doutté, op. cit., p. 166.
[5] Ibid., p. 167.

of the Berbers. Even here he remained cautious. 'This arabization, at least in the limits of our present field of observation, generally coincides with a recrudesence of fanaticism in the religious sentiments and with a considerable lowering of morality.'[1] Finally, however, his distinction between Arabs and Berbers remained founded primarily upon linguistic evidence, and he restrained his impulses to wax enthusiastic in favor of the superior virtues of Berbers over Arabs. Later students of Moroccan Berbers would not be so scrupulous.

THE CHANGING IMAGE OF THE MOROCCAN STATE, 1904–1912

The year 1904 marks an important turning point in the history of French involvement in Morocco. In this year, as a result of the *entente cordiale*, France managed to achieve a position of hegemony in Moroccan affairs—a position which it immediately sought to capitalize upon through the launching of a diplomatic offensive which was designed to achieve a *de facto* protectorate over Morocco. Suddenly the French government found that it had a vested interest in the survival of the *makhzan*, whose cooperation was necessary to the carrying out of its plans. Hitherto, discussions about Morocco in French political circles had always posed support of the *makhzan* as only one of the ways in which Morocco might be won over. The rise of a pretender to the Moroccan throne in the fall of 1902, and his continued successes against *makhzan* troops during the years which followed, suggested to some that a policy of backing him might be worth attempting. But such speculations were abandoned with the initiation of the Delcassé forward policy in 1904. With the rising importance of the *makhzan* to France, it is interesting to observe the rapid crystallization of a new, more stereotyped image of Morocco, and the gradual dropping of learned academic distinctions about the nature of Moroccan society. A new dogmatism can be observed in the writing of old French Moroccan hands beginning during this period. From this time, as well, a preference for crisp, simple dichotomous distinctions can be observed in the presentation of the realities of the Moroccan Question to the concerned French citizen. Only a clear, straightforward presentation of Moroccan society and institutions could survive the exigencies of the moment. From the start of the French colonial offensive in 1904, until the signing of the protectorate in 1912, the complicated interaction of French policy toward Morocco and French views of Morocco marks every twist and turn of the Moroccan Question.

The crystallization of a more dichotomized view of the Moroccan state from 1904 coincided and interacted with the changes in French policy toward Morocco from that date. Prior to 1904, in effect, a number of alternative proposals, each with its own supporters, existed as to how France should go about penetrating Morocco. The two major tendencies were what was called the '*makhzan* policy'

[1] Doutté, 'Troisième voyage d'études au Maroc. Rapport sommaire d'ensemble' *Rensiegnements coloniaux*, 1902, p. 158.

(because it proposed the introduction of reforms in cooperation with the Moroccan government), and what was called the 'tribes policy' (because it foresaw the gradual conquest of Morocco on a piecemeal, tribe-by-tribe basis starting from Algeria). The *makhzan* policy was largely supported by the French diplomatic corps, while the tribes policy was backed by Algerian *colon* and military interests.[1] The struggle between the two tendencies within French policy-making circles was intense and bitter, but in the end the contest was decided in favor of the adoption of the '*makhzan* policy'. This, in brief, was the origin of the policy which was put into action by Delcassé following the *entente cordiale* in 1904, except that the policy was rebaptized one of 'peaceful penetration' in order to mollify critics of the French colonial offensive within the French Chamber of Deputies. Under the rubric of peaceful penetration, France would seek to achieve a position of dominance in Morocco through the introduction of a wide range of internal reforms in cooperation with the sultan and the *makhzan*.[2] Since the policy called for a cooperative Moroccan government, and would be jeopardized by any shows of opposition by the *makhzan*, it proved to be very difficult to operate in practice. The incidents in 1905 when with German backing the sultan 'Abd al-'Aziz succeeded in blocking the reforms proposed by Delcassé (which ended with the fall of Delcassé's government), demonstrated how hard it would be to carry out. Peaceful penetration and cooperation with the *makhzan* however remained the official French policy toward Morocco even after the fall of Delcassé. The delicate nature of both the French internal political scene, and the international diplomatic front militated against a more overt and aggressive French policy.

The practical effect of the *makhzan* policy was that it gave France a vested interest in the survival of the *makhzan* (although not necessarily in the survival of any given sultan). The full advantages of this state of affairs were not seen for a while, however. When they were, it was, characteristically, General (later Marshal) Lyautey who was one of the first to see how the policy could be used. Lyautey found real cooperation to be too difficult to carry out effectively, owing to the continued resistance of *makhzan* officials to working with their French opposite numbers. Instead, he devised a means of action for the Algero-Moroccan border which fully satisfied French desires to actually control what went on in the area, without alarming the sultan's representative in the area, the *makhzan*, the European powers, or the French opposition. This *tour de force* was first conceived of during the course of 1904 and put into practice along the frontier

[1] On French policy toward Morocco before 1904, see E. Doutté, 'Les deux politiques', *Afrique française*, 1903, pp. 306–11, and R. de Caix, 'La France et le Maroc', ibid., pp. 298–306.

[2] A clear exposition of the policy of peaceful penetration, as explained by Delcassé, can be found in *Documents diplomatiques français, Affaires du Maroc*, I (1901–1905), 179–184. French penetration along the Algero-Moroccan frontier began in 1900 with the Touat oasis complex. Incidents between French troops and dissident tribesmen continued during the years which followed. Attempts were made to ease tensions in the region by the signing of diplomatic accords on the frontier in 1901 and 1902. These efforts to instill principles of cooperation failed to resolve the situation, however. For a discussion of events along the frontier see A. Bernard, *Les Confins algéro-marocains*, Paris, 1911, which includes the complete texts of the accords.

during 1905. Essentially the solution worked out by Lyautey was that France should substitute itself for *makhzan* authority in the area, choose its own tribal chiefs and obtain a *makhzan* appointment for them through pressure, and then proceed to organize groups of partisans in each tribe, collect taxes on behalf of the sultan (from which the costs of French administration and the upkeep of local forces would be deducted), and begin to develop roads, markets, and medical dispensaries to give the local population a stake in the success of the operation.[1] While claiming to be fully cooperating with the Moroccan government, France could stifle international protests and at the same time extend its political control over segments of Moroccan territory. Best of all, by substituting itself for the *makhzan*, the French government put itself in a position where it could dismiss any serious resistance which it might encounter from the local Moroccan population as the traditional dissidence of *bled es-siba*, rather than as a widespread popular patriotic response. In this way, all Moroccan attempts to oppose French penetration became readily assimilable to the normal opposition which had always met the attempts of the *makhzan* to extend its authority over unsubmitted tribes. By obtaining at least the tacit consent of the Moroccan sultans in this policy, France was able to undertake the piecemeal conquest of Morocco prior to 1912, and justify it as the patient efforts of the French government to assist the *makhzan* in imposing law and order over a recalcitrant and obstreperous group of dissidents.[2] Following the actions of Lyautey in the southeastern Moroccan frontier area, the same general strategy was followed in the operations around Oujda against the Beni Snassen (1907), the police action in the Chaouia (1907-8), and the relief of the siege of Fes (1911), each of which led to an extension of French control over still more Moroccan territory. The fact that in each instance France carefully collected taxes, respected the local religion and customs, and worked with the *makhzan* officials in the area was presented to French domestic opinion and to the European powers as a testimony of the good faith of the French government. It was this policy of substituting French control for that of the *makhzan*, but maintaining the fiction of Moroccan sovereignty which was to provide the guiding rationale for the organization of the French protectorate in 1912.

One of the most interesting consequences of the adoption of the *makhzan* policy by the French government was the way it influenced the image of Morocco presented in French scholarly publications. While there was very likely a mutually reinforcing quality about the development of a stereotyped view of Morocco and the emergence of the *makhzan* policy after 1904, the fact that France had a vested interest in the continued existence of the *makhzan* appears to have oriented French thinking about Morocco in the direction of emphasizing the importance of the *makhzan–siba* dichotomy. More carefully balanced views tended naturally to fall by the way in the years which followed. The nationalist

---

[1] The broad outlines of this policy seem first to have been suggested to Lyautey by Vaffier-Pollet, an employee of the Compagnie marocaine, in June of 1904. Cf. Lyautey, *Vers le Maroc, lettres du sud-oranais, 1903–1906*, Paris, 1932, p. 66. The policy as modified by Lyautey is explained in ibid., pp. 224–7.

[2] Ibid., pp. 224–7.

passions which were generated by the Moroccan question at its height no doubt also played a role in reinforcing this tendency. Between 1904 and 1912 a stereotyped view of Morocco began to crystallize.

The rapid development of a kind of conventional wisdom about Morocco and Moroccan society marked both serious students of Morocco like Doutté and the head of the Mission Scientifique du Maroc, Edouard Michaux-Bellaire, and pundits and policy makers in France, like Eugene Etienne, head of the colonial lobby in the Chamber of Deputies.[1] The principal characteristic which distinguished the new stereotypes from the earlier, more tentative analyses was the Europo-centric conceptual framework on which they were based. Instead of studies which emphasized that Morocco, as an Islamic state, possessed a rather different notion of sovereignty than that which European countries adhered to, such concerns were pushed into the background and a set of prefabricated interpretations were set forth. Thus, for example, Etienne could claim in 1904 that, 'the sultan is only a great religious leader. He has only one-third of the surface of Morocco under his direct and immediate authority. This is the territory to which is given the name *bled el-makhzan*, "the land of government", the other two-thirds of Morocco bearing the name *bled es-siba*, that is "the land of independence".[2] De Segonzac, in a passage devoted to exposing how the autocracy of the *makhzan* and its agents had destroyed the democratic assemblies of Berber notables, referred to the "theocracy of the sultan, emperor, and pope".'[3] It would be possible to multiply citations of this sort almost without end from the very considerable literature on Morocco between 1904 and 1912.

It is not especially surprising that a politician like Etienne should have propounded a stereotyped view of Moroccan society. But it is somewhat startling when one discovers that someone like Michaux-Bellaire, with a profound knowledge of the country based on more than twenty years residence, expressed sentiments of a similar nature. Michaux-Bellaire in fact improved on the *makhzan–siba* dichotomy. Morocco, he proclaimed in an article written in 1908, was divided into two segments, or 'organisms': these were the '*makhzan* organism' and the 'Berber organism'. Throughout history, it has been essentially the same story: 'The situation of the *makhzan* vis-à-vis this national organism [the Berber organism] is about the same as that of the ancient Phoenician and Roman conquerors; like them, it is incapable of finishing its conquest and organizing it, and it has been unable to absorb for its benefit the Berber vitality, to assimilate it; all that it can do is to resist it, to contain it within its limits and

---

[1] The Mission Scientifique du Maroc was established at Tangier in 1904 under the direction of Georges Salmon, a young graduate of the Ecole des Langues Orientales. Originally intended to gather information on Morocco to further French penetration, it was to have been modeled on the Institut français du Caire, but lack of funds prevented it from reaching its full development. On the death of Salmon in 1906, Edouard Michaux-Bellaire became the new director. On it see 'L'Institut marocain', *Renseignements coloniaux*, 1904, pp. 194–5, and the pamphlet of Michaux-Bellaire, *Le Mission Scientifique du Maroc*, Rabat, 1925.

[2] 'Discours de M. Etienne', *Afrique française*, 1904, p. 182.

[3] Marquis de Segonzac, *Au Cœur de l'Atlas, Mission au Maroc, 1904–1909*, Paris, 1910, p. 258.

to declare itself responsible for its actions *vis-à-vis* Europe in order to justify an authority which it is moreover incapable of exercising by its means alone.'[1] Michaux-Bellaire then concluded with the pious hope that the two organisms would some day be fused into one—the inference being that it was the task of France to bring about the unity of the Moroccan state. By equating Arab and *makhzan*, Berber and *siba* in an especially vivid formula, Michaux-Bellaire only brought together in a scholarly article what had been repeated often by less talented writers in plain and simple prose.

A third essential element of the composite stereotype of Morocco which began to crystallize during the years 1904–12 was the view of the nature and function of Islam in Morocco. The view of Islam was in fact the linch pin which held the ensemble of the stereotype together. If the sultan was conceived of as pope and emperor, then his spiritual and temporal authority could be distinguished analytically from one another, in a kind of updated version of the two swords theory of medieval kingship. According to this interpretation, therefore, the authority of the sultan as emperor (i.e. his temporal authority) extended only over the *bled el-makhzan*, while his spiritual authority (the sultan as pope) was recognized in *bled es-siba*. The tribes of *bled es-siba*, although they would respond to the spiritual appeals of the sultan, refused to accept his temporal authority, and refrained from paying taxes or providing military contingents. From this it followed that the *siba* populations were somehow not fully Moroccan. Lyautey was to take advantage of the distinction between the temporal and religious authority of the sultan in his dealings with the tribes along the Algero-Moroccan frontier.[2]

One of the most characteristic features of Moroccan Islam noted by French observers was the plurality of religious personages, *sharif*s and saints, and their powerful interests throughout the country. Opposing the supreme religious authority of the Moroccan sultan there existed religious notables whose influence in the provinces often rivaled that of the sultan himself. The importance of marabouts and religious brotherhoods was often emphasized by French observers anxious to find other alternatives for French policy beside supporting the *makhzan*. These opponents of official policy proposed that instead of backing the sultan, France should win over the most influential figures among this religious notability, and use them to favor French colonial penetration.[3] Such an idea was not new: it had been suggested in the 1880s by some adventurous spirits who by wishful thinking managed to convince themselves that the Sharif of Wazzan was a potential challenger to the Moroccan throne. (It must be added that they were not discouraged in this view by the Sharif himself, who was anxious to obtain a subsidy from the French government and protégé status.)[4] Most French commentators on the Moroccan scene during the period 1904–1912,

[1] Edouard Michaux-Bellaire, 'L'Organisme marocain', *Revue du monde musulman*, III, 1908, p. 43.

[2] Lyautey, op. cit., p. 127.

[3] Commandant Ferry, 'La réorganisation marocaine', *Renseignements coloniaux*, 1905, pp. 519–28, esp. p. 526.

[4] On the attempt to utilize the prestige of the Sharif of Wazzan, see the account in J.-L. Miège, *Le Maroc et l'Europe*, IV, Paris, 1963, pp. 233–49.

more closely wedded to the official policy line, tended to downgrade the importance of these regional religious interests.

As Franco-Moroccan relations became strained and embittered by the inability of French policy makers to devise a policy which would take the measure of Moroccan attempts at resistance, a significant change took place in the view of Islam propounded by French experts. Scholarly detachment and the abstention from value judgments about the Islamic religion gave way to angry and bitter statements. In this new mood, even distinguished scholars like Doutté and Michaux-Bellaire could be seen asserting that Islam was the cause of the stagnation of Moroccan society, weighing down 'like a leaden mantle over the entire country'.[1] A study of Islam could only confirm its violence and hostility to civilization and progress. 'Among the characteristics of Islam which most strike us, fanaticism is certainly in the first rank.'[2] This attitude of fear and hostility, while born of frustration in the heat of the colonial struggle, nevertheless continued to inform the stereotyped image of Islam which persisted after 1912. It is undoubtedly at the roots of one of the chief characteristics of the Berber policy which was pursued under the protectorate—the concern that France, unless it was very careful, might repeat the mistake it had earlier made in Algeria of facilitating the Islamicization and Arabization of the Berber-speaking Kabyles.[3] Even before the protectorate influential French observers could be found who claimed that Moroccan Berbers were only superficially Islamicized. Beneath a thin veneer of Islamic practices, they claimed, the 'original' Berber religion persisted, 'a mixture of fetishism, anthropolatry, and superstition, where one can find pell-mell remnants of paganism, magic, Judaism, and Catholicism'.[4] Until after 1912 this view of Moroccan Berbers remained of limited appeal, however, and no attempt was made to incorporate it in a Berber policy.

The composite set of stereotypes which composed the Moroccan Vulgate remained incomplete in one respect until after the signing of the protectorate treaty. Relatively little was known about the Berber-speaking populations of Morocco during the period of French colonial penetration, and a stereotype of the Berber never really developed. No doubt this was partly due to the fact that the bulk of French energies and attention were absorbed by the task of establishing a position of undisputed hegemony over the *makhzan*. Since the Berbers lived for the most part outside of the zone of primary interests to France there was little impulsion to think much about them. Scientific expeditions to the region south of Marrakesh had discovered the existence of a 'feudal' regime of powerful Berber chieftans in the Western High Atlas—the so-called *grands caids*. In 1905, the studies of Paul Lemoine led him to suggest the political advantages which France might derive from associating the great *caids* to the extension of French

---

[1] Doutté, 'Coup d'œil sur le Maroc', *Renseignements coloniaux*, 1909, p. 135.

[2] Doutté, 'Le Fanatisme musulman', *Renseignements coloniaux*, 1909, p. 164.

[3] R. de Caix, 'Au cœur de l'Atlas', *Afrique française*, 1910, p. 204. De Caix, it should be noted, was an original supporter of the Kabyle policy in Algeria which aimed at assimilating the Kabyles. Cf. his *Questions algériennes : Arabes et Kabyles*, Algiers, 1891.

[4] de Segonzac, op. cit., p. 266 (quote); also Michaux-Bellaire, 'L'Organisme marocain', op. cit., p. 3.

influence in Morocco.[1] The expeditions of de Segonzac among the Berbers of the Atlas brought out the anarchy of the tribes who lived beyond the range of the great *caid*s. Far from presenting an idealized image of the Berber, however, de Segonzac insisted on their religious intransigence, the anarchy of their society, the low state of their morals, and their ugliness and brutality.[2] The image of the good Berber would only develop in the years which followed the founding of the protectorate.

While there were some French experts who urged the adoption of a policy which would take advantage of the alleged differences between the Berbers and the Arabs, notably Robert de Caix, this was far from being the majority view until after 1912. More typical was the attitude of Augustin Bernard:

As for the attitude of Berbers and Arabs towards French penetration, it doesn't differ as much as is sometimes imagined. Doubtless there are differences between them which can and must be taken into account, but we should give up building a policy upon it, any more than one was built in France on the Celtic, Germanic, or Roman origin of the inhabitants, even supposing it [to be] known. The Arabs and the Berbers are too mixed, their social state especially is too similar, for one to be able to radically oppose them against one another, as we used to believe could be done.[3]

It can be assumed that in making this statement Bernard was also expressing the opinion held by Lyautey at the time.[4] Neither a stereotype of the Moroccan Berber nor a concerted Berber policy can be said to have existed until after 1912, when France for the first time came into close contact with the Berber populations of the Middle Atlas. In the end, therefore, the image of Moroccan Berbers as it emerges from French writing on Morocco during the period 1904–1912 remains unclear. Good traits were cited by some authors, who urged that France pursue a policy which would take advantage of the differences between Arabs and Berbers, while others no less insistently denied the existence of differences on which a policy might be based. This confusion seems to have derived from the fact that France did not come into close contact with the Berber bloc until after the beginning of the protectorate, and thus did not begin to consider the need for a Berber policy until after 1912.

The policy which was pursued by the French government during the period 1904–1912, and the image of Morocco which began to crystallize during the same period were on the whole mutually reinforcing. The *makhzan* policy

[1] P. Lemoine, 'Mission dans le Maroc occidental', *Renseignements coloniaux*, 1905, pp. 86–9, 92. The primacy of Lemoine in suggesting an alliance with the great caids is noted by de Caix, 'L'œuvre française au Maroc', *Renseignements coloniaux*, 1912, p. 252. This was the origin of the famous policy of the *grands qaids* pursued by France under the protectorate.

[2] de Segonzac, *Au cœur de l'Atlas*, pp. 37, 43, 68, 105, and 270.

[3] A. Bernard, *Les Confins algéro-marocains*, Paris, 1911, p. 207.

[4] Bernard generally sticks close to the Lyautey position in this book. An examination of Lyautey's writing on the policy which he followed along the border turns up no evidence of a 'Berber policy' *per se*. The general impression which one gets from *Vers le Maroc* indicates on the contrary that he did not see the differences between Berber and Arab as at all relevant to policy at this stage of his career (pre-1912).

depended upon an analysis of Moroccan society which stressed the distinction between the religious and political authority of the sultan, and between *bled el-makhzan* and *bled es-siba*. Moreover, the policy which was pursued by the French government from 1904 to 1912 encouraged the tendency to be less insistent upon nuances in the analysis of Moroccan society, and to emphasize instead the sharp cleavages which divided it. By thus seizing upon a few aspects of the Moroccan state and Moroccan society, and paying less attention to others, no less important, French scholars and politicians helped to generate a series of stereotypes about Morocco which have lasted until this day. Such stereotypes survived because they seemed to explain best the peculiarities of pre-protectorate Morocco and at the same time to provide a convincing rationale for French colonial penetration. Partially right, the interpretation has proved more lasting than the imaginative explanations of the first generation of Moroccan nationalist critics. Partially wrong as well, it is being subjected to critical scrutiny by a new set of scholars. In this way, most of the major elements of the Moroccan Vulgate were crystallized into a coherent view of Morocco between 1904 and 1912.

THE IMAGE COMPLETED: BERBER POLICY AND THE BERBER MYTH, 1912-1919

Despite over a decade of intensive study of Morocco, France began its protectorate in 1912 with a considerable ignorance of the Berber-speaking segments of the Moroccan population. This was especially true where the *thamazight*-speaking Berbers of the Middle Atlas region were concerned. In so far as French researchers had been interested in the Berbers, their attention had focused primarily upon the powerful great barons of the Marrakesh region—the famous *grands caids*. In the elaboration of a native policy, it was the need to resolve the question of the great *caids* and their rivalries which dominated the attention of French experts. The solution which was finally arrived at, it should be noted, of a kind of system of indirect rule *à l'anglaise* depended but little on any specifically Berber qualities of the political regime of the South. But in the region around the cities of Fes and Meknes inhabited by the Middle Atlas Berbers there were no great barons to capture the imagination—instead there was an acephalous society of transhumant Berbers riven by feud but fiercely devoted to the preservation of their customs and their way of life. By their strategic position astride the route between Fes and the coast, and by their warlike qualities, the Middle Atlas Berber bloc had long posed a threat to the orderly administration of the area by the *makhzan*. It was the inability of French military columns to install a durable peace in the region despite yearly expeditions into the region in 1911, 1912 and 1913 which first exposed the lack of serious information about the nature of Middle Atlas Berber society to French foreign policy makers. On investigation it developed that in 1912 there was but one French officer with any knowledge of the tribes of the region, Maurice LeGlay, and there was no scholarly research on the language, customs, or institutions of any

Middle Atlas tribe.[1] The circumstances, however, were such that region had to be rapidly brought under control because the periodic revolts of the tribes jeopardized the French position in the North. French military commanders could hardly afford to wait several years until the tribes of the region had been subjected to intense study before undertaking their conquest, yet it was evident that the traditional methods did not work. In the absence of detailed on the spot studies, at least some rough guide lines to the principles of Berber political and social organization were needed so that the earlier errors could be avoided. But where could such guide lines be found? The answer lay in a consideration of what was known about Kabyle society in Algeria, with which many of the officers and scholars serving in Morocco were already familiar from prior service in Algeria. Thus it was a natural reflex for French commanders in the field and French scholars working for the native affairs agency to draw upon Kabyle materials in orienting their thoughts about the *thamazight*-speaking bloc, and in devising policies for dealing with it.[2] Inevitably, in the process, they also incorporated in their thoughts about Middle Atlas Berbers a series of romantic stereotypes about Berbers taken from the Algerian 'Kabyle myth'.[3] Briefly, this was the myth of the good Berber, based on the supposed democratic nature of Kabyle society, its lesser degree of Islamicization, the more equal treatment of women, and the supposed assimilability of Kabyles to French culture. The introduction of the 'Kabyle Myth', it will be seen shortly, was to prove a powerful influence in shaping the image of Moroccan Berbers between 1912 and 1919. It was also to be the most influential single factor in the development of a French Berber policy during the same period. The remainder of this essay will be devoted to a study of the emergence of a Moroccan Berber myth, and of its impact upon policy during the formative early years of the protectorate, 1912 to 1919. With the addition of the stereotypes about the nature of Berbers and Berber society in Morocco, from around 1919, all of the essential features of the Moroccan Vulgate were in place.

The difficulties which French military commanders experienced in obtaining the definitive submission of the Berber tribes of the Middle Atlas depended only partly upon their ignorance of Berber society. In part, as well, they were a result of one of the major weaknesses of the system of pacification which had been worked out by Lyautey and his principal collaborators during their stay along the Algero-Moroccan frontier between 1903 and 1908. The Lyautey system of pacification (which should be distinguished from the system of administration in

[1] The lack of knowledge is frankly set forth by Lt. Col. Henrys in a report cited in G. Surdon, *Institutions et coutumes des Berbères du Maghreb*, Tangier and Fez, 1938, p. 103. 'Now, it must be admitted, what did we know at this time of the mores, customs and traditions specific to the Berbers of Morocco? Very little, if not nothing?'

[2] The tendency to look at Moroccan Berbers in terms of what was known about Algerian Kabyles was a general characteristic of the period, 1912–19. See for example, the letter of Henrys cited in Surdon, op. cit., pp. 108–9. This will be explored further below.

[3] On the 'Kabyle Myth', its origins, development and influence on French policy in Algeria see the very important article of Charles-Robert Ageron, 'La France a-t-elle eu une politique Kabyle?', op. cit. By myth I mean a mental image which determines behavior or policy, without reference to its truth or falsity.

cooperation with the *makhzan* explored above) depended upon a clever mixture of political action and force to submit a hostile tribe. By it, a French commander was expected to seek out the most influential marabouts and secular notables in the hostile tribe, and then attempt to win them over by bribes and threats, and finally to utilize their prestige to obtain the submission of the entire tribe. In this way, if the game were correctly played, a tribe could be submitted without a shot being fired. In practice, of course, it rarely worked out that way and a certain amount of force generally had to be employed to convince the last recalcitrants. One of the most characteristic features of the Lyautey system none the less remained the use of influential notables to assist in the process of pacification.[1] In the early stages of the protectorate such a policy enjoyed considerable success, because the *makhzan*, the cities, the plains Arabs, and the semi-feudal regime of the south all were characterized by the presence of notables of one kind or another. No great difficulties were experienced in gaining their collaboration in the organizing of the protectorate in return for granting them a favored position under the new regime. When, however, the problem of the Middle Atlas Berbers was posed in the spring of 1913 with the revolt of the Gerrouan, Beni Mtir (Ait Ndhir), and Beni Mguild (Ait Njild), however, the weakness of the Lyautey system was clearly revealed. For these tribes, with their loose political organization and transhumant way of life, possessed virtually no chiefs or religious leaders whose influence was able to bring about the submission of any group beyond their immediate family. The result was a continued series of failures to achieve a durable peace in the area.[2]

The failure of French policy to come to grips with the Middle Atlas Berbers was most apparent in the case of the Beni Mtir, a transhumant tribe whose lands stood atride the Meknes plain and the foothills of the Middle Atlas.[3] The Beni Mtir had been leaders of the tribal revolt which broke out against the government of Sultan Mawlay Abd al-Hafiz in the spring of 1911. A French expeditionary force sent to relieve the siege of Fes and to put down the revolt for the *makhzan* first encountered the Beni Mtir in June of 1911, when French columns marched through their territory. After their defeat, a French post was established at the main center of the Beni Mtir, El-Hajeb, and sought to insure calm in the

---

[1] On the importance of the search for notables to the Lyautey system, cf. P. Lyautey (ed), *Lyautey l'Africain*, Paris, 1956, I, 252–5. This is made clear in *Archives. Ministère de la Guerre, Maroc, Serie E-2*, Col. Henrys, Instructions politiques, 6 June 1914, No. 153z. See also the cynical observations of LeGlay on the Lyautey system: 'Lyautey et le commandement indigène', *Afrique française*, 1936, pp. 194–7. The Lyautey system of pacification had other important characteristics not of direct concern here. These included a general emphasis on political over military action where possible, and the establishment of markets and medical dispensaries in newly pacified territory.

[2] The failure of the search for notables is established by LeGlay, 'Notes contributives à l'étude de la question berbère' (unpublished paper, 1913) in *Fonds Terrier No. 5957*.

[3] On French operations in the Beni Mtir see Abès, 'Monographie d'une tribu berbère: Les Aith Ndhir (Beni Mtir)', *Archives berbères*, II, 1917, pp. 174–80. Also, LeGlay, 'Notes contributives', op. cit. The circumstances of the revolt of the Beni Mtir are dealt with in my unpublished paper, 'The Tribal Factor in North African History: the Aith Ndhir and the History of Morocco, 1900–1912', presented to the Middle East Studies Association Second Annual Conference, November 1968.

region. In spite of these precautions (or indeed perhaps because of the way they were put into operation) the tribe became active in leading resistance to the French in the region in the spring of 1912 and attacked El-Hajeb at the same time that other tribes were laying siege to Fes in May, 1912. Once again defeated militarily, the Beni Mtir resisted French efforts to subdue them, and immediately disowned the few individuals who sold out to the French. In the spring of 1913 the tribe was once again in opposition to French rule, and actively involved in organizing alliances with the other tribes of the area to attack the French posts. It was at this point that French native affairs experts became alarmed at their continual inability to come up with a viable solution to the Beni Mtir problem, and more generally with the failure of ordinary methods to obtain the submission of any Middle Atlas Berber tribes to the *makhzan*. A special military command, the Cercle des Beni Mtir was created within the Meknes region, and placed under the orders of one of Lyautey's most trusted officers, Lt. Colonel Henrys. The solution of the Beni Mtir problem was given a top priority, and Henrys was given special powers to bring the situation under control.[1]

The solution of the Beni Mtir problem was made possible by the recognition that previous attempts to subdue them had failed to take sufficient notice of the differences which separated them, as Berbers, from the *makhzan* regime. In particular, Henrys became aware that a major error of previous policies toward the Beni Mtir was that the terms of submission required that the tribe formally accept *makhzan* authority. The Beni Mtir, however, saw submission to the *makhzan* as representing not only submission to the political authority of the sultan, but also acceptance of the full panoply of *makhzan* administration, including *caid*s, *qadis*, and *sharia* law. It thus represented a direct threat to their customs, institutions and way of life. For these reasons, the Beni Mtir and the other Middle Atlas tribes would have nothing to do with any surrender terms which insisted that they recognize the jurisdiction of the *makhzan* over them. Pending further investigation of Berber social and political organization, the interim solution devised by Colonel Henrys and his native policy advisers was to modify the formula of the terms of submission. Instead of being asked to submit to the *makhzan*, the new formula specified that the Berber tribe submit to the *dawla* (state), and that the *dawla* (presumably meaning the French government) guarantee the exercise of customary law to the tribe. No *qadi* would be appointed to the tribe. Instead of a *caid*, the French appointed a *wasita* (go-between), and in other ways minor changes were made in terminology to assure that the tribe was administered with respect for the differences of Berber society.[2] This new formula proved to be successful when applied to the Beni

[1] On the organization of the 'Cercle des Beni Mtir' see P. Lyautey, op. cit., I, 220–5, and *Afrique française*, 1913, p. 118.

[2] *Archives, Guerre. Série E-2*, Henrys, Instructions politiques, 6 June 1914, No. 153z, 'The General commanding the operations recommends the use [among the Zaian] as was done among the Beni Mtir and the Beni Mguild of the word "dawla" (the government), which the mountain-folk will learn in course to respect as soon as they see the difference between the dawla of today and the makhzan of yesterday.' See also A. Bernard, 'La question berbère dans le Maroc central' (unpublished paper, 1914) in *Fonds Terrier No. 5957*.

Mtir and Gerrouan in 1913, and it was extended to the other Berber tribes of the Middle Atlas in the years which followed.

Beyond this short-run solution of the difficulties of obtaining the submission of the Berber tribes of the Middle Atlas, there still remained a pressing need for more detailed information on the basis of which permanent policy decisions could be made. Given the paucity of qualified French Berber experts, however, some general guide lines for research were required to help orient the inquiry. It is here that French experience with the Berber-speaking groups of Algeria became relevant. For there was already in existence an extensive body of ethnographic literature on the language and customs of Kabylia, and a widely diffused set of stereotypes about Kabyle society. In particular, the radiating example of the Kabyle myth, on the one hand, and of the remarkable ethnography of Hanoteau and LeTourneux, *La Kabylie et les coutumes kabyles*, on the other, exerted a powerful influence on the orientation of French research on Moroccan Berbers.[1] It was Hanoteau and LeTourneux who had first exposed and popularized the central features of Kabyle society. From that analysis two aspects seemed most relevant to the study of Middle Atlas Berbers, namely, the role of the *jamaa*, or council of elders, in deciding the most important questions facing the life of the group, and the importance of customary law, or *qanouns*, in regulating the internal life of the community according to a set of agreed norms. The discovery of the *jamaa* seemed to be especially important, for it was through the existence of this forum that the tribes, which appeared to be without rulers, were in fact governed. The great error of the *makhzan*, Henrys decided, was that it wished to impose *caids*, when in fact, 'the real authority remained in the hands of the *jamaa* and the elders . . .'.[2] It was their great knowledge of customary law, moreover, which seemed to especially distinguish the elders in the eyes of their constituents. This customary law, which differed profoundly from Islamic law, was a vital force in the life of the group and should be preserved by the French administration.[3] From 1913 onward, French policy toward the Berber-speaking populations of Morocco would be strongly influenced by the supposed importance of *izerf* (customary law) and of the *jamaa* as the central features of Moroccan Berber society. An examination of the first steps in the elaboration of a French Berber policy under the protectorate follows below. Before going on to this, however, I will look at the parallel development of a 'Berber myth' among French policy makers.

It is well known that Lyautey and his chief collaborators on native affairs prided themselves upon their clear-sighted, pragmatic, and un-ideological view of Morocco, and looked down with contempt upon what they regarded as the hopeless botch which the French administration in Algeria had made of its native policy. Certainly, if the relative success of the Lyautey administration of

---

[1] The impact of Hanoteau and LeTourneux is unmistakable. In addition to A. Bernard, 'La question berbère', op. cit., see also LeGlay, 'Les populations berbères du Maroc', in *Conférences franco-marocains*, i, Paris, 1916, p. 402, and H. Bruno, 'Introduction à l'étude de droit coutummier des berbères du Maroc central', *Archives berbères*, iii, 1917, p. 299.

[2] Henrys, cited in Surdon, op. cit., p. 106.

[3] Ibid., pp. 107-8.

Morocco is a sign of its superiority over Algeria, there was much which might have justified this feeling. But it should also be borne in mind that much more was known about North African society in 1912 when the conquest of Morocco was undertaken than was known in the early days of the colonization of Algeria, and as a consequence the native policy of the protectorate did not undergo the kind of wild oscillations which had marked that of Algeria. Members of the Lyautey *zawiya*, like Colonel Henrys, often pointed to the Berber policy of the Moroccan protectorate as an example of how their regime had managed to avoid the mistakes and excesses of the Algerian government.[1] Yet if one looks at the image of Moroccan Berbers put forward by these experts, or certain aspects of the policies which they proposed, one cannot avoid being struck by their resemblances to the romantic stereotypes about Algerian Kabyle society. How is this to be explained?

First of all, it should be noted that the majority of the early French experts on Moroccan Berber society and customs had been influenced by Algeria. Henrys, Berriau, and Simon, the principal military experts on Moroccan native policy, had all begun their careers in Algeria, and had spent some time dealing with Berberophone groups there. While there was much about the Algerian administration which they disliked (chiefly the bureaucratic inefficiency and the nefarious influence of the *colons*), there was also much they valued. Civilian scholars like the linguists E. Laoust, Biarnay, and Nehlil, law professors like H. Bruno and human geographers like A. Bernard, all of whom were to play a role in early studies of Moroccan Berbers, first began their scholarly careers in Algeria where they formed their ideas about the Berber language, society, and customs. Furthermore, both military and civilian groups developed their views about Berbers during the period when the Kabyle myth was still powerful in Algeria, and were undoubtedly influenced by it. In any event, their writings, and those of several other important figures whose earlier careers are unknown to me (notably M. LeGlay and Abès) give evidence of close acquaintance with the Algerian experience, and develop themes which closely parallel those of the Kabyle myth. It is therefore not unusual that Lyautey's Berber policy specialists, despite (or in addition to) their tough, pragmatic view of Morocco should also have developed a romantic image of Berber society, or that their policy toward Berbers should have been influenced by this image.

According to the tenets of the stereotype of Berbers which were developed by this group between 1912 and 1919, Moroccan Berbers had a number of characteristics which set them off from the Arabic-speaking segments of the population. Moroccan Berbers were, to begin with, among the original inhabitants of North Africa, and like the Algerian Kabyles they had resisted almost all invasions and in their mountains remained independent from the rulers of Morocco.[2] Moreover, although superficially Islamicized, they preserved the customs, rituals, and superstitions of their earlier faith beneath a veneer of Muslim beliefs and practices. In so far as they were Muslims, Berbers were frank schismatics who

[1] Introduction to Henrys report of 7 July 1914, cited in Surdon, op. cit., p. 106. Bernard, 'La Question berbère', op. cit.

[2] Bruno, op. cit., p. 299.

7

refused to have anything to do with *sharia* law, although the essence of Islam is the intimate union of law and religion.[1] They fought bitterly against the replacement of their customary law by *sharia* law.[2]

In their political organization, Berbers had an instinctive distrust of personal power, a kind of democratic spirit which enabled them to resist the *makhzan* and the emergence of powerful chiefs among them.[3] Through their *jamaa*s they were able to resolve most of the important problems facing the group—although it was well not to have too idealized a picture of the functioning of the *jamaa*. On questions which dealt with the honor of the group, the *jamaa* was never able to resolve the problem. Further, 'to thoroughly understand the role of the *jamaa*, it would be necessary to look at Berber family institutions, and to examine the veritable sovereignty which the chief of the patriarchal family possesses, as in ancient Rome.'[4] Finally, the Berber political system was saved from anarchy only by the strong sense of independence which the Berbers had against outsiders.[5] The customary laws by which the internal life of the group was regulated, as in Kabylia, were often written down in the form of *qanoun*s. These customs 'are more often in harmony with the spirit of our [French] code than the laws of Islam'.[6] In their social life, the Berbers were marked by a certain roughness of manner, but 'Berber mores are distinguished from Arab mores because they don't have the religious base of the Koran'. In particular, Berber treatment of women was much closer to the European than to the Arab, and Koranic prescriptions relative to women, their place in the family, and their rights were not practiced by Berbers. Indeed, their attitude was the exact opposite of what one finds among Arab Muslims.[7]

From this analysis of Berber society, a certain number of policy implications seemed naturally to flow, and while these tended on the whole to emphasize the necessity of preserving the central institutions of Berber society (or what were regarded as such at the time) from Arabization and Islamicization, they were only gradually applied by the government of the protectorate. None the less a number of important initiatives were taken between 1913 and 1919 in which can be seen the first halting development of the Berber policy which would come into full flower only later. Already by 1919 the essential traits of the Berber myth had been sketched in, and the myth itself given a wide diffusion. By 1919 as well, all of the essential policy decisions had been taken on which the completed edifice would be erected between the two wars. The foundations for France's Berber policy in Morocco were laid prior to 1919 under Lyautey.

The decision to have the Middle Atlas Berbers submit to the *dawla*, instead of to the *makhzan*, contained implicit within it the seeds of a Berber policy. By the

[1] LeGlay, 'Les Populations berbères', op. cit., pp. 388–9.
[2] Col. Berriau, 'L'Officier de Renseignements au Maroc', *Renseignements coloniaux*, 1918, p. 90. Berriau was Chef de Cabinet Politique under Lyautey, thus chief native affairs official in the protectorate.
[3] LeGlay, 'Les Populations berbères', op. cit., pp. 396–7.
[4] Bernard, 'La Question berbère', op. cit.
[5] LeGlay, 'Les Populations berbères', op. cit., p. 397.
[6] Bruno, cited ibid.
[7] Ibid., p. 397.

terms of the surrender agreement France promised that the laws and customs of the Berber tribe submitting would be respected, and that *caids*, *qadis*, and *sharia* law would not be imposed upon them. In order to make such a promise, however, French agents had to have a fairly complete idea of just what these laws and customs were. Accordingly, one of the first acts taken in the matter of Berber policy was a circular of 30 July 1913 sent out by Lyautey asking that all native affairs officers conduct an inquiry on the exact nature of the customary law practiced in their area by the Berber-speaking populations, 'in order to better fix the "formula" which is appropriate to these populations.'[1] The need to give at least some legal justification to the practice already followed in the submission of the Beni Mtir and Guerrouan in 1913, and the Beni Mguild in 1914, however, soon led to the promulgation of a decree before the results of this study were complete. The *dahir* of 11 September 1914 set forth in vague terms the principle that tribes judged 'de coutume berbère' would be permitted to keep their own judicial regime, and that further decrees would elaborate the exact terms under which customary law would be administered.[2] Initially, tribes classed as 'de coutume berbère' included the Beni Mtir, Beni Mguild, Zaian, and Guerrouan. Others were added to the list in the years which followed. For a long time no further laws were promulgated spelling out in clear terms the exact legal position of the customary law regime under the protectorate. It was this situation which the *dahir* of 16 May 1930 (the famous 'Berber *dahir*') was designed to remedy. The road to the Berber *dahir* therefore began in the early days of the protectorate.

In order to facilitate the making of policy decisions about the Berbers it was imperative that as much accurate information as possible about Berber society should be gathered as soon as possible. The Lyautey circular of 30 July 1913 was the first step in the systematization of research on Berbers in Morocco. Already Henrys had been using LeGlay, Laoust and Abès on an *ad-hoc* basis as a kind of brain trust on Berber problems. A special Berber study center was set up for them at Meknes in 1913, and outside assistance was solicited. It was the information and reports produced by this group which formed the basis for Henrys' recommendations to Lyautey and resulted in the *dahir* of 11 September 1914.[3] Since the Middle Atlas Berbers were only one of the major groups of Berbers in Morocco, however, there was a need to centralize information on Berbers in one place. A general questionnaire was sent out on 15 June 1914 to all military posts of the protectorate on the orders of Lyautey indicating the points on which further data was needed.[4] This trend was continued with the creation at Rabat of a Comité d'Etudes Berbères by a decision of 9 January 1915. The Comité was composed of Colonel H. Simon, Commandant Berriau, and Messrs Gaillard, Loth, Biarnay, and Nehlil, the protectorate officials most

---

[1] Lyautey, cited in Surdon, op. cit., p. 105.

[2] The dahir of 11 September 1914 was specifically requested by Henrys as a result of the recommendations of his native affairs staff on the question. On it, see *Afrique française*, 1915, p. 81.

[3] Surdon, op. cit., p. 109, quoting Henrys' letter of 26 January 1915.

[4] Ibid., p. 105.

directly concerned with Berber policy in Morocco, and a number of consulting members. A journal devoted to the study of Moroccan Berber society, *Les Archives Berbères*, was created as the organ of the Comité d'Etudes Berbères and its first issue came out early in 1915.[1] During the four years of its existence, *Archives Berbères* published the first monograph devoted to a Moroccan Berber tribe, and a wide variety of articles on Berber ethnology, customs, and law. It served as a means of diffusion of information about the latest research, and acted as a stimulus for further study. Something of the spirit in which this collective effort of research began can be glimpsed in the introduction of Colonel Simon, the then Director of native affairs, to the first issue of *Archives Berbères*:

> Today we find ourselves in Morocco in the presence of the largest group of Berbers remaining more or less pure. . . . We must study them thoroughly. The work done in Algeria and especially that of Hanoteau and LeTourneux will furnish us with a solid base for that; but customs vary from tribe to tribe, from village to village; the peculiarities must be carefully noted and examined to form a documentary base by means of which we will be able to fix the rules of political and administrative control to establish among these populations.[2]

The scientific study of the Berbers of the Middle Atlas proceeded at an intense pace in the years which followed. By 1919, most of the major work had been done toward unraveling the mysteries of the *thamazight* dialect, and the foundations had been laid for the development of legal studies, ethnography, and history of the Middle Atlas Berbers. The development of a French Berber policy was thereby considerably aided.

From the outset French commentators on the policy to be adopted toward the Berber-speaking populations of Morocco had been especially concerned with avoiding the mistakes which had been made in Algeria in the policy toward the Kabyles. These mistakes, it was understood, included the lack of a clear policy toward Algerian Berbers and the consequent pursuit of contradictory objectives, the favoring of the spread of the Arabic language and of Islamic law, and the unreasonable haste to assimilate the Kabyles to French civilization when a Berber policy was finally developed.[3] Care was required to make sure that there were Berber-speaking French officers attached to each post in Berber country, so that the spread of the Arabic language would not be unwittingly encouraged. A chair of Berber language was established at Rabat in 1913 as part of the Ecole Supérieure de langue arabe et de dialectes berbères (later to become the Institut des Hautes Etudes Marocaines), and M. Nehlil was named the first professor.[4]

---

[1] See the first issue of *Archives berbères*, I, No. 1, 1915, esp. p. 2, 'Décision du Commissaire Résidant Général créant à Rabat un Comité d'Etudes berbères'. Also, *Afrique française*, 1915, pp. 150–1.

[2] H. Simon, 'Les Études berbères au Maroc et leurs applications en matière de politique et d'administration', *Afrique française*, I, 1915, pp. 4–5.

[3] This concern was noted by Henrys in *Guerre, Série E-2*, Instructions politiques, 6 June 1914, No. 153z. One can find much the same fear of arabization expressed in LeGlay, 'Les populations berbères', op. cit., p. 403, and *Afrique française*, 1914, pp. 36–7.

[4] *Afrique française*, 1913, p. 22. A chair of Berber was created at the Ecole des Langues Orientales in Paris as part of the same concern, *Afrique française*, 1914, pp. 36–7.

A special supplement was added to the salary of native affairs officials for a knowledge of Berber.[1] In this manner it was hoped that enough qualified individuals would be produced that it would soon be unnecessary for political officers to have to resort to Arab interpreters and secretaries. Records of disputes, transactions, and other affairs over which the local native affairs bureau had jurisdiction were to be kept in French, rather than in Arabic, to limit the Islamicization and Arabization of the Berbers. At the same time the fact that records were written in French would enable the protectorate government to exercise some control over affairs within each Berber tribe.[2]

At the base of much of the thinking about the policy to be adopted toward the Berbers in Morocco one finds, finally, the concern that the Berbers be gradually assimilated to French civilization instead of evolving in the direction of Arabization. A sharp awareness of the demographic imbalance between colonizers and colonized lay at the origin of this feeling—if France was to successfully maintain its position in Morocco over the long run only the assimilation of at least part of the native population would enable it to do so.[3] This assimilation, the Moroccan experts thought, should be a very gradual process, however. The unfortunate results of undue haste were all too evident in the Algerian example and must be avoided. Evidently, they agreed, assimilation would be accomplished in large measure by the establishment of French schools in Berber country in Morocco. While the details are as yet unknown, there appears to have been considerable discussion between 1912 and 1919 within the protectorate administration over how this should be brought about. The preliminary decision to go ahead very cautiously with the establishment of French schools appears to have been reached prior to 1919.[4] Since most observers regarded it as unlikely that the Berbers would choose to Arabize when learning French was also a possibility open to them, they felt that there was no need to rush things. Finally, the inevitability of assimilation appeared unquestionable even to such pragmatic observers as Augustin Bernard: 'Neither the Berber language nor law can subsist in the presence of a superior organism. It will thus be necessary to give them our language and our law. In the same fashion, since they have no chiefs, or chiefs without

---

[1] *Afrique française*, 1914, pp. 36–7, notes a decision to give a supplement to the salaries of Contrôleurs Civils Stagiaires.

[2] LeGlay, 'Les populations berbères', op. cit., p. 403.

[3] This was the position of de Caix—see his 'L'Œuvre française au Maroc', *Renseignements coloniaux*, 1912, pp. 248–50. But it was shared by many others. See, for example, A. Bernard, 'La Question berbère', op. cit.

[4] It is clear from Bernard, 'La Question berbère', op. cit., that a number of studies on the education question were commissioned for the protectorate, including papers by E. Laoust, A. Bel, and Lt. Bertschi. All of the papers concluded in favor of the establishment of French schools among the Berber tribes and frankly supported the assimilation of Moroccan Berbers to French culture and civilization. Bernard unfortunately gives no idea of what decisions, if any, were taken on this recommendation. 'By a directive from Lyautey dated 18 November 1920 the creation of schools was begun. In 1923 five schools were opened in the Middle Atlas (at Sefrou, Ahermoumou, Azrou, Imouzzer, and Ain Leuh). Each was to receive one hundred students. Instruction was by French teachers. This system lasted until 1946.' Cf. Capt. Feaugeas, 'L'Enseignement dans le Moyen Atlas' (19 May 1948), Ms. No. 1336 in collection at Centre des Hautes Etudes sur l'Afrique et l'Asie moderne, Paris.

authority, the Native Affairs officer will be the real chief. This consequence should not frighten us; however, it is appropriate to mention it.'[1] The contrast between this view and Bernard's previous opinion, cited above, p. 194, is too eloquent to require comment.

The image of Moroccan society which we have called the Moroccan Vulgate was essentially completed by 1919. The set of stereotypes about the Moroccan state which had developed by 1912 were supplemented by a composite stereotype of the Berber and the place of Berbers in Moroccan society in the years which followed. By 1919 a policy which sought to capitalize upon the alleged differences between Arabs and Berbers had been elaborated, and was integrated into the wider policy pursued under the protectorate. The distinctions between *makhzan* and *siba*, and between the political and religious authority of the sultan, had been united to that between Berber and Arab in such a way that each supported the other. The Berber Myth which crystallized between 1912 and 1919 derived its principal features from the romantic stereotype of Berbers which had been developed earlier in Algeria by French observers who were convinced that the Kabyles were not Muslims in any real sense. The ultimate goal of the Kabyle policy which France had pursued in Algeria in the 1880s and 1890s had been the assimilation of the Berber-speaking Kabyles into French culture and civilization. Similarly, the policy which was designed in Morocco between 1912 and 1919 aimed at the eventual assimilation of Moroccan Berbers. Since the process was considered to be a long one, the Berber policy which was followed in Morocco concentrated in the short run on keeping the Berbers from becoming Arabized and Islamicized, and shielding them as much as possible from the unfortunate spirit of opposition which was beginning to affect the Arabs of the cities and the plains. By serving as guardian of the customs and traditions of the Berber-speaking populations of Morocco, it was thought, France could help them evolve at their own pace toward a future which would be neither French nor Arab.[2] After 1919 the final goal of assimilation gradually faded away when it was discovered that the Moroccan Berbers were in fact as Muslim as the Arabs were, but the policy of shielding the Berbers from inevitable incorporation into the mainstream of Arabic civilization continued.[3] The contradictions of such a policy in a Morocco which was beginning to stir under the influence of a growing nationalist movement were not long in appearing. The controversy over the Berber *dahir* discussed elsewhere in this volume ignited an immense opposition all over Morocco, and marks one of the first successes of the young nationalist movement. By 1930 the time had long since passed when a romantic and paternalistic image of Berbers would be quietly accepted by Moroccans. The study of the opposition which the persistence of the stereotype of Berbers excited in the years which followed belongs, however, to the story of the emergence of Moroccan nationalism and is not our concern here.

Summing up, the development of a Berber policy in Morocco prior to 1919

[1] Ibid.
[2] Robert Montagne, *La Vie sociale et la vie politique des berbères*, Paris, 1931, p. 7. (Preface by the editors of *Afrique française*.)
[3] Ibid., p. 18.

was closely connected to the crystallization of a series of stereotypes about Berbers and Berber society derived from the Algerian Kabyle myth. Early students of Moroccan Berber society tended to emphasize in their analyses the importance of *izerf* (customary law) and the *jamaa* to the social and political organization of the Berbers. In so doing, they allowed themselves to be guided by previous French discoveries about the nature of Algerian Kabyle society. The policy which was designed from these studies, therefore, tended to reflect doubly the burden of the Kabyle experience. This Berber policy was to change but slightly in the years which followed World War I, although the final aim of the policy would be altered from assimilation to a system resembling the Indian reservations established by the United States government. Later studies of Berber society in Morocco would reveal numerous inexactitudes in the analyses of the 1912 to 1919 period, but these discoveries had little effect on the general outlines of the Berber policy. Both the image and the policy toward Berbers fit together closely with the overall image of Moroccan society which developed before 1912. Thus in the end we can see how French native policy, colonial ideology, and sociology interacted in a particularly complex and powerful fashion, shaping in large measure our views of Morocco and Moroccan society to the present.[1]

[1] The research upon which this study is based was made possible by a grant from the Faculty Research Committee of the University of California at Santa Cruz during the summer of 1970.

9

Kenneth Brown

The first manifestation of modern mass nationalism in Morocco is generally
attributed to a communal recitation of the *latif*—an invocation to God—that
took place following the noon prayer in the Grand Mosque of Salé on Friday,
20 June, 1930. The recitation of this invocation was a protest against the promulgation on 16 May of that year of a decree that became known as the 'Berber
Dahir' (Arabic *zahir*—a decree signed by the Sultan of Morocco). The protest
against this decree (in matter of fact drawn up by the authorities of the French
Protectorate who had ruled Morocco since 1912) became the catalyst for
politicization of the urban masses and for the development of an ideology that
transformed what may be termed a 'pre-national feeling' into nationalism.

The ideologists of Moroccan nationalism and many of its students have
interpreted the opposition to the Berber Dahir primarily as a rejection of France's
policy of cultural assimilation.[2] However, it will be argued, only by reconstructing
the total situation preceding the movement against the Dahir in Salé does it
become possible to understand how cultural and religious sensibilities were
transformed into a nationalist movement. The Moroccan case seems to confirm
the view of Leonard Binder that 'as a minimum nationalism involved an ideological adaptation of traditional institutions to new social and economic
conditions'.[3]

THE ILLUSION OF VICTORY

To begin with, it is necessary to mention the phases of the French conquest of
Morocco following the establishment of the Protectorate by the Treaty of Fes in
1912.[4] While the plains of the country had fallen to French troops without
prolonged resistance, total 'pacification' (using the French terminology) of the
southern Atlas mountains and the fringes of the Sahara was not completed until
1934. Moreover, and of special significance, a rebellion in the Rif mountains of
the Spanish zone became a prolonged war between 1921 and 1926. Both Spanish

[1] An earlier version of this paper was presented to the African Studies Association,
Los Angeles, 1969. I want to thank my colleague Phillipe Schmitter for his comments.

Field and library research was carried out in Morocco between 1965 and 1967 through
the support of an NDEA-related Fulbright-Hays Fellowship.

[2] Cf. Allal al-Fasi, *al-haraka al-istiqlaliyya fi'l-Maghrib al-arabi*, Cairo, 1948, pp. 160–2
(English translation, *The Independence Movements in Arab North Africa* by H. Nuseibeh,
Washington, D.C., 1954); J. P. Halstead, *Rebirth of a Nation: the Origins and Rise of
Moroccan Nationalism, 1912–1944*, Cambridge, Mass., 1967, p. 266; Ch.-André Julien,
L'Afrique du nord en marche: nationalismes musulmans et souveraineté française, Paris,
1952, p. 148.

[3] *The Ideological Revolution in the Middle East*, New York, 1964, p. 2.

[4] The Spanish zone of Northern Morocco has been excluded from consideration.

and French armies were nearly defeated by the forces of Abd el-Krim and his short-lived Rifian Republic. Moreover, within five years of Abd el-Krim's defeat and before the total pacification of the countryside, the French found themselves faced with urban civil unrest. In the cities, modern Moroccan nationalism had opened a battle front where total French victory was to remain forever illusive.[1]

In Salé, French presence during the first decade of the Protectorate had caused frustration and anger, but little open resistance. On several occasions, eruptions of violence seemed imminent. Thus, when a former pasha had been exiled from the city and, again, when special taxes for trading and monopoly licences had been imposed, the shopkeepers of the city closed their doors and street demonstrations took place. The local French authorities dealt with these manifestations by a show of force, and the older generation of leaders accepted, however bitterly, the *fait accompli* of colonial dominance. Protests were sublimated into vague millennarian hopes. Rare were those who took an oath never to leave the confines of their homes again lest they see a 'Nazarene'. Most people went about their business, although at least some spent their evenings at home endlessly and tearfully repeating: *msha l-Islam; jawu l-kuffar* ('Islam has perished; the infidels have come') or muttering about the humiliation of being forced to pay the *jizya* (a tributary tax levied according to Islamic law on Christians and Jews).

The French were aware of the latent hostility in Salé toward them and its potential as a source of trouble. Thus, in 1925 Michaux-Bellaire, an adviser in Section des Affaires Indigènes (the former Mission Scientifique du Maroc), was asked by the Résidence Générale to move the Section to Salé in order 'to be in contact with and abreast of the real feelings of an especially closed segment of the Muslim population that was a sort of center of opposition, where one best finds the echo of much discontent, well founded or not . . .'[2]

SOCIAL AND ECONOMIC UNREST

Discontent in Salé had economic as well as political origins. Much has been made of the expansion of Morocco's economy from 1912 until the onset of the great Depression of 1930, with particular emphasis on the tremendous growth in

[1] A. Toynbee, *Survey of International Affairs, 1925, Vol. I : The Islamic World Since the Peace Settlement*, RIIA, Oxford, 1927, pp. 105–63; ibid., 1937, pp. 486 ff.: '. . . in Morocco . . . the transference of the struggle from the battlefield to the newspaper column and the public meeting was the most revolutionary (in the Maghreb) in its social effects, because . . . there was no chronological interval at all between two chapters of social history which were divided from one another by a vast psychological gulf.' The contrast with sub-Saharan Africa is striking: cf. T. O. Ranger 'Connections between "primary resistance" movements and modern mass nationalism in East and Central Africa', *Journal of African History*, IX, pp. 437 ff., 631 ff.

[2] Commandant Tarrit, 'La Direction générale des affaires indigènes du Maroc', *Cours préparatoire au service des A.I. Conférence 24.1.1928*, Casablanca, 1928. Cf. R. Gerofi, 'Michaux-Bellaire' in *Tinga*, No. 1, 1953, pp. 79–85; A. Khatibi, *Bilan de la sociologie au Maroc*, Rabat, 1967, pp. 13–14.

foreign trade—from 170 million francs in 1912 to over three and three-quarter billion francs in 1929.[1] However, this economic expansion favored the non-Muslim segments of what had become a plural society segmented largely along religious lines. While major economic benefits were enjoyed by the French, and to a lesser extent by some of the local Jews, the standard of living of most of the indigenous population declined. These suffered from taxation, rising cost-of-living and monetary depreciation, lack of employment for the educated, decline of the crafts and commercial instability. The urban, educated young, in particular, were held back by a colonial system in which access to both power and wealth were almost entirely in the hands of foreigners.

In the community of Salé a few individuals had profited from the early years of the Protectorate; but by 1925, the beginnings of a ten-year depression were felt by all of the population. Three years later, in 1928, an agriculture crisis in Salé's hinterland had produced a general slump. Finally, with the disastrous crops of 1929 and 1930 and the initial effects of the international depression, all economic life in Salé had become extremely precarious.

A NEW GENERATION

These worsening economic conditions particularly affected the young men of the city—increasing their bitterness toward the French as well as the tensions between them and their elders. Since the early years of the Protectorate, and especially during the 1920s, the young students of Salé had been the hope and the fear of their parents and of the French administration. A French *Contrôleur Civil* of Salé characterized the educated youth as the *enfants terribles* and the 'tainted' of the city's society and noted that 'in the eyes of their families they benefited from the prestige that their knowledge of French ways gave them, making them able to judge and penetrate the mysteries of the Christians, work with them and eventually replace them'.[2] However, by 1925, administrative careers promised to and sought after by young educated Moroccans became progressively scarcer as Protectorate policy aimed at the recruitment of more and more Frenchmen. Administrative indifference toward and often denigration of these young Moroccans compounded the economic and social difficulties of the times and produced in them a clear and conscious feeling of second-class citizenship.

The local *Contrôleur Civil*, describing the bitterness of the young Slawis, found them a 'decent and discontented group, ready to accept any propaganda for agitation'. He claimed that the young encountered difficulties both in the European milieu and at home, for their fathers—'the white beards'—viewed with anxiety what they considered the unreasonable tendencies of their sons to

[1] Cf. J. Jouannet, *L'Evolution de la fiscalité marocaine* (Institut des Hautes Etudes Marocaines. Collections des Centres d'études juridiques, I. 38) v. III, Paris, 1953, p. 89, where the period 1912–20 is called 'the phase of creation' and that of 1921–29, 'the phase of prosperity'; Halstead, op. cit., pp. 93–4.

[2] Abbadie, *Rôle joué par Salé dans l'évolution de l'opinion marocaine au cours de ces dernières années*, CHEAM, No. 340, 1937, pp. 36–7.

speak out against and take exception to everything. It was, in his view, only when the young outbid their elders in religious fervor, as defenders of Islam, that they were welcomed with sympathy and that a sense of unanimity was felt.[1]

Indeed, there was an alienated and rebellious generation in Salé. Some fifteen years after the beginning of the Protectorate, young educated Slawis ranging in age from fifteen to thirty formed themselves into a group and made their presence felt in the city. Consisting of some thirty individuals, they had all received or were in the process of acquiring a modern education—although not necessarily in French schools. A few had studied in the 'School for the Sons of Notables', opened in Salé on a small scale in 1913 and later expanded, or in the Collège of Rabat. Most, however, had received a modernized traditional education in Arabic in one of the three 'Free Schools' (free of government domination) opened in Salé in 1921 under the impetus of the older leaders of the community. These schools (whose short existence coincided with the Rifian war) had been founded by the town elders to perpetuate among their sons the culture of Islam. They aimed at counterbalancing the effects of Gallicization—namely, the neglect of the Arabic language and of religious studies.

By 1927 some members of the group were actively engaged in their own form of 'political Arabization'. They had opened a store which carried the latest books, magazines and newspapers from the Arab east, begun the publication of a weekly called *al-Widad* ('Friendship') and formed 'The Islamic Literary Club'. At their meetings the political and cultural news of colonized Muslim peoples, as reported in the French and the Arabic press, were discussed. In 1928, the members of this club favorably impressed the older generation in Salé by presenting a modern Egyptian play in verse which invoked the glories of the famous Abbasid caliph, Harun ar-Rashid. The production was highly successful, thus achieving contact with the older generation, while also forming a bond of friendship with similarly oriented groups of young Moroccans in other cities. This was particularly important in dispelling the legendary enmity between the inhabitants of Salé and those of its sister-city across the river, the capital of Rabat.

Contact with the 'Association des étudiants musulmans nord africains', founded in Paris in 1927, also influenced the group of Salé, especially by way of a young Slawi who had studied oriental languages and law in Paris (the same who directed the group's play in 1928). The Paris association, most of whose members were Moroccans, regularly discussed colonial independence movements and met with other students and intellectuals—for the most part Muslims, eastern Arabs and personalities of the French left. The Paris association influenced Salé's group by introducing them to the ideas of Ataturk and Gandhi, and these men were added to the list of local heroes—Abd el-Krim and the Egyptians Mustafa Kamil and Saad Zaghlul.

FRANCE'S COLONIAL POLICY: 'DIVIDE TO RULE'

Parallel to the coming of age of this first Protectorate generation was the

[1] Ibid.

development of French native policy in Morocco. The architect of the original lines of this policy was the first Résident Général, Marshal Lyautey.[1] The guiding principles of French rule in Morocco, as he laid them down, combined pragmatism with romanticism. Colonialism and outright annexation were thinly disguised as a Protectorate; French domination was to be practised through Morocco's traditional Islamic political structure; and Moroccan society was to be modernized without destroying its religious personality. Lyautey's disapproval of secularization comes out clearly in an interview during which he spoke of his aims for the Moroccans hand-picked for a French education. The Marshal feared a generation of Muslim atheists without respect for authority. Were Moroccans to study and mix with Europeans, they might, he believed, lose their faith and try to become lawyers and politicians, forming a Moorish party like the Young Turks or Egyptians and falling prey to Bolshevism and anarchism. The Muslims had best remain believers under the control of their own Sultan.[2]

Indeed, the 1912 Treaty of Fes recognized the suzerainty of the Sultan under the control of the French Residency and promised to uphold the traditional religious respect and prestige of the Sultan, the religion of Islam and its religious institutions.[3] But, in effect, all political, military and administrative powers were exercised by the French, albeit in the name of the Sultan. This was accomplished through decrees—or *zahirs*—bearing the Sultan's seal and carrying the force of law. Such method of government was rationalized as indirect rule, but—as more than one French scholar has pointed out—decrees were issued whenever and for whatever reason the Residency deemed necessary. Rule was direct, and it was left to the jurists *a posteriori* to ratify the *faits accomplis*.[4]

One such decree issued in 1914 went relatively unnoticed until years afterwards, despite its contravention of the Treaty of Fes. The decree concerned the Berber population of Morocco, most of whom still remained then beyond the political control of the Protectorate. Stating that 'the tribes of the so-called Berber custom are and will remain ruled and administered according to their laws and customs under the control of the authorities', it attempted to assuage Berber fears of the consequences of submission.[5] As the Berbers began to come under the control of the French, a 'Berber policy'—already influenced by ninety years of colonial experience in Algeria—was formulated. Lyautey, ignoring his

[1] For a fairly balanced English summary of this fascinating and complex figure see R. Landau, *Moroccan Drama, 1900–1955*, San Francisco, 1956, pp. 90 ff. Lyautey's Berber policy is discussed at some length and with more attention to its subtleties elsewhere in this book.
[2] The interview with Lyautey dates from *c.* 1922 and is quoted in S. M. Zwemer, *Across the World of Islam*, New York, 1929, p. 229.
[3] Cf. Appendix A, Halstead, op. cit., pp. 273–4.
[4] Julien, op. cit., pp. 48 ff.; R. Montagne, *Révolution au Maroc*, Paris, 1953, pp. 134–5; R. Le Tourneau, *Evolution politique de l'Afrique du nord musulmane, 1920–1961*, Paris, 1962, p. 176. Julien has recently interpreted the exile of Muhammad V in 1953 along these same lines: 'Le refus du Sultan Mohamed V de signer les décrets royaux (dahirs), préparés par la Résidence, créait une situation que ne prévoyait pas le traité de Protectorat et ne laissait à ceux qui ne pouvaient convaincre d'autre issue que la force' ('A propos de mon septennat de Vincent Auriol', *Le Monde*, 29 October 1970).
[5] Le Tourneau, op. cit., p. 182.

own earlier insistence on Morocco's religious personality, informed his officers
that French interests called for the evolution of the Berbers outside the framework
of Islam. A committee appointed by him submitted a report in 1924 suggesting
that by destroying the unity of the Moroccan judicial system, the Berbers could
be strengthened as a counterpoise to the city Arabs.[1]

When General Steeg was appointed to replace Lyautey in 1925, steps had
begun to be taken to separate Berbers also by means other than the judicial
system. The educational system seemed to be aimed at assimilating Berbers to
French rather than Arabic culture.[2] To the five Berber primary schools established in 1923, twelve new ones were added within the next eight years, and the
famous Berber Collège at Azrou had been opened to their graduates. In these
schools all instruction was in French and there was no attempt to teach anything
connected with Islam and its culture. These steps, however, went unchallenged.
Only during the residency of Lucien Saint, appointed in 1929, did the Berber
policy run into serious obstacles.

Early in 1930, the French prepared a new decree to further along the separation
between Berbers and Arabs. In their eyes the decree was a simple judicial-
administrative reform, elaborating the decree of 1914 by creating Berber customary tribunals and courts of appeal and establishing the competence of French
tribunals in areas of customary statute where Frenchmen were involved. In
effect, the decree placed these courts beyond the jurisdiction of Islamic law and
its experts, the *qadis*, thereby clearly contradicting the terms of the Treaty of Fes.
However, the young Sultan, apparently unaware of the implications of the decree,
dutifully signed on 16 May.[3] This 'Berber Dahir', as it came to be called, confirmed for Moroccans their mistrust of French policy. The Dahir accelerated the
politicization of the urban young and offered them an issue that could rouse the
nation to political consciousness and prepare it for a modern, mass nationalist
movement.

[1] Halstead, op. cit., p. 71. See his excellent treatment of the development of France's
Berber policy, pp. 68 ff., including the quotation from a doctoral thesis on French education in Morocco written in 1928 by a former Residency official, R. Gaudefroy-
Demombynes: '. . . (it is) dangerous to allow the formation of a united phalanx of
Moroccans having one language. We must utilize to our advantage the old dictum "divide
and rule". The presence of a Berber race is a useful instrument for countering the Arab
race; we may even use it against the Makhzan itself.' (p. 72).

The logical conclusion of this policy was the enforced exile of Muhammad V. Yves Mas,
one of the magnates of the French press in Morocco, told Julien on 7 January 1953: 'Il
faut couper la tête au Sultan . . . de chasser les Arabes, qui sont des conquérants comme
nous, et l'on s'entendra parfaitement avec les Berbères, comme le Glaoui.' (*Le Monde*,
loc. cit.)

[2] Although aware of the attachment of Berbers to the Arabic language and to Islam,
P. Moussard, an administrator in Salé was one of the proponents of assimilation: '. . . less
vain than the Arabs, less imbued with their claimed superiority over the Christians, the
Berbers will be much more docile pupils for us . . . something must be done so that . . .
they become speakers of French and not of Arabic' ('Arabophones et berbérophones au
Maroc', *Annales de géographie*, T. 33, 1923, p. 282).

[3] The text may be found in full in Halstead, op. cit., pp. 276–7; Montagne, p. 183,
claims that the Sultan's entourage discerned the anti-Islamic character of the reform, but
did not risk informing him.

'LOVE OF COUNTRY IS AN ARTICLE OF FAITH'[1]

If we emphasize one of the several attributes of nationalism, namely, the aroused feeling of identification that comes from a deep and underlying sense of community produced by generations of living together, I believe that we shall understand better these early moments of Moroccan nationalism.[2] The sense of community in Morocco—of belonging to a group having like institutions and customs and sharing a sense of social homogeneity and mutual interest—cannot be appreciated without taking into account the religious force of Islam. The importance of Islam in matters of personal and national identification has been dealt with at length in the literature on Arab nationalism.[3] Here, the religious elements in Moroccan nationalism will be described in circumstantial detail, rather than in its own ideological terms. The focus of inquiry will be on Salé during the first decades of the Protectorate.

The leaders of Salé, particularly those of the older generation, had feared that the spread of French education—whether in the cities or the countryside—would undermine the religious beliefs of young Moroccans and cut them off from the Arabic language, the vehicle of religious learning. They sensed that an education in French, just as in Arabic, transmitted a whole way of life, the one the way of life of Christianity, the other that of Islam. An example of the opposition of these two ways of life which they cited was the French insistence in their schools on the ideas of absolute personal liberty and of impartial justice. To their minds these ideas contradicted basic principles of Islam. They were not concerned with philosophical debate about these principles. For them it was a question of jurisdiction. They firmly believed that as Muslims they had absolute authority to rule their homes and courts in accordance with their religious laws and precepts, as they understood them. They were especially fearful lest their sons contest that authority and rebel against them in thought or in deed.[4] To their mind, their literary language, religious beliefs and the 'natural order' of their institutions were basic to their identity as individuals and as a national community.

---

[1] The phrase (*hubb al-watan min al-iman*) has been attributed to the Prophet Muhammad, much used by the young Ottomans and popularized by the Lebanese Christian writer al-Bustani (d. 1883). Cf. A. Hourani, *Arabic Thought in the Liberal Age, 1798–1939*, London, 1962, pp. 78 ff., 99 ff. It became a slogan of Moroccan nationalism in the early 1930s.

[2] Definitions of nationalities are, of course, debateable. I agree with Hans Kohn that objective criteria are comparatively irrelevant, that what is most essential is the corporate will of a people. Cf. his *The Idea of Nationalism*, New York, 1967, pp. 13 ff. Modern nationalism essentially builds upon this corporate will with its ideology.

[3] An excellent summary, including material on Morocco may be found in A. Hourani, loc. cit.

[4] These are the terms in which my informants, men who had grown up in Salé during the 1920s, described the concerns of their fathers. A late nineteenth-century historian of Salé expresses a similar view in regard to the European concept of freedom (*al-hurriyya*): '. . . (it) is total atheism for it necessitates the abolition of the rights of God, the rights of parents and the rights of humanity'. Ahmed b. Khalid an-Nasiri as-Salawi, *Kitab al-Istiqsa*, Cairo, 1894, Vol. 4, p. 226.

The greatest threat to these was the intrusiveness of their opposites which were embodied in the culture of the Christian colonialists.

Reports from elsewhere in Morocco and from other Muslim lands under French domination seemed to confirm their worst fears of proselytism. In Salé itself, there was much suspicion when an Algerian convert to Christianity became one of the earliest French teachers in the local school and anger when Protestant missionaries and Catholic priests contacted the young. Moreover, there was general resentment of the fact that many French teachers and translators in the Berber-speaking areas of Salé's hinterland were Algerian Berbers who had converted to Christianity and that Berber translations of the New Testament were being distributed. Many felt that there was a plot afoot. An Arabic biography of Jesus had found its way into many cities, and Christian missions boasted of their achievements among the Moroccans. Particularly scandalous to the urban bourgeois was the conversion to Catholicism of the son of one of Fes's most prominent families and his entry into a Franciscan seminar. These fears grew when the Vicariat Apostolique of Rabat in its journal *Le Maroc catholique* began openly propagating the idea of converting 'Berbers' to Catholicism and reprinted and circulated a letter written by the famous Père de Foucauld in which he urged that North Africans be Gallicized by becoming Christians, lest they become Turkish-type nationalists.[1] Earlier reports from Tunisia of demonstrations against French disabuse of Muslim cemeteries and, in 1925, against the erection at the gate of Tunis of a statue of Cardinal Lavigerie holding a cross made it seem to these Moroccans that the French indeed had a master plan aimed at destroying the religious content of national identity in each of the North African countries.

These anxieties whose causes were in part real, in part imaginary, had deeply troubled the old men in Salé who were the leaders of public opinion. In May 1930, the young of the city became equally anxious and aroused. On the eve of the promulgation of the Berber Dahir, old and young had been agitated by press reports about the preparations for and the celebration of the Centenary of the French conquest of Algiers and the public celebration by Catholics that was held in Tunis during the Eucharistic Congress in Carthage.[2]

Thus, the factors already mentioned—economic upheaval, social unrest, cultural change and resentment of colonial domination—were compounded by outraged religious sensibilities. These were all important variables in the maturation of political consciousness and the beginning of a modern national movement in Morocco. The reaction in Salé against the Berber Dahir was the immediate precipitant of that mass participation that made the movement

---

[1] The letter, dated 1916, is reproduced in full in G. Spillmann, *Du protectorat à l'indépendence: Maroc 1912–1955*, Paris, 1967, p. 57.

[2] President Bourgiba later was to write: 'The Eucharistic Congress of Carthage was in part at the origin of my combat for the independence of my country. I saw there Europeans dressed as "Crusaders", pompously walking through the streets of our Muslim city.' (Quoted by Spillman, op. cit., p. 60.) North African students in Paris telegraphed a protest, and a proclamation appearing in the press with 125 signatures asserted that 'the true aim of the Congress was a violent crusade against Islam in North Africa'. Cf. J. Berque, *La Maghreb entre deux guerres*, Paris, 1962, p. 231.

possible. A summary of what happened in Salé told in the words of one of the participants in the events of the summer of 1930 vividly illustrates and helps explain the transformation that took place.[1]

'A PENNYWORTH OF BENZOIN IS ENOUGH TO MAKE ALL OF SALÉ SMELL SWEET'
(local proverb)

In the spring of 1930, Abdellatif Sbihi was working as a translator for the Administration. In the course of his work, the text of the Berber Dahir came through his hands (in the middle of May, before anyone knew about it). After arguing with his superiors over the contents of the decree, he resigned in protest. After his resignation, Abdellatif went to the Collège in Rabat where many of the young from Salé were studying. He told them about the Dahir by which, he argued, the French were trying to divide Morocco. He didn't talk about Islamic law, but spoke of *territorial division*. Then he went to Fes and talked to people. Soon he saw that his way of presenting the threat in terms of a single territory[2] that should not be torn apart was not understood by the people. For them he had to say: 'Islam is being violated in its very being' ('Islam yumass fi jawharih'). That successfully excited people.[2]

Shortly after the promulgation of the Dahir, the schools closed for the summer. Abdellatif would come to the beach and harangue the young people, both those in French and in Arabic schools, about the Dahir and the need for action. The young would return to the city and tell everyone about the great danger menacing Islam. The old learned people began to be concerned when they saw the Berber Dahir as an issue of Islamic law, not of territory.

'The recitation of the Latif made it a matter of Islam'

On a Wednesday afternoon a group of the young met at the beach and discussed the Dahir. They were searching for some dramatic way to stir up everyone and to confront the French with an organized opposition. Then Abdelkrim Hajji suggested that they recite the *latif* (the prayer for rain). Everyone approved.[3] Returning to the city Abdelkrim found a teacher from

[1] This description is an edited translation from a tape-recorded interview with Ahmad Maaninu held in Salé in 1966. In its general lines, the information has been corroborated by other interviews and through writings that appeared in the Moroccan press to commemorate the 1967 anniversary of the promulgation of the Berber Dahir.

[2] *trab* from Classical Arabic *turab* ('soil').

[3] In Morocco the orthodox prayer for rain or natural calamities such as earthquakes or eclipses of the sun—*salat al-istisqa*—was sometimes associated with an invocation called *al-latif* ('the Benevolent'), one of the names of God in Islamic theology. After the orthodox prayer for rain and formal prayers in the mosques the *latif* invocation would be repeated several hundred times. Cf. A. Bel, 'Quelques rites pour obtenir la pluie en temps de sécheresse chez les musulmans maghrébins', *Recueil de mémoires et de textes* (XIV. congrès des orientalistes), Algiers, 1905, pp. 49–98; E. Westermarck, *Ritual and Belief in Morocco*, London, 1926, Vol. 2, pp. 254 ff. The repetition of the word *al-latif* was also part of the litanies of some religious orders; a tradition had existed in Morocco by which a determined number of *latifs* was recited by order of the Sultan in times of grave crisis. Cf. A. Peretie, 'Les Médrasas de Fès', *Archives marocaines*, Vol. 18, 1912, p. 326.

one of the Koranic schools and gave him a few coins in order to recite the *latif* for the recovery of his grandfather who, he claimed, was quite ill.

I had just returned from the pilgrimage and found everyone in turmoil.[1] Abdellatif was very active, and people were gathering around him as in the days of the Prophet Muhammad. The French *Contrôleur Civil* observed everything and wrote reports. Then he would call in the older men of the city—many of whom worked for the municipality—and warn them that their sons had been meeting with Abdellatif and that they risked punishment. These men would try to quiet their sons, but their chastisement and the rebelliousness of the young only increased the turmoil in the city.

Meanwhile, many people, both the notables and the mass, had begun to say that the French were trying to turn them into Christians: that idea got into the heads of Moroccans. The simplest and the most cultivated believed that France wanted to eliminate Islam and its Law.

On Wednesday night those of us who had just returned from the Pilgrimage went to our lodge.[2] Our family are Darqawa. By tradition whoever returns from the pilgrimage goes directly to the lodge of his religious order. There is a special meal and religious chants are sung.

Abdellatif gathered a group to come to the lodge to greet me. The lodge was full. There were about a hundred old, bearded men reciting prayers and invocations while food was served according to our customs. Suddenly all of these young men without beards entered. (At that time, whoever didn't let his beard grow was thought to have committed a sin. Whoever let his hair grow a bit was considered a Christian—a Christian-and-a-half. Whoever wore a tarbush, instead of wrapping a turban on his head was a good-for-nothing.) When they came into the lodge, everyone was startled. Some said, 'What are they doing here? They are desecrating the lodge!' Others said, 'No, they too are God's. Let them return to the Islamic way.'[3]

Abdellatif approached the head of the order, a man who was also the sermonizor of the Friday-noon prayer in one of the mosques of Salé. He said to him: 'Why are you offering praises to the Prophet while his Law is in the process of being destroyed here in Morocco? You are against Islam, against Muhammad!' He was ordered to leave the lodge. Then he told everyone that they must recite the *latif*. (It is for times of drought, an epidemic, locusts, any terrible thing such as a crisis in commerce or a bad crop.) The young dramatically left the lodge, but I remained. I was a guest and in the security of this lodge of my father and our family.

On Thursday, the *Contrôleur* learned that a teacher had recited the *latif* and that Abdellatif was trying to get others to do the same. He worried when he heard that Abdellatif (whom he knew perfectly well and liked) was praying and reading the Koran with tears pouring down his face, screaming to the people,

---

[1] It was *layla dukhul al-hujjaz* ('the night of the pilgrims' return').

[2] *zawiya*—the meeting place of a religious order.

[3] 'desecrating'—from *anjasa* ('to contaminate, defile, make impure')—the opposite of *tahara* ('cultic purity'). 'The Muslim way' (*tamsilmit*) is an abstract noun constructed according to a linguistic pattern of Berber from the Arabic *Muslim*.

'read, read, get up . . . do something . . . be brave—not a bunch of infidels,' and stirring them up against the Dahir so that they cried over the fate of Islam.

Meanwhile we had decided to organize a *latif* at the Friday-noon prayer the next day. The *Contrôleur* knew all about this from his spies. That night, on Thursday, my maternal uncle had a party honoring our return from the pilgrimage, and all of my young friends including Abdellatif were there. While we were eating, two soldiers from Rabat came to arrest Abdellatif. Before leaving he reminded us that we had not the means to leaves our homes, to revolt. If we did that we would only create anarchy. He made us promise only one thing: that when the Imam ended the noon prayer the next day, we would begin reciting the *latif*.

The *Contrôleur* learned that we planned to recite the *latif* the next day; he called in the Pasha and told him to keep a group of us (he knew exactly who the leaders were) in his house, so that we should not go to the mosque. One of the men working in the municipality, also of the Darqawi religious order, was like a brother to my father. In fact, I addressed him as my paternal uncle. He was a respected adviser of the *Contrôleur*, and therefore able to ask him to be lenient with me, since I had just returned from the pilgrimage, was a religious boy, a dervish of the Darqawa. He told him that if I were to be arrested, there would be a great scandal, crying, screaming women and so on. On my uncle's pledge, the *Contrôleur* allowed me to remain at home. At around ten o'clock next morning, 20 June (Friday) my father told me that I was to remain in the house because he had promised his friend that I would do so. However, I gathered a group of young friends and instructed them to scatter themselves throughout the Friday mosque and to spread the word that the *latif* should be recited with the Imam, if he said it, or without him, if he did not. Everyone was ready. The old people, the pious, were happy to hear that there was to be a recitation of the *latif*. They were always eager for a religious experience—without demanding why.

Moreover, the economic situation was bad. The crop had failed and there was inflation. People felt disgust.

The imam of the Grand Mosque at that time, Hajj Ali, was around eighty years old. Every Friday he would ride to the mosque on a donkey, or a horse. He also delivered the sermon, and when he spoke he was like a twenty-year-old. He had already given the sermon of allegiance for Mawlay Hasan I. I contacted his grandson who was a friend of mine and asked him to tell his grandfather that I had just come from the pilgrimage and wanted to visit him. Hajj Ali had made the pilgrimage five or six times. He loved the Prophet with great piety and emotion; often he cried when he prayed, because of the depth of his religious feeling. Just as he was ready to leave his house, his grandson presented me to him: Hajj Ali exclaimed: 'Welcome, welcome to a man of the Messenger of God. Oh God! Oh God! Oh Prophet! . . .' His turban and cloak fell to the ground in his excitement. He was crying as I bent to kiss his hand. Then I told him that in the Hijaz there was much unhappiness; everything was expensive and people were distressed. I told him that they had asked that we recite the *latif* to ask God's assistance. Hajj Ali answered: 'Have we any other way, but God's way? Of course, we'll recite the *latif*.' I kissed his hand and left.[1]

Then I went to the head of the Darqawi lodge, the prayer leader of another Friday mosque—the Shahbah. I found him at the barber's being groomed for the Friday prayer, and he greeted me heartily. (We were all Darqawa.) I told him that it had been unfair of him to ask Abdellatif to leave the lodge. I explained to him that, after all, according to Islamic Law we were all Muslims, and what we wanted was only in the interest of Islam. He answered: 'There is a Sufi proverb: "How can the shadow be straightened when the plant is crooked?" Those people . . . they shave off their beards, urinate standing up, let their hair grow and so on. They do not pray, they are impure.' I told him that what was important was that they were the sons of Islam and that they wanted to make Islam victorious. I asked him to help them to do that, like the 'Shaikh of Islam', Hajj Ali who had agreed to recite the *latif*.

Shortly after noon I went to the Grand Mosque and found it full. Everyone was there except the group which had been kept in the Pasha's house. The Pasha had gone to pray with the Sultan in Rabat. His brother, and First Assistant had come to watch over the five fellows under surveillance. He was a cousin to one of them, a brother-in-law to two others and a cousin to Abdellatif. (Here in Salé, everyone is related to everyone else. It is one big family!) One of the fellows had said to his cousin the Pasha before he left: 'You are a pasha of Islam, a learned man of the Muslims. Are you going to pray and leave us here unable to do the same? We might as well be in prison; then we would have an excuse. Do you know God, and we not?' The Pasha was a learned and modest man and did not like to upset anyone. But he lacked courage. He said: 'You have been sent here by the authorities so as not to create agitation in the mosque.' Then the Pasha told his brother that if there was a *latif* in the Grand Mosque, it would be a sign that it was not of the doing of the five youths. In that case, they should then be allowed to go to the Shahbah mosque.

In the Grand Mosque Hajj Ali, after he had pronounced the sermon, summarized it, as is the custom, by a verse from the Koran about wickedness and distress. He implied that the present situation in the city was a result of the misdeeds of the people. Then he said that if these people were to return to the right path, they should begin by reciting the *istighfar*[2] and the *latif*. It was extremely dramatic. He was an old man, but in leading the *latif* his voice cracked out across the mosque and electrified all those present.[3] After that everyone remained to recite the *fatiha* (the opening verse of the Koran). This was very unusual. It was as if something very heavy had descended on all of us. No one moved. Everyone remained sitting.

Upon hearing that the *latif* had been said in the Grand Mosque, the Pasha's

[1] Some people in Salé insist that Hajj Ali was well aware of the real reasons behind the request for the *latif*.

[2] The *istighfar* is an invocation of God's forgiveness. It is normally a part of the prayer for rain for it is believed that calamities are a form of punishment by God.

[3] According to an article from the newspaper *al-Alam* (2 April 1967) the roof of the Grand Mosque was filled with women who 'followed in all modesty the heart-rendering invocations'.

brother allowed the five youths to go to the Shahba mosque. They sat directly in front of the Imam. When he saw them, he understood that they had come to see if he would recite the *latif*. What did he do? He gave a sermon in which he spoke about the youths, their lack of prayer, how they had gone astray, and would have to recognize and abstain from abominable things. And then he led the assembly in the *latif* . . .

After that we began to recite the *latif* on every possible occasion and exchanged visits with our friends in Rabat, reciting it in each other's mosques. All of the stores closed down so that everyone could participate in its recitation. An extremely electric situation had been created.

'DO NOT SEPARATE US FROM OUR BERBER BROTHERS'

Within several weeks of these events in Salé, young men were organizing recitations of the *latif* in mosques throughout Morocco's major cities. The French reacted by arresting those whom they considered responsible.

The imprisonment of young men in several cities furthered the determination of the others to continue using a tactic which had proven extremely effective.[1] When later that summer the ritual wording of the *latif* was changed so as to invoke God's aid in the national struggle, the initial symbolic concensus expressed in the invocation had developed into a politically conscious movement.[2] As the summer of 1930 wore on and the campaign grew more virulent, many of the young urban leaders were imprisoned or exiled. In Europe, North African students and Shakib Arslan, the head of the Syrian–Palestine Committee, promoted a widespread attack against France's Berber policy. *Latif*s in support of Morocco's cause were recited throughout the Muslim world.[3]

REFUGE AND REVOLUTION

The political consciousness that emerged in Morocco in response to the Berber

[1] That the Slawis were aware of a choice of tactics is clear: later in the summer they considered holding a street demonstration but were advised by Muhammad Balafraj, vacationing in Rabat from his Paris studies, to 'continue the methods of Gandhi and offer no provocation to the French that could lead to violence'. The resemblance of the *latif* to the Indian *hartal* (a general strike accompanied by prayer and fast) was apparent to the young Moroccans, particularly those who had studies in France. Delegations of Muslims and Hindus in Europe had organized *hartals* in their countries as early as 1919. Cf. L. Massignon, 'Introduction à l'étude des revendications islamiques, in *R.M.M.*, T. 39, 1920, p. 25.

[2] 'Oh God, the Benevolent, we ask of You benevolence in whatever fate brings. Do not separate us from our Berber brothers!' Cf. al-Fasi, op. cit., p. 165.

[3] For details of the reverberations in Morocco, particularly in Fes, and the campaign abroad, cf. Halstead, op. cit., pp. 182 ff.; LeTourneau, op. cit., p. 185; Montagne (who claims that the local Moroccan reaction would have remained unimportant were it not for Arslan), op. cit., p. 184; Berque (who emphasizes the stridently religious tone of the campaign), op. cit., p. 230.

Dahir was conditioned by the colonial situation. It was, in part, a rejection of foreigners. Allal al-Fasi, the primary ideologist of Moroccan nationalism, has argued that Moroccans refused to accept assimilation to a nation of Europeans (*rumis*) whom they looked down upon. It was a refusal that emanated from a sense of pride. The French mistakenly believed that it came from a fanaticism (*taassub*) engendered by Islam rather than from a spirit of nationalism (*qawmiyya*). Thus, he argues, to further their goal of Gallicization, the Protectorate authorities adopted a policy of Christianization. Moroccan youth reacted against this policy and its embodiment in the Berber Dahir by informing public opinion and rallying the nation to oppose proselytism and assimilation.[1] This interpretation of the campaign against the Dahir and, indeed, the dominant ideology of Moroccan nationalism, emphasizes cultural and religious factors to the exclusion of those social and economic variables that have influenced the history of the movement.

To be sure, the choice in Salé of the *latif* was a symbol as well as a means of protest against colonial domination which was, at once, construed as a civilization, a culture and a religion. But people were not successfully mobilized only because of wounded national and religious pride. Without the social unrest of the period just prior to the Dahir such a politically conscious national movement would have been unlikely. The recitation of the *latif* set the tone and the vocabulary of opposition, but it should not be forgotten that the Slawis, and particularly the young among them, had chosen to employ the traditional invocation of God as a tactical weapon.[2] In this respect the *latif* had social as well as political functions. It breached divisions within society, putting an end to the strife between older and younger generations. In the account of events in Salé there is clear indication of the disapprobation of the 'vieux turbans' toward the 'jeunes tarbouches' (as the French liked to call them). The older men of the city showed an initial distrust and subtlety in their response to the evocation of religious symbols by the young. Yet, just as the theatrical production of *Harun ar-Rashid* had redeemed the young in the eyes of their fathers, so did their political dramatics—their insistence on the implicit dangers of the Dahir for Islam and their call for the recitation of the *latif*—serve to reintegrate them into the community and increase their prestige and influence. By the same token, social ties through kinship and religious orders were adroitly and opportunely brought into play by the young to further their cause.

For different reasons, then, the *latif* responded to the needs of disparate generations. While reaffirming the values of the old, compensating them for loss of authority, wounded pride and nostalgia for the past, the young had provided themselves with support for their own self-assertiveness. As one man in Salé put it: 'Although everyone participated in the recitation of the *latif*, most did not

---

[1] al-Fasi, op. cit., pp. 160–2, 165.

[2] There is little cause, none the less, to suspect the religious convictions of the young in Salé in 1930; in fact, some of them spoke of profound religious experiences in their lives and described the Latif as a 'gift from God'. However, that does not preclude awareness of the fact that they were manipulating and adapting a traditional religious symbol to secular goals.

understand what we were struggling for; they were simply relieved to see that we were, after all, actually Muslims.' Jacques Berque has phrased this differently, pointing out that the religious symbols of Islam were for many people a refuge, while for others they were a revolution.[1] In any case, in the Moroccan context it was Islam with its many symbols that acted as the midwife of nationalism.

CONCLUSION

Disruption in the social fabric of Salé nourished the response to the Dahir. Moreover, this response represented a demonstration against the disastrous economic consequences of colonialism and the dependence on the European market that came with it. The declining fortunes and prospects for a livelihood of individuals who participated in the campaign against the Dahir, in Salé and elsewhere, were important factors in their rejection of foreign domination. It was a time of economic, as well as political and social crisis. If these economic factors have not been examined here sufficiently, it is because their details remained beyond the modest limits of our immediate concern with the reaction to the Dahir in Salé. Yet even within these limits, we have tried to show that Moroccan nationalism need be analyzed in a wider sociological and economic context, one in which upheaval is not judged solely in terms of its own self-consciousness and manipulation of symbols.

The nationalist movement in Morocco began in the cities, particularly in the old, urban centers of Arabic culture. Political consensus among the inhabitants of these cities—Arabs and Berbers, young and old, rich and poor—expressed itself in religious symbols. In religion and its symbols the sense of national unity was articulated and the disagregative segments of society were pulled together. The Berber Dahir and the recitation of the *latif*, French policy of 'divide to rule' and Moroccan political tactics which aimed at finding the largest common denominator, reinforced religious sentiments and influenced the shape of the nationalist movement. The emergence of modern nationalism in Morocco, however, was never simply xenophobia or religious fanaticism. In the 1930s the meanings of Islam and its symbols were as varied and complex in Morocco as they were in the Arab East: 'a totality and an authenticity endangered by contemporary changes'.[2]

[1] 'De l'Islam refuge à l'Islam jacobin', p. 70; cf. E. Kedourie, *Nationalism*, London & New York, 1960, p. 101, where it is noted that many nationalistic movements ostensibly directed against foreigners were manifestations of strife between generations: 'nationalistic movements are children's crusades . . . stripped of their metaphysics and their slogans — and these cannot adequately account for the frenzy they conjure up in their followers — such movements are seen to satisfy a need, to fulfill a want'.
[2] J. Berque, *L'Egypte: impérialisme et révolution*, Paris, 1968, p. 527.

10

Louis-Jean Duclos

On 1 November 1955, when Berbers, still wedded to a traditional way of life, joined the war against the authorities of the French Protectorate, many Native Affairs experts were amazed and incredulous. Their surprise was to some extent understandable; for the Berbers had previously taken little part in the anti-colonialist activities pursued since the thirties by the nationalist movement. However, this was perhaps not sufficient reason for inferring that they were indifferent to the movement's goals as such.

Like all nationalist movements, it sought to reconstitute, safeguard and extend a collective personality of sufficient scope and unity to satisfy man's need to share social, cultural and political identity with as many others as possible. From a theoretical point of view, the Moroccan middle-class elite was undoubtedly in a position to fulfill this desire: linked with Eastern reformism by its Arabic culture, and with the European Left by forty years of colonial rule, the elite alone was able to formulate a doctrine, plead its cause abroad and disseminate it at home. Even in the field of direct action, its intellectual connections enabled it to devise relatively effective modern forms of resistance. Yet in addition to this ideological, or explicit, or conventional nationalism, there is an affective or implicit form (rather than 'modern' and 'tribal', or 'archaic' and 'developed'). Because of their relative cultural backwardness, presumably a product of their history, and their no doubt natural distaste for abstract speculation, the Berbers have not been adept at the former. It is my belief, however, that they have championed the latter; that leaving aside urban terrorism, they have without being aware of it steadfastly practiced nationalism, much as Monsieur Jourdain spoke prose, before, during and after the rise of conventional nationalism.

Not only did they resist foreign conquest better than others; they also reasserted Moroccan identity in opposition to such internal aberrations as the degeneration of local authorities into feudal parasites, or the adoption of denationalizing ideologies. So, at different stages of history, the specific, enduring national identity of Morocco has been maintained within the Berber world by attitudes and actions stemming from a steady and seldom resisted unconscious impulse.

In this respect, four socio-political facts, despite contradictory appearances and opinions, would seem to constitute important manifestations of Berber nationalism: brotherhood movement; state of the *siba*, the resistance to French penetration and the Army of Liberation. These are the crucial contributions of an affective nationalism to the emergence of present-day Morocco.

THE NATIONALISM OF THE BROTHERHOODS

Contrary to the *makhzan* (traditional government) institution and the basically aristocratic and feudal *caid* system, the brotherhoods, which have played an important part in Moroccan social and political life since the twelfth or thirteenth century, are of popular origin.[1] If indeed the masses were in the past imbued with nationalist feeling, its tokens should be sought in this direction, whatever conventional nationalists may say.

In their opinion, the brotherhood movement is merely a form of *maraboutisme*, that is to say adulation of a founding *marabout* (holy man) and stultifying subordination to the current *marabout* in authority. Furthermore, conditions prevailing in the past greatly restricted the sphere of influence of individual preachers and communal leaders, so that the movement was highly fragmented from the beginning; this later gave rise to political division easily exploited from the outside. The consequent hostility to the brotherhoods is motivated by two accidental factors: the influence of Eastern reformism on the first ideological nationalists, and the old rivalry between the throne (now allied to these nationalists), and the brotherhoods—especially, since 1908, that of Sharif al-Kittani.[2]

In fact, this constitutes a tendentious political interpretation of certain essentially apolitical aspects of the brotherhood movement. The fact that popular religious feeling was dissatisfied with the rigidly austere Malikite orthodoxy, imposed on Morocco by the religious advisers of the Almoravids, had little genuine bearing on Moroccan political style organization and the elaboration of a specific identity. Moreover, modern nationalist critics seem to have over-emphasized the somewhat idolatrous atmosphere of certain *zawiyas*,[3] taking notice only of some prominent individuals within the brotherhood movement, whereas it would have been more interesting to consider it from a sociological point of view as one of the few traditional institutions which have long provided the people with a strong sense of identity and active solidarity. Does it matter that consciousness of identity first developed on narrow territorial bases, if the conjunction of such areas of self-awareness provided Morocco as a whole with a means of simultaneous self-expression? The careful observer can discern in this phenomenon, at the popular level, elements of unity reflected in the convergent action[4] of spiritual leaders.

But unity does not necessarily signify the specific identity without which there would be neither nation nor nationalism. That the brotherhood movement attempted to achieve this identity, by gradually breaking away from its earlier Eastern connections and systematically stressing its (often purely imaginary) local origins, is confirmed by the popularity of certain legendary anecdotes, of which two at least are worth relating.[5] One tells how in the seventh century of the Mohammedan era, the Andalusian mystic who introduced to Morocco the teachings of the great Eastern sheikh Abdelkader el-Jilani was first required to undergo a period of 'naturalization' under a Berber anchorite named Moulay

[1] Ernest Gellner, *Saints of the Atlas*, London and Chicago. 1969 p. 8.

[2] In 1908, Sultan Moulay Abd el-Hafid captured the chief of the Kittaniya brotherhood and had him beaten to death. W. B. Harris, *Le Maroc disparu*, Paris, 1929, p. 256.

[3] In Morocco: principal or secondary seat of a brotherhood.

[4] H. Terrasse, *Histoire du Maroc*, 1949–50, p. 144.

[5] M. Michaux-Bellaire, *Les Confréries religieuses au Maroc*, Protectorat de la République française au Maroc, Rabat, 1923, pp. 38–58.

Bouazza, who is said to have enjoyed considerable prestige. The other takes place on the evening of the 'Battle of the Three Kings' (4 August 1578), when Moroccans of all regions, led by *murabitin* chiefly of Chadilist belief,[1] defeated the foreign enemy; wishing to give the victory a national character, the *murabitin* spread the belief that the Moroccan army's prowess was due to the intercession of a little-known local saint, Moulay Abdesselem ben Mechich, who suddenly acquired the reputation of having been the teacher of Sheikh Chadili.

It could be objected, of course, that from the time of the first Spanish–Portuguese attacks on Morocco, the brotherhoods constituted an Islamic movement, rather than a national one. But how then can one explain that in the sixteenth century, when the Turks threatened the eastern border of the country, the Sufi movement, unable to evoke a specifically national response in spite of its thorough local assimilation, allied itself with a cult of sharifian lineages (descendants of the Prophet) hardly permeable to Ottoman influence?

Throughout the ages, therefore, the brotherhood movement seems to have had a highly important nationalistic role at the ideological level, assimilating adaptable foreign ideas (Sufism,[2] Sharifism) and disseminating national values throughout a zone still in the process of self-definition; quite the opposite of the role of the various would-be central governments of Morocco. Although they were all, with the exception of the Idrissids, of Moroccan origin, their chief preoccupation was to denationalize their function in the name of Islam and pan-Arabism, of praetorianism and modernist reforms.

If one adds to this that at times when the monarchy was at its weakest, as during the Wattasid crisis (1420–1554), the *murabitin* and *shurfa* maintained military resistance and exercised a good deal of civil arbitration, they come to be seen as the spontaneous agents of national destiny, rather than the 'hypocritical prebendaries'[3] denounced by conventional nationalism and most observers.

It is true, nevertheless, that although the brotherhood movement, rooted in the popular classes pre-twentieth-century society folk culture and hence predominantly Berber, had been useful to the national cause, in the end it did not satisfy the needs of new nationalism, with its quite different set of symbols. The same applies to the *siba* phenomenon.

THE CIVIC '*SIBA*'

In Morocco, the term *siba* denotes the political and administrative dissidence of the tribes from the central government. Like the brotherhood movement, the *siba* is not a specifically Berber phenomenon; but it is, even more than the brotherhood movement, a rural phenomenon, and the Berbers played a major part in its inception. The *siba* is also a lasting and widespread expression of

---

[1] After Sheikh Chadili (twelfth century), reputed of Moroccan origin but buried in the East.

[2] Professor Terrasse speaks of the 'nationalization of Moroccan Sufism', op. cit., p. 145.

[3] J. Berque, *Le Maghreb entre deux guerres*, Paris, 1962, p. 74.

Moroccan popular spirit; it remains to be seen to what extent it reflects national aspirations.

Here again, conventional nationalism tends to confuse the issue; for its chief exponents, the Sultan and the urban Istiqlal bourgeoisie, had no desire to give too much credit to the tribes, even at the political level. While the balance of power remained undecided—and it was not resolved in favor of the throne until the sixties—both parties were inclined to claim credit for everything themselves; furthermore, they were unwilling to rehabilitate a style of conduct which had been a threat to them for centuries.

On the other hand, it may seem somewhat paradoxical to present a movement disputing the *makhzan*'s legitimacy[1] as expressing the national subconscious, hence as implicitly nationalistic. However, the hypothesis can be maintained, until a general sociological study proves that the *siba* is indeed something other than the following of a natural line of development or one of the higher forms of segmentation.

Numerous examples suggest that the *siba* is above all a repudiation of the lack of authenticity so often characteristic of the *makhzan*, despite its formal legitimacy. Not, however, because the *makhzan* was Arabic and Sharifian: there were many Arabs in the *bled es-siba*, integrated into tribal ethnic lineages with a majority or minority of Berbers, and the rural milieu, being deeply religious, was favorably inclined toward the *shurfa*.

Nevertheless, whenever the *makhzan* lapsed from its national duties with regard to defence, police or justice, the *siba* not only denounced such inefficiency, but also provided a context for partial alternative solutions, the conjunction of which added up to a response on the national level.

So, up to and including the first years of the Protectorate, the dissident tribes countered the *makhzan*'s conventional military defeats, and its compromises with the foreigner, with a popular militancy surpassing by far their political consciousness. For instance, after the defeat of Isly (1844), the border populations, and even those of the interior, did not resign themselves to the proximity of a dangerous and hated enemy; three years later, when Emir Abd el-Kader took refuge in Morocco for the second time, many tribesmen of the Fes region rallied round him, and sought in vain to prevent the Sultan from having him conducted by force to the border. Be it noted that by this act the Sultan must carry the major responsibility for Abd el-Kader's capture.[2]

The insecurity due to the *makhzan*'s incompetence, and the travesty of justice enacted in its name, were remedied to some extent by the traditional institutions preserved by the *siba*: customary institutions, true, and possibly of Berber origin, yet less particularistic than one might think, since they functioned fairly uniformly throughout most of the country, even in Arab tribes.

As well as compensating for the deficiencies of the *makhzan*, the *siba* supplied a '*national response*'[3] to certain domestic trends of which public opinion disapproved. The period of extreme anarchy at the beginning of the twentieth

---

[1] Cf. C. H. Moore, *Politics in North Africa*, Boston, 1970, p. 15.
[2] P. Gaffarel, *L'Algérie*, Paris, 1883, p. 246.
[3] E. Aubin, *Le Maroc d'aujourd'hui*, Paris, 1922, p. 241.

century, illustrated by the Bu Hamara episode, can be interpreted in this light. The young Sultan Abd el-Aziz, under the influence of questionable foreign elements, was then showing modernist tendencies quite incompatible with the state of Moroccan society at the time. The third national function of the *siba* seems to have been the defence of local freedom, hence the protection of fundamental social characteristics against the onslaughts of a 'domestic colonialism' devoid of any political point. To the practices of a farmed-out and 'expeditionary' administration, concerned chiefly with levying never-to-be-redistributed taxes and bolstering the precarious fortunes of personal rule, the tribes opposed aspirations for a political model allowing for a high degree of local autonomy. This model, which divided the country into numerous areas of primary identification on the basis of geographic, economic or cultural characteristics, did not *ipso facto* entail incoherency and anarchy on the national level. In fact, incoherency and anarchy were fostered by the sovereign's dividing tactics; outside his sphere of influence, attempts were being made to create vast political groupings in the form of tribal confederations. There is no proof that this system could not have spread throughout the kingdom, giving rise to a harmonious type of organization, combining alliances founded upon common characteristics with the preservation of differences.[1] This was no doubt the unconscious national ideal expressed by popular revolt against a useless despotism, which was itself devoid of philosophical content or political vision.

This hypothesis would seem to be confirmed by the fact that in their revolt against the sultans, the tribes generally refrained from attacking the specifically national functions of the *makhzan*; the 'crowned sharif' was seen as the Moroccan emblem of Islam, and by virtue of dynastic continuity or external prestige, as the symbol of national legitimacy.[2] Even when tribal dissidence was at its height, unless it was manipulated by a *rogui*[3] with national ambitions, some links were normally maintained between the tribes and the sovereign, upon whom the faithful, even in the most remote Berber areas, still called down the blessings of God.

The last quasi-traditional *siba* appeared immediately after the attainment of Morocco's independence, and seemed to express the desire of the inhabitants of the interior for a form of national unity in which the government would seek to ensure the harmony of complementary differences. Instead, the new state of affairs struck many Berber cantons as an attempt to place sole control in the hands of the often scarcely adolescent urban adherents of the Istiqlal. It was against this tendency, felt to be a kind of usurpation, that the rebels of Tafilalet (1957), the Rif and the Middle Atlas (1958) appealed directly to the king, as a national authority transcending the artificial political and administrative hierarchy.

Once more, no doubt for the last time, there prevailed the implicit conception of a 'natural' national order, such as the *makhzan* had long been entreated to ensure—in a dialogue whose prospects improved in proportion to the intensity

[1] Cf. J. Recoules, 'Siba au Maroc', *L'Afrique et l'Asie*, Paris, 1960, p. 14.
[2] Cf. Aubin, op. cit., p. 241.
[3] A would-be usurper of the throne.

of the *makhzan*'s own national orientation. This had been at a low ebb during the founding of the Protectorate, when the Berber tribes were almost alone in opposing this new national humiliation.

BERBER RESISTANCE TO THE PROTECTORATE

The tribes' twenty-seven-year resistance (1907–1934) to the penetration of the French army and administration is related in the two phenomena described above, the brotherhood movement and the *siba*. Like the former, it can be seen in part as a religious response to the preachers' call for a holy war; like the latter, it constitutes a revolt, in this case against a *makhzan* restored by a foreign army. Like both of them, it is a demonstration of nationalism: a refusal of the cultural deterioration consequent on foreign invasion, a condemnation of the highly-placed traitors who surrendered political freedom into foreign hands.

When one considers that resistance was also stimulated by economic grievances, chiefly the confiscation of pasture-land, it becomes manifest that the three chief demands of ideological nationalism: cultural identity, political freedom and economic independence, are to be found here. This is due to more than a coincidence of inspiration; at least during the initial phase, the tribes' resistance to the advance of French troops had a quality of unanimity which indicated, as it did forty years later, an authentic upsurge of patriotic feeling, the twofold nature of which has been noted by some observers.

Its first aspect is unconditional condemnation of the authorities who stooped to collaboration with the invader, chief among whom were Sultan Moulay Abd el-Hafid,[1] accused of betraying his country, and his brother and successor Moulay Youssef, who profited by this betrayal. The religious power of the sovereign, until then rarely challenged by the *bled es-siba*, seemed ripe for plucking; the two most important *roguis* involved in the resistance, El Hiba and Abd el-Krim, were granted *khalifa* status by the rural Arab and Berber populations. The people heeded their own conscience and the advice of local preachers, rather than the pronouncements made in favor of the new regime by the *ulema*, the discredited spokesmen for legitimacy, at the instigation of Field-Marshal Lyautey.

The second aspect of the almost national resistance movement animated by the Berbers, is the trans-tribal character it assumed in the Fes region, immediately after the signing of the protectorate agreement. It is indeed significant that at that time, old enmities yielding to present need, contingents of rural volunteers were drawn from all tribes without distinction, 'bearing one flag and possessed of one soul, all submitting to discipline and braving death for the sake of one idea.'[2] During the assault on Fes, Lyautey noted many signs of 'thorough

---

[1] F. Weisberger, *Au seuil du Maroc moderne*, Rabat, 1947, p. 272.

[2] M. H. Lyautey, *Lyautey l'africain. Textes et lettres*, T. 1, Paris, 1953, p. 20. Further on, he writes: 'The true order of battle found in one of the tents of an enemy camp on June 1st, addressed to more than 20 tribes, several of which had traditionally been hostile to each other, bears eloquent witness to their unity.'

organization and complete harmony'. The traditional antagonism between town and country had also undergone some changes, and one may well consider the Resident-General to be sincere and well-informed, when he notes the responsible behavior of the fighters who had infiltrated the city, and the patriotic quality of their propaganda, well suited to encourage, 'if not the wealthy and enlightened classes, at least the masses, to join forces with the attackers.'[1]

This first generation of resistance fighters was unsuccessful; but their failure is to be attributed to the defection of the elites and the disparity of technological resources between antagonists, rather than to immature national feeling on the part of the people. The desertion of the *makhzan* and its religious supporters meant the loss of the chief national symbols of the time, thus depriving nationalism of the possibility of sustained coherent action, and rendering it vulnerable to the discouraging influence of the urban and coastal Arab populations.

Furthermore, their superior strength enabled the French to keep up the war at a pace far exceeding the resisters' capacity for rapid long-distance communication, and hence for prompt mobilization.

The 1912 surge of national response seemed to hang fire; as the areas of resistance shrank, they tended to become exclusively Berber, with the paradoxical result that the milieux most favored by the colonial regime were those that had offered the most persistent resistance to colonization.

This hostility, so unyielding that many Berber tribes endured considerable loss of human life, livestock and pasture-land, lacked the coordination which would have emphasized its national scope. It did, however, achieve a certain unanimity, though spread over years. Unlike certain earlier *makhzan* attempts to recover control of the tribes, French 'pacification' almost never succeeded without a struggle in which the tribes 'exhausted all possible means of resistance'.[2]

The French Protectorate spread in concentric waves, from the *makhzan* urban areas to the rural periphery. Anticipation of its impact created acute tension; its aftermath left the tribes in a state of bewilderment. Under these conditions, the Berber cantons submitted to the local colonial authorities with seeming sincerity; for the apparent preservation of the traditional order, scarcely perturbed by the colonial presence, concealed the true extent of French aggression. Also, given the virtual disappearance of trans-tribal solidarity and the proven inadequacy of traditional, locally-based means of defence, it seemed realistic to come to terms with the invader, while remaining on the look-out for broad-based and plausible means of revenge.

One such attempt, and perhaps the only one, was Abd el-Krim's uprising. It was broad-based, because although it encompassed modernist tendencies, it was rooted in sociological conditions common to the Moroccan population, Berber and non-Berber, and expressed a general feeling; and it was plausible, because of its striking early victories, the extent of its territorial conquests, and the real danger it constituted for the Spanish and French colonial systems. Hope sprang anew in the encampments of the conquered areas, and many of the collaborating 'native chiefs' became more circumspect; even in Telouet, the center of Glawi

[1] Ibid., p. 17.
[2] G. A. Guillaume, *Les Berbères et la pacification de l'Atlas central*, Paris, 1946, p. 84.

authority, a French officer is said to have been held prisoner for some time, and taunted with descriptions of real or imaginary Riffian victories.[1]

The national reinvigoration consequent upon Abd el-Krim's exploits did not survive their disappointing conclusion. Certain authors consider, however, that the Riffian episode contributed to the political awakening of a first generation of almost modern nationalists, whom John Halstead terms proto-nationalists;[2] less because they were receptive to popular feeling, than because they were impressed by the support given the *rogui*'s cause by the French Left, which they respected and from which they hoped to receive help. In any case, however indirectly, the spontaneous nationalism championed increasingly by the Berbers alone thus made a first contribution to the conventional nationalism of the new urban political classes.

On the other hand, at a time when centers of affective nationalism were one after the other being overrun by the French, the cities provided no help whatsoever to the resistance. For want of a common language, and because of many unhappy memories, not least of which was their hasty and premature acceptance of the Protectorate, the urban elites, a vital channel for political communication between the cities and the tribes, were unable to make themselves heard. Indeed, at the time of the last flares of tribal resistance their nationalist position had barely been sketched out; in any case, even if they had been as actively patriotic as the rural resistance fighters, they would still have felt that the defeat of the tribes, by whatever means, relieved the sovereign and bourgeoisie of a long-feared menace. Furthermore, the urban elites felt little concern for the losses suffered by populations which by the urban norms of the period appeared beyond the pale, because of their remoteness from Arab culture and municipal life.

It was only at a later period that urban nationalists sought, with limited success, to enlighten the tribes. Such was the gulf between rural and urban milieux, that the institutional platform they shared was an extremely narrow one: the throne.

It is highly significant that the very year that urban ideological nationalism, with providential timing, took the place of tribal affective nationalism, Sultan Mohammed ben Youssef, who was raised to the status of a national symbol by the cries of the Fassi crowd, 'Long live the king!' (8 May 1934), was also the authority under whose jurisdiction El-Hadj Assou Baslem, the last Berber resistance in the Saghro mountains, wished to be placed, to the exclusion of all intermediaries.

THE LIBERATION ARMY

The twenty years between 1934 and 1955 were a slack period for rural nationalism in general, and Berber nationalism in particular. As a counterpart to the *trahison des clercs* and the sovereign's apathy, the tribes compromised themselves in various ways, tempted by opportunism or curiosity. A more serious matter,

[1] Cf. P. Vallerie, *La Pénétration militaire au Maroc*, Paris, 1934, p. 203.
[2] J. Halstead, *Rebirth of a Nation*, Cambridge (Mass.), 1967, p. 33.

however, for the preservation or creation of national consciousness, was the existence of a fairly sizable political clientele attached to a system, which maintained the reassuring and sedative aspects of the traditional order, while providing recourse against its individually or collectively burdensome aspects, whether these affected the group itself or its relations with the outside world.

One should not, however, exaggerate the extent of the Berbers' involvement in the institutions of the Protectorate. In fact, if they can be said to have tolerated the Protectorate rather more easily than did the intellectuals whose careers it stunted, the artisans whom it relegated to relative economic backwardness, or the peasants of the plains, driven back by colonization, the reason is that the Protectorate scarcely changed the ancestral harmony amongst men themselves and between them and their environment. It would seem, therefore, that the Berber nationalist reaction to the Protectorate appeared later than elsewhere, simply because it was less denationalizing for the Berbers than for the others. However, the inherent logic of the system meant that however lenient it showed itself initially, and however pro-Berber the policy of the Protectorate, sooner or later it had to clash with the Berbers: the nationalization of forest pasture-land, the increasing amount of forced labor required by the government, recurrent excessive taxation, inopportune government interference in matters where honor could tolerate no outside meddling, were some of the grievances which had to be countered. The most keenly-felt oppression, however, was less direct and tangible: the Berbers felt humiliated by the pro-Berber policy of the Protectorate, which frustrated their desire to share in the ever-fascinating grandeur of Islamic Arabism, as citizens of a Moroccan nation, encompassing all differences. This locally-felt alienation from the nation was compensated to some extent by the lofty far-away figure of the rehabilitated Sultan, whose opposition to the colonial authorities expressed the general need for dignity.

Among the Berbers, as among the urban masses, the coup which led to the exiling of the Sultan by the French, on 20 August 1953, contributed greatly to the surge of nationalism amongst tribes which took so many people by surprise.

Yet old hands at Moroccan domestic affairs had constantly warned: 'Keep an eye on the tribes.'[1] Indeed, symptoms of a certain inclination to challenge the colonial order had not been lacking, even in the Berber countryside;[2] if the tribes had foreborne from engaging in individual terrorism, this was because their structure does not lend itself to minority action; nothing happens until the entire group is won over.

This group conversion was perceived as a reality on 2 October 1955, when armed units from Nador, in the Spanish Protectorate, after roaming unchecked through the French zone, simultaneously attacked two posts in the Rif (Boured and Tizi-Ouzli) and two others in the Middle Atlas (Berkine and Immouzer des Marmoucha).[3] The Berber nationalism earlier expressed in the brotherhood

[1] Ascribed to the grand vizier Haj Mohammed el-Mokri by B. Desmazières, 'Meknès 1956–1961', *Archives du CHEAM*, Paris, Document No. 3726, p. 13.
[2] See my article in L.-J. Duclos, J. Duvignaud, J. Leca, *Les Nationalismes maghrébins*, Paris, Fondation Nationale des Sciences Politiques, 1966, pp. 27–8.
[3] See also my article, signed J. Ougrour, 'Le Fait berbère', *Confluent*, September-October 1962, p. 632.

8

movement and the *siba* had discovered a new mode of expression, half-traditional and half-modern: the liberation army.

Although the phenomenon took place under our very eyes, the genesis of this 'army', its organization, its channels for political and tactical initiative, the nature of its relations with the political leaders of conventional nationalism and with the urban resistance, remain obscure. One can but hope, in this context, that Aherdane and Khatib, known to have played a prominent part in the liberation army, will some day publish their reminiscences.

Perhaps we will then find out whether the liberation army was formed for purely technical reasons (in order to open a second front as a counterpart to urban terrorism) or for more political reasons. More specifically, to what extent, when, and how—unless, indeed, he played the part from the beginning—did Muhammad V become the guiding light of a force which fitted into the 'balancing act' strategy shown by Gellner to be a constant trait of the Sharifian ruling style.[1]

In any case, it will still be difficult to explain the speed and energy of the tribal uprising. It needed only the two pillars of the Protectorate to be undermined: the French army, which soon showed itself incapable of avenging the affronts of 2 October—theft of weapons and slaughter of administrators; and the native hierarchy, which had suddenly lost all Sharifian support after Muhammad V, returned from exile, did nothing to prevent the lynching, in the courtyard of his palace, of several *caid*s of the old order who had come to make amends (19 November 1955).

One could draw a striking parallel between that inaugural bloodshed and the quasi-ritual sacrifices enacted in some village settings in order to liberate occult forces. In the present instance, these two events conferred a patriotic and popular tone to the long-contained upheaval of which the liberation army was the signal and instrument.

In any case, the liberation army demonstrated anew that the Berbers could play a leading role in the defense and recovery of national legitimacy. Most of its troops were Berber, as were its chief combat zones, both in mountain areas and in flat country such as the Zemmours plain near Rabat; it was even Berber in that it incorporated Arab units at all levels, and refused to acknowledge the existence of an autonomous Berberism.

The liberation army seems to have been as nationalistic, at all levels, as the conventional nationalist elite and even the urban terrorists—if not more so. As far as actual conduct goes, it broke off all relations with the representatives of the old order, and forced the populations under its influence to do the same by force when required. Left to its own devices, it would have initiated a true revolution. Instead, many nationalist political leaders, through the contacts they maintained with the *métropole* which governed their cultural and economic thinking, were ripe for a certain neo-colonialism before they had even been decolonized.

With regard to political options and choice of allegiance, the liberation army, through its very cultural backwardness, was less a prey to partisan deviations

[1] Ernest Gellner, 'The great patron', *Archives européennes de sociologie*, No. 1, 1969, p. 63.

than the urban resistance and the historic leaders of the nationalist movement. Its political aim was extremely simple: national liberation, which they idealistically and quite disinterestedly linked with what was to their minds its highest and clearest symbol, the king. In more educated milieux, on the other hand, one often has the impression that the royal myth and the idea of the nation were merely means to gain power; if not from motives of personal interest, at least for the sake of ideological systems, of which the nation was not the center.

Finally, the highly effective role of the liberation army in the achievement of nationalist goals more than compensated for its belated appearance; ideological nationalism can be said to have paved the way, but it was the rural insurrection which ensured rapid, total and irreversible independence. Whether or not it was really 'beyond the control' of the Moroccans who were negotiating 'independence within interdependence', and notably of the throne, it had by destroying the local base of the Protectorate placed the French government in the position of having to discuss, with its back to the wall, the transformation of a state of affairs which no longer existed. On the other hand, it enabled the Moroccan negotiators to justify all their demands by asserting the need, here to ratify an accomplished fact, there to take heed of the wishes of the people, and throughout to cut the ground from under the feet of those who wished to extend their anti-colonialism to the whole of the Maghreb.[1]

The liberation army thus made gradual change impossible. Besides providing a radicalizing influence, the liberation army helped preserve the authenticity of the national(ist) movement after its victory. Without it, and in spite of the king's great prestige which would otherwise have lacked any embodiment in real force, power might well have been seized by irredentist theoreticians, internationalist ideologues, or unscrupulous Istiqlal members seeking to recolonize the country to their own advantage.

By denouncing politicians 'brought in from outside'[2] who claimed to be its spokesmen, and by attempting to form an alliance with the 'Muqawama' urban resistance—largely made up of urbanized former peasants—the liberation army laid the foundations for a strictly orthodox, if perhaps unproductive, form of popular nationalism.

Having rendered this final service, it had either to disappear or transform itself. The present king, then crown prince, made this clear after the bloody episode of the murder in Fes, by persons unknown, of one of the chief *moujahidines* (27 June 1956). During the following month, part of the liberation army joined the regular army, to pursue its mission of national defense; another dispersed itself in the arid southern region, where it proceeded to assert the 'uncontrolled' demand for a larger Morocco; the remainder returned home to serve as a reserve for the Throne. The anti-Istiqlal revolts of 1957 and 1958 contributed to the Mouvement Populaire, itself a pale reflection of the place of the Berber community in the balance of political forces in present-day Morocco.

Independence did not solve the problem of the self-definition of Moroccan political institutions and behavior. The forces which had brought about

[1] J. W. Zartmann, *Problems of New Power: Morocco*, New York, 1964, p. 69.
[2] Ibid.

independence therefore set about putting forward models corresponding to their several views and interests.

This undertaking, which was to complete the task of national reconstruction, led to a clash between the ideological nationalism of the politicians and the affective nationalism of the rural world. Their rivalry chiefly profited the monarchy, which both parties had helped to restore: by using the support of the latter against the former, it shelved for a long time to come all prospects of a conventional form of government based on an imported constitutional model. On the other hand, in the name of direct democracy, the throne claimed to restore and maintain the natural order of administrative and economic affairs, especially at the local level; thus, by flattering popular spirit and appealing to charisma, the 'Great Patron'[1] in fact gave himself a free hand.

By now, one can attempt to evaluate the contribution of Berber nationalism to Moroccan self-definition, as it appears a few years after decolonization. It must first be stressed that this Berber nationalism was never exclusively Berber.[2] The unconscious impulse which so often prompted an effort to transcend tribal barriers by asserting a wider form of solidarity, based less on descent than on geographic and historical factors, has always made the Berber community receptive to Arabs. On two occasions at least, at the time of the brotherhood movement and during decolonization, the Berbers even sought Arab support, provided that their specific identity be respected, or rather, in order to safeguard that identity.

Nevertheless, the Berber contribution to the achievements of Moroccan nationalism remains ambiguous. On the positive side, it prevented independent Morocco from straying into the waste land of ideological adventurism and verbal inflation; acting as a constant reminder of the deep-rooted social realities of the Moroccan people, the Berber community provided a resting-ground for determining the degree of adaptability of new ideas launched by the doctrinarians; in other words, it could decide whether or not to approve situations created by others, thus providing a guarantee of sorts.

Unfortunately for the prosperity and future of the Moroccan nation, the Berber contribution has also had negative effects. Their nationalism did no more than create, on the basis of some implicit territorial predestination to unity, a network of subtle relationships between ethnic groups which today still constitute separate units. This may well correspond to a necessary stage of integration; on the international scale, however, it constitutes a manner of withdrawal. This tendency to narcissism, along with the prosaic Berber spirit, which does not prevent them from becoming enamoured of some concrete (and local) myth, is manifestly opposed to the ability to draw from universal political and philosophical culture the vision without which there can be no truly dynamic development.

To conclude, and in relation with what has already been said, it may be of interest to note that national reconstruction followed completely different paths

[1] Gellner, 'The great patron', op. cit., p. 61.
[2] This is basically the contention of the discerning but perhaps excessive little book by G. H. Bousquet, *Les Berbères*, Paris, 1967.

in Algeria and Morocco. In Algeria, the leader of the time chose to rely on external military and intellectual forces, rather than the interior rural resistance. In Morocco, King Muhammad V and his son Hassan II made the opposite choice. This guaranteed them a degree of security, and still does. In the future, however, the 'crowned sharif' might do well not to take for loyalty to his person what may only have been the cult of a national myth.

11
Tribalism, Trade and Politics: the Transformation of the Swasa of Morocco[1]

John Waterbury

The dimensions of conflict and cooperation in Moroccan society are seemingly infinite, and any discussion of group contact, group interaction, group conflict and the like inevitably runs afoul of the difficulty of defining the group. Much of the ethnographic and popular literature that deals with Moroccan society was written by Europeans trying to impose some sort of analytic order upon a highly complex system of group relations, as remarkable for its ambivalence as anything else. Quite clearly certain of these attempts to put Moroccans into neat categories were designed to aid the French authorities in extending their political control through playing off allegedly rival groups.

The attempts at categorization were not wrong, but rather superficial, seizing hold of a single dimension and then treating it as if it were the only dimension. Of course, one of the focal points of all this analysis was the reification of the notion of an unbridgeable Berber–Arab cleavage. And, in exploring this theme, the French stumbled upon a vivid example that seemed to confirm their global analysis: the commercial and cultural rivalry between the 'Arab' bourgeoisie from the city of Fes (Fassis) and the Berber, Swasa,[2] petty tradesmen from the Anti-Atlas mountains. The major arena for their confrontation was and is the city of Casablanca.

The rivalry is not the figment of anyone's imagination; it does exist, but it imposes no binding constraints upon the actors involved. Its existence does not always help us predict anyone's behavior because there are so many other conflict situations, having nothing to do with Berber or Arab, in which an actor may be simultaneously involved. My central concern, however, is not so much the examination of ethnic group contact, as it is to seek the appropriate means to analyze the striking capacity of the Swasa to adapt to the urban, commercial environment. It seems to me that those explanations that insist upon Susi solidarity and group cohesion *vis-à-vis* other non-Susi groups, such as the Fassis, the French and the Jews, are essentially misleading. It has not been threats from hostile 'out-groups' alone that have driven the Swasa on to commercial success. Rather more importantly, their drive has been a function of their own internal rivalries and conflicts; that is, a function of their *lack* of solidarity, their failure to be a 'group' in our conventional sense of the word. Their success would be

[1] This paper is based on research carried out in Morocco in 1967–8. I have relied heavily on first-hand information and interviews that will go uncited. I am grateful to the Center for Near Eastern and North African Studies of the University of Michigan for making my research possible. A book-length treatment of the same subject appears as: *North for the Trade: The Life and Times of a Berber Merchant.* Univ. of California Press.
[2] Swasa is the plural of Susi, i.e. the people of the Sus region. I will use the two terms interchangeably throughout. See below for a full explanation of their geographic location.

impressive enough if one could explain it all by their solidarity and group identity. But this explanation takes much away from the far more ingenious arrangements they have devised, consciously or unconsciously, to allow them to engage in fierce internal battles for prestige all the while maintaining something resembling a common front toward outsiders. André Adam marvels at the fact that no Susi merchant has ever been declared bankrupt in Casablanca because other Swasa will always accept to absorb his debts.[1] On the other hand, Swasa talking about their own practices may cite the proverb about two brothers who run a shop together:

> We are brothers
> But when we evaluate the inventory
> We are enemies.

What weight then are we to give to ethnic group contacts in explaining group change in Morocco? What other factors are important? In the case of the Swasa, contacts with out-groups have been of considerable consequence, but one must look elsewhere to explain the transformations the Swasa have undergone. Their thrust out of the southern valleys toward the cities of the north has been the function of factors internal to the group rather than external. Primary among these is the problem of resource management in a poor land, a task carried out to a large extent through the segmentary lineages of the Susi tribes. The competition for scarce resources took place at many levels: among tribes, villages, lineages, families, and even brothers. In a manner that may be characteristic of sedentary, mountain-dwelling tribes (I think immediately of the Rif, Kabylia, Lebanon, Kurdistan, the Yemen and Hadramawt) the process was and is intense, introverted, and feud-ridden. Power and prestige were and are measured in resources, and when, almost fortuitously, new resources became available to the Swasa outside the region, in urban commerce, they packed up their rivalries and introversion and took them to the city. But there the game was no longer played among Swasa alone. Other groups were involved in the exploitation of urban resources. The Swasa have been able to react to or cooperate with these non-Susi groups much in the same way they did with tribal allies and rivals in the Sus. In the cities, however, the operative units have become patron–clientele groups rather than lineages or families *per se*. I am tempted to say, although with some trepidation, that there is nothing more or less permanent and fundamental to the Susi–Fassi rivalry than to any particular rivalry among the Swasa themselves.

The Swasa left their valleys to seek new resources and in so doing were projected into the very heart of a growing market economy and nationwide distribution system. Again, it might be tempting to explain their successful integration in this system in terms of their response to the larger process itself. Yet their own interpretation insists upon their reactions to factors internal to their communities; it was not that they were unaware of the challenge of the market

---

[1] See André Adam, *Casablanca: essai sur la transformation de la société marocaine ua contact de l'occident*, CNRS, Paris, 1968, 2 vols, Vol. I, p. 367.

economy, but simply that this was not the primary challenge. In the following pages, I will examine in some detail the inner-directed struggle for commercial prestige. The struggle always had as its referent the pecking order of power and status in the south and only took into account other groups such as the Fassis to the extent that they impinged upon the commercial arena of the Swasa.

A logical extension of Susi commercial activity was their entry into politics. It may sometimes be useful for analytic purposes to distinguish between economic and political actions, to see economic and political integration as two rather different processes. These are distinctions that are not readily made by the Swasa themselves. For after all, what the Swasa undertook in commerce was as much politically as materially motivated. Profits were not sought simply to ameliorate one's standard of living but to augment one's relative prestige. Yet to a far greater extent than in commerce, the entry of the Swasa into national politics has been at the ethnic group level and in reference to other ethnic groups. It has been in party and electoral politics that Swasa have acted as Swasa. I would be reluctant to conclude that this is a permanent phenomenon, rather than simply the product of a set of political circumstances that obtained in Morocco in the first ten years of independence. The quiet death of party politics in Morocco means that a convenient framework for Susi participation as a group no longer is available. But in the period treated in these pages, parties symbolized the development of a national political arena, and just as was the case with the market economy, the Swasa made a rapid adjustment to this situation.

In short, close inspection of Susi commercial and political behavior in Casablanca may elucidate some of the dimensions of group identity alluded to at the outset. There is another important factor that will only be touched upon, and that is the erosion of this identity in all its forms. It is too early to talk with much assurance about this process, but it is clear that for many young Swasa raised in Casablanca, or other cities, the competition among their fathers for prestige in the home valleys holds little meaning. Nor are they content to confine their commercial political or intellectual activities to the Susi arena alone which bears no particular magic for them. One may speculate that as the horizons of individual Swasa broaden, as the motives for their endeavors hinge less on struggles for prestige within the group, the group itself will lose those binding conflicts that allowed it to adapt. The need for solidarity toward outsiders seems to have varied directly with the intensity of internal rivalries, and if the latter become irrelevant, then so too the need for solidarity.

THE CORE TRIBES OF THE SWASA

The name Susi is derived from a river valley in the deep south of Morocco near Agadir, known as the Wad Sus. In fact, the Susi merchants are not from this valley, but rather from further south in the high valleys of the Anti-Atlas mountains. The other name by which they are known is Shleuh, that is those who speak the Berber dialect Tashilhit. This is no more precise than Susi, for the

8*

region in which Tashilhit is spoken comprises all of the Anti- and High Atlas mountains from the Atlantic coast eastwards to Demnat and Skoura, as well as part of the Sahara.[1]

Many tribes of the Anti-Atlas have, in recent years, begun to be drawn into commerce in the northern cities, but the pioneers and contemporary elite of the petty tradesmen consist of members of some thirteen core tribes and tribal fractions. By far the most important are the Ammiln, inhabiting a valley of the same name lying along the southern face of the Jbil Lkist in the heart of the Anti-Atlas range. To the west and south of the Ammiln are other tribes of lesser importance whose members followed the Ammiln to the north: Ida ou Semlal, Ida ou Baqil, Amanouz, Tasserirte and Igounan. On the northern face of the Jbil Lkist lies another important tribe, the Ida ou Gnidif. Further down the face of the mountain are the Ait Baha, Ida ou Ktir, and Ait Mzal who, like the Ida ou Gnidif, were close on the heels of the Ammiln in the first decades of the twentieth century. Somewhat later, the neighboring tribes of the Ait Souab, Ida ou Zekri and Ait Abdullah took their chances in trade also. It is, then, the male migrants from these tribes to whom the appellation 'Susi' has been somewhat imprecisely attached.[2]

The earliest population figures that are available for the core groups date from the 1936 census and reflect a period of accelerated emigration. Table 11.1 gives the break-down.[3] The density of inhabitants per square kilometer averaged about forty. This is a high figure considering the poor agricultural potential of the area. We cannot directly compare these population figures with those of the 1960 census as the latter are given in terms of administrative districts that do not correspond to the tribes in question. It can be safely assumed, however, that population growth in the Anti-Atlas has kept pace with the overall Moroccan increase of 2·5 to 3 percent per year. While population density has risen, average annual rainfall has continued to vary between three and twelve inches a year, well below the critical minimal level of sixteen inches needed for successful agriculture.[4]

---

[1] See Robert Montagne, *Les Berbères et le makhzen dans le sud du Maroc*, Paris, 1930. pp. 6–9.

[2] Despite the salience of these tribes in contemporary Morocco, the ethnography dealing with them is impoverished. Some useful treatments are R. Montagne, op. cit.; André Adam, 'La maison et le village dans quelques tribus de l'Anti-Atlas', *Hespéris*, Vol. 37, Nos. 3 & 4, 1950, pp. 289–362; Jean Chaumeil, 'Histoire d'une tribu maraboutique de l'Anti-Atlas: les Ait Abdullah ou Said', *Hespéris*, Vol. 39, Nos. 1 & 2, 1952, pp. 197–212 and 'Le mellah du Tahala au pays des Ammeln', *Hespéris*, Vol. 40, 1953, pp. 227–40; Eric Alport, 'The Ammeln', *Journal of the Royal Anthropological Institute*, Vol. 94, Part 2, 1964, pp. 160–71. Jacques Berque's detailed study of the Seksawa of the High Atlas deals with similar tribal groupings: *Structures sociales du Haut Atlas*, Paris, 1955.

[3] Figures are from *Répertoire alphabétique des confédérations, tribus, et agglomerations de la zone française de l'empire chérifien au Iᵉ novembre 1939*, Service du Travail, Casablanca, 1939. Direct comparison with the figures of the 1960 census are not possible because the latter are based on administrative districts that do not correspond to the tribal groupings in question.

[4] See Daniel Noin, *Population (1960) : Atlas du Maroc*, CURS, Rabat, 1963, pp. 18–23.

Table 11.1 Population of the Core Tribes: 1936

Ammiln	14,415	Ida ou Gnidif	5,438
Amanouz	4,082	Ait Baha	659
Igounan	4,819	Ait Mzal	2,921
Tasserirte	2,845	Ida ou Ktir	1,804
Ida ou Semlal	6,650	Ida ou Zekri	4,830
Ida ou Baqil	14,941	Ait Abdullah	2,977
Ait Souab	19,374		

TOTAL: 85,755

The core tribes of the Anti-Atlas have been situated in their present locations for several centuries. They are sedentary, village-dwellers who have subsisted in their over-populated valleys through goat-herding, arboriculture, and the cultivation of barley. In addition, for at least two or three centuries, there has been a trickle of male migrants to other parts of Morocco who specialized either in trade or in religious learning. Tribes are composed of agnatic lineages (*afus*; *ifassen*: Berber for hand) which inhabit villages (*muda*) or clusters of villages, generally situated along the watersheds vital to the tribes' survival. Positions of leadership were not inherited, and were achieved, to a significant degree, on the basis of performance in defending and providing for the group. The political alignments entered into by tribesmen were not wholly determined by the formal structure of tribal lineages and clans. A variety of cross-cutting, *ad hoc*, alliances and coalitions was normal at any given time, allowing for rapid internal adjustments and the movement of individuals regardless of blood.[1]

Until the twentieth century, these tribes lay beyond the fiscal reach of the Moroccan Sultan, although they generally acknowledged his spiritual authority. They were left to their own devices to regulate group conflict and to distribute the meagre resources of the region. This they did, not by authoritative rule-making, but, much as in the international system, through the very process of group interaction; the alignment and re-alignment of tribal and fractional segments. Group identity was conceived loosely enough so as to act as a consensual framework for this process, and, as in most segmentary systems, rival groups at one level of conflict might be allies at another. Identity was thus a relative quality, depending on the specific situation at hand, and, as such, acted as a permissive rather than restrictive influence. One may note here that somewhat the same phenomenon exists among the Susi communities in the north. They may be divided among themselves according to tribal identity, or within themselves according to various competing patron–clientele groups. Yet the internal rivalries are contained within a larger framework for group solidarity and sentiment. Internal tension is generally overcome in response to conflict and

---

[1] Marshall Sahlins describes agnation as being 'functional if not factual . . .', and points out that in many groups organized according to agnatic descent only a minority of adult males may in fact be true agnates. See his 'On the ideology and composition of descent groups', *Man*, July–August 1965, pp. 104–7.

rivalry with non-Susi groups, permitting coordinated community action. As we shall see, this was the case in the 1960 Chamber of Commerce elections.

SUSI EMIGRATION

The traditional cities of pre-protectorate Morocco have long been familiar with the Swasa. Frequently they were the *baqqal*s (Arabic: 'grocer') of the *medina*s of the north, retailing mostly fat-based products such as candles, soap, and cooking oils.[1] They were conspicuous but not numerous. Male migration was not yet vital to group survival in the Anti-Atlas.

The exodus intensified in the last half of the nineteenth century and changed in nature. The severe famine of 1880–82 left marginal agricultural areas like the Anti-Atlas devastated. Moreover, the northern cities were beginning to attract Europeans and liquid wealth. There was a growing clientele for retail tradesmen, and increasingly the clients were European. The first pole of attraction in this vein was the city of Oran in western Algeria where Swasa first developed their skills in what was to become virtually a Susi monopoly: *épicerie moderne*, i.e. grocery trade to Europeans or Europeanized populations. By the end of the century there were enclaves of Swasa at Oujda, Taza, and Fes, along the route to Oran, but also increasingly at Tangier, Larache, and Casablanca, seaports that were filling up with Europeans. The First World War touched off a veritable *levée en masse*, as one Susi described it, with many tribesmen recruited to work in French war industries, others going along to set up shop in the shanty-towns of Paris,[2] and still others migrating to the burgeoning urban centers of French colonization in Morocco. There is no good evidence that the traditional *baqqal*s were the first to shift to *épicerie moderne*. Initially, chance success in this branch of commerce may have set the sights of whole villages and tribal fractions on the same sphere of activity. Other tribes of the Anti- and High Atlas, and even sections of the core tribes themselves (Ait Souab), were initially successful as manual laborers and miners, thereby determining patterns of emigration for their tribesmates.

The Ammiln were the innovators in *épicerie moderne* and staked out the choicest markets: Tangier and Casablanca. By 1935, one year after the Anti-Atlas had been pacified by the French, each Ammiln household probably had at least one male member engaged in trade, and in the same year there were 1,500 of them in Casablanca alone.[3] The Ida ou Gnidif situated some of their members in the

---

[1] See, for instance, Louis Massignon (dir.), 'Enquête sur les corporations musulmanes d'artisans et de commerçants au Maroc (1923–24)', Extrait de *La Revue du monde musulman*, Paris, 1925, esp. on Salé, pp. 51–8.

[2] See Col. Justinard, 'Les Chleuh de la banlieue de Paris', *Revue des études islamiques*, Vol. 2, 1928, pp. 477–80.

[3] C. Marquez, 'Les épiciers Chleuhs et leur diffusion dans les villes du Maroc', *Bulletin économique du Maroc*, Vol. 2, 1935, pp. 230–3. The author notes that the village of Imn-Tizekht of the Afil-i-Wasif, one of the seven tribal fractions of the Ammiln, had, in 1900, sent but two tradesmen to Tangier. By 1935 the village total was 100. If Marquez is correct, then practically all males of this village big enough to walk must have been at Tangier. My own informants indicate that Imn-Tizekht is by no means an isolated example.

same cities, but had better success in Meknes, Rabat, and Marrakesh. All the other core tribes fitted themselves in where they could, a task facilitated by the steady growth of European clientele. The Ait Baha and Ait Mzal, for example, rather than seeking to crack the Ammiln networks in grocery trade, opted for retailing tobacco products and finished cotton goods.[1]

By the end of World War II, the Swasa tribes had become fully dependent upon the revenues gained in the cities of the north. Agriculture and arboriculture became activities of secondary importance carried out in haphazard fashion by Swasa women and children. Tribal competition for scarce resources no longer involved the mountain valleys, but rather the retail trade of the north. Within the space of a few decades, the Swasa had revolutionized their social and economic system. Tribesmen had become tradesmen, mono-lingual goatherds had become tri-lingual entrepreneurs without their finding the change remarkable. Although pious Muslims, they were not driven by some Islamic variant of the Protestant ethic, nor were they, in E. E. Hagen's sense, suffering from status deprivation.[2] Through trial and error, they had learned how to make the best of a new situation, something, they would claim, that they had done throughout their history.

The measurable factors necessitating male migration from the mountains can be easily summarized: increasing desiccation, soil erosion, deforestation, and population growth.[3] But individual Swasa today, looking back on this period of early migration, cite other, more subjective factors, such as feuds, local rivalries, and the maintenance of group and individual prestige. As in other heavily-populated, sedentary groups, intense rivalries were generated over questions of the use of land, water, and women. Such tensions have generally been analyzed in terms of the formal structuring of the tribes and lineages. Among the Swasa, however, conflict was not only expressed in terms of tribe *v.* tribe, and lineage *v.* lineage, but also in an *ad hoc* manner *within* lineages, villages, extended families, and even among brothers. It seems fairly clear that these rivalries were exacerbated in the late nineteenth and early twentieth centuries as the objective factors mentioned above became more pronounced.

When one of the handful of early pioneers in *épicerie moderne* would return to his valley with some cash, perhaps a new rifle, or the gleaming paraphernalia of tea preparation, his success would threaten the local power and prestige rankings and arouse the envy of rival families. Other young men, to maintain their own image and prestige, or perhaps to steal a march on their rivals, would set out for

---

[1] For more on emigration, see Marquez, op. cit.; M. Montjean, 'L'émigration berbère de l'Anti-Atlas', CHEAM (Paris archives), Vol. 26, No. 639, 1942, 8 pp.; Cne. De la Porte des Vaux, 'L'émigration dans le Sous', CHEAM, No. 1556, 1948–49, 75 pp.; Capt. de Fleurieu, 'Une tribu de commerçants berbères au sud du Maroc: les Ammeln', CHEAM, Vol. 3, No. 45 bis, 1939, 14 pp.; Robert Montagne (dir.), *Naissance du prolétariat marocain*, Paris, 1950. The latter provides a few biographies of Susi retailers as does Stéphane Delisle in *L'Evolution sociale du Maroc*, Paris, 1951.

[2] E. E. Hagen, *On the Theory of Social Change*, New York, 1962, esp. Ch. 9.

[3] The gradual atrophy of the trans-Saharan trade routes, some of which terminated near Swasa-land, may have also deprived the region of some resources. It is hard to ascertain to what extent the Swasa were involved, directly or indirectly, in this trade.

the north to try their hand at trade. The sense of competition is maintained today through various systems of village gossip. Among the Ida ou Gnidif, the old men and grocers on home leave gather at the local mosque to drink tea around the fire used to heat water for ablutions. There they discuss in front of the small boys too young to go to the city, the commercial reputations and relative skills of all the villagers in the north. Thus the young Susi is rapidly socialized into a highly competitive environment. They in turn want to set out as soon as possible and establish their own reputation. This sort of response, as I have indicated, might occur within an extended family or among brothers. It is characteristic of the nature of group ties among the Swasa, that those who first were successful in the north would be obliged to aid their rivals by giving them work in their shops, bringing them in as co-partners, or finding them shops of their own. Loyalty to the group dictated mutual aid but in no way precluded intense competition among group members. Moreover, it seems apparent that tribal rivalries were muted in the cities, and cooperation across tribal lines in matters of trade was extensive. On a day-to-day basis, the operative unit for any individual Susi might be a tribal sub-group competing with other such groups for customers. Yet, as was the case in the purely tribal situation, internal rivalries could be suspended in the name of tribal and even 'Susi' political and commercial solidarity *vis-à-vis* an out-group.

Within these new terms, the struggle for local prestige went on, and until recently trade was seen as a means to make one's mark in the valley.[1] The Susi grocer is known for his frugality and ability to live under harsh conditions, but his carefully hoarded profits are primarily designed to allow him to live ostentatiously in the valley and only secondarily to re-invest in his business. As an older merchant put it: 'We fill up in the cities and empty in the valleys. The cities may disappear but our valleys will remain.' Some decades ago, a Susi tradesman might place his first profits in the purchase of a new rifle in order to uphold his family in a local feud or to fight the French as they moved into the Anti-Atlas.[2] Today, prestige is measured in style and location of housing, and land is valued more for its potential as building sites than for its productive capacity.

In the northern cities, over a period of twenty-five years (1920–45), the Swasa came to dominate retail trade in groceries and food products, tobacco, hardware, and increasingly small restaurants, cafés, and low-priced hotels. By 1959, they were so numerous at Casablanca that they made up about ninety percent of the 7,400 members of the Union of Retailers of Food Products.[3] No other groups, indigenous or foreign, seemed able to compete with the Swasa on equal terms. Yet the strength of the Swasa did not lie in their numbers, but in the degree of

---

[1] For someone else who emphasized these same factors, see Montjean, op. cit.

[2] The Susi suffered no moral dilemmas in retailing to the French in the North and shooting at the French in the South. As mentioned earlier, it is perhaps typical of segmentary organization that an enemy is an enemy in a situational rather than a moral sense. No Swasa initially opposed the French in the North—if the French wanted to 'fill up' there, that was their business. But when the French moved in on the region where the Swasa 'empty' that called for an entirely different response.

[3] From an interview (9 November 1967). The President, Abdullah Ibrahim, is from the Ammiln. He is not to be confused with the ex-Prime Minister.

their mutual self-help relative to other groups engaged in commerce. They have never constituted a majority of the retail community in any city. In Casablanca, for instance, the bulk of the retailers come from the coastal plains (Chawia, Dukkala, Chiadma) and, once in the city, do not show any marked degree of cooperation among themselves.

SUSI COMMERCIAL ORGANIZATION: ADAPTATION TO ECONOMIC INTEGRATION

There were several ways in which the Swasa might organize their retail trades. The initial step would consist of accumulating enough capital to open a shop in a native quarter, or, for the more ambitious, in a European residential area. The seed capital could be assembled through peddling, manual labor, or working for a European or Jewish retailer. Once a shop had been acquired, a relative or acquaintance from the home region (not necessarily from the same fraction or tribe) could be brought in as an associate, co-partner, or manager. Established Swasa would help out newcomers by providing them credit, stock, or perhaps shops that they could manage while the owners were in the Sus.

In the pre-World War II period, when travel to the Anti-Atlas was difficult, a shopkeeper might spend a year at a time in his northern locale and then several months at home with his family. Today, due to improved roads and bus service, the rotation period is usually six months in the north, six months in the valley. During this period, the shop would be managed by a relative or close acquaintance, perhaps someone starting out in trade.[1] Inventory would be taken when the manager assumed responsibility for the shop and again when he relinquished it. He would reconstitute the stock, and any profits over and above this would be his. The owner charged no rent. In this way, a diligent young migrant might accumulate enough capital to open a shop of his own.

The Swasa generally lived in their shops which sometimes remained open twenty-four hours a day. They functioned with a bare minimum of clothing, food, and other amenities. Seldom would they let slip by an opportunity to sell, and it is often said of the Swasa, only half-jokingly, that they would sell matches one at a time or cooking oil by the drop, if that were the only way to make a sale. A Susi proverb states: 'Little pennies are the children of big *douros*. The grocer who chases the children from his shop will never see the mother.' In the larger shops, young boys, often the cousins, younger brothers, or sons of the owner, would learn the trade through unsalaried apprenticeship during which they delivered groceries and frequently minded the shop. The females would remain in the valley to run the family household and take care of the trees, fields, goats, the very aged, and the very young. All these practices led to minimal operating costs, maximum sales volume, and an efficient deployment of human and material resources. It should be noted, however, that some of these practices have been significantly modified in the last fifteen years. Increasingly the Swasa bring their

[1] The manager is sometimes known as *igallas*, or 'sitter', a Berberized form of the Arabic, *jallas*.

entire family to the north, stay for longer periods of time, and make some effort to send their children to school.[1]

Their frugal habits have permitted the Swasa to expand rapidly in the northern cities. By World War II, a number of them, particularly in Casablanca, had left retail trade altogether to enter into wholesaling. These men became the patrons of the Swasa trading communities.[2] Their functions were and are manifold, involving the furnishing of credit to new arrivals from the mountains, the provision from their own warehouses of an initial stock, or perhaps the loan of a shop itself. Further, the patrons have acted as intermediaries between the municipal authorities and the retailers, arranging for licenses, and explaining the municipal regulations affecting commerce. No interest was charged for the credit extended, no specific reciprocal act was demanded for services rendered. The network of obligations that any patron had, or still has, represents control over future, unspecified resources and services that the patron can activate when he feels so inclined. We should not lose sight of the fact that the power of any patron is reflected also in his prestige ranking in the tribal homeland. This, as much as material gain from commerce, provides the incentive for patrons to expand their clientele. Whatever the motives for developing them, clientelistic relations have served to bind together the Swasa tradesmen through ties of material and moral interdependence.

Credit is an instrument of control, but equally important, an instrument of competition. The retailers, after all, are the customers of the wholesalers and demi-wholesalers (*demi-grossistes*). The wholesaler-patrons *within* the Susi community compete among themselves in order to establish stable customers among the retailers. The competition has been conducted in terms of the credit, services, and protection offered.[3] Through the manipulation of these elements, some successful patrons have been able to control extensive chains of retail shops, and, for the patrons of Casablanca, control has extended to other cities. One Susi patron owned, by 1955, some 150 shops in Casablanca, rotating

[1] These trends are analyzed in John Waterbury, 'Les Détaillants Soussis à Casablanca', *Bulletin économique et social du Maroc*, No. 114 (1969) pp. 134–58.

[2] The patrons are, of course, the most successful of the retailers, but their success has often been determined by fortuitous factors. The French administration, for instance, promoted the careers of some Swasa to better control their clients. The village of Aguerdoudad, very near the French administrative post at Tafrawt, was particularly favored, the Aguerdoudadis agreeing to act as informants on what was going on in the Ammiln valley in exchange for favorable treatment in the North. A number of Susi 'moguls' in the North are from Aguerdoudad.

[3] The use of credit as the major means of competition at *all* levels of the commercial distribution system is constantly emphasized in the massive study of Morocco's internal commerce: Kingdom of Morocco, Cabinet Royal, *Etude sur le commerce intérieur*, Division du Plan et du Statistiques, 3 vols, Rabat, 1967. For an analysis of the use of credit among trading communities in other developing countries, see C. Belshaw, op. cit., pp. 68, 80–1; Clifford Geertz, *Peddlers and Princes*, Chicago, 1963, esp. pp. 37–8. There is not to the best of my knowledge anything among the Swasa closely resembling the rotating credit association, unless one were to so consider the collective use by and rotation among Swasa associates of a number of retail shops. On this problem, see C. Geertz, 'The rotating credit association: a middle rung in development', *Economic Development and Cultural Change*, April 1962, pp. 241–63.

managers among them and stocking them exclusively from his depots. Another bloc of the patron's clientele consisted of independent Susi retailers who owed their commercial start to his generosity. There are several other wholesalers, at Casablanca and elsewhere, who have risen to similar heights, and some of them have diversified their interests, entering into light industry, milling, and commercial farming in northern Morocco. Lateral mobility at the summit of the Susi hierarchy is also reflected in the fact that it is only the patrons who are able to step outside the community credit system to seek financing for their projects.

The first Susi retailers did not move into a void. There were other groups, Moroccan and foreign, seeking their place in the growing urban centers. When the Swasa first arrived in Casablanca, retail trade was largely in the hands of the Jews. After the First World War, the Jews moved vertically and horizontally in the commercial network. They entered trades ranging from tailor and hairdresser to restauranteur and garage owner. Others moved into positions in import–export, banking, insurance, and wholesaling. They ceded their place in food retailing to the Swasa, or, short of that, employed Swasa as managers in their shops. Some of the latter, in association with Jewish patrons, became wholesalers in food products and imported goods such as tea.

The financial, commercial and industrial elite of Casablanca has, since the turn of the century and up to the present time, consisted largely of French businessmen.[1] They, along with the protectorate authorities, looked favorably upon the industrious, reliable Swasa and aided certain of them in their commercial endeavors. The French were all the more solicitous toward the Swasa and Jews in that the only other indigenous group attempting to carve a niche for itself in the commercial and industrial establishment of Casablanca was the Fassi (people from Fes) bourgeoisie, and it was distinctly hostile toward the French.

The merchant families of Fes represented the native cultural and commercial elite of Morocco and had long played an important part in Morocco's external trade. Several prominent Fassi families had installed themselves in Casablanca, even before the turn of the century, in order to take advantage of the growing maritime trade handled by the port. They were involved most heavily in the importation of textiles, and they distributed finished textile goods throughout Morocco. Further, many had lived abroad in Europe, West Africa, and the Middle East. They were relatively cosmopolitan and used to dealing with the outside world. Unlike the Swasa, they could mobilize relatively large sums of liquid capital and were capable of 'thinking big'. Many tried to enter into new fields of endeavor, such as transport and industry, with varying success. Others became immensely wealthy through speculation in urban real estate.

[1] The city of Casablanca dominates the industrial, financial, and commercial life of Morocco. In 1960, 60% of all Moroccan industries were located at Casablanca, employing 58% of the entire industrial work force. Seventy-five per cent of all foreign trade was handled through Casablanca, and all banks had their central offices there also. In the same year, the total population of Casablanca was 958,000: 770,000 Muslims, 115,000 Europeans, 73,000 Jews. The next largest city was Marrakesh with 243,000 inhabitants. For more on the city see Noin, op. cit.; R. Montagne, *Naissance du prolétariat . . .*, op. cit.; and André Adam, *Casablanca*, 2 vols, CNRS, Paris, 1968.

Along the Route de Strasbourg in Casablanca, the patrons of the Swasa, the Jews, and the Fassis established their shops, warehouses and offices. Their contacts have been frequent but unpatterned, consisting of occasional common ventures across group boundaries that involve a few patrons at a time. Each community has regarded the others with suspicion and scorn, but also with some degree of respect. The Fassis picture themselves as the bearers of Islamo-Arab culture in Morocco and as the natural leaders of all Moroccans. They look down upon the Swasa as unlettered, miserly, and undistinguished, yet they cannot deny nor fail to admire Susi entrepreneurial skills. It is reported that the Fassis have even taken to using Swasa to manage their cloth shops in the Casablanca *kissaria* as Susi frugality and hard work maximizes profits. The Swasa, for their part, see the Fassis as snobs, spendthrifts, and dissipates. Berber or not, they concede to no one in piety and point out the great religious traditions of the Anti-Atlas. At the same time they do feel inferior to the Fassis in learning and sophistication, and will, for that reason, show them some deference. Both groups respect the Jews as fine businessmen while often revealing the condescension many Muslims hold for the infidel. The Jewish patrons have increasingly identified themselves with European, specifically French, norms and styles of behavior, and have taken a detached view of their major competitors typical of those who feel they are no longer really part of the game. Among all these groups, however, mutual suspicions have not precluded considerable group interaction nor have they hindered the process of borrowing and learning from one another.

TEA IN THE SYSTEM OF CREDIT, COMPETITION AND CONTROL

Even before independence in 1956, various Jewish entrepreneurs took out insurance against the future by associating themselves more closely with Muslim merchants. For the Jews the most satisfactory, or least threatening, associates were Swasa. The process of association was most noticeable in the system of tea distribution. For years, four or five Jewish families had controlled tea imports and wholesaling in Morocco. Gradually the major importers brought Swasa into the tea marketing system as wholesalers and demi-wholesalers in Casablanca and in other cities. At the same time, Susi patrons were also able to gain a favorable position in wholesaling locally-refined sugar, especially that of the French-owned Compagnie Sucrière Marocaine (COSUMA).[1] Sugar and tea, for reasons to be explained below, could be more important than monetary credit as a means of competition and control among the patrons.

With their partial grip on the distribution of these two commodities, the Susi patrons had access to a considerable part of the average Moroccan's total outlays on food products. As in many societies afflicted with low levels of nutrition, sugar in Morocco is consumed in relatively massive amounts by the poor so that they may gain enough energy to work and to take the edge off their hunger.

[1] COSUMA refines on an average about half the sugar consumed in Morocco. The company has about 800 licensed distributors.

The better-off consume large amounts also, perhaps out of habit. For Moroccans the vehicle for sugar consumption is tea, and they feel deprived if forced to forego either. It is estimated that in the rural areas twenty-five per cent of *all* family expenditures go to purchases of tea and sugar.[1] Because of these consumption habits, grocers can maintain a steady clientele among Moroccans, rich and poor, only if they are always stocked with tea and sugar of the desired qualities. In turn, wholesalers can maintain stable customers among the retailers only if they can guarantee a steady supply of sugar and tea. For those Susi patrons located at strategic points in the distribution system, their control over the supply of these two commodities represents a formidable instrument of competition *vis-à-vis* other patrons as well as an instrument of discipline among their clients. In fact, for the average retailer there might not be much to choose among the patrons in terms of the credit and services offered. But those wholesalers who can mobilize large amounts of the several qualities of tea marketed in Morocco,[2] and who are always well-stocked in COSUMA sugar, have a distinct if not over-whelming advantage in holding their clientele. The point is worth examining further, for it is essential to an understanding of the transformation of the relations of authority and control within the Swasa community and the role of the community as a whole in national and local politics.

The marketing of tea has been fundamentally reorganized since Moroccan independence. In December, 1958, a National Tea Office (ONT) was created to take over from the private sector the importation and packaging of tea. This move had followed the bankruptcy of Toledano Brothers, one of the major tea importing concerns. The new office has not undertaken the actual distribution of tea, but does fix retail prices for each of the qualities. To compensate the importers and wholesalers who had been jeopardized by its creation, the ONT offered wholesaling licenses (agréments) to 137 individuals. The licenses were grouped into six categories corresponding to the varying amounts of tea allotted to each distributor on a monthly basis. The amounts ranged from 7·3 tons per month in the first category to 0·45 tons in the sixth.

Distributors' licenses soon became an integral part of the political patronage system nationally and locally. Within a few years, the original 137 had been joined by 400 more, and by 1967 there were some 1,200 bearers of ONT distribution licenses. The Swasa patrons, among the original 137, joined by a few Fassis,[3] soon mastered the new situation. Hundreds of licensed distributors

---

[1] On tea and sugar consumption, see 'Etude sur le commerce . . .', op. cit., Vol. 2, pp. 477–547; and for their history, J.-L. Miège, 'Origine et développement de la consommation du thé au Maroc', *Bulletin économique et social du Maroc*, Vol. 20, No. 71, 1956, pp. 377–98, and 'Le commerce du sucre à Casablanca à la fin du XIXᵉ siècle', *Bulletin économique et social du Maroc*, Vol. 15, No. 53, 1952, pp. 248–58. Annual consumption of sugar averages about 77 pounds or 35 kilograms per capita, and that of tea about 2½ pounds per capita. For instance, in 1960, 12,397 tons of tea (all imported) and 350,000 tons of sugar were consumed in Morocco.

[2] Sixteen qualities of green tea are marketed in Morocco, and the qualities most con-sumed vary by region, sometimes season, and of course, income bracket. Roughly 60% of the tea is imported from China and the rest from Japan and Formosa. (1969).

[3] The Jews pretty much ceded their place to the Swasa after the Toledano 'crash' of 1958.

had no interest in or knowledge about tea marketing and were only too glad to sell their delivery coupons (*bons*) to the men who became known as the *super-grossistes*. Some legitimate dealers in the lower categories where the range of qualities supplied was limited were also willing to sell their coupons to the highest bidder. The highest bidders were usually a handful of Swasa wholesalers at Casablanca who each month were able to corner the market in tea despite the nominal control of the ONT. Fixed retail prices were ignored in what came to be for the most part a black market operation. Some of the Swasa tea barons even received official positions as advisers to the ONT on matters of suitable imports and quality control. In brief, because they were not formerly engaged in importation, the wholesalers were not directly affected by the establishment of the ONT. As the Jewish importers abandoned the field, the hand of the Swasa patrons was in some ways actually strengthened by the new office. Their relative weight within the entire distribution system of Morocco was increased as was their control over the Swasa retailers. The Susi patrons, only a few decades removed from a pastoral existence, had undertaken large-scale commercial operations uninhibitedly and with a notable degree of success. They not only readily grasped the mechanisms of marketing, pricing, and distribution, but quickly learned how to manipulate and take advantage of them. In response to the challenge of the economic integration of Morocco, the Swasa secured for themselves a strategic place in the entire distribution system.

None the less, the community control gained in this process by certain of the patrons was being counteracted in other ways. The total number of Swasa in Casablanca continued to grow after 1956, as did the city itself. Yet Casablanca (and most other Moroccan cities) was then, and still is now, undergoing a process of economic stagnation as the exodus of the French and Jews continued, and local French entrepreneurs cut back their investments and capital outlays. The average Susi retailer found that he was surrounded by an ever-growing body of competitors, and while there was no want of customers, their buying power tended to diminish over time. He contended with hordes of peddlers, push-cart tradesmen, or retailers from the shanty-towns looking for wealthier customers, and struggling to become shopkeepers. Ahead of him lay the elite of wholesalers who had grown wealthy and prestigious, but who seemed ill-disposed to make room at the top. In short, the system was saturated,[1] and the more the Susi community became stratified, the greater the strain on the long-assumed identity of interests between retailer and wholesaler. However, up to the present time, the motive of survival and security in the uncertain economic conditions of independent Morocco has sufficed to maintain a basic level of solidarity among the Swasa, and, as many readily admit, this solidarity has been the key to their success.

---

[1] Detailed figures on the retail and wholesale community of Casablanca are not available and we do not know distribution by trade. But in 1960, there were 41·4 *commerçants* per 1,000 inhabitants in Casablanca. This does not include unlicensed tradesmen and *marchands ambulants* who must easily outnumber the licensed tradesmen.

THE SWASA IN POLITICS:
ADAPTATION TO POLITICAL INTEGRATION

The Swasa tribesmen in the north have engaged in politics in recent decades for the same reasons that they engaged in tribal conflict in the past. Both periods of their development have involved the competition for the control of scarce resources. Today, however, the process is being carried out under new rules laid down by a central authority whose power can no longer be ignored nor directly contested. Within the new governmental context, those activities that we might find peculiarly political are, for the Swasa, indistinguishable from other activities—communal, social, and commercial—which they undertake as a security group. One might be tempted to characterize the political endeavors of the Swasa as those of a commercial interest group in which cohesion depends upon an identity of functionally-defined interests among its members. If this were so, we could then say that politics is a means to the end of protecting the group's commercial interests. Until the present time, however, the commercial undertakings of the Swasa have not been an end in themselves but rather a means to enhance group security. This may be expressed at a number of levels: the general feeling of solidarity among all core tribes; the more intense identification with one's own tribe and its survival in the homeland; and the bread-and-butter loyalty to a specific patron. While the different levels of concern for security are not always coincident, it is none the less often possible for an individual Susi to satisfy the demands of all three masters. What this has meant in the context of Casablanca politics will be explored in the remainder of this paper, with particular emphasis upon the 1960 elections to the Chamber of Commerce and Industry (CCI).

The Anti-Atlas was not completely pacified by the French until 1934. Within a decade of that date, many of the Swasa who participated in these last spasms of tribal resistance to a central authority had joined the nationalist movement, and in particular the Istiqlal Party founded in 1944. The leadership of the party lay in the hands of young, well-educated Moroccans from the urban bourgeoisie, whom the tribesmen tend to consider as 'Fassis' regardless of the city of their birth. In the case of the Istiqlal, true Fassis did in fact dominate leadership positions. For this and other reasons, not all Swasa were attracted by the nationalists. Some of the patrons were fearful of jeopardizing their official French protection, but most made financial contributions to the party none the less.

Instances of patron participation were, on the whole, rare, and Swasa involvement in the nationalist movement was largely confined to retailers. They proved important to the Istiqlal as it sought to penetrate the urban areas and to organize the working class and the unemployed. The retailers were ideally situated to promote this task for fairly obvious reasons. First, their tribal–commercial information networks, within and among cities, provided an effective grapevine for the movement of political information and 'intelligence' as well as the movement of personnel. This communications network, so intimately a part of the legitimate commercial activities of the Swasa, was not readily accessible to

French surveillance. Secondly, the retailers came in daily contact with workers, slum dwellers, the lower-middle classes of the *medina*s, and the European population. Their shops could serve as informal party headquarters, refuge for nationalists hiding from the police, intelligence post and sometimes arms cache. After the French exiled the Moroccan Sultan in 1953 because of his close links with the Istiqlal, a number of Swasa helped organize the armed urban resistance groups, and some, such as the Manouzi brothers, became actively involved in the rural armies of liberation. Throughout the nationalist period, the Susi members of the Istiqlal accepted, perhaps grudgingly, the 'Fassi', 'Arab' leadership of the party, deferring to the political acumen and sophistication of this elite.

In 1947, the French attempted to liberalize the political regime of the protectorate and to take the edge off the growing nationalist movement. One method employed was the holding of indirect elections to the Moroccan Section of the Council of Government, a body that acted in a purely advisory capacity to the Resident-General on economic matters.[1] The Moroccan members were chosen in part from among the members of the Moroccan Chambers of Agriculture, Commerce, and Industry. The latter, in turn, were elected on the basis of restricted suffrage among Moroccans in the same occupational category. For instance, voting in elections to the Chambers of Commerce and Industry was restricted to those Moroccans inscribed on the Commercial Register, or roughly 8,000 Moroccans for all of Morocco.[2] The limited suffrage played into the hands of the urban, commercial and industrial bourgeoisie, who, after the Second World War, identified strongly with the Istiqlal, and who were well represented on the Commercial Register. As a result, the Istiqlal took over the Moroccan sections of the CCIs in several cities, and in 1948 eleven Istiqlalis assumed their places as members of the Council of Government. There they formed a vocal and cohesive bloc to harass the Resident-General.

It was clear to the French that the elitist electoral law of 1947 had backfired because it was precisely the commercial elite of Fes, Rabat, Casablanca and elsewhere that was at the forefront of the nationalist movement. The upshot was that, in December 1950, Resident-General Juin expelled the Istiqlali members from a stormy session of the Council, and then set about re-writing the electoral law. It had already been planned that half the membership of the CCIs would be renewed through elections sometime in the fall of 1951. Without forewarning, however, the new electoral law was published on 17 October, allowing any *licensed* tradesmen or industrialists to vote. This ruling expanded the national electorate from 8,000 to 220,000. The new law also announced that the election would take place on 1 November, only two weeks after official notice, and that *all* seats in the CCIs would be up for election. The object of this maneuver was to isolate the bourgeois nationalists in a sea of new voters, and to allow the Istiqlal very little time to try to organize the expanded electorate. The French

[1] See S. Bernard, *Le Conflit franco-marocain*, 3 vols, Brussels, 1963, Vol. 3, pp. 31–5.
[2] Commercial enterprises are divided into seven categories and only Moroccans in the first three could be inscribed on the Commercial Register. See B.O., No. 735, 'Dahir du 1 septembre, 1926', 23 November 1926, pp. 2209–13. For the electoral law, see B.O., No. 1829, 'Arrêté Viziriel du 14 octobre 1947 ...', 14 November 1947, pp. 1155–6.

counted on a low turnout and hoped to mobilize on their own behalf a minimal winning coalition of their own clients in most cities. One may speculate that they expected that certain Susi patrons would help them towards this end, and that a combination of clientelistic commercial obligations and Susi antipathy for the 'Fassi' merchants would overcome the Istiqlalis. The strategy is important to understand, for while it did not work for the French in 1951, it was successfully resurrected for the elections of 1960. It should also be noted that in both 1951 and 1960, the electoral contest was, in essence, an extension of group and commercial rivalries between the Fassis and the Susis. Both communities were to some degree plagued by internal divisions, and unity of the ranks was by no means perfectly observed. Yet the overall tendency was for both groups to overcome their internal conflicts at the time of electoral confrontation.

The confrontation of 1951 did not take place. When the election date was announced on 17 October, Ahmad Lyazidi, the President of the Federation of Moroccan Chambers of Commerce and Industry and a member of the Istiqlal, denounced the French maneuver and urged all eligible voters to abstain in the elections. The appeal was successful as abstention ranged from sixty to ninety-eight per cent in Moroccan cities. In Casablanca, only 424 out of 10,364 registered voters actually voted.[1] One of the most powerful Susi wholesalers, Hajj Abbid,[2] maintained his candidacy and was elected to the CCI of Casablanca of which he became the President. It is perhaps indicative of the growing cleavages within the Swasa communities that he was unable to enlist many Susi voters in his cause.

THE ELECTIONS OF 1960: THE SWASA IN PARTY POLITICS

The 1951 elections to the CCIs were the last held until May 1960. In the interim, nationalist pressure and French preoccupation in Algeria led to the dismantling of the Protectorate regime and formal Moroccan independence in March 1956. The Moroccan king, Muhammad V, appointed a predominantly Istiqlali government in which Ahmad Lyazidi was Minister of Commerce and Industry. One of his first official acts was to dissolve the French and Moroccan sections of the CCIs, and, pending new elections, to turn over their office space to an Istiqlal ancillary organization, the Moroccan Union of Merchants, Industrialists and Artisans (UMCIA).

The UMCIA formally came into existence in March 1956.[3] Its President was Mohammed Laraqi, an important Casablanca textile importer (later manufacturer) originally from Fes. His second-in-command was Mohammed Bin Jilali Bennani, also of a Fassi family. In organizational meetings preceding the

---

[1] On this entire episode, see Robert Rézette, *Les Partis politiques marocains*, Paris, 1955, pp. 41–55.

[2] Hajj Abbid is from the Ammiln, fraction of Ait Tafrawt, village of Addad.

[3] See *Al-Alam*, 9 March 1956, pp. 1, 4.

founding of the UMCIA, only one Susi was invited to attend: Tahar Sidki,[1] a tea wholesaler with impressive nationalist credentials. He told Ben Barka, Secretary-General of the Istiqlal and the moving force behind the creation of the UMCIA, that the Swasa were no longer prepared to knuckle under to Fassi leadership and that the UMCIA had best provide ample room for his 'brothers from the valley'. Ben Barka, of humble non-Fassi origins, readily agreed, and in future meetings as many as fifty Swasa were in attendance. Sidki was even able to rehabilitate Hajj Abbid whom several Istiqlalis wanted to prosecute as a collaborator.

Sidki was entrusted with organizing unions of retailers and wholesalers in several branches of commerce. He relied heavily upon Susi colleagues in Casablanca, mostly from the Ammiln, but also from Ida ou Gnidif, Ait Baha, and Ida ou Semlal. Yet despite their formal representation in the UMCIA, Sidki and his fellow Swasa became convinced that they were being frozen out of the decision-making process by Fassi executive officers. The favors the UMCIA tried to extract from the government, and the activities undertaken in the name of its members, always seemed to be on behalf of the merchant elite and the budding industrialists. The Swasa, by 1958, had pretty much decided that in independent Morocco they no longer had to defer to the Fassis.

During this same period, a more generalized conflict was afflicting the Istiqlal as a whole, one that involved the definition of an official party position on the role of the monarchy in the Moroccan political system. It must be examined briefly before the significance of the 1960 elections, and the importance of the wasa in them, can be understood. The factional rivals within the party were the trade union and resistance leaders, later joined by Ben Barka and Bou-abid, all advocates of a restricted sphere of authority for the king, ranged against the 'old guard' of the party who wished to avoid a confrontation with the throne.[2] In the midst of the crisis (December 1958), Muhammad V appointed a new government that gave strong representation to the left wing of the Istiqlal. With governmental power at their disposal, the 'young Turks', perhaps as Muhammad V had intended, decided to break away from the Istiqlal entirely. This they did in January 1959, and the following September announced the creation of a new party, the National Union of Popular Forces (UNFP).

The new government, led by PM Abdullah Ibrahim, was charged with the preparation of Morocco's first elections as an independent nation. These were to consist of elections to the Chambers of Commerce and Industry followed by elections to local and municipal councils. The king had hoped that their political content could be minimized, but with the recent split of the Istiqlal it became became clear that the elections would entail a trial of strength between the two factions. The UNFP realized that it was in a position to score heavily against the Istiqlal bourgeoisie in the CCI elections, employing the French strategem of 1951 which had not really received a fair test. The Swasa were more than willing

---

[1] Tahar Sidki is from the Ammiln, fraction of Agunsi Wasif, village of Azruwadou.

[2] For a detailed analysis see D. E. Ashford, *Political Change in Morocco*, Princeton, 1961; and my *The Commander of the Faithful: the Moroccan Political Elite — a Study in Segmented Politics*, London and New York, 1970.

to cooperate and broke away from the UMCIA in the winter of 1959 in order to establish a rival organization.[1] As the elections approached, Ben Barka designated Tahar Sidki to draw up the list of UNFP candidates. Sidki was assisted by Mohammed Barakat, a food retailer from the Ammiln, and Ahmad al-Ayyubi, a cloth retailer from Fes. To understand more fully the tactics employed in the elections, and their outcome, we must look closely at the electoral law of January 1958.[2] It was based on French electoral procedure, and its intricacies clearly pre-supposed a literate, well-informed electorate. Having first been drawn up in 1957 and published in 1958, its authors in the Ministry of Interior were not influenced by the crisis in the Istiqlal. Rather they saw these first elections as a trial run for Interior personnel and procedures, and it was felt that low turnout would make the process more manageable.

The electorate included once again all licensed (*patenté*) merchants, tradesmen, and industrialists, twenty-one years old or older, having resided in the district of the CCI for at least one year. Originally, licensed artisans were to be included in the electorate, but when special Chambers of Artisans were created, they were no longer eligible to vote for the CCIs. This ruling was made official only two months before the election,[3] and the Istiqlal denounced the modification as a maneuver on the part of the pro-UNFP government to eliminate a large bloc of Istiqlali sympathizers. This may well have been the case for the traditional artisans of Fes, Salé, and Marrakesh who had long been staunch supporters of the Istiqlal. But in Casablanca the change may have done little to alter the Istiqlal's chances, for the 18,000–20,000 artisans of that city consisted mostly of plumbers, electricians, mechanics, etc.—who were as likely to vote UNFP as Istiqlal. For all of Morocco then, we can estimate the total number of eligible voters at 275,000 and for the city of Casablanca at 46,700.

The actual voting procedure seemed to guarantee a low turnout. For instance, at Casablanca there were 24 seats in the CCI up for election. Eventually 115 candidates presented themselves. The Istiqlal and UNFP each presented slates of 24 candidates. The other 67 candidates were unaffiliated. On the ballot, the names of the candidates were arranged in four columns and numbered consecutively. No party identification, symbols, or colors could appear on the ballot. The voter had to be able to *read* the candidates' names. He was then to draw a line through the numbers and names of the 24 candidates he wished to vote for, place the ballot in an envelope and drop it in an urn. If he crossed out more or less than 24 names, or did not cross out the numbers, his vote would be voided. Few eligible voters actually bothered to register (17,595), and fewer still voted (5,854). A determined, well-drilled minority in such a situation could provide a relative majority of votes.

Despite the financial resources and literacy of the Fassis, it turned out that in several cities they were numerically too weak to win alone and organizationally

[1] The Moroccan Regional Unions of Commerce, Industry, and Artisanry.
[2] See Dahir No. 1-57-161, 8 January 1958, 'Formant statut des Chambres de Commerce et d'Industrie'.
[3] See *Juris-classeur marocain*, Vol. 5, 1949–58, Paris. The modification of the 1958 Dahir was announced in March 1960.

incapable of activating their clientele. Where they failed, the Swasa succeeded, and in the elections of 8 May 1960, UNFP candidates swept the CCIs of Casablanca, Rabat, Kenitra, Tangier, Sidi Sliman, Settat, Ksar al-Kebir, and took all but two seats at Meknes. The Istiqlal scored heavily in its old strongholds and in cities where the Swasa were weak: Fes, Oujda, Taza, Essaouira, Marrakesh, Beni Mellal, Ksar as-Souk, Chaouan, Tetouan, Salé, and Berkane.

What went on at Casablanca is illustrative of the general process. Just prior to the elections, both the UNFP and the Istiqlal published mock ballots for the CCI. All 115 candidates were given their numerical position as it would appear on the actual ballot, but only the party's candidates' names actually appeared in print. The mock ballots could then be used by party organizers to rehearse voters in the procedure, instructing the illiterate to memorize the position on the ballot of party candidates. Although few Swasa are literate, virtually all of them handle numbers with great facility. In commerce they carry their records in their heads, and to memorize twenty-four numbers was probably child's play for them.[1] While it is not possible to verify the contention, it appears that members of the Swasa core tribes, although a minority among tradesmen, mobilized their members and won resounding victories over the Fassi bourgeoisie, an even more distinct minority. Thus, the French strategy of 1951 was successfully revived by Ben Barka in the name of the UNFP. The results of the elections for Casablanca, as presented in Table 11.2, are indicative of this success.

The table shows the heavy reliance of the UNFP upon the Swasa. Even the non-Swasa were from modest retail trades (Ayyubi, Cherkaoui). A gesture was made toward the Jewish community through Azoulay and Ibnuaysh, while 'progressive' elements of the Fassi bourgeoisie were represented by Abdelhadi Boutaleb and Moulay Ali Kittani, Mohammed Mansour, an Arab, is famous for having organized the armed resistance in Casablanca before independence. He and many of his associates were rewarded after 1956 with petty trade licenses and were thus eligible to vote in 1960. The Istiqlal, for its part, did not take the Susi threat seriously enough. Their own list of candidates shows an unmistakable bias toward the urban 'grande bourgeoisie' (Laraqi, Bennani, Sebti, Ezzizi, Manjara, Benjelloun). They matched the UNFP with two Jewish candidates (Obedia and Benisti). A small contingent of loyal Swasa, led by Bilqasim Taghawti,[2] was clearly unable to counter the efforts of Tahar Sidki in organizing members of the core tribes. Finally, the bloc voting for the UNFP is fairly evident. The spread between the most (2,632) and fewest (2,251) votes cast for any UNFP candidate is only 381. This margin might have been even narrower, but it is likely that errors in crossing out candidates, ballots cast by non-organized voters, the variations in voting preference caused by the special Jewish, resistance, and 'progressive' bourgeois constituencies, combined to increase the spread.

The results came as something of a shock in several quarters. Allal al-Fassi,

[1] For an interesting discussion of the electoral procedures in Morocco, see Octave Marais, 'Observations sur le système électoral marocain', *Annuaire de l'Afrique du nord*, Aix-en-Provence, 1966.

[2] Taghawti is from Tasserirte and had a retail trade in the Ancienne Medina of Casablanca. He helped organize the Istiqlal there prior to independence and remained a stalwart thereafter.

Table 11.2. Results of the Election to the Casablanca Chamber of Commerce and Industry, 8 May 1960[1]

Licensed *commercants*	46,700
Number registered to vote	17,595
Votes cast	5,854
Votes voided	1,920
Valid votes	3,934

	UNFP			Istiqlal	
	Candidate's name	Votes won		Candidate's name	Votes won
1	Ahmed Oulhaj (S)	2632	1	Mohammed Adnan (A)	Not available
2	Abduallah Ibrahim (S)	2623	2	Mohammed Bin Jilali Bennani (F)	,,
3	Ahmidou 'Al-Watani' Faris (S)	2612	3	Masud bin al-Haj Mamoun (S)	,,
4	Mohammed Mansour (R)	2596	4	Mohammed Laraqi (F)	,,
5	Abdullah Souiri (S)	2582	5	Mohammed Marrakshi (F)	,,
6	Ali Semlali (S)	2574	6	Ahmed Dadi (F)	,,
7	Ahmad as-Susi (S)	2568	7	Adulkader Berrada (F)	,,
8	Abdelkabir bin Omar (A)	2567	8	Mohammed Lamraani (F)	,,
9	Mbarek Semlali (S)	2546	9	Ahmed Madhkuri (A)	,,
10	Mohammed Cherkaoui (A)	2531	10	Hajj Omar Sebti (F)	,,
11	Abdullah Filali (A)	2529	11	Abbas Benjelloun (F)	,,
12	Mohammed Barakat (S)	2525	12	Maati Abakhay (F)	,,
13	Hassan BuNuh (S)	2517	13	Yahya al-Manjara (F)	,,
14	Mohammed Lahrizi	2515	14	Bilqasim Taghawti (S)	,,
15	Bouchentouf Bilyut	2514	15	Mohammed Bouzba (F)	,,
16	Brahim Benkiran	2514	16	Shalum Benisti (J)	,,
17	Saajedin Saidi	2508	17	Abdulkader Labib (A)	,,
18	Tahar Sidki (S)	2506	18	Dawi bin Dris	,,
19	David Azoulay (J)	2487	19	Meyer Obedia (J)	,,
20	Mohammed Zaghloul (A)	2479	20	Mohammed Ezzizi (F)	,,
21	Elias Ibnuaysh (J)	2460	21	Brahim Mubarki (S-Haouz)	,,
22	Ahmad al-Ayyubi (F)	2350	22	Ahmed bin Ali (S-Haha)	,,
23	Abdulhadi Boutaleb (F)	2270	23	Muhammed Zemmouri (Z)	,,
24	Moulay Ali Kittani (F)	2251	24	Abderrazaq Bennis (F)	,,

UNFP spread 2632–2251 = 381 votes

President of the Istiqlal, attributed the victory of the UNFP to the machinations of a few 'monopolists' and 'feudalists' who were able to herd the Susi grocers to the polls like slaves. Moreover, they were aided, according to al-Fassi, by a sympathetic administration and foreign capitalists who wished at all costs to stop the Istiqlal.[2] The party protested the Casablanca elections, claiming that they had been highly irregular. On 21 June 1960, the Regional Tribunal of Casablanca upheld the Istiqlali claims and annulled the elections. The court ruling required that new elections be held to the Casablanca CCI, and they were duly scheduled for December 1960.

[1] Official, detailed results of these elections were not published. The figures above are based on private sources. The Istiqlal vote per candidate was probably about half that cast for each UNFP candidate. The letter following the candidate's name indicates: S = Susi; R = Resistant; J = Jew; F = Fassi. Those not designated by a letter could not be conclusively identified.

[2] See *Al-Alam*, 15 May 1960, p. 6.

Another concerned witness to the May elections was the king. It was not comforting for him to see a recently-created and self-styled revolutionary party make substantial gains within Morocco's private commercial sector. It appeared that the UNFP might go on to score heavily in the upcoming local and municipal elections. Muhammad V, faced with this prospect, tried to deflate the UNFP balloon by dismissing the Ibrahim government on the eve of the local elections. None the less, the UNFP did quite well, again sweeping several major cities including Casablanca.[1] But what is important to note in all this is that in the pending second round of elections to the Casablanca CCI, the Swasa would be operating in a considerably different context than in May. UNFP sympathizers were no longer in power, the king had shown evident displeasure with the new party, and continued support of the UNFP might incur official wrath. Susi patrons, who encouraged a UNFP vote in May, were reluctant to do so in December. They were more vulnerable to official harassment (of which the court ruling itself might have been a forewarning) than their clientele among the retailers. The latter may not have immediately perceived the implicit challenge to the monarchy that would be read into another display of support for the UNFP, and the danger of a Fassi resurgence probably outweighed any fears of royal retribution they may have had. As a result, the vote in the elections of 18 December fell off by almost twenty per cent, but the returns did not differ greatly from those of the previous May (see Table 11.3).

The UNFP made some minor modifications in its list of candidates. Abdel-hadi Boutaleb, a UNFP militant while the party was in power, abandoned ship after May 1960. He was replaced by another 'progressive' Fassi, Karim Lamraani. Another resistance leader, Bouchaib Dukkali, was added to the list. To escape the Istiqlali charge of Susi 'tribalism', a few modest Fassi retailers, Mohammed Bouchaib and Abderrahim Cherkaoui, were also included. Otherwise it was Sidki's cohorts all over again.

The Istiqlal thoroughly reconstructed its list, holding over only six candidates from the May elections. The grandest of the 'grande bourgeoisie' were removed (Sebti, Abbas Benjelloun, Ezzizi). Several modest, though non-Susi, retailers were added, as well as five true Swasa, probably associated with Bilqasim Taghawti. For good measure, Abdulkrim Lahlou, a Fassi tea wholesaler, was included to counter the influence of the Susi patrons. Taghawti, in the weeks prior to the election, made a sustained effort to reach the Swasa of Casablanca, speaking to them in Tashilhit at various rallies.[2] The determined Istiqlali attempt to re-cast its image and appeal to the little man, especially the Susi, failed to achieve the desired results. The Istiqlal, defeated for the second time, claimed that the tradesmen of Casablanca were so disgusted with the tribal feudalists of the UNFP that they boycotted the election.[3]

It is clear that not all, nor even most, of the Swasa, participated in the elections.

---

[1] See Paul Chambergeat, 'Les élections communales marocaines du 29 mai 1960', *Revue française de science politique*, Vol. 11, No. 1, 1961, pp. 89–117.

[2] See *Al-Alam*, 16 December 1960, pp. 1, 4.

[3] See *Al-Alam*, 20 December 1960, p. 1. The UNFP interpretation appears in *At-Tahrir*, 19 December 1960.

Table 11.3. Results of the Election to the Casablanca Chamber of Commerce and Industry, 18 December 1960[1]

UNFP Candidate's name	Votes won	Istiqlal Candidate's name	Votes won
1 Ahmad as-Susi (S)	1865	1 Yahya Manjara (F)	922
2 Mohammed Lahrizi	1864	2 Meyer Obedia (J)	914
3 Moulay Ali Kittani (F)	1837	3 *Ahmad Bennani (F)*	912
4 *Karim Lamraani (F)*	1830	4 *Bouchaib Maanawi*	910
5 Abdullah Souiri (S)	1827	5 *Ahmad Benkiran (F)*	910
6 *Abderrahim Cherkaoui (F)*	1820	6 *Abdulkrim Lahlou (F)*	908
7 Abdullah Ibrahim (S)	1819	7 *Mohammed Bin Shaqrun (F)*	908
8 Saajedin Saidi	1818	8 Mohammed Laraqi (F)	209
9 *Mohammed Benjifan*	1816	9 *Lahsan Sabban (S)*	902
10 Bouchaib Dukkali (R)	1815	10 *Abdullah bin Abderrahman (S)*	901
11 Ahmad al-Ayyubi (F)	1815	11 *Abdesslam Najih (A)*	899
12 Tahar Sidki (S)	1814	12 *Brahim Sahraoui*	898
13 Abdullah Filali (A)	1813	13 *Bouchaib Mzabi (A)*	897
14 Mohammed Zaghloul (A)	1812	14 *Brahim Masluhi (S)*	897
15 Ali Semlali (S)	1811	15 Abderrazaq Bennis (F)	895
16 *Mohammed Bouchaib*	1810	16 *Joseph Amzallag (J)*	894
17 Mohammed Cherkaoui (A)	1807	17 Bilqasim Taghawti (S)	893
18 *Dris bin Ali (S)*	1806	18 *Abdesslam Abdi*	888
19 Elias Ibnu-aysh (J)	1806	19 *Ahmad Brahim Susi (S)*	888
20 Mohammed Barakat (S)	1804	20 *Mbarek al-Mahfudh (S)*	881
21 David Azoulay (J)	1803	21 *Muhammed Qarquri (A)*	878
22 Abdelkabir bin Omar (A)	1801	22 Masud bin al-Hajj Mamun	810
23 Mohammed Mansour (R)	1790	23 *Hassan Benjelloun (F)*	810
24 Ahmidou 'al-Watani' Faris (S)	1789	24 Mohammed b. Cheik Baamrani (S)	?
UNFP spread 1865–1789=76 votes		Istiqlal spread 922–810=112 votes	

Licensed *commercants*	46,700
Number registered to vote	17,595
Votes cast	4,953
Votes voided	2,139
Valid votes	2,814

It can be estimated that there are seven to eight thousand tradesmen from the core tribes in the city of Casablanca.[2] From this community, a compact bloc of 1,000–2,000 Swasa actually went to the polls. This should not be interpreted as indifference on the part of the other 5,000 Swasa. First, many of them may not have been eligible to vote, being either too young or a resident in Casablanca for too short a period, or not personally licensed in trade. Given the difficulty of the electoral procedure, the actual Swasa turnout constitutes something approximating corporate action.

[1] Vote totals for Istiqlali candidates were available for this election although official results were again not published. The italics indicate new candidates not appearing on the lists of 8 May.

[2] See note 3, p. 238. Ibrahim's figures check out roughly with my own estimates, based on 1960 census data, that the Swasa constitute *c.* 15% of the commercial community of 46,000.

The newly-elected Casablanca CCI, coached by the UNFP, took a studiously militant approach to its functions. Its first President was Mohammed Mansour, the former resistance leader, whose hostility toward the French business community was well known. His election had been recommended by Ben Barka and Basri, and was unenthusiastically accepted by the Susi members of the CCI. While they admired his nationalist exploits, he was not one of them, nor was he a 'professional' tradesman. The Swasa felt that once again, having provided the muscle of a political effort, they were to be denied the fruits of their victory. Under Mansour's guidance, the CCI antagonized the government and isolated itself from the commercial and industrial elite of the city. Denunciations of neo-colonialist economic interests may have been useful for UNFP propaganda, but were bad for business. The CCI, which many hoped would serve as a channel of communications between the Moroccan and French business communities, was virtually isolated by 1962, avoided by private interests and starved by the Ministry of Finance that funded its budget.[1]

It was not long before the Swasa became disenchanted with the UNFP, and the reasons why may help clarify the nature of their identification with that party. The declaration of socialist ideals and programs by the UNFP played a minor part in winning Susi support. In 1958–59, the Swasa were still to be found mainly in the lower echelons of the native commercial elite of Morocco, and for this reason many were attracted by the truculent UNFP pronouncements on the exploitative bourgeoisie. Moreover, their history of defying established authority predisposed some of them to the militant views of the left. None the less, the Swasa had always in the past avoided intransigence if their adversaries had a clear preponderance of force. Thus they had occasionally acknowledged the authority of the pre-Protectorate government at moments when it was powerful, and had both opposed and profited from the French presence in Morocco. After independence, their initial alignment with the left wing of the Istiqlal and later the UNFP did not entail a direct confrontation with the monarchy. The satisfactions of ideological militancy did not at first bear a high risk factor. However, after 1960, when the UNFP became an opposition party (and one that the king viewed as inherently disloyal) the price of progressivism became too high to accept for many Susis.

Individual patrons entered into politics in order to improve their individual commercial positions and the overall strength of the Swasa relative to other commercial groups. They did not enter politics to reform Moroccan society or the Moroccan regime. In this way, the patrons were fulfilling their obligations to provide security and protection for their clientele and the Swasa as a whole. It had been this sort of motivation that allowed the patrons to bury their internal rivalries and to mobilize their clientele in the name of group feeling and broad

---

[1] Moroccan and French entrepreneurs came in contact through the Moroccan National Committee of the International Chamber of Commerce. Its President for years has been Hajj Omar Sebti. Other officers and members include Driss Sebti, Omar al-Manjara, Abbas Bennani, Mohammed Ezzizi, Mohammed Laraqi (i.e. the Fassi elite), and some of the moguls of the Jewish and French communities: Gaston Baruk, Paul Ohanna, Lorrain Cruse, Nestorenko, Albert Hentschel, J. H. Kersten, etc.

community concern. Once in control of the CCIs, they had hoped to further their own interests in various cities, and, more important, to bargain directly with the governmental agencies and commissions that made policy dealing with importation, marketing, credit, and banking. It became apparent to the patrons that these ends could not be served as long as the Swasa maintained their links with the UNFP. It also seemed clear to the Swasa that the UNFP leaders were exploiting them in the name of party ideology, and were not concerned about rewarding Susi loyalty.

By August 1963, when new elections to the CCIs were held,[1] patrons in several cities were encouraged by leaders close to the palace to cut their ties with the UNFP and align themselves with a new royalist party, the Front for the Defense of Constitutional Institutions (FDIC). It was suggested that the patrons would be treated favorably by the government were they to do so. It was also emphasized that the FDIC was not only opposed to the UNFP but even more so to the Istiqlal and the Fassi interests that it represented. As a result of these blandishments, the patrons swung their clientele into line behind the FDIC, and once again the Swasa took control of several CCIs throughout Morocco. Their tacit alliance with the palace has continued ever since and is interpreted by the Swasa as a realistic adjustment to the present power balance within the national system. Once again, ideology has been of minor importance in explaining the new alliance.

The government's alliance with the Swasa patrons pre-empts the CCIs, particularly that of Casablanca, from elements with greater financial means and *savoir faire* who might try to develop the organizations into more powerful and autonomous units. Beyond this, the alliance presumably gives the government some leverage in manipulating the retail communities of Moroccan cities, communities that in the past have been politically active and somewhat dangerous. The strategy will work to the extent that the Swasa are sufficiently rewarded, and to the extent that the tribal–commercial links between patron and clientele remain firm. But, as indicated above, these links are coming under increasing stress. The proliferation of retailers and would-be retailers in the cities, the increasing lack of upward mobility within the wholesaler–retailer hierarchy, and the overall economic stagnation in the cities, may lead to the gradual loosening of community control mechanisms. The material gap between patron and client has grown in recent years, and the former solidarity between the big and the little may fall victim to the resentment of the petty tradesmen. This may take the form of searching for alternate means of credit, or moving out of trade altogether, and of cutting one's links with the home territory. It is now quite common for the Swasa to bring their entire family to the city and to send their children to school. The next generation of Swasa may have little direct contact with their tribal past and their career opportunities will be considerably different from those of their fathers. Positions of power within the Swasa groups will become more diversified, the means of control more diffused, and the pressures for group cohesion less pronounced.

[1] See Hubert Breton, 'Elections professionelles et locales marocaines', *Annuaire de l'Afrique du nord*, Aix-en-Provence, 1963, pp. 107–18; also *Les Phares,*(FDIC),23 August 1963.

CONCLUSION

The Swasa are, in twentieth-century Morocco, a regional and ethnic group with which virtually every Moroccan is familiar. Their presence outside their home region is now firmly established and is in fact essential to their popular image. In a few decades they were able to find a place for themselves in the commercial network that developed after 1912, to the point that they became an integral, if not indispensable part of it. Politicans in the broadest sense of the word— tacticians of the Resident-General, nationalists, leaders of post-1956 parties, and the Palace itself—tried to harness the political potential of the Swasa. In this way, they found themselves involved in the national political arena as a force to be reckoned with, or at least one that could not be overlooked. No other group in Morocco, starting from the same tribal origins, can cite such accomplishments.

Some of the explanations of this phenomenon can be dismissed as of secondary importance. I would not accept, for instance, that there is something peculiar about the 'Susi mentality' that lends itself to their success. They are pious, industrious, frugal, and competitive—perilously close to some Weberian Protestant ideal—but in this respect not much different from other tribes of the High Atlas and the Rif that have not registered triumphs of the same magnitude. Nor is the argument of extraordinary group solidarity convincing, for the same reasons; other sedentary tribes displaying roughly the same mix of conflict and group cohesion have submitted to a different fate. Finally, the recent history of the Swasa cannot be adequately explained in terms of a series of encounters with ethnic rivals such as the Fassis. Enemies and rivals are numerous for any individual Susi, and the ethnic label that any one may bear helps identify him but does not necessarily make the enmity more intense.

On the other hand, relative to migrants from the coastal plains who today constitute the bulk of the population of Casablanca, the Swasa have manifested a higher degree of group cohesion and self-help, or at least a lesser degree of atomization. But the phenomenon we are describing is perhaps best understood in other terms. One of the most important factors would seem to be fortuitous, that is the choice of petty trade as the vehicle for mobilizing resources outside the home area. The rapid orientation of the Swasa toward petty trade came about in an *ad hoc* manner, when a handful of Swasa several decades ago registered their first successes in trade, thereby luring their tribesmen into the same occupational patterns. Other neighboring tribes, and of course more distant ones in the High Atlas and Rif, followed different pioneers: factory workers, miners, guardians, etc. Trade, however, renders salient the very characteristics of individual responsibility and group self-help that were muted or unexpressed among the groups that took up factory work or mining. The latter harnessed their energies to the more impersonal system of salaried labor where their success depended upon employers who demanded hard work rather than ingenuity. The tradesmen had no direct masters, drew no salaries, and had to learn the intricacies of market fluctuations, credit mobilization, and the protection of tribesmates in a highly competitive situation. The Susi phenomenon may have come about through 'the luck of the draw'. We could just as easily be talking about the

Riffis, had the initial opportunities open to them been different. In fact, recently, the Riffis have become important in the trade networks of Tangier and Tetouan.

Further, having taken the trade option, the Swasa placed themselves squarely in the urban arena where the major economic and political transformations of the nation were being shaped. This salient position was likewise denied the workers in remote mining centers or the industries of Europe. Finally one may note that while there is no gainsaying 'le fait berbère', or 'le fait arabe' for that matter, the Susi–Fassi rivalry results only in part from this phenomenon. It too is a result of the luck of the draw, and had there been other actors present playing the same role as the Fassis in the commercial system, the Swasa probably would have responded in the same manner. The motivations of the Swasa as individuals and in groups have always turned on their preoccupation with the inner-workings of their own communities, rather than upon their rivalries with outsiders.

12

The Neo-Makhzan and the Berbers

Abdaslam Ben Kaddour

It is hardly possible to find an aspect of State and society in Morocco in which the impact of French colonization is not evident. Generally speaking, this impact was a modernizing one: a modern sector was introduced in agriculture, industry, and education. However, in the political field colonization had a polarizing impact since it gave birth, on the one hand, to a modern nationalist elite, and on the other hand it helped in the retraditionalization of political institutions.

Before the treaty of Fes in 1912, the political life in Morocco was marked by a dichotomy between the *makhzan* and the tribes, *bled el-makhzan* and *bled es-siba*. The French administration succeeded by 1934 in putting down tribal resistance and in subjecting *bled es-siba* to its control. Then, a new dichotomy developed; on the one hand the new nationalist elite, and on the other, the colonial power that was assured of the tribal chiefs' loyalty.[1] Some of these chiefs were merely a creation of colonialism.

After independence, a similar dichotomy appeared: neo-*makhzan*–nationalist elite.[2] Among other elements, the neo-*makhzan* inherited the loyalty of what was *bled es-siba*. As was the case under the French rule, the loyalty of the tribes was gained not by attending to their needs, but rather by satisfying the demands of rural notables, who were created by the privileges granted them by the central government. This is the framework in which the monarchy has been dealing, since independence, with the rural population in general, and with the Berber population in particular.

The monarchy's policies toward the Berbers differ, however, from those that were followed by the French colonization. While the French tried to create a division between Arabs and Berbers, in order to strengthen their rule, the monarchy used the Berbers, especially of the Middle and High Atlas, to assure its own survival, and it did so not for ethnic but for political reasons. Indeed, the

[1] Moroccan tribes generally do not have well-established hereditary rulers and dominant families. They emerge, sometimes by election, sometimes by appointment. But there is not really a name for 'chief', in the sense of hereditary leader. The *caid* is someone appointed by the government, while the *amghar* is someone elected by his fellows.
Moreover, the significance of the term *caid* changed profoundly with the coming of Independence in 1956. Under the French Protectorate, the *caid* was a tribal leader, generally selected from within the tribe and sharing tribal life, who represented the tribe *vis-à-vis* his opposite number, the French district officer, who effectively stood for the central power. After Independence, this kind of *caid*-ship was abolished, and the term was applied to the district officer, now a Moroccan, representing the Ministry of the Interior.
In brief, before 1956, a *caid* was a tribesman named by central government to be responsible for his tribe, and after 1956, he was a professional civil servant. Only very exceptionally was it possible for a man to have been a *caid* in both senses.
[2] This dichotomy was not apparent immediately after independence, and took shape only after Istiqlal left the cabinet in 1962 when it became clear that the monarchy was basing its strategy on its alliance with the Mouvement Populaire. On this dichotomy see Abdelkebir Khatibi, *Stratification sociale au Maroc*, mimeo., Rabat, 1967, p. 2.

Berbers of the areas mentioned above were the only rural populations who developed a national leadership which not merely evaded the control of the Istiqlal, but, on the contrary, was in conflict with this party. The Berber leadership was to play the role of the central group around which all traditionalist forces would be mobilized to create a strong Monarchist party.

The post-independence monarchy was the beneficiary of two policies initiated by the French administration: the creation of loyal tribal chiefs, and the prevention of the development of a Moroccan bourgeoisie. Although the Moroccan urban bourgeoisie had emerged before the advent of the French colonization and consolidated its status during the Protectorate, its economic role was limited to the fields of construction, internal trade, and part of import–export activities. The end of the Second World War brought to Morocco large amounts of French funds that consolidated the French monopoly over the Moroccan economy and relegated the Moroccan bourgeoisie to the background. The 'liberal' Resident-General Erik Labonne tried to associate the bourgeoisie to the colonial capital in the industrialization of the country, but he was opposed by the Protectorate.[1]

At any rate, the Moroccan bourgeoisie stayed, one way or another, out of modern industrial activities. Most investments were made by metropolitan groups such as La Banque de Paris et des Pays-Bas, La Banque de l'Union Parisienne, Schneider-Creusot, and Rothschild, and by 'Moroccan' groups that were either international, such as La Banque d'Etat du Maroc, in which the French participation amounted to 57·2 per cent in 1947, or French, such as La Compagnie Générale du Maroc that was related to La Banque de Paris et des Pays-Bas, and La Compagnie Marocaine that was linked to Schneider.

Conscious of certain differences between Arabs and Berbers, the French began a policy of 'divide and rule'. As early as 1928, a residency official, Roger Gaudefroy-Demombynes, wrote:

> It is dangerous to allow the formation of a united phalanx of Moroccans having one language. We must utilize to our advantage the old dictum 'divide and rule'. The presence of a Berber race is a useful instrument for counteracting the Arab race; we may even use it against the Makhzan itself.[2]

To strengthen the so-called 'Berber race', the French introduced on 16 May 1930, the Berber Dahir that legalized the customary courts in Berber areas.

The French administration also began to recruit Berber soldiers for the French army and started appointing Berber chieftains and strengthening those who existed already, such as El-Glawi in the High Atlas. This action was taken both on the economic and political levels. On the economic level, tribal notables were given land and were transformed into feudal landlords, while on the political level, these tribal chiefs were appointed as *caid*s.

At the same time, Berber schools were created for the notables' children. These

[1] Abdelkebir Khatibi, 'Note descriptive sur les élites administratives et économiques marocaines', *Annuaire de l'Afrique du nord*, Vol. VII, 1968, Centre National de la Recherche Scientifique, Paris, 1969, p. 89.

[2] R. Gaudefroy-Demombynes, *L'Oeuvre française en matière d'enseignement au Maroc*, Paris, 1928, p. 119, quoted in John P. Halstead, *Rebirth of a Nation: the Origins and Rise of Moroccan Nationalism (1912-1944)*, Cambridge (Mass.), 1967, p. 72.

schools '. . . should be organisms of French policy and instruments of propaganda . . . (In these schools) . . . all arabic instruction . . . every Islamic manifestation will be resolutely avoided . . .'[1]

The best known school was the Berber Collège, established in Azrou in 1927. Most of its students did not go beyond the Brevet d'Etudes Secondaires (equivalent to the final year in a Junior High School); many of them were appointed as interpreters in the rural administrative offices, or sent to military schools.

The other French policy, which contributed to the survival of the new *makhzan*, concerns, as we have seen, the French economic policies toward the Moroccan bourgeoisie. Despite the fact that the Moroccan bourgeoisie was very active, after the Second World War, its participation in the modern sector of the economy was very limited and amounted to only 5 per cent of the industrial investments in 1950. An apologist for the French administration well summarized the thinking of the *Residence* about the urban Fassi bourgeoisie: '. . . we always must dominate (the bourgeoisie), take its place, and transform it into an obedient caste'.[2] The bourgeoisie responded by supporting the nationalist movement.

Thus the French administration supplied the neo-*makhzan* with a source of political support (Berber *caids*—administrators—who formed the backbone of the Ministry of the Interior)[3] and with an efficient way of moderating the ambitions of the Moroccan bourgeoisie, namely, state capitalism.

Indeed, the French conceived the industrialization of Morocco as the image of their *économie mixte*, that is, as a joint effort by the state and by a number of French companies.[4] Thus the state acquired monopolies in phosphates and tobacco, while the Bureau de Recherches et de Participations Minières (BRPM) and the Société Chérifienne de Charbonnages were to control most of the mineral resources.

ECONOMIC PROBLEMS AFTER INDEPENDENCE

When Morocco became independent in 1956, 70 per cent of the population, including 80 to 85 per cent of the Berbers, was living in rural areas. The French not only had failed to solve the problems of the rural populations of Morocco; they had rather aggravated them through granting some of the *jamaas*' (communes) land to the French *colons* and the *caids*.

After independence, the inequality in rural areas was apparent. 40 per cent of the 1·6 million rural families were landless. The remaining 60 per cent were divided into four groups:[5]

[1] Paul Marty, *Le Maroc de demain*, Paris, 1925, quoted in Halstead, op. cit., p. 73.

[2] Dr Mauran, *La Société marocaine*, Paris, 1913, quoted in Khatibi, *Stratification*, op. cit., p. 18.

[3] In the early 1960s, 250 of the 320 *caids* of the Ministry of the Interior were Azrou graduates, and although the number of Berbers among these *caids* is not known, it is assumed that most of Azrou students were of Berber origin.

[4] John P. Halstead, *Rebirth of a Nation*, op. cit., p. 90.

[5] Arranged from Andre Tiano, *Le Maghreb entre les mythes*, Paris, 1967, p. 281. These figures were obtained from a rural survey carried out by the Moroccan Government in 1962.

(a) 450,000 farmers (40% of total owners) owned 7% of the land (600,000 acres).

(b) 450,000 farmers (40%) owned 28% of the land (2,500,000 acres). These two groups representing 80% of the landowners thus owned only 35% of the land.

(c) 140,000 farmers (12%) owned 24% of the land (2,000,000 acres) in lots of 10 to 20 acres.

(d) 80,000 farmers (8%) owned 41% of the land (3,500,000 acres) in lots of more than 20 acres.

In this structure of landownership lie the rural problems, problems that are sharper in the predominantly Berber areas because of their remoteness from the modern economic sector, and because urbanization in these regions was slower than in other parts of the country.

After independence, no organized political force was interested in solving the rural problems. The political elite was anxious to keep the modern sector of economy running, for it was the major source of income for the state. On the other hand, each political grouping was busy rewarding its supporters with jobs in the new administration; thus the number of administrative jobs (including the armed forces) went from 60,000 in 1956 to 165,000 in 1964 and to 230,000 in 1967.

The two major political forces of the late 1950s, the monarchy and Istiqlal, completely ignored rural problems and were not even thinking about an agrarian reform. The monarchy was not willing to antagonize the only force whose support was necessary for the survival of the *makhzan*, that is, the tribal notables who acquired land during the Protectorate. On the other hand, Istiqlal was not willing to carry out any serious land reform, for such a reform would cut its own power base in some rural areas where some of its strong low-echelon leaders were large landowners (Nejjai in the Gharb, and Kabbaj in Sous). The only type of land that both the monarchy and Istiqlal were willing to distribute was the land that belonged to the *caid*s who had collaborated openly with the French administration, and who were called traitors. It is interesting to note in this respect that a royal commission found that 14,500 acres were available for distribution in 1959.[1]

THE MONARCHY AND THE BERBERS

In this context, the monarchy was fighting on two fronts. On the one hand, it tried to undermine the importance of the bourgeoisie, and its political arm, Istiqlal, by limiting the field of its economic activities, and by creating divisions within it. On the other hand, the monarchy tried to secure the loyalty and support of the Berber population, by creating a tribal party, the Mouvement Populaire, and by granting privileges to the old and new tribal notables.

On the economic level, the monarchy followed a policy of state capitalism that

[1] William Zartman, *Morocco, Problems of New Power*, New York, 1964, p. 124.

excluded the bourgeoisie from many economic activities. The State acquired the Banque du Maroc, a majority in the Banque Nationale du Développement Economique (BNDE) and the Caisse de Dépot et de Gestion. In the field of industry, the State was the largest investor in the semi-public economic ventures. Moreover, the nationalization of a large part of the external trade in 1965 gave the State control of two-thirds of all exports. Finally, the private investments in the framework of the three-year plan (1965–67) amounted to only 10 per cent, while the State's investments reached 60 per cent.[1]

On the political level, the monarchy's Berber policy led to the creation of a Berber party, with two objectives in mind. First, it would kill any dream among Istiqlal's leaders of a one-party system (the case of Tunisia where the Neo-Destour removed the Bey—hereditary ruler—was noted with alarm in the Palace). Second, the creation of a Berber party would give the Berbers a sense of political representation while their demands would be channeled through ways controlled by the Palace. In the monarchy's plan, this Berber party was to be the backbone of a traditionalist party (Berber and otherwise) that would work hand in hand with the Ministry of the Interior in keeping the social and political structures as they are, and in preventing any social change. Furthermore, this traditionalist party would give the monarchy the 'democratic façade' that would facilitate the flow of Western economic aid.

To put this scheme into practice the monarchy sought the support of the traditionalist forces of the Middle and High Atlas regions. The question is why the choice fell on these regions and not on other Berber areas (Sous or Rif) or on other rural areas (Gharb or Doukkala). There are several reasons for this choice.

The most potent single reason was the fact that the Middle and High Atlas areas were the only rural areas that had developed political leadership at the national level. In analyzing the composition of the eleven Moroccan cabinets, we find that the only members appointed from rural areas were those from the Middle and High Atlas areas (with the exception of Mokhtar Soussi, the Minister of Religious Endowments, who was from the Sous). All of these 'rural' cabinet members were founders, leaders, or supporters of the Mouvement Populaire:

Embarek Bekkai, premier of the two first cabinets (7 December 1955 and 3 December 1956), and Interior Minister in the fifth cabinet (26 May 1960).
Lahcen Lyoussi, Minister of the Interior in the first cabinet.
Mahjoubi Aherdan, Minister of the Interior (2 June 1961 to 20 August 1964), then Agriculture Minister (20 August 1964 to 22 February 1966), and finally Defense Minister (22 February 1966).
Haddou Chiguer, in charge of Telecommunications (20 August 1964), Agriculture (22 February 1966), Defense (6 July 1967), Education (17 January 1968).

It is a well-known fact that these portfolios are reserved to the Palace's closest friends and reliable servants.

[1] Khatibi, 'Note descriptive . . .', op. cit., p. 85.

Besides this high level political leadership, there was a low-echelon leadership, expecially in the Ministry of the Interior where a large number of Berber *caid*s were operating, and in the army, where a majority of officers were of rural[1] (often Berber) origins. Most of these *caid*s and officers were the product of the Collège Berbère in Azrou, and the military school of Ahermoumou[2] in the Fes province.

The monarchy's policy was partly a consequence of the rivalry that developed between Fassis and Berbers during the first few years of independence. Mahjoubi Aherdan did not restrain himself from condemning the so-called 'Fassi dictatorship', while Istiqlal condemned 'the rural feudals'. Such a rivalry also existed between Fassis and Soussis, but manifested itself on the economic level rather than on the political level. The Sous area was known for its UNFP sympathy; thus in the 1963 legislative elections, the Agadir province cast 110,000 votes for the UNFP, 60,000 for FDIC (Mouvement Populaire and Gudira's PSD), and 25,000 for Istiqlal.[3]

All these reasons led the Palace to capitalize on the rural area in general and on the Berber area in particular, and many observers agree that the monarchy acted according to a more or less 'premeditated' plan. The first move was the spectacular royal pardon accorded to the Atlas Lord, Glawi, in France prior to independence; this move was important in assuring the network of *caid*s established by the Protectorate and Glawi that their future would not be as bleak as they might have feared.[4]

At the same time two of the four members of the appointed Throne Council were Berbers (Embarek Bekkai and Tahar Ou Assou, an influential *caid* in the High Atlas region). Furthermore, at the time of the formation of the first government, contrary to Istiqlal expectations, the party obtained only seven out of nineteen ministries, while the premiership went to a close friend of Muhammad V, a former colonel of the French army and former Pasha of Sefrou, Embarek Bekkai. The other important ministry in the Palace's strategy, Interior, fell into the hands of another Berber, Lahcen Lyoussi, the *bête noire* of the Istiqlal.

Beside the Berber 'card', the monarchy played another card against Istiqlal, namely the Democratic Party (PDI) of Hassan Ouazzani. This party filled five portfolios in the first cabinet despite the fact that its following was very limited. By 1959, the PDI became a political club rather than a party, and therefore disappeared from the plans of the Palace. Meanwhile, what Istiqlal called the 'feudal danger' was manifesting itself. In 1958, Mahjoubi Aherdan, a former officer of the French army and then governor of the Rabat province, began working for the creation of a Berber party with the help of Lahcan Lyoussi. Muhammad V, in order not to sharpen the Arab–Berber division, sent one of his reliable servants, Abdelkrim Khatib, the former head of the embryonic Moroccan

[1] Octave Marais, 'La Classe dirigeante au Maroc', *Revue française de science politique*, Vol. xiv.

[2] This school was set up in 1957, and was headed by Major Idriss Ben Omar. It trained 200 non-commissioned officers during its first year of existence.

[3] Octave Marais, 'L'élection de la chambre des représentants du Maroc', *Annuaire de l'Afrique du Nord*, Paris, Centre Nationale de la Recherche Scientifique, 1964, Vol. ii, 1963.

[4] Shortly after independence, Muhammed V married a daughter of a 'feudal' personage (the former *caid* Amehrog).

Liberation army, to share with Aherdan the presidency of the new party, the Mouvement Populaire. From 1964 to 1969, the party was represented in the cabinets by Mahjoubi Aherdan, from August 1964 to July 1967; by Haddou Chiguer, a school teacher, from August 1964 onwards; and by Abdesiam Benaissa from January 1968 to October 1969.

As far as the party's program is concerned, the only clear idea proclaimed was that of a union around the king. As far back as 1956, the real prime mover of the Berber Party, Lahcan Lyoussi, declared to the PDI newspaper[1] that the only means of unifying the country was to ban all political parties and rally round the king. The party also propagated the idea of a Muslim State under the leadership of Amir al Mouminin (commander of the faithful), Muhammad V.

The scission that occurred in January 1959 within the Istiqlal Party simplified the task of both the Palace and the Mouvement Populaire. First, the Istiqlal became weak and thus lost its capacity to threaten the monarchy. Second, the seceding party, l'Union Nationale des Forces Populaires (UNFP) was strong enough to prevent any Istiqlal's scheme of a one-party system. Third, the split left Istiqlal under the leadership of Fassi elements, since no Fassi joined the UNFP leadership. Hence, the task of attacking the Fassi hegemony became easier for the Mouvement Populaire.

The rise of Hassan II to the throne strengthened the relationship between the Palace and the Mouvement Populaire. During the constitutional referendum of December 1962 and the legislative elections of May 1963, it became clear that Aherdan's party was the backbone of the new Royalist Party, the Front pour la Défense des Institutions Constitutionnelles (FDIC), since the MP was the only organized political group within the monarchist coalition. Furthermore, by provoking the Istiqlal and UNFP into boycotting the elections which led to the formation of the Chambre des Conseillers (Upper House of the Parliament) in 1963, and the legislative elections in 1970, the Palace allowed its supporters to fill the vacuum created by such a boycott.

Indeed, the Mouvement Populaire filled 10,000 out of 11,200 seats in the Communal Councils (28 July 1963), 201 out of 281 seats in the Chambers of Commerce (election of 18 August 1963), 292 out of 312 seats in the Chambers of Agriculture (25 August 1963), 147 out of 225 seats in the provincial assemblies (6 October 1963).[2] These positions allowed their incumbents to benefit from the spoils that resulted from the recuperation of some of the land that belonged to the French administration (*lots de colonisation*) and from the transactions performed by the heads of the municipal and rural councils. These positions also allowed the elected officials of the Mouvement Populaire in particular, and the rural bourgeoisie in general, to have easy access to rural loans[3] and services performed in the countryside by the State offices such as the Office National des Irrigations (ONI), and especially by the Office de la Mise en Valeur Agricole (OMVA).

[1] *Ar-Rai Al-Amm*, 27 June 1956.
[2] Arranged from the official results published by the Ministry of the Interior, Rabat, 1963.
[3] Octave Marais, 'Les Relations entre la monarchie et la classe dirigeante au Maroc', *Revue française de science politique*, Vol. XIX, No. 6, December 1969, pp. 1172–86.
9*

However, the most important base of economic and political power was accorded the Mouvement Populaire through the 'agrarian reform'. The land that was touched by this reform came from three sources: the *lots de colonisation* that belonged to the French administration, some colons' lands, and some public lands. The first two categories represent the land that was taken or 'bought' by the French from the communes (*jamaa*) during the first two decades of the Protectorate. The agrarian reform did distribute a small part of the land to its previous owners; the largest part (600,000 acres), however, was divided among 'managers' who belonged, to a large extent, to the Mouvement Populaire.

If this trend continues, it is possible that in the future the MP will be the most important political force in the countryside, provided that the rural populations maintain their support to Amir al Mouminin, Commander of the Faithful.[1] Actually, the most potent force is the Ministry of the Interior, which is a protector of the MP but also, at the same time, a barrier to the full development of the Berber Party. Indeed, the Ministry of the Interior assumes the trusteeship of the 'collective lands' that belong collectively to the tribes; these lands amount to around 15 million acres, of which 2·5 million acres are used in agriculture. The Ministry prohibits any transactions on these lands and, therefore, prevents the rural bourgeoisie from taking them over.

Besides these economic gains, the elected officials of the Mouvement Populaire, with decisive help of the Ministry of the Interior, assure their party of a political base of power, for these elected officials acquired a role of intermediary between the rural population and the agents of the Ministry of the Interior. Such a role was played all along the Moroccan history by the *marabout* (holy man), and was a source of income, charisma and power.

In return for these political and economic advantages given the Mouvement Populaire by the monarchy, the party gives the Palace a full and unconditional support, the only kind of support that the monarchy at present requires.

Another source of support for the monarchy is the Royal Armed Forces (FAR). As was stated earlier, the armed forces, under the French colonization, were a rural, and especially a Berber affair, for most people who were recruited into the French army were from areas where land was limited and not well distributed, and where agriculture was not rewarding, and thus soldiers came mostly from the Atlas region. Besides, the Collège Berbère of Azrou was an institution that channeled students to the military schools of Ahermoumou (near Fes) and Dar al Baida (in Meknes). Most of these students belonged to modest families, for whom a military career was the only way to climb the social ladder. By contrast the bourgeoisie, especially Fassi, had the means to send its children to law, medicine and agricultural engineering schools.

The high ranking officers in the FAR went to these schools and then served in the French army, either in Europe during the Second World War or in Indochina during its struggle for independence. Most of them are Berbers (such as Medboh, the head of the Royal Military 'Cabinet' or Oufkir, the Minister of the

---

[1] The legitimacy of the king in the countryside comes in part from the belief that he is a descendant of the Prophet. On the other hand, the Moroccan king plays the *de facto* role of the Prophet's *khalifa* in leading the Muslim *Umma* in the country.

Interior). Furthermore, many of the medium-echelon army officers are called to serve in the Ministry of the Interior, as governors, or in some developmental projects, and many of them are busying themselves in land transactions, as does Oufkir in the province of Rabat.

Although the Berber hegemony in the military schools is declining, the new branch of the FAR, the Air Force, is undergoing a 'Berberization' similar to the one that characterized the military schools under the French rule.

In conclusion it can be said that the French 'divide and rule' policy has been replaced by a policy that insures the predominance of rural notables, who in return for tangible advantages have become the most dependable source of support for the regime. The fact that many of them, in the upper administration and the army, are Berbers, is almost incidental.

13

Note on the Role of the Berbers in the Early Days of Moroccan Independence

A. Coram

The Berbers have been surrounded by controversy throughout the history of the Maghreb: favored by the colonial regime, they were denied identity as a group by the Istiqlal Party after independence. Their behavior has always been contradictory, even self-contradictory; while constantly creating political confusion, they have not yet attained a stable or coherent attitude.

Nevertheless, two basic aspects of Moroccan political structure are due chiefly to the influence exercised by the Berbers from the 'fifties on. The first is the reinstatement and strengthening of the monarchy. If it had not been for the intervention of the Liberation Army, largely Berber-based and dedicated to the return of Muhammad V, the Aix-les-Bains talks between the French government and the Istiqlal which preceded independence could well have resulted in quite a different political solution, and one that by-passed the king. The second is the absence of a one-party system; the Berber-based Mouvement Populaire launched by Ahardan in 1957 put paid to Istiqlal plans for a single party, able to keep a closer check on the king.

After independence, the three main actors on the political scene were the king, the Istiqlal and the Berber movement. Muhammad V, and later Hassan II, manipulated the situation to their own advantage, by causing, first hostility between the two groups, then dissension within each party. Contrary to all the predictions made by foreign observers since 1956, the great loser has been the Istiqlal Party (both Istiqlal proper and the secessionist UNFP).

This fact is worthy of note, in view of the 1955-56 situation. Muhammad V had returned in triumph, but as a symbol rather than an actual leader. He commanded the allegiance of the Moroccan people; yet upon whom, in fact, could he rely in order to rule? The French civil servants and Moroccan *caid*s who made up the colonial administrative system had suddenly lost all power. There was no police force, no army, no system for transmitting orders. The Protectorate was no more than a paralyzed system manned by helpless spectators. For three months, millions of Moroccans milled about the Palace in Rabat, hoping to catch a glimpse of Muhammad V, while the Liberation Army surged from the Rif mountains to Taza and Fes, to the Middle Atlas overlooking Rabat, and to the High Atlas over Marrakesh.

Muhammad V was the hero of the hour, but real power was acknowledged to be in the hands of the Istiqlal; its leading figures, emerging from prison or hiding, were to be seen everywhere. Mehdi ben Barka, in particular, was amazingly active: preparing the Istiqlal Congress, addressing the international press corps, writing editorials for the party newspaper, organizing traffic by telephone when the streets of Rabat were clogged with vans of pilgrims come to see Muhammad V, holding private meetings with key figures; conversing with the king; speaking on behalf of Allal el-Fassi, then still in Cairo; and proclaiming his authority over the Liberation Army. Who could have doubted that the new Morocco was to be governed by such men?

Even then of course, the situation was more complex than it seemed. Muhammad V's choice for prime minister was a man without party affiliations, who had played an important part in reinstating the monarchy: MBarek Bekkai. He was a Berber from the Oujda region, a former French army officer and former Pasha of Sefrou, who in 1953 had publicly taken position against another prominent Berber, El-Glawi, and organized a group of *caids* faithful to the Sultan. In Paris, he had first opposed the deposition of Muhammad V, then fought for his reinstatement, thus proving that not all Berbers were backing El-Glawi against the Sultan. But Bekkai was a man of honor, not a politician; the Istiqlal felt he would be easy to manage. For instance, toward the end of 1955, Mehdi ben Barka was seen to approach in the Palace courtyard a group made up of Bekkai, his *chef de cabinet* Ahardan, and the *caid* Lahcan Lyoussi, another prominent *caid* who had remained faithful to Muhammad V. Relations between Ben Barka and Ahardan had long been tense, due as much to incompatibility of temperament as to ideological differences. Ben Barka said to Bekkai: 'Do you not think that the man best qualified to be Minister of the Interior is our friend Lyoussi?' This cut the ground from under Ahardane, who was being considered for the post, and obliged Bekkai to accept Lyoussi,[1] an elderly man, respectful of tradition, whom Ben Barka hoped to use while rapidly discrediting him. This anecdote indicates the influence wielded by a public figure devoid of official standing, and also shows that from the first days of independence, two groups representing widely differing political and social tendencies were struggling for power.

The struggle grew more violent during the months that followed; its first focus was the Liberation Army. While Moroccan ministers were negotiating independence in Paris, the Liberation Army was bringing pressure to bear on northern Morocco, jeopardizing the French army's lines of communication with Algeria. Muhammad V undoubtedly used this to induce the French government to speed up negotiations; he also used it, however, as a means of influencing Moroccan political parties, especially the Istiqlal. They were given to proclaiming that they controlled the Liberation Army, and that it would soon lay down its arms; in fact, the Liberation Army had by then completely evaded their control, if indeed it had ever been subordinate to the Istiqlal. In March 1956, Muhammad V granted a secret audience to the leaders of the Liberation Army. Not a single Istiqlal member was present.[2] The situation took a dramatic turn when Abbès, chief of staff of the Liberation Army, a Berber and a personal friend of Khatib and Ahardan, was assassinated in June 1956. Rumor had it that he had been killed by the leader of a Liberation Army group,[3] at the instiga-

[1] Lyoussi did in fact become Morocco's first Minister of the Interior.

[2] The only civilians present in an official capacity were Ahardan, Lyoussi, Guédira, Laghzaoui.

[3] This was El-Hajjaj, commanding the Liberation Army in the Taounate sector (north of Fes). A few days before, Abbès had opposed a tour by Ben Barka of Liberation Army posts, and had kept him under arrest for a night before having him taken back to Fes by force.

tion of Ben Barka. At any rate, that was the explanation favored by Liberation Army members, who took it as a sign of the Istiqlal's desire for absolute power. This was the first violent clash between Berbers and the party.

This assassination marked the monarchy's accession to full political power. It was to Muhammad V that the Liberation Army surrendered arms, in July 1956, after a month of open rebellion during which Fes had been threatened with destruction. This settlement was engineered by Ahardan, who had contributed to the creation of the Liberation Army by obtaining weapons through his Moroccan former colleagues in the French army, and who was at the time serving as a secret intermediary between the Liberation Army and the Palace. Muhammad V traveled to Nador, in the former Spanish zone, where the Liberation Army had its headquarters; on the way, he passed through Ajdir, in the Middle Atlas, a place well known to Berbers, where El-Glawi, with the support of the French authorities, had launched his movement against the Sultan in 1953.

These events also contributed to the creation of the Mouvement Populaire, which Ahardan and Khatib inaugurated in November 1957 with the slogan: 'We did not achieve independence in order to lose freedom.' In other words: the Liberation Army and the rural community did not contribute the overthrow of the colonial regime simply for the sake of being ruled by the Istiqlal.

Paradoxically enough, part of the opposition Ahardane encountered while establishing the Mouvement Populaire came from Berbers. During the two years following their initial manifesto, the movement's leaders had to fight on two fronts. First, they had to obtain legal status for the new party; the Istiqlal prevented this by blocking legislation permitting freedom of association. The Mouvement Populaire was not officially authorized until after the first Rif rebellion, in October 1958, caused by the imprisonment of Khatib and Ahardan,[1] and after the government had suffered a series of crises marked by increasingly tense relations between the king and the Istiqlal. The second concern of the Mouvement Populaire was to dissociate itself from the old-fashioned, anarchistic Berberism of Lahcan Lyoussi and Adi ou Bihi. This was a delicate operation, especially coming after Adi ou Bihi's abortive Tafilalet rebellion in 1957. Ahardan needed all his tactical skill and understanding of the Berbers to preserve contact with the traditional Berber tribes whose political consciousness had been roused by Adi ou Bihi and Lyoussi, while rejecting the political line these men represented.

From the start, the Mouvement Populaire took great care not to be seen as a purely Berber, racially-based movement, but rather as a spokesman of the rural masses neglected by the urban, bourgeois Istiqlal.[2] Ahardan's close association with Khatib, a full-blooded Arab, helped play down the movement's Berber characteristics; and its newspaper was named *Le Maghreb arabe*!

It was a strange alliance, that of Ahardan and Khatib. The one was the son of the former *caid* of Oulmès, and was once an officer in the French army; a poet

---

[1] They were guilty of the 'unauthorized' transfer of Abbès' body from Fes, where he was buried, to the Rif.

[2] One of the chief causes of rural unrest was the establishment of deputy judges, independent of the executive branch, and in fact under Istiqlal control.

and painter, ruled by intuition, he retained the bearing of his nomad forbears. The other, as tall and robust as Ahardan was slight, born at El-Jadida of an Algerian father, looked rather like a soldier turned member of a Muslim brotherhood. In 1956, it was difficult to recognize as the surgeon Khatib the bearded *maquisard* who would turn up in the futuristic villa occupied by Ahardan, then Governor of Rabat, having come secretly from the Rif in order to free some French officers or *Contrôleurs Civils* kidnapped by the Liberation Army. It was a strange time, part fantasy, part tragedy, too, in Morocco: conflict was already violent (certain urban resistance groups were physically liquidated, and members of parties opposing the Istiqlal were assassinated), yet a degree of understanding remained between the opponents.

This fragile and somewhat hectic springtime could not last; as already noted, positions soon hardened. The struggle for effective political power was under way. In 1956, King Muhammad V gave Moulay Hassan the task of organizing the army, took charge of the police himself, and retained control over the Ministry of the Interior. The Istiqlal took over Economy and Justice, and had some of its supporters named *caid*s, lacking the power to fill all governors' posts with its own men.

The army was gradually built up out of three main groups: the former Moroccan divisions of the French army (*goums, tirailleurs, spahis*), former Sharifian *mehalla*s serving in the Spanish army, and some *maquisards* from the Liberation Army once it had disbanded. The officers were mostly former French army officers; there were also some Moroccan officers from the Spanish army, and a few Liberation Army leaders, carefully selected and given lower rank. Amalgamating the troops did not prove very difficult. It was rather more complicated in the case of the officers, for both psychological and professional reasons; the French-trained officers formed a sort of elite, a fact which the others accepted only resentfully. This disparity apart, all the soldiers of this young army had one thing in common: at least 90 per cent of them were of Berber and rural origin.

Despite all its efforts and intrigues, the Istiqlal never managed to dislodge Moulay Hassan from his post as commander of the army (although Ahmad Lyazidi, one of the few former French army officers of urban origin and Istiqlal affiliations, was Minister of Defense in 1958), nor to make the army less of a Berber entity. The officers had another motive for remaining aloof from partisan struggles: most of them had served in the colonial forces, and had there been taught to be 'apolitical', and even to mistrust 'politicians'. They knew that because of their past, their only safeguard lay in loyalty to the throne. The Istiqlal alienated the army by making increasingly frantic attempts to gain control over it, and by calling it a stage army of mercenaries. The party itself thus helped consolidate the army's allegiance to the king, and exacerbated their sense of Berber identity by seeking to deny its existence.

The police, under the direction of Ahmed Laghzaoui and Driss Slaoui,[1] was largely made up of individuals and groups from the urban resistance movement, used to liquidate other more extremist groups (such as the Croissant Noir, of

[1] Director-General of the Cabinet Royal (till the aborted coup of July, 1971).

communist leanings). The Gendarmerie Royale, on the other hand, was attached to the army and commanded by Berber officers attending upon the king or the Crown prince.

The key to power over the country was the Ministry of the Interior, with its network of governors and *caids* covering the entire kingdom, even the most remote village. The ministry's role in this connection was not directly perceived by the new government. The king and the Istiqlal both viewed the *caid* system as being linked with all that was most detestable in the Protectorate. The Palace attached greater importance to the designation of Provincial Governors. The first to be named were either Berbers, former French army officers, or urban bourgeois connected with the Istiqlal, or even former Liberation Army leaders. After the unfortunate Adi ou Bihi episode, in which a provincial governor went into a kind of dissidence, Lyoussi was replaced at the head of the Ministry of the Interior by Driss M'Hammedi, a far more impressive figure. He was considered to be an Istiqlal man, but was also a friend of Ahardan and Khatib. Muhammad V trusted him, and his career as a lawyer in Meknes had given him opportunity for contact with the Berbers as well as with urban terrorists. He attempted to make his Ministry into an autonomous entity, while remaining in touch with all parties and seeming to satisfy everyone. This was a difficult task, all the more so as the situation varied throughout the country; some governors claimed virtual autonomy, and social and political conditions in the former Spanish zone differed greatly from those which prevailed in the former French zone. In some places, the *caid* from the time of the Protectorate had retained his position; elsewhere, the new *caid* had trouble asserting his authority against the Istiqlal or Liberation Army representative. At that time the Istiqlal, and especially Mehdi ben Barka, hoped to do away with the office of *caid* altogether and replace it by a new system, centered upon the head of the local party cell; Ben Barka would have liked, for instance, to transform the Centres de Modernisation du Paysannat into party cells. Thus the Istiqlal sought to control the rural masses and guide them along party lines, until such time as a sweeping agrarian reform could be enacted, by a combination of legal, economic and social tactics designed to break down traditional structures of authority.

Young Berber *cadres*, most of them graduates of the Collège d'Azrou (Collège Berbère), played an active role during these early years. Under the protectorate they had been fervent nationalists, and had often served as interpreters or clerks for the authorities supervising Berber areas. At independence, some of them were given positions of authority, either in the provinces or in the offices of the Ministry of the Interior. Although Berbers, these young men were often far from sympathetic to the traditional Berberism of men like Lyoussi or Adi ou Bihi. Most of them were attracted to the personality and modernist ideas of Ben Barka; somewhat cool toward the throne, or at least in favor of restricting its powers, they were inclined to view Ahardan's attitudes with ironic skepticism. Some of them joined the UNFP at its creation, while there were obscure struggles for control of the Association des anciens élèves du Collège d'Azrou, which long played the part of a pressure group.

Many examples could be cited to prove that Berber elites were far from a monolithic group. Thus it was Captain Medboh, who became chief of the 'Cabinet Militaire' of King Hassan (and the key figure of the coup of July 1971), then Governor of Ouarzazate, who headed the troops sent to crush Adi ou Bihi's Tafilalet rebellion. It was Hassan Zemmouri, then Under-Secretary of State in the Ministry of the Interior, who planned the installation of the *Communes Rurales* designed to destroy tribal structures. Somewhat later, it was Chbicheb, Governor of Tadla, who countenanced *caid* Bachir's rebellion against the Throne.

Studies of Morocco generally emphasize the divisive forces within Moroccan political parties, contrasting them with the monarchy's stable policies. In fact, things are somewhat more complicated. For instance, relations between Muhammad V and his son Hassan were stormy at times, largely because of their differing views of the situation, and their diverging notions of suitable methods of government. Muhammad V saw himself as an arbitrator, and was long convinced that his authority would be all the more effective for being exercised indirectly. While retaining the option of direct intervention by placing his own men in certain key positions, he was content to let the Istiqlal and even the UNFP take their chances; they were in power almost exclusively from 1957 to 1960. On the other hand, mistrust and rivalry soon characterized Moulay Hassan's relations with party men. Moulay Hassan was temperamentally inclined to the active exercise of power. He realized, no doubt much earlier than his father, that the Istiqlal could ultimately constitute a danger to the throne. As already mentioned, his role as commander of the army heightened this hostility, and both sides sought to influence Muhammad V. No one denied Moulay Hassan's ability; but he was said to have excessively close ties with the West and France, and to be responsible for disrupting the harmonious relationship between the Palace and the party. The Crown prince's private life was long a source of anxiety to his father, leading him to mistrust his ideas. It was not until the end of 1959 that Muhammad V revised his policy and drew closer to his son. Several factors helped to bring this about. In the field of foreign affairs, new developments in the Algerian War, following De Gaulle's return to power, led Muhammad V to seek to improve relations between France and Morocco. Within Morocco itself, the discovery in 1959 of a plot against Moulay Hassan shocked the king deeply, and made him conscious of the difficulties created by the UNFP government. The economic situation was disastrous, and tension was rising in rural and Berber areas. In May 1960, Muhammad V decided to rule directly, and named Moulay Hassan Vice-Prime Minister. This inaugurated a new period in Moroccan political life, which still continues today.

During these first few years of independence, what was the nature of relations between the throne and the Mouvement Populaire, and Berbers in general? Muhammad V was personally sympathetic to Ahardan and Khatib, although their impulsive tendencies rather worried him. By virtue of his position, and indeed by temperament, he attached great importance to due respect of legal process. As a political figure, he undoubtedly perceived the advantages he could derive from the existence of a force counterbalancing the Istiqlal, but he was wary of compromising himself by favoring it openly. Did he, even covertly, encourage the Mouvement Populaire? Very subtly, he assured Ahardan and

Khatib of his paternal benevolence, which meant very little, while countenancing the dismissal of the former from his post as governor in 1957, and the arrest of both in 1958. Indeed, was it not in the Sharifian tradition to avoid discouraging or favoring any one tendency, leaving the course of events to designate the stronger?[1]

Moulay Hassan would have been more inclined to support the Mouvement Populaire openly from the outset, and did indeed seek discreetly to establish relations with it. Initially, however, he committed himself no more than his father, though for different reasons. He thought that neither Ahardan nor Khatib were well enough equipped intellectually to organize a political party effectively. The Crown prince probably felt it preferable to keep the discontent channeled into the movement at an embryonic stage, as a latent source of pressure against the Istiqlal. Perhaps he was already planning to cause a split in the Istiqlal, in favor of a new distribution of political forces; for instance, by attracting some young Istiqlal moderates, who in conjunction with the Guédira group could have formed a more modernist party than the Mouvement Populaire. Finally, his uneasy relationship with Muhammad V forced him to tread warily, undertaking nothing that might serve as a pretext for dismissing him from his post at the head of the army.

It was only when the Mouvement Populaire had been legalized, the plot against Moulay Hassan discovered, and the break made final between the Istiqlal and the UNFP, that the Palace openly supported the party of Khatib and Ahardan.

By studying the behavior of the protagonists during the first five years of independence, one can perceive more clearly certain characteristics of present-day Morocco. In particular, it enables one better to understand the role and attitudes of the Mouvement Populaire and of the Berbers.

The Mouvement Populaire, or at least the group which stayed with Ahardan after his break with Khatib, is undeniably a monarchist movement. That does not mean, however, in my opinion, that its support for the Throne is entire and unconditional. Berber irreverence for authority, and independence of spirit, remained part of Ahardan's character.

Furthermore, although the Mouvement Populaire is basically Berber, it does not follow that it is wholly the Berbers' party. It should be noted, however, that many young Berbers have drawn closer to Ahardan, perhaps because the UNFP and the other parties had lost some of their strength, and power is in itself a magnet in a society of the Moroccan type.

The Mouvement Populaire is thus linked with several forces operating within Moroccan society. It serves as an intermediary between the Palace and the traditional rural masses, as well as a refuge, possibly temporary, for young people who while remaining critical have not yet found the new political structure which would express their desires. The Mouvement Populaire also makes use of its close relationship with General Oufkir to maintain and increase the number of *caid*s supporting it, as of communal and provincial candidates elected to office.

[1] Muhammed V may have been atavistically wary of the Berbers' tendency toward anarchistic autonomy, long embodied in the *siba*.

Ahardan still has many friends in the army, where the higher ranks are still mostly Berber (eight out of ten generals).

In spite of the fact that most ministerial posts, and most of the positions controlling the country's industrial and commercial activity, remain in the hands of urban families, the Berbers are once more, through the army, the Ministry of the Interior and the Mouvement Populaire, a force to be reckoned with in Morocco. True, they have no long-term political and economic outlook or program; their attitude remains basically pragmatic. Nevertheless, they have proved, to the detriment of the Istiqlal, that it is impossible to govern Morocco unless one takes heed of the Berber temperament.

14

Octave Marais

Fifteen years after independence, the Berbers' place within the Moroccan political system remains ambiguous. A simplified account would make them the chief political supports of the new *makhzan*: the new *Guich*—privileged, dynasty-sustaining tribes—used by the monarchy to counter the modernist and uniformity-imposing tendencies of urban nationalism. It should be recalled, however, that the 'Berber policy' of the French Protectorate also in the end had some most surprising results.

In 1956, the Berbers derived prestige in the eyes of urban nationalists from their active contribution to the overthrow of the Protectorate, although they still bore the stigma of their privileged position within colonialist mythology, and of their willingness to assist in urban repression.

Yet the Jacobin-style Islam of the nationalists retains its suspicion and lack of understanding of the Berbers. They considered that the only good Berbers were those who renounced their specific Berber identity. True nationalism, from the Istiqlal's point of view, meant suppressing all particularistic tendencies, abolishing customary courts in favor of judges named by the king, replacing locally selected *caid*s by civil servants appointed by the central government. Any disinclination to comply with this oppressive zeal for unification was considered a suspicious sign of nostalgia for the inherently illegitimate previous regime; little effort was made to understand the real problems involved.

Under these circumstances, the appearance of widespread discontent, followed by rebellion, is not surprising. The Berber regions came to adopt an irredentist attitude, expressed in various ways. Their dissent was influenced by historical and economic conditions; and the conflict and lack of understanding between Berbers and nationalist intellectuals in power were heightened by these divergent rhythms of development.

THE BERBERS' SITUATION

At independence, the Berber world was even more divided than in 1912. To the north, the Rif was cut off by a new border, creating a special economic system. Since the end of Abd el-Krim's rebellion, the Spanish presence had largely been accepted there, since it entailed little colonizing and administrative activity. Tribesmen could serve in the Spanish army; the administration left the shepherds and charcoal-burners free to lay waste the forests; and nearby Algeria provided the Riffians with much-appreciated seasonal employment. The Rif therefore turned its rebellious ardor against the French colonial authorities, and supported the Resistance and the Liberation Army in their struggle for independence.

In 1957, the Rif began to be somewhat anxious about the effects of unification, which integrated it into a French-style monetary, legal and cultural system imposed by the new elites educated in the south. Its own elites were even more cut off from the new government than were the bourgeois of Tetouan. In these circumstances, the revival of the legend of Abd el-Krim was not surprising.

The Middle Atlas, on the contrary, presented an ideal type of Berber national park as described by Jacques Berque. Protected from the *colons'* rapacity by the special regulations governing zones of insecurity, this part of Morocco was undoubtedly one of those least affected by change since 1912. Its prevalent life-styles, and the balance between forests and pasture-land, had been slowly adapted rather than radically transformed. The offspring of eminent members of the community were educated to serve as middle-ranking *cadres* of the Protectorate, in the army or civil service. From 1946[1] on they took part in the activities of the nationalist movement, where they came to represent the modern type of Berber who could, if they took the trouble, become an integral part of the Arab majority.

In a post-independence spirit of euphoria, many Berbers agreed to play this game, believing that the Fassi Istiqlal would also make some concessions in the interest of a modern, socialist, secularized Morocco. A group of former school-teachers, former government clerks, and students, led by Driss Mhamedi, helped the Istiqlal to regain control of regions which Addi ou Bihi or Lahcen Lyoussi had found it easy to lead into irredentism.

However, these Berber *cadres* who wished to become part of a united nation soon felt disappointed and rejected. Social factors overrode political options. They had hoped to be accepted while retaining their own language and traditions; but they soon found themselves excluded, or relegated to marginal activities, because they were unable to participate in the subtle network of family alliances, geographical solidarity and old school ties which united the urban dynasties. Thus the Berber elites from the Middle Atlas, who for various reasons could more easily than others have become part of the political system set up by the nationalist movement after independence, were rejected by that system. Some adopted a wait-and-see attitude, others a leftist position; some drew closer to the monarchy. A few wavered from one tendency to the other.

The greater number opted for the king, which brought about a reconciliation with their fellow-countrymen of the preceding generation, with whom they had at times conflicted. In various ways, this reconciliation gave rise to a new political Berberism, which was to contribute to the split within the nationalist movement.

During the Protectorate, the High Atlas had been one of the chief areas of political Berberism, characterized by the dominating influence of the great *caid*s. The urban resistance movement had gained a hold there, through the emigrants who traveled to Casablanca by way of Marrakesh.

The Souss was calmer before independence. While not remaining indifferent to the events which were causing agitation in the big cities to the north, it seems to have preserved a degree of stability, until the departure of the French administrative apparatus. The region's economic system was founded on the villages,

[1] Date of the student strike at the Berber Collège d'Azrou.

where families and traditions were maintained, and the cities where emigrants earned a living. Some emigrants became wealthy, and brought to economic life the clan rivalries which had long governed life in the region.

Independence brought an influx of Liberation Army troops, sent to recover Spanish-controlled Ifni and the Sahara, and also to rid the northern provinces of the presence of disorderly agitators. The urban resistance movement also set up a few rear bases in the areas supplying emigrants to Casablanca. The central government soon lost all real control over the province of Agadir and most of the other regions inhabited by Berbers of the Shleuh (southern) group, which entered upon a sort of left-wing *siba*. Yet this political action was never of a particularistic nature. It opposed the system as a whole, the monarchy as well as the Fassis represented by the new government officials, and by the commercial rivals of the Shleuh in Casablanca.

The role of the Berbers in independent Morocco was as difficult to determine as it was in the pre-colonial *makhzan*. Since they had played an important part in the national struggle, they could not simply be labeled collaborators and relegated to secondary status. Yet they refused, even in the name of principles which in part they accepted, to be absorbed by a uniform and highly centralized national entity which confined their elites to subordinate positions. Also, their economic situation suffered various crises, which were largely ignored by a central government more interested in the cities and industrialization. The Algerian War deprived the Rif of its main source of employment. In the Middle Atlas, the fragile equilibrium between forests and grazing-land, based partly on mutual agreement and partly on coercion, was disturbed. The commercial rivalry between Soussi and Fassi had unforeseen repercussions in the valleys of the High Atlas and Anti-Atlas.

However, no single political movement gained a monopoly of Berber discontent. During the years following independence, this discontent transcended simple refusal and rebellion, and took on various political forms.

The most obvious trend was monarchism, which attracted the majority; yet it was not alone. Rejection of the oppressive new bourgeois order also gave rise to socialist tendencies, which gained considerable ground among Berbers, although this fact was somewhat concealed by their universalistic aspects.

THE SCOPE AND LIMITS OF POLITICAL BERBERISM

Well before he came to power, Hassan II gave the impression that he was planning to refurbish the 'Berber policy'. According to a classic scheme, rural Morocco's attachment to the throne would counterbalance the traditional turbulence of the old cities and the new threat of the *bidonvilles*; the Alawite monarchy would thus take up the legacy of the Protectorate.

The real situation was somewhat more complicated. The rapprochement between the Berbers and the monarchy was directed against those nationalists who would have liked to relegate both of these aspects of Moroccan social and political reality to a museum of historical relics. The king, deprived of the prerogatives of an Islamic sovereign, would then have become a harmless sort of president, and the Berber nomads would have been transformed into peaceful sedentary farmers using modern agricultural techniques. At the time, however, Moroccan society was prey to so much tension that no single party could have abolished both Berber particularism and the monarchy. As early as the Aix-les-Bains conference, the king and the Liberation Army contracted a *de facto* alliance against those who wanted to delay the king's return to power, with the help of the colonial regime if necessary. The rebellious uprisings in the Rif, Tafilalet and Middle Atlas then enabled the king to replace the dominant party as the true symbol of national unity. The insurgent Berber regions felt that the monarchy was on their side, against the planners of the New Morocco who were announcing their intention of promoting industry and developing the main urban centers and the already prosperous irrigated zones. This policy condemned the Berbers to a crippling loss of identity, by leaving them no other choice than to stagnate in the mountains, subjected to bureaucratic interference, or to add to the population of the *bidonvilles*. Their much analyzed rebellions simply expressed an instinctive protest, exploited by those who wanted to turn the clock back. The monarchy soothed these rebellious feelings, to the extent that recourse to the king as mediator weakened their chief political opponent.

Despite this convergency of interests, Berber political leaders did not seem to have the specific power appropriate to the heads of a party. They had a certain aura of authority, making them suitable interlocutors and spokesmen for the *makhzan*; but the small favors they were in a position to grant were mere tokens of influence, rather than the basis of real power. The parties they set up always lacked structure; yet the tendencies they represented were real, depreciated but feared, and the government and administration took them into account. In organized political contests such as municipal or legislative elections, their structural weaknesses became apparent; their opponents pointed them out, while their supporters, who had relied on their strength and numbers, became indignant. In a simple referendum-type political operation, the mechanisms of adherence and participation functioned smoothly without excessive effort on the part of the organizers; the Berber regions and the former *siba*, with the exception of the Shleuh (southern) areas, voted Yes in the 1962 constitutional referendum.

In the general elections of May 1963, on the other hand, supporters of the Mouvement Populaire, then part of the F D I C—a wider monarchical group of parties—did not obtain satisfaction. The Berber political elites did not understand the rules governing politics at the national level. They thought it pointless and annoying to have to agree on a single candidate for each constituency. Conscious of forming a homogeneous majority, they failed to see why they should support candidates who were not from their own milieu; investiture by Rabat and the support of local officials did not seem a sufficient reason. Either collective decision-making procedures produced an agreed name, or there were several unconnected candidates, with results which seemed outrageous and highly suspect to their supporters, who were conscious of representing a majority. The Berbers, who had been somewhat reluctant to join a still unstructured monarchist party, soon came to feel that the government was in incompetent hands, and that there was a risk of a legal seizure of power by the opposition. They found this situation unacceptable, and were quite willing to give up the disconcerting parliamentary game when Hassan II decided, in July 1965, to suspend the constitution. The king was able to rely upon the tacit support of a large majority of the Berbers of the Rif and Middle Atlas.

Without excluding specialists from other social groups, Hassan II gave the Berbers a leading role in his political entourage. They soon formed a majority in the forces: the army, the *makhzan* militia and the *gendarmerie* became their fief. The Sûreté Nationale, on the other hand, bore for a time the stamp of its first director, Laghzaoui, a Fassi by birth. In 1960, the other forces began to weed out those whose loyalty to the king was open to doubt: often these are young Arab officers who joined the army shortly after independence and did not get on well with those of their colleagues who had been officers in the French or Spanish army. Their removal strengthened the Berbers' position, and created the impression that only Berbers could count on a successful career, which in turn affected the recruitment of officers and NCOs.

Other sectors, such as political administration, followed suit, especially at the local level. From 1960 on, an increasing number of Berbers became *caids* and *chefs de cercle*. They also constituted a majority at the Ecole de Kenitra, where future local officials were trained in the style of the Affaires Indigènes—the French administration at the time of the Protectorate. The administrative and political role of *sheikhs* also evolved toward a certain degree of local participation in the decisions made by the central government. The *sheikhs* were more effective in Berber regions, where the Protectorate had had little effect on tribal structures.

Once rid of the fear of being dispossessed by a one-party system, the monarchy did away with the technocratic tendencies opposed by the Berbers. The Promotion Nationale program provided a framework within which local administrators and rural communities could discuss the problems they actually faced. The central government was thus able to redistribute revenue, and thereby help maintain order, while laying the foundations for a degree of modernization without causing too much disturbance. A new emigration policy, directed toward Europe, reduced political tension; the regime won time, without having resolved the basic difficulties of the poor rural areas.

The political complicity between the Throne and the Berbers in the Rif, the Middle Atlas and large areas of the High Atlas, should not make one forget other Berber political trends. Although the old Istiqlal had failed to win the support of modern Berber elites, it retained some influence among Berbers. In the May 1963 elections, the Istiqlal candidate, supported by the Fassi tradesmen of Khenifra, easily defeated the Berber leader Ahardan. At Khemisset, Azrou, Midelt, the political role of Istiqlal nuclei formed by tradesmen and lower-ranking civil servants was far from negligible; they managed to create solidarity through contact with rural Berbers.

However, the Istiqlal as a whole failed to gain a footing in these areas. At most, it contrived to exploit differences between groups and individuals supporting the monarchy.

The Union Nationale des Forces Populaires—the Left hived-off part of Istiqlal—had a far more important political role. Young Berber professionals and intellectuals, symbolized by the Collège d'Azrou and its powerful Association d'Anciens Elèves, were attracted to a socialist vision of the nation's future. They were prepared to give up the particularistic leanings of their native milieu, for the sake of a government in which they could play an active part. The bourgeoisie, as represented by the Fes merchants, and the monarchy, would be the losers. They would be willing to act as mediators of the necessary changes, provided that their loyalty was not considered treated as suspect. They felt that an egalitarian and socialist nation could have dispensed with both the Fassi and the Berber traditions, and with the monarchy into the bargain.

More often than not, the only lasting effect of this ideal was a critical attitude toward the monarchy and its Berber policy, as well as toward the Istiqlal. On the whole, when perpetual opposition came to seem untenable, UNFP Berbers preferred to support the monarchy.

The attitude of the Shleuh (southern Berber) tradesmen largely fits into this category, with a few differences. During the first few years after independence, the Shleuh moved away from the Istiqlal, which was backed by their Fassi competitors, and accused the latter of deriving business advantages from their political contacts. When the UNFP was formed, the Shleuh gave it crucial support, bringing with them the provinces of Agadir and Ouarzazate, those rear bases of emigration to Casablanca. Shleuh support enabled the Moroccan Left to win Chamber of Commerce, municipal and parliamentary elections in Casablanca. From the summer of 1963 on, however, fear of going too far in opposition, and a certain deference to authority, led them to compromise.

NEW TRENDS

Whether in power or in opposition, the Berber elites have grown old. Most of the well-known figures became prominent during the years immediately before or after independence. At grass-roots level, there are still men appointed by the French or Spanish colonial authorities, who continued as *sheikh*s or presidents of rural communes after independence. Their relatives, educated to serve as middle-ranking officials in the colonial administration, simultaneously climbed the rungs of administrative and political power. They rarely occupied prominent positions in central government, but tended to hold positions of authority in such services as local administration, the police, the *gendarmerie* and the army. The government made them guardians of the Throne, and they accomplished their task faithfully, with a sense of serving the State, although they often had no illusions about the political and social order they were helping to preserve. They considered it, at most, as a lesser evil, and seemed conscious that any great upheaval would be their undoing as well as the regime's.

This generation, which remains in control of key positions, has been joined by young people educated after independence, who form a distinctly separate group. Their secondary-level schooling distinguishes them from their elders.

Attending the Collège d'Azrou is no longer the only passport to a career, as it was during the Protectorate. At present, a Berber youth is quite as likely to have been educated in the various *lycées* run by the Ministry of Education or the Mission Culturelle. Family influence plays a greater part than does geography.

Having been brought up in a national milieu where Arabic and French dominate cultural and technical fields, young Berbers will be inclined to assert their distinctiveness in a search for specific cultural values. They will not, however, go so far as to question their national allegiance. In some cases, Islam will provide them with a way of asserting both solidarity and personal identity. In other cases, this function will be fulfilled by socialism. In any case, young Berbers are not prepared to accept a passive role in the changes they know to be inevitable for themselves and their people.

Until now, the monarchy has conveniently enabled the Berbers to delay developments which would have been unfavorable to them if carried out by other forces during the first few years after independence.

At present, the young Berbers who are expected to become guardians of the Throne may feel that the monarchy is an unnecessary luxury. Some may be attracted by the notion of a pure and austere government which would ensure the country's transformation at a lesser cost, while safeguarding the interests of the regions with which they feel natural solidarity. Their goals could coincide with those of other levels of society, provided that their attitude remains sufficiently open-minded to avoid accusations of particularistic tendencies. They have the advantage, over other groups desirous of a new order, of controlling the police forces.

Berber revolutionaries today would no longer be, as in 1957, a militant handful seeking to determine a new future within the confines of nationalism, and remaining an ineffectual minority until their alliance with the monarchy. They could achieve the strength and cohesion necessary for change. Their compatriots who remain tribal would see them as just one further Berber dynasty. People of different origins would recognize in them their own desire for revolutionary change, made inevitable by the slow but sure decay of the old order, and its inability to reform itself.

15

William B. Quandt

INTRODUCTION

Political life in newly independent countries is frequently dominated by severe ethnic conflicts. Tribal, linguistic, racial and religious differences have all served as the bases of political movements that have challenged the authority of the state. Kurds in Iraq have sought autonomy within a primarily Arab state; Ibos in Nigeria fought a desperate war to establish a separate nation; Tamils in Ceylon have struggled to maintain their distinctive identity in the midst of a predominantly Sinhalese community. In Algeria, deep conflicts and divisions have also been present, but, despite the presence of a sizable Berber minority, there has not been a 'Berber problem', particularly at the level of elite politics. Why has Algeria managed to avoid conflicts rooted in ethnic particularism during its short history as an independent nation?[1]

The nature of Berber society in Algeria

Individual Berbers have played extremely important roles in Algerian politics, but they have rarely acted as spokesmen for a Berber constituency. The structure of Berber society in Algeria goes a long way toward explaining this fact. In many ways the term Berber is misleading, for it appears to refer to a relatively homogeneous ethnic group. In fact, however, several distinctive Berber subcultures exist in Algeria and have relatively little in common other than the fact that their spoken dialects are derived from a common root. Most important in numbers and influence among the Berber speakers are the Kabyles who originate in the mountainous area east of Algiers, and who have moved in large numbers to the cities of both France and Algeria in search of employment. There are somewhat less than two million Kabyles in a population of twelve million.

The second largest Berber community in Algeria are the Shawiyas who inhabit the rugged mountains of eastern Algeria. Shawiyas have had less contact with the modern world than Kabyles, as fewer have emigrated to the large cities. Their numbers are also smaller, totaling less than one million in Algeria.

While only the Kabyles and Shawiyas have been politically important in Algeria, two smaller Berber communities also exist. These are the Mozabites of

[1] Ethnic politics are well analyzed in the following sources: Samuel P. Huntington, *Political Order in Changing Societies*, New Haven, 1968, pp. 37–38; Dankwart A. Rustow, *A World of Nations*, Washington, D.C., 1967; Clifford Geertz, 'The integrative revolution: primordial sentiments and civil politics in the new states', in Clifford Geertz, ed, *Old Societies and New States*, New York, 1963; W. Howard Wriggins, 'Impediments to unity in new nations: the case of Ceylon', *American Political Science Review*, Vol. LV, June 1961.

the area around Ghardaia and the Tuareg nomads of the south. Both groups live in closed societies, resisting the pressures of modernization and striving to retain their isolated independence from central authority. The greatest threat to their way of life is the fact that they have become tourist attractions. They have little voice in national politics.

Geographical dispersion of Berber speakers has hindered the emergence of a common Berber identity. This physical separation of Berber speakers is compounded by social distinctions. Kabyles are generally more cosmopolitan and more likely to speak French than are the rather traditional Shawiyas. When Kabyles and Shawiyas do come into contact, Kabyles tend to look down on their less sophisticated cousins.

Berber particularism in Algeria might be stronger if Berbers lived in a cultural milieu that differed sharply from that of the Arab majority. But Berbers and Arabs alike in North Africa are Sunni Muslims of the Malikite rite. In the past there have been various heretical movements among the Berbers that served to accentuate their separate identity, but today only the Mozabites remain outside the ranks of Sunni Islam.

A second cultural trait that might have served as a basis for Berber separatism would have been the existence of a distinctive high cultural tradition. But the various Berber dialects have never really been written, and the absence of a literary language among Berbers has made them susceptible to the attractions of both Arab and French culture. In modern times, the mere fact that formal education cannot be carried on in the Berber language means that educated Berbers invariably learn Arabic or French.

Finally, there is no trans-national Berber movement that might attract politically conscious Kabyles and Shawiyas in Algeria. The only other large Berber community in the world is in Morocco, but there are virtually no links existing between Moroccan and Algerian Berbers. Taken together, these geographic, social and cultural facts are not sufficient to explain the lack of 'Berberism' as a political force in contemporary Algeria, but they do lower the chances that such a movement will emerge and will be sustained.

The nature of elite politics

If Berber society in Algeria has not become integrated into a cohesive political force, the nature of elite politics is at least partially responsible. The few Algerians who have managed to enter the national political elite have developed attitudes and a political style that minimize the importance of ethnic and regional origins. Algerian political leaders today were nearly all at one time involved in the anti-colonialist nationalist struggle. In a period when national independence was the one overriding objective that Algerians could agree upon, any tendency to distinguish sharply between Berbers and Arabs was seen as playing into the hands of the French *colons* whose strategy was one of 'divide and rule'. In fact, the French had tried to develop a 'Berber policy' in Algeria in the late nineteenth century, based on the belief that the Kabyles, at least, could be assimilated into

French culture, even if the Arabs could not.[1] But the success of this policy was limited, and it was soon officially abandoned in Algeria, only to be revived a generation later in Morocco. The legacy of the *colons'* strategy, however, remained, and when, on occasion, Berber separatism seemed to be growing, actions were quickly taken by the nationalists to eliminate the leaders of such movements.[2]

During the war for independence, Berbers were in the forefront of the fight against the French. The fact that the Berber areas of Kabylia and the Aures provided the first base areas for the leaders of the Algerian revolution meant that Berbers were deeply involved in the struggle from the beginning. With time, Berber leaders developed a particularly strong commitment to Algerian nationalism.

The men who emerged from the war to lead independent Algeria depended heavily upon both their revolutionary credentials and their personal relations for acquiring positions of influence. In the chaotic period following independence, political alignments were made on many bases, but common ethnic background did not prove to be a particularly strong link among competing leaders. Kabyles fought one another almost as passionately as they fought Arab rivals for power. Those who succeeded in attaining positions of influence were the politically astute individuals who managed to join one of the many groups that had support within the army. Only rarely were leaders paid deference because of their acknowledged regional backing. In part, the absense of strong spokesmen for regional Kabyle or Shawiya interests was a result of the fact that there were many aspirants to power who claimed to speak on behalf of the same community. At least half a dozen prominent Kabyles could argue that they were the legitimate spokesman for the Kabyle population, but with so many voices competing, none was paid much heed. Any political group could find a prestigious Kabyle willing to join it in the hopes of attaining power. Consequently, a Kabyle bloc closely tied to the Berber masses never developed. Personal relations at the top were far more important than the mobilization of a rural constituency in the early days of independence. Once again, the forces at work in the political system reduced the probability that 'Berberism' would emerge as an important force.

The impact of governmental policies

A third condition for the non-emergence of Berber separatism has been the absense of government policies that have alienated or discriminated against Berbers as a group. Algerian leaders are apparently aware of the potential danger that might result if Kabyles or Shawiyas strongly opposed the government. The Boumedienne government in particular has sought to avoid Kabyle dissidence by pouring vast sums of government money into Kabylia. By 1968–69, Kabylia was beginning to experience something of an economic boom, an especially

[1] See Charles-Robert Ageron, 'La France a-t-elle eu une politique kabyle?', *Revue historique*, No. 223, April–June 1960.

[2] Extreme 'Berberist' sentiments are expressed in Mohammed Arab Bessaoud, *Le FFS: Espoir et traison*, Paris, 1966.

important development in view of the stagnation and decline that had characterized the region's economy in earlier years.

In addition to the lack of economic discrimination against them, Kabyles have been relatively successful in obtaining positions in the government, which tends to temper their dissatisfaction with the regime. Within the political elite, Berbers have usually been represented in approximate proportion to their numbers in the population at large, about twenty percent. In the army, however, there appear to be relatively few Kabyle officers, but this is compensated for by the fact that Kabyles are overrepresented in the bureaucracy.

Berbers generally have little interest in Arab nationalism and are often reluctant to learn Arabic, preferring French as a second language. The Algerian government has not sought to minimize its Arab orientation simply because of Berber antagonism to such a policy, but the regime has none the less been relatively moderate in both its expressions of Arab nationalism and in its program of Arabization. Algerians in general are more likely to refer to themselves as Muslims or Algerians than as Arabs, and this helps to avoid tensions between Arabs and Berbers. Arabization will doubtless continue, but so long as French is maintained as a second language and Arabization is only gradually enforced, there is little likelihood of strong Berber resistance. Thus far, the government has acted with due regard for Berber sensibilities, and has generally sought to avoid both overt discrimination and rapid Arabization, knowing that either practice could create a Berber problem where none previously existed.

BERBERS WITHIN THE POLITICAL ELITE

The nationalist movement and the war for independence

Algerian nationalism was relatively late in producing an organized movement for independence. The precursors of the nationalists were a small group of educated Algerians who, after World War I, began to demand equality and reforms. With time, and following the failures of the reformists, more radical nationalist spokesmen emerged, so that by the end of the Second World War several groups were calling for autonomy or independence. The war for independence finally began in November 1954, and after nearly eight years of struggle Algeria became a sovereign state.

During the thirty years that encompass the period of nationalist struggle and revolution, from the 1930s until independence in 1962, the dominant goal of the nationalist elite shifted from the desire for assimilation and equality with Frenchmen to the demand for freedom from French rule. Throughout these years of profound change within the Algerian elite, Berbers, especially Kabyles, played extremely important roles as individuals. But, except for minor exceptions, 'Berberism' as such never became an issue within the political elite.[1]

The prominence of Kabyles within the nationalist movement can partially be

[1] Conflicts within the political elite are analysed in William B. Quandt, *Revolution and Political Leadership: Algeria, 1954–1968*, Cambridge (Mass.), 1969.

explained by the contacts between Kabyles and the modern world. Because of the population density and the limited resources of Kabylia, a large proportion of Kabyle men were forced to leave their mountain refuge to seek jobs in Algiers or in France. Large numbers of Kabyle workers were concentrated in the Paris region where they naturally learned French and became involved with French political movements. By the 1930s, at the onset of nationalism, Kabyles were probably the most westernized group within Algeria. Consequently, they were disproportionately likely to join political parties, trade unions, student associations, and other interest groups. Inevitably some Kabyles became prominent leaders within these movements.

Much of Algerian political life in the 1930s and 1940s revolved around the figures of Ferhat Abbas and Messali Hadj. Abbas became the leader of the liberal reformists and moderate nationalists, and Messali Hadj was the dynamic authoritarian spokesman for the radical nationalists. After World War II, a more revolutionary movement split off from the radical nationalists, and for a while was led by Ahmed Ben Bella. These three leaders, or at least spokesmen, for the liberals, the radicals and the revolutionaries were all Arabs who had spent considerable time in France. Close collaborators of each of these men, however, were Kabyles. For example, Ferhat Abbas, throughout his career, was on close terms with Ahmed Boumendjel. The movement led by Messali Hadj, the MTLD, had as Secretary General a Kabyle named Lahouel Hocine. Finally Ben Bella's associate, and occasional rival, within the Organisation Spéciale (OS) was Hocine Ait Ahmed, also from Kabylia. It is noteworthy that Boumendjel, Lahouel and Ait Ahmed had much more in common with others of their own political generation than they did with one another, despite a common ethnic background. Within each branch of the nationalist movement, Berbers played an important role, but Berbers were no more likely to collaborate with one another than they were with like-minded Arabs.

One minor exception to the absence of ethnic politics was the so-called 'Berberist' crisis of 1949. Within the radical nationalist party, the MTLD, opposition to Messali Hadj's leadership grew in strength from 1947 on. In 1949, Kabyle workers in France couched their opposition to Messali in terms that stressed that Algeria was not an Arab country, but rather a composite of ethnic groups that made up the Algerian nation. The 'Berberists' argued that the liberation movement should be open to all Algerian Muslims, whether of Berber, Arab or Turkish descent. The majority of the MTLD interpreted this as ethnic separatism rather than as a call for the unity of all ethnic groups, and in April 1949 the Federal Council of the MTLD in France was dissolved by the Central Committee of the Party.[1] Most nationalists thought that 'Berberism' was divisive and played into the hands of the French. A temporary result of the crisis was that the Kabyle, Ait Ahmed, was replaced as head of the clandestine Organisation Spéciale, by Ahmed Ben Bella. Ait Ahmed's exclusion was only temporary, however, and he was soon reintegrated into the ranks of the nationalists.

From the Berberist crisis in 1949 to the outbreak of the revolution in November

[1] See Roger Le Tourneau, *Evolution politique de l'Afrique du nord musulmane, 1920–1961*, Paris, 1962, pp. 374–5.

10

1954, the main nationalist groups nearly disintegrated. The Organisation Spéciale was broken up by the French police; the MTLD was split between followers of Messali and the members of the Central Committee; and the UDMA of Ferhat Abbas was ineffectually trying to work within the colonial system. Only in the region of Kabylia was a new clandestine organization emerging under the leadership of two ex-sergeants of the French army, Belkacem Krim and Amar Ouamrane. Kabylia, because of its remoteness, provided an ideal milieu for the growth of a small band of men dedicated to the use of violence to eliminate French rule of Algeria.

In other parts of the country there were occasional efforts to create armed cells that might one day participate in the revolution. In the Aures mountains, another Berber refuge, the isolation of the region and the absence of a large French population made it possible to organize a small nationalist group under the leadership of Mustapha Ben Boulaid.

By late 1953 and early 1954, some of the younger militants, viewing the disorder within the nationalist parties, began to talk about the need for direct armed action as a means of uniting the nationalists and, hopefully, of achieving independence. Already a group of three Algerians were in Cairo looking for international support for Algeria's independence. Among the three were Ben Bella and Ait Ahmed, the latter a Kabyle and Ben Bella's predecessor as head of the OS. In Algiers, five ex-OS members, including Ben Boulaid began to organize, and by May or June 1954 they had opened contacts with the leaders of the Kabyle underground, Krim and Ouamrane. After some initial reluctance, it was decided that Kabylia would be allowed to form one of the six autonomous zones into which the nascent revolutionary movement would be organized. Krim was recognized as the spokesman for Kabylia, and Ben Boulaid took charge of the Aures region.[1]

By early summer 1954, French intelligence sources were learning of the existence of a Comité Révolutionnaire d'Unité et d'Action (CRUA) and of its professed goal of beginning the war for independence.[2] Before any decision on launching the revolution could be made, however, further organization was necessary. In late July, five leaders of the CRUA and their closest associates met in Algiers, in the absense of the Kabyle representatives, to plan for revolution. Several organizational and tactical decisions were made at this meeting of the Comité des Vingt-deux, among them the confirmation of the agreement that the Kabyles would participate in the movement so long as they controlled their own region. By August, ties with the Kabyles were strengthened, and preparations were under way for insurrection. The Berbers of both Kabylia and the Aures were represented within the collegial directorate of the CRUA, the former by Krim and the latter by Ben Boulaid. Two of the six internal leaders of the revolution were thus Berbers, and in Cairo the external delegation of three maintained this same proportion by including one Kabyle, Ait Ahmed. Thus, three of the so-called *chefs historiques* of the revolution were Berbers, a slight over-representation in terms of the population at large, but probably a fair image of the proportion of Berbers within the nationalist elite.

[1] Yve Courrière, *Les Fils de la Toussaint*, Paris, 1968, pp. 96 ff.
[2] More detail on the CRUA is provided in Quandt, op. cit., pp. 88–94.

When the Algerian revolution began on 1 November 1954, only two regions of the country were even partially organized. Kabylia and the Aures, the two mountainous Berber areas, became the beleaguered strongholds of the revolution during its first few years of existence. The Aures, however, was soon torn by factional disputes among the top leaders following the arrest and subsequent death of Ben Boulaid. In Kabylia, by contrast, the guerrilla forces were able to grow in strength, even to the point of being able to send Kabyles to help organize and lead zones in other parts of the country.

The period from 1955 to about 1957 was one of Kabyle prominence within the revolutionary elite. The ascendance of the Kabyles within the leadership structure was based on close relations that developed between four well-known Kabyles. Belkacem Krim and Amar Ouamrane were the first military leaders of the Kabyle zone, and they soon allied with two skilful Kabyle politicians, Abane Ramdane and Dr Lamine Debaghine. Of these four, Abane Ramdane very quickly gained preeminence, and was widely acknowledged to be the most dynamic leader of the revolution, by both Arabs and Kabyles alike.

In August 1956, the first formal institutions of the revolution were created at the Soummam Congress. Executive authority was placed in a Comité de Coordination et d'Exécution (CCE) of five members, responsible to a larger Conseil National de la Révolution Algérienne (CNRA), of seventeen full members and seventeen alternates. Kabyle prominence was highlighted by the presence of two Kabyles, Krim and Abane Ramdane, among the five leaders of the CCE. In the CNRA, six of the seventeen full members were Berbers (five Kabyles, plus one Shawiya, Ben Boulaid, who was in fact already dead but whose name was included to avoid having to choose a successor). Two more Berbers, Mohammedi Said and Chihani Bachir, were among the alternate CNRA members.[1]

From August 1956 to his death in May 1958, Abane Ramdane was a key figure in the leadership of the Algerian revolution. As such, he became a bitter opponent of Ahmed Ben Bella with whom he quarreled, among other things, over the priority to be accorded the struggle within Algeria as opposed to the diplomatic efforts of Ben Bella and his colleagues in Cairo. However, when Ben Bella, Ait Ahmed and two other prestigious 'external' leaders were captured by the French in October 1956, Abane's major rival was eliminated.

New forces, however, were emerging to challenge Abane's power, but this nascent conflict did not set Arabs against Kabyles. Rather, it split both ethnic groups along the lines of those who were more politically minded and those who had been directly leading the military effort within Algeria.

These new forces came into their own at the first full meeting of the CNRA in August 1957 in Cairo. There it was decided to name a new CCE, this time consisting of nine members. Four of the nine who were chosen were Kabyles— Abane Ramdane, Belkacem Krim, Amar Ouamrane and Dr Lamine Debaghine. This number represents the largest proportion of Berbers in any national political body since 1954, but even quantity could not compensate for the divisions among the Kabyles themselves. Two Arab members of the new CCE, Lakhdar Ben

[1] Ibid., pp. 102–7.

Tobbal and Abdelhafid Boussouf, soon came to be closely linked to Krim in what was called the 'triumvirate'. This key group was able to place Abane in a minority, particularly since two supporters of Abane within the first CCE, Benkhedda and Dahlab, had been excluded from the second CCE. From September 1957 to 1962, the 'triumvirate' was the most cohesive group within the political elite. As their power increased, Abane's remaining influence and prestige must have been seen as a threat, and it is widely believed that they were responsible for his death in May 1958.

The apparent split that developed between Krim and Abane Ramdane ended whatever prospects there might have been for a cohesive Kabyle leadership of the revolution. At the time of Abane's death, Kabyles had constituted 45 percent of the top leadership, but since that date they have rarely amounted to more than 25 percent of the top elite. Divisions among Kabyles, as well as Arab opposition to Kabyle dominance of the revolution, meant that a Berber ethnic bloc within the elite was unlikely to emerge. Other sources of cleavage were simply more important than ethnicity.

As the French began to bring the military aspects of the Algerian revolution under control in 1958–59, the Algerians pressed forward on the diplomatic front by creating a provisional government, the GPRA. While legally responsible to the CNRA, the GPRA was the legal embodiment of the Algerian revolution for nearly four years. The GPRA's membership was changed twice, and in each of the three 'cabinets' Kabyles were present. Krim, of course, as a member of the 'triumvirate', was included in all three versions of the GPRA. In September 1958, three additional Kabyles were named to the GPRA—Lamine Debaghine, Omar Oussedik and Ait Ahmed. The latter, however, was in prison and was merely made an honorary member, like Ben Bella and three other prisoners, in all of the GPRAs.

In December 1959, when the GPRA was reshuffled, two Kabyles were dropped and Mohammedi Said was brought into the government. Mohammedi had led the guerrilla forces in Kabylia for a while after Krim and Ouamrane had departed, and eventually he came to share authority with Colonel Houari Boumedienne over the Algerian forces stationed in Morocco and Tunisia. But as Boumedienne moved to consolidate his control over the army, Mohammedi Said was 'promoted' to the GPRA, where he had few clear functions and little authority. While in the GPRA, however, Mohammedi developed a strong antipathy toward Krim, so that the three Kabyles within the last two GPRAs of 1960 and 1961 were all hostile to one another.

Following Abane's death in 1958, for the duration of the revolution there was no 'Berber problem' at the level of elite politics. It was not until independence was achieved in July 1962 that what appeared to be a serious Arab–Kabyle split arose. Despite the complexity of the lines of cleavage within the revolutionary leadership, there is no denying that ethnic considerations did count for something in the crisis that immediately broke out after independence had been won. (See Figure 15.1 for a summary of Berber representation within the elite during the revolution.)

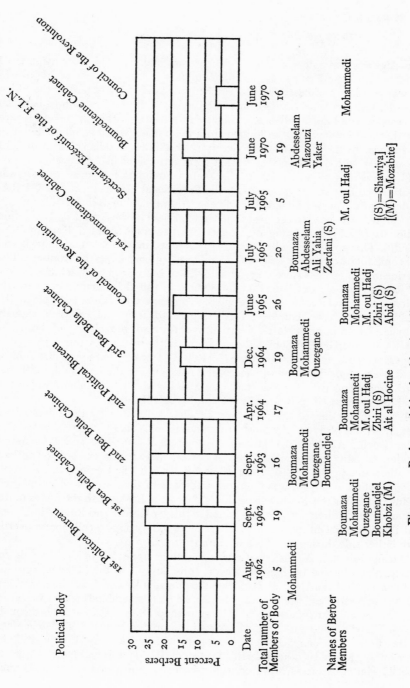

Fig. 15.1 Berbers within the Algerian elite: the revolutionary period

Political Body	1st Political Bureau	1st Ben Bella Cabinet	2nd Ben Bella Cabinet	2nd Political Bureau	3rd Ben Bella Cabinet	Council of the Revolution	1st Boumédienne Cabinet	Secrétariat Exécutif of the F.L.N.	Boumédienne Cabinet	Council of the Revolution
Date	Aug. 1962	Sept. 1962	Sept. 1963	Apr. 1964	Dec. 1964	June 1965	July 1965	July 1965	June 1970	June 1970
Total number of Members of Body	5	19	16	17	19	26	20	5	19	16
Names of Berber Members	Mohammedi	Boumaza Mohammedi Ouzegane Boumendjel Khobzi (M)	Boumaza Mohammedi Ouzegane Boumendjel	Boumaza Mohammedi M. oul Hadj Zbiri (S) Aït al Hocine	Boumaza Mohammedi Ouzegane	Boumaza Mohammedi M. oul Hadj Zbiri (S) Abid (S)	Boumaza Abdesselam Ali Yahia Zerdani (S)	M. oul Hadj	Abdesselam Mazouzi Yaker	Mohammedi

[(S) = Shawiya]
[(M) = Mozabite]

The Ben Bella period

The Algerian struggle for independence was finally ended by a negotiated settlement, for the French, despite their military successes, were unable to win the war politically. A cease-fire was reached in March 1962 as part of the Evian Accords. Independence finally came on 5 July 1962. In the few months between the cease-fire and independence, conflicts and tensions within the revolutionary elite that had previously been hidden from the outside world suddenly burst to the surface. In the midst of their victory celebrations, Algerians began to fight one another with a passion that rivaled their anti-colonialist sentiments.

Three major groups within the elite were contenders for power in post-war Algeria. The first was represented by the Provisional Government, the GPRA, headed by Benyoussef Benkhedda and the 'triumvirate' of Krim, Boussouf and Ben Tobbal. Opposed to them was the General Staff of the Armeé de Libération Nationale (ALN) consisting of Houari Boumedienne, Ahmed Kaid and Ali Mendjli. This group controlled the forces stationed in Morocco and Tunisia and had some followers in the *willayas*, or military regions, along the frontiers. The interior military forces were themselves divided, but none had much use for the GPRA. Of the six *willayas*, the Aures, Oranie and the Sahara were strongly opposed to the GPRA, but were willing to support the General Staff of the ALN. The *willayas* that were further removed from the frontiers, namely Kabylia, Algerois and North Constantine, rejected the claims of both the GPRA and the General Staff, although for tactical reasons they were disposed to cooperate on a limited basis with the GPRA. The two Berber areas, it should be noted, were aligned on opposite sides, the Aures under the leadership of Tahar Zbiri supporting the General Staff, while Kabylia, led by Mohand oul Hadj, was bitterly opposed to Boumedienne and his ALN forces.

A new dimension to the intra-elite conflict was added by the release from French prisons of five of the most prestigious revolutionary leaders, Ahmed Ben Bella, Hocine Ait Ahmed, Mohammed Boudiaf, Rabah Bitat and Mohammed Khider. Lacking independent bases of power, these men were obliged to look for allies among the existing forces. Ben Bella, who had gained considerable prestige while in prison, was the most ambitious of the five as well as the most useful ally. After considerable bargaining, he cast in his lot with the forces under Boumedienne's direction, and was joined in this by Khider and Bitat. Ait Ahmed and Boudiaf pursued more independent courses, refusing to collaborate overtly with either side during the crisis of summer 1962.

During July and August, two major coalitions appeared in the struggle for power. The bloc led by Ben Bella came to be known as the 'Tlemcen group', and consisted of the General Staff plus the guerrilla leaders from the *willayas* of the Aures, Oranie and the Sahara. The second bloc, assembled around Belkacem Krim, came to be known as the 'Tizi Ouzou group'. Since Tizi Ouzou is the main city of Kabylia, the name itself underlined the predominantly Kabyle character of this force. The name, however, was somewhat misleading, for the Kabyles were intially joined by other guerrilla leaders of the Algerois and North Constantine. The latter two areas, however, were eventually neutralized by Boumedienne's troops, leaving the Kabyles as the main armed force opposed to Ben Bella and Boumedienne. Standing between these two groups were the remnants of the GPRA under Benkhedda and the Provisional Executive that had been formed to oversee the transition to independence.

While the Tizi Ouzou group naturally relied primarily on Kabyle support, it denied having any regionalist objectives. Nor was it able to claim to speak for all Kabyles, since Ben Bella's 'Tlemcen group' had managed to gain the support of such prominent Kabyles as Amar Ouamrane, Ahmed Boumendjel and Mohammedi Said. Ait Ahmed, another prestigious Kabyle, refused to back either side.

During August and early September, both occasional fighting and constant negotiation took place. The Kabyle region itself never became an arena of battle, for Boumedienne's forces concentrated instead upon gaining control of the Algerois and North Constantine, thus isolating Kabylia. Ben Bella, who was generally willing to seek negotiated settlements rather than confrontations, was in contact with the leaders of the Tizi Ouzou group and reportedly offered Krim the post of Minister of Foreign Affairs within a Ben Bella-led government. The Ministry of Justice would have also gone to a Kabyle, Arezki Bouzida. The offer was rejected, however, since the Kabyles preferred to retain their freedom of action as members of the National Assembly. Ben Bella was willing to allow the Kabyles, and in particular Mohand oul Hadj, to draw up the list of deputies to the National Assembly to be elected in September. On this basis, the crisis was brought to an end, and elections were held nearly on schedule. Among the hand-picked deputies, there was, as agreed, a substantial Kabyle bloc that was generally hostile to Ben Bella.[1]

Kabyle representation in the five-man Political Bureau was virtually non-existent, since Ait Ahmed had refused to join and Mohammedi Said, the only Kabyle member, was generally viewed as pro-Ben Bella. In addition, Mohammedi was a fervent believer in Arabization, and was in fact given responsibility for promoting the use of Arabic in the administration and in the schools. He was bitterly opposed to Krim and other members of the Tizi Ouzou group, for, in his words, 'C'est moi, Tizi Ouzou!' But his authority in Kabylia had waned since the days when he and Krim were both leading the guerrilla war in the rugged mountains surrounding Tizi Ouzou.

Ben Bella's first government included five Berbers out of nineteen ministers. Four were Kabyles, Mohammedi Said, Bachir Boumaza, Amar Ouzegane and Ahmed Boumendjel, and one was a Mozabite, Mohammed Khobzi. Of the four Kabyles, each came from a totally different political background. Boumaza had been with the FLN in France until his arrest in the late 1950s. Ouzegane was an ex-Secretary General of the Algerian Communist Party, who, since his ouster from the party in the late 1940s had been an active nationalist with a

[1] Kabyles in the Assembly included Ali Yahia, Mohammed Boudaoud, Ahmed Boumendjel, Abderrahmane Fares, Slimane Dhiles, Lamara Hamel, Belkacem Krim, Salah Louanchi, Ahcene Mahiouz, Mohammedi Said, Amar Ouamrane, Amar Oudni, Tayeb Seddiki, Mohammed Yazourene, Hocine Ait Ahmed, Mabrouk Belhocine, Arezki Bouzida, Ahmed Feddal, Hadj Ali Boubekeur, Mourad Oussedik, Arezki Hermouche, Mouloud Gaid, Sfaya, Aoudjhane, Slimani and Bouaziz.

confused ideological perspective. Boumendjel was a close friend of the moderate nationalist leader, Ferhat Abbas. And Mohammedi had been with the GPRA since 1960. None of the four had close links with either Krim, Mohand oul Hadj, or Ait Ahmed, all of whom retained some independent bases of support in Kabylia.

During Algeria's first year of independence, many of the groups that had initially agreed to accept Ben Bella's leadership began to turn against him. First to defect were older revolutionaries such as Khider and Boudiaf. By June 1963, the moderates around Ferhat Abbas were also becoming disillusioned with the regime. Soon thereafter two prominent Kabyles, Ait Ahmed and Belkacem Krim, spoke of the need to oppose the government. During the summer, Ahmed Francis, a close friend of Abbas, quit as Minister of Finance and was replaced by one of the few Kabyles in the government, Bachir Boumaza, who became responsible for an enlarged Ministry of National Economy. Boumaza's promotion did nothing to satisfy Kabyle grievances, however, and in late August a largely Kabyle opposition group formed around Ait Ahmed. The Front des Forces Socialistes, or FFS, as the movement was called, rejected the Constitution that Ben Bella was trying to force through the Assembly. In the Constitutional referendum held on 8 September, the region of Kabylia had the lowest level of participation in the entire country.

An open clash between Ben Bella and the FFS now seemed unavoidable. On 19 September, Ben Bella formed a new government, retaining four Kabyle ministers, Boumaza, Ouzegane, Mohammedi and Boumendjel, but dropping the Mozabite Khobzi. A few days later both Ait Ahmed and Krim were expelled from their positions in the National Assembly and the FFS was banned. In reaction, FFS demonstrations were held in Tizi Ouzou and were addressed by such national figures as Ait Ahmed, Mohand oul Hadj, Ali Yahia, Mourad Oussedik and Arezki Hermouche. With Mohand oul Hadj's support, Ait Ahmed had acquired a military force to back his dissident movement. Mohand oul Hadj was immediately relieved of his command of the seventh military region, and was replaced by a younger officer, Said Abid, a Shawiya from the Aures region. At the same time, Ben Bella took advantage of Boumedienne's absence to appoint Tahar Zbiri, also a Shawiya, to the position of Chief of Staff.

Despite this apparent demonstration of Kabyle separatism, half of the Kabyle deputies in the National Assembly opposed the actions of the FFS. Declaring that '. . . there is no Kabyle problem; Kabylia is a region like any other in the country', thirteen Kabyles voted a resolution condemning the uprising.[1]

During the month of October there was scattered fighting between the FFS and the regular armed forces, but Ben Bella sought to avoid an armed showdown. Instead, he played for popular support by announcing dramatic decisions, such as the nationalization of French lands, while at the same time creating a war-scare on the Moroccan–Algerian border. When fighting did break out on the border, Ben Bella appealed for national unity, and managed to convince Mohand oul

---

[1] Kabyle deputies opposing the FFS dissidence were Belhocine, Bouzida, Gaid, Ouamrane, Hamel, Mahiouz, Sfaya, Yazourene, Aoudjhane, Slimani, Bouaziz, Feddal and Hadj Ali.

Hadj to abandon Ait Ahmed, thereby succeeding in depriving the FFS of its military capability. Ait Ahmed, although isolated, managed to continue the struggle on a small scale until his arrest a year later, in October 1964.

In order to gain Mohand oul Hadj's support, Ben Bella was obliged to agree to reintegrate some of the opposition into the FLN and to hold a Party Congress within six months. In addition, Mohand oul Hadj is reported to have demanded that the Kabyle cabinet members be dropped, along with Boumedienne and his followers. Whether Ben Bella initially agreed to this demand is unknown, for no such action was ever taken.

In April 1964, a Party Congress was held, and large numbers of opponents of the regime were allowed to attend and to speak, among them Belkacem Krim. The most tangible result of the Congress was the election of a new Political Bureau and a Central Committee. Kabyle representation on the powerful Political Bureau was increased somewhat with the inclusion of Mohand oul Hadj and Ait al Hocine, in addition to such reliable standbys as Boumaza and Mohammedi. One other Berber, Tahar Zbiri, was named to the Political Bureau as well.

In the fall of 1964 there were new elections for the National Assembly. In the first Assembly, Kabyles had been the most active members, as well as the most anti-regime in their voting.[1] In the new assembly, many of the dissident Kabyle deputies were replaced with more docile ones. Only Mohand oul Hadj and Ait al Hocine stood out as prominent Kabyle leaders among the newly elected deputies.

Ben Bella's last change of government took place in December 1964, at a time when it appeared that the regime was increasing its ability to control events throughout the country. Active dissidence had been virtually eliminated by the efficient efforts of Boumedienne's army. Kabylia had returned to its normal state of reserve toward central authority, and fighting had stopped. In his third government, therefore, Ben Bella felt no particular need to make overtures to the Kabyles, and in fact dropped one Kabyle minister while retaining Mohammedi, Ouzegane and Boumaza, the latter two in somewhat less important posts than they had previously occupied. The proportion of Kabyles in top government positions was lower than it had been at any time since 1954.

Kabyle problems were of relatively minor importance as Ben Bella prepared to confront his most important antagonist, the army led by Houari Boumedienne. Ethnic politics faded from the scene as Ben Bella and Boumedienne maneuvered to gain support for an eventual confrontation. Once again, conflict within the top elite developed along lines far removed from simple ethnic considerations. Ben Bella and Boumedienne were both able to find Berber supporters.[2] The masses of Berbers in Kabylia and the Aures were either ignorant of, or indifferent to the quarrels of their self-appointed leaders. When Boumedienne launched his surprising and successful coup against Ben Bella on 19 June 1965, there were few within either the elite or the masses who reacted strongly.

[1] Quandt, op. cit., pp. 190-9.

[2] Just before the *coup*, Ben Bella had reached an agreement with the FFS, through the intermediary of Mabrouk Belhocine, which is said to have provided for Ait Ahmed's release from prison and his eventual inclusion within the government as Foreign Minister.

10*

The Boumedienne period

Houari Boumedienne came to power in June 1965 with the backing of the professional military, the ex-guerrilla leaders and many of the technically competent cabinet ministers. The little opposition to the coup came from students, trade unionists and some of Ben Bella's close associates. The coup aroused neither enthusiasm nor particular hostility in the Berber areas. Little was known about Boumedienne, for he had never sought popular support. Consequently, most Algerians adopted a wait-and-see attitude toward his regime.

Boumedienne showed himself to be a careful politician who concentrated on developing ties to members of the elite rather than seeking the backing of the masses. In view of the instability of the Ben Bella period, the search for a reliable ruling coalition marked a major departure in political style from Ben Bella's confusing practice of playing off factions against one another. Boumedienne and his colleagues of the so-called 'Oujda group', none of whom was a Berber, seemed aware of the potential for regional dissidence in areas such as Kabylia and the Aures.

In creating new ruling bodies, posts were allocated to Berbers in exact proportion to their numbers in the population at large, about twenty percent. The Council of the Revolution, the supreme authority within the governing structure, consisted of twenty-six men, five of whom were Berbers. Boumaza, Mohand oul Hadj, and Mohammedi were Kabyles who had served the Ben Bella regime previously, and Zbiri and Said Abid were Shawiyas who had also been part of the former government.

Within the Council of Ministers, there were several new faces, including three Berbers. Belaid Abdesselam, a Kabyle, became Minister of Industry and Energy, and was soon acknowledged to be one of the most dynamic leaders of the regime. Abdennour Ali Yahia, also a Kabyle, was made Minister of Public Works. Abdelaziz Zerdani, a Shawiya who was close to Zbiri, was named Minister of Work. In addition, Boumaza was retained in the cabinet, but this time as Minister of Information.

To head the party, a five-man Secrétariat Exécutif was named. The FLN had never amounted to much after independence, and it was unclear whether there would be an important place for the party within the new state structures. In many ways, the party's primary purpose seemed to be that of providing positions within the regime for the ex-guerrilla leaders whose prestige was great, but whose technical competence was lacking. Of the five members of the party directorate, one was the venerable Kabyle leader Mohand oul Hadj.

Rather than relying on accommodations with prominent Berber political figures to prevent dissidence in Kabylia or in the Aures, the Boumedienne regime determined instead to pursue policies that would help the underdeveloped Berber areas. Even during Ben Bella's rule great efforts had been made along these lines, especially in the field of education. Both Kabylia and the Aures had received special attention, and primary school attendance between 1962 and 1965 had grown much more rapidly in these two areas than in the rest of the country.

Boumedienne continued and amplified this policy under a program designed to reduce regional disparities in level of development.

As in the past, however, government initiatives to promote economic and social development were hampered by the continuation of conflicts within the top elite. The first signs of these internecine disputes came in the fall of 1966 with the defection of two ministers from the cabinet. One of the dissidents was a Kabyle, Boumaza, but his reasons for leaving the government were totally unrelated to Berber problems. A minor cabinet reshuffle occurred, and the former Minister of Public Works, the Kabyle Ali Yahia, was transferred to the head of the Ministry of Agriculture.

A more fundamental conflict was beginning to develop within the elite during 1967. Proponents of two contrasting methods of economic organization began to clash with one another in public. One faction, headed by Abdelaziz Zerdani, favored the decentralized, 'self-management' approach to agricultural and industrial development. Zerdani, who was known to be something of a Marxist in his ideological perspectives, was thought to have the backing of his fellow Shawiyas, Tahar Zbiri and Said Abid, both of whom held important posts within the army. A second school of thought was identified with the Minister of Industry and Energy, the Kabyle Belaid Abdesselam, who favored a centrally organized form of state capitalism. Boumedienne tried to mediate the dispute, but by November 1967 Zbiri was preparing for a display of force against Boumedienne. The Minister of Work, Zerdani, was reported to have offered his resignation, as did the Kabyle Minister of Agriculture, Ali Yahia. In mid-December, the covert struggle erupted in the form of an attempted coup led by Zbiri. The coup was rapidly put down by the professional army officers loyal to Boumedienne. Zbiri's supposed friend, Said Abid, played an ambiguous role during the crisis, apparently trying to prevent an armed clash. His mysterious suicide following the failure of the coup raised numerous questions concerning his actions. None the less, it is apparent that the little support that Zbiri did manage to find came primarily from other Shawiyas, but the issue for which they fought had little to do with problems peculiar to the Berber regions. Rather, in the highly suspicious atmosphere of Algerian elite politics, Zbiri and Zerdani had found few reliable allies other than those who shared with them a common origin and, more important, a common political past.

Following the coup attempt of December 1967, the elite was purged of other potential dissidents, primarily the ex-guerrilla leaders, including the Kabyle Mohand oul Hadj. Berber representation within the elite dropped to an all-time low. The Council of the Revolution had initially included five Berbers, but, with the defection of Boumaza and Zbiri, the elimination of Mohand oul Hadj, and the death of Said Abid, only Mohammedi Said remained as a minor Kabyle figure on the Council. The Cabinet was slightly altered following the attempted coup, and one prominent Kabyle, the former Prefect of the Department of Kabylia, Mohammed Mazouzi, was appointed Minister of Work. No other changes occurred until June 1969, when Layachi Yaker, also a Kabyle, was named Minister of Commerce. (See Figure 15.2 for a summary of Berber representation within the top elite since 1962.)

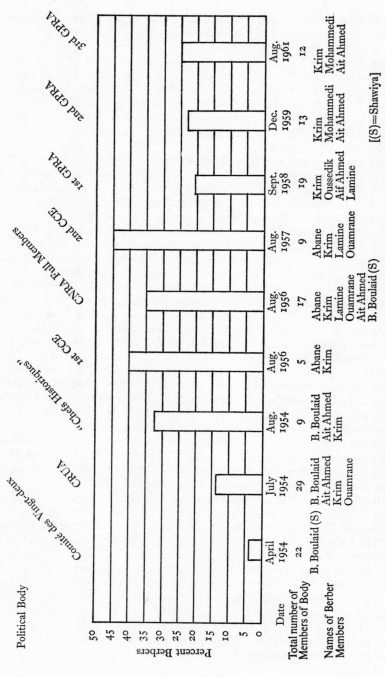

Fig. 15.2 Berbers within the Algerian elite: the Ben Bella and Boumedienne periods

After the December 1967 crisis, the Boumedienne regime began to show more signs of confidence and dynamism. No longer as threatened by internal divisions, the government began to attack fundamental social, economic and even political problems. Meetings of the Council of Ministers were held in both the Aures region and in Kabylia in order to demonstrate concern for those backward areas. Massive government credits, reportedly exceeding $100 million, were designated for agricultural and industrial development in Kabylia. By 1970, something of an economic boom was under way in that region. Part of the success of the government's program in Kabylia was attributed to the actions of the energetic and competent Prefect of the department, a Kabyle educated in the Middle East, M. Ghozali.[1]

The political returns to the government from its policies in both the Aures and in Kabylia were evident in the departmental elections of May 1969. It is difficult to judge the accuracy of election statistics, but at least in Kabylia the figures seem plausible. Of the three elections since independence for which data are available, the level of support for government-approved candidates in Kabylia was 54 per cent of registered voters in 1963, 57 percent in 1964 and 70 percent in 1969. In the Aures region, fewer eligible voters were registered, but of those registered 79 percent approved government candidates in 1969, a lower figure than during Ben Bella's rule, but a bit above the national average of 74 percent none the less.

The results of the 1969 elections in Kabylia reveal that the government was at least partially successful in introducing party officials as representatives in the departmental assemblies. Many party functionaries were among the candidates, who numbered two per seat, but only 50 percent were actually elected. This compares to an election rate of 100 percent for the few party officials running in other departments. The elections resulted in party officials occupying 19 percent of the seats in Kabylia, compared to 4 percent elsewhere. In addition, acting members of the communal assemblies were elected in large numbers, totaling 23 percent of all members of the new departmental body in Kabylia. Compared to other regions, however, there were relatively few government administrators elected. (See Table 15.1.)

In general, it seems as if the Boumedienne regime is succeeding in gaining some popularity among the Kabyles, as demonstrated by the unusually warm reception the President received in Kabylia in the fall of 1968 and by the election results of May 1969. In addition, governmental authority is extending into the region, as evidenced by the government-sponsored programs directed by the Prefect and by the large numbers of party officials elected to the departmental assemblies.

If successful, this policy should prevent serious dissidence in the major Berber area of the country by both reducing grievances and by expanding governmental authority. It seems likely that the 'carrot and the stick' will both be used to ensure that a Berber problem does not arise in the near future.

---

[1] A more extensive analysis of developments in Kabylia is available in 'Nationalisme et provincialisme Kabyles', *Maghreb*, No. 33, May–June 1969.

Table 15.1   Departmental Assembly Election Results in Kabylia

	Occupations of winning candidates	
Occupation	*Kabylia*	*Other departments (Algiers, El-Asnam, Medea)*
	%	%
Teachers	26	23
Communal Assembly representatives	23	10
Party officials	19	4
Workers	13	19
Administrators	9	17
Liberal professions	4	7
Peasants	4	9
Directors	2	9
Others	0	2
	100	100
	(*n* = 47)	(*n* = 139)

CONCLUSION

Conflicts within the Algerian political elite have been both frequent and intense, but with rare exceptions they have not revolved around issues of regionalism, separatism or ethnicity. While Berbers and Arabs in Algeria are aware of their distinctive identities and often express hostility to one another, at the level of elite politics ethnic background has been a minor source of friction. In part this has been due to the impact of the nationalist movement and the war for independence, both of which created lines of cleavage within the elite that were far more important and complex than those indicated by mere regional origins. But with time, it is likely that the legacy of the past will weigh less heavily, and new sources of conflict may arise within the elite. Under some circumstances ethnic group politics could become more important in the future than they have been in the past.

It is frequently argued that ethnic particularism is itself a product of modernization rather than a relic of traditional society.[1] With increased social communication, linguistic, religious and racial groups become aware of their distinctive identities and find in their particularism a basis for political organization. Ethnic politics can develop in stages, beginning with limited cooperation among leaders of the same ethnic background. As the above survey of Algerian

---

[1] Huntington, op. cit., p. 37, argues that, 'The breakup of traditional institutions may lead to psychological disintegration and anomie, but these very conditions also create the need for new identifications and loyalties . . . Modernization means that all groups, old as well as new, traditional as well as modern, become increasingly aware of themselves as groups and of their interests and claims in relation to other groups.'

politics has shown, there have been instances of this form of political behavior in the past, but thus far no cohesive Kabyle or Shawiya leadership bloc has emerged.

A second stage in the development of ethnic politics would be the creation of a Berber leadership with links to the masses. Such a movement might work within the ongoing political system, or might press for autonomy from the central government. In an extreme case, armed dissidence might begin in the Berber areas with the objective of overthrowing the government. A third form of ethnic politics would be the demand by a well-organized Berber movement for a separate state and the use of force to achieve such an objective. While stages one and two seem plausible and even have some historical precedent, stage three seems out of the question in Algeria.

Under what circumstances might ethnic politics develop at least to the stage of constituting an important political movement capable of threatening the central government? A major impetus toward ethnic politics would be the adoption by the government of policies actively hostile to the Berber minority. These might include rapid Arabization, the neglect of economic development in rural Berber areas, and the exclusion of Berbers from political and administrative positions within the government. Under a weak and unenlightened government, such policies might be pursued, but thus far Algerian leaders have consciously avoided these measures.

A second means by which ethnic politics might grow in importance in Algeria could come, ironically, through the liberalization of the political system. If a multi-party system with competitive elections were to be adopted, there would be strong incentives for politicians to seek support in the countryside. In response to the demands of constituents, leaders might be obliged to cater to regionalist and ethnic sentiments to a greater degree than is now the case. A Kabyle and a Shawiya 'party' might emerge, and could conceivably join together to form a larger Berber party. The objectives of such a political movement, however, would almost certainly not be independence for the Berber population, but rather would be limited to demands for equality and for special favors from the central government. A Berber party would quite likely seek to cooperate with other groups concerned with development of the rural areas.

While it is possible that ethnic politics could develop in Algeria, it seems more likely that for at least the next decade Algerian political life will not be seriously colored by Berber–Arab rivalries. Conscious government policies will probably avoid overt discrimination against Berbers. Equally important, the Algerian political system will probably remain relatively centralized and bureaucratized, thereby providing few opportunities for the emergence of rural-based political movements. If the government is successful, Berbers will be integrated into the Algerian nation without major conflicts, and in time Berber particularism, which is already virtually absent within the elite, will probably decline among the masses as well.

Part 3 Ethnicity and Social Change

16

Jeanne Favret

Theoretically there are no dividing lines between political science, sociology, and anthropology, but in practice we seldom see any field studies that make use of all three disciplines at once. Theoretically social groups have no substantial existence; in practice, researchers always forget that they exist only as relational systems. The study of local politics in rural Algeria is a good cure for these academic failings; to persist in them would be to miss the point.

I

This paper attempts to explain two empirical facts—two rural rebellions that have occurred since Algeria became independent—which at first seem to concern anthropology:

(a) It is not surprising that *bandits d'honneur*, dedicated outlaws, should still be roaming the countryside in the remotest Algerian region—Aures—where 130 years of colonial rule did not suffice to stamp out the anti-government tradition; nor that a sub-prefect, tired of playing an inept role in local society, should marry into a powerful marabout family; nor that when he was sent for to settle a minor conflict, he handed his revolver to the victim and told him to defend the honor of his tribe; nor that he rounded up a jury from among the combatants' own lineage to decide who was guilty; nor that party officials should be planning to join forces with the *bandits d'honneur* in the hills: all this shows that *siba*—civil defiance of the central government—has been all but openly declared. But what are we to make of this revival of long-forgotten political forms when we know that the purpose of the insurrection is to protest against the regional government? And why revive a segmentary political organization whose traditional aim[2] was, on the contrary, to avoid being controlled by any central government?

(b) A few months after independence, the Kabyle military leaders went back into their mountains. They reactivated the *maquis* and organized the civilians so as to make it impossible for the national army to occupy the region without setting off a civil war. A deputy, one of the 'historic revolutionary leaders', joined them there, followed after a few weeks by his brother-in-law, the General Secretary of the Political Bureau, who thus abandoned a position that, in theory, could be considered more important than that of the head of the government himself.

Reporters and commentators on current Algerian affairs proceeded to issue

---

[1] First published in *Archives européennes de sociologie*, VIII, 1967, pp. 71–93.
[2] 'Traditional' as used here means simply 'pre-colonial'.

learned pronouncements on Kabyle particularism and on the impossibility of getting despotic Arabs and democratic Berbers to live together peaceably under a single government. If they had read Clifford Geertz's paper,[1] they would have noted in addition that independence often leads to the re-establishment of traditional political divisions: the new citizens are for the time being unable to comprehend the notion of belonging to an abstract State, devoid of historical traditions, otherwise than through participation in more familiar groups (ethnic, religious, linguistic, etc.). Consequently, the revival of primordial feelings is a result of independence—unexpected, but not necessarily dysfunctional for the unity of the State.

How then can we explain why this Kabyle insurrection has no primordial or nativistic ideology?—why the 'historic leader' doesn't make use of his kinship with a prestigious marabout lineage, and prefers to quote Goethe rather than the Kabyle laws (*qanun*s)?—why traditional language, culture, and methods of organization are not being promoted?—and why on the contrary the slogans, official orders, and indictments of the 'central' government are those of some centralist pressure group supported by a modern military organization? The insurgents, unlike the classical dissidents which they used to be for hundreds of years, do not in fact hope to prevent a State from being set up, but rather to conquer it, or at least play an important part in developing its economic policy.

Under the guise of a Berber insurrection, to use the terminology of French ethnographers of the nineteenth century, we find in reality two different things: in the first case, the reaction of peasants neglected by a distant government; in the second, threatened disruption of national unity by a fraction of the political elite. In neither case is it really a matter of nativistic demands.

This statement casts no doubt upon the value of Geertz's analysis, which accurately sums up the situations he is considering: in Indonesia, Burma, Malaysia and even Morocco, the primordial groups are without a doubt alive and functional. We suggest rather that in Algeria, where social discontinuity is more marked than in any other country recently freed from colonial rule, the primordial groups survive today not as unconscious anachronisms but as the result of deliberate reaction. The anthropologist seeking to investigate traditional political phenomena therefore risks a monumental error by taking them at face value, since today they appear in a totally different context. For the heirs of the nineteenth-century segmentary tribes the choice is no longer between taking part in the central government and institutionalizing their dissent, for henceforth the former is the only alternative; the choice—or the fate—of the peasants in the underdeveloped agricultural sector lies between the various means of attaining this end, among them, paradoxically, dissidence.

Moreover, criticism of these traditional political institutions from the inside confirms their character of secondary or reactive manifestations. It is hard to find a hamlet without any pre-colonial elements, but it is just as rare to see these elements forming institutions of a lasting kind. For the most disconcerting thing to an anthropologist is undoubtedly their volatility: born through the lack

[1] Clifford Geertz, 'The integrative revolution, primordial sentiments and civil politics in the new states', in C. Geertz (ed), *Old Societies and New States*, Glencoe, 1963.

of a State, they disappear when the State asserts itself. In any event they have only a semi-official, informal existence which limits their development; and their marginal character is attested by the peasants, who explicitly dismiss them as a mere makeshift.

The explanation of this pseudo-traditionalism is thus not to be sought at the level of the local group (lineage, hamlet, tribe), but rather in the relation between the State, the peasants of the underdeveloped agricultural sector, and the other social categories. For ultimately, what counts with the anthropologist is not that the traditional culture has become debased, but that 130 years of centralized government have not eradicated every form of segmentary organization. A difficult conquest and the demands of colonization had indeed convinced the French authorities of the need to wipe out tribal organization and replace it by a strong administrative system; it could be said that as early as 1880, tribalism was dying out.

This situation is unusual, since no traditional society has been disrupted so totally by colonization; yet the same effect will be achieved in other similar societies by its ethically less loaded equivalent, modernization. And this leads us to question the performance of anthropological method: what becomes of it, when the society under consideration no longer carries within itself its motive force?—when the factors that lead to social change originate elsewhere?—when what used to be a society (the *Beni X*) becomes instead a social category (small farmers)?

Too often, anthropologists evade the problems of modernization by proceeding as if there were two societies—one modern and the other traditional—exactly as there are two disciplines in the Social Sciences Faculty of their university, anthropology and sociology; and to make the analysis easier, these two societies are considered separate, one rural and the other urban, each classified according to the ethos of the researcher's academic discipline. To anthropologists, peasants appear sound and townspeople anomic; to sociologists, on the other hand, peasants are backward and will always drag their feet against the civilizing forces of the city. Plainly, however, there are not two societies; there is only one, even if there are two separate disciplines in Social Sciences departments.

Another way of avoiding this problem—academically less elegant, and therefore usually shunned—is to liken the relations between peasants and townspeople to a genealogical model: the former are the survival from the past of the latter, and in the local official, hospital attendant, or teacher, the peasant beholds his own future. But this distinction raises a question that even the least gifted functionalist learns to ask concerning evolutionist hypotheses: why are past and present, traditional peasants and modernized townspeople, living at the same moment in history, and what is their present relation to each other? Apparently a relation of dominance and subordination: the peasants do not constitute a separate metaphysical entity just because some anthropologists looking for examples of otherness have chosen them to study; they are first of all a social category, technically, economically and politically subordinate to the urban elites. We cannot, therefore, ascribe social change to the latter and stability to the former; from the condition of a relatively independent society to that of a dependent social category entails serious consequences for the peasants, even where change seems to have been most stoutly resisted.

What then is the status of the traditional political culture in present-day Algeria?—or again, what is the status of the small farmers in the political society, and how are we to interpret the two rebellions, Kabyle and Auresian? Finally, what is the nature of primordial groups in Algeria? Do they not constitute a modernist reaction, of which the cases discussed below represent the extremes? These may seem difficult questions, but in trying to answer them we shall find that we will have to consider several new findings, and that we can question the methods of anthropology with greater clarity since we are dealing here with an extreme case.

II

The first type of insurrection (Aures) can be explained with reference to the situation of the small farmers, who think of themselves as socially (that is economically, politically, and culturally) marginal, although statistically they are a majority;[1] the only social categories whom they consider non-marginal are those enjoying the occupations, life-style, and the values of industrial society. They differ in this respect from the peasants of other underdeveloped countries, who never refer exclusively to the values of the industrial society. Indeed, the frame of reference of traditional culture seems unable to endure without one or the other of the following conditions: (a) the profession of farmer is not too degraded economically; this is the case, for example, among the Turkish peasants described by P. Stirling;[2] (b) urban development is so limited that there is an unbridgeable gap between city and country; modernization is not only beyond the financial means, but also beyond the imagination of the country-dwellers such as, for example, the marsh people of Iraq described by S. Salim,[3] or certain peasants in India.

Neither condition exists in Algeria. (a) agriculture contributes much less to the peasants' total income than it used to; (b) the country way of life can be preserved only because so many workers have moved away; emigration has convinced many peasants that city ways are better, yet most of them are unable to leave their village.

A comparison of the stratification of two hamlets vividly illustrates these two phenomena. Hamlet X is located in the Ouarsenis mountains. All the men work at home; their natural wealth comes from growing grain and vegetables and breeding cattle, and their monetary wealth from working in the nearby zinc mine, which employs one-fourth of the men of the hamlet at an average monthly salary of 220 Algerian dinars. Thus the hamlet is better off than neighboring ones whose income is derived solely from farming and who are therefore begin-

---

[1] In 1954 when the last but one census was taken, they constituted 62·5% of the working population.

[2] Paul Stirling, *Turkish Village*, London, 1965.

[3] S. M. Salim, *Marsh Dwellers of the Euphrates Delta*, London, 1962.

ning to feel the effects of emigration. Hamlet Y is located to the south of the high plateau of the Setif. The people live almost entirely by raising livestock, since they were dispossessed of their land by colonization. Since independence, more than one-fourth of the men work in France, in rotation.[1]

Table 16.1 shows the restricted contribution of farming to the income of peasants. One-third of the population is poor because it has no other resource but farming. In Hamlet X, a 'rich' landowner might have 3.5 hectares that could be worked by one man working full time almost the year round for a net gain, at

Table 16.1

Annual per capita income, 1964 (Source: direct inquiry)	Hamlet X			Hamlet Y		
	Popula-tion %	Cumula-tive population %	Cumulative resources and their origin %	Popula-tion %	Cumula-tive population %	Cumulative resources and their origin %
(i) Less than 500 DA[2]	37.6	37.6	9.5 Public relief, farming, stock-raising	31.8	31.8	7.0 Public relief, stock-raising
(ii) 500 to less than 1000 DA	42.1	79.7	42.9 Farming, stock-raising, mining wages	26.3	58.1	25.8 Ditto, and irregular income
(iii) 1000 to less than 1500 DA	11.3	91.0	57.9 Ditto, and regular income	7.8	65.9	36.4 Ditto
(iv) 1500 DA and over	9.0	100.0[3]	100.0 Ditto, and government wages and trade	34.1	100.0[4]	100.0 Ditto, and emigration

[1] The investigations of these two hamlets were made respectively by Jacques Lizot and Simone Lempereur.

[2] One Algerian dinar equals one new franc.

[3] 9% of the population has 42% of the sources of income. This privileged category is mostly made up of people belonging to Marabout families who collaborated with the French government; their regular practice of marriage between parallel cousins (unknown in the non-clerical families of the region) has made possible the preservation and enlargement of hereditary lands, the founding of most of the businesses, and the monopoly of government jobs, even since Independence. The Mayor has an annual income 280 times that of the poorest person under his jurisdiction.

[4] 34% of the population has 64% of the sources of income. The most ambitious emigrants belong to the lineage of the *caid*, the patriarch who brought the French army into the region and to whom *lots de colonisation* were distributed—the only cultivated land belonging to the hamlet. His descendants were the only Algerians admitted to the communal school, and hold most of the government jobs today. In short, the 'wealth' of the two hamlets is produced by the accumulation of limited resources, the most important of which are of political origin.

current rates, of 525 Algerian dinars. Naturally, this man can call himself rich because his net yield (10 cwt of wheat) is not sold, but consumed at home, where it feeds six persons for one year. In market value, the equivalents would be:

525 Algerian dinars = the return from 3·5 hectares = 300 days of farm work;
= the market price of one cow or nine lambs = 100 days of work for a teenager;
= wages for 75 days' work in the mine;
= savings from 40 days' work in France.

Grain-raising is therefore the least profitable work available to the peasant.

A 'good' farming estate includes two hectares of grain, half a hectare of garden, one or two cows, and five or six sheep or goats. It employs two families: the men for the grain crops and the heavy work; the women to look after the garden, the wood, and the winter feeding of the livestock; the children to take care of the sheep. In an average year, the farm produces two-thirds of the family's food; the sale of the young animals makes up the rest. The produce of the farm does not allow for storage of reserves to offset a poor harvest; its net yield (900 Algerian dinars for two families) precludes any chance of saving money or adding to the number of animals. Its produce for a whole year is equivalent to what a hard-working emigrant can save in two months—and only 12 percent of the farms in Hamlet X enjoy this privileged position.

Table 16.2

	%	%
Publicly Employed, total		10·2
Permanent farm labor	6·3	
Government work	1·4	
Army	2·5	
Privately Employed, total		54·6
Non-farm, unsalaried	2·4	
Non-farm, salaried	3·7	
Farm, now working	24·2	
Emigrated to Europe	24·3	
Unemployed		35·2
Total		100·0%

It is hardly surprising that 75 percent of the Algerians questioned during the current census said they were unemployed; nowadays work on the land is considered not a job, but a non-job.[1]

[1] This phenomenon has already been noted by Pierre Bourdieu and Abdelmalek Sayad in *Le Déracinement, la crise de l'agriculture traditionnelle en Algérie*, Paris, 1964.

Our estimate,[1] shown in Table 16.2, of the present distribution of working males in the rural areas offers certain less discouraging indications.

Hence, if emigration were not limited by agreement between Algeria and France, it could attract more than a third of the male rural population without detriment to agriculture, and without noticeably affecting the balance between town and country. For economic reasons, the savings of emigrants are mostly invested in the farms, unprofitable though they are, instead of being invested in the city. Such savings will buy livestock, or build a house, for example, because the family's livelihood is already assured at home by the labor of other family members. However meager and unprofitable the farm may be, it does at least provide a living to those who work it.

Emigration is thus limited to rural regions that are strongly integrated socially. It has often been observed that in this respect the war of liberation completed the destructive work of a long-lived colonialism. Direct investigation and examination of government records show that family structures have hardly changed at all during the past hundred years; the same alignments persist, and the lineage is the individual's frame of reference. Undoubtedly it has lost its political significance, which was once all-important, to the extent that the peasantry has lost its independence and, more broadly, its political status. But its economic function is rather strengthened by the new material insecurity which the traditional foresight cannot allay. Insecurity diminishes as more men join forces economically; the presence of only one man in a household is a sign of indigence or poverty, whereas three men means the hope of security, that is, 'wealth'. This is why, contrary to the current opinion which sees in emigration an important cause of social change for the Algerian peasantry, it can be said that its main result is to preserve the rural ways of life. Even though these ways may not make sense economically, they are likely to persist for a long time, till industrialization can absorb the surplus manpower of the rural areas. Wage-earning in Europe nevertheless has ideological consequences whose significance is hard to judge, since it has made the small farmers painfully aware of their real situation.

This economic and cultural frustration has been accentuated by the achievement of independence. The burden of the war of liberation fell mainly on the peasants: livestock decimated, houses and food reserves destroyed, able-bodied men lost, etc. The State has offered only limited economic relief. The new jobs available affect a ridiculously small percentage of the working population in the country (3%); pensions to families of soldiers killed in the war and foreign aid from America in the form of food—or that part of it which actually reaches the hamlets—scarcely suffice to stave off the threat of famine for the most severely deprived groups. In fact, it is the emigration of rural workers to Europe, which has almost quadrupled in twelve years, that has provided the monetary resources that have made it possible to get the farms back into working order.

Thus, the comparison of their lot with that of the town-dwellers, and especially

---

[1] Based on a combination of predictions from the 1954 census, the 1960 census, the first returns from the 1966 census, and the estimates of Samir Amin in *L'Economie du Maghreb*, Paris, 1966, 2 vols.

of their former politico-military leaders who went down to the city after liberation, is a subject of continual amazement to the peasants, if not to economists. Whereas independence meant new jobs for 3 percent of them, almost 25 percent of the city people benefited by jobs created or left open by the departure of the Europeans. Since most of these are held by men, about half the male population of the cities has found jobs in this way, especially in the civil service (see Table 16.3).

Table 16.3   Distribution of employed males in cities

	%
Civil service	12·0
Army	8·6
Industry and trade, including self-employment	26·0
Total	46·6%

Whereas the urban population suddenly found itself better off, the rural population had to exert itself just to keep going. An administrative bureaucracy was set up in the cities, thanks partly to the important educational effort of the past decade, of which the city-dwellers were the chief beneficiaries. Unquestionably the reduction of inequalities in schooling is a high-priority objective for the new State, but in this field the usual difficulties crop up, such as the unwillingness of qualified teachers to leave the cities, and the limited results of teaching in French among populations that speak nothing but Arabic, etc. For the rural population, the channels of social mobility will remain for a long time individual, that is to say exceptional.

The reinforcement of this economic and cultural marginality which still characterizes two-thirds of the Algerian population can partly be explained by the role the peasants have played in the nationalist movement. As in most colonial lands, they have had nothing to do with the development of the nationalist ideology, nor with the establishment of the political parties. Here as elsewhere, the cities have been the only source of political innovation. But when the urban militants tired of the factionalism and ineptitude of the nationalist parties and went out into the *maquis* to enlist in a war of liberation, they were much surprised[1] to find that the peasants, who were supposed to have been tamed by the traditional culture, poverty, and the colonial government, were much more radical than they were themselves, and ready for immediate rebellion. People often speak of a 'peasant revolution' in Algeria. The term is accurate if it means that the revolution consisted in ridding the country of a dominant foreign minority, and that the instrument of this liberation was an army made up largely of peasants, officers included. But this military role of the peasantry had no decisive political implications. The loss of the only leader who would have given

[1] E. J. Hobsbawm would have been less surprised than these urban 'cadres' brought up in the political tradition of the French Revolution. Cf. E. J. Hobsbawm, *Primitive Rebels*, Manchester, 1959 (French translation, *Les Primitifs de la révolte dans l'Europe moderne*, Paris, 1966).

the *maquis* a deciding voice in the leadership of the FLN, together with the impossibility of a French military defeat in the field, brought to the foreground the diplomatic aspects of the struggle for liberation, especially after the establishment of a provisional government and military headquarters outside the country. Although they did play an important military role, which distinguishes them from the stereotyped 'backward' peasantry, the Algerian peasants have played almost no part politically in organizing the movement for national liberation, nor in the negotiations with the French government, nor in what has followed liberation.

Since independence, the State, which has become the dispenser of all bounties for the city dwellers, is a necessary middle-man to the peasants. It is almost the only employer, providing jobs for a tenth of the male rural population; it is the only source of income for the poorest segment of the population, thanks to pensions and relief in the form of food supplies; all essentials of economic life— in particular, the emigration of workers to Europe—depend upon it.

What stirs up rebellions is not so much the fear of being overrun by big-city ways as the fear of not being sufficiently overrun. The peasants don't mind the State's being in charge of all economic activity; they resent its failure to be the driving force of the local economy. To them there is only one calling, that of *fonctionnaire*—a title with which all government employees adorn themselves— all else being mere eyewash and pretence.

Thus, we can see what the traditional institutions mean to the small farmers. They are what hold these marginal members of the majority together and enable them to make a living while they wait for industrialization. For example, in hamlets that have no judge cases are tried by co-opted juries. The Koranic school can at least teach moral principles to people who will never hold a French qualification, nor, consequently, a government job, and insurrection is one of several ways to attract the concern of the administration—that is, of industrial society— since the government is the only employer who counts. So we find the reasons for both the existence and the instability of these institutions, and we can see how the homogeneous culture that distinguished the segmentary tribes of pre-colonial Algeria has undergone an upheaval without entirely disappearing. Each of the surviving cultural traits seen today is completely functional, but in a different way from what would have impressed a nineteenth-century anthropologist; for in each hamlet[1] these institutions are a function of its relations to industrial society.

Thus, according to the 'social bandits', as Hobsbawm calls them, certain hamlets in the Aures break out into rebellion because the local officials cut down their income by limiting emigration, by misappropriating pension money and the money orders sent home by emigrants, and by distributing food relief to friends and courtesans. For the local government offices are crawling with former collaborators of one type or another; they give jobs to men who used to serve in the French army and thus learned the language of the bureaucrats, or to youngsters who owe their education to their parents' collaboration. These facts, that are common enough, point to a truth of broader significance: of all the regions in

[1] The basic social unit of the small farmers.

Algeria with a potential for revolt, the Aures is undoubtedly the most neglected by the modern economy, and correspondingly the one most remote from government control. Its distance from the capital, its pastoral economy oriented toward the desert rather than the coastal plains, and finally its extreme poverty, kept the colonial authorities from ever trying to develop it. That is probably why it became the cradle of the war for liberation. But independence hasn't done the Aures must good. Although it headed the list of disaster areas, the Aures has had where look on helplessly while funds for economic rebuilding went to Kabylia, to political hostility to the government was incomparably more dangerous. It has also suffered more than the coastal regions for want of administrative officials; it could not supply them itself, nor could it attract any but the mediocre ones.

If the causes of insurrection are to be sought in the relations between local groups and industrial society, the actual forms that the rebellion takes are nevertheless traditional. The 'social bandits' are called *mujahidin*, fighters for the faith. Women save up perfume to put on their hair in case they might seek refuge in their houses. Young men, who in this region have no jobs and therefore no wives and no social standing, leave home to join forces with them. And when a *mujahid* comes into a hamlet at night, he knows whose door to knock on: somebody who belongs to the old village assembly (*jamaa*) if it still exists unofficially, or anyhow some middle-aged man who practices the traditional virtues and is therefore a former fighter or the father of a fighter, and is also necessarily economically marginal in Algerian society.

The aim of the *bandits d'honneur* is in part similar to that of the Sicilian Robin Hoods described by Hobsbawm: to restore justice, that is to get rid of the former collaborators now holding office in the local government; but whereas the Sicilian bandits want plenty of distance between the central government and the small towns so they can keep to themselves, the Auresian bandits are trying to make the central government take notice of them the only way they know; since no political elite represents them in the government, they are showing their courage and virility so that the industrial society that they helped to liberate will treat them justly.

If this hypothesis is confirmed, it will lead to two predictions about the Algerian society. (*a*) Any political regime that performs its functions as entrepreneur, that is provider of jobs, has the small farmers' support no matter which way it leans politically. This amounts to saying that despite—or because of—their military role in the war of liberation, these farmers are notably unpolitical and are only interested in economic modernization. (*b*) The peasants' traditionalism is no obstacle to modernization, since it is actually caused by an excess of modernity compared with the means at their disposal. It can already be observed that education is now highly valued throughout the rural areas,[1] and that any chance for local development is eagerly grasped by the peasants, if not by the town government.

---

[1] Because of its essential role in the mechanism of social ascension—every primary school graduate being virtually assured of a government position—it furnishes an excellent pretext for rural uprisings.

III

The insurrection of small farmers in the Aures was due to a combination of insufficient economic integration and an all-too-perfect identification with the ideology of industrial society. In Kabylia it was a different matter altogether.

The first thing to observe is the political discontent of the urban middle class, especially in Algiers. These are business men, whose 'ill-gotten gains' were confiscated by the national government; landowners dreading agrarian reform; office-holders dissatisfied with the insecurity of their standing and with financial austerity, culturally frustrated by the de-gallicization of administrative methods; democratic intellectuals, ill at ease in the only political party in existence; trade-union leaders displeased with the party's disciplining of their organization; etc.

Such discontent cannot be expressed by modern political means (parties and pressure groups) for two kinds of reasons, those relating to government, and those that concern society.

(*a*) As often happens in new states, the opposition, if there is one, lacks the institutional means of action or even of self-expression because the power of the executive branch is unchecked, either by Parliament, from which opposition members were quickly excluded, and which in any case has not been convened for the past two years, or by the trade union movement, periodically 'restructured', either because its authority is needed to assure the participation of the workers in the government's economic plans, or just to bring it into submission. As for the party, which is supposed to be the moving force in political decision-making, its Political Bureau is an adjunct to the activities of administrative personnel rather than the center of political decision. Since the liberation, moreover, the young graduates of European universities have had no qualms about how to divide responsibilities; they themselves have plunged into administrative jobs, leaving the political posts to Arabic-speaking militants incompetent to work in a French-speaking administration. This explains to some extent the rigidity of the party, its mistrust and hostility toward high officials who, even without having fought for independence, now monopolize knowledge, power and the best-paying jobs. And it is correspondingly impossible for a political opposition to be organized within the administrative staff, since every official is by definition subject to transfer or dismissal.

The president is the one who can make decisions, but he shirks the responsibility as much as possible. Now that socialistic legislation[1] has been enacted in an atmosphere of ideological intoxication—one-fourth Leninism and three-fourths *philosophie des lumières*—he governs the country by calling administrative work political, a practice inherited by the military regime from the civil regime that preceded it. The problem it is trying to solve is, however, not the same one that confronted the colonial authorities, which was to politicize the administration so as the prevent the development of a (nationalistic) political organization. Today the situation is practically reversed; the new State has to 'bureaucratize'

---

[1] These laws have to do with the nationalization and self-management of European agricultural and industrial undertakings.

politics because the society lacks oppositional tendencies strong enough to give birth to political movements.

(*b*) The political and cultural ambivalence of the urban middle class had brought it into disrepute even before the war of liberation got under way. This middle class has been torn too long between the claim to assimilation within French society proposed by the '*évolués*'[1] parties and the nationalistic demands made through the movement of religious reform. As for the working-class party, it fell victim to irreparable schisms when some of its leaders, the '*chefs historiques*', left the party in order to work underground. Of course this lack of organization of political parties is connected with the attitude of the French administration, which was responsible for confining the working-class party and trade union to urban groups, as well as for over-representing the Europeanized bourgeoisie among the elected representatives in the French Assemblies.

Another reason for lack of organization is the nature of social stratification. In 1954 when the war of liberation began, the urban population made up only 12 percent of the total, with the group generally labeled 'bourgeoisie' constituting less than 2 percent. This was really a land-owning bourgeoisie, since industrial and even commercial capitalism were almost nonexistent.[2] The intellectual elite was insignificant. Only 5 percent of the working population could read and write in Arabic or French; upper and middle 'cadres' and members of the liberal professions accounted for only 0·6 percent of the total. The middle classes (4·3%) included salaried workers (0·5%) and small and medium tradesmen and artisans (3·8%), a good third of whom were really unemployed. The working class (31·5%) was made up of two groups; full-time farm laborers and skilled industrial workers on the one hand (5%), and agricultural day-laborers (14·5%) who were most of them unemployed or underemployed farmers, together with semi-skilled and unskilled urban workers on the other. But this class was plainly heterogeneous, because the situation of the farm hands was different from that of the city workmen: their pay was poor, they received no 'fringe benefits', and they were not unionized. The small farmers constituted a clear majority (62·5%) but counted for nothing politically. Thus, any class struggle inside the Algerian society was almost impossible, for wage-earners were the exception and not the rule; only 2 percent of the population were employed in indigenous enterprises. Yet social inequality was striking, as in the two hamlets mentioned above, especially as regards land ownership; 5 percent of the farming estates[3] accounted for 54 percent of the arable land. In other words, social inequality was marked, but did not serve to divide people into classes, since the possibilities of economic exploitation were limited.

To a certain extent the political parties reflected the interests of the different urban 'classes' as they used to be under the colonial regime. Yet these parties

---

[1] The lower classes in Algiers still use the word *boulitique* to designate the mockery of political activity practised by Algerian delegates who were recommended by the colonial government.

[2] One percent of all firms, European and Algerian combined, employed more than fifty persons; only 9% of the business jobs were held by salary-earners.

[3] 9,000 of these belonged to Europeans and 25,000 to Algerians, with each of the two ethnic categories owning about the same acreage.

could not free themselves from the legal restrictions imposed on them by the French administration, which brought the multi-party system into disrepute. This confirms Worsley's thesis:[1] since independence, the 'monolithic' character of political life is also an expression of the lack of social differentiation.

This political discontent of the urban middle class, which cannot find expression in any modern political forms, is strongest in Kabylia, whose social composition is very much more diversified than that of other rural districts in Algeria. There seem to be no figures showing the distribution of the Algerian elites (political, economic, intellectual, etc.) by language or ethnic groups. It is known, however, that Kabylia is the only rural area that does supply the nation with members of such elites, and that a considerable percentage of the Algerian political and administrative personnel, as well as the industrial and business community and the intellectuals, is of Kabyle origin. The 1954 census does tell something about this group: 18·3 percent of the population living in the Algiers metropolitan area were born in some Kabyle township; no other rural area sends so many of its natives to the capital. The Aumale arrondissement ranks second with 9·3 percent of emigrants, but its population is decidedly less diversified, as shown in Table 16.4, which compares the distribution of the working population by type of employment in the townships referred to in this study.

Table 16.4

Township	Livestock & Farming	Business
	%	%
Djurdjura (Kabylia)	68·0	12·0
Aumale	97·7	0·2
Aures	95·4	0·2
Teniet el-Haad (Hamlet X)	97·3	0·3
Rhira (Hamlet Y)	97·8	0·3

Finally, of all the rural arrondissements we are considering in this study, the one with the least illiteracy, approaching that of the big coastal cities, is Tizi-Ouzou, in the very center of Kabylia (see Table 16.5).

Table 16.5

Arrondissement	Number of illiterates over 6 years of age, per 1,000 population
Tizi-Ouzou (Kabylia)	807
Aumale	931
Batna (Aures)	873
Orleansville (Hamlet X)	946
Setif (Hamlet Y)	884

[1] Peter Worsley, *The Third World*, London, 1964.

This markedly differentiated social composition has an interesting result: Kabylia is the only place in Algeria where discontented peasants constantly rub elbows with the urban political elite.

The Kabyle farmers, although much better off than other small farmers in Algeria, are more frustrated because their standard of comparison is not these other small farmers, of whom they know nothing, but their own relatives who have moved to the cities; and this 'subjective' privation of the Kabyle peasants has more important political consequences than the 'objective' privation of peasants elsewhere in the country, because the former have close ties with the urban political elite, many of whom came from their own neighbourhood and social stratum.

Such, at any rate, is the explanation given by the leaders of the insurrection, who pride themselves on being socially responsible enough to rush to the defense of peasants oppressed by the administration, war widows forced into prostitution, and so on, even when defending these unfortunates means risking their own respectable and well-paid jobs. Elsewhere in the country the hard-up peasants in underdeveloped regions have no such influential and close contacts even to help with things like applying for a government pension. This is probably why the poorest regions constantly undergo rebellions and wildcat strikes in which the agitators have no objective estimate of their chances of getting satisfaction.

In the case of Kabylia, however, we must ask ourselves whether another interpretation is possible: whether the elite have not simply used the defense of the peasants as a tool for the furtherance of their goals at the national level (for instance, steering the government's economic policy in another direction). The question may be asked whether in Kabylia the bourgeois make common cause with the peasants, as the revolutionary leaders insist, or the other way around; whether insurrection succeeds because the peasants feel close to the bourgeois, who are not only their standard of comparison but the only means they have of getting anything done locally. Discontent among the peasantry is not in itself a danger to political stability in Algeria, as shown by the case of the Aures. There, the peasants consider the Kabyle insurrection and conclude that they themselves are fools to think that by sitting still and behaving themselves they can get economic help from the government. 'The Kabyles rebeled, and now they have everything', they think. Naturally they assign the wrong reasons for this victory; the Kabyles didn't get what they were after just by rioting, but by rioting under the impulse and expert direction of a political elite. For the government to disregard the mood of the Aures peasants is to allow the kind of unrest that leads nowhere and is settled by installing some local military leader in the political bureau of the party. On the other hand, to disregard the mood of the urban bourgeoisie is to encourage a rural uprising in Kabylia that threatens the political balance precisely because it involves first and foremost the political and administrative cadres, the intellectuals, the business men, etc. The Kabyle peasants thus provide the permanent pretext for all opposition—their comparative poverty being by definition impossible to relieve[1]—as well as its ideological 'point of

[1] However the government may try to help the region with roads, hospitals, and schools, it will always fall short of the peasants' expectations, since they demand nothing less than an idealized France brought to reality in Algeria.

honor' and potential pressure group; the opposition, in turn, is necessarily made up of urban elites, who for a long time to come will continue to be mostly Kabyles.

In fact, insurrections that pose a real threat to the stability of the government cannot arise elsewhere than in Kabylia. (*a*) The other urban elites have no peasants at their disposal: this was demonstrated when the president had to be protected from the threat of a military *coup d'état*. Even though he described himself as 'the president of the peasants and the unemployed', he was arrested without any protest from the country-dwellers, and his militants, including those in charge of agrarian reform, found refuge in the cities. (*b*) The other primordial groups are less diversified,[1] so that the government can displease them without danger; they are just as numerous, but farther away from the capital.

We must now consider the reasons for the comparative economic success of the Kabyles. Why should they succeed and nobody else? Here we cannot turn to traditional culture and social organization for an explanation; in these respects Kabylia is not unusual compared with the rest of Algeria, except in having been the subject of most of the ethnographic studies carried out by the French, for reasons which we shall presently see. The explanation is rather to be sought in the special relationship between the Kabyle society and the colonial economy:

(*a*) Before the French conquest, the Kabyles did not think of themselves as a people, much less a nation, but as members of tribes. They would call themselves 'Ait X' as opposed to 'Ait Y'; they have a segmentary rather than a state tradition,[2] like other tribal groups in the Maghreb. The word 'Kabyle' was then used by city-dwellers, especially in Algiers, to define a linguistic area. But this linguistic differentiation was inadequate then, as it is today, as basis of a separatist ideology; this language is secondary (secular, vehicular, and unwritten) and does not prevent the integration of the Kabyles into an Arabic-Moslem cultural whole. If the Kabyle opposition today is hostile to the Arabization of education and administration, this means that it doesn't want these institutions de-gallicized because French is the language of an industrial society, not because it is seeking equal status for the Kabyle language. The latter is however very widespread; in 1954, 48 percent of the men and 69 percent of the women knew no other.[3] In principle this alone would form the basis for a primordial group; yet the opposition bases itself on other things, its members being modernists even though they appear to be traditionalists.

Finally, the economic ethic of the Kabyle culture is not favorable, any more

---

[1] In the Mzab, for example, 20% of the employed population are in business, not counting emigrants who have gone north; but the Mzab has only business people and farmers, whereas Kabylia has also industial workers, intellectuals, government officials, etc.

[2] The ethnography of the Maghreb owes much to the thesis of Ernest Gellner, *The Role and Organization of a Berber Zawiya* (Ph.D. University of London, 1961), for the use of the segmentation concept in connection with the social organization of this region. This is now published in *Saints of the Atlas*, London and Chicago, 1969.

[3] In the Aures, the second Berber-speaking region of Algeria, 14% of the men and 17·4% of the women spoke nothing but *chaouîa* (local Berber dialect) in 1954.

II

than it is elsewhere, to a capitalistic outlook. In 1830, this society was just as traditional in the Weberian sense of the term as the other rural groups. Its trading tradition, although ancient, has not succeeded in urbanizing the Kabyles. On the contrary, the emigrants of any one family take turns working in the city, have no contacts with anybody but fellow-tribesmen, and look upon their absense from home as a necessary purgatory, their Paradise being the hamlet where they left their land, homes, and social base. For centuries emigration has served to keep tribal structures intact, not to destroy them; and for the townsman of Algiers, the Kabyle is the epitome of the austere and tireless countryman who thinks only of returning to his native heath.

(b) At the time of the conquest,[1] the dissidence of the tribal society in its relations with the Turkish government and its refusal to join the resistance movement headed by the Emir Abd el-Kader resulted in its being less disrupted by the French military operations in Kabylia than was the case in the neighboring regions (Mitidja, Titteri). This society seems to have regarded the Emir merely as a new candidate for the Sultanate, and the French army as a special kind of tribe, with which or against which it would be possible to fight other segmentary tribes. This may explain why the Kabyles were the only natives to fight the French in battle even while doing business with them, at the time when the tribes subject to the rule of the Turks or of the Emir were avoiding all contact, and people were moving out of the cities. The Kabyles were also the only ones who went to work as farm laborers for the colons. This was doubtless the origin of the stereotype necessary to colonial ideology whereby the Kabyle is seen as different from the Arab (as austerity differs from slackness, work from idleness, and self-discipline from carelessness). The Kabyles were thus the first of all rural groups near the capital—the source of wealth and of economic and political innovation—to adapt themselves to the colonial economy, precisely because they were political dissidents in their own 'nation'.

(c) The colonial policy is not a negligible but a secondary factor, in so far as from 1870 on it was no longer developed by army officers, as it was in Morocco, but by colonists eager to get hold of tribal lands. In Algeria there was no Berber policy in the sense of promotion of Berber forms of organization and Berber values at the expense of modernist values, although there were important Berber minorities. In particular there was no special legislation for the Kabyles except in minor matters; and the experiment in the indirect administration of the tribes by officers of the Arab Bureaux met with a crushing defeat due to the power of the colonists' party, which dominated politics in Algeria almost without interruption from 1870 to 1958. The colonial ideology in Algeria therefore differs from that developed in Morocco exactly as the ethos of sociologists differs from that of ethnologists. In Morocco, the officers in charge of 'native affairs' were always setting the tribes of the interior—the real country, whose social structures were frozen but not destroyed, and whose spirit was unbroken—in opposition to the decayed cities, an artificial world swarming with detribalized people who

[1] Some of the following points are based on a study made by a rural administrator in Kabylia which is less mythological than its title suggests: Jean Morizot, *L'Algérie kabylisée*, Paris, 1962.

were politically uncontrollable. In Algeria, the colonists contrast the city sophisticates, of whom the Kabyles are the most typical exrmples, with the refractory and unassimilable primitives who occupy the countryside and whose land the Europeans have benevolently moved in to improve. Since 1870, the very character of Algerian politics, determined less by the metropolis than by a broadly autonomous colonial society, has not tended toward the glorification but rather the debasement of the traditional rural society. This is probably one reason for the low standing and general mediocrity of the local administration in Algeria, since the military administrators together with the pro-tribal policy had yielded to the hostility of the colonists.

Although there has been no Berber policy in Kabylia similar to that in Morocco, there has been educational policy of the missions and possibly of the French government, encouraged by the stereotype of the Kabyle, the only native capable of being assimilated to the economic and political values of the industrial society— reasonable, hard-working, and enterprising like a Protestant; democratic like an American. Before public education was set up in the rest of Algeria, Kabylia was already enjoying primary and secondary schools organized by missionaries and a public school to train Algerian teachers. From 1891 to 1950, practically all the Algerians recruited by the State Normal School for teachers in Algiers were Kabyles.

Thus, several decades before the other rural regions, Kabylia had an intellectual and an administrative elite, as well as a tradition of emigration of workers and tradesmen. The importance of the latter is now apparent: the Kabyles, who together with the Mzabi were the first native businessmen, served as middlemen between European producers and Algerian markets, a role formerly played by the Jews, who became progressively assimilated into the French society after 1870.

CONCLUSION

1. We have here a special type of traditionalism, that of an underdeveloped society which has been so thoroughly exposed to the ideals and the economic realities of the industrial society that it has lost its identity; its traditional institutions no longer serve the purpose they were designed for, but from now on are just a way of encouraging, or awaiting, modernization.

2. The elements of the 'traditional' culture that the peasants are now manifesting are not something created *ex nihilo*, but a selective reactivation of aspects of the pre-colonial culture. On the one hand there are certain traditional elements neither entirely functional nor entirely forgotten; on the other, there are some situations[1] in which this plethora of traditional elements can be seized upon and used as part of the strategy of different social groups in their struggle for modernization.

3. This situation remains an exceptional one in the Third World, but in one way foreshadows what is going to happen elsewhere.

[1] I have described the two extremes, the 'objective' frustration of the small farmers of Aures, and the comparative deprivation of those in Kabylia.

4. To explain this phenomenon it has been necessary to use both micro- and macrosociological factors, as well as diachronic and synchronic ones, since research on any one of these levels by itself has proved misleading. If we study nothing but hamlets or villages, we run up against insuperable contradictions that can't be explained just by invoking the decapitation of their political organization: changes at the top do bring significant changes at the lower levels. Likewise, macrosociological analysis remains sketchy because of uncertainty about the cultural variables: what function does tradition serve, what precisely are socialization and political integration, etc. In this perspective, studies like those of Almond and Coleman[1] appear promising, but only in the context of a myth that social science knows what it is talking about.

5. In principle, anthropology cannot be defined empirically by the kind of facts—that is, 'traditional' facts—that it deals with. Yet when it comes to a different kind of facts, such as those we are examining here, anthropology has neither a conceptual framework nor any techniques that make it possible to study a society simultaneously at the macro- and microsociological levels and in synchronic and diachronic perspective. Although contemporary sociology and especially political science are not of much help, a thorough study of the concepts used by the 'founding fathers'—Weber, Tocqueville, and the inevitable Marx—will perhaps give us some idea what a true social science might amount to. Structural-functionalism is not superseded *in principle* by the process of development in the 'backward' societies, but as long as it offers an empty framework—a general methodology without the corresponding aggregate of concepts and techniques—it is of little use in the actual situation where we find ourselves today.[2]

[1] Gabriel A. Almond and James S. Coleman (eds), *The Politics of the Developing Areas*, Princeton, 1960.

[2] The data on which this article is based were gathered in Algeria between 1962 and 1964. Thanks are due for a grant from the Wenner-Gren Foundation for Anthropological Research in 1965, which helped materially in the completion of this work.

17

André Adam

The industrial development of Morocco, which began when the protectorate was established in 1912, has caused a considerable increase in urban population. Cities arose from nothing, like Kenitra (formerly Port Lyautey); others have grown out of all recognition, like Casablanca, which had 20,000 inhabitants in 1907, nearly one million in 1960, and is probably now approaching 1,300,000. In this great city, the economic capital of the country, a large part of its activity is concentrated: the harbor alone handles approximately 75 percent of the tonnage of all Moroccan ports, and industry in Casablanca represents 60 percent of all Moroccan industry, excluding the mines. It is therefore not surprising that Casablanca should absorb a considerable part of the rural exodus in which, during the past half-century, country-dwellers unable to live by agriculture have moved to the cities. Between 1936 and 1952, Casablanca absorbed three-fifths of these emigrants; in 1965, approximately 36,000 people moved there.

This emigration does not affect all Morocco to the same extent. All the cities contribute to the exodus toward Casablanca; but the rural areas which contribute most heavily could roughly be delimited by a triangle of which the apex would be Casablanca, one side the Atlantic coast to the mouth of the Oued Dra, the other a line drawn to the bend of the Oued Dra, and the base the boundary of the Sahara, roughly indicated by the lower reaches of the Dra.

This triangle encompasses both Arabs and Berbers; or rather, Arabic-speakers and Berber-speakers, for the language spoken is the only certain element, ethnic origin being impossible to determine nowadays. It would seem that few Arabs were transformed by Berber influence, whereas many large Berber tribes were subjected to Arab influence in the course of history. Arabic-speakers form the majority in Casablanca, but Berber-speakers constitute a sizable minority: a fairly large-scale survey, conducted in conjunction with the 1952 census, enabled me to estimate it at 20 or 22 percent. This proportion seems especially large in view of the fact that the Berber-speaking region of the triangle, made up of mountainous or subdesertic areas, has a far lower population density than the Arabic-speaking region, which is essentially made up of the Atlantic plains with the most fertile land in all Morocco. This means that emigration is particularly frequent among the Berber, as is only to be expected of a rural population dwelling on unproductive soil.

It should be noted, however, that the triangle of heavy emigration toward Casablanca includes only part of the areas at present occupied by Berbers. The Berbers of Morocco are distributed among three dialectal groups: *zenatiya*, chiefly spoken in the Rif and the Berber-speaking enclaves of eastern Morocco; *tamazight*, spoken by the Imazighen or Beraber, largely pastoral tribes of the Middle Atlas and the central and eastern High Atlas; lastly, *tachelhit*, the language of the Shleuh, who inhabit the western High Atlas, the Anti-Atlas and the plains or valleys of southwestern Morocco.

There are few representatives of the first two groups in Casablanca. Most of the Riffians, before independence, were cut off from the rest of the country by the inter-zone boundary, as if by a national frontier. If they emigrated at all, it was to Tangier or Tetuan. Their chief sources of income were smuggling across the border, serving in the Spanish army, and seasonal labor in Algeria. Independence did away with all three; but the disappearance of the boundary-line enabled them to seek employment in the former Southern Zone. They went first to the nearest cities, Oujda, Fes, Meknes but they are beginning to emigrate to Casablanca.

The Imazighen rarely emigrate. They seem to have achieved a relatively satisfactory balance between demography and natural resources. Pastoral economy remains prosperous, in spite of the extension of cultivated land and the increasing difficulty of traveling with the flocks. The birth rate seems much lower than that of the country as a whole for obscure reasons seemingly of a psycho-sociological nature.[1] Surplus population is absorbed by the nearby cities, Fes, Meknes, even Kenitra, and by the mines of the region. Statistics for Casablanca list them under 'miscellaneous'.

The Shleuh are a different matter altogether. They have been sedentary for a long time, although they occasionally raise sheep, especially in the western High Atlas. However, agriculture is difficult for them; although the High Atlas receives adequate rainfall, soil is scarce, because of the mountainous terrain; the Anti-Atlas and the adjacent plains, close to the Sahara, often suffer from drought. The birth rate is high. Islam in these regions has long had a puritanical cast; the Almoravid and Almohad religious reform movements were born here in the Middle Ages, and although they disagreed violently over dogma, they both involved an austere moral code. Family structures today remain markedly patrilineal and patriarchal. This is why 24·7 percent of the 60,307 heads of households in Casablanca included in my 1952 survey were born in the *tachelhit* zone.[2]

It should be noted that there are two distinct groups among these Berber-speakers: black and white. The black men cultivate the Dra and Bani palm-groves; they are somewhat contemptuously termed *haratin*, the plural of *hartani*,[3] by the white men, and in Casablanca and the rest of the country, they are called *sahrawa* or *drawa*. By contrast the white men of the area call themselves *harrar*, 'free men'. The Haratin were not slaves, but they always paid tribute to Arab or Berber nomads, who granted them their protection in return; and the aristocrats of the desert considered that men who paid tribute were not really free.

[1] The women of these tribes have long enjoyed greater freedom by far than those of other Berber tribes. This may be linked to a degree of birth control. The Moroccan government chose to conduct its first 'pilot experiment' in birth control in this region; no doubt because it anticipated less opposition there than elsewhere.

[2] There are a number of Arabic-speaking enclaves in the area, especially in the valley of the Oued Sous. This helps to explain why the proportion of Berber-speakers in Casablanca has been evaluated at only 20 or 22 percent.

[3] This word has sometimes been linked with the Arabic root *hrt* ('to plough'); it would seem, however, that it derives from the Berber adjective *ahardan* ('black').

Little is known about the origin of these people. Some of them are the descendants of slaves captured by nomads south of the Sahara, and made to work in the oases. It is likely, however, that most of them are the descendants of black populations which once lived in the Sahara, and were driven to the north or to the south by increasingly desertic conditions; those same people whom the author of the well-known *Hannon's Journey* encountered at the mouth of the Dra, and called 'Ethiopians'. Even today, their physical type differs from that of the other Blacks, the descendants of sub-Saharan slaves.[1]

Of course, these men cannot, properly speaking, be considered Berbers. We do not know when or how they adopted the Berber language. Indeed, some of them came under Arab influence instead. Their behavior differs from that of the white Berbers; and although they share the same language, the Haratin are not considered equals or brethren. Muslims are not inclined to racial prejudice; furthermore, the Haratin are modest people, content with a subordinate position and unlikely to provoke strong antagonism; they do not need to be put in their place, for they keep to it of their own accord. Nevertheless, the amused smile with which white Berbers respond to the word *Haratin* is full of condescension. Although they are numerous in Casablanca (10% out of the 24·7% mentioned earlier), I shall leave them aside[2] and deal only with white Berbers.

The emigration of Moroccan peasants takes various forms. The vast majority practice permanent family emigration, the most common form throughout the world. A man leaves home with his wife and children—emigration almost always means breaking up the extended family—and returns home only on temporary visits, if at all. First-generation emigrants maintain close economic and emotional ties with their birthplace. The second generation, however, usually makes the break final; I have more than once met youths in Casablanca who did not know where their father was born. This is the type of emigration practiced by most Arabic-speakers, even though their tribe of origin is often fairly close to the city, thus making frequent visit possible.

The Berbers have long practiced, and sometimes still practice, temporary masculine emigration: a man departs alone, leaving wife and children in the village, and returns after a certain length of time—periods of absence were longer in the past, when travel was slow and costly—being meanwhile replaced by a brother or cousin in his shop or occupation.[3]

This type of emigration—found not only among the Shleuh, but also among

[1] See, on this subject, a good discussion by Gabriel Camps, 'Recherches sur les origines des cultivateurs noirs du Sahara', in *Revue de l'occident musulman et de la Méditerranée*, Aix-en-Provence, 1. semestre 1970, No. 7.

[2] I have written a paper on the subject, 'Les Sahariens à Casablanca', in *Le Sahara, Rapports et contacts humains. Colloque organisé par la Faculté des Lettres d'Aix-en-Provence*. Publication des Annales de la Faculté des Lettres, Aix-en-Provence, 1967, pp. 169–92.

[3] The *drawa* sometimes practiced an intermediate form of emigration, both family and temporary; a man would leave, with his wife and children, when drought made it impossible for him to till his plot of land, but he would return as soon as rain fell, the *oued* began to flow again, or the level of the well rose, enabling him to cultivate the land with some hope of harvest.

the Kabyles and Mozabites, also Berbers—seems to be linked to specific social and judicial structures. That a man should feel able to leave his wife and children behind, implies the existence of an extended domestic family which encompasses individual households, so that his departure, even though felt as a loss, does not affect his family's economic and social condition. Indeed, the man who emigrates does not do so on his own initiative, in the sole interest of his family in the narrow sense of the word; he is the emissary of the family group as a whole, which sends him afar in order to compensate for the temporary or permanent inadequacy of family resources. In southern Morocco, after a few years' drought, grain reserves are exhausted. How are the vital supplementary resources to be obtained? There is no employment to be had in an egalitarian society where everyone lives off the same barren land, within the same economic system. The only solution is to emigrate to the cities, the mining centers or the large shipyards, where money can be earned by trade or wage-labor. That the individual who emigrates is a delegate of the family group, is shown by the fact that on his return, a brother or cousin will leave in his stead.

Why has this type of emigration never, or rarely, been practiced by Arabic-speaking peoples? Obviously, language has nothing to do with it. One must remember that until recently, Berbers differed from other Moroccans not only by their language, but also by their judicial system. Most of them continued to observe the old customary law, which had inevitably been more or less influenced by Koranic law, but still differed from it on several points: especially with respect to inheritance. The Koran, it will be recalled, contrary to Arab law, allows women to inherit, although their portion is restricted to half that of a male heir. Berber custom, adhering to the spirit of the patrilineal system, denies women this right, for in leaving their family for another, as marriage requires, they would alienate part of the family inheritance, which is intolerable within the logic of the system. The Imazighen have stood firm on this point: women are debarred from inheritance. The Shleuh, more devout, and influenced to a greater extent by the Sharia, have accepted the principle of female inheritance, but have devised all manner of legal subterfuges to annul its effect, thus, in practice, keeping the entire patrimony within the male lineage. This is not the case among Arabs, or those subject to Arab influence, who have long observed Koranic law; there, female inheritance divides or at least breaks into the patrimony in each generation.[1]

In order to maintain its solidarity, the extended family requires an economic substratum: an undivided patrimony. If it is divided up, ties between conjugal families are necessarily weakened, and they tend to become autonomous. This is what has happened among the Arabic-speaking tribes. Berber-speakers, on the other hand, by keeping their inheritance intact, have preserved the extended family. Of course, this is only a hypothesis; but it seems to me more likely than explanation by some 'tendency' or other, the scientific value of which is doubtful.

[1] The Arabs dislike this process no less than the Berbers. For several centuries, they have attempted to halt it or at least slow it down by various practices such as joint tenure of inheritance (often during several generations) or marriage with the father's brother's daughter, which has the advantage of doing away with the problem.

The importance of keeping the patrimony intact is illustrated by the motives which first led Shleuh peasants to emigrate: their purpose was often to acquire the means to recover a part of the patrimony temporarily surrendered in adversity. Temporarily only; for the Shleuh rarely consent to out-and-out sale, at least in the case of land; they perform *rahen* (or *rahnia*), sale with privilege of repurchase, which allows the seller to buy back his land when he is in a position to do so. Sale was often the only expeditious way to obtain cash, which was then scarce in rural Morocco; and emigration was the only way to recover that part of the patrimony which had been alienated out of need. To resign oneself to its loss would have been a dishonor.

Within this form of temporary emigration practiced by the Shleuh, a further distinction must be made between trade and wage-labor.

Like the Djerbans in Tunisia and the Mozabites in Algeria, the Soussi (*Swasa* in Arabic) have a quasi-monopoly of the grocery trade in the cities of northern Morocco.[1] Although one finds grocers from various tribes, including, of course, non-Berber tribes, an impressive number of shops are run by Shleuh belonging to a few specific tribes of the Anti-Atlas: those situated immediately north and south of the highest range of mountains, the Jbel Lkest: Ait Souab, Ida ou Gnidif, Ait Mzal, Ida ou Ktir, Ait Abdallah to the north, Ammeln, Igounan, Amanouz and Tasserirt to the south. Shopkeepers are to be found elsewhere; here, almost all the emigrants are shopkeepers.

There has been speculation on the reason for this phenomenon. It seems difficult to attribute it to some special 'vocation'. In Balzac's Paris, water-carriers and coal-merchants were almost all from Auvergne, chimney-sweeps almost all from Savoie: it has never been suggested that they possessed a specific 'gift' for these occupations. Some observers have noted that according to tradition, there were once large Jewish communities in this area, which were subjected to persecutions leading to a large number of forced conversions. It is true that neighboring tribes are inclined to call men from the trading tribes 'Jews', but envy caused by their success is probably a contributing factor in this case. Here again, I am reluctant to explain a social phenomenon by something called 'hereditary aptitude'; the Jews were tradesmen (and artisans: this is often forgotten, although they were in fact more numerous than tradesmen) because they were denied the right to own land; where this was granted (in certain valleys of the High Atlas, for instance among the Ait Bougmez) Jews became farmers. Even supposing that they had Jewish ancestors, the Shleuh tradesmen of the Anti-Atlas had been farmers for generations; it is difficult to imagine a 'gift for trade' which remains dormant for a century or two, then suddenly to reappear. Such explanations are based on pure imagination; not on sociology or psychology.

In a more scientific vein, reference has been made to the social conditions

---

[1] For the French, *Sous* denotes the valley of the *oued* of the same name, which flows into the Atlantic a little to the south of Agadir. For Moroccans, however, the term designates Shleuh country as a whole; the expression *Sus el-aqça* ('the Far Sous') is often used to refer to the Anti-Atlas.

prevalent in the tribes concerned at the time when emigration began.[1] Neighboring tribes were all governed by near-feudal chiefs, who appropriated a considerable part of the money sent home by emigrants; whereas the Ammeln, for instance, had been able to avoid the emergence of personal power, which was common at that time among the Berbers of southwestern Morocco, and to retain the old *jemaa*, which ensured a minimum of order and justice. It is suggested that the Ammeln were therefore able to accumulate capital freely, whereas their neighbors could not. This is an ingenious theory, but it is contradicted by fact. Although the Ammeln are the main 'grocer tribe', they are not alone, and many of the others were under the control of rapacious *murabitin* or an *amghar*; the Ammeln themselves paid tribute to Merebbi Rebbo, brother of El-Hiba, who had settled in the Kerdous after the failure of the 'Blue Sultan' in 1912.

One could also—as has been done—attempt a Weberian interpretation of the *tabeqqalt*,[2] basing oneself on the puritanism of the Ammeln and their neighbors, and comparing it with that of the Mozabites and Djerbans, also Berbers who emigrate to the cities of the north, in Algeria and Tunisia, and have a near-monopoly of the grocery trade there. However, the Mozabites, and some of the Djerbans, are Ibadite Kharijites, that is to say Muslim heretics, which is not the case of the Shleuh; there were once Kharijites in Morocco, but they all disappeared a long time ago. All Moroccan Muslims are Sunnites, and moreover of the Melikite rite. True, the Shleuh are fairly devout, more so than the Imazighen at any rate, and there are so many *tolba* (Koranic scholars) among them that their training has been termed in jest the national industry of the Sous. But this applies to tribes other than those which specialize in trade, and is therefore not an adequate explanation.

Granted, the latter tribes are more stringently puritan, especially with regard to women, who are strictly veiled and cloistered in the manner of the traditionalist city-dwellers. It would seem, however, that this is a consequence of emigration and trade, not a cause: just as the Swasa, grown wealthy, copy the urban middle classes' housing conditions and way of life, they copy their attitude toward women—with a certain time lag, since while the Shleuh are veiling their women, the Westernized bourgeoisie are unveiling theirs.

In *Le Cousin Pons*, Balzac draws a parallel between 'the Jews, the Normands, the Auvergnats and the Savoyards; these four races have the same instincts, they grow rich in the same way. Spend nothing, make a small profit, and pile interest upon profits—that is their charter'. Leaving aside the Jews, who constitute a different problem, and the words 'race' and 'instinct', which denote an outworn biological determinism, the common trait of Normands, Auvergnats and Savoyards is that they are all peasants; and the latter two farm barren rocky soil, as do the Shleuh of the Anti-Atlas. The qualities required for survival in such circumstances—industry, frugality, thrift, parsimony—are also highly

---

[1] C. Marquez, 'Les Épiciers chleuhs et leur diffusion dans les villes du Maroc', *Bulletin économique du Maroc*, Rabat, July 1935.

[2] The trade of a *beqqal*: this term, used exclusively in Morocco, denotes the 'grease-merchant' as opposed to the *attar* or spice-merchant, *épicier* in the strict sense of the word.

successful in urban activities, whether industrial or commercial. In the mines of Morocco, the miners who work hardest, but also, through production bonuses, receive the highest salaries, are often Berbers, especially from the Anti-Atlas.

Of course, this does not explain why, within the Anti-Atlas region, some tribes provide miners or waiters, and others tradesmen. This further problem requires only the introduction of two factors, one of which is determined by chance: the success of a few tribesmen, and traditional tribal solidarity. We shall never penetrate the motives of the first ones (Ammeln, apparently) to attempt commerce. Their success spread, not only by imitation or contagion (it should not be forgotten that these are social phenomena, even though sociologists disapprove of them . . .), but also by virtue of the Berber individual's integration into the concentric circles of the domestic family, the clan (*ikhs* or *afus*), the village and the *taqbilt*.

This process also explains the different forms of occupational and geographical specialization of the various tribes: the Ammeln are usually grocers, the Ait Souab greengrocers, the Ait Tasserirt tobacconists, the Ait Mzal carriers;[1] the Ait Abdallah are to be found chiefly in Salé, Meknes and Fes, the Igounan in Marrakesh, the Ait Tasserirt in Rabat, and the Ammeln in Casablanca, Tangiers and Larache. Casablanca, however, is so large that it offers opportunities for everyone, and members of all tribes are to be found there. To give some idea of the number of emigrants: in 1950, the Ammeln alone already had 1,290 tradesmen in Casablanca and 363 in Tangiers, to mention only their main centers of activity.

The same phenomena of contagion and solidarity explain the specialization of emigrant workers, and the presence in some factories of what Robert Montagne has termed tribal 'swarms'. The Compagnie Sucrière Marocaine in Casablanca employed for some time a large number of Ait Ba Amran workers (from the former Spanish enclave of Ifni); not, obviously, because this tribe had a particular vocation for sugar production, but because a few Ait Ba Amran whose services were appreciated used their credit with the company to have relatives and fellow-tribesmen taken on.

It is essential here to remember the role of temporary emigration. A man returning to his home will not thereby deprive the family group of resources, if he arranges to be replaced by a brother or cousin. Furthermore, in a developing society where would-be workers largely outnumber available jobs, it is risky to give up one's position. The risk disappears if one is replaced by an *alter ego* who will return the favor when he leaves. This particular type of turnover is quite the contrary of instability. European manufacturers in Morocco soon understood this, and since Shleuh workers had a good reputation ('hard-working, docile and non-political', the last only up to a certain period), they willingly took them on. Individuals often changed, but the turnover regularly brought back the same faces.

---

[1] Towards the end of the last century, they were caravaneers, and could travel safely among the *siba* tribes by paying the *zettata*, a form of insurance. Since the Protectorate, they have acquired buses and trucks, and now enjoy a quasi-monopoly of transport between the Sous and the big cities of the North.

A specific institution of Moroccan industry favored this recruitment by 'swarms': the *caporal*, or 'corporal'. This term (*kobran* is its Arabic version) designated, under the Protectorate, a sort of foreman's assistant. The foreman was always a European, the *caporal* always a Moroccan; since the foreman often did not speak Arabic, let alone Berber, the *caporal* was usually made responsible for relations with the workers outside the purely technical sphere. He played an especially important part in hiring new workers. Since jobs were rare, one can easily imagine the consequent abuses of power: some *kobran* levied not only a 'hiring fee', but also a tax on each wage packet; workers who refused to comply would be dismissed on some pretext or other. Among the Shleuh, the abuse— if it can be so termed—was of a different nature: each *caporal* hired, first the men of his family, then those of his clan, then those of his tribe. The foreman had no cause for complaint; the work team was more cohesive, and discipline was easier. When certain large concerns, such as the mining companies, were faced with a rapid increase of production after World War II, they systematically sought to recruit workers among the tribes of the Sous which had already provided them with 'swarms'.

This preferential recruitment of Berbers (which, I hasten to add, was by no means a general rule) has sometimes been ascribed to French 'Berberophilia', to the myth of the 'good Berber' as opposed to the 'bad Arab' held responsible for all the Protectorate's difficulties. True, after the phase of military pacification, there was a period during which the Berbers did not cause the French any serious political problems. But this was true of the rural population in general, not only of the Berbers; nationalism was initially an urban phenomenon, and did not affect the rural areas until the colonial period was drawing to an end. Casablanca, city of new urban dwellers, became the capital of nationalism at a fairly late date; before 1952, Fes held this position.

The 'Berber policy' is one thing; hiring policy in industry is another. Employers, and still more foremen, were practical people (although no more free of prejudice than other Frenchmen), and their preference for Berber workers was based on practical motives. Quite apart from their involvement in politics (which in fact did not cause any trouble until the last years of the Protectorate), many Arab workers were extremely unstable; they would work for a few days, then disappear. Why? There are many plausible reasons: aversion to regular work at fixed hours; a taste for variety; the illusion that one will be better off elsewhere; physical deficiencies due to malnutrition, which make sustained effort difficult; above all, the absense of needs, which meant that a man who had earned a small sum of money preferred to rest, rather than continue working.

True, this lack of stability satisfied a few short-sighted small employers: it enabled them to avoid such extras as length-of-service bonuses, and sometimes even the legal minimum wage. But well-established firms, concerned with maintaining production levels, preferred a stable work force; and the Shleuh, who were glad to spend their two years' exile in one place, provided this. Furthermore, as delegates of an extended family group which depended on them for support, their life remained centered on their home, and they considered their work as a sort of precious lode, to be exploited as intensively as possible during their stay. They therefore sought out the most difficult tasks, because they were better paid, and tried to supplement their wages with all the production bonuses offered by their employers.

The above analysis indicates the characteristics of temporary emigration, and its sociological background. It should be added that temporary emigration does not explain everything, and that the Berbers are not the only exception to the characteristic instability of Moroccan labor. Among the Arabic-speakers—or rather, since language is irrelevant in this context, among permanent emigrants to the city—there are some who adapt themselves to the conditions of industrial labor quite as well as the Shleuh. They usually come from tribes which have long been sedentary, either Arabs or Berbers having undergone Arab influence. It would seem that nomads, or former nomads still unused to sedentary life, find it much more difficult to come to terms with industrial activity. It is not easy to make a modern factory worker out of a peasant accustomed to a traditional agricultural system: even such basic mental categories as space and time must be radically transformed in the process. But at least the farmer, even if the only tool he knows is the hoe, is already *homo faber*; by his work, he acts upon a substance, the soil, in order to obtain that which it would not produce spontaneously. The nomad who travels with his flocks can only take what the land offers. When one stretch of pasture-land is exhausted, he simply moves on elsewhere. Caring for his flock takes up little of his time, and he has leisure for dreaming. It is not surprising that the pastoral life has evolved a specific poetic *genre*, the eclogue, whereas there is none for farmers: the latter have no time to dream. It is easy to understand that a man accustomed to a nomadic way of life should find it extremely difficult to conform to the fixed schedules, sustained effort and prolonged concentration required for industrial work.

The nomad finds stability more difficult than the sedentary farmer; economy, too, is more of a novelty for him. Unlike the farmer, the shepherd cannot practice thrift; the farmer has known for thousands of years how to store grain in silos, but meat could not be preserved before the invention of industrial cold storage.[1] Traditionally, the shepherd feasted during a good year, and could only tighten his belt when drought decimated the flock. Hence one of the best-known traits of Bedouin custom, extreme munificence, which does not stem from pride alone; for what better use to make of God's gifts when they are plentiful, than to squander them lavishly, since they cannot be set aside for the future?

The spirit of economy, more natural to sedentary peoples, no doubt explains the vocation and success of those small capitalists, the Soussi shopkeepers. I also believe that it contributes at least as much as the nature of temporary emigration to the Shleuh worker's desire to earn as much as possible; whereas the former nomad, accustomed to making immediate use of what he has, be it much or little, is less inclined to economic rationality, which implies both calculation and the emergence of needs more pressing than the desire for leisure. The shepherd lives in the present, and does not attempt to foresee the future, since he cannot provide for it. The farmer thinks of the future, since he can

[1] If not meat, men have long known how to preserve fodder; but this is irrelevant to extensive sheep-farming, almost the only form known to Moroccan shepherds.

prepare for it and take precautions against possible mishaps; this attitude contains the seeds of 'capitalist enterprise', but also of the mechanism of economic development, which increases production by needs and needs by production.

The stage of temporary emigration is now over, or soon will be. Before moving on to the second stage, however, let us consider the life of emigrant Berbers and some of the problems they face.

While working extremely hard, during a limited period of time, to supplement or restore the family economy, the Shleuh lead an incredibly frugal life. They keep their personal expenses to a minimum, in order to save as much money as possible to send home. For a long time, Soussi shopkeepers had no residence: they lived in their shop, sleeping on a mat kept under the counter during the day. They ate their customers' leavings, wilted vegetables or spoiled tinned food they could no longer sell. City-dwellers tend to be sarcastic about what they term Soussi avarice: as in the story of three brothers who ran a shop together and lived there day and night; they had only one pair of shoes between them, for they went out only one at a time.

Workers will crowd, as many as possible, into one room, in order to pay the least rent possible. They too eat badly. After the war, when rationing was still being enforced in Morocco, a Casablanca factory-owner told me that while he was greatly pleased with his Shleuh workers, he felt that they spent too little on food, which lowered their productivity. He had offered to provide them with a meal, the extremely low price of which would be deducted from their wages. They refused his offer, and insisted on being paid their entire salary in cash, maintaining that they were free to use their money as they liked, and that it was none of their employer's business.

The way of life of these bachelors (ruwwasa), or young men living as bachelors, inevitably created sexual problems, for which continence could only exceptionally provide a solution. Of course, the city's many prostitutes, professional or occasional, offered the easiest way out; but it was an expensive way. Muslim law provided some prosperous shopkeepers with another possibility, more consonant with morality and economic rationality: in addition to the wife they had left at home (Berbers are generally monogamous), they took another, whom they repudiated when they returned to the village, or who was willing to stay behind in town during their brief if frequent visits to the village. This second wife sometimes knew about the first wife, but the reverse was never true; and male solidarity could be relied upon to conceal the matter from the Berber wife. This system had two advantages over resorting to prostitutes: it did not infringe God's law, and it provided a woman to keep house for the exile. It sometimes had disadvantages as well, as in the case of the Soussi who was led to ruin by marrying a Fasiya, who made him pay heavily for the honor of having married a city-dweller.

Their meager resources and desire to economize led some Shleuh workers to create an original institution: the garsuna.[1] This woman, usually widowed or

[1] Feminine form of garsun, from the French garçon (as in garçon de café or garçon de restaurant).

divorced, kept house for several *ruwwasa*, and satisfied their other needs. The sharing of expenses, and the twofold role of the *garsuna*, made the institution a highly profitable one, if somewhat at odds with traditional morality. One might think that it would give rise to quarrels, jealousy and other disturbances; apparently this was not the case. The management of the Khouribga phosphate mines, where the institution flourished, tolerated it in their housing centers, considering that all in all, it provided the least pernicious solution to an almost insoluble problem. A puritanical governor suppressed the *garsuna*; one cannot tell whether public order, as well as morality, profited thereby.

Although they do not always belong to the same tribe, Shleuh shopkeepers and workers do not form separate groups; they are solidary. First of all, the shopkeeper gives credit; the worker buys what he needs every evening, and pays his debts on Saturday night, when he has received his weekly wages. There are shopkeepers who can only write figures; they have a drawer full of slips of paper each bearing a column of figures, but they can put a face to each one, if not a name. The shopkeeper also serves as letter-box, bank and employment agency. If he is not illiterate, he will write letters for the workers, or read out those which are sent to his shop because he is the only one to have a fixed address. He often holds the worker's savings in trust, and even takes them to his family when he travels to the village. The post-offices of Sous, like those of Kabylia, receive large sums of money-orders; but these represent only a small part of the total amount conveyed there. The Shleuh especially have always trusted messengers, known to them personally, more than the impersonal administrative channels. I have seen travelers arrive in Sous literally padded with bank-notes; the next day, there was a queue in front of their house, waiting for the money to be distributed. Because he comes from the same area, the shop-keeper is often asked to find employment, especially domestic employment in the European quarters; the housewives with whom he deals often ask him to find them a cook or a gardener. Lastly, in the evenings, after work, his shop serves as a meeting-place, where workers can talk about home, obtain news from those who have just been there, and entrust messages to those who are about to go there; verbal messages, far more precise and detailed than if they were consigned to paper in a foreign tongue, Arabic or French, and in the stilted style of the uneducated.

Of course, the solidarity characteristic of these relations also governs the organization of trade. The shop, whether large or small, belongs neither to an individual, nor to a company, but to a family; all the male members of the family who work there have a share in it. The commercial concern is thus an extension of the family's patrimony. However, the two do not merge completely; one often finds in the shop, not as co-owners but as managers or employees, uterine kinsmen who are excluded from the family patrimony.

Some Shleuh tradesmen who 'started small' have acquired a further two, three or more shops; a few own over a hundred. The owner of several shops runs one of them himself. For the others, two possibilities are open to him: he can either rent them by the month to an *agellas*, who pays all the expenses and keeps all the profits, or—as is more frequently done—entrust them to a tenant-manager with whom profits are equally shared, a sort of transposition of the *métayage* system from rural to urban life. Solidarity also governs the choice of these tenant-managers, who are taken from within the *afus*, the village or the *taqbilt*. Since saturation-point was fairly quickly reached, other groups were called upon; thus interest in trade slowly spread from the main founding tribes, Ammeln, Ida ou Gnidif, to their neighbors.

I have kept for the last the most remarkable token of solidarity among Shleuh tradesmen. In the bankruptcy register of the Casablanca law-courts, there is not a single Soussi shopkeeper. A few may have had difficulties, but the clan always intervenes in time to save them, if necessary by placing them under the supervision of someone more capable.

Since independence, and especially during the 'sixties, Berber emigration to Casablanca has changed a great deal. It has not decreased,[1] but its nature has been transformed. Although temporary masculine emigration has not entirely vanished, permanent—hence family—emigration has become more and more frequent. The reasons for this change differ slightly, according to whether one considers shopkeepers or workers.

One can still find the small *beqqal* who lives on scraps and sleeps in his shops, but he is a relic of a former era. The Soussi's unrelenting hard work and frugality have borne fruit. Middle-sized and large commercial concerns are as frequent as small ones. Not only do some own a large number of shops, a Soussi version of the 'chain store'; others have become wholesalers. In the vicinity of the Place des Alliés in Casablanca, there are unprepossessing little shops which are in fact the anterooms of huge warehouses, supplying the thousands of Shleuh shopkeepers of the city and province.

Not content with reigning over the grocery trade, the Berbers attacked the Fassi monopoly over the fabric trade. The Ammeln of Tangiers started this trend before World War II. In Casablanca, which was for a long time the exclusive preserve of the large merchants from Fes, many Soussi entered the fabric trade; first as retailers, then as wholesalers, and not without success: in 1964 they owned most of the shops in the Kissaria Menjra and 25 percent of the Kissaria Haffari, two of the largest centers of the textile trade in the New Medina of Casablanca.

After independence—and especially since 1960—many European shopkeepers left Morocco, their customers, especially European, having greatly dwindled in number. They were usually replaced by Soussi. The collective nature of their concerns, the clan and tribal solidarity between them, enabled them to take over European businesses. One need scarcely add that the operation was highly profitable, since a man who is known to be obliged to sell is in no position to ask a high price. Between 1 January 1963 and 31 March 1964,

---

[1] Emigration since 1960 cannot be evaluated until the results of the 1970 census are known. I do know, however, that whereas there were about 51,600 emigrants from the Tiznit Territory (including the Anti-Atlas) between 1936 and 1952, their number is estimated at 96,500 for the period between 1952 and 1960. As to the proportion emigrating to Casablanca, one can derive some idea of it from the fact that in 1949, the Agadir authorities estimated that 14,200 male emigrants out of a total of 34,500, or 41 percent, had gone to Casablanca.

878 Moroccans, of whom 765 were Muslims, were entered in the Casablanca commercial register; judging by birth-place, 42 percent of the Muslims were Shleuh. During that period, the number of Europeans leaving the country rose.

Nowadays, some of the most important businessmen in Casablanca are Soussi. Some of them have already been granted the ultimate seal of commercial success: presidency of the Chamber of Commerce. What importance do these full-blown capitalists attach to the family plot of land on the stony slopes of the Anti-Atlas? From the sentimental point of view, undoubtedly, a great deal. But from an economic point of view? As early as the 'forties, black-market profits were being invested in palm-groves in the Bani oases, or in fields in the *ma ader* (flood-lands) of the Dra. During the past fifteen years, all available funds have been invested in apartment buildings in Casablanca or farms in the Chaouia, both more profitable than the arid land of the far south.

In this context, one can no longer speak of temporary emigration. Shop-keepers will only return to their place of birth on holiday, as it were, just as a Paris businessman will spend Christmas or part of August in the family dwelling in Auvergne or Normandy. The houses of the 'grocers' villages' of the Anti-Atlas are transformed into fully-equipped holiday villas. Even so, a Place des Alliés wholesaler, a native of Tafraout, told me once that he had not been home for eight years; he had been too busy. Instead, he sent his wife and children, on the occasion of the chief Muslim holidays. At such times, there are twice or thrice as many buses as usual leaving Casablanca, and cars laden with families and gifts for relatives travel the narrow winding roads of the Anti-Atlas.

Soussi grocers no longer live in their shops. The smaller shop-keeper rents a modest apartment in the neighborhood; the wealthier one buys a villa in the more fashionable quarters. Their wives and children live with them. This is no novelty; in 1951, Robert Montagne indicated that 20 percent of Ammeln emigrants took their wives with them, and that the proportion rose to 40 percent in the vicinity of Tafraout. Nowadays the percentage is undoubtedly much higher. The problem of children's education has played an important part in this development.

In earlier days, a man's son would join him in his shop at a fairly early age, to learn the business and generally be of use. They sometimes spent a short time, no more than three years, at the neighborhood school, in order to learn the rudiments of reading, writing, and above all arithmetic. Those who prospered soon realized that this sketchy education was inadequate in a modern economy. These self-made men were too intelligent not to be conscious of their deficiencies, and too ambitious not to want to give their heirs a better chance. The chief rivals of the Soussi in the commercial world of Casablanca are the Fassi. The Fassi's strength, however, is not merely financial: by alliance or kinship, they have access to important posts in the civil service, or even in the government. The reason is that the bourgeoisie of Fes was the first to send its sons, and later its daughters, to the primary and secondary schools established by Lyautey. The Shleuh are behind the times in this respect. The more far-seeing know that only education will enable them to catch up; already, many of their sons are attending the Casablanca *lycées*.

Among the workers, the causes of change are necessarily different, although not radically so.

Turnover rates in Moroccan factories have markedly decreased during the past fifteen years. For various reasons, one of which is undoubtedly the rise in unemployment, new jobs are not created at a rate sufficient to keep up with, let alone outstrip, the rapid growth of population. A man lucky enough to be employed, however modestly, would be most unwise to leave; workers are therefore much more stable than before. However, this explanation seems inadequate. After all, twenty years ago, it was no less risky for a Moroccan worker to give up his job; yet thousands did so every day. If they no longer do so, the reason must be that they have greater needs. Workers are no longer content with day-to-day subsistence for themselves and their families; they want to be adequately housed, to be free from hunger, to educate their children, etc. Only stable employment will make this possible. Those who are not so employed, through ill-luck or their own fault, sink into the sub-proletariat of the slums and the shanty-towns, where they subsist through occasional menial labor and the supplies distributed by the government. This class of unfortunates, long resigned to its fate, is now far less inclined to accept it, as was shown by the outburst of March 1965, caused by a sudden rise in unemployment.

Temporary emigrants, who paradoxically were highly stable in spite of an abnormally high turnover during the 'fifties, no longer dare to leave their jobs; competition is so fierce that they would stand little chance of recovering them. A *caporal* of one's own tribe is no longer a sufficient guarantee; there are increasing numbers of Moroccan foremen, and few of them are Shleuh, because of Shleuh educational backwardness. Blood ties still play a part in hiring practice, but they no longer favor the Berbers; the post-war 'swarms' have all gradually disbanded.

For tradesmen, the relative importance of emigrant earnings in the family economy has increased to such an extent that revenue from the land is negligible; much the same is true for workers. Here we approach the problem of the economic dualism characteristic of developing countries: traditional subsistence agriculture coexists with a modern economy which provides standards of living which may seem low in relation to more advanced countries, but are incommensurately higher than traditional levels. Fifteen years ago, a worker in the mines of eastern Morocco could earn in one month the equivalent of his yearly income as a *khammes* (one-fifth tenant-farmer) tilling the arid soil of the same region;[1] and the soil of the Anti-Atlas is no better. Since family life, and a decent existence according to changing norms, require emigration and steady employment, it is not at all surprising that temporary masculine emigration should have yielded to permanent family emigration.

Nowadays, the Soussi shopkeeper dreams of sending his son to the Ecole Supérieure de Commerce; the Shleuh worker dreams of sending his to the Ecole Industrielle or technical school, which is not possible in the Anti-Atlas. He knows that his earnings as an unskilled worker, however relatively high they may seem, will always be less than those of a skilled worker, let alone of a technician; and

[1] See Jean-Paul Trystram, *L'Ouvrier mineur au Maroc*, Paris, 1957.

that the latter, still scarce on the employment market, are often overpaid and need not fear unemployment. Economic calculation appears when standards of living rise and employment is more stable; Shleuh workers, who have long been the least unstable, and often the most hard-working and thrifty, were not slow to reflect on the future.

Changes in modes of emigration evoke two types of problem. The first has to do with the Berbers' adjustment to modern urban society; the second, with their integration to society as a whole, of which they would seem to constitute a marginal element.

We have noted that European employers and foremen showed a marked preference for Shleuh workers. This preference was due chiefly to their moral qualities: stability, diligence, docility. Not that the Shleuh were better than others; but temporary emigration had spared them the dismantling of traditional structures which affected permanent emigrants. The latter were suddenly taken from their traditional social environment, and exposed without adequate preparation to the temptations of individualism. The Shleuh, on the other hand, being merely 'on loan' to the city for a limited time, remained part of their traditional milieu, and continued to adhere to the values instilled by custom and education. Being uprooted was not so dangerous for them, as for the others.

This very fact, however, set limits to their adaptation to modern life. No doubt this adaptation can take place only after a breakdown of traditional structures, with all the consequences that entails. The old must die, that the new may be born. In spite of all their qualities, Shleuh workers did not accede to the upper strata of labor, the qualified workers. The type of emigration they practiced meant that they lacked the necessary training and experience; this elite could not include part-time city-dwellers.

Merchants, too, were successful only within a traditional field: the bourgeoisie of Mecca was already active in trade in the days of the Prophet, and the bourgeoisie of Fes, which still maintains its hold on trade, has dynasties dating from the thirteenth century. The problem facing all under-developed countries, unless they have opted for socialism, is that of creating a class of capitalist entrepreneurs similar to those who, for selfish ends but with great efficiency, ensured the industrial development of the West during the eighteenth and nineteenth centuries. The major Fassi merchants, with their abundant capital and social influence, seemed designated to play this part. In fact, however, they did not wish to, or were unable to. With a few rare exceptions, they hesitated to make the long-term investments required by industry, and preferred the short-term speculative investments of commerce, whence they had derived their fortunes.

Would the Soussi compensate for their rivals' inactivity? It seemed likely at one time, when a man of exceptional ability, Lahoussine Demnati, a Berber from the High Atlas, head of several large concerns mostly connected with the mining industry, decided after independence to establish an industrial investment bank. The government, then dominated by the Istiqlal, denied him permission; but most of the many subscriptions already made came from Berber tradesmen and farmers. The official reasons given for this refusal were connected with Demnati's political past: at the time of the national crisis, he had suggested that both French and Moroccan inhabitants be given double nationality. It seems fairly likely, however, that the Fes bourgeoisie, highly influential within the Istiqlal, were opposed to the emergence of a rival financial power in the hands of an active leader who might have endangered their economic and political preeminence.

It is impossible to tell whether this project would have been successful. In any case, the attempt was not renewed. Like the Fassi merchants, the Soussi tradesmen have not yet begun to venture their capital outside the traditional investments—goods, land, buildings, gold, jewels—the only ones they trust. When the State, despite its official liberalism, was obliged to remedy this state of affairs by creating an industrial development bank, financed chiefly by State or foreign capital, 10 percent of the shares were set aside for the local market, in the hope of attracting Moroccan private subscriptions; this was to such an extent a failure that the foreign financial group involved had to buy up the 10 percent. It is difficult to blame the Soussi for abstaining: being new to big business, less well-educated, and strangers to the inner workings of politics and high-level administration, they have excuses the Fassi lack. Now that they are rid of the handicap of temporary emigration, and have grown accustomed to handling large amounts of capital; now that their sons are attending secondary school and university—will they venture into the *terra incognita* of modern industry? Time will show; but it is already late in the day, and history, unlike the postman, does not always ring twice.

The problem of integration to society as a whole does not exist in political terms, at least not if it is taken to refer to a possible Berber separatist movement. Such a movement does not exist now and has never existed in the past. There may be a Kurdistan, but there is no 'Berberistan', whether in Morocco or in Algeria. True, there were upheavals among the Berbers of Morocco after independence (in the Rif and Middle Atlas). Ernest Gellner has shown, however, that far from expressing separatist feeling, these stemmed from a desire for acceptance as full-fledged citizens of the unified State.[1]

The Shleuh differ from other Moroccans only by their language; the others do not speak it, whereas all emigrant Shleuh necessarily speak Arabic. Their distinctive judicial system has practically disappeared, now that Moroccan legislation has been unified and Berber customary law abolished. This measure caused some turmoil among the Imazighen, but the Shleuh readily accepted it; indeed, it meant little change for them, since their customs have long been deeply influenced by the Sharia.

However, this common linguistic personality creates a high degree of solidarity among the Shleuh. There are other contributing factors: the persistence of tribal structures, which in Arabic-speaking tribes have been dismantled by migration, intermarriage and the influence of the *makhzan*. The clan or tribal nature of commercial ventures has already been noted: in Casablanca, I know of no instance of partnership between a Shleuh and a non-Shleuh. The 'swarms' of factory workers resulted from the same conditions.

[1] 'Patterns of rural rebellion in Morocco: tribes as minorities', *European Journal of Sociology*, 1962, pp. 297–311. Reprinted as Chapter 19 of this volume (pp. 361–74).

This solidarity extends beyond tribal boundaries, to encompass all those who speak *tachelhit*. This is a form of behavior characteristic of minority groups, who must struggle for recognition and are aware that solidarity is the condition of success. The emotions aroused forty years ago by the 'Berber *dahir*' (which marked the beginning of the nationalist movement in Morocco) should not obscure the fact that the Berbers have long been objects of veiled contempt on the part of city-dwellers, especially the bourgeoisie. Contempt on religious grounds, for Muslims who do not obey Koranic law were not considered true Muslims; contempt, mingled with fear, for those who flouted the authority of the Sultan, commander of the faithful and symbol of national unity; contempt on the part of those who spoke the Arabic language, which is also the language chosen by God to reveal his Truth to mankind, for an idiom considered 'barbaric' and incapable of expressing a culture.[1] This environment, not actively hostile but distinctly unfavorable, could but knit closer together all those who were exposed to it. Clan or *leff* quarrels, so frequent among Berbers in their native land, tend to disappear among emigrants, by virtue of the rule that one's enemy's enemy is one's friend. Furthermore, the Soussi's commercial success, by constituting a threat to the trading empire of the Fes bourgeoisie, necessarily made the latter more hostile, and heightened group solidarity among the Soussi.

This unit, or particularistic feeling, was for a time given religious expression. Not that Shleuh religion deviates in the least from Malekite Sunnite orthodoxy; they have had no inclination to Kharejism for several centuries, unlike the Mozabites or Djerbans. But the religious brotherhoods they favored were not those of Arabic-speakers; even emigrants remained under the moral and religious influence of Sous *murabitin*, and continued to pay them the traditional tithe.

Such is the decline of the brotherhoods and *murabitin* throughout the country, that this form of particularism cannot be considered significant. A more interesting phenomenon is the attitude of southern Berbers toward those modern brotherhoods, political parties. Without going back as far as the Protectorate (which the Shleuh opposed along with the rest of the country, although less forcefully than the Riffians or the Imazighen), one can ascertain the political behavior of emigrants on the basis of the various elections held during the past ten years.[2]

One negative characteristic is worthy of note. There is a Moroccan party, the Mouvement Populaire, which enjoys widespread Berber support;[3] but only in the *tamazight* and Riffian linguistic zones, not among the Shleuh. This shows

[1] The contemptuous etymology of the word 'Berber' invented by an Arab annalist centuries ago (according to which the first Arabs to hear Berber spoken devised the term *ber-ber* in imitation of the incomprehensible babble) is still current in traditional urban milieux.

[2] With the exception of the most recent elections (September 1970), following revision of the 1962 Constitution, the results of which have not yet been analyzed with sufficient precision to serve as a basis for political sociology.

[3] This is no doubt due to the personality of one of its chief leaders, M. Mahjoubi Ahardan, from the Oulmès area (*tamazight* dialect), who addresses the Berbers in their language and never fails to assert that the Berber language should have a place in the national educational system.

once more, if need be, that there is absolutely no 'Berber nationalism' in Morocco, and that the feeling of solidarity which gives rise to particularistic tendencies is restricted to a regional or dialectal context.

It is difficult to determine for whom the Soussi of Casablanca voted in the May 1963 Chambre des Représentants elections: the victory of the UNFP (Left) candidates (six out of ten elected) was determined by heterogeneous constituencies, in which the Shleuh were a minority, and widely scattered at that.[1] The electoral map indicates, however, that support for the UNPF was at its most intense, not only in the industrial cities of the Atlantic seaboard, but also in the province of Agadir, which stretches to the Anti-Atlas valleys; this is precisely the zone which has the greatest number of emigrant Soussi workers and tradesmen. It seems obvious that those resident in Casablanca voted no differently from those at home.

This is not surprising on the part of the workers; but rather more so on the part of the tradesmen. Surely these men, who operate within capitalism like a fish in water, ought to feel some aversion for a political program explicitly based on socialism. Nevertheless, they voted as did their fellow-tribesmen among the workers: witness the 1960 election to the Chambres de Commerce et d'Industrie, where they ensured the victory of the UNPF candidates, often chosen from among them, over the UMCIA candidates, affiliated to the Istiqlal. However, their behavior in the same election three years later, in August 1963, indicates the limits of their political commitment, and their true reasons for supporting the UNFP: the latter having decided not to present any candidates, the Soussi tradesmen voted for the FDIC (Government front) against the Istiqlal. There were even Shleuh among the FDIC candidates who had been elected on the UNFP ticket in 1960. One can but wonder at an opposition which prefers to support the majority, rather than allow the other opposition group to triumph. There is no need to be deeply versed in political science, to understand that the basic and enduring objective of the Soussi tradesmen is to defeat, by whatever means, their rivals the Fes merchants, who support the Istiqlal: if the best way to counter the Istiqlal is to vote for the UNFP, then let us do so by all means, but if the UNFP is abstaining, why not vote FDIC! The workers' motives may be more political; the link between the Istiqlal and the highly influential Fassi *grande bourgeoisie* can in any case but strengthen their opposition. Thus Shleuh solidarity and particularism would seem to be the basic factors determining Shleuh political attitudes.

Futurology is a difficult science, and still far from being an exact one. I shall therefore not attempt to predict the future of the Shleuh of Casablanca and the rest of Morocco. It seems permissible, however, in looking back on the past, to indicate apparent trends.

Temporary masculine emigration, long the prevalent form among the Berbers of southwestern Morocco, enabled them to preserve their distinctive characteris-

[1] The UNFP (Union Nationale des Forces Populaires) resulted from the 1958 split in the Istiqlal; it represents its left wing, and has links with the Union Marocaine du Travail, the large trade union group.

tics: language, judicial system, customs, family and tribal structure. This type of emigration, however, is fast losing ground, for the reasons, chiefly economic, already indicated. If permanent family emigration becomes the rule, it will necessarily, although perhaps slowly, blur these specific traits and weaken their particularistic spirit. The first generation of permanent emigrants will no doubt preserve its character; but what of the second, or the third?

Will children attending primary and secondary school, where they learn classical Arabic and French and speak vernacular Arabic among themselves, still speak Berber? Yes, no doubt, so long as they learn it at their mother's knee; but will their mother always be Berber? At present, all Soussi emigrants return home to find a wife. But what will those born in Casablanca do?

The life of the Shleuh of Casablanca will center less and less on a barren plot of land in the Anti-Atlas and the rustic dwelling of his ancestors, and more and more on his shop or warehouse, the regular job where his services are appreciated, the luxurious or modest home to which he returns every day.

Minority groups struggling to conquer a place in the sun, remain closely-knit. When they have won that place, the ties between them are inevitably loosened. The Shleuh are struggling peacefully, as the Berber rebels of 1957 did violently, not for separatism, but for full participation in Moroccan society as a whole. This undertaking, which in the present case does not have to overcome the formidable barriers of race or religion, is fated to lose its *raison d'être*, and the specific forces which sustained it, as soon as it succeeds. Modern urban and industrial civilization, Morocco's goal, is a fearsome leveling and assimilating force. It crushes even those it rejects. It will not reject the Berbers; their talents guarantee them success. Perhaps, in a few decades, it will be meaningless to speak of the Shleuh of Casablanca, save to the extent that one now speaks of the Auvergnats of Paris, or the Scotsmen of London.

18

Jeremy H. Keenan

**Social Change among the
Tuareg of Ahaggar[1] (Algeria)**

The Tuareg inhabit an extensive area of the Western Sahara and Sudan: that is, in terms of modern state boundaries, the southern part of Algeria, much of Niger, northern Mali and southwestern Libya. They are divisible into seven main groups or political units which comprise a total of between 240,000 and 300,000 people. The two northernmost groups, the Kel[2] Ajjer and Kel Ahaggar, are found almost exclusively within the mountainous massifs of Ajjer and Ahaggar in southern Algeria. The French military census for the years 1948 and 1949 gives a nomadic population of 6,048 and 6,013 respectively, but this census probably includes several slaves and members of certain tribes resident in Niger, for Lhote, using census figures for 1950, gives the number of Ahaggar Tuareg as 4,611.[3] The Algerian census in 1965 did not consider ethnic groupings but one can estimate the number of Tuareg in Ahaggar in 1970 at about 5,000. Throughout the last century the Tuareg population in Ahaggar seems to have risen only slightly, but whereas before the mid-nineteenth century they were the majority group in Ahaggar, they are now a minority due to the influx of sedentary cultivators who settled increasingly in the region after about 1861, and the later growth of Tamanrasset as an administrative and commercial center with the consequent demand for labor which was drawn largely on succeeding generations of *harratin*,[4] ex-slaves, and the increasing Arab population that has accompanied the development of Tamanrasset.

Until the end of the nineteenth century, many of the Tuareg's material needs were obtained by raiding outwards from Ahaggar. Raiding, and the control on caravan routes, were the mainstay of the Tuareg economic organization and the traditional tribal differentiation and social organization were well adapted to it, but the increasing French control of the surrounding regions during the latter part of the nineteenth century limited raiding and necessitated the development of salt caravans to Niger. These caravans, in conjunction with stock-breeding and the use of 'slave' labor, largely formed the basis of the economic organization throughout the French period. But, the loss of the slaves, the restrictions imposed on caravan movements, and the relatively poor grazing facilities over the last eight years, along with Algeria's policy of sedentarization, means that the proportion of true nomads is continually decreasing. Most Ahaggar Tuareg are now semi-nomadic while several groups have become completely sedentarized.

French colonization of Ahaggar lasted from the final battle of conquest of the

---

[1] *Ahaggar* in Tamahaq (the language of the Tuareg), *Hoggar* in Arabic.

[2] *Kel* in Tamahaq = 'people of'.

[3] Henri Lhote, *Les Touaregs du Hoggar*, 2nd edn, Paris, 1955, p. 157.

[4] *Harratin* (sing. *Hartani*) in Arabic (*Izeggaren* in Tamahaq): Caste of agricultural Negroes of mixed origin and thus frequently bilingual, speaking both Arab and Tamahaq. They are generally less negroid than the slaves.

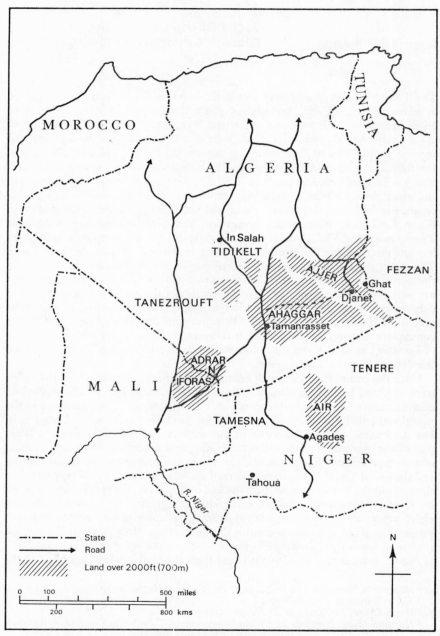

MOROCCO

TUNISIA

ALGERIA

In Salah
TIDIKELT

AJJER

FEZZAN

Ghat
Djanet

TANEZROUFT

AHAGGAR
Tamanrasset

ADRAR
N
IFORAS

MALI

TENERE

TAMESNA

AIR

Agades

NIGER

Tahoua

R. Niger

—··—··—   State

——▶   Road

////////   Land over 2000ft (700m)

0   100   500   miles
    200   800   kms

N

Map 18.1   West-Central Sahara

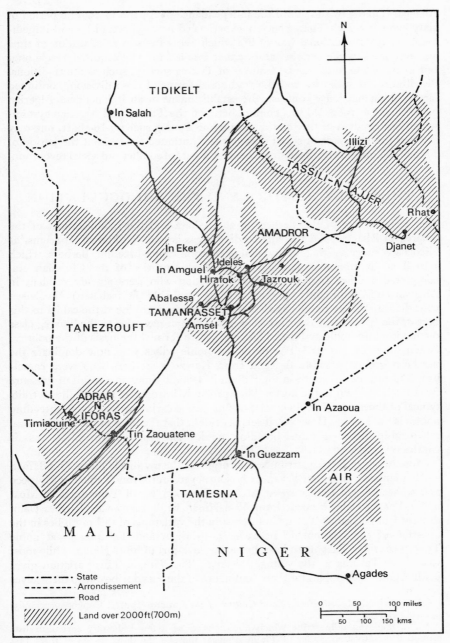

N

TIDIKELT

In Salah

Illizi

TASSILI-N-AJJER

Rhat

AMADROR

Djanet

In Eker

In Amguel   Ideles

Hirafok   Tazrouk

Abalessa

TAMANRASSET

Amsel

TANEZROUFT

ADRAR
N
IFORAS

Timiaouine

Tin Zaouatene

In Azaoua

In Guezzam

AIR

TAMESNA

MALI

NIGER

Agades

State
Arrondissement
Road
Land over 2000ft(700m)

0   50   100 miles

50   100   150 kms

Map 18.2   Ahaggar

Ahaggar Tuareg in 1902 until the independence of Algeria in 1962; a period of sixty years in which Tuareg society experienced new opportunities and impediments to their traditional way of life which necessitated a re-allocation of time and resources, while certain values either lost meaning or acquired a new one; but many of the fundamental features of Tuareg society, such as the traditional distribution of authority and the traditional forms of class division, continued largely unchanged. By contrast, the establishment of an independent Algerian government in 1962, led to a conflict between the Tuareg and Algerian systems which has resulted in the total disruption of Tuareg society. In short, one may say that the processes of social change that continued throughout the period of French colonization has been superseded by a state of conflict and social revolution.

THE EARLY HISTORY AND FRENCH OCCUPATION

The early history of the Berbers in the Sahara and the establishment of the Tuareg in Ahaggar and the surrounding areas is not well known. It seems, as Nicolaisen suggests[1] that an invasion of pastoral camel-breeding Berbers, which started at an unknown date during the first centuries of the Christian era, conquered another Berber-speaking population who were already resident in Ahaggar and lived mainly by goat-breeding (probably the Isebeten). Nicolaisen considers that these noble camel-breeding Berbers introduced the camel to this part of the Sahara and their invasion into Ahaggar gave rise to the Tuareg class distinction into noble and vassal Tuareg, which formed the basis of the political system in most groups.[2] The particular noble tribes who now dominate the northern groups possibly descend from Hawwara Berbers who were camel-breeders and moved south in the Sahara in Islamic times as a result of pressure from Arab bedouin in the north. They probably introduced many cultural traits typical of the Arabs, but their relationship to the earlier arrived camel-breeding nobles is not known. However, it seems evident that the basis of the noble–vassal relationship between camel-breeding nobles and the goat-breeding vassals continued.

Most Ahaggar Tuareg attribute their origin to the mythical Queen Ti-n-Hinan and her female companion Takama who journeyed south from Tafilelt in Morocco and whose alleged tombs are at Abalessa (100 km W. of Tamanrasset). Most noble Tuareg claim descent from Ti-n-Hinan while many vassal tribes claim descent from Takama. The main interest in the variations of this myth lies in the question of the relationship between Ti-n-Hinan and Takama. Most noble Tuareg consider Takama to have been the slave-girl of Ti-n-Hinan, while most vassals see Takama as the younger sister of Ti-n-Hinan. This variation gives justification to the nobles for their dominance of the vassal tribes, who themselves

[1] Johannes Nicolaisen, *Ecology and Culture of the Pastoral Tuareg*, Copenhagen, 1963, pp. 411, 479 ff.
[2] The Ikadeyen noble tribe which now consists of a few sedentary agriculturalists around the cultivation center of Tit in Ahaggar may be the descendents of these first nobles.

see their relationship with the noble tribes as entailing the same degree of respect that a younger sister would give to an older sister. This present lack of consensus among Tuareg is of interest.

The beginnings of the present-day tribal organization can be dated from about 1660. At this time, the Berbers who inhabited the region between Rhat and Tin Zaouatene, that is the region of Ajjer, Ahagger, and Adrar n Iforas, were dominated by the noble Imenan tribe who claimed relationship to the Prophet. The Imenan chief lived at Rhat and Djanet and it was during this period that the noble Uraren tribe rose up against the Imenan. The supreme chief of the Imenan, Goma, was assassinated and control of the Ajjer region, Rhat and Ghadames, passed into the hands of the Uraren. There is little mention of the Kel Ahaggar at this time.

It seems that a state of anarchy continued among the Kel Ahaggar until the end of the seventeenth century when Salah took upon himself the title of 'Amenukal'[1] which had previously been held by the supreme chief of the Imenan.[2] We know virtually nothing about Salah although Gast[3] does suggest that his 'election' was encouraged by outside religious leaders, and it is perhaps of interest to note that the first four Amenukals of the Kel Ahaggar are credited with Arabic names.

We find the present political groupings of the Kel Ahaggar being formed during the reign of Sidi ag Mohamed El-Khir (Grandson of Salah) at around 1750. The Kel Ahaggar were divided into three major groups centered around the noble tribes of the Kel Rela, Taitok, and the Tegehe-Mellet. Until this division, the Kel Rela and Taitok were one single tribe. (Today their respective members often claim matrilineal relationship.) The Tegehe-Mellet probably descend patrilineally from Arabs (possibly Chaamba). There were two other noble tribes in Ahaggar at this time but they were very small with few or no vassals. Vassal tribes were referred to as 'Imrad' or 'Kel Ulli', meaning literally 'the Goat People', due to their traditional dependence on goat herding as distinct from the camel-breeding nobles. The division of vassal tribes between the three noble tribes resulted in certain vassal tribes being split; for example, the Imessiliten tribe was split into the Kel Ahnet attached to the Taitok and the Dag Rali to the Kel Rela. Most vassals went to the Kel Rela, but several were allotted to the Taitok, while the Tegehe-Mellet received so few that they could never become politically important. Apart from the Kel Ulli or Imrad vassals, there is a second group of vassal tribes—the Isekkemaren tribes. They descend from Arabs, or from union between Arab men and Tuareg women and have a slightly different status from the true vassals (Kel Ulli or Imrad) in that their dependence was not on any member of the noble tribe but only directly on the drum-chief, whose position will be explained subsequently. On this basis they were apparently considered a superior type of vassal but I have never heard

---

[1] Nicolaisen states that the 'Amenukal' is a title used for supreme and independent chiefs of large political units (Nicolaisen, op. cit., p. 393).

[2] After losing their supreme authority it seems that they retained the titles of *Imenikalen* (sing. *Amenukal*).

[3] Marceau Gast, *Alimentation des populations de L'Ahaggar*, p. 402.

present-day Tuareg refer to them in this manner. In the past they rarely engaged in raiding and warfare and are now sometimes spoken of as being physically weak.

Each of the three noble tribes with its respective vassal tribes formed a political unit with a chief whose authority was symbolized by a drum. Thus the 'Drum-Chief' held supreme political and judicial authority in the 'drum-group'. These three drum-groups jointly formed a sort of federation, but whereas the chiefs of the Taitok and Tegehe-Mellet drum-groups were called *amrar* (pl. *imraren*),[1] the drum-chief of the Kel Rela drum-group took the title of Amenukal as chief of the whole federation. His authority over the other two drum-chiefs was never strong, except perhaps in matters which concerned the whole federation, if the three groups united to fight other groups.[2] In fact, throughout the nineteenth century there were long periods of quarreling and fighting between the Kel Rela and Taitok.

Of particular importance for the analysis of the social revolution that has occurred in the past decade is the use of slaves that continued throughout the colonial period. These slaves (*iklan*, sing. *akli*) who were brought mostly from the Sudan region, began to form an extremely important and numerous social class within Ahaggar. Although raiding had stopped a long time before independence, this large class of slaves formed a fundamental part of Tuareg social organization in 1962.

During the nineteenth century *akli* certainly fitted the meaning of slave. However, the *iklan* had certain rights and privileges which they were able to exercise more and more after slave raids gradually ended. The status of the *akli* before independence was more akin to that of a permanent domestic servant.

Until the impact of French influence in the latter half of the nineteenth century, the division of Tuareg society into 'nobles' and 'vassals' corresponded well to their economic interdependence. An analogy to a feudal system had good foundations. While the nobles indulged almost solely in warfare, raiding, and the control of the caravan routes, the vassal tribes were engaged in goat-herding and to a considerable extent in their own caravan trading in cereals and dates. The 'vassals' had few of their own camels but were rich in goats whose products were essential for the nobles, while on the other hand the many camels that the nobles left in the care of their 'vassals' could be used by them for their own caravan trading and raiding. But, to appreciate the relationship between the two classes, it is necessary to examine the 'functional' unit, the relationship of *temazlayt*, meaning literally 'the root of the nail'. These relationships have now virtually ceased to exist and are consequently difficult to describe. The *temazlayt* group imposed certain rights and obligations between a small noble matri-lineage with its leader and a larger matrilineage of 'vassals'. The rights of the noble were much less than those of the drum-chief or Amenukal. He had no judicial authority and could not summon his 'vassals' to war or raid unless they themselves were interested. He was obliged to offer them protection from any other raiding groups, and while he was away the 'vassals' had rights to use his

[1] Today in Ahaggar, the title *Amrar* is used very loosely to mean 'chief' as well as 'old man'.

[2] As in the case of the war with the Kel Ajjer between 1872–78.

camels for their own raiding and caravans. In return, the noble was almost entirely dependent on this relationship for his food and many other supplies. The noble could make any request of his 'vassals' but they in turn could refuse. It was, therefore, in the noble's interest to ensure that his particular *temazlayt* group was rich. But as raiding diminished, and the vassals increased their caravan activities and ownership of camels, the justification of the 'vassals' obligations diminished.[1]

The second half of the nineteenth century saw two major impacts on this traditional Tuareg system. The first was the introduction of sedentary agriculturalists. The Kel Ajjer had profited from their gardens for a long time, but the Kel Ahaggar, being violent and intolerant fighters, could not endure the presence of cultivators on their territories. Being themselves scornful of all manual work, it took a clear and foresighted chief, namely El-Hadj Akhmed, to realize the economic need for cultivation within Ahaggar. Some diffident gardening had been attempted by Tuareg slaves in the vicinity of Ideles at about 1840, but they proved to be unsatisfactory cultivators, and, at about 1861 we see El-Hadj Akhmed extending the gardens of Ideles and creating a new cultivation center at Tazrouk. In this task he was short-handed and under his protection gardeners, white Ahl Azzi and black Harratin from Djanet, Tuat, and Tidikelt were invited to become the gardeners for the Ahaggar Tuareg. The newcomers found a new land with areas of good soil and relatively abundant water. They progressively installed themselves with their families and began to spread and multiply throughout the region.

The gardens which developed throughout Ahaggar were owned by the Tuareg but worked on a contract system by the sedentary agriculturalist. There were three types of contract which were all variations of the '*khamessa*' system, entitling the cultivator to one-fifth of the harvest and the Tuareg owner to four-fifths. In fact, the Tuareg tended to fare even better than this arrangement would imply, for at harvest time he would invariably camp in the vicinity of the garden and stay there several weeks while living on the 'hospitality' of the cultivator. At the end of this period he would withdraw with his four-fifths!

The second major impact on the traditional Tuareg system was the increasing influence of France. Before the middle of the nineteenth century, Tuareg had had considerable contact with the outside world through their raiding and commercial activities, but Ahaggar was their domain; the outside world had not yet found a foothold in it. Contact with the outside world had been external. The agriculturalists brought the processes of cultural contact into Ahaggar. The French began their push into Ahaggar at the turn of the century and the biggest defeat of the Kel Ahaggar came in 1902 at the battle of Tit—a defeat which shattered the Tuareg's assumption of their invincibility and opened the way for French control in Ahaggar. The Tuareg were conquered; they became a colonized people.

The end of the nineteenth century also saw the beginning of a new commercial activity—the salt caravans to Damergu in Niger. The development of these caravans is perhaps the best example of the adaptability of the Tuareg system.

[1] Nicolaisen, op. cit., pp. 403–4 (for details of tribute, division of booty, etc.).

The need created by the loss of revenue from raiding led the 'vassal' tribes and *iklan* to extract salt from Amadror[1] and go south to exchange it for millet in Damergu. The first caravan seems to have set out in 1896. The results were encouraging; one load of salt resulting in up to fifteen or twenty loads of millet. With the development of the salt caravans, and with the later establishment of a class of 'shopkeepers' in the newly created administrative center of Tamanrasset, the introduction of money as a means of exchange, and the opportunity for labor and wage-earning, we can see a re-allocation of time and resources within the Tuareg system.

The French military administration became established at Tamanrasset in 1920. In retrospect, one can say that the continuity of the fundamental structures of Tuareg society was largely dependent on the French support and policy of *laissez-faire* toward the Tuareg. The French administrative system, although superordinate, developed alongside rather than in dominance of the Tuareg system. Admittedly, raiding and slave 'trading' were officially stopped and as a result the noble–vassal relationship was threatened, but the French made no serious attempt to alter the position of the *iklan* already found in Ahaggar. The *iklan* were undoubtedly the mainstay of the Tuareg economic system. They provided much of the labor required by the Tuareg for their domestic and commercial needs and thus provided the Tuareg with the resources needed to adapt to the economic changes.

The French would have had great difficulty in administering Ahaggar without gaining the support and cooperation of the Tuareg in positions of power and authority. But, in Ahaggar, at the time of the conquest, the distribution of authority no longer found absolute justification. We have already discussed the position of the *temazlayt* relationship, given the diminution of raiding. The greater economic initiative taken by the 'vassal' tribes, the psychological effect of the Tit defeat, were all factors leading to social leveling. It was in French administrative interests to support and reinforce the traditional distribution of authority. They installed Moussa ag Amastene (the Tuareg commander at the battle of Tit) as Amenukal, and invested him with authority that no previous Amenukal had been able to maintain. The position of the Amenukal within the Tuareg system became stronger than at any other time within the preceding century and a half. Through his military leadership and his political sense in dealing with the French, Moussa had gained the respect of both Tuareg and French. Today only fifty years after his death he is regarded as the greatest of all Tuareg chiefs and has become a legend.

This reinforced and sanctioned authority of the Amenukal gave the dominant Kel Rela tribe a status which perpetuated certain of the noble–vassal rights and obligations. But, in spite of the continuation of the noble, vassal, and *iklan* classes, the feudal system had gone. Particularly toward the end of the French period, only vestigial traces of the *temazlayt* relationship remained, and the favored position of the noble Kel Rela owed much to the support by the French administration.

[1] Amadror—salt mines at Tisemt along the Oued Amadror—plain of Amadror (approx. 400 km NNE of Tamanrasset).

Let us now make a brief examination of the economic regime between 1905 and 1962 and some of the major social changes that it brought about. The French built a military post at Fort Motylinski in 1908 and then moved to a military fort constructed at Tamanrasset in 1920; the final transfer of the Saharan Company[1] from its original base at Ft Motylinski to Tamanrasset focused in 1929, with the result that the whole French administration and military became centered at Tamanrasset. The centralization of this new administration gave rise to new developments in the economy. The small group of French military were paid regularly in money, thus bringing a money market into a region in which commerce had been traditionally carried out in barter. This need to buy locally led to the introduction of a new kind of merchant, the shopkeeper, who originated either from Tidikelt or the Mzab. In a way, the growth of Tamanrasset was a measure of French control and development of the region. But, for the Tuareg it represented the outside world and had always been repressive for them. Tamanrasset belonged to the administration, the sedentarist, and the shopkeeper; it was not part of the Tuareg world.

From the beginning of this period we can see a great demographic change. In 1860 the population of Ahaggar had consisted of approximately 3,000 Tuareg nomads with a certain number of *iklan*. With peace and the growing importance of Tamanrasset there was a rapid increase in the sedentary society. By 1960 the sedentarists numbered about 5,500—more than the number of Tuareg, and consisted of gardeners who had settled in increasing numbers, around the water points, merchants attracted by the growing importance of Tamanrasset, the military and administrative personnel, and the workmen of Tamanrasset. The numbers of workmen grew in relation to the constantly increasing demand for manpower.

Gast says that the nomad society hardened during this period and lived on the memories of the past.[2] What is meant by hardened? Revenue from raiding had stopped and Tuareg were dependent on the revenue from their herds (goats and camels), caravan trade, and from the gardens. But with the exception of the gardens, these sources showed a continual decline. The deterioration of pasture by overgrazing on the one hand, and the decline of the revenue from caravan trading on the other, led to a greater dependence on the gardens. The salt of Amadror which had at one time been exchanged for 15 or 20 loads of millet, had by 1962 acquired little more than an equal rate of exchange. Caravans taking wheat from the gardens and various products of stockbreeding northwards to Tuat, in exchange for dates, had been almost totally replaced by mechanized transport. Nevertheless, despite the apparent economic lack of viability, the caravans are still an essential part of the Tuareg life.

In view of these drastic economic changes, it seems odd to say that the French did not cause an upheaval. Rather I believe that the forces that impinged on the Tuareg during this period caused a series of adjustments and were largely

---

[1] The Sahara Company was the *mehariste* (camel mounted) *gendarmerie* comprising a few French officers and sergeants with Arab soldiers and NCOs (mostly Chaamba).

[2] Marceau Gast, *Revolution de la vie économique et structures sociales en Ahagger de 1660 à 1965*, Travaux de l'Institut de Recherches Sahariennes, Paris, 1965, Vol. xxiv.

absorbed, whereas the impact of the independent Algerian administration could not be absorbed and led to a social revolution.

In looking at the French administration we see it as superordinate to the Tuareg system, but rarely ever manifesting this superordinate position; perhaps it would have found difficulty in its justification. The French attempted to preserve Tuareg culture; the administrative link was the Amenukal whose authority was reinforced and sanctioned by the French. Thus, all Tuareg judicial matters and the regulation of their internal affairs were carried out within their own system according to traditional means. The Tuareg did not see the French as quite such a superordinate force, but rather as a system which impinged alongside their own and in which they saw their identity confirmed.

As the new impediments to their traditional way of life affected them, they were forced to seek alternatives. As raiding stopped, so resources had been directed toward caravan trading, and as caravan trading became less economically efficient so the new opportunities of wage-earning were explored. But these decisions had been made 'voluntarily'—they were made within the Tuareg social organization and in terms of their own values and their own appraisal of the situation.

The fundamental traits of Tuareg society can perhaps be seen in terms of their assumptions concerning the rights of the groups with which they identify. These three crucial assumptions concern the ownership and rights to land, the distribution of authority, and above all the position of the *iklan* within the Tuareg system.

Previous to the French conquest Ahaggar had been undisputedly Tuareg territory. For the Tuareg, the concept of a region could not be more easily defined. The agriculturalists who came into Ahaggar after about 1861 had been invited to work the land for the Tuareg. There was no question as to their ownership of the land; they cultivated it on a contract basis for their Tuareg masters. The arrival of the French did not destroy this basic assumption. After all, the French created their own center at Tamanrasset; a center that was geographically in the heart of Ahaggar but, for the Tuareg, it belonged to and was part of the outside world. The cultivators continued to work on their various contract systems while tribal and section land rights were regulated under the authority of the Amenukal. Not only did Tuareg assume rights of ownership over Ahaggar, but over much of northern Niger as well—in particular the plains of Tamesna. This region was the natural pasturage for Ahaggar; Tuareg considered it as merely an extension of their rights of Ahaggar. The presence of a frontier between the two French territories was meaningless for the Tuareg.

But of crucial concern is the position of the *iklan* throughout the French period. One must stress that the Tuareg considered the *iklan* to be an integral part of the Tuareg system; they could not conceive of a Tuareg society without them, and if there is any one issue that one can consider as being critical or indeed symbolic of the Algerian-Tuareg conflict it is undoubtedly this question of the *iklan*.

According to Lhote[1] there were 1,552 slaves owned by 3,960 pastoral Tuareg in Ahaggar in 1949, and among the Kel Rela and Dag Rali tribes there were more

[1] Lhote, op. cit., pp. 224 ff.

slaves than Tuareg. This figure probably does not include a number of *iklan* who had become free. The ownership of slaves was organized predominantly upon a kinship pattern whereby the *iklan* were normally the fictive children of their masters. According to Nicolaisen,[1] Tuareg of both sexes owned slaves individually so that a Tuareg man was the 'father' of his slaves and a Tuareg woman the 'mother' of her slaves. This position of slaves as 'children' of the slave-owner meant that the owner's brothers, sisters, and parents were considered as classificatory mothers and fathers by his slaves.[2] This results in young slaves being considered a kind of 'brother and sister' to the slave-owner's children.

An important point is that slaves did not form a political class so that a noble could marry a slave whereas the marriage between a noble and a vassal would have cut across the political division of society.[3]

The legal inability for slave-owners to sell or trade slaves came in with the French, but even in pre-European times it was extremely unusual to do so; the slaves were inherited within the same family. It does seem that *iklan* were relatively well treated, and the relationship between slaves and their masters were usually good.[4] For the Tuareg, the slave was a part of Tuareg society; he did not belong to the outside world. His rights, obligations and relationships were not determined by any political class system as was the case of the nobles *vis-à-vis* the vassals, but were seen as an extension of the organization of the Tuareg family unit. The *iklan* were also a 'buffer' to the economic forces impinging on Tuareg society from the outside world. It was by means of the reallocation of resources that the Tuareg society was able to adapt to the economic pressures which they experienced during the French period. Resources could largely be measured in terms of *iklan*; herds were looked after by them, the salt caravans were largely manned by them, and much of the domestic work was carried out by them.

These three value assumptions provide us with a measure of the continuity of the Tuareg system throughout the French period. The traditional distribution of authority was sanctioned; the land of Ahaggar was 'Tuareg', and little attempt was made by the French to alter or abolish the position of the *iklan*.

---

[1] Nicolaisen, op. cit., p. 442.

[2] When a slave marries, his owner is obliged to pay the bride-wealth which goes to the owner of the slave-girl with whom the slave marries.

[3] The position of the children of a mixed marriage varies considerably. In Air, if a Tuareg man marries his own slave-girl the children have a right to be considered true Tuareg, whereas if he marries a slave-girl who is not his, the children will not become true Tuareg. This general rule is the same in Ahaggar, but as in Air, it seems that the right of a child to be considered a true Tuareg depends largely on his standing and relationship with other individuals. The rule is often the exception and status is more achieved than ascribed.

[4] A slave had the right to change masters. An ill-treated slave could cut the ear of a camel of another Tuareg whose slave he wished to be. In consequence of the 'damage', the owner of the camel was obliged to take the slave in recompense, for the owner of a slave was responsible for his actions. To lose a slave in this way was a great loss of prestige. The owner of a slave could demand his return if he ran away, but if badly treated the Amenukal might intervene on his behalf.

INDEPENDENCE

The Algerian administration that took over in Tamanrasset in 1962 was faced with numerous problems. The Algerians who filled the administrative posts, the Sous Prefecture, the Gendarmerie, etc., were men who came from the north, some 2,000 kilometers away, and were thus foreigners to the region. Ahaggar, with its different language and customs was a strange country for them.[1]

We can see this difficulty on the individual level. Algerians from the north had little feeling for this country, which was desolate and hard. They were a great distance from their homes and families and in a land about which they knew and understood relatively little—least of all perhaps did they understand the Tuareg themselves. Most Algerians posted to this quarter of Algeria wanted nothing more than to see the end of their posting.

Critics of Algeria and certain 'sentimentalists' have criticized Algeria for her 'colonization' policies in Ahaggar. If the social revolution that has taken place in Tuareg society during the last eight years is the beginning of the 'annihilation of a culture', then one has a moral duty to put forward the 'case for the annihilation', for no country in the world is more sensitive to, and aware of, the meaning of colonization than Algeria. This is not a defense of Algerian policy. It is merely that one cannot make an objective analysis of a conflict situation unless both sides of the situation are understood. In this case one must put the Algerian policy in Ahaggar into its national context.

The Algeria which emerged from the revolution was in a state of disarray, its institutional structures were in total disruption. The greatest need in Algeria during these formative years was trained cadres. In 1954, 92 percent of the intellectual cadres had been Europeans, while of the technicians occupying subordinate positions 82·4 percent were Europeans.[2]

Ahaggar presented Algeria with its own singular problems. In many aspects it was not part of the new Algeria. The war had not disturbed it and the connections of the Ahaggar Tuareg were far stronger with the south (Tamesna and Air) than with the north. But the socialist ideology and nationalism committed Algeria to the assimilation of minority groups into Algeria and to the welding of the north and the south into a unified State. The opportunities of the socialist system were to be made available to all Algerians, thus including Tuareg, *iklan*, and *Harratin* alike.

A detailed account of Algerian policy falls into three periods, 1962–65, 1965–1969, 1969–. These three periods coincide with the periods of office of the three Sousprefets who have administered Tamanrasset since independence. In general terms the aim of this policy has been to assimilate the Tuareg into an Algerian system; a system whose socialist values of equal opportunity and freedom from class distinction are almost totally incompatible with the traditional values of Tuareg society.

[1] Arabic has been the official language of the administration, and several Tuareg men are bilingual. However, Tamahaq is the mother tongue of the Tuareg and few of their women speak Arabic.

[2] G. C. Gordon, *The Passing of French Algeria*, Oxford, 1966, pp. 81–2.

The first period of Algerian administration in Ahaggar, until 1965, can be thought of as a 'testing' period; the Algerians could not feel totally in command of the region, in view of the continued French presence at the atomic base of In Eker, and of their unfamiliarity with the region and the Tuareg. On the other hand, Tuareg resentment of the Algerian increased as the future Algerian policy began to reveal itself to them. Both societies were unsure of the other, each testing the relative strengths and weaknesses.

The Tuareg institution most abhorrent to Algeria was that of slavery; it was totally incompatible with the principles of any government that was 'Démocratique et Populaire'. The gendarmerie of Tamanrasset scoured through all the encampments within the region and led the *iklan* away with their few belongings to Tamanrasset and their freedom. A few found work as laborers in Tamanrasset, established themselves in a quarter of Tamanrasset and began to mix with the free *Harratin*. But for many, there was no work, and they could not establish themselves in a nomadic way of life for they had no herds, tents, or equipment, nor the money with which to buy them. They began to huddle around the outside of Tamanrasset in what Gast[1] describes as a *bidonville*. The creation of agricultural cooperatives did to some extent assist these freed slaves; the cooperative at Otoul (20 km N. of Tamanrasset) for example, consists almost entirely of ex-Dag Rali slaves (1967, 14 members) and has resulted in the establishment of a new 'village', populated almost entirely by families of ex-slaves.

The liberation of the *iklan* could be described as removing the mortar from the brickwork of Tuareg society. The mere sight of armed gendarmerie coming into the encampments turned many Tuareg's resentment into fear and hate.

During the French period, economic forces had made the Tuareg even more dependent on their gardens which were cultivated by the *Harratin*. But, in Algeria, is not the earth free? Does it not repay those who work it? With independence the *Harratin* began to show their hostility toward the Tuareg. They began to refuse to pay their contract dues, but this refusal varied according to how far they thought they could depend on support from the administration. Naturally, this dependence on government support often varied according to the distance and accessibility of the gardens from Tamanrasset. With some gardeners a degree of collaboration took place in that the nomad paid for the motor for pumping water, or cost of irrigation channels and then came to an agreement with the cultivator. But several cultivators began to cultivate virgin land so as to free themselves completely from the Tuareg. The *Harratin* were beginning to feel confidence in their independence; they were beginning to stand up to the Tuareg, but nevertheless, even in 1964–65 many cultivators were still giving half their harvest to their Tuareg masters. The Tuareg themselves were free to cultivate any land, indeed they were encouraged to do so. A few did, but they are still a small minority.

This first period of independence also meant a total reorganization of the political system. The French administration was linked to the Tuareg through the Amenukal. The Algerian administration effected a complete change in the

[1] Gast, op. cit.

distribution of authority. The Amenukal lost his official status of traditional chief, and nominally became a chosen representative in the new popular democracy and took a salary as deputy. One should add that the position of the Amenukal as a deputy in the republic was honorary and to my knowledge he has rarely, if ever, exercised this role. Officially the tribes no longer pay tribute to the Amenukal. A few tribes continued to pay their tribute in the immediate post-independence years but this has now diminished. His traditional authority no longer found sanction in the administration of Tamanrasset and Tuareg increasingly took their disputes and problems to the Mairie or Judge in Tamanrasset in preference to the Amenukal. In this new political system the *Harratin* and ex-slave became the majority; the nomads who were the minority looked more and more to Hadj Moussa, the half brother of the Amenukal, as their political leader.

During this first period of Algerian administration there were countless examples of antagonism, fear, resentment, opportunism, and so on. There is no space for them here; it is only necessary to emphasize the degree of conflict and tension that existed. Tuareg now realized that their system was being attacked directly; the *iklan* had been taken away and the rights to Tuareg land were given to those who had originally been invited into the region to cultivate it on contract to the Tuareg owners. These two issues in particular, combined with the lack of clarity in the distribution of authority, the jealousies arising within Tuareg society, and the serious state of the pasturage had led the Tuareg into an easily exploitable political position.

In the spring of 1964 there was a skirmish between a group of Tuareg and the ex-slaves at Otoul (20 km N. of Tamanrasset). The precise details of the skirmish are obscure, both to the administration and the Tuareg themselves. The number of individuals involved was small and about a dozen people seem to have been injured, and coincidence seems to have played a large part, for two of the five Tuareg concerned had never met each other before the incident. It seems that certain Tuareg, on arriving back from the winter caravan, were led to believe that they could retake their former slaves. Part of the explanation may have been a political conflict simultaneously going on amongst the Algerian leadership, one of whose members, Chaabani, may have wished to use the Tuareg in support of the rebellion of his own based at Biskra. The investigations resulted in five Tuareg being sent to detention prisons.

The full establishment of Algerian authority in Ahaggar did not really become evident until during the period starting in 1965 with the installation of Aktouf as Sousprefet. Aktouf was a brilliant administrator who was given the enormous task of integrating the Tuareg and Ahaggar into Algeria, or, what his successor called 'the establishing of the preconditions for socialism'. The success of his administration in achieving this goal can perhaps be measured by the fear and respect that he evoked from the Tuareg, in contrast to his predecessor.

Aktouf's policy toward the Tuareg was one of sedentarization. It meant the development of agricultural cooperatives, the protection of the *Harratins'* interests and restrictions on the nomadic way of life.

The construction of most cooperatives began in 1966; the agreements were signed in 1967.[1] These cooperatives are faced with numerous difficulties in terms of marketing, transport, techniques, etc., which make their economic efficiency extremely low. But their advantages cannot be measured only in terms of their economic value, but rather by the political and social transformation that they have helped bring about. The cooperatives, for both *Harratin* and Tuareg alike, symbolize the increasing control that the government is maintaining throughout Ahaggar. The cooperatives do not consist solely of *Harratin*; the Amenukal Bay has set an example to Tuareg with his own cooperative at Asliskine, which is worked by four noble Tuareg. At the pilot cooperative at Amsel one finds a close association between the cooperative and nomadic activities.

Monetary exchange had become established with the French presence, but few Tuareg had accepted the idea of work until the last few years of their occupation and even then the circulation of money within the Tuareg system was minimal. Most of their money had been earned by laboring at the atomic base set up at In Eker in 1959.[2] The closure of the base in 1966, which decreased the small circulation of money among the nomads still further, combined with Aktouf's protection of the *Harratin* from Tuareg demands of a share of the harvest, made them even more dependent on the revenue of the salt caravans, returning with millet from Damorgu. Though the exchange rate between salt and millet was low in comparison with former years, it enabled Tuareg to obtain millet without having to depend on money.

However, the motivation for these caravans was not entirely economic. Tamesna, in northern Niger, had always been the main pasture for the herds of Ahaggar. Since independence rainfall in Ahaggar had not been adequate to maintain good grazing and herds were relying more on these southern pastures which were a 'staging post' for the caravans. Caravans would rest in Tamesna for a month or more on their way south and often take on new camels, leaving the weakened camels from Ahaggar to regain their strength on the richer pastures.

A further consideration was that many Tuareg had left Ahaggar after independence and were living in Niger. There was thus the social motivating of these caravans which formed the link between the Tuareg of Ahaggar and their fellow tribesmen now living south of the frontier.

In line with Aktouf's sedentarization policy, the frontier restrictions that Algeria began to impose on these caravans became stricter, particularly after 1966. An agreement was signed between the Niger and Algerian authorities which fixed a quota, based on the estimated surplus of millet, of caravans that could be allowed to leave Ahaggar. Permission for every caravan must now be obtained from the Sousprefecture in Tamanrasset while Customs officers demand that the Tuareg check their caravans through Tamanrasset—a demand which is often

[1] Twenty cooperatives were registered. Timaiouine (700 km from Tamanrasset) has proved to be unable to operate effectively on a cooperative system, while the village of Hirafok has produced organizational problems of its own which have hindered cooperative development. Excluding these two there are 360 members and 258 hectares of cooperative land.

[2] In 1964 the two companies of the base employed an average of 350 and 750 workmen respectively. These 1,000 jobs represented an annual turnover of 2,000–3,000 workers as at the end of each month, one group would be replaced by another.

impossible for the Tuareg and not easy for the Customs to enforce. In 1967–68 and 1968–69 there were officially no caravans, although a few did cross the frontier. In the winter of 1969–70 approximately 200 men and 1,000 camels were checked through Tamanrasset. This particular year was critical for many nomads; not only was there a shortage of food in the encampments but also a dire shortage of pasture within Ahaggar.

By the middle of Aktouf's period and particularly after the winter of 1968–69, when there were no caravans and the final revenue from the previously owned gardens had gone, the Tuareg were faced with no alternative but to accept and assimilate themselves into the Algerian system. Aktouf himself once said that the Tuareg of Ahaggar could either sedentarize as Algerians or leave the country and go to Niger. What is perhaps surprising is the speed in which most Tuareg have been prepared to accept this process of assimilation. One can argue that the forces of 'Algerianization' have been so ruthless that Tuareg have had no other choice but to accept them or leave the country.

The Amenukal Bay has often been criticized for not making a stand against Algeria. My own opinion of Bay, which is shared by several other 'outsiders' and now by an increasing number of Tuareg themselves, is that he has shown considerable shrewdness and perception. He realized the force of Algeria in Ahaggar and has made efforts to discourage open resistance. His authority is now, however, minimal and responsibility for Tuareg affairs is in the hands of the Mairie.

The Algerian government now considers the traditional Tuareg system as broken and anticipates the complete political, social and economic integration of the Tuareg through the processes of education and industrialization.

19

Patterns of Rural Rebellion in Morocco during the Early Years of Independence[1]

Ernest Gellner

During the early years of Moroccan Independence in 1956, there occurred a number of relatively minor rural rebellions, in the main in Berber regions, Morocco is an independent country which had undergone a fairly brief colonial period (1912–1956), and with a social structure which is a strange amalgam of a pre-industrial but partially urban society, with a modern sector which had emerged rapidly during foreign rule. Something under a half of its population (no one knows exactly) are Berber-speakers, rural tribesmen whose tribal organization is fairly well preserved. The rest are Arabic-speakers, urban and rural (disregarding Jewish and European minorities)

This paper will attempt to throw some light on the place of such tribesmen, whose language is not that of the state in which they live, within the wider society of which they are now part. It will do this through trying to explain the odd and surprising features of the tribal risings mentioned above. These oddities are considerable:

(*a*) The uprisings collapse fairly easily. This is very surprising in view of the past history of Morocco.

(*b*) Its leaders, when captured, are treated with leniency. Though generally imprisoned for indefinite periods, they are not killed. This, likewise, is odd.

(*c*) The uprisings generally simply do not make sense, quite literally. For instance: tribesmen who proclaim themselves supporters of X, stage a rebellion— *whilst X is in office* as Prime Minister. Or again: a rural leader who proclaims himself supporter of dynastic personage Y stages a rebellion—which is then suppressed *by Y himself*, whose supporter the rebel claims to be, and in whose very support the rebellion was made.

Feature (*c*) is manifestly and genuinely puzzling. We should be puzzled if we found a bona fide Fidelista rebellion against Castro, a Titoist uprising suppressed by the Marshal himself, etc.

Features (*a*) and (*b*) may not seem quite as puzzling to someone not acquainted with Morocco's past: but, at least for the sake and duration of the argument, I must ask that it be accepted that, in the light of even very recent Moroccan history, these features are *most* odd, and indeed just as odd as the self-contradictory feature (*c*).

[1] First published in the *European Journal of Sociology*, 1962.
12*

SOME SUPERFICIAL AND MISTAKEN EXPLANATIONS

(*a*) The listener or reader may suspect that where alleged or self-proclaimed followers of X rebel whilst X himself is in power, or where Y suppresses a rising made on his own behalf, all is not what it seems: that the supposed followers of X are not such really, but only falsely claim the appropriate label. Or, that Y is suppressing rebels who only wished to use his name, but who are in fact his enemies. The movements invoking the name of X or Y, he may suspect, are not united but profoundly divided internally.

Now it is certainly the case that all is not as it seems. But it simply is not the case that the followers-of-X are not such really, or those proclaiming allegiance to Y do not really feel it. I must ask that this to be accepted as a fact[1], and in any case, I propose to put forward an explanation which does not require the assumption of the spuriousness of apparent loyalties.

(*b*) A favourite explanation with journalists commenting the Moroccan scene: do not attempt to make consistent sense of Moroccan affairs. It *never* makes sense. It is all a matter of personalities, irrational passions, accidents, etc., etc. No explanations are possible or required for the conduct of these people.

This is facile and false. But the frequency with which journalists are forced to invoke such pseudo-explanations, when pressed to attempt any kind of coherent account, is significant.

(*c*) Another favorite explanation, particularly amongst European residents in Morocco: the tribes have gone soft. Their fathers, a mere twenty-five years or so ago, fought fiercely against all comers; and the central power had to stick their heads onto the ramparts of Fes, *pour encourager les autres*. But today . . . the fact that tribal revolts collapse, and that when they do, no heads adorn the walls of the new Ministry of the Interior—whose modern plaster and extensive glass windows are admittedly ill-suited for such decoration—simply indicates degeneracy all round. This explanation is also false.

(*d*) There is an explanation which is often favored by observers from outside Morocco, and which is also enshrined in a serious study of post-Independence Moroccan politics,[2] and which sees in these occasional rural risings attempts by tribesmen to recover their erstwhile tribal independence. This explanation owes its superficial appeal to fitting in with a widespread and popular stereotype of Berbers and tribesmen generally, as ferocious near-Noble Savages devoted to

---

[1] When the *Royalist* Governor of Tafilalet province, Addi u Bihi, rebelled and was suppressed by the Crown Prince and the Royal Army, the explanation was *not* that he was not really Royalist after all. When the members of the Ait Abdi tribe, affiliated through their leader Haddu u Mha to the Leftist party, rebelled at the time when the Leftist leader Abdallah Ibrahim was Prime Minister, the explanation was *not* that they were not 'truly' Leftist, i.e. genuine and loyal clients of the Leftist party. (Of course, in a sense they were not truly 'Leftist', i.e. they have no idea of what 'Left' and 'Right' mean in the contexts from which these terms are borrowed. But that is hardly relevant. They do not need to understand to be loyal: and that they were.)

[2] Douglas Ashford, *Political Change in Morocco* (Princeton University Press, 1961).

tribal ways, anxious to preserve them in their purity for a kind of ethnographic zoo, and resentful of all outside interference. In part, this explanation also appeals to those who are hostile to the new independent Morocco (though this is not true of the author of the volume cited), and who would welcome a demonstration of its incapacity to retain the loyalty of its subjects.

In fact I am confident, in the light of the characteristics of these rural risings, of field observation, and of general considerations, that this explanation is false. When, in connection with the biggest of the risings, the Rif tribesmen submitted a list of complaints to the central government, the list contained the complaint that the region was *under*-administered and neglected. When confronted with the alternatives of tradition and of the benefits of modernity and industrialism, Moroccan tribesmen behave in conformity to the views of Lord Snow rather than those of Mr Leavis: given the option, they prefer modernity. These risings, whatever they are, simply are not nativistic movements.

(*e*) There is also an explanation very favorite with Moroccans themselves. It runs as follows: Morocco is a monarchy. Hence any rebellion is really an act against the King. But all Moroccans love their King. Admittedly, they nevertheless, in moments of folly and forgetfulness, commit rebellion. But when they realize what they are doing, they are sorry, and desist. (This explains the early collapse of rebellions.) The King, however, loves all his subjects, and is all too glad to forgive. (This explains the relative leniency towards the culprits.)

I do not propose to discuss the merits of this explanation.

Before an adequate sociological explanation can be offered, the background must be sketched in. Moroccan history, and hence also the history of its urban/rural, governmental/tribal relationships, has gone through three phases: [I] traditional society, till about 1912 (later for some regions); [II a] the French period; [II b] the period of Independence, since the winter of 1955–56. II a and II b can be lumped together for many purposes as two substages of the 'Modern' period. They have far more in common with each other than either has with I.

TRADITIONAL MOROCCO [I].

Islam obtains throughout (with only a Jewish minority, which can be disregarded for the present purpose). A dynasty rationalized in terms of Islam: the monarch is a descendant of the Prophet. (This however is not a very strong validation in as far as Morocco is full of people believed to be so descended.) In name, religious unity is complete: not only were all Moroccans Muslims, but they are all *Sunni* Muslims and, moreover, they are all Sunni Muslims of the Maliki rite.

The central power was dynastic. It was based on the walled towns—garrisons as well as centres of learning and trade—and on varying kinds of supporting sheepdogs: foreign mercenaries, slave armies, but above all on priviledged (tax-exempt) tribes (which in earlier times were often also the tribe from which the dynasty had sprung: but later, dynasties had non-tribal, Prophet-originating genealogies). Apart from these special, tax-exempt and tax-extracting tribes, the rest of the country was divided into tax-paying and tax-resisting areas: into *blad makhzan* (land of government) and *blad siba* (land of dissidence). The latter fluctuated in size but covered something close to half the territory of the country. The loose and fluctuating division of the land into *makhzan* and *siba* was the central fact of Moroccan history: the United States had its moving frontier, Morocco had a static one. Most mountainous and desert terrain, and most but not all Berber areas, were *siba*.

One might well ask whether a country, about half of which is permanently outside the political order and moreover speaks in the main a different language, should be called *one country* at all. Although of course the modern nationalist territorial notion of 'country' was absent, nevertheless I think the answer is Yes. The lands between the Sahara, Atlantic and Mediterranean have a considerable geographic unity (only to the East is the frontier somewhat more arbitrary), and they were united by Islam. Dissidence, though accounting for one half of this territory, was geographically discontinuous, and it was self-consciously a *dissidence from* something, something which was tacitly recognized in various ways, including the use of the notion of *siba* in self-characterization.

The relationship between the central power and the tribes of this kind of 'external proletariat' were as follows: the latter were in a permanent *state* of dissidence. (Rebellion, in the language of linguistic philosophers, was a dispositional, not an episodic concept.) They were a threat to the central power; a kind of political womb of potential new dynasties; a moral scandal, being addicted to brigandage, heterodox practices and, allegedly, sexual licence, etc. Similarly, central power was a threat to them: a strong monarch would periodically mount expeditions against them. The essence of government, in fact, was a highly peripatetic court and army, with a multiplicity of 'capitals', and local officials, who were really local power-holders who were ratified by the monarch and had made their submission to him.

Nevertheless, the political bifurcation of the country (*makhzan/siba*) was compatible with unity in other senses. Economic and religious life moved across the (often vague and fluctuating) border between the two kinds of area. Regular pilgrimages took pilgrims across it; markets existed on either side; religious orders had lodges on either side, and local 'saints' had followers drawn from either side. Indeed an important function of the various local religious centres was precisely to facilitate and guarantee contact across septic frontiers, not merely between *makhzan* and *siba*, but also between various tribes.

This aspect of Moroccan history—the existence of a large penumbra of anarchy surrounding the political community—is very well documented, for the following reason: the French policy in Morocco was accompanied and supported by highpowered and highbrow historiography and sociology, and the French case was not so much that modern Morocco was a colonial creation, like some tropical African states, but rather that the overcoming of *siba*, and hence national unification, was a French achievement. Whatever the ideological uses of the historic fact of *siba*, there can be little doubt that it was indeed a fact. Moroccan nationalist writers who react against French interpretations do not deny it, but merely re-interpret it (as indicative, for instance, of democratic rather than absolutist traditions).

To sum up: the traditional power set-up was a mildly unstable stalemate between dynastic central power, based on towns and the plain, and hill and desert tribes who successfully defied it.

THE FRENCH PERIOD [II a].

This situation changed with the coming of the French in this century. The colonial period in Morocco took the form of a 'protectorate', i.e. the French ruled 'in the name of' the old dynasty. The *ancien régime* continued, in name. The French *nouveau régime*, however, which effectively ruled, did not also perpetuate the old stalemate with the marginal tribes. It subdued them. (As we have seen, the territorial unification of the country, for the first time, was one of its proud claims.) *All* the tribes were now, by 1934, incorporated in the state. And although the *nouveau régime* had taken some time to subdue the tribes, it was fairly successful in coping with them and administering them subsequently. The antithesis, and the ultimate doom, of the old *makhzan*, i.e. the tribes, was not an insuperable problem for the new, French *makhzan*.

The *nouveau régime* found its doom elsewhere. This part of the story is pure Marx. With the French administration providing security and an infrastructure of transport, communications, etc., a modern economy mushroomed at great speed and generated a typical proletariat of an early stage of industrialization— recently sucked off the land, uprooted, unspecialized, extremely ill-housed, severely underemployed, and politically explosive. *This* was the dissidence of the new régime. The termination of French rule came when this new internal proletariat went into active dissidence ('terrorism') in the early 'fifties, led by a new intelligentsia and in alliance with the symbolic head of the *old* régime. They were joined, when the battle was virtually won, by parts of the countryside as well. They were, of course, helped by the favorable international situation, and in particular by the situation in neighboring Algeria.

It is interesting to note that each of the two successive régimes was quite capable of coping with the doom, the generated antithesis, of the *other*: as in chess, each could 'take' diagonally, but not straight. The new power could cope with tribes through superior technology and organization; the old could always cope with an urban mob, mainly by not needing it—rather the reverse, for townsfolk needed the government for defense against the tribes.

But the new proletariat and the recent political history of Morocco as such are not our concerns here: tribal/governmental relations are.

One feature of the French Protectorate period was that the previous wolves-beyond-the-pale became the latest sheepdogs: the central power used the Berber tribesmen to keep order, both through native troops and through tribal tyrants such as the famous Glawi, Pasha of Marrakesh. This was a fairly good way of controlling one of the traditional, walled towns: an ad hoc levy of tribes-men would be camped under the walls, and let inside them unless rioters inside desisted. But it was not usable against the new dissidence, the new proletariat, in its shantytowns, *bidonvilles*. Bidonvilles have no walls, so that there is no way of using a levy as a threat without letting it loose, and in any case, there is not much to loot inside.

Another important feature of this period was that, in one sense, the tribesmen continued to be insulated. It is true that the Pax Gallica reigned, and tribesmen could go and seek work in the plain, etc. But for those who remained in their villages and encampments—who, after all, were the majority—political life remained, in a new way, as local and circumscribed as before, perhaps more so. This was for a number of reasons:

(1) The *Dahir berbère* And All That. This is one of the most well-worn themes in the discussion of modern Morocco: it is not, in fact, as important as some other associated factors, but in view of its notoriety I shall take it first.

This *dahir* (degree) was promulgated in 1930 and underwrote the retention by Berber tribes of their tribal customary law, if they chose to retain it, as opposed to Koranic Law administered by Koranic judges, and to centralized, national law. Tribal law is differentiated from Muslim law by being, of course, secular; and (contrary to a widely held stereotype of the tribal mind) it is seen and held to be secular, as emanating from the traditions of the tribe and changeable by consent. It differs from Muslim law in content on various points, of which the most interesting perhaps are (*a*) method of proof, tribal law recognizing and favoring proof by collective oath with supernatural sanctions at traditional shrines, etc., and (*b*) concerning family matters, notably by frequently excluding female inheritance in these severely patrilineal tribes, whereas Koranic law, *in theory*, ensures that the daughter inherits one half of the share of the son. But the most important differentiation of tribal law is not to be found in its content or in its meta-legal theory, but in (*c*) the fact that it invokes local lay tribunals rather than trained, specialized, individual judges.

The historic significance of the promulgation of the *Dahir berbère* was that it triggered off modern Moroccan nationalism, and bridged the gap between old Islamic feeling and the modern national one. The *Dahir* provoked violent protests from the learned guardians of Islam in the old towns, and these protests were echoed in Muslim lands as far as Indonesia. It was seen as the official underwriting of scandalous heterodox practices: it was also seen as a prelude to an attempt at converting the Berbers to Christianity: and it was *also* seen as a Divide and Rule measure destined to alienate the mountain tribes from the national community. The history of modern Moroccan nationalist movements begins with the protest movements against the *Dahir berbère*.

(2) The tribal regions were now administered by military officers or civilians (according to region) and, in practice, every region lived a political life fairly insulated from the others. It is true that all regions were united with each other in one political system: but unifying links between them were modern, not only on the physical plane (cars, jeeps, and telephones, which in rural areas were most precarious), but, more significantly, they were such on the human plane. They were connected by a network of bureaucrats, Frenchmen, in French, related by a modern bureaucratic hierarchy and procedures. All these were of course a

mystery to the tribesmen: as far as they were concerned, the local district officer was the representative of a power whose principles and inner mechanics they did not understand and could not hope to influence. There was hardly any question of playing off someone at the center of the hierarchy against its local representative: the tribesmen would not have known how to find, how to approach, or how to influence such a personage at the center. Hence each administrative district was, for the tribesman, a complete world on its own, whose battles and problems were worked out locally.

All this is a slight exaggeration. Some exceptional, really big tribal chieftains could play a political game at a more than local level. The Glawi, friend of Winston Churchill, lived a cosmopolitan life in the political as well as other senses[1] with town houses in Paris and Casablanca as well as a palace in Marrakesh and a castle in the tribal homelands amongst the Glawa tribe. Occasionally, and notably under the Glawi's leadership, local rural leaders might form a political movement active on the national level. Again, a local tribal dignitary might resist the French administration's pressure on a point of national policy,[2] but these were exceptions. Basically, local life was local life, self-enclosed and self-sufficient. The links which united the regions were beyond the reach or the comprehension of illiterate tribesmen.

The theory of power during this power was that of *reduplication*: just as, at the top (in theory) power was shared by the Sultan and the French proconsul, so at each level a Moroccan and a French official were paired off (excepting, of course, at the lowest levels—village headmen did not have an attendant Frenchman—and in technical services). The reality was however affected by different factors. Take any administrative region: at its head, a French captain and a tribal *caïd*, such dignitaries being imposed on (and chosen from) even those tribes who did not traditionally have any permanent chiefs, but elected them annually. The two men, captain and *caïd*, faced each other: but their positions were very different. The captain was at the bottom end, at the end of the antennae, as it were, of a hierarchy reaching up to the proconsul, assisted by many specialist technical agencies, and endowed with genuine means of communication, moral and physical, and a discipline. The *caïd*, on the other hand, was at the top of a local hierarchy, leading up from village or clan headmen to himself, with whom he in turn could communicate perfectly. One of the men, the caïd, was as it were at the ceiling of his world, the other, the captain, on the floor of his: yet they were at the same level, both supervising the same number of people and the same area, and even, roughly, with similar power. The consequence was this: for the tribesmen, political life was the conflict of local groups, alignments, lineages, families, for local power, and the game was played out within the region: it was of course important, indeed crucial, to gain the support

[1] One of his mistresses was a French actress of distinction, who was duly rewarded by a handsome piece of landed property in Morocco. In her declining years, in an administrative theatrical post in France, she charged one of the district officers, an army captain, to look after her Moroccan land. In her case gallantry, if not Muslim law, ensured some female inheritance, as it were.

[2] The chief of the Ait Atta of the Shadow (i.e. of the Northern slopes of the Atlas) did so in the early 'fifties, and suffered exile in the South in consequence.

of the administration, but this meant, essentially, its one local regional representative. There was not much point—nor the means—to look towards the provincial or, still less, the national capital. Each administrative district was politically, very nearly, an island unto itself—despite the fact that roads were clear of bandits and one could cross tribal frontiers in security[1]

TRANSITION FROM [IIa] TO [IIb].

Independence came during the winter of 1955–6, as a result of a number of factors, including the international situation, urban 'terrorism', etc., and, towards the end, rural uprisings. Only these last concern us.

First of all, it is interesting that the rural troubles for the French came only towards the end, when the direction of events was becoming clear, and contained an element of band-waggon-jumping. I am not suggesting that the tribesmen were basically pro-French: but what does follow, I think, is that a reasonably intelligent and well-organized *nouveau régime*, a modern administration which is well-staffed, well-informed and well-trained, does not have too much difficulty in controlling tribal populations in areas where the tribal organization is well preserved. These rural social structures, like some kind of scaffolding, are easy to perceive: there are no large anonymous, amorphous, uncontrollable masses. It is not difficult to operate a 'prefect system' which utilises internal local divisions and provides sufficient spoils for some to control the others. A squirearchy of *caids* was supported, and if necessary invented and created.

When rural troubles did come, they varied in kind, along a spectrum whose extremes were the following: (*a*) fully planned, 'modern' operations, based in this case on Spanish territory; these were in no sense tribal, but manned rather by 'politically conscious elements'; (*b*) totally unplanned, genuinely tribal and extremely violent outbreaks of hysteria, such as that of the Smala tribe on August Twentieth 1955, leading to the massacre (and multiple retaliatory counter-massacre) of Oued Zem. Other risings were between these extremes: for instance, they might be led by a nucleus of 'politically conscious' men who had received instructions from the underground political party, but who led men who still acted in local kin units.

Those groups of rebels who were at all organized continued to exist, and indeed to multiply, even after the French had given in and fighting had ceased. Indeed the number of such groups multiplied, and many were by them locally organized and drilled. They were known as units of the 'Army of Liberation'.

An important fact for the present argument is the following: during the negotiations between nationalist leaders and the French in the autumn of 1955, and indeed earlier, an important argument on the French side—sincere or not—

---

[1] One of the factors in the decline in importance of rural holy lineages was precisely this: their settlements on inter-tribal borders lost their function of facilitating inter-tribal trade and movement.

was to query the standing of the opposing negotiators, or would-be negotiators, and to cast doubts on their qualification to speak for their fellow-nationals. A frequent argument from the illiberal French Right was always that there are no valid representatives, that the 'agitators' are not entitled to speak for their contented or misguided fellow-nationals, that there are no *interlocuteurs valables*.

The answer on the part of the national leaders was this: we prove that we speak for our nationals, that *we*—and not this or that political rival or French stooge—are the recognized leaders, by the fact that *our* order for a cessation of hostilities will be observed. For, as stated, the countryside was full of growing armed or militant groups, some of them engaged in hostilities. Some of them were certainly organized by the nationalist leaders who claimed authority over them; others had arisen in all kinds of semi-spontaneous ways. It is doubtful whether anyone could be quite sure whose order they would take. In the end, these groupings were disbanded or incorporated in the new Royal Army: but only in the end, and after several years of continued activity.

The point which is crucial here is this: there was a situation where no one really knew clearly whose authority counted. There had been no election conferring a mandate on this or that man or party, and if there had been, it would not have been very relevant. The only demonstration—or, indeed, disproof—of a claim to leadership and authority by a man in the capital was that *his* voice was heeded by some reasonably formidable organized group in the countryside. Very crudely, the weight of a man's, or party's, voice in the capital was a function of the number of men willing to lay down their arms at his orders in the countryside. The self-identification of the *interlocuteurs valables* in the face of the French set up a model for the demonstration of influence in the subsequent years of Independence.

INDEPENDENCE [II b].

Independent modern Morocco came into being in the Spring of 1956. In theory, this was a restoration of the pre-French-protectorate, pre-1912 state. Theoretically all power was vested in the Sultan,[1] who however now, significantly, decided to have himself called King, '*malik*', thus hinting at the shift of image from theocratic empire to national state. So much for theory. The realities had changed since 1912. There were now modern towns alongside the old and vast shantytowns alongside the new towns, a modern administrative machinery and

---

[1] There is a rival, Left theory which denies that this was traditionally the case. It maintains, instead, that traditional, pre-1912 Moroccan government was based on consent. Part of the evidence for this thesis is precisely the existence of dissidence, *siba*, of opting-out by regions and tribes, and of recognized ritual acts for opting-in, for submission. The thesis goes on to maintain that the absolutist interpretation of the past of the Moroccan state was a French invention, designed to rationalize the Sultan's abdication of power in favour of his 'Protectors'. Cf. M. Lahbabi, *Le Gouvernement marocain à l'aube du XXe siècle* (Rabat, 1958), and E. Gellner, 'The Struggle for Morocco's Past', in *The Middle East Journal*, winter 1961.

economic infrastructure, a small modern élite. Also, as indicated, there was no longer a penumbra of dissident tribes.

The political situation of the tribes was now determined by the following factors: Abrogation of the *Dahir berbère*. The 'Rural Communes'. Abolition of the 'feudal class'. The Administration. The Separation of Powers. The Emergence of Political Parties. Each of these must be considered in turn.

THE ABROGATION OF THE *DAHIR BERBÈRE*

Tribal customary law and tribunals were now abolished, and replaced by national law administered by appointed, non-local judges. As far as the actual content of law was concerned, this made less profound a difference than one might suppose. For instance, collective tribal lands (pastures, forests) were the concern of the Ministry of Interior, not of Justice, and its agents were free to adjudicate or decide disputes according to traditional local criteria. Judges were also aided by 'assessors' whose role was not all that different from that of members of Customary Law tribunals under the French. But it did mean the termination of the customary tribunals and their sessions—which used to be prolonged, regular, and canalized much local energy into cheap and enjoyable litigation—and this termination incidentally stimulated a greater recourse to informal arbitration, which in a sense was closer to the real, pre-French traditional situation than was the embalming of 'custom' in the ice-box of indirect rule.

Whilst tribal separatism was to be abolished, new 'rural communes' were to be set up, as forms of local democracy and aids for development. In fact, however, these were a long time coming, and when they were set up and elections held for them in 1960, they did not amount to much: their powers and resources are too limited. They may yet—especially if the Left came to power—become institutions of importance; but as yet, they are not very significant.

THE CLASS OF TRIBAL *CAIDS* WAS ABOLISHED

The *name* was transferred to the bureaucrat, a non-local official, who now replaced the French district officer. The only locally recruited officer-holders were headmen at village level, or at most clan level where the groups involved were not very large. This did have an enormously important consequence: there was no outlet, in the *official* hierarchy of the state, for the ambitious local who wished to operate locally, or whose local interests or lack of formal education prevented other than local activity. Admittedly, there were the village headmanships—but the power, prestige and perks attaching to these are not significant.

The essence of Independence was the continuation of the administrative machine, but with Moroccan personnel replacing the French. But: as indicated, the old dualism was gone. A district no longer had an official, representing central power, facing a tribal leader, representing the local groups: there was only *one* administrative hierarchy, which down to and including the level of district officer consists of appointed, non-local professional officials, and which below that level consists of local, non-professional, part-time headmen, etc.

But if the central/local duality disappeared, another form emerged. One of the big slogans of post-Independence Morocco was the 'Separation of Powers', a Good Thing which characterizes all forward looking nations. There are various reasons why this excellent eighteenth-century ideal should have been so much invoked in Morocco: opposition to the usurpation of powers by the French previously, the 'confusion of powers', as the Moroccan press called it; the fact that it was a slogan cherished by the Left as a future lever against royal power, and also by the monarchy against party power; and as a diversion of interest from the failure to implement some other anticipated reforms which were expected from a constitutional, democratic, progressive state. The separation of powers meant a number of things, and some of its manifestations were odd.[1]

But in the rural tribal areas it had primarily the following meaning: previously, the district officer, whilst facing the tribal leader, was himself the undisputed and complete master of the administrative outpost and all the important and manifold activities emanating from it. The administrative outpost, one should say, is a striking and important enclave in tribal lands, standing for the central power and modernity. Now, however, authority within it came to be divided: the administrator and the new judge were distinct, and each had his own Ministry to answer. Each tended to be 'modern' at least to the extent of understanding what went on in the capital. This opposition was not one between a man who could appeal to the center and one who could not (but on the contrary based his power on a local following and understanding), but between two men neither of whom was a local and both of whom could appeal to the center. Ironically, and inconveniently if they were in conflict, both these capital-oriented officials depended on the same solitary and highly precarious telephone line, the same telephone operator, etc., and hence were liable to have some difficulty in keeping things secret from each other.[2]

The recruitment of the new administration was from (*a*) men who had held subordinate positions as clerks, interpreters, etc., to the French, (*b*) men distinguished in the Resistance against the French, and (*c*) men literate in the traditional, Arabic-urban sense. It was the first of these classes, with their prior

---

[1] The police, for instance, remained under the direct control of the monarchy and not the Ministry of the Interior.

[2] The matter was of course further complicated by the trilingual situation. The administration continued to work in French. Some administrators were Arab, some Berber. Some were literate in Arabic, some in French, some in both, and some in neither. Thus many needed interpreters, either to read documents in one of the two written languages (Berber is not written), or to communicate with locals. For instance, a document marked 'Confidential' would reach an administrator who happened to be illiterate (the man I have in mind, I should add, is otherwise very able, and was given his post as a reward for ably organizing a very daring rebellion during the final months of French rule). He would, of course, be at the mercy of some of his subordinates when it came to reading the document: these subordinates might be politically opposed to him.

knowledge and experience of the administration that was to be kept going, who were the most important.

THE POLITICAL PARTIES

These organized widely immediately after Independence, setting up cells throughout the country. In the immediate post-Independence wave of enthusiasm, recruitment was enormous, and it has been calculated that the total claimed membership of all the parties was larger than the total population of the country. But even subsequently, cells and organization and affiliation survived. This is the crucial fact. The parties provided an organization, a hierarchy, and a channel of information leading right up to the provincial and national capitals. The rural regions were now incorporated in the national community, and local politics were not, as under the French, locally circumscribed.

Hence it was now important to have a line to the capital, to have a friend at court. Moreover, there was no outlet other than political parties for the ambitious local: the official hierarchy was now single-track, or at least not divided on the local/central principle, and all posts in it at attractive levels, i.e. at all levels above the very lowest, were reserved for full-time non-local officials. These factors explain the incentives for the locals to be active in the parties; and there were equally incentives for 'men at court', i.e. politicians at the national level, to be willing and anxious to organize these channels and antennae leading into the recesses of the countryside. This was not merely because it was always possible that the much-announced national elections would really be held one day: but also, as explained earlier, influence at the center was in part a function of what rural support a man could claim or mobilize. This was a game of poker in which generally hands were not shown, and in which frequently the participants themselves were not sure, and not in a position to be sure, what cards they held. What locals *said* was not of much consequence: they might proclaim a lot of things (notably an unwavering love of the King), or cautiously keep quiet;[1] what mattered was whom they would obey in a crisis, and this could not be ascertained in advance.[2]

This is not the place to trace the history of the parties. Suffice it to say that, by the end of the 'fifties, three important parties emerged and had their antennae

---

[1] Locals were positively irritated when the fission in the major party forced them to make overt avowals of loyalty in one direction or the other, and often evaded this, certainly in the open. The political structure, both of traditional tribal organization and of the present Moroccan state, makes anticipatory full political commitments, prior to the final result, undesirable and disagreeable. Tribal elections, for instance, *end* in unanimity, however hard-fought or hard-negotiated they may be. In the end it is a matter of sheer courtesy to vote for the victor.

[2] There is an Arab story about a man who went into the desert. His equipment, carefully checked, included matches. To make sure that the matches would prove reliable, he tested and struck each one. . . .

Similarly, those blessed with rural followers cannot test the loyalty of all of them in advance of actual *use*.

of patronage and organization reaching out into the country: the Right, the Left, and the allegedly Berber-Separatist party.

The material must now be drawn together and set against its background. Morocco is a transitional country, which means, amongst other things, that most of the people involved know that fundamental changes in society are coming, and that most of the present social environment—political, economic, social—is extremely precarious and temporary. Hence, the political struggle is played for enormous stakes: not for marginal advantages, or for top positions in a stable structure, but, on the contrary, for control of the direction of the fundamental changes: and the winner takes all. The struggle has not been played out: at present, the parties are jockeying for position and awaiting the suitable moment.

In the meantime, influence is a matter of followers, and followers are those who will follow you in a crisis, or when *the* crisis comes, rather than simply those who will vote for you. (There have in any case been no elections other than local ones.) The incorporation of the countryside in the political life of the nation has meant, in effect, the burgeoning of a number of systems of patronage and support, of a *number* of central nervous systems whose nerve ends reach into the villages. The systems rival the official hierarchies—those, in particular, of the Ministry of Interior, and of Justice—and indeed cut across them and intertwine with them: an official's political loyalty is, in the end, more important than his loyalty to his formal superior, at any rate in a crisis. This complex wiring does of course lead to short-circuits of the currents of power.

These systems of patronage and support are, however, necessarily in part covert, and also extremely loose-jointed, so to speak. They are anchored onto local situations by being connected with local rivalries: the local Montagues join party X, and the Capulets become the branch secretaries of Y. But the local issues dividing the Montagues and Capulets have a good deal of autonomy, and are not necessarily connected with national ones: *one* of the things which is liable to happen is that they erupt into violence, as local strife in rural Morocco habitually has done in the past, and take on the appearance of political violence. But this is not the only thing which happens. The local rural pressure organizations must, if they are to be useful to their patrons at the center, remain fairly ready to be activated for overt action at short notice. They are there, so to speak, with detonators in place and barely a safety catch on. From time to time, they are triggered off: it may be, through one of the local quarrels which really have nothing to do with national issues; or again, it may be that some patron wishes for once to strike a match to see whether it will work when the day comes, or he may wish to show opponents what good matches he has.

When some of this politically explosive material in the countryside is set off in one of these ways, if it does not spread into a national conflagration and trial of strength—which, so far, has not happened—it is put out rapidly. The patron continues to sit in the capital, he may even have to take part in the suppression of a tribal rising which for the time being he cannot commend overtly; but when its leaders are brought to gaol it is his task to see to it that they do not face the full consequences of their transgression. And in as far as alignments at the center are complex and manifold, it is generally not to the interest of those who could exact full retribution to antagonize some group definitively by doing so.

All this, I believe, explains the strange patterns of rural risings, with their rapid collapse and lenient aftermaths—relatively—since Independence. The national political battle has not been fought, and until it is, these little rural dress-rehearsals, the limberings-up of the limbs of patronage and support, are played with restraint: a flare-up, then everyone looks around for reactions, the positions held are analysed as in chess, and the weaker side resigns in a civilized manner—for the time being. Hence it is quite wrong to see these risings as atavistic reversals to tribal independence: they are the very reverse, being a participation in a national game. There is of course some historical connection between the lands of the old dissidence, and the areas of activation of 'armies of liberation', etc.; but the phenomenon is quite different.[1]

---

[1] The contrast I am drawing is not the same as the one drawn, by for instance students of Algeria, between old tribal and new national rebellions. That is a different contrast, and no doubt the crucial one for Algeria. But here, we are contrasting old tribal dissidence with new revolts which are not 'national' either—they are *not* attempts at setting up regional independence—but are a move in a new national type of politics.

20

C. C. Stewart

Mauritania is a country divided between the Maghreb and the Sudan, culturally dominated by the former and, until independence, economically and administratively a part of the latter. It is at the western end of a belt of states which link white North Africa with black Africa, and it shares with these countries many of the same explosive social, ethnic and religious problems which are perhaps most dramatically and tragically illustrated today in Chad and the Sudan. The country and people of the *vide*, as Mauritania was known to the French, were only marginally affected by the colonial period in comparison to the imprint left by France on the neighboring states of Algeria and Senegal, and even Morocco, and because of this the legacy of the colonial period in Mauritanian social history appears in bold relief against the background of traditional society. The French colonial experiment did produce some alterations to the Moorish social structure, but the bases of political authority and social class in nineteenth-century Mauritania have undergone remarkably little change.

These points are all related, and one object of this essay will be to demonstrate this in a discussion of political authority and social stratification in Mauritania. The theme of this story is the continuity of nineteenth-century political concepts and social institutions in contemporary Moorish society. This theme has been considered in the context of the emergence of a Mauritanian state in which traditional Moorish society finds itself in competition with a sizable minority of other ethnic groups as well as the apparatus of a modern state. My own perspective is that of an historian who has studied nineteenth-century Mauritanian history and lived in the camps and the capital of the country, during which time many of the impressions reported below were formed; this is obviously a very large and complex subject, and only the highlights of it can be traced below.

THE LAND AND THE PEOPLE

The Islamic Republic of Mauritania encompasses a vast stretch of the western Sahara, known in the Arab world as Shinqit, which is bordered on the south by the Senegal river and Mali, on the east by Mali and Algeria, and on the north by Algeria and the Spanish Sahara. Apart from two series of ridges and plateaux in the north (Adrar) and southeast (following a line from the Tagant plateau to Oulata) there are few distinguishing geographical features; most of the country is made up of 'live' or semi-stabilized dunes aligned in a northeast–southwest pattern, punctuated by occasional *aftouh* (plains), *aouker* (plateaux formed by dunes) and *sebka* (hillocks and high dunes). As one moves from the southeast of the country and the Senegal valley, which is the granary of Mauritania, to the great ergs of Adrar the depth of water tables increases and the amount of rainfall decreases rapidly as does the amount of vegetation, and as a result some 80 percent of the population today live on 25 percent of the land in the eastern and southernmost sections of the country.[1] The Moors are cattle and camel herders and it is by their livestock husbandry, their keen commercial sense and, from the late eighteenth century onwards, through the selling of gum (*acacia senegal* and *acacia verek*, mainly) to European traders along the Senegal river and the Atlantic coast, that they have traditionally supported themselves. Today, mineral discoveries in the north of the country (iron ore) and in the center and south (copper and rare earths) which are being exploited by international consortiums are altering this traditional economy, at least in the nation's import and export statistics. But well over 90 percent of the population, variously estimated as being between 500,000 to 1,500,000, continues to lead a traditional nomadic or semi-nomadic life or to cultivate lands in the Senegal basin; for them rainfall, spring herbage, water tables or summer floods are far more weighty concerns than fluctuations of the world iron or copper markets.

It should be stressed that Shinqit encompasses a vast geographical area, and within that area there are wide variations in the social and political institutions which will be described here. This is particularly apparent as the 'Moorish social structure', which will be referred to below, merges in the east with Tuareg peoples and in the north with Berber tribes south of the High Atlas, more or less marked off by the Reguibat and Tekna in northern Mauritania and the Spanish Sahara. Within Mauritania we will be dealing with the peoples in the southwest corner of the country, or regions of Trarza and Brakna which are known collectively as the *gebla*, where, today, 53 percent of the Moors live. The population density of the *gebla* is 4·8 per square kilometer; the national average is 0·8 per square kilometer. Largely because of the population density and economic affluence of this area much of the politics of modern Mauritania tend to intimately concern the *gebla* and out of the *gebla* have come the greater part of the country's principal political and historical figures.[2]

The inhabitants of the *gebla* in the nineteenth century were regarded by themselves as comprising two broad ethnic groups: the *bidanis* or 'whites' who claimed Arab or Berber origins and who were so distinguished by a more or less elaborate genealogy to prove their claims, and the *sudanis* or 'blacks'. This latter group, like the *bidanis*, was of mixed social origins but dominantly Sarakolé, Bambara, Wolof or Toucoulor and Fulani, most of whom had been absorbed into the camps of the *bidanis* and were generally subservient to them. The terms

[1] The demographic statistics here and below, unless otherwise stated, are drawn from the *Enquête démographique, 1964–65, résultats provisoires*, Paris, 1966, prepared for the Ministère des Finances, du Plan et de la Fonction Publique de Mauritanie, by the Société d'Etudes pour le Développement Economique et Social.

[2] The chief exception is, of course, Shaikh Ma al-Aynain, whose activities in the north of Mauritania, Rio de Oro and southern Morocco in the early twentieth century certainly were external to the gebla, but even this episode in Mauritanian history can be interpreted as a reaction to the politics of Sidiyya Baba in the gebla and it did intimately concern that region.

'Moor' and 'Moorish'[1] will be used below to describe jointly those *bidanis* and *sudanis* who have lived traditionally in a symbiotic relationship in Mauritania and shared the common Hassaniyya tongue. Among the Moors, noble *bidanis* represented in the nineteenth century about 20 percent of the population and the *bidani* tributaries and *sudanis* 80 percent, although it must be stressed that these categories are not based on color so much as class. A man, black in color but with a noble genealogy which is socially acceptable may be a *bidani*, just as some *bidanis* in the nineteenth century held social positions on a level with *sudanis* for lack of a noble genealogy. This ratio of *bidani* nobles to their *bidani* and *sudani* tributaries is mentioned to emphasize that the descriptions below involving *bidani* nobles will be dealing with a very small, albeit important, fraction of Moorish society and an even smaller fraction of the Mauritanian population today.

By way of background for the story which follows a brief historical note will be necessary because mid-nineteenth-century Moorish social structures and relationships repeatedly refer, for points of reference, to either the sequence of the arrival of putative ancestors in Shinqit or the role played by tribes in an event known as Shurr Bubba. The peopling of Mauritania is an exceedingly complex subject and one on which considerable study has been and continues to be given by Moorish historians. Several broad waves of immigration into Shinqit can be discerned from the numerous and often conflicting accounts in popular history.

Reputedly, the first ancestors of the present inhabitants of the country came into Mauritania with the Almoravid chieftain Abu Bakr ibn Umar when, in the eleventh century, the Almoravids invaded the western Sahara and occupied the ancient empire of Ghana. Other Moors claim to have descended from peoples who came from Morocco or Touat during the following two centuries, and a third influx of peoples began to filter into Shinqit from the fifteenth century onwards who trace their descent from Hassan of the Bani Maqil. It is from this last group that the Hassaniyya language takes its name; oral literature suggests that the peoples who preceded the hassanis, as the descendants of Hassan have become known, spoke a Berber dialect, Znaga, which is still found in small pockets in Trarza.

There have been, of course, other waves of immigration and emigration to and from Shinqit which have followed these earlier migrations, the most dramatic recent ones being the impact of the Moroccan Ouled Bou Sba in the gebla in the late nineteenth and early twentieth centuries and the exodus from Shinqit, at the time of the French arrival, of individuals and families who felt their religious or political views threatened by the incoming French administration. Most of the migrants into Shinqit gradually moved toward the south, either pushing ahead

---

[1] The appellation 'Moor' comes from Latin and has been applied at various times to Muslim peoples from Andalusia to the Senegal basin. Its use in describing the inhabitants of Shinqit was formalized at the time of the French conquest of the western Sahara, although it had been in use at least since the eighteenth century, and it is used today by Mauritanians. A Moorish noble, however, until recent times would be more likely to identify himself as a*bidani* rather than the less precise term 'Moor'.

of them or incorporating the previous inhabitants who are known today only as the 'Bafours'. The attractions of southern Mauritania have been mentioned above; pasturage was relatively abundant, the banks of the Senegal offered limited cereal cultivation, gum harvests provided, after the late eighteenth century, a medium of exchange for the purchase of European luxury goods—cloth, firearms, paper, tobacco, etc.—and the negro population on both banks of the Senegal provided an inexhaustible supply of labor. It was in this manner that sudanis were incorporated into Moorish society, as hewers of wood and drawers of water, but because of their low social status, their origins or point of entry do not figure conspicuously in the history of the peopling of Shinqit.

The watershed in the image of Mauritanian history is an event known as 'Shurr Bubba' or the War of Bubba, which is remembered as having taken place between the embittered autochthons, i.e. the pre-hassani, Berber inhabitants of the country and the hassanis themselves. Recent research suggests that there may have been two (or more) such major battles between newly arrived peoples and established tribes, separated by several centuries, and that these have become telescoped into a single event, which is dated as taking place or concluding in about 1672. However this new data, which has only recently come to light, does not alter the importance of the event which has taken on the significance of a foundation myth and which has been widely recognized until recently as *the* event of Shurr Bubba.

Shurr Bubba was launched by a group of the autochthons and, according to oral literature, the battle lasted thirty years. At its conclusion the hassanis were victorious and the defeated peoples swore to renounce warfare, live by the Book (Koran) thereafter, and make available to the hassanis certain defined services such as water rights, hospitality, tribute and religious and legal counsel. In this way the origins of the two major divisions of Moorish nobles are explained. Those who renounced the use of arms after Shurr Bubba were known as *tulba* (literally 'students') or the *zawiya* (people of the religious establishment), called by the French *marabouts*; the victors became known simply as 'hassanis', called by the French *guerriers*.[1]

What is of equal interest to the event itself for the writing of history in Mauritania is that Shurr Bubba marks the earliest time at which written documents appear in Shinqit. To my knowledge no manuscript has yet been uncovered in Mauritania which dates from before the time of Shurr Bubba, but thereafter a few eighteenth-century manuscripts have been uncovered and from the nineteenth century onwards there is a wealth of Arabic materials of very considerable historical value. Many interpretations may be placed on this phenomenon, but for the moment it will suffice to note the importance of Shurr

---

[1] Further refinements of these categories do exist and are socially functional; among the major ones are the distinctions of *zawiya al-zill* and *zawiya al-shums* (zawiya of the shade and sun) between zawiya tribes which fought in Shurr Bubba (and thereafter have lived under the 'shade' of hassani demands on them) and those who were neutral during the war (and thus bask in the sunshine of independence from the hassanis). Also among the zawiya tribes there are distinctions between the older units, the formerly hassani units which 'converted' to zawiya status before Shurr Bubba, and the *tiab* who have become zawiya units since the time of Shurr Bubba.

Bubba as a foundation myth and the emergence of a literate tradition at about the time of Shurr Bubba which, to some extent, documents the war, and, of greater importance, begins to preserve and broaden our accounts of social relationships in Moorish society. In the light of this rather unusual tradition of literacy and scholarship in a nomadic society a few words ought to be said in qualification of its use.

Writing and, indeed, scholarship in Shinqit were the occupation of learned men and women among the zawiya; the purpose of this scholarship was primarily religious—to learn or describe what God's will might be in particular circumstances, but especially in legal matters. However, genealogists and, occasionally, historians did emerge, and the efforts of some of them may be considered as supra-tribal in scope, i.e. they sought to keep track of the pedigrees and history of neighboring or rival units for the purpose of advantageous marriages or for challenging the trumped-up credentials of a rival tribe. It is particularly this latter ramification of the Moors' literate tradition with which we will be concerned here, largely because of its tendency to preserve non-functional social relationships. However, the source of this data must be appreciated for what it is; lengthy genealogical accounts in the post-Shurr Bubba period are available for zawiya tribes, particularly the larger and politically active ones, but comparable data on the hassanis or on tributary bidani groups is definitely weak. For the sudanis and other subordinate classes it is almost non-existent. As a result any effort toward an understanding of authority patterns or stratification in the nineteenth century which is based on this literature, must be recognized as a zawiya-oriented account of Moorish society which can only imperfectly be qualified by the use of French archival sources and contemporary oral data.

SOCIAL ORGANIZATION IN THE GEBLA IN THE EARLY NINETEENTH CENTURY

Standard accounts of the social stratification of Moorish society written by the first 'generation' of French administrators in Mauritania picture a hierarchy of classes, led by the politically dominant hassani tribes which were commanded by an 'amir' in each region (Trarza and Brakna in the *gebla*, Adrar in the north and Tagant in the east). Subordinate to the hassanis were zawiya tribes and several strata of tributaries: the *zenegha* or *lahma* who were bidanis, *haratine* or freed slaves, *abid* or slaves, *mallemin* or smiths, and *iggawen* or musicians and bards. These classifications are based on noblesse, e.g. genealogy, and the infrequency of intermarriage between strata, certainly between bidanis and sudanis, contributed to the impression of at least one observer who has written of the 'Moorish caste system'.[1] Although this presentation of the Moorish social hierarchy is both simplistic and misleading it served well as a model for the early French administrators, as it evidently did for their informants, generally nobles from the

[1] See Constant Hamès, 'La Société maure ou le système des castes hors de l'Inde' *Cahiers internationaux de sociologie*, XLVI, 1969, pp. 163–77.

zawiya tribes who were frequently called upon to explain and interpret Moorish society for the French officials.

However, contrary to this model which sets hassanis over zawiya, the direction of Moorish society was, in actual practice, shared between these two groups which maintained separate identities, economies and cultural traditions. A brief examination of the powers held by the nobles of each of these two groups in the nineteenth century may clarify their bases of authority and lay a foundation for understanding the alterations which have taken place in Moorish society in the colonial period and more recent times.[1]

THE HASSANIS

According to the terms of settlement of Shurr Bubba, certain dominant hassani lineages became the temporal leaders of their society. This took the form of bearing arms, levying taxes and, under particular circumstances, acting as superior mediation authorities in conflicts involving other hassani and occasionally zawiya tribal units within their sphere of influence. What, in fact, this sphere of influence may have been for any one dominant lineage must be redefined in geographical and social terms for each generation and leader.

The means by which a dominant hassani lineage exerted its authority was through its ability to raid rivals or to protect allies, and this ability was dependent upon the strength, fighting ability and loyalty of the dependents and tributaries of the dominant lineage. These dependents and tributaries were only in part made up of blood relations and the greatest part of any raiding force was generally composed of allied zenagha units. The reputations of zenaghas as warriors varied considerably and the loyalty of such support was not always predictable.[2] For each dominant hassani lineage there existed a nearly equal opposing lineage, also served by zenagha warriors, and as a result of this opposition and complementarity in hassani leadership, the sphere of influence and political power of a particular hassani chieftain was extremely variable.

Within Trarza and Brakna the dominant hassani personality was generally addressed by his followers as 'Sultan' or 'Shaikh', which was an acknowledgement of the temporal authority which lay in his prerogatives to lead those who bore arms and to collect taxes. The French addressed these men as 'amirs', a title which has since been popularly adopted and which we will use here but which, as with the title 'Sultan', bears little resemblance to the classical Arabic use of the term. In spite of the prerogatives of the amir in each region, he was no more than the first among equals in his own family and tribe, and with his hassani cousins in his region. The hassani amir was elected by the *jamaa* or council of

[1] The description below has been drawn from an analysis of nineteenth-century correspondence between several politically dominant lineages in the gebla.

[2] H. T. Norris (*Shinqiti Folk Literature and Song*, Oxford, 1968, p. 21) notes that there is a difference in the status of the haratine and zenagha tributaries between Trarza and Brakna; in the former region tribes show more regard for the haratine than for zenagha units, and in Brakna the zenagha are held in higher esteem than haratine.

his tribe which was made up of elders in that unit. He was not a man of great personal fortune and his authority was dependent upon his personality and the power which was vested in him by other hassani colleagues; as an individual he could not take independent action on behalf of his tribe.

The forms of hassani taxation were varied and the mechanisms by which the levies were imposed are unclear; however some general points can be made about the types of levies and the method in which the principal tax, *hurma* or *gharama*, was collected. *Hurma* was a form of tribute paid annually by subservient zawiya or zenagha families to specific families within the dominant hassani lineage in each region, or to the hassani unit to which they were attached. *Hurma* rights could be inherited or sold and, if they lapsed, they could not be collected retroactively. The origins of *hurma* payments are generally traced back to the settlement of Shurr Bubba when certain zawiya and most zenagha families ('tents') were required to pay to their protectors, on demand, an annual sheep, or two calves, or one piece of *guinée* cloth, etc. Another, similar form of tribute was the *ghafar* which could either be tribute paid by subservient hassani families to the dominant families in their region, or protection money paid by caravans for the assurance of an uninterrupted passage through the hassani's sphere of influence. There were also numerous types of levies on agricultural produce and lands, although the most widespread appears to have been *abbakh* which was set according to the size of the palm grove or agricultural land under cultivation and was paid in *mudds* of dates, millet, etc. In each region in Mauritania the form that each of these levies took had slight variations, and when a new source for revenue was found, which tended to be in connection with stranger groups such as Europeans, travelers and non-Moorish sudanis, the types of taxes which became applicable to them illustrate well the flexibility of the system.

Instances of hassani mediation among tribes within their sphere of influence were limited; this sort of activity was usually left to the shaikhs from among the people of the zawiya. Where the amirs did become involved in arbitration, it generally involved their immediate families and dependents and only very rarely zawiya tribes.

THE ZAWAYA

In contrast to the post-Shurr Bubba stereotype of hassani tribes as being somewhat ruthless, exploiting their tributaries by numerous forms of taxation and extracting protection money wherever possible, the stereotype of the zawiya is one of pacific tribes engaged in pastoral activities and pious meditation. According to the settlement of Shurr Bubba, the zawiya tribes were to renounce the use of force in disputes and to act as the guardians of the Moors' spiritual and cultural heritage. To this role, assigned to them in the foundation myth, which some of them did fulfil, must be added their guardianship of the physical resources of their society, their exploitation of those resources and their own systems of gathering revenue.

The people of the zawiya, generally, were better educated than the hassanis and their observance and application of the *sharia* is perhaps their most distinguishing feature by comparison to the hassanis. As the spiritual guardians of the society they conceived themselves as imposing the discipline of the *sharia* upon hassanis, wherever possible, and this is frequently demonstrated in their mediating disputes, acting as *qadis* for hassani units and acting as spiritual counsellors to hassani figures. It was among the zawiya that literacy flourished and because of this the Moors' culture and, indeed, the very structure, i.e. genealogical records, of their society was in the hands of the zawiya scholars.

Emphasis ought to be placed here on the zawiya scholars; just as the character and spirit of the hassanis as a group were personified by the amir and his lineage, so too the embodiment of the zawiya 'type' was a small number of erudite men whose libraries, literary works, religious influence and students represented the ideal of zawiya achievement. In this respect the learned zawiya figures resemble in their scholarship and mediation activities, the *igurramen* described by Ernest Gellner in the central High Atlas of Morocco.[1] The vast majority of the zawiya were not, of course, mediators and scholars, although there was a firmly established tradition of literacy among the zawiya tribes generally. In Gellner's terminology, most of the zawiya tribes were lay units.

The zawiya tribes have been described as controlling the economic resources of the country; the exploitation of salt and its marketing and the gathering and selling of gum were among their responsibilities. Hassanis were thus dependent upon the industry of the zawiya tribes for their salt revenue (in Trarza where the amir levied a tax on salt extraction) and for customs duties paid by European traders on their gum purchases. Only zawiya tribes could create and maintain wells, but hassanis were permitted to use them during specified hours; commercial caravans were organized by the zawiya, but the protection of those caravans rested with the hassanis. Although the greater part of the livestock in the gebla was in the hands of the zawiya tribes and the total population of the zawaya was much greater than that of the hassanis, most zawiya tribes were divided into small, dispersed herding units for the purpose of pasturage and they were highly vulnerable to attacks by those hassani units which were not bound to protect them or to honor their protection by another hassani tribe.

Among the zawaya there was also a system of gathering revenue, not unlike the taxation of the hassanis. This centered around various forms of religious offerings such as the *zakat* which could be entrusted to noble families or shaikhs of apparently either hassani or zawiya descent. Revenues which were exclusively the prerogative of the zawaya were the *ghabd*, paid to shaikhs and their families, *hadiyya*, or religious offerings to *shurfa* or, in Trarza, shaikhs in general, and *tajharbit*, given to a teacher, *qadi* or scholar for their *baraka* or upon a son's completion of the Koran. Other revenue came from *hubus* or gifts in the form of endowment presented to religious figures.

In contrast to the hassani chief as a *primus inter pares*, the shaikh of a zawiya tribe held very real authority. Large zawiya tribes were frequently divided in leadership between temporal and spiritual authorities, but the balance of power appears to have rested with the spiritual head. Although the consent of the

[1] Ernest Gellner, *Saints of the Atlas*, London and Chicago, 1969.

jamaa was advisable for a zawiya shaikh, his authority and influence were derived in large part from Allah, and because of this he could and often did initiate affairs on behalf of the *jamaa*. This might involve admitting new tributary units to the tribe or committing the tribe, independent of any authority vested in him by his *jamaa*, to the defense of a non-tribal unit.

Something ought to be said here about the interdependence of the hassani and zawiya bidanis and the lower classes of zenagha tributaries, haratine smiths and *iggawen*. Most noble hassani families were served by a number of tributaries whose services—fighting or herding—depended upon the status of their master, and whose food, clothing and general welfare were the responsibility of the head of the noble family. The master–servant relationship which existed between the nobles and their subordinates, however, did not preclude an obligation among the people of the zawiya to educate their attendants, at least in the fundamentals of Islam; the noble children joined in circumcision ceremonies and camaraderie with their contemporaries from these lower classes. This is not to assert that all masters looked upon their tributaries and haratine with benevolence and care, or that the tributaries faithfully and consistently served their masters' interests. The shifting of alliances, particularly by zenagha groups, was common and in some instances zenagha or haratine groups had a great deal of independence from their nobles and could negotiate their rights with their masters or seek advice and counsel outside the tribe to which they owed allegiance. These maneuvers by groups subordinate to hassani and zawiya leadership tended to be motivated by a number of factors, among them the burden of tribute and the geographical proximity of a bidani clan which was capable of defending their interests and which might consent, for example, to the purchase of their *hurma* rights or to pay a gift to their abandoned masters. Other factors include the prestige or greater degree of security or wealth which might be obtained by joining a neighboring tribe, and, for bidani tributaries, the genealogical connections which might be discovered or which might already be known to exist between themselves and their new masters.

In brief, lateral mobility for zenagha and haratine families existed within the social organization of the gebla. As far as the tributaries of hassani tribes were concerned this lateral mobility could determine the balance of physical power between opposing hassani units, while in zawiya tribes the addition of dependents, i.e. labor, meant economic wealth. On a smaller scale, there also existed a limited vertical mobility for zenagha or haratine individuals; a particularly gifted man, either by his service to his shaikh or amir or by virtue of his erudition, could be elevated through marriage or fabrication of his genealogy, to the status of a noble bidani or a bidani. However, such genealogical legitimations do not seem to be a regular occurrence during the post-Shurr Bubba period.

From these descriptions certain conclusions may be drawn about the exercise of political power in Moorish society in the gebla during the early nineteenth century. Traditional Moorish society was directed by two, theoretically separate segmentary, patrilineal groupings, each dependent upon the other for its physical or spiritual security. Nobles from the zawaya enjoyed a life of greater ease and comfort than did the hassanis, yet they were in constant need of hassani protection.

The hassanis, whose security was assured by their allies and their fighting ability, but who were in a minority, lived a more mobile life, yet were dependent upon the zawaya for their water, gum revenues and religious instruction. Strong leadership was in the hands of the zawiya shaikhs who exercised, in theory, no temporal authority; temporal authority was the prerogative of the hassani chiefs, whose only power lay in the directives given by their *jamaa*. Thus the segmentary principles of opposition and complementarity balanced the numerically superior zawaya against the militant hassanis, the pastoral against raiding economies, and spiritual against physical protection.

The separateness of these two groups is perhaps best illustrated by the infrequency, historically, of conflict between hassanis and zawaya. In spite of their pacific ideals, battles between zawiya units were common, and fighting between hassani tribes was frequent; but, very few instances of conflict between a hassani tribe and a zawiya unit are known. This can be interpreted in structural terms. The zawaya did not stem from a single ancestor but rather from a host of 'founding fathers', and few of the zawiya tribes were large enough to militarily challenge an amir and his tributaries. Conversely, the hassanis were dependent upon the zawaya for their revenues and spiritual protection, and it was in their interests to protect rather than make war on the zawaya who were geographically close to them. Also cognatic links between hassanis and zawaya were not unknown, and where these existed they served to ally specific groups.

Finally, it ought to be stressed that the dominant principles of social cohesion in Moorish society, in spite of nominal chieftains in both hassani and zawaya camps, were those of a segmentary society. We have noted the opposition and complementarity at work in determining spheres of influence and political power among dominant hassani lineages, as well as between the hassani and zawaya tribes in the direction of the society. Similarly, within individual tribes competing forms of relationship were subordinate or parallel to the segmentary model. The social hierarchy, the presence of literacy (which tended to preserve non-functional relationships) and the important role played by bidani women and maternal kin (maternal uncles generally were as influential as paternal kin in a child's early years) did not upset this segmentary structure. Within groups of bidanis or sudanis the sense of ethnic or class identity was subordinate to the bonds of family, clan and tribe; and haratine, slaves or smiths living within noble camps were affiliated, in their tributary status, to their bidani nobles, not to their respective tributary strata. Supra-tribal bonds of geographical region, class, ethnic group, language or religion were, for the most part, not functional in the early nineteenth century and therefore did not interfere with the segmentary hassani and zawaya social structures in Moorish society. However, the separateness of these hassani and zawaya traditions should be stressed. Although some hassani units had renounced their militant past and become zawaya, which in effect confused even further an already vague, and historically inaccurate, division between 'Berber' zawiya and 'Arab' hassani traditions, the fiction of these separate identities was kept alive in the nineteenth century. Tensions did exist among the zawiya units between those which traced their origins back to Almoravid times, for instance, and those who had hassani origins, but these tensions were subordinate to the ethnic unity represented by the Berber zawiya tradition in opposition to the Arab, hassani peoples.

CHALLENGES TO THE NINETEENTH-CENTURY SOCIAL AND POLITICAL STRUCTURES DURING THE COLONIAL PERIOD

French commercial interests, along with those of other European powers, had been in regular contact with the Moors of the gebla from the late eighteenth century, but the first serious involvement on the part of French authorities in the internal politics of the region dates from the mid-nineteenth century. We cannot detail here the many ramifications of the efforts made toward the imposition of *la civilisation française* on the rich Arabic/Islamic culture of the Moors, but some French administrative policies, particularly after the 'pacification' of Mauritania got underway in 1903, can be highlighted as being particularly instrumental in challenging the early-nineteenth-century concepts and institutions of political authority and social stratification described above.

From the time of their early contacts with the Moors in the nineteenth century the French formulated and preserved certain misconceptions about how the Moors governed themselves and, in turn, misconceptions concerning the ways in which the French commercial interests and later the government might manipulate Moorish politics to their own advantage. Perhaps their most basic misunderstanding of Moorish society involved its authority structures; 'amirs' were accepted as absolute, if somewhat incompetent sovereigns, and it was to the office of the amirate that treaties were directed, customs duties for the gum trade were presented, and political manipulations were effected. During the first twenty or thirty years of serious French commercial and governmental activity on the Senegal river (1846–66/76), this policy had little real effect upon the internal politics of the gebla. Amirs did not rise above their positions as *primus inter pares* within their hassani coalitions, nor was the succession of amirs noticeably influenced by French policy. But eventually the regular subsidies and 'customs' paid to the dominant hassani lineages did have the result of enlarging their scope of patronage and their ability to command an increasingly more predictable following than had been possible prior to the arrival of the French. This had the dual effect of stabilizing the office and regularizing succession to the office of 'amir' within the families which held the amirate in the mid-nineteenth century. French control over the actions of the amirs was likewise increased and the notion of a somewhat centralized authority structure—which closely approximated what the French thought they had been dealing with for nearly a century—was introduced.

When the French 'pacified' the country between 1903 and 1934, and administered it until independence in 1960, the amirate system was institutionalized as the only possible alternative to direct rule in the gebla. It was in this period, as intermediaries between the French administration and tribes in their regions, that the amirs did, finally, take on the roles which justified earlier French belief

13

386 C. C. Stewart

in the hassani political domination of Moorish society. It was not until 1934, when a particularly thorny dispute over succession to the amir of Trarza required a thorough administrative study of that office, that it was discovered that the amir's authority was not traditional, and it was debated whether the amirate system should be abandoned on these grounds. This was, of course, after the institution of the amir had become firmly implanted, albeit artificially and with limited effect, in local and regional politics.

In direct contradition to this policy of treating exclusively with the amirs in the gebla, Xavier Coppolani began his 'pacification' program in Mauritania, the cornerstone of which was the 'maraboutic' or zawiya tribes, to whom he offered protection against their hassani 'expoiters'. Short-lived as it was, from 1903 until Coppolani's assassination in 1905, his policy did introduce a technique of dealing with the Moors, i.e. balancing the hassani powers, which had been built up as agents of indirect rule, against their zawiya counterparts, which was to be employed in varying forms throughout the colonial era. However, unlike the amirate system which remained an artificial creation, especially after being incorporated into the French administration of Mauritania, this particular divide and rule policy was a close reflection of traditional divisions within Moorish society and it was very effective in maintaining the identity of each group in the face of very profound alterations to the bases of the economic life of the bidani nobles.

The French presence meant, in principle, an end to razzias and, in fact, a greater degree of security for the non-hassanis. However, internal security was only one element in the French effort to correct what they conceived to be a feudal society. In order to free the tributaries from their masters, the administration systematically purchased *hurma* rights from the hassanis and at the same time sunk wells for them. In effect this eliminated most traditional sources of income for the hassanis; although direct subsidies to the hassani nobles were introduced, they were obliged to take up livestock husbandry and commerce. Elsewhere wells were cemented (thus retracting and regularizing nomadic patterns of hassanis and zawaya alike), and communications were improved; motorized transport contributed to the decline of camel breeding and the caravan industry while at the same time expanding markets for European goods.

Ahmed Baba Miské notes that one effect of French rule on the zawiya was that educational standards dropped, and he suggests that this may have been due to a reduced pressure to maintain scholarship as a mark of zawiya status in opposition to the hassanis. The colonial period, he argues, marked a dramatic break with the past and all that the zawiya tradition and influence was built upon—legal scholarship, mediation activities and the maintenance of the archives of civil order.[1] In the light of important functions which the zawiya nobles continued to play during the colonial era, this line of argument may be challenged; but Miské's evaluation is significant, since this decline came at the time of the dramatic shift in the bases of power and economy within the hassani tribes.

Another effect of the French colonial experiment in Mauritania was the

[1] Ahmed Baba Miské, 'Al-Wasit (1911), Tableau de la Mauritanie à la fin du XIXe siècle'. *Bull. IFAN*, No. xxxB, 1969, pp. 138-9.

introduction of western education, although it affected only a small number of Moors. Madarsas were established in four regions of the country between 1920 and 1936 (at Boutilimit, Kiffa, Atar and Tembedra), in which both Arabic and French were taught. At its height the most successful of these schools, at Boutilimit in the gebla, had a staff of five professors—French, Algerians and Moors. For the most part these schools were short lived and were regarded with great suspicion by the noble families, with the notable exception of the Boutilimit madarsa. But the madarsas and the 'Ecole de fils de chefs' at St Louis in Senegal, through which a few Moorish nobles passed, did serve to consolidate the economic and political positions of some noble families *vis-à-vis* the French; because of this the meager French educational effort among the Moors cannot be entirely dismissed as insignificant. However, the zawiya tradition of scholarship in the Islamic sciences remained until independence the basis for evaluating a man's *adab*, or culture, among the nobles, constituting a standard quite apart from the French madarsa system. In contrast, the emancipated sudanis and former tributary classes were far more receptive to the French education and, indeed, had far more to gain by it than the bidani nobles. The ramifications of this in independent Mauritania, led by bidani nobles and a Moorish majority, which depends in large measure upon the technical services of sudani bureaucrats, will be discussed below.

Another important impact of French administration on Moorish society in the post-independence period was the drawing of the frontiers of the 'Territoire Civil' and later the Colony of Mauritania. Prior to the carving out of the territory which is known today as Mauritania, the Moors inhabited an area vaguely known as Shinqit, and the lands to the south of Shinqit, inhabited by Wolof, Toucoulors, Bambara, and Sarakolés, marked the beginning of the *bled es-sudan* which was beyond the pale of Moorish politics and only marginally involved in the historical tradition of Shinqit. This was, of course, of no particular consequence in Paris when the frontiers of the 'Territoire Civil de Mauritanie' were drawn up, nor did it cause any particular problems during the colonial period when ethnic unities were observed for administrative, if not political, convenience. However, today, roughly one-sixth of the country's population which the minority ethnic groups—Toucoulour, Peul, Sarakolé and Wolof—represent has become a major political factor which has had a profound effect on the domestic and external politics of independent Mauritania.

Finally, the emergence of modern political parties in Mauritania may be considered as a last contribution of the French colonial effort toward the creation of a viable political entity in that country. Mauritania was administered by the French from St Louis in Senegal, but the constitution of the Fourth Republic granted the country a separate identity and the representation of a deputy in the National Assembly. Mauritania's first deputy was M. (Ahmedou ould) Huorma ould Babana who, as a member of the French Socialist Party (SFIO), was instrumental in promoting SFIO candidates (and his relatives) in the local elections of 1946 for the Conseil Général and, later, in elections for the Senate and National Assembly. The first Mauritanian parties were created in 1948, when Hurma broke with the SFIO to create the 'Entente Mauritanienne' which was opposed by a party formed in the same year, the 'Union Progressiste Mauritanienne' (UPM), led by Ahmed Saloum ould Haiba, Sidi Ahmed el-Hbib, Mohammed ould Salem and Malik Dyko. The cleavage between these two parties in the late 1940s and early 1950s may be characterized as the opposition between supra-tribal, progressive elements and traditional political authorities, although this is a gross over-simplification. The 'Entente Mauritanienne' was only sporadically active in this period and its policies on domestic and external matters were frequently inconsistent, but it was committed to a replacement of traditional authority structures, and because of this the UPM drew its support from traditional bidani authority figures in alliance with a few sudanis. Honorary presidents of the UPM included Charles de Gaulle, Abdallahi ould Shaikh Sidiya, Ahmedou Mamadou Ba, and Abd al-Rahman ould Bakr, and the party, as this list might suggest, was favored by the French administration. Through their successes in the elections of 1951 and 1952, the UPM emerged as the dominant party in Mauritania. Four years later a split in the UPM drew off some of the more militant members who were pressing for immediate independence and who created the 'Association de la Jeunesse Mauritanienne' (AJM). This was a short-lived splinter party which served to divide the Entente Mauritanienne vote in the 1956 election and helped to return the UPM encumbent, Sidi al-Mokhtar N'Daiye, to the French Assembly.

The next two years, 1956–58, were particularly important for the emergence of political parties and platforms in Mauritania as, indeed, throughout French West Africa, as the French Community was created and prospects of independence became apparent. In Mauritania the party platforms crystalized around several domestic and external issues. Internally, tensions between political leaders of the ethnic minorities in Mauritania and the Moorish politicians and their platforms were evident. They were manifested by the apprehension with which the pan-Arab statements of the AJM were regarded in the Senegal basin, by the emergence of non-Moorish, regional parties such as the 'Bloc Démocratique du Gorgol' (BDG) in 1956, and by efforts made at the same time to establish 'l'Union des Originaires de la Vallée du Fleuve'. A second internal division, mentioned above, was that between politicians representing traditional authority structures—whether of the zawaya or hassani traditions—and those politicians who were less firmly implanted in these traditions and were pledged to their dissolution.

Externally, two issues dominated this period: the claims voiced by Allal el-Fassi in 1956 that Mauritania (along with sections of Algeria, Mali and all of Rio do Oro) constituted an integral part of Morocco, and the question of economic and political union with Senegal and Mali. The cause of a Greater Morocco was taken up by Hurma ould Babana who drew support from some tribal groups in the north of Mauritania, and who was eventually expelled from the 'Entente Mauritanienne' and went to Paris, Cairo and finally Rabat to champion the irredentist movement. Although this active support of Morocco's claims represents an extreme in the spectrum of attitudes taken by individuals and parties in Mauritania during the later 1950s, there were other, more moderate stances represented by the al-Nahda al-Wataniyya al-Muritaniyya party, created in 1958, toward Mauritania's role in the Arab world or her *rapprochement* with Morocco (and immediate independence). All these northern and eastwards-looking movements were regarded with an equal suspicion by the non-Moorish non-Arabic speaking population. Equally intense emotions on the part of the Moors came out of the issue of Mauritania's links with Mali and Senegal, which led to the creation of the BDG in 1956, and, three years later, to the creation of the 'Union Nationale Mauritanienne', which was affiliated to the Senegalese 'Parti de la Fédération Africaine' and which proposed federation with Mali.

In 1958, the 'Entente Mauritanienne' and the UPM united, forming a center group, the 'Parti du Regroupement Mauritanien' (PRM) which attempted to avoid the extremes of alliance with either Morocco or Mali and Senegal, and to maintain a balance between the Moorish population and the black minorities in the newly emergent Islamic Republic of Mauritania. The Secretary General of the party, Mokhtar ould Daddah, was a new figure in Mauritanian politics, and their representative in the National Assembly, Mokhtar N'Daiye, was the former UPM delegate. The balance between the strong PRM on the one hand and Nadha and UNM on the other continued through the declaration of Mauritanian independence on 28 November 1960, during which time the Moroccan irredentist claims intensified, only to subside gradually after independence. In an effort to broaden the base of the PRM as well as to press for more radical policies in development and foreign policy, the party was dissolved in December 1961, to form the 'Parti du Peuple Mauritanien' (PPM) or Hizb Chaab, which dominated Mauritanian politics in the 1960s and became the only political party in the country after 1964. Until August 1964, other efforts to create a viable opposition party continued, including the creation of 'Parti du Front national démocratique' (PFDM) and of the 'Parti démocratique Mauritanien' (PDM) which were led by the same persons (former UNM and Nahda organizers). Neither of these parties got beyond the drafting stages.

In brief, political parties in Mauritania are a post World War II phenomenon, born within the context of AOF (Afrique occidentale française) politics and initially nurtured by the French. The present single party, the PPM, traces its origins back to the first two political parties in Mauritania. In spite of the growing importance of political parties in the late 1950s, the increasing use of them by Moors and non-Moors, and the hiving off and union of separate factions, the personalities leading these parties, factions and unions have been remarkably consistent, and their political platforms remarkably pragmatic. The central themes have not been ones of traditional versus modern authority structures, or of a gradual move toward independence in opposition to immediate independence, although these have been important issues at different times. What appears to have had a far more profound effect on the fortunes of individual parties is the balance they were able to maintain between the increasingly intense fears on the part of black minorities of the possible incorporation of independent Mauritania into North Africa and the Arab world, and the equal apprehension with which association with the *bled es-sudan* has been viewed by the Moorish majority.

In the light of these themes, the colonial experiment in Mauritania reflects many of the same features of colonial administration and politics which are found in other countries in North and West Africa. These include indirect rule, a policy of divide and rule, the creation of new, broader political entities by the incorporation of minority groups under a single administrative unit, the introduction of the metropolitan language and culture, the consolidation of colonial administration and the undermining of traditional authority. Also relevant is the nurture of political parties which are likely to cooperate with the metropolitan country, while at the same time building up a more or less effective apparatus for the administration of an independent state. What remains to be examined are the results of these policies in the post-independence period and in the light of nineteenth-century patterns of social stratification and political power.

CONTINUITY AND CHANGE IN SOCIAL STRATIFICATION AND POLITICAL AUTHORITY

Until the emergence of the independent Islamic Republic of Mauritania in 1960, relatively few alterations to traditional patterns of political authority and social stratification had taken place, and this may be explained in terms of contradictory and self-defeating colonial administrative policies, the vigor of the Moorish cultural tradition, and the indifference with which the French viewed internal politics and social organization in the country. An example of two important French administrative policies which in effect cancelled one another out is the system of indirect rule through amirs (who were no more readily accepted as French administrative spokesmen by their society than other agents of European indirect rule in other colonial societies) and the policy of divide to rule, which served to reinforce traditional divisions between zawiya and hassani units. The economic bases of power for the bidani nobles were theoretically undermined, but this stratum of Moorish society was supported through direct subsidies and alternative economic opportunities. A pastoral economy for the hassanis, commerce, and employment in minor positions in the administration and security forces were provided for a limited number of zawaya and hassanis. But there was no effort to create any infrastructure in the country that might provide an opportunity for 'freed' tributaries to take up other means of livelihood. One cannot even speak of an urban tradition in Mauritania prior to independence[1] and thus the primacy of traditional hassani and zawaya leadership was not challenged by competing political units with a supra-tribal, urban or salaried base. Zawiya tribes did emerge as the economically dominant groups in Moorish society during this period, because of their numbers, their already established tradition as merchants and as exploiters of the country's economic resources, and the dramatic shift in the hassanis' economic bases, probably the most profound effect that the French colonial effort had on Moorish society.

The effort toward introducing French education and the French language had

[1] At independence Mauritania had no capital, and only two of the ten towns in the country had a population in excess of 5,000 persons.

little impact. At the creation of the Islamic Republic of Mauritania, there was only one *lycée* in the country and Mauritania had only a handful of university graduates. Although French administrative units in Mauritania, theoretically, cut across nomadic and sedentarized populations, in fact it would appear that these two sectors of the population (which may be roughly divided into Moors and non-Moors, respectively) were subject to differing degrees of administrative supervision; in the colonial period, as in the nineteenth century, the non-Moorish population was largely beyond the pale of Moorish tribal life.

In their early years of development, political parties represented only a continuation of nineteenth-century patterns of authority in Moorish society. A few very noteworthy exceptions might be cited, but for the most part these parties were formed by bidani nobles, largely from the zawiya tribes, whose alliances—perhaps best illustrated by the honorary presidents of the UPM—frequently were direct transfers of nineteenth-century political coalitions. Even the 'Entente Mauritanienne', which had the most progressive, supra-tribal platform among the early parties, was founded by bidani nobles from the respected Idaw Ali zawiya tribe. Similarly, leadership of successor parties to the UPM and Entente has rested with families whose positions can be traced directly to dominant *fractions* and tribes in the gebla during the nineteenth century.

In spite of this overall continuity in patterns of political authority and social stratification, severe challenges to nineteenth-century institutions and conceptions were absorbed by Moorish society during the colonial period. As a result, gradual change can be observed in the Moorish social structure particularly since independence. Perhaps the most graphic proof of this is the emergence in the twentieth century of an extremely prolific group of bidani, zawiya historians whose chief purpose may be interpreted to be the preservation and codification of a precolonial social order which has come under increasingly severe attack and which is seen to be eroding around them.

This change is particularly apparent in the new capital of Mauritania, Nouakchott, but is also reflected in the northern port of Nouadibou (formerly Port Etienne) where the iron mining interests have established their base, and in other, smaller urban centers. Although Nouakchott, as an administrative center, is little more than ten years old and remains an artificial creation in the eyes of most Moors, the politics of Mauritania (as well as the tensions in Mauritanian national life) have been increasingly focused on the towns and capital of the country. With this nascent urbanization the beginnings of supra-tribal associations can be seen, such as trade union developments (the 'Union des travailleurs mauritaniens'—UTM) and women's organizations which will eventually alter the present primacy of tribal loyalties.

The educational system, too, is encouraging supra-tribal bonds between classmates, although the system itself is a long way from fruition. It has given rise to the 'Syndicat des enseignants de Mauritanie' (SNEM) which, in spite of divisions between Arabic- and French-speaking members, is another example of the supra-tribal organizations which have begun to compete with traditional tribal loyalties and established patterns of political authority. In addition, a 'second generation' of students is now returning to Mauritania which has studied abroad and which views traditional social and political institutions with a greater detachment than the present political leadership in the country. As this increasing influx of graduates becomes greater and more vocal, it would seem a safe assumption that more radical solutions to Mauritania's social and political problems will be sought. Another recent factor that is beginning to have an effect on traditional patterns of social stratification and political authority is the emergence of a Moorish class of entrepreneurs that includes representatives of the lower social strata, thus contributing to a shift in economic resources to a new class of *patrons*.

Finally, perhaps the most profound changes in Moorish social organization in recent times have come as a result of the incorporation of non-Moorish and non-Mauritanian sudanis into the independent Islamic Republic of Mauritania. It has been noted above that, during the colonial period, as in the nineteenth century, Moorish life continued to be divorced from the sedentarized, non-Moorish Wolof, Toucouler, Sarakolé and Bambara populations in the Senegal basin. The numbers of these non-Moorish agriculturalists increased under the protection of the French administration. Immediately before independence, this minority population became a major force in Mauritanian politics, which has been described above in connection with the evolution of pre-independence political parties and accompanying tensions. These tensions have been intensified by the influx of a sizable number—set by some at over half of the 27 percent non-Moorish black population in the country today—of vocal, non-Mauritanian blacks who saw economic opportunities in coming to the new state, since it was sadly lacking in experienced bureaucrats, entrepreneurs and skilled labor. One result has been a deeply felt division between Hassaniyya-speaking Moors and the non-Moors. The latter are divided by the Moors between black Mauritanians, i.e. cultivators who have lived on the right bank of the Senegal river in recent times and who pose no real economic threat; and non-Mauritanian blacks whose social mobility, disproportionate numbers in the government, and indispensible services in the national economy are regarded as a very real threat by the Moorish majority.

This division between Moors and non-Moors has come to center on the use of the Arabic and French languages. When Arabic was made an 'official' language along with French in 1965 (Arabic had formerly been the 'national' language and only French had the status of being 'official'), this decision sparked off a series of disturbances which have occurred periodically ever since in the schools and urban centers across the country.

The tension between Moors and non-Moors, which penetrates every sector of national life has had two effects on Moorish social stratification and Mauritanian politics. From the point of view of ethnicity, the most interesting development has been the evolution—largely since the mid-1950s—of a sense of Moorish identity. The former fictions of Arab and Berber origins and the hassani and zawiya/bidani divisions have been subordinated to the new cohesion of bidanis in opposition to non-bidanis, and to the emergence of a socially and politically functional Moorish group opposed to non-Moorish (and non-Hassaniyya-speaking) blacks. While the emergence of a Moorish identity has served to intensify tensions between themselves and the non-Moors, it is significant that this is the first time that such a unity has been created in Shinqit, and as such it is having an effect on traditional Moorish social stratification. The arena in which these tensions have been played out has been a national one, and the leaders of opposing factions have, for the first time in the history of Shinqit, become national figures, speaking for major segments of the population. Although the price which is being paid, and which will continue to be paid, for this emergence of a Mauritanian nation from a divided Mauritanian people is very high, it is perhaps the most significant political and social development in that country today, and it may prove to be the point from which the gradual disappearance of nineteenth-century patterns of social stratification and political authority can be dated.

Part 4 The Coup of 10 July 1971

BACKGROUND TO THE PUTSCH

The immediate reaction of foreign observers to the recent attempted coup d'état in Morocco was to place it in the context of a general radicalizing trend throughout the Arab world, perhaps best represented by the military régime in Libya that overthrew the monarchy in September 1969.[2] King Hassan II, who nearly lost his life in the bloody massacre at his summer palace, encouraged such commentary by implicating the Libyan government in the effort to topple his régime. Moroccan politics do not fit easily into the general patterns of the Arab world, however, and what is now abundantly clear is that the coup manqué was generated entirely within Morocco and its objectives were based solely on factors peculiar to the Moroccan régime and political system. There is no need to implicate the Soviet Union, the C.I.A., the Libyans, or any number of other possible foreign meddlers to understand, at least in its broadest aspects, what transpired on 10 July at Skhirat.

The attack on the King's summer palace at Skhirat was organized by some of the highest-ranking officers in the Moroccan Army, including four generals. Their plot was one in a series of events during 1970–1 that demonstrated the gradual collapse of a civilian-military alliance—or perhaps more accurately, a clientele relationship—that King Hassan had carefully constructed over the decade since he acceded to the throne in February 1961 upon the death of his father Mohammed V. Moreover, the officers that betrayed him had been hand-picked by King Hassan when he was made Heir Apparent and Commander of the Royal Armed Forces in 1957. At that time the Moroccan Army barely existed as an organized force, inasmuch as the country had won its independence from the French protectorate just one year earlier, in March 1956. King Mohammed V designated Prince Hassan as his successor, and, as many a sultan in the past, placed his heir in control of the military apparatus of the dynasty so that he could guarantee his succession, if need be by force. It was after 1957 that Prince Hassan promoted the careers of many of those who were involved in the coup, either as rebels or loyalists. If there was one sector of the Moroccan power structure that King Hassan felt he knew individually and collectively, it was the high-ranking officers of his Army. This is not to say that he felt they were and are all blindly loyal and trustworthy. The King is too canny a leader to rely on transitory and emotional sentiments such as personal devotion. Rather he felt

---

[1] This article (originally published as *American Universities Field Staff Report: Africa: North Africa series:* Vol. xv, No. 1) was written immediately after the coup, in July 1971.
[2] See for instance Raymond Anderson, *New York Times*, 11 July 1971. Causes that may be ruled out as having any major bearing on the coup are: the Arab-Israeli dispute, socialism or leftist ideology, United States military installations and personnel on Moroccan soil.

that the men in whose careers he took a direct and constant interest were in a sense presented with a 'unique alternative': loyalty to the throne and the Alawite dynasty. This was so for two reasons. One, most of the senior officers had first been commissioned in the French Army (with the exception of Marshal Mezzian, who served in the Spanish Army and as Governor of the Canary Islands). None of these officers resigned their commissions during the nationalist period, particularly between 1953 and 1955 when Mohammed V was in forced exile in Madagascar and Moroccan nationalists launched an armed movement, both in the cities and the countryside, to force the French to bring him back. After independence was attained, these officers did indeed resign their commission in the French Army in order to take over the command structure of the newly-created Moroccan Army. While they were able to rise rapidly in rank, both the King and the Prince, as well as the officers themselves, fully realized that they would have no political constituency in the country, that they would in effect be highly trained, reasonably competent janissaries with no choice but loyal service to their royal benefactors.

The unique alternative had a second facet that linked the military elite directly to the civilian elite that emerged in the 1960s. The monarchy wanted an efficient military establishment, and a contented officers corps. At the same time, functional commands among the officers were changed rapidly so that no single officer was so long in one place as to build a loyal following or power base among those under his command. The degree of shifting was augmented during the past fifteen years by the use of high-ranking officers in the Ministry of Interior as provincial governors. It can hardly be flattering to the ego of an officer to know that his career pattern is structured to discourage any personal ambitions for personal power he may have. To compensate for the lack of power in terms of stable commands, the palace saw to it that the officers corps was materially well treated and integrated into the expanding royal patronage system. Many of the officers were already wealthy men, but as European *colons* and businessmen sold off their interests after 1956—often illegally—many farms and enterprises found their way into the hands of the officers with the active connivance of the Palace. These emoluments of the patronage system were not in any way 'earned' but were contingent gifts from Morocco's chief patron to some of his important clients. If the client's services became superfluous or unsatisfactory, the gift could be reclaimed (the farm or enterprise simply confiscated). The client could not protest, for in accepting the gift in the first place he had destroyed any moral ground for protesting its withdrawal.

It was precisely in this way that King Hassan gained control of the political and civilian elite over the decade of the 1960s. After four years of party politics between 1956 and 1960, when the great nationalist party, the Istiqlal, could bargain head on with the King, the monarchy gradually reduced the arena for party politics. This trend first started with a split in the ranks of the Istiqlal, nominally between young radicals (Mehdi Ben Barka, Mohammed Basri, Mahjoub Ben Seddiq, Abderrahim Bouabid) and older conservatives (Allal al-Fassi, Omar Abdjelil, Ahmad Balafrej). Aided and abetted by the Palace, the split effectively crippled the nationalist movement as well as the alliance between the Moroccan Union of Labor and the leftist leaders of the new radical party, the National Union of Popular Forces. The ill feeling generated by the party split caused many Moroccans to drop all affiliation with any political organizations. It was precisely these unattached individuals that King Hassan drew into his new governmental and administrative elite. While a number of parties still existed in name, the real politics of the country became concentrated in the competition for patronage among various ministers and their protegés. This kind of competition was and is far easier for the King to manage than that of political organizations and political ideology. Actively-ruling kings tend to fare badly in nationalist politics; sooner or later some important groups find them superfluous and do away with them. However, by becoming the chief dispenser of spoils and patronage in a highly individualized political arena, King Hassan sought to establish his indispensability to the system. He was the arbiter who could turn the tap on and off at will in a game where ideas and programs counted for little and the competition for material advantage became everything. Like the officers, a civilian minister or director could not take satisfaction in his work as a result of his power to generate a program or translate an ideological viewpoint into action. He too would have to seek gratification in momentary and essentially unearned access to all the forms of graft, kickbacks, embezzlement, and trading in favors that any administration can generate for its masters. Access to this patronage system was again controlled by the Palace, and once in it no participant could protest being eased out of it. Nor could any participant honestly criticize the system whose accomplice he had become. In this sense, the civilian elite had likewise a unique alternative; to serve the system or remain silent, and the material advantages offered were such that few refused to serve. Over the years, of course, more and more educated Moroccans sought access to the system and to the extent that they were absorbed into it, the amount of resources consumed by the patronage system grew apace. During this time, the economy grew little at all, while the population grew at a rate of 3.2 per cent per annum. To an outside observer it was clear that something had to give, but no one predicted that the King's own janissaries would be the first to act.

The King's alliance until 1971 was thus composed of a civilian wing that administered the commercial and technical affairs of the country and a military wing that kept law and order and was always present to remind any civilians of the folly of recalcitrance vis-à-vis the régime. This alliance began to come unstuck just when the system seemed to have reached its peak of perfection. In the summer of 1970 King Hassan had the country approve a new Constitution giving the throne virtually unlimited powers. The referendum was followed by elections to a unicameral Parliament, only a third of whose members were chosen by direct suffrage. The Istiqlal and the National Union of Popular Forces boycotted the elections so that once again unaffiliated individuals filled its seats, many of whom were handpicked by the Ministry of Interior. In fact, as well as constitutionally, the King was the unchallenged master of the system.

Then dramatic changes occurred. In the fall of 1970 two ministers who had been mainstays of the governments of the 1960s were fired, allegedly for corruption. Mohammed Imani of Public Works and Mohammed Benhima of

Agriculture were both dropped. It is said that the real reason for their firing was that they did nothing to help campaign for the new Constitution nor for desirable candidates for the Parliament. It should also be noted that Benhima, as Minister of Agriculture, was involved in a land dispute that resulted, officially, in the death of six peasants. A *colon* farm in the rich Gharb plain north of Rabat was to be sold. Villagers close by who had owned the land before the coming of the French went to the Ministry of Agriculture to request authorization to buy the land in the name of the village. Instead, as had happened over the years, permission to acquire the land was given to a wealthy Moroccan closely tied to the administration. When he took over the farm he also refused the neighboring peasants access to some pasturage on the farm that the *colons* had granted in an ad hoc manner over the years. The peasants were enraged, occupied the land, and then confronted the gendarmes who were sent to drive them off. Six peasants were shot and killed. Other incidents of a similar nature were reported unofficially in the region of Beni Mellal, Marrakesh, and the Sous. It may have been events such as these that indicated even to the most privileged members of the elite that the system was under severe strain. Benhima and Imani may have been the first among the principal civilian allies of the throne to take their distance from the center of power.

Others were not long in following, but in a different manner. In a very real sense the illicit benefits of the patronage system were and are an essential aspect of the King's control over the elite. He has always been aware of the traffic in privileges in which the governmental elite has indulged. Only once was a minister ever fired publicly for curruption; Ali Benjelloun, former Ambassador to the United States, was removed from office as Minister of Justice in 1967 for kickbacks he had taken when Director-General of the Sherifian Office of Phosphates. He was never tried, simply retired with most of the spoils he had amassed. His sin apparently was not so much the kickback but the fact that he did not share his winnings with certain key personalities. Benjelloun was, in any event, the exception that proved the rule that corruption is seminal to the entire system. It was something of a shock, therefore, when in April 1971 Mamoun Tahiri, the Minister of Finance, Mohammed Jaidi, the Minister of Commerce, Mohammed Kriem, the Minister of Tourism, the Yahya Chefchaouni, Director General of the Bureau of Mines (BRPM) were all fired for corruption. Of these men, the removal of Tahiri was the most astounding for he had been Minister of Finance for nine years during the crucial decade in which the King built his civilian clientele. Tahiri's departure was the end of an era.

The cause of the removal of these men leads us directly into causes of the attempted coup. In April, General Mohammed Nedbuh, since 1967 Director of the Royal Military Household (Maison Militaire Royale), was dispatched by the King to prepare his state visit to the United States. As to other aspects of Medbuh's mission, opinions and rumors vary widely. What is certain is that during his visit to the United States he gathered information from American sources that implicated all the men who were eventually fired in a large-scale operation involving enormous kickbacks and illegal currency transfers outside

Morocco. It has been said that the King specifically asked Medbuh to find out why Pan American Airways had shown no interest in contracting for the construction of an Intercontinental Hotel at Casablanca. Other observers argue that Najib Halaby, President of Pan Am, passed on the information through the C.I.A. or Secretary of State Rogers. This version has been categorically denied by American officials. It is fairly certain that in the spring the C.I.A. prepared an intelligence report on Morocco for the information of interested congressional committees in which the gravity of corruption in Morocco was stressed.[1] But as for the specific complaint of Pan Am, it probably was General Medbuh who sought out the information on his own initiative, to be used to convince the King of the deterioration within his own elite. What Medbuh found was the copy of a letter signed by Omar Ben Messaoud, an important Moroccan entrenreneur and speculator and at one time an attaché in the Royal Cabinet. The letter stipulated that if Pan Am wished to build on a particular plot of land in Casablanca, over a million dollars would have to be apportioned among the foreign bank accounts of the above-mentioned ministers as well as that of the King himself.

General Medbuh returned to Morocco and showed the copy to King Hassan who was suitably annoyed for this was one ministerial escapade about which he knew virtually nothing. Ben Messaoud was arrested and in the course of his interrogation he revealed similar affairs, several dating back over many years and involving some of the King's most 'trusted' servants. One involved a dummy company in Switzerland set up by Moroccan administrators to buy ore from Morocco. The metallic content of the ore was to be underdeclared and then sold in Europe at its proper content; the profits realized by the dummy company in Switzerland would be deposited in local accounts. This particular operation led to the shakeup at the BRPM. As for Mamoun Tahiri, ex-Minister of Finance, the rumor mill in Rabat has it that he traded his influence over the years for a personal fortune of over $14 million.

The King, as is his habit, took only halfway measures in dealing with people who had violated his rules by trafficking behind his back. Although they were removed from office throughout the month of April, and the crisis was severe enough to oblige the King to call off his trip to the United States, they were never charged nor brought to trial. Even Ben Massaoud, after a month of questioning and detention, returned to his villa in the plush ministerial quarter of Souissi in Rabat. General Medbuh, it appears in retrospect, was very unhappy with the King's leniency, so much so that he decided the King would only see the light by direct pressure from the Army.

What motivated a handful of high-ranking officers to take matters into their own hands? Because all of those who have been officially designated as having taken part in the coup are now dead, one can only speculate as to what prompted them to action. One may at least note the official explanation. Prime Minister Laraki explained to Parliament on 21 July the General's putsch: 'Its unique aim was to seize power for power's sake and satisfy their vile and egotistical appetites.' Given the fact that all the officers involved were already quite powerful,

[1] See Raymond Tournoux, 'Les Secrets du coup d'état manqué contre Hassan II,' *Paris Match*, N.1163, 25 August 1971.

and that not all of them could become head of state, we must look somewhat further to understand their goals.

General Medbuh's career may shed some light on the matter. In late 1958, Medbuh was made Minister of Communications in a government that was controlled by men of the Moroccan left, in particular the National Union of Popular Forces. He was appointed to this position not because he had leftist sentiments himself, but because there was a rural insurrection in the Rif mountains where Medbuh was born and it seemed wise at the time to include a Riffi in the cabinet in order to placate the local populations. Still Medbuh had the chance to rub elbows with civilian politicians of the left, a number of whom remember him with respect. It may have been this brief and indeterminate contact with the UNPF that led to Medbuh's implication in a plot against the King's life in 1963. In that year over 100 members of the UNPF were arrested on charges of plotting against the régime. A key piece of evidence in the trial was a taped conversation between 'Fqih' Basri, member of UNPF and former urban terrorist, and Medbuh, during which Basri tried to convince Medbuh to join the plotters. At that time Medbuh was the King's aide-de-camp. It is said that Medbuh strung Basri along until he had adequate evidence to lead to the arrest of the other plotters. While the UNPF denied the authenticity of the tape, contacts between Basri and Medbuh were not denied, which is some indication that Medbuh was considered to be a man with political ideas.

Some of those who know Medbuh well claim that for several years he had been trying to convince the King to keep the patronage system under control. Not only was its economic cost too high, Medbuh believed, but it was also leading to Morocco's disgrace internationally.[1] Despite the fact that he was probably the most powerful man in the military establishment after 1967, Medbuh was unable to convince the King. His information gathering operation in the United States may be seen as a last attempt to see if the King would act. He did not.

Less is known about the other rebel officers. Lt Col Ababou, Commander of the Non-Commissioned Officers School at Ahermoumou and a personal friend of the King's brother, Prince Moulay Abdallah, was born at Aknoul in the Rif, and Medbuh's home town. This fact may explain the contacts between the two men. Most people who remember Ababou, including the cadets at Ahermoumou, speak of him as a militant, silent, tough, dedicated man. Few, however, can attribute any particular political ideas to him. It is important to note that Ababou, at 35, was the youngest officer participating in the coup. Most of the others were in their middle or late forties (Medbuh was 44) and General Amahzoun Hammou was 56.

General Hammou was a close relation of the King's official wife, a Berber

---

[1] In the fall of 1970 some Army officers in charge of supplies and matériel were discharged for corruption. The editor of *L'Opinion*, the French-language daily of the Istiqlal party, commended the government for its resolve in this matter. He was tried and sentenced to six months in jail for having insulted the Moroccan Armed Forces. Officers not involved in the scandal could not have taken much pride in the regime's handling of the affair.

woman of the once-powerful Middle Atlas tribe of the Zayyan, and of the tribe's principal family, the Amharoq. It is difficult to explain his participation except that he was known to be a very pious man who, like some of the others including Medbuh, may have been revolted by the degree of decadence manifested by the civilian elite and Palace entourage.

The other officers executed after the coup failed were Generals Bougrine, a Riffi from the Ait Warain tribe, 47 years old; Habibi, from the Middle Atlas tribe of the Beni Mtir, 48 years old; Mustapha Amharech also of the Zayyan, 48 years old. Bougrine was the Commander of the Fes-Taza Military Region, Hammou was Commander of the Rabat-Kenitra Military Region, General Amharech was Director of Military Schools under whose jurisdiction the Ahermoumou Non-Commissioned Officers School fell. Finally, General Habibi was Commander of the Marrakesh military region. Joining these men, or perhaps leading them, were the above-mentioned Lt Col Ababou of the Ahermoumou School, Colonel Chelouati, born at Ahermoumou, 46 years old and of the Royal Gendarmerie, Colonel Fenniri, Director of the Kenitra Military School, Colonels Bouberri, Ammi BenBrahim, and Leksir Belabsir, whose roles in the coup remain obscure, and Commandant Manouzi. Finally, General Abdesslam Benamar, Commander of the Casablanca Military Region, was arrested after the coup as a possible sympathizer with the rebels. He was not, however, executed.

Commandant Manouzi's puzzling presence among the rebels warrants further mention. He was from the village of Amanouz, deep in the Anti-Atlas Mountains of southern Morocco, and was, along with his brothers and several other villagers, a participant and leader in the Moroccan Liberation Army that fought the French in 1955 and 1956. After Mohammed V returned from exile, many leaders of this army were inducted into the new Moroccan Army and given officers' rank for their nationalist sacrifices. Others went on to organize the Liberation Army of the South whose nominal task was to liberate the Spanish presidio of Ifni. However, the southern Liberation Army more or less con-controlled Agadir province until the early sixties at which point several of its leaders were brought into the Moroccan Army. Thus Commandant Manouzi was from the old Moroccan macquis, a group that had fought in the name of the King but never ceased to worry the throne. In 1963, several of those arrested in connection with the plot of that year were from the Liberation Army. Again, in 1970, widespread arrests occurred among the former resistants and the UNPF. Again the charge was plotting to overthrow the régime. These arrests gave rise to the so-called Marrakesh trial. While the King eventually denied that there was any connection between those on trial at Marrakesh and the coup attempt at Skhirat, it is a more than curious fact that Commandant Manouzi's brother, Said Bounaillat, was one of the two principals accused at Marrakesh. Some Moroccans believe that the officers in the Moroccan Army who were once in the Liberation Army may have pressured their superiors for action. Indeed, such nationalist officers were and are in no way presented with the unique alternative that limited the possibility of political intervention for the French-trained officers.

Without being able to assign weights and intensities to the motivations shared by the putchists, we can identify the following factors: (1) Most of the officers, with the exception of Chelouati, were known for their honesty relative to the rest of the elite. Michel Legris writing in *Le Monde* noted:

> The leader of the plot (General Medbuh), as well as several other officers . . ., had, even among those who condemned their machinations most vigorously, an established reputation of honesty and moral rectitude.[1]

Disgust and despair with the degree of corruption elsewhere in the military and in the civilian elite must surely have moved these men to act. (2) There is some evidence that certain officers—perhaps Chelouati and Ababou—felt as if they had been 'bought' over the years, that they had become the mercenaries of the régime, placated for their unglorious role by royal patronage. When Chelouati was Governor of Oujda Province, for example, he was known for his heavy-handedness and rapaciousness. He benefited as much as anyone from the system. It is also alleged by some that as a close confidant of General Oufqir, Minister of Interior, he had played a sordid role in the kidnapping and assassination in 1965 of Mehdi Ben Barka, former leader of the National Union of Popular Forces. (3) Along with their reputation for honesty, some of the participants were said to be disturbed from a religious and moral viewpoint by the decadence of the régime and its poor public image. (4) From the perspective of career advancement, some of the officers were upset by the constant shifts in position to which they were subjected and the clear lack of confidence that such transfers implied. (5) Lurking behind all explanations of the coup is the notion of pre-emptiveness. These were not leftists, nor young junior officers, nor did any of them have any known links with civilian politicians and parties. It is quite probable that they had no political program whatsoever other than a brutal military housecleaning. It may be that the officers observed the economic stagnation in the country, the growing spoils system, the disintegration of the civilian elite, took note of the widely-reported discontent, militancy, and politicization in the junior ranks of the Army, and decided to act before younger and more radical men seized power, eliminating the King *and* his senior officers.

Another factor must be given separate and detailed consideration. With three exceptions, all the major actors among the rebels were Berbers from the Rif and Middle Atlas Mountains. Commandant Manouzi was from the Anti-Atlas Mountains but nonetheless a Berber, and Colonels Ben Brahim and Belabsir were both Arab. Was the putsch somehow a reaction of the old Berber-speaking, mountain-dwelling populations against the Arabic-speaking, urban bourgeoisie that dominated the civilian sectors of the government and the private commercial sectors of the economy? There is some meagre evidence to this effect but in the final analysis it must be regarded as of secondary importance. In its favor is the attitude of the urban bourgeoisie itself, particularly those from the

---

[1] Michel Legris, *Le Monde*, 14 July 1971. *Le Monde*'s reporting was, as usual, exceptional. Other sources worth consulting on the coup are: *Paris Match*, No. 1159 with its extraordinary photographs of the rebel generals before execution; *Jeune Afrique*, n. 550, 20 July 1971 with 11 pages on the coup attempt; *Africasia*, 19 July 1971; and *L'Express* n. 1045, 19–25 July 1971.

merchant families of Fes and their offshoots in Morocco's economic capital, Casablanca. They were ready to see in Medbuh's action a Berber reaction to their privileged position in the patronage system. The Istiqlal party, dominated by urban, Arabic-speaking elements, while in loyal opposition to the throne, severely condemned the coup attempt as a manifestation of retrograde Berber particularism.

It is true that after the coup there was much talk in all quarters of a building resentment against the so-called 'Fassi (bourgeoisie of Fes) Mafia' that had dominated the administrative system virtually since independence. It is not surprising that mountain Berber officers might feel contempt for the effete, easy-living city bourgeoisie. It is said that when Colonel Chelouati was led before the firing squad, he crudely questioned the virility of Prime Minister Ahmad Laraki, scion of a famous Fes-Casablanca family, who came to watch the executions. In a similar vein, it is worth noting that in the winter of 1970 an incident occurred that aggravated tension between the two groups. Three high-ranking officials—a personnel director for the Ministry of Interior, the Head Prosecutor for the city of Casablanca, and the Minister of Labor—all of them Berbers, concerted to close down a French-owned enterprise in Casablanca and then to buy it themselves at a cut rate. Their plan worked except that the French owner had access to President Pompidou, who, having heard the sorry tale, protested to the King through the French Ambassador in Rabat. The King fired (secretly) all three officials and jailed them. At that time a petition was circulated throughout the Berber members of the Ministry of Interior and the Army protesting the arrests and arguing that if the offenders had been Fassi nothing would have been done to them.

Nonetheless, it must be kept in mind that cleavages and animosities among Berbers are often as severe as between Berbers and Arabs. Surely, had the coup succeeded General Oufqir, himself a Berber, would have been executed. General Gharbaoui, Director of all the King's aides-de-camp, was executed by the rebels, although a Berber. Other Berber officers who lost their lives to the rebels were Generals Bachir Bouhali, Chief of Staff; Boulhims, Commander of the Royal Gendarmerie; Colonel Khiari-Bougrine, a cousin of the rebel general, and Colonel Mekki, aide-de-camp of the King. Colonel Loubaris, Commander of the Paratroopers and a close personal friend of General Medbuh, was severely wounded at Skhirat. General N'michi, Commander of the Air Force, was the only Arab (from Fes) among the loyal officers who were killed.

There are at least two reasons why the Berber identity of the rebel officers is of secondary importance in explaining their motivations. Beyond the fact that Berber officers were found both among the putschists and the loyalists, as a group they had come to share the same privileges as the civilian, Arabic-speaking elite. General Medbuh was related by marriage to some of the wealthiest Fassi families of Casablanca. He had married the daughter of Marshal Mezzian and two of his sisters-in-law had married, respectively, Othman Benjelloun and Jalil Tazi, powerful merchants and industrialists of Casablanca. One may speculate that the Berber officers wanted to protect the interests they shared with the rest of the elite rather than abolish their privileges entirely in some sort of puritanical purge. Second, the fact that the rebel officers were Berber is to some extent fortuitous. With the exception of four or five men, almost all Moroccan officers are Berber.[1] For the Army to act at all, Berbers would have to make it move. This in turn is the result of French recruiting practices whereby during the years of the protectorate young Berbers from powerful rural families were brought into the French Army as junior officers. French military experts always felt that Berbers made good soldiers and officers. But for a quirk of French recruitment, therefore, the leaders of the 10 July putsch could easily have been Arab.

The predominance of Berbers in the Army is bound to change in the near future. Since independence in 1956, recruitment into officers candidate schools has been carried out by competitive examination. This selection process favors the urban, literate, Arab middle classes which in fact have packed the junior officers corps with its offspring. These young officers, apparently frozen in rank for a number of years,[2] have been closely watched by the King and his senior officers. It may have been that the rebel officers sensed or were informed of the rising frustration in the junior ranks, and acted in the pre-emptive manner alluded to above.

THE PUTSCH AND ITS AFTERMATH

The attempted overthrow of the Moroccan monarchy, if it was that, is doubly obscure, for witnesses to it are confused as to what went on and those who could explain the immediate objectives of the rebels are all dead. One can only speculate on both counts, and while there are many improbable stories floating about Rabat, none is more improbable than those incidents and explanations that have been made public.

First, it would seem that the conspirators were prepared to act much earlier, on 14 May in fact, just after the firing of the civilian ministers in April. The plan was to use certain armed units (the cadets of Ahermoumou who were not far away?) to intercept the royal cortège on the road from Fes to al-Hajeb. For some reason the itinerary of the King was changed at the last minute and the ambush failed. The plan was then changed to capture and/or kill the King, his brother Prince Moulay Abdullah, the entire governmental elite and unsympathetic Army officers at the King's forty-second birthday party. The latter was to be celebrated as usual at the summer Palace at Skhirat, a beach resort about fifteen miles south of Rabat. General Medbuh was intimately involved in the preparations for the party as Director of the Royal Military Household. He helped prepare the invitation list which included over one thousand Moroccan and

[1] The most notable exceptions are Marshal Mezzian, General Driss Ben Omar, Colonel Ahmad Dlimi (head of National Security), General N'michi (killed at Skhirat) and Colonel Housni Ben Slimane, former Governor of Tangier Province. General Kittani, Morocco's first Chief of Staff, died in the early 1960s and was likewise an Arab.

[2] See 'X' 'le Maroc' in Leo Hamon (ed.) *Le Role extra-militaire de l'armée dans les pays du Tiers Monde* (Paris, 1965).

foreign guests. He was also responsible for the security arrangements at the Palace. An easy target and practically indefensible, the King's summer residence is nothing more than a sprawling beach house set back from the main highway by about three hundred yards of brush and golf course, and built directly upon the dunes of the beach. At this isolated spot the entire elite could be taken in one fell swoop while other rebel officers rallied the capital and the regional commands at their leisure. Presented with the *fait accompli* of the King's arrest or demise, most officers would have come around. The plan was so simple and straightforward that the rebels concentrated on trivia and failed to pay sufficient attention to details of importance.

For example, the conspirators went to some pains to display normal behavior. General Medbuh played golf with the King at the summer Palace the morning of the coup. Col Chelouati and his French wife offered a gala reception the night before the coup and even invited hundreds of people to another one that would have taken place the night of the coup itself. General Hammou made a routine visit to a hospital for a checkup and cardiogram the day before the coup. It was later alleged that the rebels agreed to wear yellow shirts at the party so that the attacking cadets would be able to identify them; this latter appears a bit far-fetched because, at a summer party with a thousand guests, hundreds are likely to be wearing yellow. General Oufqir later acknowledged that he had planned to wear a yellow shirt until his wife told him that the shirt did not go with his pants.

Taking the Palace by force required more planning. The only armed unit used in the coup attempt consisted of the 1,400 cadets from the Ahermoumou school, all between 18 and 20 years old. Despite the fact that several officers had regular units under their orders these were not used. One can only conclude that they would not have been reliable in carrying out orders. The problem then was to transfer all the cadets from Ahermoumou, deep in the Middle Atlas Mountains, to Skhirat without the King and loyal advisers being alerted. General Medbuh was again well placed in this respect. He saw to it that the necessary authorization was given for the cadets to be moved on 10 July from Ahermoumou to Ben Slimane on the road from Casablanca to Marrakesh where the cadets were to carry out maneuvers. The normal itinerary would be to take the Meknes road to Rabat, the coast road to Casablanca, and thence on to Ben Slimane. The Skhirat Palace is on the coast road. In addition, because it was a question of maneuvers, the cadets were issued rifles, machine guns, bazookas, grenades, and ammunition. The truck convoy that departed in the early morning of 10 July, from Ahermoumou under the command of Colonel Ababou, passed through two military regions under the command of rebel officers— Bougrine at Fes-Taza and Hammou at Rabat-Kenitra—and was supposedly to go on to that of a third, General Habibi's at Marrakesh. In theory the convoy would have passed through Casablanca Military Region as well, and it may be for that reason that General BenAmar was suspected of complicity after the coup aborted.

The convoy approached Skhirat at midday. About five miles away the convoy stopped and lunch rations were issued to the cadets. It was later claimed that the coffee served to the cadets at this time was drugged. At this moment, General Medbuh, having left the party, drove up to the convoy and announced to Ababou and his men that the King's life was in danger at Skhirat and that the cadets should go to his aid. Ababou was said to have then issued instructions to his men as to how to take the Palace and save the King. The official version

Map 21.1. Morocco and the coup of 1971

would thus have it that the attacking cadets were both drugged and duped. Once having arrived at Skhirat, the cadets moved in on the Palace in two bodies: one frontally from the highway and the other from the beach. Oufqir later argued that one group fired off a few rounds while the officer in charge of the second told his men that the shots came from the people trying to harm the King. He then supposedly told his thoroughly whipped-up charges to go and kill in the name of the King.

It is possible that some of the cadets had no idea what they were doing. It is equally clear that an important part of them knew quite well the objectives of the operation. As for being drugged, the haggard looks and glazed eyes of the cadets could be explained as easily by the fact that they had been up since 2.30 a.m. and were clearly involved, whatever their understanding of it, in a pitched battle.

Those who knew the rebel officers, particularly Medbuh, cannot believe that from a moral or a practical point of view he would have ordered the massacre of over one hundred people, including foreign diplomats. It is not upon such a note that a new régime can be smoothly launched. Yet a massacre did occur, and the mysterious figure of Colonel Ababou is sometimes evoked to explain it. He was said to have harangued his men, both at Ahermoumou and the day of the coup, about the corruption and decadence of the régime. At the Palace, as his cadets took control, he was said to have stalked about shouting that 'We have had enough of this garbage and filth'. Later in the day, wounded, and lodged at General Headquarters in Rabat, he moved among the units of cadets holding the radio building and the Ministry of Interior, urging them not to lose their resolve and to hang on to the power that was in their hands in order to cleanse Morocco. It is for this reason that several observers, including General Oufqir, have suggested that there may have been two plots; Medbuh's plot to take power in the name of the Army with a minimum of bloodletting, and Ababou's to liquidate the entire elite if not the King himself. At some future date Ababou would have retired Medbuh in a Moroccan version of the Nasser-Neguib tandem. The King, while comparing Medbuh to Charles Manson and calling him schizoid and paranoid, has suggested that Medbuh wished him no personal harm. In fact the issue of *Paris-Match* in which Raymond Tournoux declared that the alternatives the rebels were to have offered the King were (1) fully to accept to govern with the Army (2) to accept a role for the monarchy similar to that in Spain (3) to go into exile—was on sale throughout Morocco.[1] What went wrong?

Once the firing started—and no one is quite sure how it did start, it could not be brought under control. With the exception of some Army officers, the cadets were apparently under orders to kill no one. Having met some resistance, how- ever, the cadets opened fire on the Palace. Several people who were unfortunate enough to be still on the golf course were cut down. Some victims staggered into the Palace and created a panic there. Hundreds of guests made a break for the front gate where their cars were, only to be mowed down by the group leading the frontal assault. Others leapt through windows onto the beach where they met a hail of fire from the group attacking from the beach. It was in that manner that Mohammed Lazrak, Minister of Tourism, was wounded. He died sometime later because during the five or six hours that ensued before any calm was restored, no one could attend to the wounded, and several simply bled to death.

Once the cadets gained control of the Palace, they were in a trigger-happy state; the guests, needless to say, were in a total panic, the two states combining to cause more carnage. Guests and servants were herded from one room to

[1] Tournoux, op. cit.

another. Those that moved too slowly or tried to break away were shot. The scne as described evokes images of traditional tribal *razzia*, the sweeps against decaying régimes so preceptively analyzed by Ibn Khaldoun centuries ago. Young mountain Berbers from poor families, having undergone spartan training for several months, are led into a setting that their own leader could hardly have described. The diplomatic corps and Moroccan elite in gaudy sports shirts and bell-bottoms, rings and watches aglitter, their Mercedes and Cadillacs parked outside with chauffeurs waiting, are lunching from tables laden with caviar, shrimp, lobsters, pate, wine, and whiskey. The only thing lacking was women. Men alone were invited to the King's birthday party; the women of the elite were to celebrate the following day.

The instinct of the cadets was to smash all that they saw. The Ambassador of the People's Republic of China and the Libyan Ambassador, both of whom proclaimed their revolutionary ardor, were treated with contempt. The Pakistani Ambassador identified himself and noted that he was Muslim. A young cadet retorted, 'I'm the Ambassador of Ahermoumou. Shut up!' Watches were ripped off wrists and stamped on. Tables were overturned. Some guests offered the cadets money only to have it torn up and thrown in their faces. At one point all the guests were herded outside and made to stand and then to lie in the sun with their hands on their heads. Witnesses noted that the cadets and their officers had conducted the entire proceedings in French. One guest whispered to the French cultural attaché that he should be very proud of the progress the French language had made in Morocco.

The King from the early moments of the attack disappeared into a bunker, or bathroom, depending on the source. He was accompanied by Prime Minister Ahmad Laraki, the Director General of the Royal Cabinet, Driss Slaoui, General Oufqir, and some other dignitaries. It may have been that Medbuh led him there himself. In any event the notion that the cadets did not know where the King was all this time does not hold water. Some important segment of the cadets knew the King's whereabouts, for he was in essence being held prisoner. Medbuh tried to negotiate with him at that time, and according to the King the General said 'that madman Ababou is leading them. Will you talk to him?' There is now, however, only one version of that conversation available. The King, at one point peering through a keyhole, saw Ababou walking about among the cadets and said in total bewilderment, 'I don't understand, I don't understand.'

During the King's imprisonment, some planned executions took place. Names of officers were being called from a list. After Generals Gharbaoui, N'michi, and Abdelhai were called and executed, others did not answer to their names. It was thus, reportedly, that General Driss Ben Omar survived. It is a disputed point whether or not Oufqir's name was ever called.

All accounts agree that the assailants lost all sense of direction when General Medbuh was severely wounded. How this came about is also disputed. The official version has it that Dr Fadel Benyaich, one of the King's physicians who was with him in the bunker, found his way into a bedroom where he discovered an old machine gun that had been given to the King long in the past. He emerged from the room and confronted Medbuh, who tried to disarm him. He fired, wounding Medbuh, and was in turn shot and killed by some cadets. Another version has it that Dr Benyaich was about to be executed by the cadets who thought he was the King's Chamberlain, Ali Benyaich. Medbuh tried to intervene to save him but was wounded by the volley that killed the doctor. Medbuh, who had a heart condition and was a hemophiliac, apparently bled to death. For some inexplicable reason, Ababou, apparently wounded himself, decided to return to Army GHQ in Rabat to join the other generals, leaving the Palace and the King in the hands of the cadets. By this time they had lost all sense of discipline and cohesion. Albert-Paul Lentin, writing for *Africasia* reports the following, rather improbable conversation. General Oufqir was somehow able to talk separately to some of the leaders of the cadets. He said to them: 'What do you want? To assure the full authority of an Army capable of fighting corruption and these rotten civilians effectively? The Army here is me, and in the name of the Army I declare that your demands are just.' Then he turned to Hassan II to say, 'That is why, your Majesty, I ask you to delegate to me immediately and in writing all military and civilian powers.'[1]

No other observer reported any such conversation, but it is a fact that at the end of the day General Oufqir had been delegated all civilian and military powers. After two hours of captivity, the King was led out of his bunker to where the other guests were still being held. He was made to stand with his hands on his head like all the rest. After a while a cadet approached him and told him gruffly to follow him around a corner. The King was sure that he was to be executed quietly out of eyesight. Once around the corner, the cadet snapped to attention. The King, showing his remarkable presence of mind, immediately recognized that the situation called for daring. He looked at the cadet and said, 'At ease'; the cadet relaxed and the King snapped 'Attention!' The cadet stiffened, and the King asked 'What are you waiting for to kiss my hand?' The cadet kissed his hands and his feet, and told the King that he had been misled. The King led him off to find other cadets. Soon a little group formed shouting 'Long live the King'. Hassan II led them in reciting the *fatiha*, the first verse of the Koran. They all went back to the guests who were astonished to see the cadets acclaiming the King. At about this time the King vested full powers in Oufqir who had found a uniform somewhere. An untold number of cadets tried to stop those who had suddenly turned loyalist, but they were subdued quickly. It was then discovered that the leaders of the coup had neglected to cut telephone communications between Skhirat and the outside. With the principal leaders in Rabat, the King began to organize the countercoup at Skhirat.

A makeshift headquarters was set up at Skhirat and plans were laid to retake the radio building, GHQ, and the Ministry of Interior in Rabat. General Bouhali, it would seem, went to Rabat to direct operations. The Rebels by this time were broadcasting proclamations in Arabic and in French to the effect that the régime had been overthrown. It is disputed whether or not the rebels announced that the King was dead, although that news immediately found its way into world news coverage. The announcement that was repeated most

[1] Albert-Paul Lentin, *Africasia*, 19 July 1971.

frequently went as follows: 'Attention. The Army has just conducted a revolution for the people. The royal régime is abolished. Remain vigilant.' The loyal officers at Skhirat were able to contact Tangier radio station and deny the news. Later in the evening, Europe No. 1 was able to reach King Hassan for a telephone interview at the same time that the counterassault reached its peak at Rabat.

In the early evening General Bouhali gained access to Colonel Ababou at GHQ and told him that the coup was hopeless and that he had best surrender. Ababou tried to convince Bouhali to join the rebels. Bouhali produced a machine gun and shot Ababou. Ababou's men immediately killed Bouhali. Other important rebel leaders had already left Rabat to return to their regional commands and declare their support for the new régime. General Bougrine tried to fly to Fes, but the airport would not let him land. He flew back to Meknes, and upon landing was arrested by junior officers who had remained loyal. General Habibi made the mistake of returning to Skhirat on his way to Marrakesh. Instead of finding the King a prisoner, he found him in charge. Habibi tried to bluff his way out. He told King Hassan that he was on his way to Marrakesh to rally his men in defense of the régime. The King let him go, and then issued orders that led to his arrest upon arrival in Marrakesh. By 8 p.m. or so the rebellion was leaderless. It was then a question of dislodging the cadets from their positions in Rabat.

With Bouhali dead, General Oufqir took direct command of the attack, using paratroopers and the Light Mobile Security Unit, a crack riot control and internal security outfit that had first been organized by Colonel Boulhims. It is interesting to note that neither the rebels nor the loyalists were able to use regular Army units in their operations. Like the overwhelming majority of the population, the Army took a wait-and-see attitude throughout the day of 10 July. No one, civilian or military, rushed to the defense of the King or of the rebels. Some students went into the streets to announce their support of the revolution, and the following day when the King was back in control, a 'popular' demonstration was held in Casablanca. Other than that, the Moroccan population observed the bloody game at the summit impassively and inscrutably.

The mopping-up operations went on throughout Saturday night (the tenth) and Sunday. The re-taking of the radio station proved an arduous affair, and it is reliably reported that after most of the cadets had surrendered an untold number were summarily executed. The following day, cadets were flushed out all over Rabat where they had hidden. It was announced officially that over 150 cadets had been killed in the fighting, but it was rumored in Rabat that over 600 of the 1,400 cadets were missing, either killed or in prison. Relatives of the cadets were unable to obtain any news whatsoever of the missing cadets and their fate has been a closely guarded secret.

On Sunday and Monday, while the King and General Oufqir were giving out their version of the events, the rebel officers were being interrogated. In his 11 July press conference, King Hassan announced that an emergency tribunal set up at Skhirat immediately following the coup had decided that the officers should be executed after they had revealed all the details of the plot. There would be no public trial, no interviews, and, the King noted, the officers should probably have been executed on the spot. The same day King Hassan presided over funeral ceremonies for the victims of the coup.

At midmorning on Tuesday, the thirteenth, the rebel officers were taken to an empty field south of Rabat overlooking the Atlantic Ocean. Their interrogation over, they were led and tied to eleven stakes in the ground. Soldiers tore off their insignia. There were no blindfolds. The reactions of the condemned varied: Habibi protested his innocence until the end; Hammou was said to have died shouting long live the King; Chelouati, on the other hand, exited defiant, heaping his scorn upon the Prime Minister who stood nearby. Commandant Manouzi was also defiant. He shouted that there was only one King but eighty Manouzis, or so the rumor mill would have it.

The King asked that each family that had lost a member at Skhirat send a representative to watch the executions. Several cadets, their hands on their shaven heads, were made to sit close to the area where the executions were taking place. The entire government was there, and the King watched at a distance through binoculars. The firing squad fired several rounds into the eleven men. The soldiers then rushed forward to spit on the corpses. Shortly thereafter bulldozers unceremoniously pushed the bodies into an open trench. Lye was poured over them and the trench bulldozed over. There was to be no marking on the rebels' communal grave. The coup was over, in fact and symbolically. In a few weeks the local press would refer only to the 'events' of Skhirat.

Immediately following the executions, an inventory of all the ill-gotten gains of the rebels was published. The intention was clearly to demonstrate that these men were moved by no noble sentiment, that all the talk of corruption having something to do with the coup was nonsense. But, like describing Medbuh as mentally ill, showing how venal these men supposedly were reflects directly on the King. If Medbuh were deranged why had the King given him such power? If an inventory of the patronage accumulated by the rebels could be produced in twenty-four hours, why hadn't this property been seized long before? The tactic of the unique alternative had failed for it was designed to keep elite members from acting. If, however, they were driven to action, then revealing their complicity with the system was like closing the gate after the horse was out of the barn. One may note at the same time that the strategy was eminently successful in another sense. Had Medbuh, *et al.*, actually succeeded, the rebels would have been terribly isolated without any constituency or of political credit in the country.

Instead, it was the King who emerged isolated from the experience. His Army had betrayed him and it was impossible for him to know if there were any trustworthy officers other than those who had died for him. His civilian elite had been crumbling over the preceding months. The political parties that he had reduced to impotence, while hostile to the rebels' cause, were no warmer to the régime. The population was at best indifferent. In this situation the King had only one man to rely on, General Oufqir.

General Oufqir's appearance and the reputation lend themselves to facile stereotypes. His hawk-like face and ominous dark glasses are paired with his counterinsurgency experience with the French in Indochina and his well-documented cruelty in putting down the Rif rebellion of 1958-9 and the Casablanca riots of 1965. As head of the security police after 1960 and then Minister of the Interior from 1964 to the summer of 1971, he was instrumental in dismantling the Moroccan left (including the kidnapping of Mehdi Ben Barka) and in bringing the entire political arena under effective police control. Oufqir had so few allies and so few friends among the Moroccan elite that scarcely anyone thought he had any choice but to place all his ruthless skills in service of the King.

Yet a very different image of Oufqir emerges from the events following 10 July. First, all Moroccans have at least considered the possibility that Oufqir was in on the coup attempt, and many are convinced that if he did not support it, he had at least assured its organizers of his neutrality. It was Oufqir who announced that the plot had been brewing for at least a year (the King claimed two). Is it conceivable that this man whose intelligence system was deservedly renowned knew nothing? Could someone as close to him as Chelouati have participated in the conspiracy without informing Oufqir? If so, then Oufqir's sources are not as omnipresent as he would like others to believe. If not, then he was at least prepared to stand idly by while the régime was overthrown. Whatever his role, the King can hardly regard him with confidence today.

Further, there are persistent reports that Oufqir opposed the executions of his former camarades but that the King overruled him. This could explain in part his extraordinary performance in a cabinet meeting in early August. Raymond Tournoux reports the following scenario, verified through other sources. General Oufqir arrived at the meeting obviously depressed. He slumped into his chair, then arose trembling, drew his revolver, and blurted: 'If nothing is going to change, if none of us is willing to draw the necessary conclusions, I prefer to finish myself off now than to see a second Skhirat and to be shot down in my bathing suit.'[1] The King was shocked and moved. He talked privately with Oufqir for two hours and a few days later announced the formation of a new government that was charged with devising a program of national reform. What Medbuh had tried to do by making the King prisoner, Oufqir achieved by threatening to commit suicide. Yet it was Medbuh who was dead and Oufqir who became Minister of Defense in the new government. Whatever the King's misgivings about him, he had decided to give Oufqir the authority to purge and rebuild the officers corps just as he had purged the civilian elite.

The pattern of King Hassan's reactions following 10 July is similar to that following the riots in Casablanca in 1965. The riots represent in effect the last major threat to the régime before the events of 10 July. At that time a strike of secondary school students in Casablanca led to rioting with the police in Casablanca, rioting that soon involved thousands of workers who had been laid off during an economic recession in 1964. Casablanca was paralyzed, the King denounced by name, and hundreds of people wounded or killed in the ensuing repression. King Hassan at first tried to blame the disturbances on certain Syrian Ba'athi high school teachers and other outside troublemakers. He later

[1] Tournoux, op. cit.

shifted ground to pin blame for the riots on the then bicameral Parliament which spent so much time pontificating that it failed to do anything about the economic situation in the country. Finally, the King admitted that measures undertaken by the Ministry of Finance that affected imports, as well as the raising of the price of sugar, had caused a great deal of discontent in Casablanca.

So too in 1971, King Hassan at first denounced the Libyans in an initial outburst and even went so far as to say that he expected more such 'under-developed' coup attempts in the future. Later, he suggested that it was the unabashed power hunger of the officers that explained Skhirat. He also claimed that unfounded party propaganda from civilian politicians had goaded the generals into action. But then in a speech to the nation on 4 August, following Oufqir's performance, the King changed his tone dramatically:

We have often said that our socio-economic policy is aimed at enriching the poor without impoverishing the rich.

Unfortunately, for reasons for which there is no need to set forth now, we have seen that while the poor have not been enriched, the rich have increased their fortunes. Thus the gap between the two categories has only widened. This situation is intolerable in a country like Morocco, blessed by God and of which the Koran is the real constitution. The Koran in fact teaches the practice of egality and equity.

The next government must devote itself to establishing an equitable distribution of national income.

The new government was given 12–18 months to undertake new policies in the fields of education, economic development, administrative reform and the fight against corruption, and justice. It was announced that for the first time Moroccan ministers would have regulatory powers, and that the King would delegate his powers of decree. As a symbolic gesture the King abolished the post of Director-General of the Royal Cabinet whose incumbent, Driss Slaoui, had ranked higher than any minister. Karim Lamraani was made Prime Minister in charge of economic development. Throughout the month of August the new government went about its tasks with much fanfare. Several measures were announced that can only be seen as sops to assuage or rally public opinion.

The new Minister of Agriculture (and former Secretary-General of the Ministry of Interior) Maati Jorio announced that nearly 300,000 acres of land the state had taken over from French farmers in 1963 would be distributed in 1971 and 1972. Having waited eight years, the state said it was ready to distribute 100,000 acres within a month. Along the same lines it announced that salaries in the civil service would be increased in October and that a new pension system would be introduced to allow civil servants to retire with benefits before statutory retirement age.

In a move that revealed much about the general economic situation in the country, it was declared that beginning in September the price of sugar would be reduced by 18 per cent (35 francs) per kilogram. The new Under-Secretary of State for Finance estimated that this reduction would result in a loss in revenues to the government of some $28 million a year. On the other hand, he noted that Moroccans on the average consume 25–30 kilos of sugar each year per capita and that the reduction in sugar prices is equivalent to 3 per cent of the annual income for 15 million Moroccans. To compensate the revenue loss it was decided to raise income taxes in the upper brackets, i.e., for some 100,000 people. Following my own calculations this would mean that these 100,000 people would have to pay $280 each in additional taxes to fill the gap. If this is feasible, and at least on paper it may well be, then each additional tax bite is more than the entire annual average per capita income of $150–180. 100,000 individuals paying additional income taxes can compensate in effect for 3 per cent of the per capita income of 15 million Moroccans.

Finally, the new Minister of Interior proclaimed his intention to fight corruption wherever it exists but somewhat blunted his popular appeal by declaring that those who bribed an official would be as guilty as the official who demanded a bribe. As for the realms of justice and education, at the time of writing no new programs had been announced.

While the new government went into action, King Hassan was having severe problems in rounding it out. First, through Driss Slaoui he made contacts with certain prominent civilian politicians such as Reda Guedira and Dr Khatib, who refused to serve in the new government. Moreover, in the search for under-secretaries of Tourism, Finance, and Commerce, the King met with several refusals among men who had always served in the past. Before 10 July, these men, all of whom had or have business interests, could ill afford not to serve if they wished to prosper later. But 10 July changed all that; like Oufqir, most members of the elite feared going down in their bathing suits at some future Skhirat.

No one in Rabat is quite sure how the King has appraised the attempt to overthrow his régime. Is he really prepared to undertake bold new initiatives and perhaps associate the semimoribund political parties with his government? His public statements have emphasized his determination to move ahead decisively. Addressing his new council of ministers, the King explained their mission:

> If our ancestors were able to cross the Straits of Gibraltar and then burn their ships, saying 'the enemy is in front of us, and the sea behind,' then we must remember these words and repeat them, knowing that the enemy lurks in the problems of underdevelopment, corruption, and others that we wish to avoid in the future. If we decide to burn our ships, to convince ourselves that it is impossible for any of us to turn back; if we decide to arm ourselves with faith and to prove our sense of judgment, we are convinced that in combatting this enemy, we shall win a great victory for all the generations to come.

The King's oratory, however, was met with skepticism both by those whom he tried to associate with the government, and the leaders of the political parties. The Istiqlal reacted to the King's new program by arguing that Morocco's problems could only be solved by the election of a truly representative parliament and the revision of the constitution so as to give real powers to the parliament and the council of ministers. The National Union of Popular Forces, through its spokesman Abderrahim Bouabid, allowed that it could not see how a government consisting of holdovers from the decade of the 'sixties or inexperienced young men could carry out the housecleaning with which the King had charged it. With several UNPF members on trial in Marrakesh (in late August the prosecutor demanded the death penalty for forty-nine of the accused), it is practically impossible for the party to consider cooperation with the Palace.

The King may feel that his isolation is temporary and that he will be able to reconstitute his military-civilian clientele once the memory of Skhirat is not so fresh in the minds of Moroccans. He may well be right. Doubters must remember that when he succeeded to the throne in 1961, many observers felt that Hassan, having none of his father's charisma, would not last more than a year. After his fashion he was eminently successful in establishing his authority in the country, and he may feel that the same methods can succeed again.

On the other hand, his officers corps is decimated and it became clear that relations of friendship, marriage, and service were so profound that to cleanse the Army would require the elimination of the entire senior officers corps. Added to this is the undeniable fact that the brutal execution and dishonoring of the rebel officers, many of whom were very popular throughout the Army, has left a bad taste in the military establishment, not to mention their families and tribal cohorts. The King has created a very real problem of personal vengeance.

To the extent that the Army is unreliable, the King no longer has a convincing instrument to keep the civilian elite in line. One of the most striking changes to follow the events at Skhirat is the widespread feeling among civilian elite members that profound and perhaps violent changes are imminent. In such circumstances Moroccans habitually withdraw into *attentisme*, and unless the King is able to change this wait-and-see mood, he will have to engage in a cat and mouse game with the Army without the benefit of any sort of civilian counterweight. It is for this reason that he would very much like to have political parties formally participating in his government. But the question is upon what terms and after what concessions would they be willing to associate themselves with the throne? The King's program in the coming months will be to determine those terms as well as their acceptability.

In retrospect, the Skhirat putsch was an appropriate climax to a decade in which Palace politics replaced party and ideological politics. Morocco returned to something resembling the old *makhzan* or sultanic system that existed before 1912. In both instances the Palace elite consisted of men hand-picked by the King and whose recompense for service would be the amount of goods they could accumulate while in office. Elite clans competed for access to spoils and the strategic placement of their own members rather than for the application of programs, the defense of ideological stances, or the interests of political organizations. Elite politics became divorced from the masses who simply observed the struggles at the top and then paid the winners' price. In 1971, instead of the régime being challenged by leftist subversion, invasion from socialist Algeria, or guerrilla warfare in the countryside, it was threatened by its own janissaries in a classic Palace coup. The King's reaction was that of all Moroccan sultans; any threat to the monarch's person must be met with the utmost severity and public

14

humiliation. The execution of the rebels, and the defilement of their bodies— all of which was later shown on Moroccan television—reminds one of the execution of the pretender, al-Rogui, captured by the Sultan in 1908, paraded for days through the streets of Fes in a cage for public amusement, thrown to the lions who mangled him, and then finished off with a bullet in the head.

But Morocco of 1971 is not the Morocco of 1908; it now has a modern military and administrative apparatus that has effectively controlled the country for several decades. It has the class structure of an industrializing nation, with hundreds of thousands of literate citizens, an urban proletariat and urban unemployed, sprawling cities and sprawling slums, and 15 million inhabitants, half of whom are under 20 years old. The politics of the sultanate are no longer appropriate and can be recreated only at great cost. The King may now realize this, but it will be difficult to undo the policies of a decade.

BIOGRAPHICAL SKETCHES

REBEL OFFICERS

General Mohammed Medbuh; born 1927 at Aknoul in the tribe of the Igzinnayen. His name, which means the slaughtered one, came from the fact that his father fought against Abdelkrim in the Rif War of the mid-1920s. Abdelkrim came from the neighboring and rival tribe of the Aith Waryaghar, and it was natural that Medbuh's father would side with the French against his rival. There is no love lost among Berbers. At one point Abdelkrim's men captured the elder Medbuh and slit his throat, leaving him for dead. The French were able to save his life but he was known thereafter as the slaughtered one. Under French auspices he became a powerful *caid*, or rural administrator, and the family acquired considerable wealth during the protectorate.

Mohammed Medbuh was schooled, interestingly enough, at Morocco's Eton, Moulay Idriss, the bastion of the Fassi urban elite. In 1943 he was admitted to the military school at Meknes (Dar al-Beida) and was inducted into the French Army as a second lieutenant in 1948. He served in the forces of occupation in Germany and then in 1949 was moved out to Indochina where he remained until 1952. In 1954 he joined a regional command in Morocco, still within the French Army. After 1956 he was appointed Governor successively of the provinces of Ouarzazat, Rabat, and Taza. In September 1958 he was made head of the Royal Gendarmerie and in December he became Minister of Communications. In August 1959 he resigned as minister to become aide-de-camp of Mohammed V. On 9 October 1967, he was appointed Director of the Royal Military Household and in March 1968 was promoted to Brigade-General. He was married to the daughter of Marshal Mezzian, whom he led to safety during the coup attempt, and who is now reportedly under house arrest.

General Amahzoun Hammou; born 1915 at Khenifra, in the tribe of the Zayyan. He is from the great Zayyani family of Moha ou Hammou 'Amharoq', which,

like the Medbuh family, became powerful rural administrators for the protectorate. This family literally gave one of its daughters to Mohammed V, and
Prince Hassan in turn married her. General Hammou served with French
forces in World War II, and then later in Indochina. After 1956 he commanded the Forces Auxilliaries, was appointed Governor of Rabat. He was
also Commander of Meknes Military Region, and at the time of the coup,
Commander of the Rabat-Kenitra Military Region.

General Bougrine; born 1924 in the Riffi tribe of the Ait Warain. His career,
like that of Medbuh and Hammou, included duty in France and Indochina.
His father was also *caïd* under the French and died fighting Abdelkrim. He
was governor of three provinces after independence, and in July 1971 was
Commander of the Fes-Taza Military Region.

General Mustapha Amharache; born 1923 at al-Hajeb in the tribe of the Beni
Mtir. He, like Chelouati, had a French wife. His career pattern resembles that
of the others. At one time he was Director of the Military Academy at Meknes
and in 1971 was Director of all military training schools.

General Abderrahman Habibi; born 1923 at al-Hajeb in the tribe of the Beni
Mtir. He served in the Royal Gendarmerie and in 1971 was Commander of the
Marrakesh Military Region. He too served in France and Indochina before
returning to Morocco at independence.

Colonel Larbi Chelouati; born 1925 at Ahermoumou in the Middle Atlas.
Married to a French woman, Chelouati had been Governor of Oujda Province
and Regional Commander at Kenitra. He was known to be a close friend of
General Oufqir. Moreover, he was related to Mohammed Ben Allem, Under-
Secretary for Interior who acted as Oufqir's right-hand man in the ministry. Ben
Allem, it should be noted, was removed from the ministry following 10 July.

Lt Col Mohammed Ababou; born 1936 at Aknoul, in the tribe of the Igzinnayen.
Because of his relative youth his career was necessarily different from those of
the others. At the time of the coup he was Director of the Non-Commissioned
Officers School at Ahermoumou.

LOYAL OFFICERS

General Mohammed Oufqir; born 1924 at Ain Cheikh in the tribe of the Ait
Yafelman. He went to the famous Berber high school at Azrou and then to the
military academy at Meknes. In 1943 he was part of the Allied expeditionary
corps in Italy. From 1947 to 1950 he was in Indochina as a commando officer.
He returned to Morocco in 1950 and served in the general staff of the French
Army in Morocco. Mohammad V appointed him as aide-de-camp in 1955 and
in 1960 he became Director of National Security. In 1964 he was appointed
Minister of the Interior. In the same year he was promoted to the rank of
general. After the events of Skhirat he was moved from the Ministry of Interior

to the Ministry of Defense and promoted to Major General of the Army. Died, allegedly by his own hand, after the second abortive coup in August 1972. His family history is like that of Medbuh, Bougrine, and Hammou. In 1907 his father facilitated the French invasion of southern Morocco and the Tafilelt valley and was suitably rewarded after 1912 with the caidate at BouDenib.

General Driss ben Omar al-Alami; born 1917 at Moulay Idriss. Graduated from the military academy at Meknes as a second lieutenant in 1939. He served in the French Army throughout World War II and was decorated five times. He later served in the forces of occupation in Austria. Later he served in Indo-china and returned to Morocco at independence. In 1956 he was made Governor of Meknes Province, and then after a period of command in southern Morocco, was made head of the school at Ahermoumou. He was made Commander of the Royal Gendarmerie in 1960 and then in 1961 Governor of Casablanca Province. He attained the rank of General in 1963 and was also made Inspector-General of the Moroccan Armed Forces. In 1967 he became Major-General of the Army. At the time of the coup attempt he was Minister of Communications. He comes from one of the famous sherifian lineages of Morocco, the Idrissids, sometimes rival of the currently reigning lineage of the Alawi.

General Mekki Gharbaoui; born 1930, Ain Leuh, Middle Atlas. His secondary schooling was at Azrou. He graduated from the Meknes military academy in 1952 and served thereafter in Germany. After independence he became aide-de-camp to Mohammed V and then to King Hassan. At the time of the coup attempt, he was director of all the King's aides-de-camp. After 10 July the King appointed Colonel Hassan Hamou, the rebel General's cousin, to that post.

Colonel Bouazza Boulhims; born in 1917 at al-Hajeb in the tribe of the Beni Mtir. He graduated from Meknes and then went to the General Staff College in Paris from which he graduated in 1956. He was responsible after independence in Morocco for the organization of the Light Mobile Security Group which first saw action in the Congo in 1960 under his command. In 1967 Boulhims was made Governor of Casablanca Province and in 1970 he was appointed Commander of the Royal Gendarmerie. After his death, the King appointed Lt Col Arzouz al-Hajj to head the Gendarmerie.

SOME IMPORTANT VICTIMS OF THE ATTEMPTED COUP

Killed

Dr Fadel Benyaich	Personal physician to the King
Boubker Sbihi	Attache in the Royal Cabinet; brother of one of the founders of the Moroccan nationalist movement

Ahmed Ben Souda	Director of Planning, 34 years old and one of Morocco's most promising technocrats
Ahmad Bahnini	President of the Supreme Court and brother of M'hammed Bahnini
Omar Chbouki	Lawyer, member of the Berber party, the Popular Movement, and from the same tribe as General Hammou, the Zayyan
M. Abdennebi	Director of the Moroccan School of Administration
Dr Abdelmalek Faraj	First Moroccan Minister of Public Health
Mohammed Lazrak	Minister of Tourism
Marcel Dupret	Ambassador to Morocco from Belgium

Wounded

Belhassan Wazzani	President of the Democratic Party of Independence
Bahreddine Senoussi	Minister of Labor and Youth
Mahjoubi Ahardane	President of the Popular Movement
Dr Adelkrim Khatib	President of the Democratic Popular Movement
Prince Moulay Abdullah	King's brother

A SELECTIVE CHRONOLOGY OF MOROCCAN EVENTS

1912	Establishment of French protectorate in Morocco
1944	Founding of the Istiqlal party
1953	Exile of Sultan Mohammed bin Youssef (later King Mohammed V) and his replacement by the puppet Sultan, Bin Arafa
1954–55	The launching of urban terrorist groups and a rural Liberation Army fighting for Moroccan independence and the return of the Sultan from exile
November 1955	Mohammed V returns to Morocco
March 1956	Morocco becomes formally independent
November 1958–January 1959	Widespread insurrection in the eastern Rif mountains; during the same period the Istiqlal party splits and left wing elements found the National Union of Popular Forces

December 1962	Morocco's first Constitution is approved in a national referendum
March 1963	Morocco's first, bicameral, Parliament is elected
July 1963	Over one hundred Moroccans are arrested for plotting against the régime
September 1963	Warfare with Algeria breaks out over disputed border areas
March 1965	Severe worker/student riots occur in Casablanca and elsewhere
June 1965	The King dissolves the Parliament and proclaims a state of emergency that lasts until August 1970
October 1965	Mehdi Ben Barka of the UNPF is kidnapped and presumably murdered in Paris
August–September 1970	A new Constitution is approved in a national referendum and a new unicameral Parliament is elected. The state of emergency is declared over
April 1971	Three ministers fired for corruption
10 July 1971	Rebel officers try to topple the régime
4 August 1971	King Hassan constitutes a new government

RECENT MINISTERIAL STAFFING IN MOROCCO

	Fall 1970	Spring 1971	20 August 1971
Agriculture	Mohammed Benhima replaced by Ahmad Lasky	Abdelhadi Sbihi	Maati Jorio
Interior	Gen. Oufqir	…	Ahmed BenBouchta
Finance	Mohammed Lazrak	Karim Lamraani	Mohammed Mdaghri (dead in auto accident Aug. 30)
Prime Minister	Ahmad Laraki	…	Karim Lamraani
Tourism	M. Kriem	Mohammed Lazrak	Abdelkamil Reghai (also Dir. Gen. of the Caisse de Depot et de Gestion)
Commerce	M. Jaidi	Mohammed Tahiri	Abdelaziz Benjelloun (also Dir. Gen. of the Bureau of Mines)
Justice	Ahmad Benbouchta	…	Mohammed Bahnini (also Sec. Gen. of the Gov't.)
Foreign Affairs	Youssef Bel Abbes	…	Abdelatif Filali
Public Health	Dr. Bel-Mahi	…	…
Defense	Mohammed Bahnini	…	Gen. Oufqir
Public Works	M. Chami replaces Mohammed Imani	…	Mohammed Bernoussi (Chami becomes Dir. Gen. of the Export Office—OCE)
Information	Ahmad Senoussi	…	Abdelkader Sahraoui
Labor and Youth	Badredin Senoussi	…	Arslan al-Jadidi
Primary Education	Haddou Chiguer	…	…

	Fall	Spring 1971	20 August 1971
Secondary and Higher Education	Mamoun Tahiri	Ahmad Lasky	Arslanal-Jadidi
Habous	Ahmad Bargache	...	...
Communications	Gen. Driss Ben Omar	...	...
Administrative Affairs	Ahmad Osman	...	Ahmad Majid Benjelloun
Under-Secretary for the Plan	Mustapha Faris	...	...
Under-Secretary for Education	Mohammed Chafiq	...	...
Secretary-General of the Government	M'hammed Bahnini	...	...

... = no change

During the aftermath of the bloody day at the Skhirat Palace, Morocco, still shell-shocked, drew up the balance sheet of the putsch—in terms not merely of its dead and wounded, but also of its political consequences. The royal façade, notwithstanding the abortive nature of the coup, was now visibly shaken, and with it all conventional wisdom concerning the bases of the régime. The origins, ideological aims and full extent of the plot still remain unknown. The chiefs of the rebellion were killed or executed without trial. The King and Oufkir, for their part, have taken care not to disclose whatever they may have learnt. It is not my intention to deal with these issues,[1] but merely to attempt to elucidate one aspect of the matter, namely its bearing on the Berber question. In effect, five of the generals of the revolt, and two at least of its most active colonels, were Berbers. Had the uprising succeeded, Morocco would, without any doubt, have been ruled by Berbers. Yet it does not follow that it was a Berber plot. Numerous Berbers were also victims of the rebels, including three generals (Gharbaoui, Boulhims, Bachir), and two outstanding Berber personalities, Oufkir and Ahardan, were reduced to the role of mere spectators of the massacre. The rebels were officers as well as Berbers, and it was in the former capacity that they acted. But having stressed all this, the fact remains that the abortive coup did have a kind of Berber colouring, and it is this that I shall try to analyse here.

I shall not discuss again Morocco's characteristic Berber problems, which have already been explored in this volume, but let us recall three facts: the series of rural rebellions which took place soon after Independence (Tafilalet, the Rif, Middle Atlas, the South); the troubled inception of the Mouvement Populaire party; and the growing importance of the Army, among whose leaders and men the Berbers formed a strong majority. These three factors in a way reinforced one another: it was the Army which had to contain the rebellions and administer the more troublesome provinces, and it was the Mouvement Populaire which came into being in response to rural discontents, while at the same time being closely linked to both the Army and the Ministry of the Interior (which is in effect responsible for provincial administrations).

The Monarchy knew how to make use of the rebellions, of the Mouvement Populaire, and of the Army, first to counterbalance and then progressively to diminish the influence of the political parties. One may just note a certain developmental sequence: during the first period (1957–9), the rebellions, partly a sequel of the Army of Liberation, were the dominant feature; subsequently it was the Mouvement Populaire which provided the star turn, until it itself became one further party of the old type, at which point it simultaneously

---

[1] One of the best analyses of the coup and its political and socio-economic aspects is to be found in John Waterbury: 'The coup manqué'. *American Universities Field Staff Report*, Vol. xv, No. 1. Reprinted as preceding chapter.

became a potential threat to the Monarchy and was weakened by its own internal divisions. As the years went by, it was the Army which emerged as the most important piece on the Moroccan chessboard. But throughout and behind these transformations, the Berbers were there.

Given the policy of weakening the parties, conducted by King Hassan II, observers had long ago noted that the Army had become the only organized force capable of changing the direction of national policy.[1] It controlled arms and territory. At the same time, discontents fermented, and rivalries and ambitions emerged within the Royal Armed Forces. It is in this context that one may recall the abortive attempt at a rebellion attempted by young officers in 1970. But the deeper and more fundamental question asked in Rabat concerns the nature and importance of General Oufkir's role at the King's side.

In one sense, the putsch of 10 July 1971 came as no surprise. What was surprising was its personnel. Where one might have expected to see unknown and radical young captains, or Oufkir himself, in fact one saw basically royalist officers. Hence, the first question: who were the rebels?

The most conspicuous personality of the plot was General Medboh. As Director of the Royal Military Establishment (*La Maison Militaire Royale*), he controlled the whole Army in the King's name, and was the King's closest collaborator. He was 43 years of age, a native of the Rif, son of a *caid* (governmentally endorsed tribal leader) who had supported the French against the rebellion of Abd el-Krim. Until Independence, his career was typical of so many young Berber notables of the Protectorate period, and indeed of the majority of senior officers who participated, whether as rebels or as loyalists, in the events of 10 July: he had been educated at the Military College of Dar el-Beida at Meknes, and had seen active service in the French Army. After 1956 (the coming of Independence), his career took an interesting turn. He was named Governor of Ouarzazate Province, and as such found himself obliged to direct a column sent against his rebelling fellow-Governor, the old Adi u Bihi, in the neighboring province of Tafilalet, and also to restrain the turbulent gangs of the Army of Liberation, still operating in the South. In 1958 he was called to succeed Ahardan as Governor of Rabat, Ahardan having been dismissed for the illegal foundation of the Mouvement Populaire, and subsequently he was briefly in charge of his own native region. In these semi-civilian, semi-military posts of the troubled early years of Independence, Medboh was in a position to acquire first-hand knowledge of the problems and aspirations of the rural world, and to assess the importance of provincial control, at the very time at which he also became sensitive to political issues. In brief, from this point on he found himself at the meeting-point of the three Berber contributions to the situation— rural rebellions, the Mouvement Populaire, and the Army. His political role became more marked in 1959 when King Mohamed V named him Minister for Postal Services and Communications in the UNFP party's government led by Abdallah Ibrahim. Within a year, he resigned in protest against the attacks made on the Army by both the Istiqlal and UNFP parties. 1958–9 were crucial

[1] See for example J. & J. Aubin, 'Le Maroc en suspens'. *Annuaire de l'Afrique du Nord*, 1964.

years for Morocco, during which there occurred the fission of the Istiqlal party (UNFP being the seceding segment), the Rif rebellion, the official recognition of the Mouvement Populaire, the growth of hostility between the UNFP and Prince (as he then was) Moulay Hassan, and the political rise of the Prince and in his wake, of the Army and Oufkir. Following his resignation, Mohamed V made Medboh Commander of the Royal Guard, and after that he came to be ever closer to the royal center of power, with Hassan II in 1967 making him Director of the Royal Military Establishment (Maison Militaire Royale). It is noteworthy that throughout these years, Medboh succeeded, in his discreet, exceedingly courteous, not to say courtier-like, manner, in maintaining his contacts with all persons of influence in the Kingdom, his successive appointments having brought him in close touch with diverse sections of the country. There is an interesting portent in the fact that in 1963, Medboh was involved in an attempted plot against Hassan II, organized by ex-members of the Resistance. The conversation was recorded and was of assistance in the arrest of the plotters. Two facts emerge—his then loyalty to the King, and his contacts with extremists. As Director of the Maison Militaire, he was ever more closely involved in the King's game and its innermost secrets. He frequently carried out missions of importance, abroad and at home, in an official or a private capacity. It was in consequence of a mission to the United States early in 1971 that Medboh brought back to the King shattering and conclusive evidence of corruption in the royal inner circle. It was this episode which led to the dismissal of several ministers, but it also precipitated the July 1971 coup. Medboh was better placed than anyone, with the possible exception of Oufkir, to know the thoughts, plans, and inner state of mind of Moulay Hassan II. He watched the development of the King and Kingdom with growing anxiety and, given his character and past record, it must have been despair at what he beheld which drove him to act.

Little is known about Commandant-Colonel Ababou, the second personality of the putsch. He was Medboh's junior by ten years, and, like Medboh, was born in the region of Aknoul. Unlike his seniors in the plot, Ababou is an officer of the post-Independence generation, and has no personal experience of the French Army. As Commander of the School for NCOs at Ahermoumou, he led the assault group of the operation and was in charge of the attack on Skhirat Palace. He is certainly responsible both for the massacre which took place there and for the death of Medboh. Had he not in turn been killed by General Bachir, he might today perhaps be the Nasser or the Khadafi of Morocco. No doubt he stands for the new generation of officers, without a colonial past or special links to the Monarchy, who aim at the establishment of a military régime similar to that which prevails in so many of the states of Africa and the Middle East.

The presence of Colonel Chelouati amongst the plotters highlights a series of puzzles, typical of the complexity of Berber affairs and of the relationships that obtain within the Army. Chelouati was born at Ahermoumou, the hinge linking the Middle Atlas to the Rif chain. He belongs to the Medboh and Oufkir generation and like them served in the French Army till the coming of

Independence. He held important posts in the Royal Army, commanding its Engineers in succession to General Oufkir's father-in-law, and was subsequently in charge of the Officers' School at Dar el-Beida, before becoming Governor of Oujda province in 1965. It is said that he was retired from this post as a result of his profiteering from transactions in irrigated land of this region, despite the support he received from Oufkir. This however helped him to obtain a good position on the General Staff and, subsequently, the command of the Armoured Units at Kenitra. Before the event, there was simply nothing to indicate that Chelouati would take part in the plot whose spokesman he was very briefly to become. He was a typical cavalry officer, in no way puritan or austere, intelligent but with limited vision. He had the reputation of being a faithful client of Oufkir's, and moreover one of his brothers was Bel Allem's brother-in-law. Bel Allem, a Berber from Oujda, was Oufkir's ADC, and one of the most cryptic and influential personalities in the Ministry of the Interior. Hence it is difficult indeed to find a logical explanation of Chelouati's adhesion to the plot. The whisper has been heard in Rabat that where Chelouati was present, Oufkir could not have been so very far away.

Concerning the other rebels, let us note simply that all the Generals were Berber, and shared both a past and a reputation for loyalty to the throne with Medboh and Oufkir, that General Hammou was related to the King's wife, and that they occupied strategic posts in the Army (commands of Military Regions and of Military Schools).

This rapid survey of the dramatis personae brings us to the heart of our problem, the relationship between the King and the Berbers.

The first point, which has been argued by others before, concerns the ambiguity of the relationship between the King and the Berbers. The Berber leaders (military and civilian alike), were royalist in as far as they found themselves in conflict with the political parties, considered to be non-Berber or non-rural. For the Berbers, the Monarchy represented above all a bulwark against domination by an urban bourgeoisie. A number of the rebellions of the early period of Independence had a slogan—the King is prisoner of the parties, let us free him. (This was also a theme invoked by some of the cadets arrested in the aftermath of the July 1971 coup.) This helps to explain why the regions of erstwhile tribal dissidence, of *siba*, had become a pillar of the régime. This support however did not imply total devotion, nor the disappearance of that sense of honor and independence which are inherent in the Berber character. No doubt Hassan II had forgotten this, and hence he now faces the double self-questioning: how had my army been able to do this? How had my officers, covered with honors and riches, been able to provoke a rebellion?

In effect, we have no reliable knowledge of the aims of the rebel officers. The long term aims of Medboh, Ababou, and Chelouati, could hardly be identical. But their shared short term view of the situation can be summed up thus: the royal set-up, based on corruption and a contempt for men and institutions alike, is leading the country into ruin and dishonor. Nothing further can be hoped for from the King—so we had better act now, before others do so and sweep us away along with the Monarchy.

After the coup, Hassan II took trouble to publish details concerning the 'wealth' of the rebels, so as to bracket them with the corruption, whose perpetrators were now all of a sudden to be called to account or imprisoned. But in doing this he ignored at least two facts: the wealth of the rebel officers, though not contemptible, was modest in comparison with that of other personalities of the régime, and hardly shocked anyone, notably when contrasted with rumored figures of the wealth of others. Secondly, the style of thought of the rural masses continues to bear the imprint of tribalism: a man counts more than an ideology. The rurals have more confidence in one of their own number, even if his riches are ill-gotten, than they do in townsfolk, who are corrupt by definition. Here one may remember the fury which seized the cadets of Ahermoumou at the display of luxury at the feast of Skhirat. What they saw before them was, in their eyes, the very picture of corruption and dishonor: they overturned the loaded tables, tore up the currency notes, crushed the gold watches, in a mad frenzy which recalls the great movements of Reform that have on earlier historic occasions shaken Berber and Muslim North Africa.

We have described the ambiguity in the relations between the King and the Berbers, an ambiguity which led to and culminated in the coup of 10 July at Skhirat. But after all, the relations amongst the Berbers themselves are no less ambiguous. As we have stressed, there is no Berber consensus, any more than there is a consensus of Berber officers. The putsch cannot be reduced to a Berber uprising. Besides, there are considerable divergences of character, opinion, and interest, between a Medboh, an Oufkir, or an Ahardan. These differences had become more marked over the past ten years, and were accentuated in as far as the régime itself hardened its position. The entry on the scene of a younger cohort, men such as Ababou, complicates the situation further. It is but rarely and for brief periods that Berbers have attained an unity of ideas or of action, lacking as they do a shared inherent outlook. By contrast, they have a basically similar temperament which brings them together in adversity, and which allows them to retain a thread of secret complicity that transcends even bloody confrontations: it is their shared speech.

It is our view that a certain solidarity did play its part in the events of Skhirat, at a number of levels, notwithstanding the little matter of butchery for which one of its perpetrators made his excuses to the French writer Benoist-Mechin. Oufkir after all was not killed that day, and it is hard to believe that this was a matter of chance. We have spoken of his close links to Chelouati. Ahardan, a guest of the King on that day, perhaps owes his life to the fact that he is indeed Ahardan and a Berber. But what were the inner thoughts of Oufkir and Ahardan when they were shooting, ignominiously and without trial, their old friends and colleagues, their 'cousins' in Berber fashion, Chelouati, Mustapha, Habibi, Hammou, Bougrine? What are the thoughts of hundreds of officers and NCOs, not to mention those under arrest? What are the thoughts of the Berber Governors and Caids, many of whom were dismissed? What are the thoughts of the inhabitants of the Rif and the Middle Atlas, the rebels' home regions? Whatever their outward comportment today, one may well wonder about the depth of their devotion to the King.

In the end, one cannot but be struck by the parallels between the 'Berber policy' of the French Protectorate, and that of Hassan II. Both were based on the rural-Berber milieu and its military elite, and in each case it turned against them in the end.

The abortive coup of July 1971 was not a Berber enterprise, notwithstanding the fact that certain members of the Moroccan elite, having survived the massacre, now assert, with loathing tinged with fear, that it was all the fruit of Berber duplicity, savagery and madness. These same speakers might have been heard, not so very long ago, enthusing about the 'faithful Berber ramparts of the Throne . . .'

John Waterbury[1] has well demonstrated how little one may conclude from the fact that nearly all the participants were of Berber origin. But the failed coup left its mark on the Berber milieu, in the Army, the civil service, the countryside. The myth of loyalty, of an elective affinity and solidarity between the Berbers and the Monarchy, is crumbling, and it would seem even that it is being replaced by a furtive distrust.

While General Oufkir, equipped with special powers, takes the Army in hand, the favored place which General Medboh had occupied at the King's side is now taken by Colonel Dlimi. Dlimi is a native of the Gharb (the Arabic-speaking western Atlantic plain of Morocco), and the warmth of his relationship to Oufkir has diminished since the days when he was his ADC as chief of Security. It appears that a number of young officers of Arab origin have received commands, thus filling the gaps left by the casualties of the abortive coup.

Moreover, it seems that the administrative network centered on the Ministry of the Interior was brought back under full control by agents of the old Laghzaoui team at Security (Sûreté Nationale). The rapid recovery of control of the provinces had been made possible, in July 1971, by the loyalty of the Sûreté. Its new Director General, Hassar, is a member of one of the old-established bourgeois families of Salé, and has close family links with the Istiqlal party. (The Royal Secretariat—le Cabinet Royal—once again played a most active role in the dismissals and promotions, whether in the Army or among the officials of the Ministry of the Interior, who of course occupy local administrative positions up and down the country.) It is hard to draw up an exact balance sheet, but it is certain that Berber office-holders were adversely affected by the aftermath of the coup, and suspicion continues to attach itself to those who have remained.[2]

Even if the Berbers are no longer the privileged allies of the Monarchy, they continue to occupy a position in the country and its government which requires that they be treated with respect. Excessive displays of hostility towards them

---

[1] See pp. 397 et seq.

[2] The Istiqlal party made its own contribution to the diffusion of a perhaps somewhat retrospective idea of a 'Berber plot'. After the coup, the petty townsfolk of Rabat were heard to say, 'Had they succeeded, they would have crushed us like caraway seed . . .'

might provoke dangerous rural reactions.[1] The clemency of the post-coup verdicts indicates an attempt to appease the rural population. The King is planning a grand Royal Progress through the mountains behind Beni Mellal (Central Morocco), in a region which had hardly been affected by the rebellion, and which will make a sumptuous show of the display of its loyalty to the Sovereign, no doubt with less bitterness than will be felt by the Zaian tribesmen of the Middle Atlas.

The new Minister of the Environment, Hassan Zemmouri, had been a member of the erstwhile Abdallah Ibrahim (left) government, and had been president of the important Association of Graduates of the Azrou College, the crucial Berber educational institution in the Middle Atlas. Since 1960 he has been Secretary General of the Casablanca Chamber of Commerce, and he knew how to use this position to establish close contacts with the Soussi trading community, whose support assisted his election to the Presidency of the Casablanca Town Council in 1970. But Zemmouri on his own cannot constitute a gage for the Berber world. Ahardan has displayed an unfriendly reaction to the new Constitution, and the UNFP party meaningfully plans to hold a colloquim in the autumn of 1972 on Abd el-Krim and his Rifian Republic.

Feared, courted, and unloved, the Berbers who are also members of the elite fall back on a wait-and-see attitude. No doubt they would have welcomed a government led by Abderrahim Bouabid. It would seem that the government need fear no plots from them. But can it seriously rely on their aid, should there be urban outbursts such as the Casablanca riots of March 1965, or rural rebellions? Despite the purge, the Berbers remain present in good numbers in the Army, the local administration, in the Courts of Justice. The diffuse hostility, which they cannot but sense, reinforces their cohesion. Will they remain forever the willing and unconditional guardians of a Monarchy and a bourgeoisie whom they, in their turn, also despise?

[1] Such as inscriptions which could be seen in the Middle Atlas, proclaiming 'Ababou, thou shalt be avenged!' Cf. *Maghreb*, No. 48, Nov.–Dec. 1971, p. 18.

There is a remarkable consensus among the contributors to this volume concerning the absense of a serious 'Berber problem', at least in the present and foreseeable future. In North Africa there appears to be no 'simultaneous development of both national and sub-national solidarities' as in many of the new states,[1] but rather the coexistence of the traditional outlook centered on village, clan, or tribe, with an Algerian or Moroccan sense of national identity. The same is true of Tunisia where the Berber-speaking minority is less than 1 percent but where a strong sense of national identity does not preclude local and regional forms of patriotism.

There are a number of reasons for this lack of Berber identification and aggressive ethnic affirmation. William Quandt points out that there are only widely separated islands of Berber-speaking people with different dialects and no written language, who share the same religion as the Arab-speaking majority. They have therefore looked up to higher cultures, whether Muslim-Arabic, or French, and many have been partly Arabized or Gallicized.

Other contributors have shown that Arabs and Berbers identify and apprehend each other by a variety of characterizations besides that of language and customs.[2] There are a series of cleavages and areas of differentiation that help blur ethnic differences, such as the opposition of city dweller and sedentary peasant, and nomad; regional, tribal and sub-tribal loyalties; class, educational, and occupational differences.

It can also be pointed out that many Arabs are conscious of being Arabized Berbers, that there is no myth of common ancestry among the major Berber groups,[3] no historical memories to substantiate the presence of a deep antagonism between the two ethnic groups since no central political system, specifically Arab or Berber, tried to impose its rule on the other group. On the contrary, the Berber islands were largely autonomous under the nominal rule of the Sultan in Morocco and under that of the Turks in Algeria. They were by-passed by the French colonizers who did not settle there and were content with establishing an administrative superstructure that left almost intact the traditional way of life.

This does not mean that frictions have not continued to exist among the two language groups and that mutual contempt is not often expressed. But this is not

---

[1] Charles W. Anderson *et al.*, *Issues of Political Development*, Englewood Cliffs, 1967, p. 28. See also Clifford Geertz, 'The integrative revolution', in C. Geertz (ed), *Old Societies and New States: The Quest for Modernity in Asia and Africa*, Glencoe, 1963.

[2] See especially Chapter 7, by Lawrence Rosen.

[3] Such myths seem to have existed in the distant past or at least are credited by Ibn Khaldun.

translated into a 'gut drive for ethnic affirmation'[1] and does not preclude solid working relationships. In fact animosities among Berbers along tribal and sub-tribal lines are just as intense, if not more so, than those between Arabs and Berbers. It was French colonialism that attempted—with little success—to emphasize the notion of Berber separateness in Morocco, as it had attempted to do in Algeria decades earlier, and to spread the belief that Islam was not an essential aspect of Berber identity. During the years immediately following independence, some political leaders also tried to play upon primordial sentiments and to mobilize Berbers in a struggle against the central government. But these revolts were not motivated by a drive for ethnic affirmation, much less for a desire for independence or even autonomy.

Anthropology and sociology offer what is perhaps the most important insight into the absense of a militant ethnic, or regional, sense of identity. This is the perpetuation of traditional structures and values in a fragmentary type of society that emphasizes fierce loyalty to the village or clan and by both encouraging and regulating conflicts among neighboring units does not lend itself to a broader type of identification, except under exceptional circumstances.

In some areas, as in the Rif, the Atlas mountains and the Aures, modernization has hardly penetrated the traditional society. In other areas such as Kabylia and Mzab, temporary male migration to Algerian cities, then to France, brought the indispensable supplementary income that allowed the traditional way of life to survive. Jean Morizot points out that local production furnished only 25 percent of the per capita income in Kabylia in 1950, that few men were left in the villages, agricultural and artisanal occupations having been largely abandoned. A family with two wage-earners in France was relatively well-off; with three, it was almost wealthy. But whereas wage earning elsewhere in Algeria had helped destroy the old social equilibrium by undermining the authority of the local notables and of the heads of the families, in Kabylia and Mzab temporary male migration was largely responsible for maintaining intact the traditional social structures in communities enjoying relative economic well-being as well as real autonomy.[2]

He showed how the traditional village organization kept coexisting with the French-created administrative structures. Thus as late as 1953 the candidates to municipal elections were selected by the 'Kharoubas' (fractions of villages grouping all families claiming a common ancestor). Side by side with the official administration, the unofficial *jama'a*s continued to exist with their own funds and their own agents who generally had greater authority than the official agents and saw to it that the traditional rules (Quanoun) were respected. He emphasized the extraordinary solidarity of the village republic and the sense of duty toward the collectivity that was inculcated very early in childhood and kept guiding the behavior of adults working in France whose *code de l'honneur* demanded that they send a monthly money order to their families.

The temporary male migrants adopted a purely functional approach to

[1] This and the following remarks are taken from John Waterbury's unpublished paper delivered at the Middle East Institute Conference held in Washington, D.C.
[2] *L'Algérie kabylisée*, Paris, 1962, pp. 112 ff.

modernity—making money for the family, at home—while they remained emotionally attached to their village and to the values they had been socialized into. They were eminently adaptable to their conditions as city dwellers but not subject to the uprooting effect of dual and conflicting sets of values. Their self-confidence and self-reliance may be viewed as a result of their strong sense of self-identity that did not permit the erosion of traditional values even in the most modern surroundings. Once back in the village, the readjustment to old ways was easy. Their village-centered view blended with whatever cosmopolitan outlook had been acquired in their self-imposed exile.

Had there been early mass migration by whole families to the cities, a sense of ethnic identity cutting across lineage and village ties might well have developed as differences in language, customs, and values between Berber and Arab communities would have tended to broaden the sense of identification from the village to the ethnic group. Ethnic identification and tensions with the outer group could then have allowed masses to be mobilized by political leaders capitalizing on the painful cultural transition imposed on the migrants. By contrast the male immigrant, single, inconspicuous and adaptable, did his best to avoid ethnic tensions. For him the challenge of city life was an individual, not a collective one, and, above all, it was temporary.

Yet the fragmentary society that did not lend itself to ethnic identification, did not prevent a sense of national solidarity to develop, as soon as the first winds of liberation began to blow. For one thing the male migrants were keenly aware of their economic dependence on the whole of Algeria. For another thing they could easily equate their lot with that of their Arab-speaking brothers since they suffered the same petty humiliations and discriminations, whether in Algiers or in Paris. Their resentment could influence others in the village despite its relative insulation from colonial rule and the benefits it derived from the colonial situation. The more successful migrants, particularly those with higher education, were quick to see the obstacles to social promotion deriving from their inferior status as *indigènes*. Some had been tempted by assimilation and had become French citizens. Many more opted for independence and the possibility of fulfilling their potentialities in an independent state where they could replace the French in the important positions reserved for them. They had an educational headstart on most Arabs—in French, if not in Arabic—no inferiority complex and no fear of being discriminated against in the newly independent state that would need their talents. Berbers held leadership roles from the beginning in movements for national liberation. There was no reason why they could not some day hold key positions in the government as well as in the administration and in business.

Organized resistance to foreign occupation could not start in the *colons'* lands of western Algeria, anymore than in western Morocco or Tunisia where traditional structures had been in the process of disintegration and where passivity prevailed. Mountainous areas or the regions populated by independent farmers and artisans, whether the Sahel in Tunisia, or Kabylia, were the logical starting points for organized revolt. In Algeria it started some two years earlier in the east than in the western part of the country. Once started, the dialectics of war led to total involvement of the population in the Berber-speaking areas. Traditional structures and values, as much as the favorable terrain, made for successful armed revolt in the Willayas (province) controlled by Berber leaders. Their tactical autonomy in military matters was balanced by a centralized political organization operating outside the country, where Berber leaders played a major, if not preponderant, role. But they formed no united front—they opposed one another in jockeying for positions of control as much as they opposed Arab-speaking leaders. The same situation prevailed in the hectic days following independence, where Berbers and Arabs were found in all contending factions during the bitter fratricidal struggle for power.

Once Ben Bella had won and established his authority in Algiers, Kabylia remained a relatively autonomous military enclave, a bastion that the central government could not easily control. But the insurrection of 1963–64 under Ait Ahmed showed the limit of Kabyle expectations. Not only was it condemned by half the Kabyle deputies at the national assembly and not followed by a sub-stantial fraction of local troups, but it petered out as soon as the border war between Algeria and Morocco had started. Colonel Mohand then led his Kabyle warriors to fight the Moroccan army, proving rather conclusively the strength of Algerian nationalism among the Kabyles. In fact the revolt had had no separatist objective; Kabyle peasants were used by some Kabyle leaders in Algiers as a power base to increase their authority in the central government. There was no attempt at opting out of the political system—but rather at demanding greater participation and integration in the new nation-state. The problem was to warn against discrimination and call attention on local grievances, as Jeanne Favret demonstrated in the case of the spontaneous upsurge in the Aures. It was not a case of regional patriotism opposed to Algerian nationalism and calling for some degree of autonomy.

The same is true of Morocco in the period immediately following indepen-dence. John Waterbury spoke of the ambiguous period after 1956 in which politicians tried to mobilize as large a constituency as possible and to play on group feelings and fears. There was once again no attempt to opt out of the political system. He pointed out that the Rif uprising of 1958–59, triggered off by the founding of the Mouvement Populaire, a group created to counter the Istiqlal, was launched to cut into the patronage system dominated by Istiqlal. The move got out of hand and led to a general uprising that had to be suppressed by the army (made up mainly of Berbers). Waterbury points out that the MP was a counter-coalition encouraged by the Palace to face the monolithic Istiqlal and to serve as a channel for patronage from leaders to tribal notables who constituted their clientele.[1] The same can be said of the patronage system instituted by the Ministry of the Interior, also controlled by Berber leaders.

Thus the king continued to use the 'divide and rule' policy of the French by gaining the support of tribal notables, mainly Berbers, as a counterweight to the Fassi-dominated Istiqlal. He did not try to discourage the notion of a cleavage

---

[1] This is taken from the unpublished paper mentioned above. See also his recent book *The Commander of the Faithful*, New York, 1970, for a good description of the Mouvement Populaire.

between Arabs and Berbers, wanting to appear as the symbol of the bridge above this cleavage. This policy is partly a reflection of the pluralistic nature of Moroccan society. It also reflects the traditional style of leadership based on the patronage system and a deliberate search for a rural base of support, although the monarchy did little to modernize the countryside and improve the living conditions of peasants and nomads. Thanks to the patronage system, the rural notables are to keep the rural masses quiescent.

Here the difference with Algeria is obvious. The ideology and, to a lesser extent, the strategy of the Algerian government are resolutely modernist, populist and egalitarian. Despite the rather heavy dose of Muslim puritanism that colors its modernist stance, the political system is establishing a legal-rational, rather than a charismatic, type of leadership, supported by a large administrative class in which the spoils system is discouraged. Efforts are made to transform economic and social structures and to equalize conditions in at least parts of the country, particularly in the Berber-speaking areas that could be a potential source of trouble. Algeria is thus gambling on establishing the conditions for the lasting legitimacy of the regime, even if this includes the strengthening of the one-party system and the discouraging of any type of opposition.

Although Algeria is making efforts at modernizing some rural areas, mass migration to the cities cannot be avoided any more than it can in Morocco. This presents serious dangers if rapid industrialization does not take place. But the unemployed and semi-employed are more likely to aquire a new class consciousness than to be mobilized along ethnic lines.

In both countries Berber elites have been used as beneficiaries and guardians of the political system, in which they have held a fair proportion of top political positions. But it is not irrelevant to notice that in Morocco the Berbers are overrepresented in the army, while in Algeria they are overrepresented in the administration; army and administration representing respectively the main institutional support of the regime.

Among the Western-educated elites, particularly university students, the problem of ethnic origin seems to play only a minor role in both countries. The unifying elements seem to be both political opposition, however different the ideology of the opposition in each country, and paradoxically the preponderance of French as the *lingua franca* of Westernized elites. French acts as a cultural bridge that transcends other differences. This does not preclude a certain romantic pride on the part of some intellectuals in their Berber origin. But so long as no discrimination is shown against them, their pride is not likely to lead to aggressive self-assertion and alienation.

In both countries social mobilization would seem likely to bypass the sub-national variety of identification and to work toward the goal of nation-building. This is particularly so since the State has become the great provider of the necessities of life and since there is no salvation outside of it. One may threaten it, fight for a larger share of its bounties, but no one would dare to cut loose from it and risk economic suicide. In the long run the growing role of the State—particularly in the countryside—should facilitate the process of nation-building, as the notion of class or interest group tends to replace the tenuous one of ethnic identification; an hypothesis that is probably more valid for Algeria than for Morocco, where the modernizing role of the State in the rural areas is at best erratic and unconvincing.

Notes on Contributors

ANDRÉ ADAM. Professor at the Sorbonne. Spent many years in Morocco, of which his knowledge is both many-sided and intimate. In his teaching capacity and as Director of the National School of Administration, he acquired a profound knowledge of the Moroccan elite. For a time he administered a Berber tribal region which is noted for supplying migrants to Casablanca, and has published scholarly work on it. But his outstanding contribution is to the sociology of modern urban Morocco. His main work, a two-volume study of Casablanca, appeared in 1968.

E. A. ALPORT was a sociologist living in Oxford, who specialized in North Africa, to which he had made frequent visits. He continued working bravely on his researches despite a tragic and crippling illness, to which he succumbed in February 1972.

KENNETH L. BROWN. A young American scholar, now lecturer in Social Anthropology at the University of Manchester, England, previously at the University of Chicago. Has written a thesis on the social history and structure of the town of Salé, soon to be published.

EDMUND BURKE III. A young American scholar who has specialized on the immediate pre-protectorate period of Moroccan history, on which he has written a thesis. Has published various articles, including a comparative study of North Africa and the Middle East. At present teaching at the University of California at Santa Cruz.

ANDRÉ CORAM. A Frenchman who has spent many years in Morocco both before and after Independence. A friend of the principal political figures, has participated in their struggle for Independence, and in the subsequent social reconstruction. Was technical adviser on the rural economy. Author of various articles.

LOUIS-JEAN DUCLOS. Spent many years in North Africa, especially Morocco. Now research associate at the Fondation Nationale des Sciences Politiques, is the author of numerous articles on Maghrebin politics.

ROSS E. DUNN. Ph.D. from the University of Wisconsin, now Assistant Professor at San Diego University. His thesis on the Moroccan far South-East, the oases between the Atlas and the Sahara, combines the approaches of an historian with those of a social anthropologist, and illuminates the inter-relationships between tribes, traditional state, oasis-dwellers and foreign penetration.

JEANNE FAVRET. Grew up in Tunisia and had close experience of Algeria both during the war and after it. Taught at the University of Algiers from 1959 till 1964. With various publications to her credit, now works at the French Centre National de la Recherche Scientifique.

ERNEST GELLNER. Educated at Prague and Balliol College, Oxford, has carried out intermittent research in central Morocco between 1953 and 1961. Professor at the London School of Economics. Author of *Saints of the Atlas* (1969).

DAVID MONTGOMERY HART. An American with extensive Moroccan field experience, notably in the Rif and among the Ait Atta. Worked with the help of a Ford

Foundation grant from 1952 till 1955, and under the auspices of American Museum of Natural History from 1959 till 1967. His work on 'The Aith Waryaghar of the Moroccan Rif' is due to be published soon.

JEREMY H. KEENAN. Educated at the Universities of Cambridge and Exeter, England, acquired his Ph.D. for a thesis on the Algerian Taureg, based on four prolonged field trips between 1965 and 1970. At present teaching social anthropology at the University of Witwatersrand.

ABDASLAM BEN KEDDOUR. A young Moroccan social scientist who voices the viewpoint of one important segment of Moroccan intellectuals.

OCTAVE MARAIS. Researcher at the French Fondation Nationale des Sciences Politiques, with extensive experience of Morocco as teacher and technical adviser, and with many articles to his credit.

CHARLES MICAUD is Professor at the Graduate School of International Studies, University of Denver. He spent several years in Tunisia and is co-author of *Tunisia: the Politics of Modernization* (1964) as well as of several books on French politics.

WILLIAM B. QUANDT. Author of *Revolution and Political Leadership: Algeria 1954–68* (1969), a study of Algerian politicians based on field research carried out during 1966–7. Now on staff of the Rand Corporation, has taught courses on North Africa and the Middle East at U.C.L.A.

LAWRENCE ROSEN. A young American who has carried out social anthropological field research in Morocco, centering on problems of urban social structure, Berber tribal organization and the operation of local law courts. Has published numerous articles and is at present completing two books based on his North African material, as well as dividing his time between anthropology and law.

DAVID SEDDON. Educated at Cambridge and the London School of Economics, has taught archeology in Africa, and social anthropology at the School of Oriental and African Studies in London. Is now lecturer at the University of East Anglia. Carried out extensive field research in North Eastern Morocco.

CHARLES C. STEWART. D.Phil. from the University of Oxford for a thesis on the social structure of the Moorish society of the Western Sahara and the adjoining parts of the West African Sudan. The thesis combined the use of historical and social anthropological methods and ideas. He now teaches in the History Department of the University of Illinois at Urbana.

AMAL RASSAM VINOGRADOV. Educated in Iraq, the American University of Beirut, and the University of Chicago, has taught at the University of Alberta. Previously associated with the Center for Near Eastern and North African Studies at the University of Michigan, she now teaches at Queens College in New York. Her dissertation was based on field work amongst Berber-speaking tribes in the Middle Atlas.

JOHN WATERBURY. Ph.D. from the University of Columbia. He previously taught political science at the University of Michigan, and is now resident in Cairo as local representative of the American Universities Field Staff. He is the author of the study of post-Independence Moroccan politics *Commander of the Faithful: the Moroccan Political Elite—a study in Segmented Politics* (1970), and a further volume, a contribution to the social history of the Moroccan south, is due to appear shortly.

INDEX

Ababou, Lt. Col. M., 402, 403, 407, 408, 409, 410, 412, 419, 427, 428, 429, 432n
Abbadie, 203n
Abbas, F., 289, 290, 296
Abbasids, 204
Abdel Kader, (Abd el Qader), Emir, 19th century Algerian leader, 119, 230, 322
Abd el-Krim, 27, 36, 37, 39, 43, 44, 45, 47, 49, 50n, 114, 131n, 202, 204, 222, 223, 224, 277, 278, 426, 432
Abbes, Chief of Staff, Army of Liberation, 270, 271n
Abès, 67, 77, 190n, 193, 195
Abou Zakaria, 142n, 150
Adam, A., 14, 15, 20, 232, 234n, 241n, 325–343
Adams, Robert O. Mc. C., 155n
Adi u Bihi (Addi Ou Bihi), governor of Tafilelt, 271, 273, 274, 278, 362n, 426
Africa, 11, 15, 21, 26, 202n, 241, 364, 375, 388, 389, 390, 427
Agadir, 57, 279, 280, 282, 329, 336n, 342, 403
Ageron, Ch.-R., 177n, 189n, 287n
Agurram, Pl. Igurramen, Berber hereditary saint, 59, 60, 61, 64, 65, 66, 123n, 382
Ahaggar (Hoggar), 345 et seq.
Ahardan (Aherdane), Mahjub, 41, 55, 56, 226, 263, 264, 265, 269, 270, 271, 272, 273, 275, 276, 281, 341n, 425, 426, 429, 432
Ahermoumou, 264, 266, 402, 406, 407, 409, 410, 419, 427, 429
Ait Ahmed, (Algerian politician), 289, 290, 292, 294, 296, 297, 300, 436
Ait Atta, 14, 25, 28, 30, 32, 37, 38, 41, 43, 51, 52, 53, 54, 55, 56, 85 et seq 367n
Ait Atta, 14, 25, 28, 30, 32, 37, 38, 41, 43, 51, 52, 53, 54, 55, 56, 85 et seq, 367n
Ait Atta n-Umalu (Ait Atta of the shadow, i. e. North) 51, 54, 367n
Ait (Beni) bu Ifrur, 109 et seq
Ait bu Iknifen, 52, 55
Ait Hadiddu (Hadiddou), 38, 55, 78n
Ait Harzalla, 71, 72, 78, 80
Ait Izdig (Izdek, Izdeq), 55, 78, 90, 92n, 93, 95, 96, 98, 101, 104, 105
Ait Khabbash, 87, 90n, 91, 92, 93, 96, 97, 98, 99, 100, 101, 102, 103, 104, 105, 106
Ait Mguild (Beni Mguild), 55, 67, 74, 76, 190, 195
Ait Murghad (Merhad, Merghad), 32n, 52, 53, 55, 89, 90, 93, 102, 104
Ait Seghrouchen, 67, 78, 105
Ait Siddrat (Seddrate), 32n, 52, 53, 55
Aith Waryaghar (Beni Ouriaghel, Ait Waryaghel), 25, 28, 31, 32, 33n, 36n, 41, 43, 44, 45, 46, 47, 48, 49, 50, 51, 52, 53, 54, 55, 110n, 130, 418
Ait Yafilman (Yaffelmane, Yafalman), 55, 89, 90, 93, 101, 102, 103, 104, 106, 419
Aix-les-Bains, 269, 280
Ajdir (in middle Atlas), 271

Ajdir (in the Rif), 45
AJM (Association de la Jeunesse Mauritanienne), 388
Al-Alami, Gen. Driss Ben Omar, 410, 420
Alawites, (Alaouites), 67, 94, 102, 162, 279, 420
Albeniz, V. R., 131n
Al-Bustani, 207n
Algeciras, Act of, 113, 130
Al Fassi (El-Fassi), 201n, 213n, 214, 250, 270, 388, 398
Algiers, 294, 302, 321, 322, 436
Al-Kittani, 218
Almohads, 178, 326
Almond, G. A., 324n
Almoravids, 85, 178, 218, 326, 377, 384
ALN (Algerian Army), 284
Al-Nahda Al-Wataniyya Al-Muritaniyya party, 388, 389
Al-Nasiri, historian, 67n
Alport, E., 13, 20, 26n, 32n, 141–154, 234n
Amat, C., 152
Amenukal, 349, 350, 352, 354, 356, 358, 360
Amghar (Amhrar), Pl. Imgharen, elective chief, old man, 62, 76, 77, 78, 79, 81, 87, 88, 105, 330, 350
Amharache, Gen., 403, 419
Ammeln (Ammiln), 26n, 32n, 57, 234, 235, 236, 237, 238n, 247n, 248, 329, 330, 331, 336, 337
Amzzyan, Muhammad nj-Hajj Sillam n-Muh, Rifian leader, 46, 48, 49, 50n
Andalusia, 218
Anderson, C. W., 433n
Anderson, E. R., 131n
Anderson, R., 397n
Anti-Atlas, 32, 33, 34, 57, 143, 231, 233, 234, 235, 236, 238, 239, 242, 245, 325, 326, 329, 330, 331, 336n, 337, 338, 342, 343, 404
Antoun, R. T., 162n
Anual, Spanish defeat at, 114
Aqqa Boubidmani, leader of Beni Mtir, 77, 78
Arensberg, M., 36n, 117n
Army of Liberation, 45, 114, 132n, 133, 135n, 162, 217, 224, 226, 227, 246, 265, 269, 270, 271, 272, 273, 277, 279, 280, 368, 403, 412, 425, 426
Arnaud, Cmmdt. Ed., 67n
Arnaud, L., 128n
Arslan, Shakib, 213
Ashford, D. E., 25n, 132n, 133n, 134n, 135n, 136n, 137n, 138n, 248n, 362n
Assu u-Baslam (El-Hadj Assou Baslem) Chief of Ait Atta, 54, 56, 224
Ataturk, 204
Atlantic, 27, 35, 42, 86, 234, 325, 329n, 342, 364, 376, 413
Aubin (Descos) E., 106n, 128n, 179, 180, 221
Aubin, J., 426n

Aurès, (Range), see also Shawiya, 143, 146
150n, 285, 287, 290, 294, 296, 298, 301,
304, 310, 315, 316, 321n, 323n, 434
Auriol, V., 205n
Azrou (*see also* Collège Berbère), 206, 261,
264, 266, 273, 278, 281, 282, 283, 419,
420, 432

Bachir, Gen., 425, 427
Bailey, F. G., 122n
Balafraj, M., 213n, 398
Balzac, H. De, 329, 330
Bambara, 376, 392
Bani Hilal (Beni Hillal), 86
Banton, M., 121n, 126n, 132n
Barth, F., 122n, 124n, 125n
Barabish, 89
Baraka, 60, 68n, 99, 107, 382
Basri, M., 398, 402
BDG (Bloc Democratique de Gorgol), 388
Bekkai, E., 263, 269, 270
Bel, A., 197n, 209n
Belgium, 51, 421
Belkacem Krim, 290–300
Belshaw, L., 240n
Benabdallah, M., 176n
Ben Allem, Oufkir's A D C, 428
Ben Barka, M., 134, 248, 249, 254, 269, 270,
271, 273, 398, 404, 414, 422
Ben Bachir, S., 137n
Benet, F., 36, 117n
Ben Bella, A., 289–301, 436
Benkhedda, (Ben Khedda), 292, 294, 295
Ben Boulaid, 290, 291, 300
Benhima, M., 399, 400, 421, 422
Ben Kaddour, A., 20, 259–267
Beni Mellal, 25, 51, 54, 55, 250, 400, 432
Beni Mtir, also Ait Ndir, also Aith Ndhir,
67 *et seq*, 190, 191, 192, 195, 419, 420
Benoist-Mechin, 429
Ben Seddiq, M., 398
Berchem, M. van, 145n
Bernard, A., 97n, 98n, 144, 145n, 146n, 179,
182n, 187, 191n, 192n, 193, 194n, 197,
198
Bernard, M., 103n
Bernard, S., 246n
Bernstein, B., 169, 170n
Berque, J., 32n, 173n, 208n, 213n, 215,
219n, 234n, 278
Berraber (Beraber), Central Moroccan term
for Berber, 14, 325
Berriau, Col., 97n, 103n, 193, 194n, 195
Bertschi, Lt., 197n
Bessaoud, M. A., 287n
Biarnay, 193, 195
Binder, L., 155n, 201
Blanco Izaga, Col. E., 29n, 33n
Bouabid, A., 398, 432
Boudiaf, M., 294, 296
Bougrine, Gen., 403, 407, 412, 419, 420,
429
Boukili Shurfa, 71, 78

Boulhims, Col. B., 412, 420, 425
Boumedienne, Col. H., 287, 292, 295, 297,
298, 299
Boumendjel, A., 289, 293, 295, 296
Bourdieu, P., 124n, 312
Bourguiba, President, 208
Bousquet, G.-H., 26, 93n, 228n
Breton, H., 255n
Brignon, J., 118n, 176n
Brown K., 12, 19, 116n, 155n, 201–216
Brown, L. C., 172n, 173n
Brunhes, J., 141n
Bruno, H., 93n, 192n, 193, 194n
Bu Gafr (Bou Gafer), Battle of, 54, 56, 103
Bu Hmara (Al Rogui, Pretender), 46, 113
128, 129, 221, 418
Burke III, E., 13, 18n, 106n, 155n, 175–
200
Burma, 171, 308
Byzantine(s), 11, 143, 144

Cairo, 47, 184n, 270, 290, 291, 388
Caix, R. de, 182n, 186n, 187, 197n
Calvin, J., 144, 152
Campoamore, J. H., 131n
Camps, G., 327n
Canavy, Capt., 98n
Capot-Rey, R., 147n, 150n
Carthage, 143, 208
Casablanca, 46, 55, 57, 113, 231, 232, 233,
236, 238, 239, 240, 241, 242, 243n, 244,
245, 246, 247, 249, 250, 251, 252, 253,
254, 255, 256, 278, 282, 325, *et seq*, 367,
401, 405, 407, 412, 414, 415, 420, 422,
432
Casanova P., 142n
Castro, Fidel, 362
Cauchemez, 101
C C E(Comite de Co-ordination et d'Execu-
tion), 291, 300
Central del Ejercito Estado Mayor, 131n
Ceuta, 119, 143
Ceylon, 285
Chaamba, 141, 349, 353n
Chad, 15, 375
Chadili, Shaikh, 219
Chambergeat, P., 135n, 138n, 252n
Chapelle, F. de la, 89n
Charlet-Cozon, Lt., 150n
Chaumeil, J., 234n
Chelouati, Col. L., 403, 404, 405, 407, 413,
418, 419, 427, 428, 429
Cherkaoui, A., 135n, 137n
Chiapuris, J., 78n
China, 243n, 410
Churchill, Sir W., 367
Christianity, 11, 12n, 13, 14, 59, 144, 151,
186, 202, 207, 208, 210, 348, 366
C.I.A. (Central Intelligence Agency), 397,
401
C N R A (Conseil National de la Révolution
Algérienne), 291, 296
Cohen, A., 124n

Coleman, J. S., 324n
Colin, G. S., 86n
Collège Berbère, 206, 261, 264, 266, 273, 278, 282, 283, 419, 420, 432
Congo, 420
Constantine, 284, 295
Coon, C., 175n
Coppolani, X., 386
Coram, A., 14, 20, 269–276, 425–430
Courrière, Y., 290n
Crown Prince Mulay Hassan, *see* Mulay Hassan II
CRUA, (Comité Révolutionnaire d'Unité et d'Action), 290
Current Anthropology, 109n, 155n
Curtin, P. O., 175
Cyprus, 116n
Cyrenaica, 28, 29n, 121n

Dads (Dades), 53, 89, 104
Dadda Atta, 14, 52, 86, 87
Dahir Berbère, (Berber Decree), 39, 40, 54, 156, 195, 198, 201 *et seq.*, 260, 341, 366, 370
Damascus, 143
Dastugue, H., 92n
Dawi Mani, 90, 93n, 99, 100, 102, 103n, 104, 105, 106, 107
Deffontaines, P., 141n
De Gaulle, Ch., 274, 388
Delamarre, Mme. Jean-Brunhes, 141n
Delcassé, 181, 182
Delisle, S., 237
Denoun, Officer-Interpreter, 96n, 97n
Denmark, 26
Derro Project, 47
Desmazières, B., 225n
Des Vaux, de la Porte, 237n
Djerba (Jerba) 11n, 149, 329, 330, 341
Dlimi, Col., 431
Doury, 90n
Doutté, E., 106n, 141n, 173n, 178, 179, 180, 181n, 182n, 184, 186
Dra (Draa, Draoua, Draua), 37n, 53, 86n, 89, 93, 100n, 325, 326, 337
Duclos, L.-J., (*see also* Ougrour), 11, 15, 19, 217–230
Dunn, R., 14, 15, 86–108
Durkheim, E., 121n, 178
Duvignaud, J., 225n

Egypt, 47, 86, 143, 145, 204, 205, 215n
El-Hajeb, 79, 190, 191, 406, 419, 420
El Hiba, 222, 330
El-Hoceima (al-Husaima), 25, 43, 45, 48, 49, 50n
El-Mukri, Haj Mohammed, Grand Vizier, 225
England, 12n, 51, 119, 188
Entente Mauritanienne, 387, 391
Esslaoui, Ahmed Ennasiri (as-Salawi, A. ben Khalid an-Nasiri) 92n, 100n, 207n
Etienne, E., 184

Europe, 11, 14, 15, 18, 97, 100, 103n, 107, 110, 113, 114, 116, 118, 119, 120, 130, 134, 141, 152, 175, 178, 180, 182, 183, 194, 205, 207n, 208n, 213, 214, 217, 231, 236, 239, 241, 315, 323, 331, 332, 335, 336, 337, 339, 355, 356, 361, 362, 382, 385, 398
Evans-Pritchard, E. E., 28, 29n, 30, 121n, 122n
Ezziani, Aboulqasem ben Ahmed, 92n

Fallers, Lloyd A., 155n
Fatimids, 145
Favret, J., 14, 20, 121n, 122n, 307–321
FDIC (Front for the Defence of Constitutional Institutions), 162, 255, 265, 280, 342
Feaugeas, Capt., 197n
Ferry, Commdt., 185n
Fes (Fez), Fassi, 38, 67, 71, 72, 79, 97, 101, 102, 103n, 106, 112, 113, 114, 117, 124, 127, 128, 131, 157, 183, 188, 190, 191, 201, 205, 206, 213n, 220, 222, 227, 231, 232, 233, 236, 241, 242, 243, 245, 246, 247, 248, 249, 250, 251, 252, 255, 256, 259, 261, 264, 266, 269, 270n, 271, 278, 279, 281, 282, 326, 331, 332, 336, 337, 339, 340, 341, 342, 403, 405, 406, 407, 412, 418, 419, 437
FFS (Front des Forces Socialistes), 296, 297
Figueras, T. G., 120n, 131n
Firth, R., 121n, 127n
Fleurieu, Capt. de, 237n
FLN (National Liberation Front), 295, 297, 298, 315
Fogg, W., 35n, 117n
Formosa, 243n
Foucauld, Ch. de, 89, 178n, 208
Franco, Gen., 114, 132n, 133
Frazer, Sir James, 178
Fulani (Peuls, Fulfulde), 376, 387
Fulbright-Hays, Fellowships, 201n
Fumey, E., 92n, 100n

Gaffarel, P., 220n
Gaillard, 195
Gallagher, C. F., 172n
Gandhi, 204, 213n
Gaudefroy-Demombynes, R., 206n, 260
Gast, M., 349, 353, 356
Gautier, E. F., 141n, 150
Geertz, C., 155n, 156n, 167n, 240n, 285n, 433n
Geertz, H., 155n, 159, 164
Gellner, E., 11–24, 25, 28, 34, 36, 37n, 41, 42, 49, 54, 55n, 58, 59–66, 69, 70n, 76n, 86n, 87n, 88n, 89n, 93n, 106n. 109, 116n, 121n, 123n, 155n, 176n, 218n, 226, 228n, 321n, 340, 361–374, 382
Gerlings, J. H., Jager, 52n
Germany, 51, 54, 100n, 120, 182, 187, 418, 420

Gerofi, R., 202n
Gerouan, (Guerrouan), 67, 68, 77, 192, 195
Ghana (Ancient), 377
Gharb (Western Plain of Morocco), 49, 263, 400, 431
Gharbaoui, Gen, Mekki, 405, 410, 420, 425
Ghardaya, 141, 145, 146, 151
Gheris, 89, 95
Ghmara, (Ghomara), 31
Glawi, (Glaoui), 31, 36, 40, 206n, 223, 260, 270, 271, 365, 367
Gluckman, M., 33n
Goichon, Mlle. A.-M., 150, 151n
Goliath, 13
Gordon, G. C., 356n
GPRA (Provisional Algerian Government) 292, 294, 295, 300
Great Britain, 100, 120, 175
Greece, 143, 146
Guedira, R., 270n, 275, 416
Guennoun, Said, 62n
Guillaume, G. A., 223
Guillen, P., 100n
Guir, 90, 92, 98, 104, 105
Guish (Guish), Tax-privileged tribes, 68, 69, 71, 277
Gumperz, J. J., 170n
Gundafi, 31

Habibi, Gen. Abderrahman, 403, 407, 413, 419, 429
Hadramawt (Hadramaut), 232
Hagen, E. E., 237
Halpern, M., 38, 39n
Halstead, J. P., 201n, 203n, 205n, 206n, 213n, 224, 260n, 261n
Hamès, C., 379n
Hammou, Gen. Amahzoun, 402, 403, 407, 413, 418, 419, 420, 428
Hamon, L., 406n
Hannon, 327
Hassaniya language, 192, 196
Haroteau, 192, 196
Haratin (Harratin), Sing, Hartani, see also Negro, Black, 27, 53, 54, 55, 95, 96, 98, 105, 326, 327, 345, 351, 356, 357, 359, 383
Harik, I., 162n
Harris, W. B., 102n, 218n
Hart, D. M., 14, 15, 25–58, 62n, 86n, 88n, 91n, 110n, 121n, 122n
Henriet, 97n
Henrys, Lt.-Col., 189n, 190n, 191, 192n, 193, 195, 196n
Hobsbawm, E. J., 314n, 315, 316
Hoffman, E. C., 116n, 123n
Holland, 51
Holt, R. T., 109n
Houdas, O., 92n
Hourani, A., 207n
Howe, M., 133n
Huguet, J., 146n
Huntington, S. P., 285n, 302n

Huot, Lt., 98n
Horma ould Babana, 387, 388
Hymes, D., 170n

Ibadi (Abadi), see also Mzab, 13, 142, 143, 145, 330
Ibn Khaldun, 13, 14, 142n, 144, 410, 433n
Ibrahim, Abdallah, 42, 248, 252, 362n, 426, 432
Idan-Gnidif (Ida ou Gnidif), 57, 234, 235, 248, 329, 336
Idrissids, 219, 420
Ifni, 279, 403
Igharm (Igherm, Irherm) Amazdar, 37, 52, 56
Igzinnayen, 40, 45, 47, 418, 419
Ikniwn (Iknioun), 54, 56
Imazighen (Central Moroccan Berbers), Speakers of Tamazight Dialect. See also Berraber, 59–108, 325, 330, 340, 341
Imzuren, Post of, 48, 49
India, 121n, 213n, 310, 379n
Indochina, 414, 418, 419, 420
Indonesia, 308, 366
Institut de France, 90n
Iraq, 285, 310
Islam, Muslim, 11, 12, 13, 14, 15, 21, 21, 25, 26, 34, 38, 39, 42, 44, 54, 59, 65, 85n, 95, 96, 99, 106, 142, 143, 144, 145, 151, 156, 159n, 161, 166, 167n, 177, 178, 184, 185, 186, 189, 193, 194, 196, 197, 198, 202, 203, 204, 205, 206, 207, 208, 209, 210, 211, 212, 214, 215, 221, 225, 237, 242, 261, 265, 266n, 272, 277, 280, 286, 321, 326, 327, 330, 337, 341, 348, 363, 364, 366, 367n, 375, 385, 389, 390, 392, 410, 429, 434, 437
Isly, Battle of, 113, 230
Istiqlal Party, 34, 38, 40, 41, 45, 48, 49, 114, 132n, 134, 135, 138n, 162, 220, 221, 227, 245, 246, 247, 248, 249, 250, 251, 252, 253, 259n, 260, 262, 263, 264, 265, 269, 270, 271, 272, 273, 275, 278, 281, 282, 339, 342, 399, 402n, 405, 416, 421, 426, 427, 431, 436, 437
Israel, 53, 124n, 145, 397
Italy, 54, 146, 147, 172

Japan, 243n
Jaques-Meunié, D., 53n, 89n, 95n
Jamous, R., 109n, 121n, 124, 138n
Java, 156n
Jbala (Jebala), 27n, 31
Jbil Hmam, 43, 48, 49
Jbil Saghru (Jebel Saghro), 25, 37, 52, 54, 56, 86, 87, 89, 103, 104, 224
Jews, Judaism, 13, 14, 15, 53, 95, 96, 141, 143, 144, 146, 151, 159n, 161, 167n, 186, 202, 203, 231, 239, 241, 242, 243n, 244, 250, 251, 323, 329, 330, 361, 363
Jmaa, (Jema'a, Jama'a), Tribal Assembly, 69, 73, 75, 76, 79, 80, 82, 177, 192, 194, 199, 261, 266, 316, 330, 380, 383, 384, 434

Jongmans, O. J., 52n
Jonnart, 90n
Jouannet, J., 203n
Juin, Resident-General, 246
Julien Ch.-A., 142n, 201n, 205n
Justinard, Col., 236n

Kharejites (See also Ibadis), 14, 142, 143, 330, 341
Kabylia (Kabilia), 19, 121n, 122, 124n, 146, 150n, 177n, 180, 186, 189, 192, 193, 194, 196, 198, 199, 232, 285, 286, 287, 288, 289, 290, 921, 292, 294, 295, 296, 297, 308, 298, 299, 301, 302, 303, 304, 307, 310, 316, 321, 322, 323, 328, 335, 434, 435, 436
Kairouan, 144
Kedourie, E., 215n
Keenan, J., 15, 20, 345–360
Kel Ahaggar, 345, 349, 351
Kel Atter, 345, 349
Khadafi, Col., 327
Khatib, Dr. A., 226, 264, 270, 271, 272, 273, 274, 275, 415
Khatibi, A., 202n, 259n, 260n, 263n
Khider, M., 294, 296
Kohn, H,. 207n
Koran, 12, 13, 14, 37, 38, 60, 68, 74, 82, 142, 143, 144, 151, 194, 210, 212, 315, 328, 341, 366, 378, 415
Ksar es-Souk, 25, 51, 78, 250
Kunstadter, P., 171n
Kurdistan, 124n, 232, 285, 340

Labonne, E., 260
Lacouture, J., 172n
Lacouture, S., 172n
Lacroix, N., 97n, 178n
Laghzaoui, 270n, 272, 281, 431
Lahbabi, M., 28, 106n, 176n, 369n
Lahouel, H., 289
Lamalif, 138n
Lamartinièri, H. M. P., 178
Landau, R., 133n, 205n
Laoust, E., 193, 195, 197n
Laraki, A., 405, 422
Lavigerie, Cardinal, 208
Lazrak, M., 409, 410, 421, 422
Lebanon, 207n, 232
Leca, J., 225
Le Chalelier, A., 103n
Leffs (Soffs), Moieties, 18, 19, 41, 80, 120, 121, 122, 124n, 125, 126, 127, 146, 148, 177, 341
Le Glay, M., 128n, 188, 190n, 192n, 193, 194n, 195, 196n, 197n
Legris, M., 404
Lehman, F. K., 171
Lektaoua, 53n, 89n
Lemoine, P., 186, 187n
Lempereur, S., 311n
Lentin, A.-P., 411
Lenz, O., 95n

Lesne, M., 85n, 93n
Le Tourneau, R., 142n, 205n, 213n, 289
Le Tourneux, 192, 196
Lewis, B., 142n
Lewis, W. H., 26n, 32n
Leys, C., 163n
Lhote, H., 345, 354
Libya, 345, 397, 410, 415
Linares, Dr., 96n, 101, 102
Lizot, J., 311n
Llanos y Alcarez, A., 120n
Loth, 195
Lyautey, Marshal, 90n, 175 *et seq*, 205, 222, 337
Lyautey, P., 190n, 191n
Lyazidi, A., 247, 272
Lyoussi, L., 263, 264, 265, 270, 271, 273, 278

Madagascar, 40
Ma al-Aynain (Aynin), 376n
Madrid, 133
Makhzan, (Makhzen), Traditional Central Government, 26, 67, 68, 69, 92, 99, 100, 101, 106, 107, 109, 112, 113, 116, 117, 118, 119, 124, 125, 128, 129, 130, 132, 133, 134, 135, 136, 137, 138, 139, 173n, 175, 176, 177, 179, 180, 181, 182, 183, 185, 186, 187, 188, 190, 191, 192, 194, 198, 206n, 217, 220, 222, 223, 259 *et seq*, 277, 279, 280, 281, 340, 364, 365, 417
Maitrot de la Motte Capron, A., 128n
Maldonado, E., 128n
Mali, 15, 345, 375, 388, 389
Maliki (Meliki) Rite, 11, 218, 286, 330, 341, 363
Manouzi, Cmmdt., 403, 404, 417
Maqil, Group of Tribes, 86, 90, 96, 377
Marais, O., 14, 20, 250n, 264n, 265n, 277–283, 431–432
Marcais, W., 150
Marcy, G., 82n, 93n
Marquez, L., 236n, 237n, 330n,
Marrakesh, 40, 55, 56, 68n, 97, 102, 106, 113, 131, 178n, 237, 241n, 249, 250, 269, 278, 331, 365, 400, 403, 407, 412, 417, 419
Marty, P., 261n
Martin, A. G. P., 98n, 99n, 100n, 103n
Marx, K., 324, 365
Mas, Y., 206n
Masqueray, E., 142n, 143, 146n, 150, 151n
Massignon, L., 213n
Mauran, Dr., 261n
Mauritania, 15, 85, 86, 375 *et seq*
Mawlay. . . , see also Mulay . . .
Mecca, 339
Medbuh (Medboh), Gen., 47, 266, 274, 400, 401, 402, 404, 405, 406, 407, 408, 409, 410, 411, 413, 414, 418, 419, 420, 426, 427, 428, 429, 431
Mehamid (M'hamid), 53n, 89n

Meknes, 35, 67, 68n, 72, 188, 195, 225n, 237, 250, 266, 273, 326, 331, 407, 418, 419, 420, 426

Melilla, 113, 114, 115, 116, 117, 119, 120, 128, 129, 131

Mennesson, 115n

Mercier, L., 90n, 97n

Mercier, M., 149n

Messali Hadj, 289

Meyer, A. C., 126n

M'hammedi, D., 273, 278

Micaud, C., 21, 433–438

Michaux-Bellaire, E., 184, 185, 186, 202, 218n

Middle East, (Near East), 11, 14, 18, 18n, 26, 39, 124, 175n, 241, 301, 427

Middleton, J., 30

Miège, J.-L., 100n, 118n, 119n, 120n, 185n, 243n

Mikesell, M. W., 35, 36, 117n

Miské, A. B., 386

Mjatt, 68, 71

Mohand oul Hadj, Col., 294, 295, 296, 297, 298, 299, 436

Mokhtar ould Daddah, 389

Montjean, M., 237n, 238n

Montagne, R., 32n, 33, 36, 40n, 86n, 125, 198n, 205n, 206n, 213n, 234n, 237n, 241n, 331, 337

Moore, C. H., 220n

Moors (Mauritanians), 375 *et seq*

Morand, M., 147n, 148n, 151n

Morizot, J., 322n, 434

Motylinski, A. De C., 145n

Moulay..., See Mulay...

Moussa ag Amastene, 352

Moussard, P., 206n

Mouvement Populaire (Popular Movement Party), 41, 55, 56, 135, 162, 227, 259n, 262, 265, 266, 269, 271, 274, 275, 276, 280, 425, 436

Mozabite, See Mzab

MTLD Party, 289

Mtuggi, 31

Muhammed V, King, 40, 46, 49, 114, 133, 135, 136, 205n, 206n, 224, 226, 229, 247, 248, 252, 264, 265, 269, 270, 271, 272, 273, 274, 275, 397, 398, 399, 403, 418, 419, 420, 421, 426, 427

Mulai..., See Mulay

Mulay (Mawlay) Abd al-Aziz, Sultan, 107, 113, 129, 182, 221

Mulay (Mawlay) Hafid (Hafiz) Sultan, 113, 190, 218n, 322

Mulay (Moulay) Abdallah, Brother of Moulay Hassan II, 402, 406, 421

Mulay Hasan II, King, 48, 49, 56, 107, 114, 133n, 135, 136, 227, 229, 265, 269, 272, 273, 274, 275, 279, 281, 362n, 397, 398, 399, 401, 404, 406, 407, 408, 409, 410, 411, 412, 413, 414, 415, 416, 417, 418, 419, 420, 422, 425, 426, 427, 428, 429, 430, 431

Mulay Hasan, Sultan 1874–94, 68, 79, 96n, 100, 101, 106, 113, 128, 211

Mulay (Moulay, Mulai, Mawlay) Ismael, 99, 100

Mulay (Mulai) Yussef, Sultan, 113, 222

Mzab, Mzabite, Mozabite, 11n, 141 *et seq*, 285, 293, 296, 321n, 323, 328, 329, 330, 341, 353, 434

Mzzyan, Marshal, 47, 398, 405, 418

Nador, 35, 47, 109, 110, 111, 112, 114, 115, 116, 132n, 134n, 135, 137n, 138, 225

Naroll, R., 155n

Nasser, Gen., 409, 427

Negro, Black, see also Haratin, 14, 15, 46, 54, 89, 145, 147, 148, 326, 327, 392

Neguib, Gen., 409

Nehlil, M., 193, 195, 196

Niclausse, 89n

Nicholas, R. W., 121n

Nicolaisen, J., 348, 355

Nicosia, 116n

Niger Republic, 345, 351, 354, 359, 360

Niger River, 89, 149

Nigeria, 285

Noin, D., 234n, 241n

Norris, H. T., 380n

Norway, 26

Nouakchott, 391

Nuer, 28, 30, 121n, 122n

Nuseibeh, H., 201n

Oran, Oranie, 44, 93n, 129n, 183n, 236, 294

Ottomans, 11n, 18, 207n

Ouarsenis, 310

Ouamrane, A., 290, 292, 295, 300

Ouarzazate, 25, 51, 56, 274, 282, 418, 426

Oued Zem, Massacre of, 368

Oufqir (Oufkir, Ufkir), General, 49, 266, 267, 275, 404, 405, 406n, 407, 408, 409, 410, 411, 412, 413, 414, 415, 416, 419, 422, 425, 426, 427, 428, 429, 431

Ougrour, J., (see also Duclos, L.-J.) 42n, 225n

Oujda, 113, 117, 120n, 129, 183, 236, 250, 270, 298, 326, 404, 419, 428

Oulmes (Ulmas), 41, 271, 341n

Pakistan, 135n, 410

Paris, 204, 208n, 213n, 270, 329, 337, 343, 367, 388, 420, 435

Palestine, 213

Pascon, P., 123n

Payne, 117n, 120n, 131n, 133

Pathans, 122n, 124n

PDI (Democratic Independence Party), 46, 264, 265, 421

Pearson, H. W., 36n

Peretie, A., 209n

Peristiany, J., 124n

Persia, 12

Peters, E. L., 121n, 122n, 124n, 125n, 126n

Peyreigne, C., 131n

PFDM (Parti du Front National Démocratique), 389
Phoenicians, 11, 184
Pitt-Rivers, J., 25n
Polanyi, K., 36n, 117n
Pompidou, President, 405
Portugal, 14, 219
PPM (Parti du People Mauritanien), 389
Prophet Muhammed, 27, 60, 65, 69, 94, 144, 145, 148, 207n, 210, 211, 218, 266n, 339, 349, 363
Protectorate, 28, 35, 104, 107, 113, 131, 133, 155, 173n, 181, 202, 203, 204, 205, 207, 208n, 217, 222, 223, 225, 227, 255, 262, 266, 269, 277, 278, 279, 281, 283, 331, 332, 341, 365, 369, 421, 426, 430
PRM (Parti du Regroupement Mauritanien), 389

Qabila (Taqbilt) Tribe, 25, 70, 73, 88, 91, 146, 147
Quandt, W. B., 14, 20, 285–306, 433

Rabat, 35, 40, 41, 42, 46, 56, 85, 106, 109, 133, 134n, 195, 196, 204, 208, 209, 211, 213, 226, 246, 250, 267, 269, 272, 280, 331, 388, 400, 401, 405, 406, 407, 409, 411, 412, 413, 418, 419, 426, 431n
Ramdane, A., 291, 292, 300
Ramos, G., 131n
Ranger, T. O., 202n
Recoules, J., 221n
Regnault, Capt., 93n
Réunion Island, 47
Rézette, R., 133n, 247n
Rgibat, (Reguibat), 27n, 89, 376
Riera, A., 131n
Rif, 25, 26, 27, 29, 31, 33, 34, 35, 36, 37, 38, 40, 42, 43, 44, 45, 46, 47, 48, 49, 50, 51, 58, 62n, 110n, 112, 113, 114, 115, 117, 118, 119, 122n, 130, 131, 132, 134, 138n, 179, 201, 202, 204, 221, 224, 225, 232, 256, 257, 263, 269, 271, 272, 277, 278, 280, 281, 325, 340, 341, 363, 402, 404, 414, 418, 419, 421, 425, 426, 427, 429, 432, 434, 436
Rio de Oro (Now Spanish Sahara) 376, 388
Robin, N.-J., 150n
Rohlfs, G., 95n, 96n
Rome, Roman, 11, 146, 184, 187, 194
Rosen, L., 12, 14, 155–174, 433n
Rosenfeld, H., 124n
Rousseau, J.-J., 28
Row, E. F., 141n
Rustow, D. A., 285n

Sahara, 11, 13, 15, 25, 27, 32n, 37, 85, 86, 88, 90, 91, 92, 95n, 97, 98, 99, 100, 101, 103, 104, 142, 145, 149, 150, 178, 201, 202n, 237n, 279, 294, 326, 327, 345, 348, 353, 364, 375, 376, 377
Sahlins, M., 132n, 235n
Saint, L., 206

Sais, Plain, 68, 71
Sale, 15, 85, 116n, 201 *et seq.* 249, 250, 331
Salim, S., 310
Salmon, G., 106n, 184n
Samir Amin, 313n
San Diego State University Foundation, 86n
Sanusi (Senoussi), 29n, 121n
Sarakole, 376, 387, 392
Sayad, A., 312n
Schlumburger, 102n, 103n
Schmitter, P., 201n
Schutz, A., 167
Scotland, 144, 343
Seddon, J. D., 15, 19, 20, 109–140
Sefrou, 157, *et seq.*, 264, 270
Segonzac, Marquis de, 179, 180, 186n, 187
Seksawa, 32n
Senegal, 387, 388, 389
Senegal River, 375, 376, 377n, 378, 385, 392
Setif, 311
SFIO (French Socialist Party) 387
Sharia (Shra'a), Koranic Law, 39, 44, 54, 68, 156, 194, 328, 340, 382
Sharif (Sherif), pl. Shurfa, 60, 72, 76, 79, 82, 85n, 92n, 94, 95, 96, 98, 99, 100, 101, 102, 107, 116, 119, 127n, 162, 177, 185, 218, 219, 220, 221, 226, 275, 382
Shaw, G. B., 59
Shawiya, see also Aures, 285, 286, 287, 293, 296, 298, 299, 300, 303
Shinqit (Arabic for Mauritania) 375 *et seq*
Shleuh (Chleuh) Southern Moroccan Group of Berbers, and their Language, 321–258, 325–344
Shurr Bubba (Conflict) 377 *et seq*
Siba, 26, 27, 28, 67, 106, 107, 109, 117, 132, 173n, 175, 177, 179, 180, 183, 185, 188, 198, 219, 220, 222, 259, 275n, 279, 280, 331, 364
Sidi Muhammad, 18th c. Sultan, 92n, 100
Sidi Mumhamed Ben Arafa (Puppet Sultan, 1953–55) 421
Sidi Mohamed Ben Yussef, Sultan, See Muhammed V, King
Sidi Said Ahansal, 55, 86n
Simon, Col. H., 193, 196
Skhirat (Palace, also by extension, abortive coup located there), 397, 406 *et seq*
Slane, Baron M. de, 142n, 144n
Smith, A. D., 20n
Smith-Mundt Foundation, 33n
Soffs see Leffs
Soummam Congress, 291
Souss, see Sus
Soviet Union, 397
Spain, 25, 26, 28, 32, 35, 39, 40, 41, 43, 44, 45, 46, 47, 48, 50, 54, 111, 113, 114, 115, 117, 119, 120, 129n, 130, 131, 132, 133, 134, 138, 144, 148n, 201, 219, 225, 271, 272, 277, 279, 281, 282, 326, 368, 375, 376, 398

Spillmann, G., 37, 52n, 86n, 87n, 89n, 91n, 92n, 97n, 100n, 102n, 104n, 208n
Steeg, Resident-General, 206
Stewart, C. C., 15, 375-393
Stirling, P., 310
Sudan, 15, 89, 149, 345, 350, 375
Sufi, 177, 212, 217, 218, 219
Sunni, 11, 27, 286, 330, 341, 363
Surdon, G., 189n, 192n, 193n, 195n
Sus, (Souss, Soussi, Swasa), 26, 32, 57, 179, 231 *et seq*, 263, 264, 278, 279, 326n 329, 400
Sweden, 26
Sweet, Dr L., 11
Switzerland, 401
Syria, 213, 414

Tafrawt (Tafraout), 57
Tait, D., 30
Tafilalt, (Tafilalet), Ancient Sijilmassa, 42, 85n, 90, 91, 92, 93, 94, 95, 97, 98, 100, 101, 102, 103, 104, 107, 221, 271, 274, 280, 348, 362n, 420, 425, 426
Takama, Slave-girl, 348
Tamahaq (Language) 345n, 356n
Tamanrasset, 345, 352, 353, 354, 356, 357, 358, 359, 360
Tangier, 57, 179, 184n, 236, 250, 257, 326, 331, 336
Taraf, 67 *et seq*
Tawney, R. H., 149n
Taza, 117, 128, 129, 236, 250, 269, 403, 407, 418, 419
Terrasse, H., 106, 107, 177, 218n, 219n
Terrier, A., 90n, 190n, 191n
Tetuan, 40, 45, 50n, 119, 133, 250, 257, 278, 326
Tiano, A., 261n
Tichoukt, 78
Timbuctu (Timbouctou), 95n
Ti-n-Hinan, Queen, 348
Tit, Battle of, 351, 352
Tito, Marshal, 362
Tizi Ouzou, 294, 295
Tlemcen, 294
Tocqueville, A. de, 324
Touat, Tuat, Oasis of, 85n, 90, 92, 97, 98, 99, 100, 103, 104, 107, 178, 182n, 353, 377
Toucoulor, 376, 387, 392
Tournoux, R., 401, 409, 414
Toynbe, A., 202n
Tripolitania, 143
Troin, J.-F., 35, 115n
Trystram, J.-P., 338n
Tuareg, 90, 286, 345 *et seq*, 376
Tuat, see Touat
Tunis, 67n, 69, 208
Tunisia, 11n, 13, 14, 18, 135n, 149, 208, 263, 292, 329, 330, 433, 435
Turkey, 19, 205, 208, 219, 289, 310, 322, 433

UDMA Party, 290
Ulad Stut, 109 *et seq*
UNFP Party (National Union of Popular Forces), 38, 41, 55, 114, 134, 135, 136, 248, 249, 250, 251, 252, 253, 254, 255, 265, 269, 273, 274, 275, 282, 342, 362n, 399, 402, 404, 416, 417, 421, 422, 426, 427, 432
United States of America, 25, 46, 199, 364, 397n, 427
University of California, 116n, 199n, 231n
University of Illinois, 145n
University of London, 117n, 321n
University of Michigan, 67n, 231n
University of Minnesota 109n
University of Winsconsin, 86n
UMCIA (Moroccan Union of Merchants, Industrialists and Artisans), 247, 248, 249, 342
UNM Party, 389
UPM (Union Progressiste Mauritanienne), 388, 389, 391
Urf, Customary Law, also Qaida, also Abrid, also Izref, 68, 72, 76n, 192, 199, 370, 434

Vaffier-Pollet, 183n
Val D'Eremao, J. P., 120n
Vallerie, P., 224n
Vicard, 103n
Vidal, E., 131n
Vigourus, L., 149n
Vincent, J., 162, 163
Vinogradov, A. R., 15, 19, 67-84
Voinot, L., 120n

Wahabi Movement, 142
Waterbury, J., 14, 20, 109, 110, 116n, 123n, 124n, 125n, 126n, 132n, 133n, 134n, 135n, 136n, 138n, 231-258, 397-423, 425n, 431, 434n, 436
Wattasids, 219
Weber, M., 149n, 256, 322, 324, 330
Weisberger, Dr F., 128n, 222n
Wenner-Gren Foundation, 324n
Westermarck, E., 96n, 209n
Wolof, 376, 387, 392
Woolman, D. S., 131n, 132n
Wriggins, W. Howard, 285n

Yemen, 232

Zartman, I. W., 48n, 227n, 262n
Zawiya Ahansal, 55, 66n, 86n, 89n
Zayan (Zaian, Zayyan,) 31, 55, 191n, 195, 403, 418, 432
Zemmouri, H., 274, 432
Zenatiya, language group, spoken mainly in Rif, 325
Zeys, E., 152
Ziz, 89, 90, 91, 92, 93, 94, 95, 98, 101, 104
Zummur (Zemmour), 85, 226
Zwemer, S. M., 205n